INDUSTRY GOVERNANCE AND REGULATORY COMPLIANCE

A Theoretical and Practical Guide to European ICT Policy

Guido Reinke

London – Brussels – New York
GOLD RUSH Publishing 2012

Industry Governance and Regulatory Compliance:
A Theoretical and Practical Guide to European ICT Policy

ISBN-10: 1908585021
ISBN-13: 9781908585028

For further information or if you wish to submit any comments or ideas for future publications, please email to the email address below.

GOLD RUSH Publishing® books may be purchased for educational, business, or sales promotional use. We are an independent publishing house promoting innovative publications.
For information please email: info@GoldRushPublishing.org.

Industry Governance and Regulatory Compliance:
A Theoretical and Practical Guide to European ICT Policy
Includes text, diagrams and tables. First Printing, 2012
978-1-908585-02-8 (ISBN 13) paperback
Available for sale in bookshops, online at Amazon.com, and other channels worldwide.

GOLD RUSH Publishing

Information technology and business

are becoming inextricably interwoven.

I don't think anybody can talk meaningfully

about one without talking about the other.

Bill Gates (1955-)

FOREWORD
BY PETER ENGSIG-KARUP

This book, *Industry Governance and Regulatory Compliance – A theoretical and practical guide to European ICT Policy*, is an excellent tool to industry professionals seeking regulatory influence and to students of politics who want to get insight to public governance and related complex networks with public and private stakeholders.

The book provides a comprehensive structural theory based on the policy governance processes experienced during the build-up of the European Union´s Information Society agenda, as it took place over more than a decade from around 1995 to 2010.

Today the policy agendas of the European Union ICT industry have shifted. Key agendas are Europe 2020[1] and the Digital Agenda for Europe.[2]

If, as reader, you want to go directly to the conclusive essence of this book, I shall recommend you to focus on Chapter One, where the author, Guido Reinke, presents his *New Governance Theory* and *Policy Making Model*. This theory and model may help policy stakeholders to understand and seek influence into the EU ICT policy governance processes today: Europe 2020 and the Digital Agenda for Europe.

Peter Engsig-Karup
President, CEO at Nuuk Sky Net A/S

Peter Engsig-Karup is an ICT Industry professional of 21 years, a graduate in political science and social economics from Roskilde University, and in business management from Copenhagen Business School. He has worked for the European Commission and Tele Danmark, and is currently President and CEO of Nuuk Sky Net.

1 Europe 2020. Please refer to http://ec.europa.eu/europe2020/index_en.htm.

2 Digital Agenda for Europe. Please refer to http://ec.europa.eu/digital-agenda/node/1584.

PREFACE

This book contributes to a better understanding of policy influence and regulatory compliance in the context of European regulatory governance and the European information society. It is addressed to organisations seeking influence or compliance strategies, regulators initiating "better regulation", and scholars wanting insight into the "new thinking" of both. It is the perfect guide for professionals and business personnel involved in regulatory consultation proceedings, such as project managers, corporate public affairs officers, and technical experts; as well as those responsible for regulatory compliance, such as compliance managers, data protection officers, COOs and CIOs. It will interest regulators, scholars and other policy stakeholders no less. The book provides insight, concepts and approaches particularly helpful for simplifying and clarifying the complex and dynamic role of Information and Communication Technologies (ICTs) regulation across all its fields and sectors.

European regulation has become much too complex for most stakeholders. It operates on multiple levels, is extremely fast-moving, and mutates from industry to industry. Businesses struggle to implement cost-efficient compliance programmes. Perhaps the greatest difficulty is to prioritise efforts according to risks and non-compliance impact. Regulators face similar challenges: they need to avoid issuing conflicting regulations; to ensure that the costs of regulation do not outweigh the benefits (*e.g. via* impact assessments); and to gain adequate insight into the regulated industry so as to avoid a heavy hand. To achieve their common objective of "better regulation", businesses and regulators have recently entered into a symbiotic relationship.

This book was written to assist business organisations and other stakeholders to participate successfully in the new consultation-style regulatory governance. By revealing informal stages of policy making where the stakeholder is likelier to exert maximal influence over the end-result, rather than rehashing the formal stages of EU legislation as usual, it provides practical tools and models for wielding influence in the decision-making processes of European regulation. It also comes to the practitioner's assistance in the aftermath of regulatory decisions, to provide cost-efficient ways of crafting and implementing an organisational compliance programme.

Amongst the book's many effective tools for maximising influence over regulatory decisions is a descriptive catalogue of over 600 international, EU, national and sub-national stakeholders, who have been recently involved in shaping ICT regulation. All of these are listed by name with weblinks. They are aggregated into a *Stakeholder Action Matrix*, a typology which maps stakeholder influence at all levels of European governance, showing the characteristic channels of consultation each type of stakeholders uses to make the deepest impact on regulatory decisions.

Other tools contained in this book are meant to serve the compliance efforts of business and other organisations. These include the *Regulatory Compliance Matrix*, a synoptic framework that for the first time ever categorises over 1,000 applicable laws, regulations and norms into domains of general and ICT-specific policy, then maps these categories to applicable standards, frameworks and guidance. Last but not least, a guide toward picking one's way through the minefield of regulatory compliance is given in the form of a *Regulatory-Compliance Maturity Model.*

In addition, this book has a strong theoretical component that should interest scholars. The *Industry Governance Theory* reveals that the pro-active role of industry in the new consultative regulatory governance has resulted in industry's predomination in shaping public policy, which it uses to further its business objectives of enhancing innovation, competitiveness, and consumer satisfaction. This inference is grounded in social scientific methods of statistical survey, participant observation, policy paper review, and case study. At its broadest it helps explain why mutually beneficial relationships between industry and regulators have emerged.

This book is based on many years of experience working first for and then with regulators and standards institutes, professional service firms and business organisations, seeing them from the inside and the outside. Having acquired multiple perspectives on regulatory challenges while being actively involved in many stakeholder activities over the years, the author understands how all sides think and has gleaned some unique first-hand insights. The concepts herein presented have been verified by application to multiple contexts by lawyers, auditors, operational risk managers, compliance officers and other stakeholders.

The models and matrices contained in this book will serve to guide both practitioners and researchers through the entire European regulatory process, from policy initiation and consultation through to stable monitoring of organisational compliance. Whoever is affected most especially by ICT and ICT-related issues will find this book a quick and easy reference guide to just that part of the regulatory framework applicable to you.

ACKNOWLEDGEMENTS

Working on a publication is a bit like climbing a mountain. With every step the view gets wider and one's view and one's own knowledge more humble. My professional and academic friends encouraged me to climb higher and discover new horizons in the "European policy and regulation" sky. I would like to express my gratitude to everybody who speeded my journey with emotional support and/or intellectual stimulation. It is essential to have an experienced "Sherpa" in order to avoid getting lost on one of your most challenging climbs. I was lucky to have Prof. Andrew Chadwick to supervise me in the arduous research that laid the foundation for this publication. He provided stimulation, guidance and challenge.

I also wish to acknowledge the important role played by the officials and experts who graciously allowed themselves to be surveyed and interviewed. They gave me access to first-hand information and valuable input without which my fieldwork would have been impossible. Special thanks go to two scholars for their guidance: Kyriakos Hatzares (eHealth expert, Imperial College, London, formerly at Worldcom) and Dr. Klaus Meyer (Oracle, Paris). The following legal experts and regulatory professionals provided sound advice on various aspects of this book: Gilbert Germain (PwC, Head of European Public Affairs Group, Brussels), Dr Hannah Ellin (PwC, Global Methodology Group, Boston), Marc Sel (PwC, Information Security Group, Antwerp), Ada Muirhead (Shepherd and Wedderburn LLP, Edinburgh; formerly at Ofcom), Prashant Joshi (Ernst & Young, Information Technology Advisory Services, London), Jack Nagle (Verizon, IT security specialist, Dublin), Peter Engsig-Karup (CEO at Nuuk Sky, ex-Head of Corporate Regulatory Affairs at Tele Denmark, Copenhagen; former Regulatory Expert at the European Commission, DG XIII A1, Brussels), Mark Windy (Belgacom, Telecoms Strategy, Brussels), Ermina van Hoye (United Nations, New York), Cor Berben (European Commission DGXIII A1, former Head of "Telecommunications Regulation", Brussels), Claire Hobson (DTI/BERR, Head of UK Telecoms Policy, London), James Hughes (Department for Innovation, Universities and Skills, London), Robbert Fisher (Joint Institute for Innovation Policy, Managing Director, Luxembourg), Glenn Meeks (ABN Amro, IT security, London) and Lee Lee Oh (HSBC, IT Risk and Compliance, London).

I would next like to extend my thanks to the librarians who offered advice and assistance at the British Library, the LSE Library, the Department of Trade and Industry library in London, the UK National Statistical Office, and the European Research Centre in Brussels.

This book was written with the invaluable support of Royal Holloway University and the London School of Economics and their excellent research facilities. My participation at conferences and workshops was made possible by several institutions and organisations: Ernst & Young LLP, PricewaterhouseCoopers LLP, European Electronic Messaging Association (EEMA), now the Forum for Electronic Business, and Intellect UK.

Finally, the intellectual stimulation of Jerry W. Bains and Osmond D'Silva challenged my basic concepts and through revision ultimately validated them, and the former's sharp pen saved me from the embarrassing typographical and grammatical errors that continued to evade my eye no matter how many times I reread this book. And my special thanks go to Ben Veal (Statistical Department, LSE), the statistician who helped me analyse my survey results and who provided guidance on SPSS testing.

ICT is a fast-moving area, and for this reason commentary on regulations and standards can quickly become outdated. I shall try to avoid this by timely updating my Regulatory Compliance Matrix, and making it available to a larger audience. Updated versions of the Matrix will be published in the form of handbooks in the near future. This will enable me to address a wider community consisting of practitioners, regulators and academics who share my interests and concerns, and to further develop solutions in this area.

Above all, I am thankful for all my friends and family who have supported and encouraged me, particularly in dark moments when I feared drowning in the flood of information. This book is dedicated to all my friends, who have always supported me in my publications and research, and given me their advice, their encouragement and their enthusiasm.

Guido Reinke

TABLE OF CONTENTS

FIGURES AND TABLES

List of Figures

List of Tables

GLOSSARY OF ABBREVIATIONS AND ACRONYMS

ACTS	Advanced Communications Technologies and Services
Article 169	Article 169 of the EU Treaty enables the EU to participate as an equal partner in R&D programmes conducted by several Member States, combining various national and regional programmes into a single joint programme.
BER	Better Regulation Executive
BERR	Department for Business, Enterprise and Regulatory Reform (replaced DTI in July 2007)
BIS	Department for Business, Innovation and Skills (created in June 2009 from the merger of the Department for BERR and the Department for Innovation, Universities and Skills)
B-ISDN	Broadband ISDN
BEREC	Body of European Regulators for Electronic Communications
BEUC	Bureau Européen des Unions de Consommateurs (The European Consumers' Organisation)
CBI	Confederation of British Industry
CEC	Commission of the European Communities (European Commission)
CCITT	Comité Consultative International Télégraphique et Téléphonique (International Telegraphy Consultative Committee; previous name for the ITU)

CEN	Comité Européen de Normalisation (European Committee for Standardisation)
CENELEC	Comité Européen de Normalisation Electrotechnique (European Committee for Electrotechnical Standardisation)
CEN-ISSS	Information Society Standardization System
CEO	Chief Executive Officer
COM	Commission policy document: Communication (of the European Commission)
CORDIS	Community Research & Development Information Service
CREST	Comité de la Recherche Scientifique et Technique (Scientific and Technical Research Committee)
DG	Directorate General (of the European Commission)
DG XIII	1986-1990: DG Information Market and Innovation 1990-1994: DG Telecommunications, Information Industries and Innovation 1994-1998: DG Telecommunications, Information Market and Exploitation of Research 1998-2006: DG Information Society (DG INFSO) 2006-2012: DG Information Society and Media 2012: DG Communications Networks, Content and Technology (DG CONNECT)
DG III	Directorate General Enterprise and Industry (DG Enterprise)
DIR	Directive of the European Commission (policy document)
DNS	Domain Name System
DTI	Department of Trade and Industry (replaced by BERR in July 2007)
EAAC	European Academies Advisory Council
EBU	European Broadcasting Union
EC	European Community
ECOSOC	Economic and Social Council
ECSC	European Coal and Steel Community
ECMA	European Computer Manufacturers Association

EEA	European Economic Area
EEC	European Economic Community
EIB	European Investment Bank
EP	European Parliament
EFTA	European Free Trade Association/Area
EMU	Economic and Monetary Union
ERA	European Research Area
ERG	European Regulators Group (replaced by BEREC)
ESA	European Space Agency
ESPRIT	European Strategic Programme for Research & Development in Information Technology
ETSI	European Telecommunications Standards Institute
EU	European Union
EU15	European Union 15 Member States, 1995-2004
EU27	European Union 27 Member States, since January 2007
EUREKA	European Research Coordination Agency
EUROCHAMBERS	Association of European Chambers of Commerce & Industry
EUROSTAT	European Community Statistics Office
EUTELSAT	European Telecommunications Satellite Organisation
FP5/6/7	Fifth/Sixth/Seventh Framework Programme (of the European Community for research, technological development and demonstration activities)
FTC	Federal Trade Commission (US)
FTP	File Transfer Protocol
G-7 Summit	Group of the 7 most developed industrial countries: Canada, France, Germany, Italy, Japan, United Kingdom, United States
G-8 Summit	Group of 8 (leading industrialised countries): G-7 and Russia

G-20 Summit	Group of the 20 major economies: Argentina, Australia, Brazil, Canada, China, France, Germany, India, Indonesia, Italy, Japan, México, Russia, Saudi Arabia, South Africa, Korea, Turkey, the United Kingdom, the United States and the European Union.
GATS	General Agreement on Trade in Services
GATT	General Agreement on Tariffs and Trade
GBDe	Global Business Dialogue on E-Commerce
GDP	Gross Domestic Product
GIIC	Global Information Infrastructure Commission
GSM	Global System for Mobile Communications
GPRS	General Packet Radio Service
3G/4G	Third/Fourth Generation wireless Telecommunications
HLEG	High Level Expert Group
i2010	European Information Society 2010 initiative for ICT research and innovation
ICANN	Internet Corporation for Assigned Names and Numbers
ICC	International Chambers of Commerce
ICT(s)	Information and Communication(s) Technology(ies)
IDA	Institutional Analysis and Development
IEC	International Electrotechnical Committee
IETF	Internet Engineering Task Force
INFSO	Information Security
IPv6	Internet Protocol (Version 6)
IRAs	Independent Regulatory Agencies
IS	Information Society
ISO	International Organization for Standardization
ISP	Internet Service Provider

ISDN	Integrated Services Digital Network
ISPO	Information Society Project Office (closed in 1998)
ISO	International Organization for Standardization
IST	Information Society Technologies
IT	Information Technologies
ITU	International Telecommunications Union
JRC	Joint Research Centre
JTI	Joined Technology Initiative
LAN	Local Area Network
MEP	Member of European Parliament
MoU	Memorandum of Understanding
N/A	Not Applicable
NGO	Non-Governmental Organisation
NRAs	National Regulatory Agencies
OECD	Organisation for Economic Co-operation and Development
OJ	Official Journal
OJ/S	Official Journal/ Supplement
OJ/C	Official Journal/ Court of Justice
ONP	Open Network Provision
PC	Personal Computer
PKI	Public Key Infrastructure
PR	Public Relations/Press Release
PROMISE	Participative Research labOratory for Multimedia and Multilingual Information Systems Evaluation (Multi-annual Community programme to stimulate the establishment of the Information Society, 1998-2002)
RCM	Risk and Control Matrix
R&D	Research and Development

RTD	Research and Technological Development
RACE	Research & Development in Advanced Communications Technologies for Europe (1990-1994)
SEA	Single European Act
SMEs	Small and Medium-sized Enterprises
TCP/IP	Transmission Control Protocol/Internet Protocol
TEN	Trans-European Networks
UMTS	Universal Mobile Telecommunications Standards
UN	United Nations
UNCTAD	United Nations Conference on Trade and Development
UNDP	United Nations Development Programmes
UNESCO	United Nations Educational, Scientific and Cultural Organization
UNICE	Union of Industrial and Employers' Confederations of Europe
UNCITRAL	United Nations Commission on International Trade Law
W3C	World Wide Web Consortium
WEF	World Economic Forum
WIPO	World Intellectual Property Organisation
WiFi	Wireless Fidelity
WRC	World Radiocommunication Conference
WSIS	World Summit on the Information Society
WTO	World Trade Organisation
WWW	World Wide Web
XML	eXtensible Markup Language
£	Pound Sterling
$	Dollar
€	Euro

DEFINITIONS OF TERMS

This book introduces some new definitions, resulting from the innovative concepts presented:

Industry Governance Theory: The pro-active role of industry in the new participatory governance of the regulatory regime, resulting in industry's predominating influence in shaping public policies, regulations and standards, in order to achieve the business objectives of enhanced innovation, competitiveness and consumer satisfaction. Industry governance has emerged because of massive changes, in particular, an entirely new approach by regulators to governance [of the ICT sector]; new market dynamics caused by the economic liberalisation of the Single Market, combined with the rapid technological advances unleashed by this development; and the emergence of a gamut of new market players with innovative new business models.

Regulatory Compliance Matrix: A comprehensive inventory of regulations currently in force and applicable to the ICT industry. It maps the principal domains of legislation, regulation and norms, and their content, together with all ancillary standards, frameworks and guidance.

Policy Influence-Timing Model: A *dynamic* model based on a Stages Heuristic idea, which analyses the policy-making process into seven distinct Phases (issue emergence, policy initiation, agenda setting, discussion and consultation, policy formulation, adoption and implementation, and review), which may be distinguished by their distinct acts and purposes. By tracking the variable participation of two main actor categories (stakeholders and regulators) through the Phases, the primary importance of agency to our understanding of EU regulatory policy is made manifest. The model enables a holistic view of the policy cycle as well, revealing that the influence of private stakeholders (especially large business organisations) predominates until Phase 3, when paramount influence over the policy process changes hands and public officials come more to the fore.

Four-Level Model: A *static* model describing stakeholder interactions and influence on EU policy at four Levels: Sub-national, National, European and Global. This multi-level governance concept defines the vertical structure of the Stakeholder Action Matrix.

Advocacy Coalition Typology: A scheme classifying advocacy coalitions into four main types; *viz.* Individual advocates, Public-sector and non-profit organisations, Industry-focused associations, and Project groups. It synergises with the Four-Level Model, greatly simplifying the stakeholder behaviour and belief systems across all Levels of governance. The reader should note that the term "advocacy coalition", a term found in the literature of interest groups, is herein used in a modulated sense. The Advocacy Coalition Framework (ACF) originally propounded by Paul Sabatier and Hank Jenkins-Smith resembles political coalitions in being constantly in flux. By contrast, the Typology herein presented features precisely rather those aspects of stakeholder behaviour that are permanent and characteristic; so that the "Coalitions" in question constitute durable communities of mentality and therefore self-interest, at a high level of generality.

Stakeholder Action Matrix (Four-Level Model by Advocacy Coalition Typology): This Matrix is a scheme of simplifying and classifying the participatory action of stakeholders both by level of governance and by stylised motivation. It is the synthesis of the Four-Level Model and the Advocacy Coalition Typology also presented hereinbelow. The resulting Matrix contains sixteen characteristic stakeholder action modes.

Regulatory Compliance Maturity Model: A model for estimating how far an organisation has progressed in meeting its regulatory objectives. It maps out maturity over four ontological pillars (governance, controls, people, and technology) interacting with five levels of compliance (nascent, initiative, established, advanced, and perfected). Refer to Section 8.5.3 for further details.

Received terms used in this book:
Other terms used in this book are to be understood in the sense received from the relevant literature. The reader is referred to Appendix One in case any confusion arises as to the precise meaning or scope of the following terms:

- Information Society
- Information and communication technologies (ICTs)
- Industrial policy, policy-making, regulation, and standards (including *de facto* standards)
- Actors, stakeholders, interest groups, lobbyists, and decision-makers
- Governance

THE PRACTITIONER'S OUTFIT: HOW THIS BOOK ADDS VALUE IN THE FIELD

In matters of European industry regulation, most businesses and practitioners feel inadequately prepared just to deal with (let alone influence) state and quasi-state regulatory bodies. Many do not even contemplate participation or direct involvement, but (if they do anything at all) delegate responsibility to "expert" consultants, or hire public relations agencies, or outsource functions to specialist contractors, or rely implicitly on professional bodies and industry associations to handle such matters. It is too widely assumed that the daily workload leaves no time left over, or that no private action can avail. Actual experience refutes this misconception.

This book furnishes a practical toolkit that may applied to achieve pro-active "regulatory intelligence" and policy influence. If applied consistently so as to become in time an integral part of "business as usual", it is a powerful route to success. Attending stakeholder events and talking to regulators (or just listening to them) can teach participants incredibly much about upcoming and likely costly regulation *before* it is even drafted. Then one can work pro-actively to influence the outcomes of the regulatory policy process, while also undertaking compliance preparations far in advance of implementation.

Toolkit One: *Stakeholder Action Matrix*
(Four-Level Model by Advocacy Coalition Typology)
The Stakeholder Action Matrix has remarkable potential leverage for planning strategic decisions about regulatory governance. Often practitioners in the field of regulatory compliance and risk management feel overwhelmed by the apparently bottomless complexity of Europe's multi-level governance structures, and may end up missing the "big picture" and focussing too narrowly on just some aspects of it. The role of one's own organisation in this governance is not self-evident and is certain to seem smaller than it actually is. Practitioners need to know more than just the obvious; many are the unforeseen ways by which even small and medium-sized organisations might take action in regulatory matters. The Matrix reveals which "stakeholder action modes" (or elemental collective-action channels) exist. From this it is possible to choose an overall *configuration* of such modes of action that best fits one's own organisation in the pursuit of its political goals.

Toolkit Two: *Stakeholder Directory*
The Stakeholder Directory in Appendix Six is another tool of enormous potential leverage. It is the gamut of active stakeholders, from which one may choose a whole range of new allies (while becoming aware of likely rivals) in the competition for regulatory outcomes. Attending events sponsored by industry associations or regulators is not only "educational", it may also be one of the best opportunities to mingle with influential peers. It may even lead to new business opportunities and partnerships, particularly for public-sector funding. There is also evidence that *thought leadership* originating with private business organisations may bring about state action toward profitable regulatory reforms.[3] A business that knows which channels of communication and networking are the most influential for the purpose is better positioned to disseminate valuable information to the most interested audiences.

Toolkit Three: *Policy Influence-Timing Model*
One of the most difficult problems in the strategic management of compliance and risk consists of determining the priority and the timing with which one's own organisation must address regulatory governance issues. The Policy Influence-Timing Model empowers companies wishing to influence the outcomes of upcoming regulatory policy initiatives to identify where their minimally costly and maximally beneficial intervention would lie in the policy lifecycle, *i.e.* when and how resources are best deployed to try and achieve the desired effects. (As any such resources need to be cost-justified, this model may also aid in planning the allocation of resources to participation in the policy cycle.)

The combination of this toolkit with the Stakeholder Action Matrix empowers the user to plan, execute and monitor their engagement with the regulatory governance of the industry, from participation to compliance, at the highest strategic level. Regulatory knowledge can then be developed in-house and strategic multi-level networks built at lowest cost.

Toolkit Four: *Regulatory Compliance Matrix*
The complex, dynamically mutating European regulatory environment necessitates that business organisations, especially, must quickly and intelligently adapt. The universe of potentially applicable regulations is vast, poorly documented and intimidating. The Regulatory Compliance Matrix comprehensively maps this universe, bringing simplifying structure to the whole by dividing it into thematic clusters for quick and comprehensive identification of areas of non-compliance risk. A corollary benefit is that the Matrix matches regulatory obligations with best practice guidance and solutions.

Toolkit Five: *Regulatory Compliance Maturity Model*
This book also provides practical advice and tools for business organisations on how to manage compliance programmes effectively (see Chapter Eight). This Chapter in particular, helps the reader with an understanding of the challenges that businesses have when it

3 As an employee in the assurance services for twelve years, the author has been a participant observer of many surveys, commissioned by private third parties and quoted in the press, the results of which exposed weaknesses in state organisation and galvanised the state concerned toward improvements.

comes to compliance, whom does it benefit most, the key benefits of using the herein-presented approach and the four compliance domains (governance, policy and processes, people, and technology). This Chapter then presents compliance phases and practitioner toolkits, including the widely used Risks and Controls Matrix (RCM) for compliance risk identification and assessment, a newly developed Regulatory Compliance Maturity Model (a detailed model for immediate use is included in Appendix Seven), and the concept of Heatmaps and Roadmaps that plan the way forward.

A STRUCTURAL OVERVIEW OF THIS BOOK

In an increasingly regulated world Eurosceptics claim that EU politics follows a supra-national state logic dominated by Eurocrats in Brussels who override at will national, citizens' and company preferences. They claim that national interests risk being ignored, with an often negative impact on the control by European peoples over their own economies, finances and even cultures. However, Europeanisation is more complex than that and calls for a more balanced view.

This book finesses these widespread populist claims. It offers empirical evidence and theoretical modelling that, in the field of Information and Communication Technology (ICT) at least, policies and standards have been shaped through a consultative process in which European regulators, the Member States, independent national regulatory agencies (NRAs), standards institutes, global organisations, business interests and other stakeholders interact with each other quite intensely. It is demonstrated that business is the crucial factor in this process, especially industry experts and industry associations. Commercial stakeholders have experience of and insight into whether and how the EU's legal and regulatory interventions actually benefit the market, businesses and consumers. This book investigates the variety of strategies that ICT and other companies have adopted and deployed in order to participate effectively in the policy-making processes that are now influencing the direction of Europe's Information Society.

A comprehensive review of policy papers, the analysis of a Europe-wide survey, and insights into stakeholder participation in the new Regulatory Framework for Electronic Communications (*a.k.a.* eCommunications Framework) has revealed that European ICT policy does not follow a simple supra-national state logic, but is shaped by a combination of international initiatives, global market factors, public consultation processes, interest groups, and Member-State influences. Here is evidence that stakeholder interests, particularly large business interests, predominantly influence European regulators. Also highlighted is the importance of the EU economic legal framework, in pursuance of which European legislators have adopted an approach to Europe-wide ICT policy that requires stakeholder input. Nowadays ICT policy development cannot succeed without commercial stakeholders' involvement in the policy process.

This book is divided into four Parts. The first Part (titled *Core Concepts*) presents the author's contributions to the better understanding of the EU policy process, especially as it relates to the ICT industry. This consists of an *Industry Governance Theory*, a *Policy Influence-Timing Model*, and a *Four-Level Model*-cum-*Advocacy Coalition Typology* yielding a Stakeholder Action Matrix. These original concepts should be understood as supplementing, not contradicting the standard theories of EU governance that fall under the rubrics of intergovermentalism, supranationalism and neofunctionalism. They explain in part the emergence, as the ultimate outcome of the complex relationships between stakeholders at all Levels of governance, of *industry governance* over the entire policy cycle.

The second Part (titled *Theory and Methods*) outlines the main conceptual sources of the author's ideas as well as the methods applied to develop them further. It reviews existing theories of business influence and "new governance", policy processes, multi-level governance of the EU, and policy networks and communities. It also discusses policy-process and business-influence models derived from studies of politics, all in Chapter Two. This laid the foundation for the core concepts presented in Part I. The ways and means of validating these concepts are then presented in Chapter Three, including methods of collecting primary and secondary data, and how data reliability was achieved through triangulation and saturation. Explained too are the "abductive" methods of logical inference brought to bear; the Grounded Theory precepts governing the processing of the large amount of information gathered in the field; the ways of handling primary and secondary data; and how models were assessed for explanatory power, relevance and completeness.

The third, an empirical Part (titled *Core Findings*) furnishes to the practitioner a ready-to-use synopsis of European ICT regulatory and standards policies. Chapter Four introduces the concept of the European Information Society, and provides background information on European ICT policy and regulation, examining their impact on the industry. A detailed list of all current regulations and standards (see Appendix Five) was compiled into a *Regulatory Compliance Matrix*, presented in Chapter Four. Next, the main actors (regulators and stakeholders) in European ICT policy making are identified, and their involvement in a multi-level decision-making process is discussed. Various forms of stakeholder participation are described in Chapter Five, including committees, consultations, studies, framework programmes, and other vehicles. The data collected have yielded a directory of the Sub-national, National, European and Global stakeholders involved in ICT policy (see Appendix Six, Stakeholder Directory). This Part continues by analysing the data collected from a Europe-wide Survey of practitioners, presented in Chapter Six. From a case study of the EU eCommunications Framework (2006) emerged Chapter Seven, which examines at the National, European and Global Levels the involvement of industry associations in policy-making, both "active" (*viz.* hosting workshops and collaborative events, coordination of responses to public consultations) and "passive" (*viz.* showing up at stakeholder events, dissemination of information to members).

The fourth Part (titled *Applications Theoretical and Practical*) provides in Chapter Eight the tools and guidance needed to implement in-house regulatory compliance programmes. Chapter Nine concludes by bringing together all the results of the author's empirical and theoretical contributions, and draws from them the master lessons. These lessons are offered in hopes of showing practising stakeholders how to manage regulatory compliance more effectively, while also advancing our understanding of the EU's actual ICT policy processes.

PART I

Core Concepts: Industry Governance – Models and Matrix

The noblest pleasure is the joy of understanding.
(Leonardo da Vinci, 1452-1519)

CHAPTER 1

A NEW GOVERNANCE THEORY AND POLICY-MAKING MODEL

A new understanding of regulatory governance is here presented. It has emerged from the author's practical experience of the challenges stakeholders face in complying with complex regulation, combined with his participation regulatory processes on multi-levels. All of the findings are supported by scientific research methods. The fruits of these labours have been presented in this Chapter in the form of practical interactive models of the European Union regulatory policy-making process. At the most general level, these new conceptions rest on an interactionist framework that assumes the primary importance of individual and corporate agency. The actors involved are assumed endowed with certain capabilities and specific cognitive and normative orientations, and although they act within a given institutional setting and a given external policy situation, these settings are assumed to leave room for entrepreneurial initiative.

In order to explain stakeholder influence over ICT policy, these new concepts must show how diverse stakeholders may affect the regulatory agenda of the EU. Chapter Two presents ways of theorising stakeholder relationships. Bear in mind that these theories complement rather than contest each other; for example, the process approach (*viz.* the Stages Heuristic) theorises policy as steps in a process, the interest-based approach (*viz.* Epistemic Communities) ignores process as such to view stakeholder influence in a timeless way.

This Chapter consists of six Sections. The first and second introduce the reader to the importance of the ICT industry for Europe's economy and the basic rules of European governance. The third Section expounds the Industry Governance Theory applicable to the ICT (and presumably many another) industrial sector of the Single Market. The fourth Section introduces the analysis of decisional processes over time, and uses the analytical results to theorise a Policy Influence-Timing Model. The fifth Section expounds the Four-Level Model, a point-in-time perspective on the "levels" of EU governance. It then proceeds to generalise about the overarching motivations and characteristic modes of action of certain stable coalitions of stakeholders, which yields an Advocacy Coalition Typology. This Typology is synthesised with the Four-Level Model to produce a Stakeholder Action Matrix, and the synergy effects of the collaboration of diverse stakeholders within this scheme are noted. The last and sixth Section presents an assessment of the models, based on standard criteria for evaluating the goodness of models. The purpose of all of these concepts is to improve our understanding of the interaction between private and public interests in the EU policy arena.

1.1 THE IMPORTANCE OF THE ICT INDUSTRY

The "Information Society is evolving at an increasing speed. The accelerating convergence between telecommunications, broadcasting multimedia and information and communication technologies (ICTs) is driving new products and services, as well as [new] ways of conducting commerce" (Ducatel, Webster and Hermann, 2000:12). Globalisation and market liberalisation are also contributing to these developments. Former Microsoft Chairman Bill Gates has noted, "Business is going to change more in the next ten years than it has in the last fifty" (Gates, 1999:xv), due to the implementation of new ICTs across all sectors of the European space. The changes include: the importance of knowledge resources; mutually encroaching industrial sectors; the importance of economies of time; the growth of micro-businesses and self-employment; network-like structuring of companies; the need for a global presence; and the rise of service clusters (Bosch, Webster and Weissbach, 2000:99-118).

ICTs have occasioned an industrial revolution more world-changing than all that have come before; one based not on material goods, but on information. Global liberalisation and the exploitation of information has opened the floodgates of opportunity to competition, foreign investment and the creation of new services in previously closed societies. The World Summit on the Information Society characterises this phenomena as follows:

> This dynamic promises a fundamental change in all aspects of our lives, including knowledge dissemination, social interaction, economic and business practices, political engagement, media, education, health, leisure and entertainment. We are indeed in the midst of a revolution, perhaps the greatest that humanity has ever known. (Working Group 1 on Civil Society Participation in the WSIS, 2002:2)

The rapid progress of information and telecommunications technologies, and its impact on the workplace and society, is a background assumption of this book (Apgar, 1998).

The importance to the Single Market of ICTs and of (even individual segments of) the ICT sector can hardly be exaggerated. "The e-communications services sector continues to represent the largest segment ... accounting for 44.4% of the total value [...] The [whole ICT] sector was worth €614 billion in 2005, €273 billion of which derived from e-communications services [...] The production and use of ICT accounts for around 40% of productivity growth and one quarter of overall growth in Europe" (CEC, 2006p:2). Estimated to be fluctuating between 3.8% and 4.7% *per annum*, the growth of the ICT sector is very strong.

The evidence indicates that capital expenditure in the European ICT sector (measured in terms of capital expenditure) has been as high as or higher than in other world regions. Having increased by 6% over 2004, total investment stood at €45 billion in 2005, the third consecutive year of expenditure growth (CEC, 2006z:12). The European Commission found a correlation across Member States between their broadband investment and the competitiveness of their electronic communications infrastructure. Higher broadband penetration was found where telecoms incumbents[4] were competing with newcomers more fiercely (CEC, 2006aa). It is

4 The term "incumbent" in the European telecommunications sector means: "Telecommunications organisations granted special and exclusive rights by Member States" (CEC, 1990b) or public operator(s) which enjoyed a *de facto* monopoly before liberalisation.

thus no surprise that the Commission has spotlighted research and investment in the ICT sector as one of its top priorities, constituting one of Europe's main chances for economic development and job growth. This on-going growth has continued even during the recent economic slowdown. For example, business broadband penetration in the EU27 continued to increase steadily from 45.6% in 2004 to 89.2% in 2012 (OECD, 2012; OECD website – Key ICT indicators, 2012).

The Information Society is challenging the standards of businesses and regulators with new practices like teleworking, developments compounded by the new regulatory governance framework which features a strategic commitment to fostering new modes of production. Homely things like regulations and technical standards have emerged as important success-factors for the ICT industry (Pelkmans, 2001:432-453). Issues of competition, information security, intellectual property protection have become critical, and must be addressed by self-regulation if not by law. The centrality of governance is now universally acknowledged (Wendy, 2000: 38-39, 48-87).

Regulatory governance affects business in mundane ways as well. In the sub-sectors of telecommunications and broadcasting, for example, operating requires a licence from the state. More subtly, the market is likelier to resist non-standard products. ICT companies realise that the government must determine how they operate. Although acknowledging the general helpfulness of regulations and standards, business has always understood the need to assert itself lest regulatory proposals hinder growth and development.[5] A pro-active, precautionary, preventative strategy is indicated that sets high-level goals and pioneers policy-input pathways for stakeholder participation in issue emergence, agenda-setting, and policy consultation – the formative stages of policy-making. Many companies now recognise the desirability of developing a strategy for participating in the policy processes of regulators and standards institutes. This book shows how business organisations and other stakeholders have been forging working relationships especially with regulatory officials and standards institutes, who are more willing than ever to view policy from a business perspective.

The main incumbents in today's market for eCommunications services are telecommunications network operators enjoying some structural superiority (*e.g.* infrastructure, coverage of services) and competitive advantage (Significant Market Power) in the market over new market entrants. This relates to the operators' legacy position, deriving from their former exclusive rights as monopolists to serve an area, which often led to the assumption of extensive market powers by the regulated and state-owned (*i.e.* traditional) monopolies.

In the case of mobile telephony, however, the term "incumbent" may refer to a subsidiary of the incumbent in the fixed telephony market.

The term is also used in media, where it refers to television or radio stations that have benefited from government-granted broadcast licenses.

5 For example, the International Chamber of Commerce (ICC), having become an advocate for thousands of its member companies and associations from about 130 countries, is promoting minimal government intervention. Their preferred option is self-regulation through codes of conduct (Farrell, 2003, Hassan, 2003; ICC Commission on E-Business, 2003).

1.2 THE GENERAL NATURE OF EUROPEAN GOVERNANCE

The policy-making processes of the EU institutions have sparked much criticism. The debates swirling around the Maastricht Treaty and, later, the Constitution, alleging the excessive policy-making of the European Union (EU),[6] have usually singled out the Commission. The anti-Maastricht position was that the EU has been overregulating the economic and social life of Member States. Certainly the locus of decision-making has shifted dramatically. Cowles estimated that in 1995 some 60% of all legislation addressed to European industry was stamped "made in Brussels" (Cowles, 1995:225-236). Ten years later "the EU set over 80% of the rules governing the exchange of goods, services and capital in the member states' markets" (Hix, 2005:4; Coen, 2009b:147-148). A huge corpus of EU law now affects the gamut of policy sectors; according to Hix, "on average more than 100 pieces of legislation pass through the EU institutions every year – more than most other democracies" (Hix, 2005:4). It is a complex edifice of policy-making, encompassing policy actors operating at multiple levels (Richardson, 1996a:2). International treaties and EU law have both introduced a complex dimension to policy making (Sewell, 1999:15). This book will focus more on EU regulation than national or international regulation.

ICT regulation is mostly in the hands of the European Commission and its Directorates General. Nugent suggests that "EU decision-making processes are strong on sectoralisation [specialism by Directorates General] but rather weak on coordination [of the DGs' sundry jurisdictions]" (Nugent, 1999:141). One would think that the scholarship on EU governance would have investigated the several DGs for insights into their concrete features; instead, it has contented itself with fuzzy generalities "from the top down" as it were. Much of this scholarship is, moreover, unsolicitedly prescriptive in nature, addressing perceived shortcomings of EU institutions, oversimplifying problems while underestimating the conflicting demands and pressures these institutions face from Member States and abroad. This book takes a different approach, beginning from the bottom up with the empirical facts, then generalising from there (but see Section 2.1 below).

It is not intended to criticise the EU legislative process itself, or to question their jurisdiction. The former has been settled for practical purposes by the Treaties and the Constitution, and the latter is assumed *arguendo*. The question this book takes up is how ICT regulation and standards-setting is carried on in actuality; in particular, given what has been found by previous research, how external stakeholders influence specific decisional processes. The importance of this for the European regulator itself – "opening up the policy process to get more people and organisations involved in shaping and delivering EU policy" – is highlighted by White Paper COM(2001/428final) on "European Governance".[7]

The key questions this book answers are, firstly, does the existing body of scholarship give due consideration to the ICT sector, probably *the* most important industrial sector of

6 The author acknowledges the important formal distinction between "European Community" (EC) and "European Union" (EU). However, as the distinction is not very relevant to ICT policy, for the sake of simplicity 'EU' and 'EC' will be used synonymously.

7 A large body of literature exists on institutionalism, institutional design and institutional reform, the debates of which lie beyond the scope of this book.

the European economy? Secondly, who are the stakeholders participating in regulatory governance, and are they driving the outcomes? Thirdly, is it possible to understand in simple terms the complex multi-level governance process? Fourth, what have stakeholders done to achieve success? Fifth and lastly, how have those subject to ICT regulation approached compliance?

1.3 INDUSTRY GOVERNANCE: A NEW RELATIONSHIP BETWEEN REGULATOR AND INDUSTRY

Before the EU telecommunications market was liberalised, telecommunications and postal services had been assumed to be a State responsibility. Consequently, the Member States' legal regimes were designed to suit the convenience of State-owned telecoms monopolies, leaving little room for competition. The State directly managed or "governed" State-owned telecoms operators or *régies*. At the end of the 1990s this State-dominated regime of State-ownership was transformed into an industry-driven and merely State-*regulated* regime. Three determinants are considered responsible for bringing about this massive change: first, the adoption by both European and national regulators of an entirely new approach to the governance of the ICT sector; second, new market dynamics caused by the economic liberalisation of the Single Market, and the rapid technological advances unleashed by this development; and, third, the emergence of a gamut of new market players in lieu of the former monopolistic *régies*.

1.3.1 The EU's new regulatory governance principles

The first determinant is the adoption by European and national regulators of a sea-change in their approach to governance itself, adopting principles of good governance outlined in the European Commission's European Governance White Paper(CEC, 2001d).[8] These included openness, participation, accountability, effectiveness, and the conformation of policies to the EU's Action Plans and other socio-economic agendas. The policy objectives defined in the Lisbon Agenda, and in key White and Green Papers stemming from the Information Society project, called for regulatory policies that enhanced European competitiveness and economic growth, creating value for consumers and citizens. Building confidence in the Single Market necessitated "economical [*i.e.* thrifty] policy objectives" that would feature fair competition, investment, accountability, and consumer choice, in lieu of the continuing defence of state-owned monopolies.

The data collected for this book clearly evidences that this new "economical thinking" forms an essential part of European-integration policy. For example, the Commission's Staff Working Documents SEC(2006)816 and SEC(2006)817 assessed whether the eCommunications Framework would encourage the transnational investment and innovation that could lead to higher pan-European economic growth. This economical regulatory impact analysis was supported by recent studies undertaken for the Commission (CORDIS, 2006b);

8 The European Governance White Paper made the provision that the Commission should develop, by the end of 2002, a more systematic and pro-active approach to working with key stakeholders and associations to enable them to contribute to decision shaping and policy execution.

statistics from EUROSTAT;[9] other sources such as the OECD (*e.g.* OECD Regulatory Reform Index for the Telecoms sector); as well as stakeholder input gathered *via* consultation. The Commission's view was that "competition drives investment, and that investment occurs even where [network-]access regulation is imposed, but that slow implementation of regulatory reform and poor application of the framework hold back investment" (CEC, 2006y:11). This led to the conclusion that "the framework is flexible enough to handle new and volatile markets, and allows regulators to take account of the need for risky investments to generate an adequate return on capital when imposing pro-competitive access obligations" (CEC, 2006y:11).[10]

The EU's eCommunications Framework is founded on the concept of regulating *markets* rather than technologies. This new market-based approach answers to the technological convergence still happening, and its technology-neutrality should bring about more competition between the players within each industry sector; whilst avoiding the contradictions (post-convergence) of the too technology-specific regulations that arise when networks and equipment are made the object to be regulated. The Article 7 procedure of the eCommunications Framework Directive on "a common regulatory framework for electronic communications networks and services" has now been implemented. It aims to: (1) promote regulatory harmonisation across the Member States on the basis of EU competition law principles; (2) limit EU regulation *to* the competition principles; and (3) furnish a transparent process for formulating and implementing these regulations.

The new governance principles and the market-oriented approach necessitate close co-operation with policy stakeholders, especially those close to the market who provide its services and products, lest regulators should fail to understand the real economic impact of their rules. This concept goes far beyond offering participation in research programmes, studies and pilots. The European regulator has taken ownership of its responsibility for stimulating competition and economic growth through better regulation (CEC, 2005e).

One important observation made at the 2006 eCommunications Review – the *ex post* evaluation of the Framework Directive – was that expanded powers and autonomy had to be given to National Regulatory Authorities (NRAs). The Commission's 2006 Impact Assessment confirmed that "the implementation of the framework depend [*sic*] heavily upon the work of the independent national regulatory authorities in each Member State while the processes created by the framework aim to ensure coordination and harmonisation of national efforts to create a consistent European market" (CEC, 2006z:33). The delegation of national regulatory powers to public bodies insulated from the influence of politicians (*i.e.* "quasi-governmental organisations", the so-called "quangos") is a trend that may be observed in

9 European Community Statistics Office. It gathers and analyse data from the different European statistics offices in order to provide comparable and harmonised data to the EU institutions so they can define, implement and analyse Community policies.
EUROSTAT website at http://epp.eurostat.ec.europa.eu (2012).

10 A vast body of evidence suggests that competitiveness has become the main driver of the Better Regulatory Agenda. Günter Verheugen, for example, the Vice-President of the European Commission and Commissioner for Enterprise and Industry, stressed the importance of competitiveness for Europe's innovation and economic growth (Verheugen, 2004, 2005a, 2005b, 2005c).

many industry sectors since 2000; *e.g.* the financial services and energy sectors.[11] But the trend has reached a new level of pervasiveness for reasons to follow.

Article 7 of the Framework Directive gives the Commission power to oversee national regulatory measures by holding "consultations" and "transparency proceedings". These proceedings require an NRA to conduct not only a national but also an EU-wide consultation on its own proposed regulatory measures, before it may adopt them. Consultees are to be provided with a definition and analysis of the relevant markets susceptible to the NRA's regulation and of the proposed imposition or removal of regulations on "undertakings" (*i.e.* profit-making businesses) that provide electronic communications networks or services. Article 7 delegates to the NRAs powers which traditionally lay within the jurisdiction of the European regulator. This delegation is a new development and a recurrence of the principle of "subsidiarity", that decisions are to be made as close to "home" as possible. The Commission has power to comment on an NRA's draft measures and, in certain cases, to veto its decisions. Out of more than 410 notifications as of 2006, however, the Commission has vetoed only a handful of cases (CEC, 2006g). One surmises that the Commission and the NRAs have worked so closely together since 2002 that both agree on the realities of the marketplace in each Member State.

"Delegation to independent regulatory agencies (IRAs)[12] has resulted in the emergence of a new mode of governance in Europe" (New Modes of Governance Project website, 2007). IRAs perform the following critical roles: implementing national and European law; exercising their regulatory powers and corresponding discretion; providing expert advice to national policy makers as well as supranational institutions like the Commission; and keeping stakeholders informed (New Modes of Governance Project website, 2007). Because of these innovative functions, IRAs are considered by policy advocates to be more responsive to the industry's calls to heed economic growth, competition and consumer rights than their statist predecessors.

The European standards institutes which are "official" (because the Commission's delegatees) have likewise been given more responsibilities by the Commission than before

11 For example, in the UK the powers of NRAs have been strengthened since 2000 through the restructuring of existing and the establishment of new regulatory authorities. These include, in 2003, the Office of Communications (Ofcom), combining five previously separate regulators; the Financial Services Authority (FSA), which replaced eleven financial regulators in 1997; the Office of Gas and Electricity Markets (Ofgem), established in 2000; the Information Commissioner's Office (ICO), replacing the Data Protection Commission in 2001; the Civil Aviation Authority (CAA), converted from a public corporation to an NRA in 2001; and the Medicines and Healthcare-products Regulatory Agency (MHRA) set up in 2003 to merge the Medicines Control Agency with the Medical Devices Agency. Additionally, consumer watchdogs have been set up to protect, promote, and develop the interests of consumers. Such are Postwatch, EnergyWatch, the Financial Ombudsman Service, and London Travelwatch.

12 *N.B.*: National Regulatory Authority (NRA) and Independent Regulatory Authority (IRA) are two different terms for one and the same thing. NRA is the term mostly frequently used on the European Level of governance in order clearly to distinguish these bodies from any EU supranational institutions; whereas on the National Level IRA is preferred as pointing out their special legal status respecting Member State governments. Both terms are used interchangeably in the academic literature.

the new governance, having now a central role in identifying, drafting, and implementing technical standards and guidance on behalf of the European regulator. This development has opened these institutes up to stakeholder participation. Many have even created vehicles specially for participation, such as working groups, and pro-actively invited stakeholders to participate in them.

1.3.2 New market dynamics

The second determinant of ICT sector governance has been changes to the telecoms market itself and by technical advances. Market liberalisation was instigated by advances like wireless and data communication. Economic data also suggest that mobile telephony will continue to grow strongly, boosted all the more by third-generation systems and their convergences. The convergence of telecommunications, IT, and broadcasting technologies will continue to reshape the industry, blurring the boundaries between data-, voice- and image-transmission, and impacting previous pricing models and challenging regulation of these sectors. These changes call for a coherent, consistent and integrated European regulatory approach.

Market- and technological globalisation is accelerating in breadth and intensity, creating new regulatory, technical, and commercial challenges demanding a global response. It has forced open the European ICT market to global competition, and has driven changes in European regulatory culture. Globalisation has enabled ICT service providers to shift their operations with ease to jurisdictions offering a regulatory approach more favourable to achieving their business objectives. Thus, industry-favourable regulation is crucial to attracting global businesses that contribute to competitive economic growth and job creation. Ian Bartle too has identified what he calls "techno-economic forces" as an important influence on the EU telecommunications policy process (Bartle, 2005:19-27, 190-191). He found that the European Commission had embraced a neoliberal regulatory culture as a necessity and a precondition of the competitiveness of European firms in the global telecoms market (Bartle, 2005).

If business and industry are driving globalisation, and globalisation is driving regulatory reform, it is then abundantly clear that business and industry have been governing at the most fundamental level of all, that of "globe-changer". It may be argued, however, that competition and globalisation have empowered consumers no less, who are demanding better quality at lower cost. If industry is not acting in consumers' interest, then at a minimum an opportunity would arise for independent consumer watchdogs and/or the Commission to intervene; as witness Directive 2002/65/EC on "Distance marketing of financial services", or Directive 1997/7/EC (the "Distance Selling Directive"), or Regulation (EC) No 717/200 on "International roaming". Industry Governance is not autocracy; the new governor must respond to the demands placed on it.

1.3.3 The emergence of new business models

The third determinant is the impact of technological change on business strategy. Not merely new service providers but even whole industries have emerged (*e.g.* wireless telecoms) that call for the removal of market distortions caused largely by incumbents. The IT industry needs free access to fixed (or local loop) and wireless networks in order to develop and enhance the services it offers. This situation has led to the founding of new associations representing the interests of industry and the strengthening of certain existing ones. These associations have not merely contributed to and influenced policy debates, but have also wrought changes in the ways their memberships perceive their own interests. Both Europe-wide and global liberalisation is causing an increasing number of mergers and acquisitions, unheard-of business alliances, and public-private partnerships. These profound changes have driven the development of European and global services in the ICT sector. The incumbents, that is, the former state-owned monopolies, have been forced to innovate and adopt new technologies, from telecoms equipment to IP services, in order, by becoming more competitive, to avoid being overtaken and taken over by other national telecoms-operators or by private consortia.

It may be argued that Member State governments had financial motives for making drastic changes to the regulatory landscape and for market liberalisation (Dunford and Perrons, 1993:9-35), in that the privatisation of state-owned companies generated tax and fee revenues for them. As the telecommunications market becomes entirely privatised, governments can find new sources of revenue. For example, European telecoms operators paid €109 billion in licence fees in the UMTS/IMT-2000 License Auctions for spectrum allocations. Indeed, many telecoms operators have been struggling under the financial burden, given also their infrastructure investment expenditures for 3G services, estimated to have fallen within the range of €148-224 billion by 2010 (McKinsey & Company, 2002). Thus, governments have adopted commercial principles, *viz.* maximising their own profit, in charging licence fees, meaning that regulator-initiated changes can negatively impact markets, if the additional costs and administrative burdens result in misallocation of resources. Deregulation is not guaranteed to promote efficiency.

1.3.4 The Industry Governance Theory

The data to be presented clearly shows that a conjuncture of renovated policy processes, redefined interests, and redesigned business strategies has overtaken ICT policy-making to alter the relations between the regulator and stakeholders, stimulating and redirecting them toward co-operation. The regulator and the industry both have strong incentives toward mutual co-operation, even to the point of becoming what has been called "symbiotic" (Cram, 1997:75).

It is contended that industry has become the dominant force not only in revising regulations and standards, but even in setting the policy agenda and defining regulatory objectives. One reason for this is that industry is closer to the "ingredients" that make for better regulation. Perpetually obliged to innovate services and products; to be accountable to shareholders for long-term objectives; to deal with consumers' dissatisfactions; and to face competition at all Levels – National, European and Global, – industry have a better understanding of market dynamics, of the products and services that consumers want, of emerging technologies, and of the overall "state of competition" inside and outside the European Union. But because business organisations create employment and are a major contributor to national and European wealth, it is also true that the new governance is purposely oriented toward accommodating the needs of business within the overall regulatory plan.[13]

The empirical research conducted for this book has also revealed a link between regulation and standards-setting. European and national regulators have the same interest as industry in the setting of common standards supporting regulatory implementation and allowing interoperability between products and services.

Based on the results of research and observation, a new term, *industry governance*, is here introduced. Industry governance may be defined as:

> the pro-active role of industry in the new consultative governance of the regulatory regime, resulting in industry's predominating influence in shaping public policies, regulations and standards, in order to achieve the business objectives of enhanced innovation, competitiveness and consumer satisfaction. (Reinke, 2009)

Indeed, industry can be seen as the driving force behind the new regulation. The principal players amongst industry stakeholders are not only corporate directors but also, surprisingly, other actors directly affected by regulations and standards, such as product and service managers, as well as technical staff and researchers (*cf.* Survey Question 2 in Chapter Six).

Other stakeholders include customers, employees, suppliers, and creditors. Of these, it might be supposed that the predominance of industry would shortchange consumers the most, as their participation in the regulatory process is much lower than business's. To the contrary, the liberalisation favoured by business interests has benefited consumers as much as producers. A macroeconomic survey reveals that the uptake of new technologies and interrelated services by consumers is very high. As one example, broadband penetration in the EU has risen almost 20 million to nearly 53 million fixed telephone lines in 2005, and average mobile phone penetration in the EU reached 92.8% in October 2005 (CEC, 2006p). By 2008 mobile phone penetration had topped 100% (CEC, 2009b). A microeconomic survey ought to show that competition amongst market players has increased, and has led to price reductions and the innovation of new services.

At its broadest the industry governance concept explains why "governance" (*i.e.* regulatory processes, rules and laws) has evolved toward a mutually beneficial relationship between industry and regulators. But whilst industry is of course the driving force behind

13 *N.B.*: this view chimes with classical economics, widely regarded as the first school of modern economic thought, and neoclassical economics. The publication of Adam Smith's *The Wealth of Nations* in 1776 is usually considered to mark the beginning of *classical economics*. Classical economists attempted (with partial success) to explain economic growth and development based on their investigation of factors such as prices, product demand and supply, and wages. The school was active into the mid-19th century, until it was discredited by Socialist thinkers, notably Marx. But its basic tenets made a comeback with the neoclassical school, beginning in Britain around 1870 with the marginality revolution of Stanley Jevons and others. *Neoclassical economics* is a general approach to economics focussing on individual and group choice based on preference relations. In neoclassical economics people always exchange things they value less highly for other things they value more highly ("prefer"). This activity is typically explained in terms of rational utility (relative happiness or satisfaction) and/or profit maximization. Collective enterprises are formed to earn profits, with some exceptions like cooperatives, non-profit organisations and (supposedly) government institutions.

industry governance, the theory should also explain why regulatory bodies are responsive to and dependent on the industry. Concrete instances corroborating the concept range from EU-sponsored initiatives that recruit industry experts to identify and resolve policy issues to the now-institutionalised participation of stakeholders in consultative policy-making. The following diagram summarises the key elements comprising the Industry Governance Theory.

Figure 1.1: Industry Governance Theory

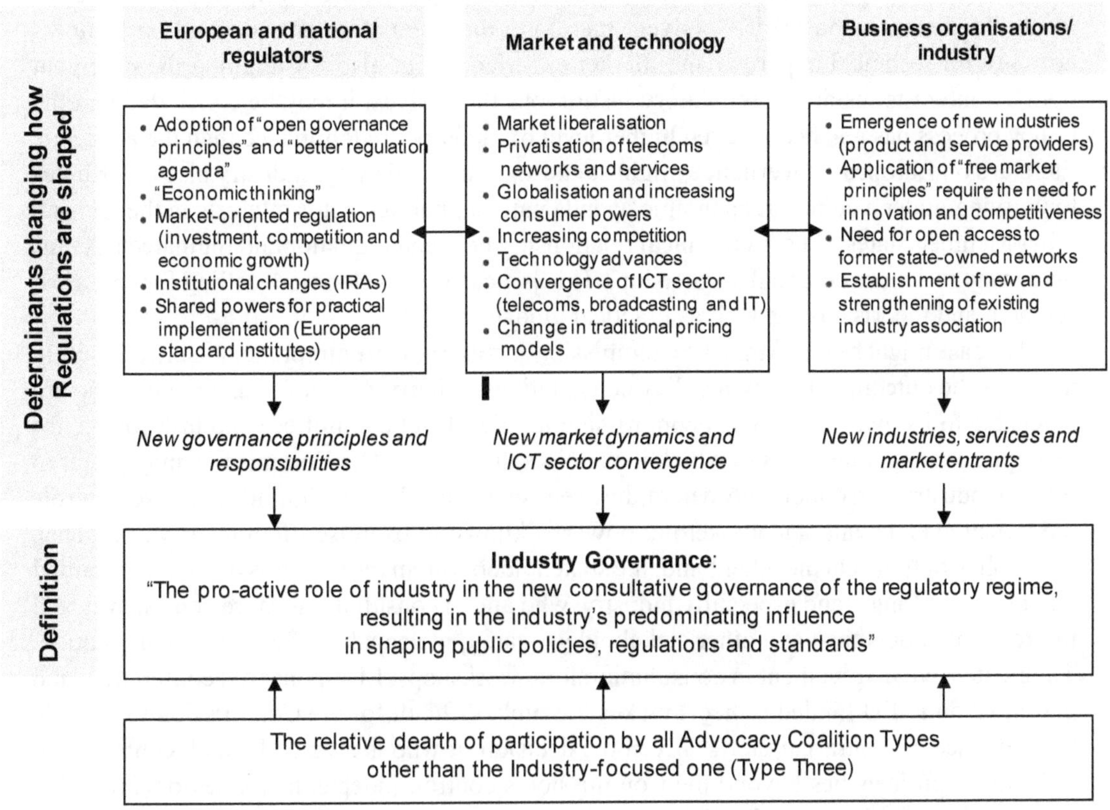

This new theory expands the debate on European governance by recognising the role of business organisations and associations in shaping policy, regulations and standards. As the evidence presented in subsequent Chapters will show, business organisations and their associations dominate the debate and formulation of ICT policies. Regulators, standards organisations, and other bodies responsible for developing and implementing ICT policies find themselves obliged to get into alignment with industry if their work is to be effective and benefit the market. Indeed, even their internal processes may not function properly without such an alignment.

One concern raised (by UK stakeholders) about EU regulation was the lack of "joined-up thinking between different European [Commission] Communications" and their policy proposals (BERR website, 2007). The EU's ICT-related policy outputs come from sundry

Directorates General: DG Information Society, DG Competition, DG Internal Market & Services, and DG Enterprise & Industry. This state of affairs recommends the utility of stakeholder participation in multi-level regulatory governance. Based on the evidence yielded by the Survey in Chapter Six, as well as on the author's personal experience working in the Commission and his participant observation in the decisional processes of CEN and BERR, it is concluded that businesses and other stakeholders who get involved in the activities and initiatives of unjoined-up DGs – which often do have different policy motivations and agendas – act as "glue" unifying toward a common economic objective the divergent political actors inside the Commission itself.[14] Given, therefore, that regulators now depend on business not only for technical expertise and market experience, but also for aligning the divergent political interests inside the regulatory institutions themselves, it may be concluded that the policy process has reached an even higher level of industry predominance than the academic literature on European governance might suggest. In the same way, industry also contributes to unifying under a common economic agenda national public-sector interests in the UK and other Member States. The hierarchical relationship between regulator and regulatee has thus given way to a more co-equal partnership. This is clearly a development calling for empirical research and theorisation as well as practical guidance.

The case might be made that the Commission acts as a policy entrepreneur itself, and subtly manages the outcome of its own policy consultations, "cherry-picking" stakeholders who are amenable to its own views when commissioning high-level committees and task forces, for example, over appointments to which it exercises discretion. The Commission may prefer to rely on industry personnel with whom they see "eye to eye". The Commission also controls the policy agenda, and agenda-setting power is known to exercise often decisive influence over policy output. On the other hand, the stakeholders whom the Commission has committed itself to consulting – and especially industry, who attend consultations more consistently and in greater numbers than any other stakeholders – are quite capable of counter-manipulation. Their extensive involvement in consultation fora, workshops, EU-sponsored conferences and participation in EU funded projects makes it doubly difficult for the Commission to exclude the influence of contrarian views. Even the decision of who is awarded which contracts for EU-funded projects lies beyond the Commission's control: independent assessors are relied on to evaluate such proposals. The new transparency regime and the widespread access to information that it fosters also empowers many more stakeholders than ever before to try their hand at policy entrepreneurship. These circumstances conspire to circumscribe the Commission's policy-making discretion more than sufficiently to open the door to systematic

14 This illustrates the thesis of Streeck and Schmitter (1985:121) that the interest-intermediating Association has become in the contemporary age an ordering principle at least as important as the classical principles of Community, Market and State. It vindicates too their insistence, in particular, that associations contribute as much order to the State as disorder. The author is aware that Community as defined in the social sciences – which includes family, clan, bloodline and ethnicity or nationality – is a principle of social order equally as important (in theory) as the regulator [State], the liberalisation agenda [Market], and business organisations [interest Association]. But it has been left out of account in this book because, in the context of ICT regulation, Community forms a uniform backdrop that harbours no distinctive dynamic properties bearing on the outcome of the new governance project.

influences which it can hardly master. It has become manifest that the Commission does not even try to make itself the undisputed master of policy.

The net result is a new alignment between regulators and industry in pioneering a less adversarial and more productive relationship which fosters the innovations, investments and technological developments conducive to European integration. Better services and products will be manufactured and offered to the public in a market that has been made stable and robust through the removal of barriers to investment and innovation; through the promotion of compatibility and interoperability in service- and product markets; and through pro-active co-operation between regulators, standards bodies, and industry.

In support of the Industry Governance Theory, and to introduce additional evidence of its explanatory power, the following Section presents two complementary constructs: the Policy Influence-Timing Model and the Stakeholder Action Matrix, two new approaches to the understanding of policy-making that describe better than previous theories the relationship between regulators, industry and other stakeholders.

1.4 POLICY INFLUENCE-TIMING MODEL

The following section summarizes the assumptions and the eight distinct phases of a new policy-process model, herein called the *Policy Influence-Timing Model.* Its components are brought together synoptically in the "Phase diagram of ICT stakeholder influence over the policy cycle" below, which graphically illustrates the waxing and waning of ICT stakeholder influence in the EU regulatory process, and in the diagram, also below, charting the phases of the EU policy process.

1.4.1 Assumptions of the Policy Influence-Timing Model

The Policy Influence-Timing Model is based on the theory of Stages Heuristic, which is described in more detail in Section 2.2.2 below. Although analytic rather than realistic,[15] this heuristic allows critical reflection over the policy process. The waxing and waning of stakeholder influence from stage to stage may thus be theorised, with practical conclusions derivable to the extent that stages exist in reality. The aim is to identify at which notional or actual stage of the process stakeholders may exert the most influence. The Four-Level Model of stakeholder influence, deriving from the concept of multi-level governance, lacks a temporal dimension, and is correspondingly well complemented by a Policy Influence-*Timing* Model.

As the case study presented in Chapter Seven illustrates, the policy process typically involves discussions, meetings, research, consultations, and coordination. Policy strategies are developed; compromises bargained and concessions made; and policy proposals reiteratively revised. The decisional process is essentially non-linear. Problems and

15 The originators of the Stages Heuristic called it such in acknowledgement of the fact that the real policy process is complex and does not proceed by neat, sequential stages. Nevertheless, even its severest critics (cf. Sabatier and Jenkins-Smith, 1993a, 1993b, 1999) admit that the concept has a definite "heuristic" value in breaking down an otherwise impenetrably complex process into manageable parts for analysis' sake.

solutions are constantly being defined and redefined. Often the actors are driven by strategic considerations of self-legitimisation – the necessity of mobilising support for a proposed course of action. Support may be conditional; compromises may be reached; actors may withdraw their initial policy initiatives from the process; and the information flow may be strategically controlled. Often several alternative courses of action may be formulated to try and resolve problems in one and the same policy domain.

To date it has been little investigated empirically how the EU's ICT regulation is shaped in actual practice, or where in the policy process and with what intensity and effect stakeholder input is likeliest to materialise. The case study in Chapter Seven demonstrates how complex the decisional processes may be; stakeholders are embedded in (nearly) every stage. Based on this deep empirical source, the author has constructed a model that stylises (accurately enough for the purpose) the iterative nature of the EU policy process, as follows:

(1) When new regulation is to be initiated and/or existing regulation reviewed, the EU regulator usually offers stakeholders opportunities for participation, both active (*e.g.* consultations, workshops) and passive (*e.g.* surveys). The EU's own principles of new governance and Better Regulation have effectively rendered stakeholder involvement mandatory.

(2) Shaping regulations requires of stakeholders a medium- to long-term commitment; to succeed best, stakeholders must: keep abreast of the policy direction (as by digesting the latest Green Papers, White Papers and policy Roadmaps); understand the economic and normative issues that drive the Commission (which at the core are competition, innovation and consumer benefit); and take advantage – consistently, if possible – of all opportunities for participation.

(3) Influencing the scope and form of regulation is best done in the earlier "stages" of the policy process. By the time the Commission submits a draft policy proposal to the consideration of Parliament and the Council, only very limited opportunities (if any) are left for stakeholders to influence outcomes. Moreover, compromises between industry, consumer groups, the regulator, and other parties are intrinsically easier to achieve during these early stages.

1.4.2 The Policy Influence-Timing Model: eight Phases of policy-making

It will be advantageous in developing this model to use accurate analytical labelling for the stages. The literature theorises, rather broadly, the stages of "formulation", which yields a policy proposal, and "legitimation", which induces adoption and implementation. It has been found empirically that this elementary dichotomy actually breaks down into *seven* distinct stages. Because this finding is unique (as far as the author knows), he has deemed it best to designate as "Phases" the stages peculiar to his own model.

As expounded by Lasswell (1951), Brewer (1983), and deLeon (1999), each stage (or phase) is distinguished by different acts and purposes. The beginning phases are the most interesting for the Policy Influence-Timing Model herein presented. The origination/ emergence of topics and issues occurs at the stage I have labelled "Phase 0". It is an activity typically pursued by industry players, consumers and regulators who are not acting in concert. By contrast, Phases 1 through 3 (*i.e.* policy initiation, agenda-setting and consultation) are typically driven by concerted advocacy coalitions and engaged epistemic communities. Strong evidence derived from the Survey, case study and literature reviews suggests that advocacy coalitions, especially industry associations, are the most influential actors during these three Phases. The later Phases (4, 5 and 6) of policy-formulation, -adoption and -implementation are typically performed by an entirely different set of actors, the EU institutions in co-operation with Member-State regulatory bodies.

These Phases need to be elaborated in depth for the Policy Influence-Timing Model to be rigorously defined. This undertaking is based on the evidence presented in Chapters Five through Seven.

Issue emergence (Phase 0)

Actors must perceive the existence of an issue and define the problems arising from it even before initiating policy making. Topical matters especially if negatively impacting economic growth, consumer confidence, or the previous regulatory objectives, generate controversy. The case study illustrates how the emergence of topical controversies is driven by many factors, amongst which are the Commission's Green Papers[16] that take note of recent developments and pose questions to stimulate debate. These Papers and other means of emergence such as open fora and annual conferences may draw upon recent research (studies, pilot projects and statistical data-gathering) that has presented new knowledge about a specific policy field and its evolution. Issues may emerge from prior agendas, even such as the broad political framework of the Treaty of the European Union of 1993, or the subsequent European Councils (*e.g.* the Lisbon Agenda agreed at the Lisbon Council in 2000),[17] which define the strategic direction of the EU as a political community. If an emerging issue captures the imagination of enough political actors, transition to the initiative Phase of consultation is characterised,

16 Green Papers are documents published by the European Commission to stimulate debate on a particular topic at the European level. A Green Paper usually presents background information and/or a range of ideas; raises questions; presents possible policy options; and outlines a proposed timetable for further action. The Commission invites relevant and interested parties (organisations, associations and individuals) to participate in consultations and discussions over the proposals it has put forward. A Green Paper and its aftermath may give rise to legislative developments which are then outlined in a White Paper. Examples are COM(97/623/EC), the Green Paper on "The Convergence of the telecommunications, media and information technology sector, and the implications for regulation: towards an information society approach", COM(98/596/EC), the Green Paper on "Radio spectrum policy in the context of European Community policies such as telecommunications, broadcasting, transport, and R&D", and COM(2005/576/EC), the Green Paper on "A European programme for critical infrastructure protection".
A complete list of Green Papers published since 1984 is available at: http://ec.europa.eu/comm/off/green/index_en.htm.

17 The Council of the European Union, or "European Council" for short, came into being in 1974 and was given formal status by the Single European Act. It meets at least once every six months under the chairmanship of the Head of State / Government of the Member State which holds the Council's Presidency, which also rotates twice a year. Article 4 of the EU Treaty provides, "The European Council shall provide the Union with the necessary impetus for its development and shall define general political guidelines thereof".

on the Commission's side, by White Papers[18] and Communications, which start up the new policy cycle.

Graphically illustrated in Figure 3.2 is the point in the policy cycle where the influence of private stakeholders (predominantly large business organisations, as evidenced below in Chapters Five, Six and Seven) begins to wax. Believing that regulation has a "big impact" on them (see Survey, Question 7), big business are more active, more continually than any other private stakeholders throughout all Phases of the process, although the absolute magnitude of their influence typically begins to wane after Phase 3. Most large business organisations operate a medium- to long-term strategy and take a holistic view of the policy cycle – involvement does not begin with the initiation of a new policy cycle; large businesses constantly monitor and interact with the regulator and are constantly embedding regulatory requirements in existing business practices. From the perspective of big business, it is not they who bring resources to the regulator, but rather, it is the formal public institutions like the Commission or national legislatures that bring critical resources to business, especially the authority to co-create decisions that will be binding on all.

Policy initiation (Phase 1)

Once an issue has emerged and become salient, formal initiation of the policy cycle ensues. An issue may not become "official" until it becomes recognised by *public* officials, but it is increasingly likely that it will have become political even before officials of the EU institutions have taken cognizance of it. The Industry Governance Theory indeed suggests that policy initiation may be take place outside the Commission, notwithstanding its role as initiator of EU policy; having emerged from the boardrooms of private corporations or other fora not usually recognised as "political".

In the EU, the Commission primarily has the responsibility of setting the policy agenda; however, it may well delegate this in detail to private stakeholders selected by itself. For example, the i2010 High-Level Group, who published the discussion paper titled *The Challenges of Convergence* (i2010 High-Level Group, 2006a). This Phase culminates in demands[19] being made on political authority, and with preliminary conclusions drawn and offered for official consideration. The initiative is then submitted by the Commission to the Council, so that formal endorsement may be secured.

---

18 Commission White Papers "are documents containing proposals for Community action in a specific area. They sometimes follow a Green Paper [previously] published to launch a consultation process at the European level. When a White Paper is favourably received by the Council, it may lead to an action programme for the Union in the [policy] area concerned" (Europa Glossary – "White Paper", 2008). Examples are COM(93/700/EC), the White Paper on "Growth, competitiveness, and employment: The challenges and ways forward into the 21st century", and COM(2001/428/EC), the White Paper on "European governance". A complete list of White Papers published since 1985 is available at: http://ec.europa.eu/comm/off/white/index_en.htm.

19 Demands may eventuate in the formal adoption and "translation" of issues into policy papers issued by the Commission. Multiple and often conflicting policy issues may be raised by various stakeholders. These issues need to be reconciled and formalised in policy papers, because these have the potential to lead to practical policy measures.

Agenda setting (Phase 2)

The Commission regularly uses White Papers to draw up a comprehensive agenda for a given policy domain. White Papers provide factual background based on recent regular reports and commissioned studies in the relevant policy domain. They also introduce new terminology to ensure that all actors speak the same language. White Papers provide reasons for the importance of a policy issue; present a checklist of policy ideas; and define "Action Points" formalising policy actors' responsibilities, along with timelines for the consultation, formulation and implementation Phases. White Papers often solicit the public's views and initiate a consultation process to confirm the agenda and, if required, to amend or enhance the objectives of the policy proposal.

The Council having endorsed the initiative, it proceeds to set a definite agenda by imposing an official timetable with deadlines. At this agenda setting Phase 2 the actors acknowledge the issues in question are redressable politically, and command that the process toward redress should commence on the European Level. The agenda is the definitive beginning of a new regulation or regulatory review.

Discussion and Consultation (Phase 3)

Once the clock begins ticking on the policy timetable, the door is opened for the official involvement of private stakeholders. As the case study reveals, the consultation stage takes place at both European and National Levels. After consultation is complete, the Commission publishes a Communication summarising the comments received on the main policy proposals and regulatory actions suggested by itself in the White Paper. The Commission then offers an evaluation of the consultation; sets priorities based on stakeholder input; and may even propose a tentative timetable for enactment and implementation.

The consultative process greatly stimulates debate. Survey Question 4.1 revealed that ICT stakeholders most preferred conferences and workshops (88%) and consultations (74%) of all the ways of participating in regulation and standards-setting. Stakeholders *ex hypothesi* have a strong interest in policies that affect them once implemented; therefore, they are also interested to provide the Commission with feedback, backed up with their experience, in advance of implementation. The Commission depends on input from stakeholders, not only because of their experience and expertise, but also because of the Commission's own set commitment, under the new governance principles[20], to work with stakeholders and to promote their participation.

Policy formulation (Phase 4)

Once all relevant consultations have been brought to a close, then official documentation, such as Commission Staff Working Documents, is usually published to communicate in-depth information about the proposed new policies. This may furnish statistical information and market data; summarise the findings of recent studies, not only commissioned by the

20 COM(2001/428final), the European Governance White Paper of 25.7.2001 mandates the European regulator to take all measures necessary for (1) better involvement and more openness, (2) better policies, regulations and delivery, (3) a European contribution to global governance, and (4) a re-focussing of staff efforts on policy revision.

Commission but also by other institutions and organisations; and outline the economic and normative rationales behind the proposals. The Commission may also publish impact assessments examining how well similar or previous regulation has achieved its objectives, and what the amended or new regulations should cover in light of technological and market developments. These assessments may also present policy options and alternative scenarios involving changes or no changes.

This is the Phase where the influence of stakeholders begins to wane and that of public officials waxes. Figure 1.1 illustrates graphically the general trend of stakeholder influence over the whole policy cycle. The reader should note that there is a crossing-point where the paramount influence in the process changes hands; this happens on the cusp of Phases 3 and 4. The literature mistakenly assumes that the politically appointed or career civil servants who officially initiate the action on public issues are the "engine" of policy formulation; but the fact of the matter is these actors do not begin to drive the policy process forward until it is already well underway. At this point, too, the legislator may also wax influential in formulating policy, especially when problems have been identified in existing legislation or have arisen from its implementation.

Adoption (Phase 5)

Once the Commission has drafted a legislative proposal for the European Council and Parliament, and finalised the corresponding Council Directives, external stakeholder influence declines rapidly (*cf.* Table 7.1: Roadmap for the 2006 Review of the EU Regulatory Framework). It may be that on matters that require clarification, European Parliament committees or Council working groups request expert hearings that lead to changes to the proposal, but major amendments owing to external influence are unlikely by this late stage.

Implementation (incl. Transposition) (Phase 6)

During the implementation phase the EU Member States must transpose the new EU law into the terms of their national legal systems. The most rigorously binding form of EU law is the *Regulation*, which is not transposed but is implemented "as is" throughout every Member State. *Directives* set common norms and policy goals for the Member States, but are indefinite enough to require "transposition" or adaptation to the national legal system. *Decisions* are legal instruments addressed to individual Member States and other legal entities subordinate to EU law, including even private companies.[21] Transposition normally ought to be completed within 18 months after the EU law was enacted by the Council and the Parliament.

Review (Phase 7)

Once a new regulation has been enacted and transposed into national law (and presumably implemented), the Commission may initiate a post-implementation review. However, as witness the 1998 Telecommunications Framework, which was not reviewed until 2004,

21 For further information on EU Regulations, EU Directives and EU Decisions, see Appendix 1.2.

up to six years may pass after enactment by the European Parliament, or four years after implementation by the Member States, before this happens. Often, such a review serves to initiate a new policy cycle that amends existing regulations or re-structures and revises them within a new Regulatory Framework.

As argued by Sabatier and Jenkins-Smith (1993a; 1993b), policy evolution entails multiple cycles involving diverse actors. Based on these research findings, the following diagram has been created to graphically display the waxing and waning influence of ICT stakeholders over, and the involvement of the EU regulator in the policy process.

Figure 1.2: Phase diagram of ICT stakeholder influence over the policy cycle

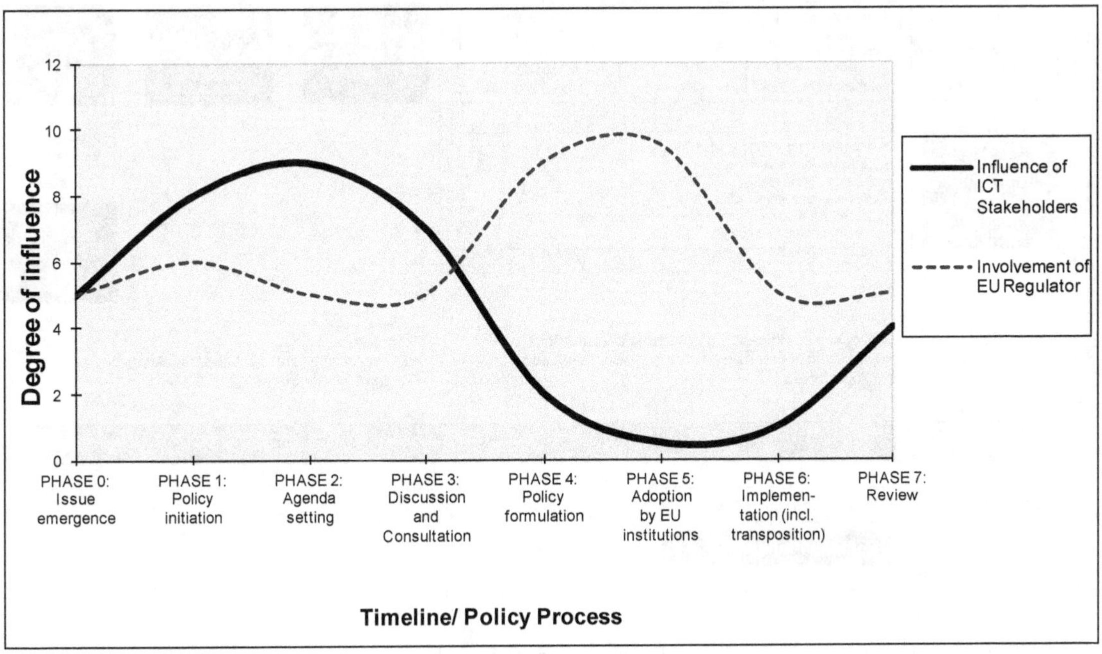

Up to four years may pass from the emergence of a policy issue to the enactment of a solution by the European Parliament. The whole cycle, then, including transposition and post-implementation review, typically takes nine to ten years; although it should be noted that considerable differences in the willingness of Member States to transpose EU Directives exist. This may occasion long delays in the actual implementation of the affected EU law, which cannot have effect before transposition into national law. For many businesses, particularly SMEs who struggle to see beyond the next quarter, it is difficult to get involved in such a complex, long-drawn-out policy process (Konings, 2007:38). This does not mean that SMEs have no influence on European policy, but it does mean large businesses' efforts at policy influence, exemplified by the birth of the European Round Table of industrialists, shifted to the European Level more readily than small businesses', who had no one to rely on except national business associations and ECOSOC, the EU's Economic and Social Committee (Coen and Dannreuther, 2003:255-275).

When we summarise ICT stakeholders' and the EU regulator's activities through the several Phases of the policy process, we obtain the following Policy Influence-Timing Model.

Figure 1.3: The Policy Influence-Timing Model

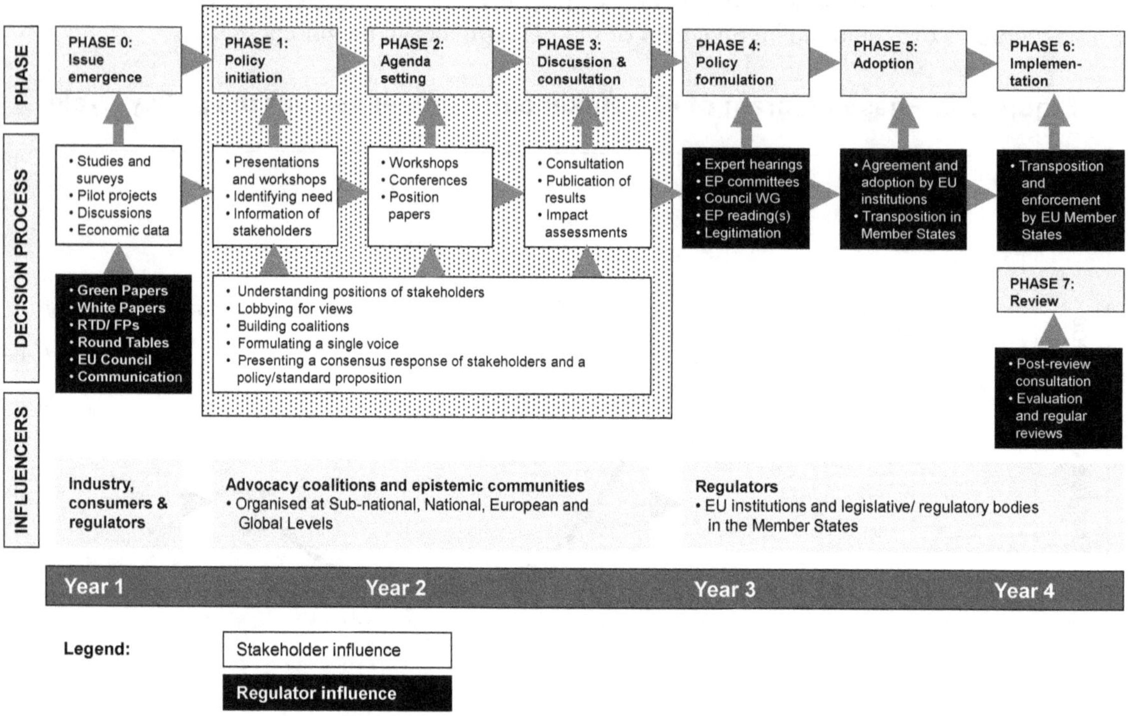

The *Policy Influence-Timing Model*, by tracking the variable participation of the two main actor categories throughout the policy cycle, implies the prime importance of actors to our understanding of how EU regulatory policy is shaped. One of these two categories – private policy stakeholders – is systematised in the following Section in order to perfect this theory of the policy process. This stakeholder model, which the author has named the Stakeholder Action Matrix, exhibits which "advocacy coalitions" typically coalesce to influence the opinions, views and directions of the officials – (the other main category) – who are regularly involved in the policy process.

1.5 THE COMPONENTS OF THE STAKEHOLDER ACTION MATRIX

1.5.1 Causality and the Four-Level Model: Multi-level governance

Most European scholars accept that the European Union operates at several administrative levels which exhibit all the features of "governance"; however, they disagree, often fundamentally, about the nature of the relations between the several levels of governance. The term "multi-level governance" which has swept through European studies in the last ten years has opened up debates and inquiries, as analysts have begun to compare the (official) policy dynamics between these levels. It remains none the less obscure how external stakeholders are involved in these processes, and how they influence EU policy at all the Levels identified in the author's model: Sub-national, National, European and Global.

Jeremy Richardson and like-minded scholars accept that a complex array of actors and institutions are involved in the policy processes at each of these Levels. He stresses that "the rapid internationalisation of agenda setting, and the internationalisation of policy solutions, has been an enormously powerful dynamic which has shown no more respect for nation states than it has for other policy actors" (Richardson, 1996a:2). Richardson talks of the steady Europeanisation of national policy processes, which has challenged the power and political organisation of national actors. Fritz Scharpf, who questions the legitimacy of EU rule-making, states that "the European Union is not, and cannot become, a unitary nation state; it can at best become a multi-level political system in which national and subnational units must retain their legitimacy and political viability" (Scharpf, 1994:12). This means the deconcentration of powers onto multiple levels, a development sets the stage for both private and public stakeholders to participate in EU policy making.

Multi-level governance must not be considered a theory proper, but merely a heuristic that helps us understand that policy is being influenced complexly (*i.e.* on multiple levels), but postpones rigorous explanation of the entire phenomenon. European governance is a complicated set of interconnected institutions that operate on sub-national, national, and supranational levels. Without addressing the issue of state sovereignty directly, multi-level governance simply asserts the probability that sub-national and supranational actors have been and continue to be creating a network-like governing structure that reaches beyond the formal bounds of state sovereignty.

1.5.2 Vertical structure of the Model: the Four Levels

The four Levels on which stakeholders wield influence, which together constitute the vertical structure of the model, derive from the "multi-level governance" concept. This follows Snyder's logic of law in distinguishing, in terms of hierarchical precedence, between National ("State"), European ("inter-State"), and Global ("international") Levels (Snyder, 2004). The case study and Questions 2, 3, 4 and 10 of the Survey also confirm that ICT stakeholder activities take place at all of these Levels.

A fourth Level (Level 1) of governance, however, additional to these three, was found to exist, whereon private, non-state stakeholders' activity originates. A well-rounded theory like Industry Governance cannot do without this Level. Its typical actors are described in detail in Section 5.1.1 "Sub-national Level". Private and public organisations at this Level have in common that they are governed (at that Level) not by the law of the state, but by their own operating policies, procedures, codes of conduct, and well-defined business objectives. Business organisations, especially, have internal rules that all employees agree to follow.

Actors on Level 1 communicate and bargain – whether business-to-business or business-to-consumer – predominantly with stakeholders on the same Level.

The National Level (Level 2) features actors who interact primarily in the arena of national policy, *i.e.* no higher than the jurisdiction of national law. Individual actors like politicians represent national interests. National regulators, local (*viz.* sub-national) and national governments, and trade unions are only able to enforce their wishes on other actors at these two Levels. National associations include members coming from the Sub-national Level while interacting in the first instance with other associations on the same National Level.

The European Level (Level 3) is populated by pan-European interest groups, Europe-wide industry-focussed associations and cross-sectoral business groups, fora connected to the EU organs, as well as to all-European standards institutes with and without EU links. Also included are European Project groups involved in programmes and initiatives funded by the European Commission to support EU policy objectives.

The Global Level (Level 4) is characterised by actors who represent multinational business interests, or who formulate and police international laws and standards. International law is "horizontal", *i.e.* lacking a hierarchically superior third-party enforcer. All stakeholders (primarily states and international organisations) are theoretically equal, and thus participate voluntarily in the formulation, observance and enforcement of international law. Most states and organisations, therefore, "enter into legal commitments out of self-interest rather than adherence [to anything higher]" (Tofan, 2008). "International law has no established compulsory judicial system for the settlement of disputes or coercive penal system" (Snyder, 2004). As discussed in Chapter Five, other international organisations active at Global Level, such as OECD, ICC, ISO and IETF, issue voluntary guidelines and recommendations, and promote industry best-practice standards.

The diagram below presents the Four Levels of stakeholder influence.

Figure 1.4: The Four Levels

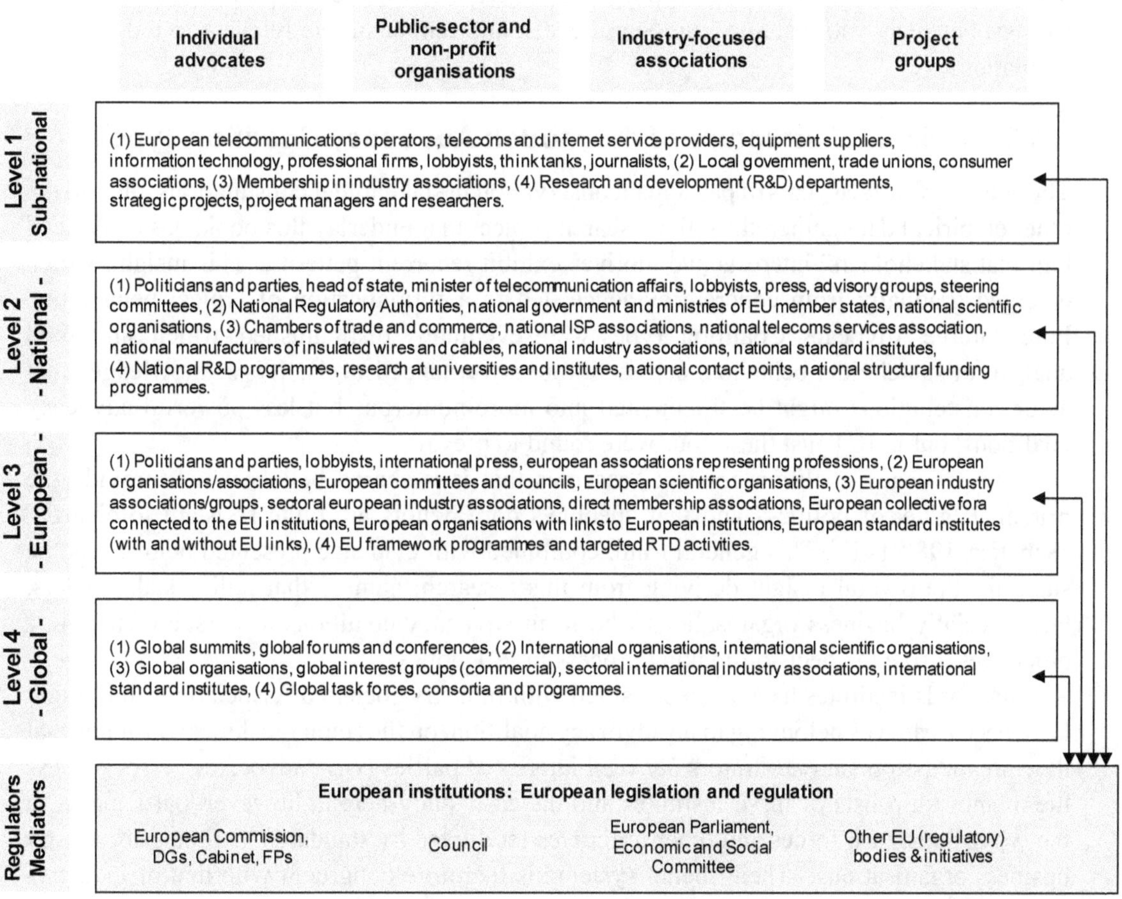

At this point the question arises, Why does this model recognise just four levels? Why not three or six or some other number? For example, a case could be made that the Sub-national Level might be broken down into several levels. A Private Level might be distinguished, which unlike all the other levels would not be territorially limited. Alternatively, the Sub-national Level might be sub-divided territorially into *e.g.* sub-national "regions", "metropolitan districts", "provinces", and/or "counties". Although such a detailed breakdown might bear on other policy domains, it would involve needless complications irrelevant to ICT regulation in particular. The relevant fact that all of these sub-national levels have in common is that they are subject to national and European governance, where ICT policy is actually made; therefore, it was decided to subsume everything below those two Levels under a "Sub-national" category.

Equally, a case could be made that the European and National Levels might be "fused" in the sense theorised by Wessels, and therefore be counted as one (Wessels, 2004, 2009). The EU's ultimate goal is to integrate the nations into one Europe, integrating national and

European ICT policy along with it. However, this goal lies far in the future; European integration is very much a work in progress. Therefore, for present purposes a distinction subsists between National and European Levels, and remains quite relevant to today's ICT regulation.

1.5.3 Horizontal structure of the model: Advocacy Coalition Types

The author's fourteen years of participant observation in stakeholder consultations, plus all the other empirical data gathered for the research project that underlay this book, has convinced him that stakeholders' interests and motives exhibit recurrent patterns. This insight, which emerged gradually from concrete evidence, led to a formalisation of typical behaviours. Four durable Advocacy Coalition Types were eventually distinguished, which simplified analysis of stakeholder behaviour across all four governance Levels. It is acknowledged that actor constellations might be fragmented into more numerous but less powerful advocacy coalitions, but in ICT just these four were found to prevail.

The advocacy coalition concept "assumes that it is shared beliefs which provide the principal 'glue' of politics" and that "people's core beliefs are quite resistant to change" (Sabatier, 1988:141). This general truth, combined with evidence presented below, sets the stage for the pivotal insight deriving from this research, namely that policy stakeholders, but especially business organisations who form advocacy coalitions to pursue their policy objectives, drive the decision-making process in ICT policy.

Standards institutes have been classified with Industry-focussed Associations, but might have been treated as belonging to no advocacy coalition, on the (rather technical) grounds that they are mediators and arbitrators *between* interested parties (*viz.* "advocates"). As witness the membership lists of these institutes and the case study herein, however, participants in the workshops, task forces and other initiatives facilitated by standards institutes are mostly business organisations. Their "belief system" is therefore congruent with that of industry-focussed associations (see Figure 1.5 below). Standards institutes were consequently classified with the "Industry-focussed Associations" Coalition Type. Standards institutes provide channels for industry input into the setting of standards pertinent to policy-making, thereby greatly facilitating industry participation therein. Thus, it was found by trial and error that the typological structure herein presented is the simplest, yet without sacrificing theoretical sufficiency.

The following characterisations of the belief systems of the four Coalition Types were distilled from the Survey data as well as from years of personal participation in EU-funded projects and stakeholder events at all four governance Levels. The National Level, for example, included eCommunications Review stakeholder meetings with BERR; the European Level, development of online privacy guidance with CEN; and the Global Level, participation at the ITU's Annual Conference. These examples are but a smattering of the depth and breadth of personal experience with both stakeholders and regulators and how they interacted at these and other events, which could be drawn upon directly as well as brought to bear on interpreting the Survey data. The belief systems of participating stakeholders were quite transparent, and vividly transpired in their remarks made at these and similar events.

The four main types of advocacy coalition were arrived at inferentially through logical methods which closely resemble those which Charles Sanders Peirce called abduction and abductive induction (see Chapter Three). All of these data and other supports are analysed in depth in Chapter Five, and manifested in the compendious Stakeholder Directory presented in Appendix Six.

I term *Advocacy Coalition Type One*: "Individual advocates". These may be employees, middle managers, lobbyists, journalists, "decision-makers" at committees and conferences, and certain other influencers such as researchers and technical experts. Type One comprises influential individuals whose belief system features a strong faith in Information Society technology. This Advocacy Coalition harbours more diverse views than the others, because individuals present individual opinions, rather than seeking consensus within a group, or following a formal process. Oftentimes views are extreme and unbalanced; for example, a politician or party activist involved in a re-election campaign will stress the achievements of their term, while the opposition and critical journalists will highlight the failures.

Advocacy Coalition Type One does not hang together because of any formal organisation or incentive structure, but through a common belief in the following tenets: (1) technology benefits society in a fundamental way; (2) business organisations cannot operate optimally, nor consumers and shareholders be protected, in an unregulated market where no standards, guidelines or rules of conduct exist; (3) a causal assumption that small business organisations and new market entrants will be operating in highly competitive environments and need some protection from the regulator; (4) monopolies and dominant market players are deeply to be distrusted; and (5) open market principles that incubate technological innovation are strongly preferred to over-regulated markets where economic initiatives are typically directed and subsidised by government (*a.k.a. dirigisme*).

Advocacy Coalition Type Two, which has been labelled "Public-sector and non-profit organisations" , is dominated by trade unions, consumer associations, governments, and certain European and international organisations. Differences of size and other heterogeneities of these stakeholders weaken the cohesion of this Advocacy Coalition Type over all four Levels, and on some controversial issues it may well break down. Consumer associations may disagree with national governments, and national governments may not support certain aspects of EU policy,[22] hence discovering a consistent belief system for this Type is difficult. All members do have in common that they are governed by formal organisations, and that their main concerns arguably fall within some "public interest" that features "social" responsibility and protection of the consumer.

Advocacy Coalition Type Three is "Industry-focused associations" . This group includes industry associations, commercial special interest groups (*e.g.* the Internet Service Provider Associations), professional associations, and employers' organisations, all defending the common interests of their members. The beliefs of this Advocacy Coalition Type

22 For example, so far no agreement between the European regulator and national governments has been able to be achieved on the social aspects of the European Information Society. Also, due to the diversity of economic and technological development amongst Member States, their views on the speed of market integration and market liberalisation may vary widely.

characteristically include: (1) a focus on commercial and technological needs, with the technical problems of production coming to the fore; (2) a general disapproval of strong regulation, on the assumption that the industry is capable of governing itself (*viz.* through industry standards, codes of conduct, and schemes of self-regulation); and thus (3) a preference for the flexibility and cost-effectiveness of economic incentives over universal legal commands. The academic literature contains some evidence to suggest that industry associations are declining in influence. This is seen most clearly in the "company state" debate (Grant 1999). The empirical data presented below, however, suggests that industry associations are still powerful influencers of ICT-sector policy at least; for example, the author found industry associations to constitute the second most numerous class of stakeholder participants in policy consultations, second only to individual companies (see Section 7.3 below). Given that, in the nature of things, companies greatly outnumber associations of companies, this is a noteworthy finding. Moreover, the data show that companies preferred participation in industry associations to any other vehicle for influencing ICT regulatory policy at both National and Global Levels, and even at European Level (see Figure 6.4 below); only lucrative EU-funded programmes was preferred to industry associations. The implications of these data will be discussion in greater detail below (see Chapter Nine).

The International Chamber of Commerce is the classic exemplar of the Industry-focussed Association. The ICC represents "business views" to governmental organisations and regulators and aims to create a business-supportive regulatory environment. It is dedicated to business self-regulation and has developed a number of *de facto* standards, such as the INCOterms and the ICC Model Contract for Privacy Protection in Transborder Flows. Moreover, ICC has defined alternative dispute resolution (ADR) rules, and set up an International Court of Arbitration for resolving international commercial and business disputes, thereby offering faster, cheaper fora than formal legal proceedings and litigation (ICCa, 2002).

The last Type to be treated, *Advocacy Coalition Type Four*, is "Project groups", consisting of teams of stakeholders bound together by contractual obligation (a "project" of finite duration) and tasked with implementing both private and public initiatives. Such are company research departments, national research programme units, research project staff at universities, working groups, workshop participants, and task forces. The belief system of this Advocacy Coalition Type centre around: (1) the primacy of the technological over the regulatory dimension of ICT; (2) the conviction that technology increases social welfare; and (3) a strong disapproval of regulations that are not technology-friendly. Typically, "projects" are accompanied by conferences and presentations, a consensus-building mechanism that brings disagreements and issues into the open and poses them for resolution, so that harmony may be conserved or restored by the coalition.

Not everyone active in the policy process will belong to an Advocacy Coalition Type or share any of its major beliefs; some Coalition Type members who are otherwise indifferent to policy disputes may participate in the policy process simply because they have certain skills to offer (Nelson, 1987:49-91; Meltsner, 1986). Those enjoying a high reputation may influence the beliefs of others by indirectly and unintentionally exerting pressure on their thought patterns (Meltsner, 1990). Those bureaucrats who actually do adhere to the tradition of "neutral competence" may have a similar effect (Knott and Miller, 1987).

The following diagram presents the four Advocacy Coalition Types identified.

Figure 1.5: The Advocacy Coalition Types

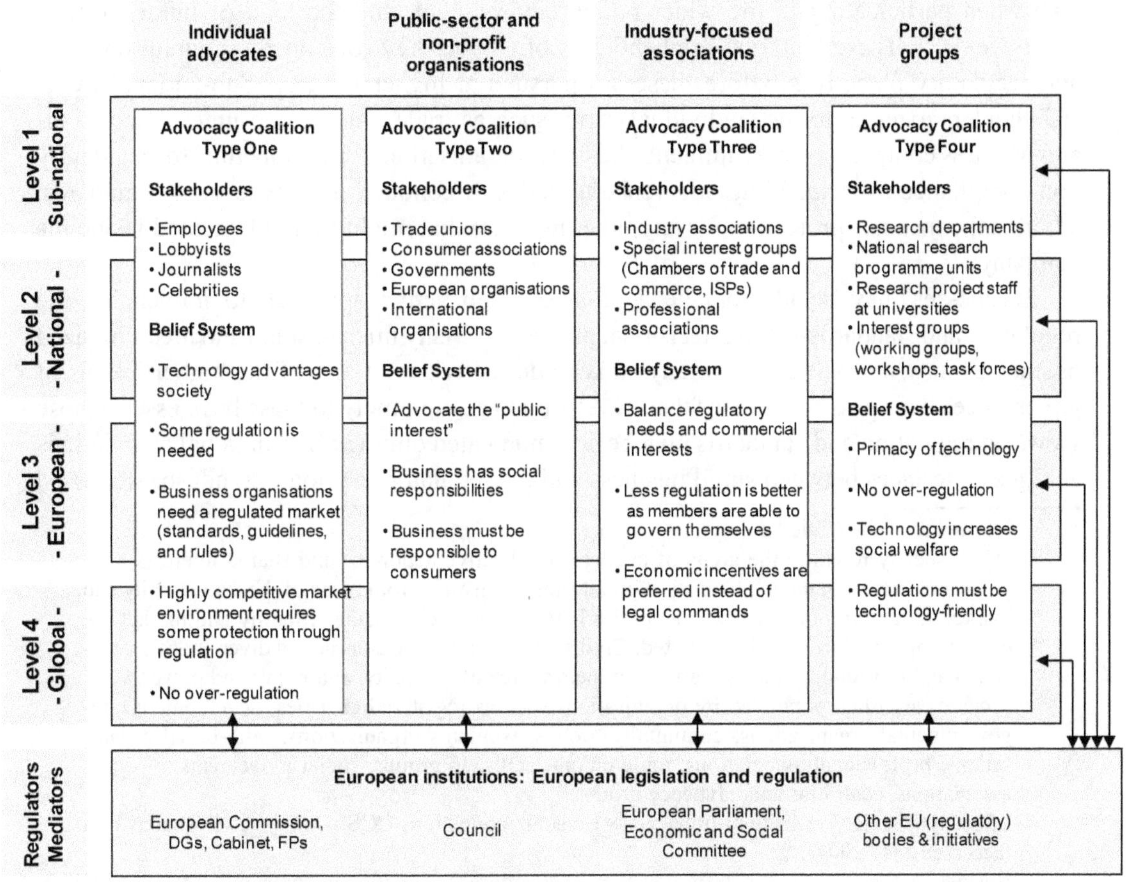

1.5.4 Developing the model: the Stakeholder Action Matrix

This Section demonstrates the practicability of mapping the (vertical) Levels of governance onto the (horizontal) Advocacy Coalition Typology, perfecting these components' utility through their combination into one holistic Stakeholder Action Matrix.

Level 1: The Sub-national Level

The first Level of the Action Matrix comprises business and other civil society[23] organisations. Although business was found operative at all Levels of governance and has representatives in

23 The London School of Economics Centre for Civil Society provides the following definition (also

each of the Advocacy Coalition Types (not just Industry-focussed Associations), a separate Sub-national Level is nonetheless a vital basis for the Matrix's integrity. The discussion, formulation and (inter-firm) communication of business concerns over regulatory compliance and technical standards typically emerges at this Level. Furthermore, the solutions developed inside business organisations by employees, management, policy experts, compliance managers, researchers, and technical personnel determine the approach that companies take when participating in the wider policy environment, and the kind of influence they exert over it.[24] These "internal" stakeholders often play key roles in formulating opinions and regulatory objectives before these are pursued at higher Levels. Sub-national Level stakeholders external to the (individual) firm, such as trade unions, consumer associations and business competitors, may influence business organisations' "risk appetite" for regulatory non-compliance by demanding adherence to codes of conduct, employee safety standards, additional consumer protection, or any other measure that might be implemented inside the company.

Businesses may decide to take a passive or an active approach to influencing the regulatory and standards-setting decisional processes. Many micro-, small and medium-sized businesses may not participate in any stakeholder activities at any of the higher Levels of governance. This passivity means that Level 1 matters supremely to these businesses, whose views on regulation and standards may be communicated only *via* Sub-national associations acting as interfaces between small business and the regulator. By joining industry-focussed

referred to as the Civic Society):

"Civil society refers to the arena of uncoerced collective action around shared interests, purposes and values. In theory, its institutional forms are distinct from those of the state, family and market, though in practice, the boundaries between state, civil society, family and market are often complex, blurred and negotiated. Civil society commonly embraces a diversity of spaces, actors and institutional forms, varying in their degree of formality, autonomy and power. Civil societies are often populated by organisations such as registered charities, development non-governmental organisations, community groups, women's organisations, faith-based organisations, professional associations, trade unions, self-help groups, social movements, business associations, coalitions and advocacy groups."

LSE Civil Society website at http://www.lse.ac.uk/collections/CCS/what_is_civil_society.htm (accessed May 2007).

Business associations in the definition above have more the function in contributing to public policy issues, and less in shaping specific industry regulations or standards. Usually the civil society focuses on policy areas with a social, political or public economic dimension. Typically examples of civil society institutions are: non-governmental organisations, private voluntary/ charity organisations, non-profit organisations, community-based organisations, community development programmes, civil clubs, trade unions, cultural and religious groups, social and sports clubs, environmental groups, academia and consumer associations. This is why the Civil Society is a phenomenon, which has drawn a lot of attention from international organisations such as the United Nations (http://www.un.org/issues/civilsociety/, http://www.unep.org/civil_society), the World Bank (http://www.worldbank.org/civilsociety), the Organisation for Economic Co-operation and Development and the European Commission.

European Commission Civil Society website at http://ec.europa.eu/civil_society/index_en.htm (accessed May 2007).

24 *Cf.* Survey Question 9: "Who is involved in reviewing and assessing the potential threats and opportunities presented by regulatory initiatives for your organisation?"

associations at Level 1, they may at least send delegates to participate in these activities. Association members having formed a common policy view, this is then presented to the higher-Level regulator.

One assumption about the "Industry-focused associations" Advocacy Coalition Type at Sub-national Level is that companies prefer to partner with organisations having similar policy goals, either on a single, pivotal issue or on an entire agenda. The formation of advocacy coalitions can help maximise a company's (indirect) investment in the policy process by maximising the attention regulators give to its own and like-minded actors' viewpoints. Companies can wage cost-effective and successful governmental and inter-organisational (business-to-business networked) relations by finding out when to partner with other companies that share regulatory goals. As some social scientists argue, "there will be many linkages between various policy communities in each sector [...] but there will be also some linkages between sectors" (Jordan and Richardson, 1982:89-90). Indeed, policy networking takes place not only between ICT businesses but also between the ICT and other industry sectors.

The author contends that the most successful advocacy coalitions consist of companies able to support one and the same policy position and present that to the regulator as one body. They are also more likely to succeed when everyone uses the same line of reasoning, since this delivers a unified and consistent message to the regulator.

Industry-focussed advocacy coalitions are an ideal way to increase individual organisational influence over policy processes without investing the additional time and money it would take to act individually. Lawmakers respond more favourably to whole groups of companies whose advocacy represents broad economic interests, rather than the self-interest of just one company.

Empirical research identified the following Sub-national Advocacy Coalition Types:

Figure 1.6: Four-Level Model: Level 1 – Sub-national Level

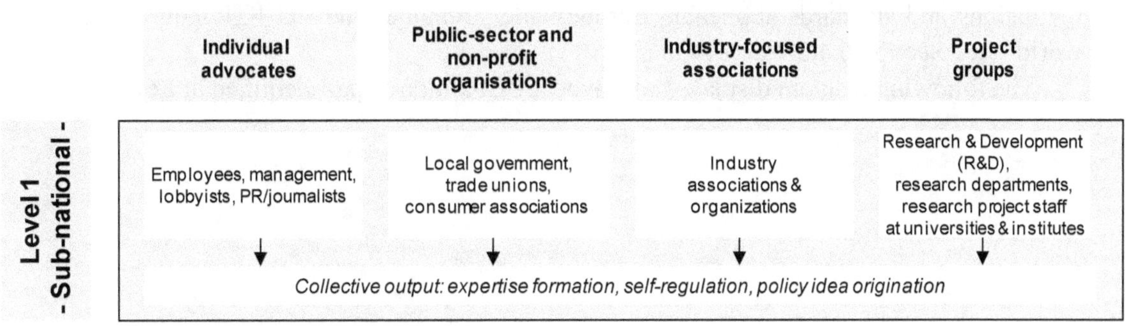

Level 2: The National Level

The Survey in Chapter Six indicated that participation in national industry associations was one of the most widely preferred pathways for ICT policy-making participation (see Section 6.4.1, Survey Question 2, below). Participation in national R&D programmes and initiatives was also strongly preferred. By contrast, stakeholders were rather dissatisfied with the outputs of politicians and governments at this next-up (National) Level.

At Level 2 it was possible to identify the following Advocacy Coalition Types:

Figure 1.7: Four-Level Model: Level 2 – National Level

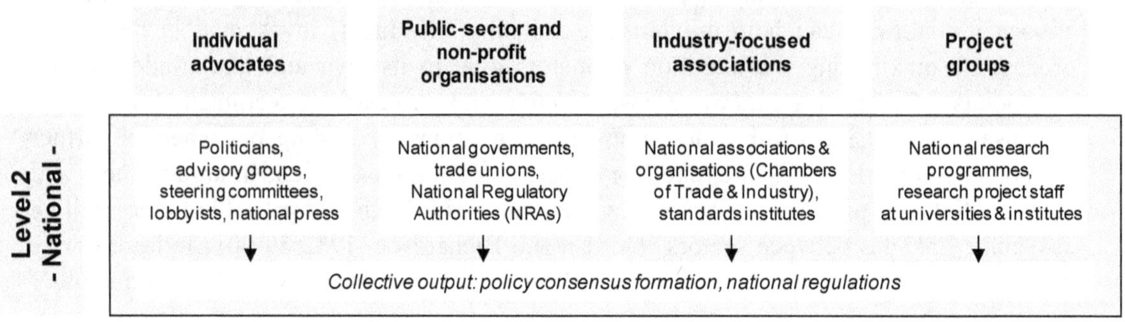

Level 3: The European Level

The Survey results show that European programmes and initiatives are considered by respondents an effective way to influence decisional processes on ICT issues (Survey Question 2). Survey respondents believed, moreover, that EU-funded programmes contribute to their understanding of regulations and standards, and help them influence the policy making and standards development process at the very early stages where their influence is the highest (Survey Question 6).

Even though ICT-stakeholder participation in the activities of European standards institutes was only moderate (Survey Question 2), the degree of satisfaction with these institutes' output was high (see Section 6.4.4, Survey Question 3). This appreciation of the European standards institutes was reinforced by the respondents' strong belief that "EU regulations and standards applicable Europe-wide strengthen the EU ICT industry in the world" (see Section 6.4.2, Survey Question 11).

The following diagram displays the Advocacy Coalition Types identified at Level 3:

Figure 1.8: Four-Level Model: Level 3 – European Level

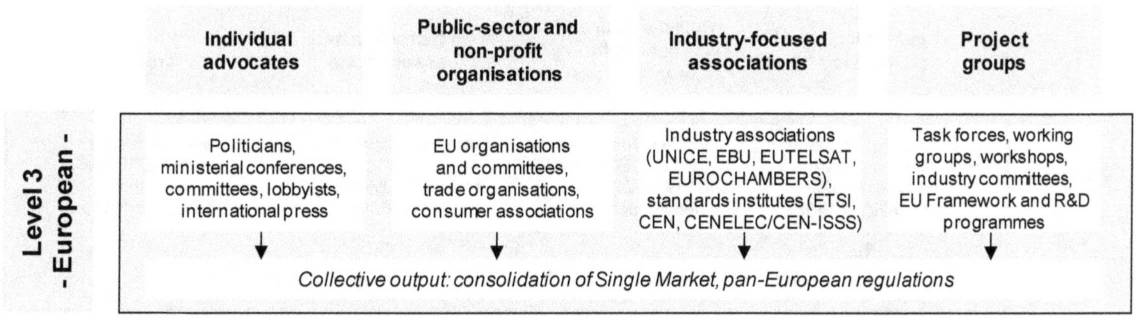

*) Please refer to the Glossary of Abbreviations and Acronyms

Level 4: The Global Level

Due to the global nature of ICT there is a need for international co-operation. For example, addressing the issue of spam at an OECD meeting in Brussels, EU Information Society Commissioner Erkki Liikanen stressed that "effective legislation also means that countries have the necessary investigation and prosecution powers, as well the ability to co-operate internationally" (Anonymous, 2004b:10). Chapter Seven below shows how international organisations such as the OECD, ITU and WSIS coordinate anti-spam activities globally. On the other hand, Rex Parry, Eversheds LLP's [the law firm's] Head of IT and e-Commerce, is sceptical of the likelihood of consistency in global legislation. "Just as certain countries are tax havens, I do not believe that all countries in the world will adopt the same legislation", he concludes (Thomas, 2003:28). Most international initiatives provide international guidelines, frameworks and recommendations, but lack enforcement and penal powers if parties do not comply. When operating at the Global Level to define strategies for influencing regulators at this and other Levels, stakeholders must consider the total political framework.

The international situation of standards institutes is much different from intergovernmental organisations. Most technical standards are in fact global; *viz.* ETSI/ITU/ISO standards, Internet standards, software standards, and operating systems standards. Even if global e-Commerce or eCommunications regulations were unlikely to be adopted by every jurisdiction in the world, international technical standards already have been widely adopted.

The Survey shows that international organisations show the lowest stakeholder participation (Survey Question 2); nevertheless, their work is highly valued (Survey Question 3). Many Survey respondents affirmed the importance of global initiatives and international guidelines for enabling technical interoperability.

The key stakeholders at Global Level in the four Advocacy Coalition Types are:

Figure 1.9: Four-Level Model: Level 4 – Global Level

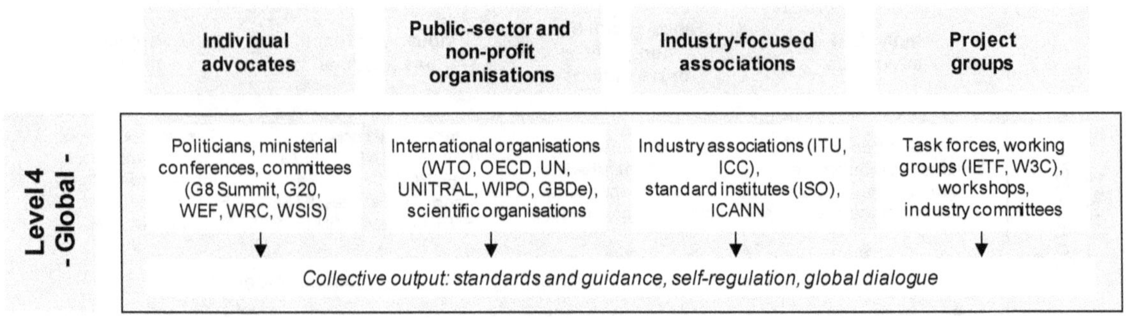

*) Please refer to the Glossary of Abbreviations and Acronyms

1.5.5 The Stakeholder Action Matrix

We are now in a position to bring all dimensions of the model together and present a holistic ICT-industry Stakeholder Action Matrix. As explained above, this is a point-in-time model, which nonetheless shows the complexity of stakeholder participation in, and influence over (European) ICT policy-making. The Policy Influence-Timing Model complements the Stakeholder Action Matrix with another dimension: the timing of stakeholder participation over the life-cycle of the policy process.

Additional research might be conducted to observe and analyse the interactions between the four Levels; more specifically, between the sixteen Stakeholder Action modes comprising the Matrix. However, in this book it has been assumed that all of the Stakeholder Action modes shape the EU's ICT regulation, actively or passively; hence, the interactions between the stakeholders – without reference to the regulator – are of secondary interest. Accordingly, the author has left this issue to future governance and stakeholder research.

Figure 1.10: The Stakeholder Action Matrix

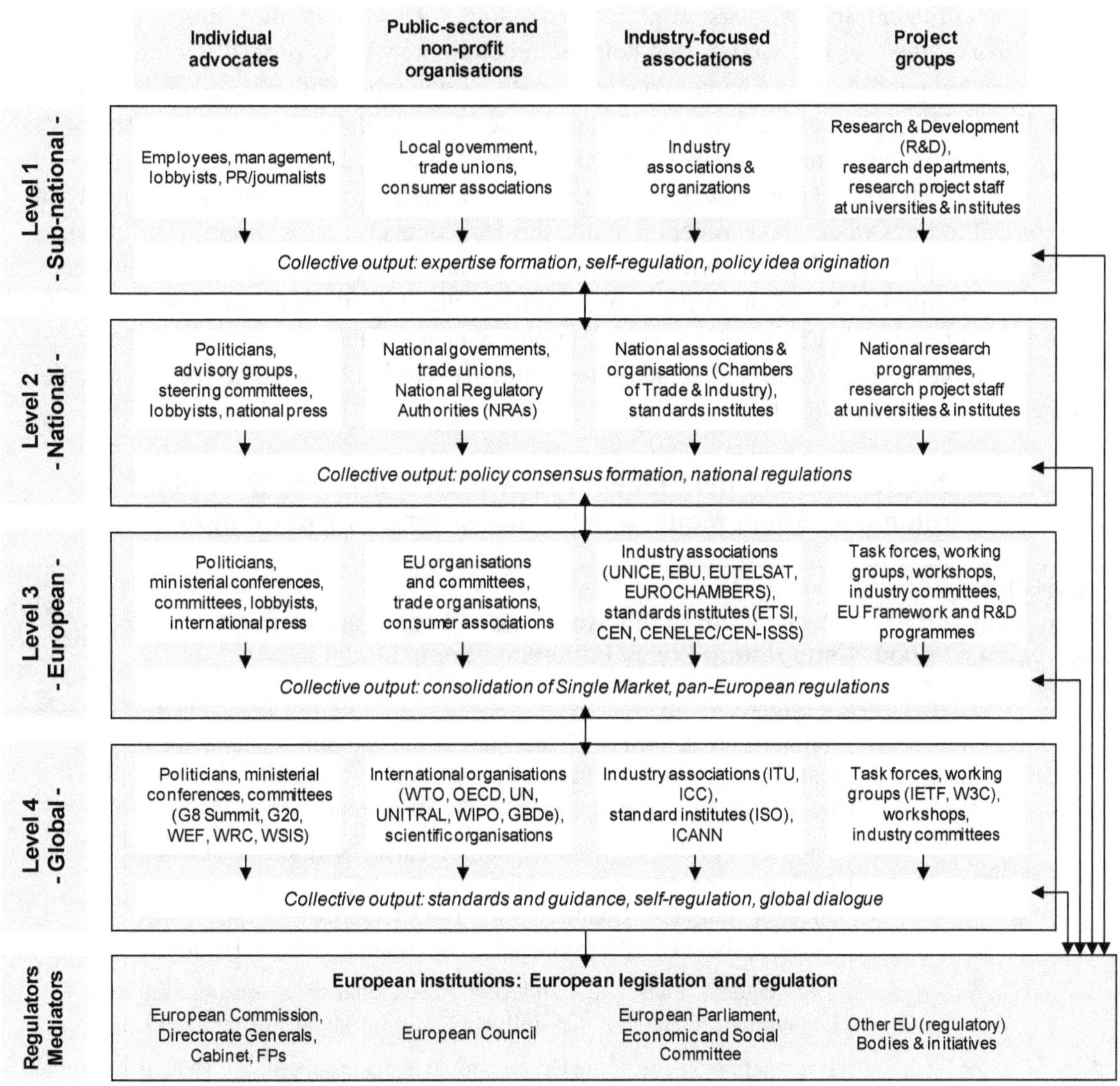

The Four-Level Model combined with the implicit belief systems of the Advocacy Coalition Types may be adapted to other regulated industry sectors, like the pharmaceutical or financial services industries. Additional research might provide further insights into the interactions of Advocacy Coalition Types both within and between regulated industries. A good example might be electronic payments, where the financial services sector collaborates with ICT providers to develop international standards for payment systems (*e.g.* the SET and PCI DSS payment standards).

1.6 ASSESSMENT OF THE MODELS

Both practitioners and scholars want understanding. To gain it, they need conceptual frameworks, theories and models that help them determine what is probably important and what can be ignored. This Chapter concludes with a review both of existing models and of the Policy Influence-Timing Model and Stakeholder Action Matrix, with an assessment of how far these models meet the specifications of good causal models.

The Stakeholder Action Matrix which has been presented can be applied to a variety of empirical settings where stakeholder input into the decisional process is strong. It synthesizes some major findings of the knowledge-utilisation literature, especially that about advocacy analysis. While developing this model, care was taken that the criteria for formulating a good model, as presented in Chapter Three (see Section 3.8.1), were met. An assessment that maps the Stakeholder Action Matrix and the Policy Influence-Timing Model onto the good-model criteria is presented in the following table.

Table 1.1: Testing the Stakeholder Action Matrix and the Policy Influence-Timing Model against the criteria of a good model

Criteria for formulating and developing a "good model"	Application to the Stakeholder Action Matrix and the supporting Policy Influence-Timing Model	Criterion met (Y/N)
(1) Concept and propositions must be relatively clear, internally consistent and falsifiable.	Variables are defined (individual actors and epistemic communities) and assumptions made before the actual development of either the Policy Influence-Timing Model or the Stakeholder Action Matrix. The four Levels were derived from organisational, local, national, European and international laws, regulations, by-laws, standards and guidelines (see Chapter Four). The structure of the model was further elaborated by introducing an Advocacy Coalition Typology. The Stages or Phases, the underlying decisional processes, and the key influencers in the Policy Influence-Timing Model are explained. If regulation on one of the Levels should become superfluous (which is unlikely), adjustments to the model might be required.	Yes
(2) Model must have been subject to recent conceptual development and/or empirical testing.	The literature review, Survey results, and case study, which form the empirical foundation of the models, are recent and were conducted specifically for developing a decision-making model. The models have been discussed with ICT policy stakeholders, and constructive criticism was taken into account. Furthermore, the author himself has participated in stakeholder consultations and activities on all four policy Levels.	Yes

Criteria for formulating and developing a "good model"	Application to the Stakeholder Action Matrix and the supporting Policy Influence-Timing Model	Criterion met (Y/N)
(3) Model must be a positive theory seeking to explain much of the policy process.	The Stakeholder Action Matrix in conjunction with the Policy Influence-Timing Model reflects current policy developments and stakeholders who shape policy. The review of current scholarship in Chapter Two and the case study in Chapter Seven describe and analyse the development of European Information Society policy over the last 20 years, as well as most of the recent developments related to the eCommunications Framework. Policy processes and patterns of successful stakeholder input were identified and analysed.	Yes
(4) It must address an important set of factors affecting diverse aspects of policy making.	Key elements, such as agency; multi-level dimensionality; the factor of time; policy Stages, values and belief systems; and other factors (*e.g.* policy debates) have been addressed.	Yes
(5) Descriptive language that allows a practical application of the model.	The terms defined for this publication were subjected to intense cross-examination and revision to ensure the level of semantic accuracy and generality that researchers everywhere in the field of policy modelling should find both handy and lucid.	Yes
(6) Economical in elements and assumptions.	The causality of the models and the methodology used is explained in detail. Basic assumptions are presented for both models before their development. However, it is acknowledged that the complexity of external stakeholder interactions seemed to require a number of assumptions, some of which may prove superfluous upon further research and theoretical refinement. Furthermore, as the Stakeholder Action Matrix deviates from Sabatier's own advocacy coalition model, additional explanation and reasoning seemed to be called for. For this reason, there may be room for further reductionism. A re-evaluation of the model might also lead to modifications and simplifications (yet equally well, perhaps complications) of the structure – in particular, the number and nature of the Levels of Governance and the Advocacy Coalition Types.	Partly met

Criteria for formulating and developing a "good model"	Application to the Stakeholder Action Matrix and the supporting Policy Influence-Timing Model	Criterion met (Y/N)
(7) Model must be "productive": have power to predict future policy outcomes.	The two models have not been developed with the intention to predict the outcome of a specific ICT policy or standards initiative. They only predict, in general, what are the best timing and the most successful pathways stakeholders may take to achieve their policy objectives. The models have explanatory power to illuminate the policy process in the abstract, rather than to predict the outcome of a given policy initiative. The Policy Influence-Timing Model should prove useful to practitioners in gauging at which processual Stages their involvement is most likely to succeed. The Advocacy Coalition Typology is useful for assessing which potential coalition partners (out of all stakeholders) are most likely to speed one's own policy objectives.	No
(8) Model ought to be "contributing to a better world"	The models explain the policy process, describe the actors that are involved in it, and analyse their influence over decision-makers – furnishing some quite valuable information to whomever it may concern. Additional guidance is provided in form of a Regulatory Compliance Matrix that exhaustively lays out ICT regulatory and standards domains. The compendious Stakeholder Directory of more than 600 stakeholders at all Levels may be used to identify current and future actors shaping ICT policy. All of this data is immediately and highly useful to ICT stakeholders themselves.	Yes

It is the aim of this book that the Policy Influence-Timing Model, which is an enhancement of the Stages Heuristic, and the new Stakeholder Action Matrix will join the existing models of the policy process in the literature. As the models herein presented, combined, factor-in the latest developments in regulation – particularly the reform mandating external stakeholder participation in the policy process, – it should be defensible and of practical use for the foreseeable future. The Stakeholder Action Matrix, however, will have to become established by being applied to many more empirical settings than the instant one, and its utility cross-examined by diverse scholars. Examples of other policy domains to which combined models might be applied include finance and accountancy, competition policy, and environmental policy.

In order to test the Stakeholder Action Matrix and develop its characteristics in further detail, both Chapter Five on actors and forms of participation and the case study in Chapter Seven explore some of the stakeholder fora and the regulatory bodies that the European regulator has set up to maintain and improve the regulatory regime for electronic communication services.

PART II

Theory and Methodology

It is the theory that decides what can be observed.
(Albert Einstein, 1879-1955)

CHAPTER 2

CONCEPTUAL ORIGINS

The following Sections review the existing sources which have inspired the development of the new concepts and models presented herein. The first Section considers business influence and the new governance concept, while the second focusses on the processes of policy making. This is followed by an review of the concepts of multi-level stakeholder participation and advocacy coalitions. The Chapter concludes with some observations about why the unique concepts and models presented in this book are needed.

2.1 BUSINESS INFLUENCE AND THE NEW GOVERNANCE

This Section reviews the contemporary literature on business influence, on the EU policy regarding ICTs, and on external stakeholder influence over EU decision-making processes. Sub-section 2.1.1 reviews the scholarly work on general business power and influence. Sub-section 2.1.2 describes how scholars of European regulation of ICT view the European Information Society project. Sub-section 2.1.3 reviews the scholarly literature dealing with external stakeholder influence over ICT policy. Sub-section 2.1.4 analyses the most recent debates over regulatory reform, which was supposed to lead to a "new governance" of Europe. It reviews the official policy papers that introduced these fundamental changes, commencing with the White Paper on European Governance in 2001, and their consequences in the "better regulation" initiatives now being rolled out at Member-State level. Attention is given to the efforts of European and national regulators to engage professionals, businesses and industry associations in regulatory policy making in order to improve its transparency, accountability and effectiveness. The last Section 2.1.5 covers the new Independent Regulatory Agencies, their genesis and their role in the "regulatory ecology". The focus is on the theories and evidence that sparked the author's interest in this topic and his development of the Industry Governance Theory.

2.1.1 Industry self-governance and business influence over government

Claire Cutler investigates inter-firm co-operation and the emergence of "private authority". Rather than being mutually isolated units of competition and never co-operation, she claims that "firms, singly and jointly, construct a rich variety of institutional arrangements that structure their behavior" (Cutler *et al.*, 1999b:333). Competition is often modulated, even strategically managed by international co-operation between firms, which consists of joint manoeuvres like "rule-making, standard-setting, and organization of industrial sectors". This

New Competition or "alliance capitalism", as it has also been named, is characterised by Brian Portnoy as "the governing of competition … through the use of networks, especially transnational strategic alliances [TSAs] among multinational corporations … if networks are a distinct form of economic governance, and [TSAs] are an important form [thereof], then the growth in [TSAs] over the last couple of decades constitutes an increasingly important source of governance in the global political economy" (Portnoy, 2000:157). The resulting state of affairs is accepted after the fact by governments, which, not in the best position to dispute these outcomes of massive private co-operation (Cutler *et al.*, 1999a:4 *et passim*), try to accommodate themselves to them. This structured behaviour of whole industries, with its stable and persistent co-operation capable of coordinating autonomously with governments and intergovernmental organisations amounts to a form of "governance without government" (*Cutler et al.*, 1999:ix). Firms possess massive material wealth that often dwarfs that of nation-States; they cooperate as much as compete with each other in deploying it. The norms that arise from these interactions significantly affect the opportunities faced by other societary actors. This phenomenon has been called "private authority", as it shares many features of government proper. A new form of governance has thus emerged (Cutler *et al.*, 2002:23 *et passim*), such that "in areas where technology is complex or information plays a significant role, the private sector is sometimes viewed by participants as more capable than governments in designing appropriate rules and procedures" (Cutler *et al.*, 1999a:4-5). Nowhere is this more evident than in the ICT sector, where the standards-setting regime, for example, has evolved from a public activity to one performed by a far-flung network of private actors. Liora Salter sums it up in the case of ICT standards: "[I]n the old era, standard setting appeared to be very much a public or governmental activity … [e]veryone now agrees that standardization should be industry-led. In the new world of [ICT] standards, industry reigns supreme and virtually everyone agrees that this is as it should be" (Salter, 1999:111-112). These conclusory assertions, which often typify academic discourse about difficult and complex phenomena like policy-making, chime with my own conclusions which, however, stem from actual empirical research (see Section 4.6.2 below).

Cutler *et al.* claim that this "industry self-governance" forms the basis of the industry's dominant interactions with public government, traced empirically in this book. The phenomenon that Cutler describes from the top down indirectly supports the Industry Governance Theory of this book, which was inferred from multiple sources of data gathered in the field.

David Coen and Wyn Grant, who acknowledge the "increasing complexity of business political strategies" (2006:13), confirm Cutler's conclusions, suggesting that "large firms have in recent years … come to play a large role in EU public policy" (Coen and Grant 2006:14; see also Coen, 1997b and Coen, 1998). They speak of "business associations" – a category apparently including what herein is called "industry associations" plus associations that appear to be trade and professional ones; concluding that they "vary considerably in their organizational effectiveness from country to country and sector to sector" (Coen and Grant, 2006:22). Coen notes that "internationalization" and capital-intensity are factors helping industry associations effectively represent their members at the policy table; whereas, greater market fragmentation leading to large numbers of SMEs hinders effective associational representation overall, which then yields individual big businesses a competitive advantage in influencing policy. The ICT sector exhibits both of these factors – certainly capital-intensity and internationalization characterise the industry; – nevertheless, the complexity of the ICT sector allows large numbers of SMEs to find specialist niches. If Coen and Grant's rule held up in the ICT sector, then the effectiveness of associational representation should vary noticeably within the sector. However, it was actually observed that associational representation was quite effective across the sector for all sizes of business. It follows that factor(s) other than size – or else some conditions upon size, making it relevant in other ways – must explain the lack of variation in associational effectiveness found by Coen and Grant in other industrial sectors.

Coen has asserted that the largest firms, which managed to "develop a broad political profile across a number of issues and to participate in the creation of *collective* political 'goods'", were those that benefited the most from the Commission's "gradual 'closing down' of the Commission in the face of interest overload in the 1990s" (1997b:19). The result, according to Coen, was that the EU policy process has become an elite pluralist system wherein "access is generally restricted to a few policy players, for whom membership is competitive and strategically advisable" (Coen 1997a: 98–99).

However, by the time the author began to gather data on stakeholder involvement in 1996, as a *stagière*, this closing-down trend had begun to be reversed, at least in the ICT sector. The Commission accommodated large numbers of lobbyists by inviting their participation in the inclusively designed consultation fora and other stakeholder-participatory facilities described in greater detail in this book (see Section 5.2 below).

The Commission, needing to overcome the "legitimacy deficit" of being lobbied by an exclusive club of insiders, imposed on itself the European Transparency Initiative, contained in its Communication COM(2008)323, to enhance the transparency of its own policy processes, and to institutionalise processes of more inclusive stakeholder participation (see Section 5.2.3). Broscheid and Coen reach a similar conclusion, that the Commission has chosen a more consultative style – *viz.* "committees, working groups, conferences, and other policy fora" (Broscheid and Coen, 2007:348) – when making regulations for highly technical sectors like ICT, "where technical policy input defines the policy legitimacy and [Commission] staffing numbers are low", forcing it to rely on outside expertise (Coen, 2009b:152). Coen acknowledges that the extent of "elite pluralism" in EU-lobbying regimes differs significantly across policy domains (Broscheid and Coen, 2007:348). This raises the question whether the findings in this book about the lobbying regime of the ICT sector are exceptional – in the sense of being exceptionally egalitarian, – or whether they reflect (or herald) a broader trend away from elite pluralism (toward inclusive corporatism) throughout the Commission's policy processes.

Coen also found that "the most favoured political channel was to lobby the Commission directly … [because] businesses recognized that some 80 per cent of single market regulations and standards were initiated and formulated at the Commission" (Coen, 2009b:147-148). This finding chimes with the author's finding that stakeholders exert the most influence over the content of regulations at the very beginning of the policy cycle, a stage dominated by the

Commission's policy processes, when the Council and the Parliament have hardly become engaged.

Wyn Grant propounds three models systematising business-State relations: (a) the company State; (b) the associative State; and (c) the [political] party State (Grant, 1993:13-17). Grant claims that, the party State having been everywhere undermined or scrapped (Grant, 2000:10-11), and the associative State becoming obsolescent under the forces of globalisation, the future belongs to the company State. The company state features direct relations between the State and individual business organisations. The associative state was characterised by the mediating role of overarching, all-encompassing business federations – even federations of federations as in Germany: the BDI (Bundesverband der Deutschen Industrie [Federation of German Industries]) and BDA (Bundesvereinigung der Deutschen Arbeitgeberverbände [Federation of German Employers' Associations]) – in managing and negotiating business-State relations (Grant, 1993:15). The associative State is doomed partly because of the persistent national orientation of the big trade associations. According to Grant, "[a]lthough there is some evidence that trade associations are themselves becoming international in scope ... their response lags a long way behind that of the leading transnational firms" (Cawson *et al.*, 1990, quoted in Grant, 1993:18).

It would appear, however, that ICT-sector associations are ahead of the learning curve compared with the trade associations studied by Grant. The author's data show that companies in the ICT sector collaborate extensively with industry associations on all Levels of governance. In particular, for SMEs, membership of industry associations is often the only way of being heard on the European and Global Levels. Of course, big ICT companies inevitably use industry associations more extensively than small ones.

Wyn Grant also typologises "interest representation" regimes and how they characterise the influence of business over the State, with particular attention to Charles Lindblom and his elite pluralist theory of contemporary business-State politics. According to him, pluralism is an interest representation regime where a multitude of interest groups compete with each other on more or less equal footing for the favours of government. A pluralist regime is where the interest groups are not only equal but also are in adversarial relationship to each other, more than to government (Grant, 1993:21-27). Corporatism, by contrast, is where potentially competing interest groups bargain not only amongst themselves but also with the State, to the end of *its* reconciling (more than compromising) their adversarial interests; thereby forestalling adversarial relations from arising *ex ante*, or allaying them *ex post* (Grant, 1993:28-32). Interest groups are inexorably drawn into implementing the Grand Reconciliation, which goes beyond representing their members' interests.

Wyn Grant points out that business will be privileged, regardless which way private interests are handled by the State (Grant, 1993:32 *et passim*). This is because "[c]apital is different from other interests [in that] it [exerts] influence in two ways – directly through interest groups and structurally because of the crucial role boards and managers exercise over the production, investment and employment decisions which shape the economic and political environment within which Governments make policy" (Marsh and Locksley, 1983:59, quoted in Grant, 1993:32).

Charles Lindblom introduced elite pluralism as an evolution of pluralism (Lindblom, 1977). Specialised elites bargain with each other over politics and market position. After discovering shortcomings to elite pluralism, Lindblom then theorised elite corporatism as an evolution of corporatism (Lindblom, 1980:91). Lindblom ended by theorising that business enjoys intrinsic privileges in any consumer-capitalist society, regardless whether the representation regime is pluralist or corporatist; having started with the simple question, *How does it come that business should have a privileged position in public policy?* Pointing out that businessmen collectively wield as much power as government officials, maybe more on a purely practical level, Lindblom concluded that they are as needful to our civilised condition as government. But implicit in this needfulness is that the rest of society, including government, is obliged to cater for businessmen – even in the teeth of clear and persistent majority preferences for alternative policies. This means that the public policies businessmen prefer – claiming they are necessary for carrying on business – will prevail (Lindblom, 1980:71-82; 2001). This clash of preferences constitutes an intrinsic, ineluctable and everlasting contest, which contrasts control of government by businessmen (capitalism) with democracy or popular self-determination. This contest is bound to arise in any society that brooks freedom of enterprise and expects economic growth, including the EU and its Single Market agenda. A good example was reported in *Time* magazine in 1975:

> Unless the British government agreed to provide massive aid to Chrysler's troubled British subsidiary, Riccardo (chairman of Chrysler) said, the company would be forced to shut down its five major plants in Britain and cashier its 25,000 employees there ... [Prime minister] Wilson denounced the Riccardo ultimatum; angrily protesting that Chrysler had left the government 'with a pistol at its head.' But last week in a startling, if characteristically Wilsonian, about-face, the Prime Minister agreed to help out Chrysler after all. (*Time*, December 29, 1975, p. 61, quoted in Lindblom, 1980:75)

Nothing has changed in more than 30 years – as witness the current German government of Chancellor Angela Merkel (2005-), which found itself in 2009 obliged to of subsidising and financially guaranteeing the sale of General Motors' Germany-based Opel subsidiary at a cost to the German taxpayer of €1.5 billion, – nor will it ever change so long as democracy depends on business enterprise for its prosperity.

Lindblom points out that this privileged position comes to big business without its having to "try". The rest of society, in order to enjoy the fruits of free enterprise, must at all costs keep business in business.

The ICT industry exhibits some features of all of these interest representation regimes. Elite pluralism for example is evinced by the European Round Table, a "direct membership association" (in the words of Wyn Grant) initiated by Volvo and a few other industry giants, to which only a select few large businesses are invited. Probably every policy-making regime in reality exhibits something of every possible configuration of interest representation, the predominance of one of them being the real basis of typification. The author's observation is that, at least in the regulation of the ICT industry, *the interest representation regime to which the Commission aspires* s a corporatist state of affairs masquerading behind a façade of pluralism. The principles of the Commission's new governance – especially the "deliberative democratic" principles[25] of transparency and "public" consultation – imply the State-mediated reconciliation of adversarial interests in the "public" interest; also manifested in the European Union's general culture of consensus (Warleigh, 2002:171; Heisenberg, 2005:65 *et passim*; see also CEC, 2009a). In the fora set up to embody these principles and this culture the Commission would knit together adversarial interests, finding a place in the policy system for every major interest group.

The capstone of this interpretation of the Commission's new governance is the strongly corporatist flavour of its efforts at recruiting the regulatees themselves to help implement and enforce the regulatory output, through having previously captured their loyalty by taking them on as partners in making the regulations that will bind them. This *démarche* is probably dictated as much by the European Union's dearth of enforcement powers as by any intrinsic preference of the Commission for corporatism.

The Commission's aspirations and the reality on the ground, however, are two different things. In theory, and to the eye of one who does not trouble too much to "look behind the scenes", the policy input of civil society follows a non-elitist mode: input is solicited from all interested stakeholders, not just from the ICT industry. Consumers, trade unions, NGOs, the public sector: – the demands and the comments of all are welcomed into the new public consultation fora. It was discovered, however, that, although the ICT policy process may exhibit "populist" trappings as a Potemkin Village, behind the variety of Advocacy Coalition Types lurks the reality that one Coalition – the one labelled "Industry-focused associations" – wields more power than all other Types put together. The reality, then, is a novel variant on elite pluralism, in the analysis of David Coen (1997a:98-99).

Such is the situation within the ICT policy domain. Whether this represents a trend or not is one of life's little conundrums. Nevertheless, the Industry Governance Theory as such needs to assume nothing more than the generally privileged position of business interests in the EU polity – a position already implicit in the liberalising agenda of the Treaties of the European Union and in the Single Market principles.[26]

Streeck and Schmitter actually defend the "associative" mode of business-State relations, seeing in it a new, lasting and unique principle of social order. According to them, the Associative principle of social order has been subjected to one-sided criticism by political scientists and economists as bringing dysfunction to the other principles of social order; *viz.* Community, Market, State (1985). But they point out that dysfunctional effects flow

25 For more on the principles of deliberative democracy see Bessette, Joseph M. (1980), "Deliberative Democracy: The Majority Principle in Republican Government", in Goldwin, Robert A. & William A. Schambra (eds.) *How Democratic is the Constitution?* (American Enterprise Institute: Washington DC).

26 See in particular TEU, Arts. 25, 39, 49-55, 73, 95, 215; but also Commission Directive 2002/77/EC of 16 September 2002 ("Framework Directive") on competition in the markets for electronic communications networks and services.

from the other ordering principles; Association, while not perfect, is no more intrinsically dysfunctional than the others. On the contrary, Association makes its own unique contribution to the establishment and maintenance of social order. As Streeck and Schmitter put it, "there are specific problems of order that each of them [*viz.* community, market and state] is better equipped to resolve than the others. The same, we submit, can be said of associations" (1985:120). Essentially the same point is driven home in the context of "industrial districts", a device of multi-level, and especially sub-nationally regional governance:

> [Interest associations] play an indispensable part in the negotiation of distributional compromises, the building of growth and productivity coalitions, the formation of public-private interfaces, the provision of a protective institutional exoskeleton for small, innovative firms, the generation of collective factor inputs, and [in general] the creation of institutions that allow for nonzero-sum cooperation among firms as well as between capital and labor at the workplace and beyond. (Streeck and Schmitter, 1991:153).

In what they call Association Streeck and Schmitter seek to establish the reality of an autonomous source of social order. It is a system of organisational concertation: "The background of our argument is the emergence in Western societies of systems of bargained interest accommodation and policy concertation in the 1960s and 1970s" (Streeck and Schmitter, 1985:120).

The author's evidence shows that industry associations are those vehicles of interest representation and intermediation which ICT business organisations resort to the most on all Levels of governance. This means that the association, together with the forces of the marketplace, is the glue that holds the multi-level governance system together more than the State or the Community. It may be said, then, that the Association as a principle of order is probably even more important in the governance of the ICT industry than of society in general.

Others who have investigated the importance of policy networks in influencing public policy have also found evidence that not only industry associations, but also individual large business organisations, in particular, were dominant (Schneider, 2006:115). The author's empirical research, presented below (*cf.* Sections 6.3.1 and 7.3 below), found evidence of the same phenomenon. Volker Schneider, whose policy research is restricted to the National Level, reviewed nine case studies, spanning 20 policy areas, that others had written-up between 1987 and 2002. He concluded that industry dominance is not confined only to the ICT sector. In about a third of the 20 cases, the "number of business actors exceeded 50 percent of policy actors" (Schneider, 2006:113-115). He also concluded that variations exist not only amongst actors across industry sectors, but also across host countries, with the US and Canadian firms seeming to be more active than European or Japanese firms (Schneider, 2006:115). The inference from these figures chimes perfectly with the inference the author drew from his Survey: that *industry governs*.

Susan Strange identifies technological advances as one of the prime causes of the "shift in the State-market balance of power" (Strange, 1996:7), and criticises social scientists for their neglect of this factor. The importance of technology as a political-economic cause is frequently overlooked; the author's research, however, singles out advances in technology and their intrinsic dynamism as one of three primary causes for the emergence of Industry Governance. Indeed, Strange herself singles out telecommunications as "[a] classic, extreme example of one process by which authority has shifted massively away from the governments of states to the corporate management of firms …" (Strange, 1996:100). If telecoms is an "extreme" example of industry influence, where authority has shifted "massively", then from this it is natural to infer that industry governs that sector – regardless what may be the state of affairs in other sectors.

To explain the impact of technology Strange distinguishes between *relational* power and *structural* power.[27] The former is the power to command obedience: "the power of A to get to [*sic*] B to do something they would not otherwise do" (Strange, 1988:24). Structural power is something altogether different; it includes but is not limited to the classical instance of agenda-setting. Strange elaborates that structural power is "more than the power to set the agenda of discussion or to design … regimes of rules and customs that are supposed to govern international economic relations … [like the American invention of corn futures or the Lloyds system of reinsurance, it] confers the power to decide 'how things shall be done', the power to shape frameworks …" (Strange, 1988:25 [inverted commas added]). The latter kind of power is what the ICT industry wields according to Industry Governance Theory. The EU supranational organs retain the relational power – that of giving legislative consent – together with the legitimation which that confers.

Strange identifies the incompetence of the contemporary national State to remedy certain "failures" of international scope as an insoluble problem (Strange, 1996:3 *et passim*), but in fact the EU was created precisely to overcome this very "Westfailure" as Strange terms it (Strange, 1999). It has been quite successful, so far, at compensating for the weaknesses of the national States of Europe. The author agrees that the Westphalian State[28] is in retreat, but profoundly disagrees this is something to be lamented.

Stephen Gill believes that a new constitutionalism, as he terms it, has emerged: "a doctrine and associated set of social forces which seek to place restraints on the democratic control of public and private economic organisation and institutions" (Gill, 1993:10). The liberalisation agenda of the Treaties of the European Union and the implicit pro-capital bias of Europe's new Constitution[29] – (which caused its repeated rejection by referendum) – are instances of Gill's new constitutionalism. Gill is highly critical of this elite political strategy, saying that its "discourse" (in the sense of Foucault, *cf.* Gill, 1992) "attempts to embed the hegemony of 'disciplinary' neo-liberalism, of the type associated with the attempts to restructure the

27 This distinction has been criticised by Fuchs (2004:8) and others as inadequate.

28 Named after the system of State sovereignty, the creation of which is conventionally attributed to the Treaty of Westphalia of 1648 which brought the Thirty Years' War (putatively over religion) to an end.

29 As of 1 December 2009.

post-communist states under IMF and Western tutelage" (Gill, 1993:10). This is supposed to "reconstruct the terms through which political action is possible in a capitalist society", thereby redefining politics itself; that is, the art of the possible. This is also the structural power cited by Susan Strange, which the ICT industry has been wielding in the EU policy process, and which is proving so much more effective than the classical "relational" power of the EU institutions (Gill, 2002:48).

Doris Fuchs analyses the nature of power to greater depth than Strange, distinguishing within Strange's "structural" power both structural and discursive power in addition to "relational" power (which Fuchs calls "instrumental"). Fuchs identifies the political activities business is typically engaged in – lobbying, capital mobility, "quasi-regulation"[30], self-regulation, public-private partnerships (PPPs), privatisation (such as the telecoms industry), and public relations and communication (Fuchs, 2005:87-90; 2004:9) – and constructs a table mapping these activities onto the modes of power through which they are pursued. This table exhibits what the field of researchers needs to investigate to fully fathom the role of business in the "political economy" of governance in the contemporary age. The author's contribution to this research programme is this investigation of stakeholders in the ICT industry, which observed the instrumental and (to a slightly lesser extent) structural influences they exert over the EU's policy process. "Discursive" power was more elusive. It is the power of social institutions to determine values and norms of behaviour, as reflected in the form and content of verbal and non-verbal communications; it is the kind of power that *constitutes* legitimate authority rather than merely "influencing" it, that *creates* an interest rather than merely pursuing it (Fuchs, 2004:6-7; 2005:83-87). This mode of power is accounted for herein only through the Advocacy Coalition Typology (see Section 2.3.3 below), which typologises stakeholder beliefs and the behaviours typically driven by them. Of all three modes of power the "discursive" is the most invisible, in that it is "taken for granted" by everyone. It is not generally visible to observers of political processes, yet the author managed to note something of it amid the myriad stakeholder events participated in.

Fuchs's theorisation supports a deductive inference similar to what the author was driven to by exhaustive data-gathering. Fuchs's survey of the field shows that "business clearly has become a pivotal political actor" (Fuchs, 2007:4) in global governance in all three modes of power (structural, relational and instrumental) and at all levels of governance (Fuchs and Lederer, 2007:11-12). Fuchs concludes that commercial actors may already have the power to "rule the world", but she notes that this aggregate power is both contested by scholars and to some extent self-limiting anyway. The power of business to shape through discourses what "everybody" considers normal and legitimate is well attested, and perhaps the form of business power that potentially holds the most sway. But it is pointed out that the intentionality of business-backed discourses has not been fathomed. It is likely that many of the discourses businessmen deploy are sincerely held and not "Machiavellian" attempts at strategic manipulation. The author, for his part, did not approach the study of business

30 Fuchs defines this as actions and activities by business actors that have the effect or side-effect of influencing governments' choices when defining policy rules.

influence as an activist, but took a disinterested view which acknowledges that good and bad actors exist amongst all stakeholder categories.

The self-limiting nature of business power is evident in the unrelenting competition between businesses and between businessmen. As Fuchs points out, "[i]n numerous political controversies, business actors are lined up on both sides" (Fuchs, 2004:25). This leaves much "tipping room" for other actors to tip the scales to one side or the other. Nevertheless, on certain overarching principles businessmen find themselves in complete harmony, such as avoidance of government regulation and liberalisation of trade and investment. The research presented herein ignores the many differences in detail between stakeholders classified under the same Advocacy Coalition Type, and instead concentrates on the "big picture", the better to develop a *comprehensive* model of stakeholder involvement.

Fuchs asserts that business appears to wield so much power, which is growing in tandem with the progress of globalisation, that it is a cause for concern for traditional democratic values (Fuchs, 2005:193-195). Nevertheless, she acknowledges that the involvement of business in global governance shows many positive aspects that ought to be conserved (Fuchs, 2005:187 *et passim*). Although the author is more sanguine about the participation of business in governance, this conclusion essentially chimes with the Industry Governance Theory.

2.1.2 The development of European ICT regulatory regime

Regulation of the European Information Society is a topic that has stimulated interest in a range of disciplines. As boundaries between academic disciplines, including economics, politics, law, and political science, must often be crossed, interdisciplinary approaches are better able to account for the complexity and international dimensions of this topic.

Regulation is often described as an intervention that directs and/or restricts certain behaviour which the regulating authority considers un/desirable. This is called the "red light"[31] concept of regulation. However, regulations need not always direct or restrict; they may on the contrary function as a "green light"[3] or enabler. A topical example would be regulation of electromagnetic spectrum allocation, which frees competitive operators to carry-on mobile telephony in an orderly fashion, while avoiding the wasteful and expensive duplication which a lawless free-for-all would impose. The circumstances said to justify regulation are often instances of what is called "market failure" by economists, who point out that the free market, especially where oligopolised, may evoke behaviour harmful to "third parties" (those not parties to the buyer/ seller bargain) without compensating them for their losses (Francis, 1993).

Generally, the scholars "associate regulation with the post-privatisation control of the utilities by [EU] Directors-General and their offices" (Baldwin and Cave, 1999:2). Before privatisation, utilities were commonly state-owned and thus the issue of "regulation" did not arise; the state had all power to manage its own property as it saw fit. Moussis identifies three broad EU regulatory objectives in the wake of privatisation: (1) to enact a legal framework

31 On "red light" and "green light" rules and regulations see Harlow and Rawlings (1997), chapter 2 "Red light theories" and 3 "Green light theories".

fomenting the development of enterprises in the EU; (2) to create an economic environment helping enterprises reach their full potential in the Single Market; and (3) to promote co-operation between enterprises (*e.g.* in regards to research) situated in different regions of the Union (Moussis, 2001:389).

In most areas of ICT regulation the main source of regulatory law is Europe, the driver of privatisation, not the Member States, even though the latter have in theory the jurisdiction to regulate the newly privatised industries. In the telecom sector alone, "well over 100 different directives, decisions, regulations, recommendations and resolutions, relating to every aspect of the industry, have been adopted since 1994" (Walden and Angle, 2001:279).[32] Mark Thatcher identifies six factors that have driven the expansion of EU regulatory activity, grouped under the following six themes: (1) the Commission's central role in broaching new ideas, pressing for action, and proposing specific measures; (2) the EU legal framework, which provides incentives for regulatory initiatives, together with the European Court of Justice's tendency to expand EU competencies and regulatory purviews; (3) the acceptance by national governments of increased EU regulation; (4) the readiness of national policy-makers to adopt EU regulatory principles when faced with difficulties in domestic markets; (5) the participation of interest groups and business firms in legislative activity at both EU and national level, whereby they have sought to expand regulation; and (6) the complexity of interactions between policy actors in EU policy-making, especially the interaction between national governments and the Commission, which fuels EU regulatory expansion (Thatcher, 2001b:307-312).

ICT policy is an increasingly important part of EU industrial policy, as witness the average annual growth rate of the ICT industry from 1995 to 2006 which was 6%, but rose to 10% in the period 2004-06 (CEC, 2007g, CEC, 2007m); making it one of the fastest growing sectors in the whole European economy. During the economic downturn in 2008, the annual growth rate of the EU ICT sector declined (to 5.6%); however, it was still much higher than the annual growth rate of EU GDP (2.2%) (Turlea et al., 2011). Thus, it is all the more needful for scholars to have a basic understanding of the regulatory objectives and actors involved in the ICT sector.

In the 1980s the European Commission saw so much potential in the ICT sector and its economic and technological development, that it developed a vision of the sector's future which purported to foresee and encourage but also to manage its broad impact on the whole economy and society of Europe. This vision it named the "European Information Society". In Chapter Four there is presented an overview of the Commission's high concept; of its evolution from the 1980s to the present; and of the Commission's responses to the challenges posed by its so-far incomplete implementation.

The Commission acknowledges that the implementation of the Information Society has not been without complication. In the beginning, especially, the uptake of Internet usage, notably e-Commerce, was disappointing. Internet usage then became a European public policy priority, the remit of which encompasses online provision of public services

32 Actually, 1984 can be considered as the beginning of the liberalisation of the telecommunications sector, starting with Council Recommendation 84/549/EEC "concerning the implementation of harmonisation in the field of telecommunications" (1984), OJ L 298/49.

(e-Government), faster Internet access (broadband), and the adoption of e-Business practices by SMEs (Verrue, 2002). Marsden confirms that the regulator faced difficulties in regulating the Information Society, which is "both necessary and highly demanding, in that the complexity, dynamism and globalisation of the markets often render traditional top-down regulation obsolete" (Marsden, 2000:15).

Since the early 1980s a convergence of computing and communications has been observed, which has made regulation even more difficult. Samuelson identifies five main challenges in regulating the Information Society: (1) estimating the extent to which new regulation is needed (*e.g.* because existing laws and policies are inapplicable); (2) ensuring reasonableness and proportionality in the new regulatory response; (3) building into the new regulations flexibility and adaptability to rapidly changing conditions; (4) conserving timeless human values before the onslaught of economic and technological pressures; and (5) harmonising regulations to create a globally consistent legal environment (Samuelson, 2000:316-330).

There is a danger of over-regulation. The Chicago School accuses Europeans of seeing market failures everywhere, although this accusation seems aimed more at EU competition policy (Marsden, 2000:18) than at industry-specific or interventionist regulation. With respect to telecommunications policy, everywhere in the world, including the EU, "the regulator progressively withdraws from detailed intervention and becomes more like a competition authority" (Cave, 2000:93). That this development took place even in Europe tends to vindicate the Chicago School's strictures against the European regulatory style. The Commission saw a need to regulate the overall process of liberalising telecommunications in 1998, lest the market becomes distorted and monopolistic, or market-dominant structures emerge. Now, more than ten years later, the Commission is slowly coming around to the Chicago School's view, and is trying to re-introduce free competition *via* less regulation. This explains the Commission's emphasis on economic rather than regulatory policy. The Commission created a feedback mechanism (*i.e.* fora for stakeholder participation) which enables industry to comment on new regulations, and to alert the Commission if they have overregulated.

2.1.3 Interest groups and the EU's decisional processes

There is an extensive body of literature on the role played by interest groups[33] in EU policy-making, *viz.* Jeremy Richardson (1996a, 1996b), Marius van Schendelen (1994b, 1994c), Robin Pedler (1994, 1996), David Coen (1997, 1998, 2007), Justin Greenwood (1994, 1997, 2000b, 2001a) and Laura Cram (1995, 1997). Scholars have developed diverse approaches and models to conceptualise and explain how actors shape policy. The concepts which proved most relevant for this research project were *the policy networks*,[34] propounded by

33 Interest groups are defined as "a group of individuals and/or organisations who hold specific, often sectoral, social or economic interests in common" (Philip and Gray, 1996:x).

34 A policy network is the whole collection of actors and organisations, whoever they may be, that influences decision-making in the public sector. Types of policy network include *policy communities* (a restricted set of actors and organisations) and *issue networks* (loose collections of actors and organisations) (John, 1998).

Charles Raab (2001), Jeremy Richardson (1994b), David Knoke (1990b, 2001), and Hubert Heinelt (1996); *advocacy coalitions* and *epistemic communities*,[35] in particular as expounded in the works of Peter Haas (1992, 1997), Paul Sabatier (1988, 1993a, 1999), and Hank Jenkins-Smith (1993a, 1999). The theories that contributed to the development of the ICT policy-making model propounded in this book, in particular the categorising of stakeholders according to their beliefs and policy objectives, is discussed in detail in Sub-sections 2.3.3, 1.5.2 and 1.5.3.

Perhaps the most important concept that has contributed to the theories and models herein was given by Jeremy Richardson, that the EU is a complex, unique policy-making system: "the extreme openness of decision-making to lobbyists, and the considerable weight of national politico-administrative elites within the process, create an unpredictable and multi-level policy-making environment" (Richardson, 1996a:2). Richardson concludes that the most fruitful approach to analysing the EU policy process is to focus on sets of actors as stakeholders in the policy process. In this attempt he developed a model of the EU policy process consisting of four stages: agenda setting, policy formulation, policy decision, and policy implementation (Richardson, 1996a). This intertemporal approach to the policy process is what suggested the desirability of complementing the Stakeholder Action Matrix with a "perpendicular" dimension of time (the Policy Influence-Timing Model) which models policy-making in stages.

McCormick shares the view that the EU policy process is complex, and the forces engaged are not fully understood; especially as the EU is still evolving, so that the correlation of forces among the players is constantly in flux. McCormick's attempt to reduce this complexity to its key elements recognises the pivotal importance of agenda-setting and policy formulation. He argues that the European Commission largely drives the origination of proposals and the formulation of new laws, hence the Commission must be the cynosure of private interests seeking to influence EU policy (McCormick, 2001:7-26).

"[I]t is estimated that more than 50% of our national legislation derives from decisions taken at EU level, with this number increasing to 95% in certain areas" (Konings, 2007:38). For stakeholders, then, it is important to engage with those Directorate(s) in the Commission which have the most influence in the policy domain in question. Although the Commission does not take the final decision on enacting most of its proposals, the power to table ideas is crucial in the policy process. The importance of early involvement in tabling ideas is confirmed by Hull, who states that typically the final proposal adopted by the Council conserves at least 80% of the original Commission draft proposal (Hull, 1993:83).

Just the right timing for involvement in the policy process is also crucial. Mazey and Richardson argue that the best time for a lobbyist is *before* the policy proposal has even been drawn up. The most effective way for a group or business to get involved in agenda setting is to provide a Commission official with a policy idea worthy to be turned into a proposal. Getting into this position is hard, but it helps if the policy stakeholder understands *how* the agenda is influenced – *viz.*, through participation in public consultations, working groups,

35 An epistemic community consists of actors who share common values or solutions to policy problems. It is similar to a *policy advocacy* coalition (a coalition of actors within a policy sector who share and advocate common ideas about how to solve public problems) and a *policy community* (John, 1998).

and task forces. It also helps if the stakeholder belongs to an existing policy network that is known and trusted by the Commission (Mazey and Richardson, 1993). Time is an essential dimension of policy making, which the author investigated in great detail in developing the Policy Influence-Timing Model (see Section 1.4 above).

Both Van Schendelen and Pedler investigated how companies influence EU public affairs *via* the total political environment, which includes a "political black market" (informal and especially inside influence) in addition to the formal decision-making procedures. They both believe that the study of public affairs[36] provides insight into the role private organisations play at the input end of politics – how they develop networks in order to influence the outcomes of policies under consideration; why the voice of business is listened to; why some private organisations are more politically successful than others; *etc.* (van Schendelen, 1994c:3-20; Pedler, 1994:303-311). Van Schendelen stresses that lobbying the EU can also boost company profitability; *viz.* new market opportunities for their goods or services, the desired standardisation, avoidance of the necessity of adapting to varying national standards in other Member States, or wangling a comparative disadvantage for competitors (van Schendelen, 1994b:5). In his view, "lobbying is the lifeblood of any political system" (van Schendelen, 1994b:1). In investigating stakeholder influence, van Schelden concludes that the swift growth of EU issues, competing interest groups, and informal relationships have led to the "declining effectiveness of national government coordination, and the rise of more sophisticated or professional EC [EU] lobbying by many private and public organizations" (van Schendelen, 1994a:283).

This claim is confirmed by empirical studies that have investigated the strategies of business associations striving to expand their influence within the EU policy process. David Coen conducted a survey of the political representation of Europe's top 200 firms.[37] He concludes that "multinationals have established a sophisticated political capacity that allows them to develop new multi-level and *ad hoc* political alliances and that this new political co-ordination has standardised political responses across issues and altered national public policy systems" (Coen, 1998:75). Coen suggests that this new, distinctive, EU-led "forum politics" has created a new élite pluralism and new institutional arrangements between businesses and the EU institutions. At the same time, the Commission benefits from the improved input into the European policy process and from a broadening of its constituency of pan-European firms. (However, a similar relationship does *not* appear at National Level.) In a new 2004-05 survey Coen confirmed the growing sophistication of private as well as public interests in negotiating the complex multi-level environment, and their improved access to the Commission (Coen, 2007a:333-345).[38] Coen suggests that the creation of business policy

36 Public affairs refers to operations within private organisations, including industry associations, that manage the relationship of the organisation to public officialdom, with its power to influence or draft legislation and regulation.

37 Between 1993 and 1997, Coen conducted interviews with 50 company European affairs directors, and with officials of the European Commission, the European Parliament and the European Trade Federations. 94 survey replies where received. The results are presented in Coen (1998).

38 Coen's survey results show "that large firms have adopted multiple lobbying strategies when seeking

alliances at the European Level may be also attributable to general globalisation trends faced by all democracies. Indeed, global business networks are one of the main drivers of these very globalisation trends, an enabler that brings together and can even intermediate interests and discourses from multiple Levels of governance. Businesses are "well-connected" not only between themselves, but with all who partake in the marketplace: a vast assemblage of suppliers and demanders amidst whom business is centrally or "nodally" placed. This nodality demands that businesses find ways of conciliating the self-interests of a diverse throng who transcend national boundaries. Industry not government drives the globalisation which drives government itself (*cf.* Section 2.1.1 above). This home truth forms the basis of both the Industry Governance Theory and the Stakeholder Action Matrix.

Greenwood, a major researcher into business alliances and how these interact with the European regulator, conducted a large-scale research project on European-level interest groups (Greenwood, 1997). He concluded that "business is more intensively organised at the EU level than at any other transnational level in the globe" (Greenwood, 2000b:77). The Commission has counted over 600 formal European-level business associations – a vast gamut of informal business public-affairs clubs and alliances, – and at least 250 individual firms with representative offices in Brussels.[39] The largest cross-sectoral business interest-groups working in Brussels include UNICE (Union of Industrial and Employer Confederations of Europe) which represents the industry as a whole; EUROCHAMBERS (Association of European Chambers of Commerce and Industry), representing 800 local Chambers of Commerce, and through them, some 14 million enterprises; European Round Table (ERT), a "rich club" consisting of 45 chief executive officers (CEOs) of some of the largest European firms with combined revenues exceeding €550 billion a year; AMCHAM-EU (EU Committee of the American Chamber of Commerce), created to represent European firms with American parentage. European interest groups are described in depth by Greenwood (2000b:81-89). Based on the results of this research, he concluded that they concert their actions within more collectives and through more channels than anywhere else in the world. Interests are organised at European Level in various ways, including individual- and/or firm membership groups and fora, federations of national associations, and transnational networks (Greenwood, 1997:4-5). This adds a further dimension to the complexity of the European policy process, which the theorisation presented in this book attempts comprehensively to explain.

to influence the European policy process" (Coen, 1997b:21). However, the favoured option of the respondents was "to deal directly with the Commission, with approximately a quarter of the average large firms' political resources dedicated to this channel. Such action appears to be consistent with the effectiveness rankings that firms awarded the Commission and was no doubt facilitated by the good access that 80 per cent of the companies surveyed believed they had to the Commission" (Coen, 1997a:100).

39 This figure has been arrived at by a calculation derived from Directory sources, using the editions of 'European Public Affairs Directory' (Landmarks, 1999); the Directory of 9300 Trade and Professional Associations in the EU (Euroconfidential, 1999); EURO-GUIDE: Yearbook of the institutions of the European Union and the other European organisations (CEC, 2001a); EURO Lobbying: Directory of European Union Trade and Professional Associations (CEC, 2002b); the European Commission web-directory of interest groups (CEC, 1999a); and Justin Greenwood's own calculations (Greenwood, 2001b).

Greenwood also investigated the political effectiveness of EU business associations, organising a conference in September 2000 that set up an "academic-practitioner dialogue" on this topic in Brussels.[40] Its main goals were investigating: the *milieu* in which associations function in order to discover anything that might be impeding their capacity to reach coherent policy positions in a timely manner; the impact on performance of the leadership and institutional design of associations; and factors relating to associations that function across industry sectors. Greenwood's study proved to be a major contribution toward understanding how business associations provide accurate information and sound policy-making advice, and how they build consensus on behalf of their member-organisations, who wish thereby to participate in the EU policy process.

Marina Green Cowles pioneered further investigations in the *European Casebook on Business Alliances*, concluding that the European Round Table of Industrialists (ERT) has not only influenced public policies, but has actually set the European agenda and defined fundamental economic issues. Rather than the ERT having to pressurise the Commission to come to the meeting table, Green Cowles found evidence of the reverse, *i.e.* of the Commission actually courting ERT for policy formulations (Cowles, 1995:225-236).[41] Sandholtz and Zysman support the view that the Commission actively seeks collaboration and acts as a "policy entrepreneur". The Commission, with the help of a transnational industrial coalition favouring the Single Market, has managed to persuade national governments of the benefits of collaboration (Sandholtz and Zysman, 1992:95-128).

David Coen investigated the Commission's motives in espousing the creation of permanent business fora and alliances *ad hoc*. He concluded, firstly, that the Commission originally decided to supersede "mutual recognition" between Member States with the direct implementation of the EU's own directives and technical standards, so as to enforce a Single Market more efficiently; secondly, that the Commission saw in business a channel of communication to the Member States that could facilitate intergovernmental negotiations in the EU; thirdly, that Brussels believed membership of political fora credentialised and legitimated business participation, which should no longer be seen as exclusively self-seeking (Coen, 1998:70). Coen demonstrated the creation of a "permanent" vehicle for industry participation in the EU's decisional processes which made them more effective and consistent.

A further argument for the involvement of businesses in regulatory design is that it contributes to business-friendly regulation (Baldwin, Hood and Rothstein, 2001:117-121). Coen elaborates, arguing that "this business friendly agenda explicitly recognised the importance of entrepreneurs as a means to growth and job creation and attempted to create

40 A selection of keynote contributions to the conference on "The Effectiveness of EU Business Associations" held in Brussels, 18-20 September 2000, is published in Greenwood & Westgeest (2001a).

41 "The ERT is an informal forum bringing together around 45 CEOs and chairmen of major multinational companies of European parentage, covering a wide range of industry and technology sectors. ERT Members are situated in 18 European countries and have a combined turnover of around €1,600 billion, employing around 4.5 million people" (European Round Table website, 2007).

an innovative environment through the reduction in compliance costs and coordinated and benchmarked regulation within the internal market" (Coen and Dannreuther, 2003:268). It follows that the predominating influence of the ICT industry over the EU's ICT regulatory regime is not an outcome that the industry forced on a weaker Commission, but something the Commission itself invited for its own good and sufficient reasons.

This is not to suggest, however, that the Commission could have done otherwise, as the words of Coen quoted above might be interpreted to imply. The Commission's increasing dependency on external advice leaves them no choice, as is concluded below.

2.1.4 The New Governance in Europe: participation and subsidiarity

The reader should note that this Section reviews and summarises those developments since 1998 which have had the strongest influence on the research agenda and the theories and models in this book. Perhaps the most important is the European Commission's Better Regulation initiative, which promises salutary reforms in many respects, such as new kinds of Impact Assessment and mandatory consultations of those affected by regulatory policies. It is of paramount importance to understand the regulatory changes that have taken place in the last decade before analysing stakeholder influence on policy-making.

The inspiration for this new EU governance thinking originated with the United Nations. In June 1998 the European Commission signed the United Nations Economic Commission for Europe (UNECE) Convention on "Access to Information, Public Participation in Decision-Making and Access to Justice in Environmental Matters", also referred to as the Aarhus Convention. This demonstrated the European Commission's commitment to initiate at the European Level reforms enhancing policy-processual transparency and adequate public consultation. The ratification of the Aarhus Convention put public involvement in the policy process atop the Commission's agenda (UNECE, 1998).

In February 2000 Commission President Romano Prodi identified the promotion of new forms of governance as one strategic objective of his term in office (CEC, 2000b). A work programme for the preparation of a White Paper was agreed, and twelve working groups set up focussing on six "working areas"[42] (CEC, 2000f). The programme was accompanied by a public consultation (European Governance Team, 2001) and two case studies (Castillo, 2001; OPTEM, 2001). Before releasing the White Paper, the Commission also consulted non-governmental organisations (NGOs) in depth to produce a discussion paper on "the Commission and NGOs: building a stronger partnership" (CEC, 2000a).[43] These results were presented in the form of a 420-page Preparatory Work for the White Paper (CEC, 2002u).

42 The work programme focussed on the following six work areas for European Governance: (1) Broadening and enriching the public debate on European matters; (2) Handling the process of producing and implementing Community rules; (3) Improving the exercise of European executive responsibilities through decentralisation; (4) Promoting coherence and co-operation within a 'networked' Europe; (5) Strengthening Europe's contribution to world governance; and (6) Strengthening the interaction and strategic dimension of policies across the continent.

43 The aim of this paper was to give an overview of existing partnerships, suggest possible ways of developing these relationships, and provide a coherent framework for co-operation across a Commission that had thitherto been organised on a sector-by-sector basis (NGO Discussion paper website,

On 25 July 2001 the Commission adopted this White Paper on "European Governance" (CEC, 2001d),[44] which proposed to realise the new "principles of good governance" by imbuing the policy process with openness, participation, accountability, effectiveness, and the joining-up of policies and actions. The Commission admitted that the proposed changes should apply first and foremost to the Commission itself, on top of other internal reforms already embarked on (such as preparation for a Treaty establishing a Constitution for Europe). The White Paper aimed to modernise the EU policy process, increase the accountability of EU Executive organs to elected assemblies, and open up the EU's decisional procedures to concerned and interested citizens and other stakeholders. The publication of this White Paper intensified the governance debate at the European Level.

The lessons to be drawn from the consultation, together with an assessment of the progress achieved with the implementation of the White Paper's recommendations, were published in a 2003 report (CEC, 2003d).[45] The consultation confirmed the strong desire of stakeholders to participate in EU policy-making and implementation.[46] To improve communication and make information more easily available to private-sector and non-institutional stakeholders, the Commission agreed a list of measures[47], including principles and standards for involving non-traditional, "outsider" policy participants (CEC, 2002s). The overall idea was to determine in advance who ought to be consulted whenever a new policy was to be initiated, to the end that all those affected might become (more) involved.

Interestingly, the White Paper also documented and analysed, at both European and Global Levels, the ascendant influence of policy networks over governance in Europe. It recognised, in particular, that business organisations are increasingly organised in networks which interact with other organisations, such as regional and local authorities, the DGs in Brussels, and research centres. The Commission recognised that networks operate in a non-hierarchical way, yet all participants are committed to a common objective. The Commission

2007).

44 The proposals for change cover: (1) better involvement and more openness; (2) better policies, regulations and delivery; (3) Europe's contribution to global governance; and (4) a refocus of policies and institutions (European Governance website, 2007; Better Regulation website, 2007).

45 260 written contributions were received as the result of the consultation process that ran over an eight-months period from 25 July 2001 to 31 March 2002. Contributions are accessible on the European Commission's governance web site: http://europa.eu.int/comm/governance/index_en.htm.

46 Further evidence for a strong interest in this matter was the consultation response rate to this topic. Most of the contributions to the White Paper received were about the theme "participation of actors and consultation" (310), followed by contributions for "better lawmaking, application of community law" (224) and "refocussing of policies and institutions" (113) (CEC, 2003d:42).

47 The following actions were identified by the European Governance White Paper consultation as needful for enriching the flow of information and communications that inputs into the Commission's decision-making process: Publication of all policy proposals on EUR-Lex; the set-up of a central service accessible both by phone and *via* the Internet (Europe Direct); enhancement of web portals (*e.g.* the interactive policy-making website "Your voice in Europe": http://ec.europa.eu/yourvoice/index_en.htm); and a commitment by all the supranational institutions to greater openness of proceedings and availability of documentation.

aspired to "retool" itself to pro-actively and systematically collaborate with key stakeholders and facilitate their contributions to policy-making and -implementation. "As a general rule, horizontal European federations are consulted on all matters and the professional organisations are consulted on sector-specific matters" (CEC, 2003d:19). The importance of business associations to the policy process is at the centre of the present research. The case study presented in Chapter Seven on the eCommunications Framework analyses in detail how business associations and other stakeholders have pro-actively participated in the consultation process underlying the Framework.

These governance reforms were strongly supported by the Convention on the Future of Europe, or European Convention, which initiated the drive toward a European Constitution (European Convention website, 2007). The Göteborg European Council had initiated discussion of reforms to modernise EU governance in June 2001 (Göteborg European Council, 2001). In December 2001 the Laeken European Council adopted the "Laeken Declaration on the Future of Europe", which established the European Convention. It was acknowledged that EU citizens were "calling for a clear, open, effective and democratically controlled Community approach" requiring the EU to submit to renewal and reform (European Convention/Laeken Declaration on the Future of the EU website, 2007). The Convention, which met for the first time in February 2002, and thereafter in plenary sessions once or twice a month, laid the foundations for such a renewal. Even though the Treaty establishing a Constitution for Europe was rejected in May 2005 in French and Dutch referenda, and the Treaty of Lisbon of December 2007 was crafted to salvage as much as possible of the unratified Constitution. The regulatory reforms the Convention process had initiated were continued.

The European-level governance debate led to targeted actions. Communications, including an Action Plan on "better lawmaking",[48] were adopted and an *Internal Market and Consumer Protection Committee Report* was published (Committee on the Internal Market and Consumer Protection, 2006). With the support of the Council and the European Parliament, the Commission concluded that Community legislation should be simplified and its volume reduced[49] (CEC, 2002n:13-14). The EU had rediscovered the home truth uttered by

48 The main policy papers that supported the Action Plan on "better lawmaking" include: COM(2002)275 "European Governance: Better lawmaking", 5.6.2002 (European Commission: Brussels). COM(2002)276 Communication from the European Commission on "Impact Assessment" (European Commission: Brussels). COM(2002)277 "Consultation Document: Towards a reinforced culture of consultation and dialogue-proposal for general principles and minimum standards for consultation of interested parties by the Commission" (European Commission: Brussels). COM(2002)278 "Action plan: Simplifying and improving the regulatory environment", 5.6.2002 (European Commission: Brussels).

49 It was estimated that the body of Community law runs to over 80,000 pages applicable to companies and consumers. To reduce and simplify the volume of legislation, consolidation (grouping regulatory instruments scattered over the first act and subsequent amending acts), codification (adopting a new legal instrument that integrates a previous instrument and its amendments into a superseding instrument which, however changes nothing of substance), redrafting (making required substantive changes and repealing the previous act), and simplification (making the legal substance simpler and more appropriate to users' requirements) were proposed as options (CEC, 2002n:13-14).

Winston Churchill as long ago as 1931: "If you have ten thousand regulations you destroy all respect for the law". The Commission continually monitors progress and initiates legislative and work programmes for Better Regulation initiatives (CEC, 2006u, CEC, 2006v; Better Regulation website, 2007). These principles, designed to bring about more transparency and openness in decisional processes, have been endorsed by international organisations; the OECD, for example, which publishes reviews of regulatory reform in various OECD countries, has been monitoring the reforms' progress[50] (OECD, 2002c, 2003c).

The better to implement these principles, the European Parliament, Council and Commission reached in November 2005 an "Inter-institutional agreement on better lawmaking", which laid out a common approach to regulatory-impact assessments". This common approach considers "how to assess the potential impacts of the legislation that [the three EU institutions] process and adopt, so that decisions are made after giving careful consideration to the available evidence"[51] (Council of the European Union, 2005b). The agreement also requires that all regulatory initiatives must be accompanied upon submission by a regulatory impact assessment describing and justifying the initiative.

In practical policy terms, this means that "the Commission needs to carry out both *ex-ante* and *ex post* impact assessments on legislation to test whether key policy objectives have been met, [in order] to assist with the regulatory review process" (CEC, 2002l:2). The new impact assessment procedures are intended to "contribute to an effective and efficient regulatory environment, and further, to a more coherent implementation of the European strategy for Sustainable Development" (CEC, 2002l:2). The Parliament and Council agreed to take the Commission's impact assessments fully into account, and to commission impact assessments prior to the adoption of any substantive amendment. The 1998 Aarhus Convention guidelines and the recommendations contained in the Commission's Communications for "better regulation and lawmaking" were rolled out nine years later at Member State level, affecting even the local level of government.[52] In early 2008 the Commission announced a Strategic Review of Better Regulation. Besides announcing further measures to refine the regulatory impact assessment procedure, including its inter-institutional aspects, this review also covered simplification, codification, screening and withdrawal of pending regulatory proposals, and action for the reduction of administrative burdens (CEC, 2007n). This new governance initiative is clearly a long-term strategy that goes beyond "better regulation and lawmaking" to aim at a more partner-like relationship with stakeholders, in which the Commission fancies itself *primus inter pares* [first among equals] (whether that is the reality or not). If successful, the new partnership will reshape the whole way of doing "business" in

50 Other publications in this area include the annual OECD "Economic Policy Reforms: Going for Growth" (OECD, 2005, 2006, 2007).

51 See also SEC(2005)791 "Impact Assessment Guidelines", 15.06.2005 (European Commission, Brussels).

52 For example, the UK Cabinet Office launched a Better Regulation Executive "to minimise bureaucracy for businesses and front-line staff in the public sector and to help charities and the voluntary sector to make a greater contribution to society" (Better Regulation website, 2007).

Brussels, moving the practice of policy influence away from lobbying (behind closed doors) to a form more transparent and open to all stakeholders.

Seven years after Romano Prodi announced his European governance reforms, their implementation has entailed a policy objective for "better regulation and lawmaking" at Member State level as well. These changes are most conspicuous in the UK, one of the most advanced Member States in regulatory reform.[53] Tony Blair initiated the reforms in 2002 with a "Regulatory Reform" Action Plan (Cabinet Office, 2002). In 2005 the Government commissioned a report from Philip Hampton "for promoting more efficient approaches to regulatory inspection and enforcement" (Hampton, 2005); followed by a detailed progress report that drew on Hampton's recommendations (HM Treasury, 2006). The Hampton Report proposed a Local Better Regulation Office (LBRO), a Regulatory Enforcement & Sanctions Bill, and a Regulators' Compliance Code (Cabinet Office & Better Regulation Executive, 2007a, 2007b). The resultant Regulators' Compliance Code requires regulators to promote a "positive" (*viz.* business-friendly, non-punitive) approach to regulatory inspection and enforcement so as to improve net regulatory outcomes without imposing unnecessary burdens on regulated entities.

In July 2007 the new Prime Minister, Gordon Brown, laid out his follow-up strategy of the regulatory reform. Herein, the government committed itself to "tackle unnecessary regulatory burdens on the private, public and third sectors", which he considered "a key element of keeping our society fair and our economy strong in an increasingly competitive and global environment" (BERR, 2007a). Unsurprisingly, the UK government identified many of the same areas needing improvement as the European regulator had done, including simplification, easy and understandable regulations, and the accountability of the regulator.

In 2007 the government went so far as to reconceptualise the Department for Trade and Industry (DTI), renaming it the Department for Business, Enterprise and Regulatory Reform (BERR) (BERR, 2007b). The Reform in question aimed "to create the conditions for business success through competitive and flexible markets that create value for businesses, consumers and employees. BERR's main objective is to drive regulatory reform, and work across Government and with the regions to raise levels of UK productivity" (BERR website, 2007). John Hutton, who headed BERR, announced that he would "provide a strong voice for business and regulatory reform at Cabinet" (Hutten, 2007c). In particular he promised to "listen to business needs" and "to do everything possible to open up new business opportunities in emerging markets" (Hutton, 2007a); as well as "to constantly review and re-evaluate the approach to regulation" and "to deliver big reductions in the administrative burdens of regulation" (Hutton, 2007b). William Sargent, Executive Chair of the *Better Regulation Executive* (BRE) works with the government "to reduce and remove unnecessary regulation for the public, private and voluntary sectors" (BER website, 2007). His first responsibility in 2007 was to work with the National Audit Office (NAO), with regulators, and with business to develop a process of external review of regulatory performance. The resulting assessment

53 The UK commenced de-regulating and liberalising its telecommunications sector ahead of all other EU and OECD countries except the United States, beginning in 1982. Gradually, form 1990 onwards, the UK has had to implement an increasing number of EU telecommunications directives.

process was based on Hampton's principles.[54] To develop and communicate best practice among businesses, BERR also works with the Trade Association Forum and Business Link, which support mainly small and medium sized companies (Trade Association Forum website, 2007; Business Link website, 2007), and cooperates with the Department for Innovation, Universities and Skills (DIUS), which has set the vision to make Britain one of the best places in the world for science, research and innovation.[55]

To further these efforts, the government set up the Business Council for Britain to advise the government in crafting a long-term strategy for economic growth through industrial policy, technology and state subsidies. The Council comprises fifteen highly influential business leaders,[56] with enough clout between them to affect regulatory reform in the UK and even in the EU. This evidences the increasing dependency of National-level public authorities upon private stakeholder advice.

The preparation of a "Regulation and Business Advice" report, undertaken and published by BERR to "educate" business organisations,[57] together with other steps taken by the UK government, show that the UK has taken regulatory reform a step beyond the European Governance agenda. Both the European Commission and the UK regulator stress that good regulation can foster economic progress and lower business costs.[58] Moreover, the risk

---

54 Better Regulation Executive and National Audit Office (May 2007) "Hampton Implementation Reviews", Guidance for Review Teams.
Five major UK regulators have been assessed with help of these regulatory performance indicators by the end of 2007. These were the Health and Safety Executive, Food Standards Agency, Financial Services Authority, Environment Agency and Office of Fair Trading.

55 DIUS are the UK counterparts with both DG Research and DG Education and Culture, and the new UK Department for Children, Schools and Families (DCSF). The policy team at DUIS will be responsible for managing the EU's 7th Framework Programme (FP7).
Meeting with James Hughes (27 July 2007): Department for Innovation, Universities and Skills, London.

56 The 15 members of the Council are: Sir Richard Branson: Founder, Virgin Group; Damon Buffini: Managing Partner, Permira; Sir William Castell: Chair, Wellcome Trust; Mervyn Davies: Chairman, Standard Chartered Bank; Sir Rod Eddington: Director, News Corporation; Dr Jean Pierre Garnier: Chief Executive Officer (CEO), Glaxo SmithKline; Stephen Green: Chairman, HSBC; Tony Hayward: CEO, BP; Sir Terry Leahy: CEO, Tesco; Sir John Parker: Chair, National Grid; Sir John Rose: CEO, Rolls Royce; Stuart Rose: CEO, Marks and Spencer; Arun Sarin: CEO, Vodafone; Dame Marjorie Scardino: CEO, Pearson; and Sir Alan Sugar: Chair and CEO, Amstrad. The Council is chaired by Mervyn Davies of the Standard Chartered Bank and attended by the Prime Minister and Secretaries of State of the main economic departments. Other Secretaries of State can attend the meetings at the invitation of the Council.

57 This report finds that businesses spend at least £1.4 billion each year on advice about how to comply with regulations. It recommends that, with better communication and guidance, costs to business could be substantially reduced. The five key drivers of external costs incurred by business identified in the report were: volume and complexity of regulation; low awareness of government guidance; regulatory change; poor quality of government guidance; and uncertainty, risk, and lack of confidence (Better Regulation Executive, 2007).

58 The "Next Steps of Regulatory Reform" report (July 2007) mentioned commitments to deliver a 25% reduction in administrative costs both at UK and EU level. Interestingly, the same reduction target for administrative burdens of 25%, to be achieved by 2012, has been also identified in COM(2006)689

assessments that are supposed to forerun all UK national regulatory initiatives must expressly consider the potential impact of non-compliance on regulatory outcomes and the likelihood that non-compliance will occur. This refines the methods of the "better-regulatory" practice still more.

The Conservative opposition under the leadership of David Cameron joined the regulatory debate even before coming to power, noting especially the "growing burden of regulation". They summarised their new approach in a commissioned report titled "Freeing Britain to Compete", which detailed the failings of the regulatory regime; the successes of past deregulation; the desirability of self-regulation; removal of burdensome regulators; a Conservative deregulation bill; the European Union's legislation and its tendency to overregulate; and the sufficiency of substituting competition policy for bureaucratic command (Redwood and Wolfson, 2007). The Conservatives proposed an action plan which has been partially carried out since the Coalition took office in May 2010. Already by November 2009 the Conservative Party had published a policy paper titled "Regulation in the post-bureaucratic age", promoting a reduction in red tape and reforms cutting the costs and burdens of regulatory schemes. Since the Conservative-Liberal Democrat Coalition acceded to Downing Street in 2010, more than 100 so-called QUANGOs (quasi-autonomous non-governmental organisations) have been axed. In addition, government departments have been streamlined and merged, notably the Department of Business, Innovation and Skills (BIS), which was created in June 2009 out of BERR and the Department for Innovation, Universities and Skills (DIUS). The Coalition Government also promised further regulatory reforms, such as sunset provisions for all regulators, and a "One In – One Out" rule whereby new regulations may not be issued without simultaneously withdrawing old ones; resulting, it was claimed, in a 5% reduction of the total regulatory burden (Conservative Party, 2009:15). The need for these reforms had become obvious to nearly everybody: "In 2007, more than 3,000 separate pieces of legislation, totalling some 29,000 pages of text, became law in the United Kingdom. 18,000 pages originated domestically and 11,000 came from the implementation of over 2,000 EU Regulations and Directives. The Government's own figures show that, in 2008, all this new regulation cost the British economy £663 million in increased administration alone" (Conservative Party, 2009:6).

It may be argued that the UK has merely adopted ideas already developed at the European Level, and so has added little value to the European agenda. However, by implementing measures like BERR and the Better Regulation Executive to reduce and simplify regulation, the UK has taken a leading role in pursuing the agenda of better governance and industry regulation. Participatory institutions like the Business Council for Britain enable private stakeholders not only to influence the national but also the European policy agenda.

on "A strategic review of Better Regulation in the European Union". COM(2006)691 on "Measuring administrative costs and reducing administrative burdens in the European Union" estimates that economic benefits from such action can increase GDP up to 1.5% or €150 billion *per annum*. As with other European policy initiatives, economic arguments are often used to promote speedier adoption and implementation of EU initiatives at national level. Governments can "sell" these policy initiatives more easily to stakeholders in general, and to businesses in particular.

Regulatory reform is no longer an academic debate: policy-makers at the Global, European, and National Levels are at the forefront of defining and implementing it. It was for this reason that the foregoing policy papers that led to these changes have been reviewed. It is a good example of how multi-level governance works in practice. Let us now turn to the scholarly output concerning this new and ambitious agenda for the governance of Europe.

The transition from deregulation to regulatory reform and, more recently, to regulatory management is still underway, and the results have been variable.[59] In 2000 the Prodi Commission initiated a new Europe-wide regulatory reform known in the EU and OECD Member States as the Better Regulation agenda. However, when this reform was launched there was arguably no consistent and clear way forward for it. "The Commission itself was struggling both in ensuring public and stakeholder participation, attempting to promote social and environmental concerns raised at the European Council of Göteborg while at the same time arguing for greater EU competitiveness" (Lofstedt, July 2006:2). The EU's Better Regulation agenda in general, and the new governance in particular, has topped the agenda in recent years owing to three main difficulties: competitiveness, sustainable development, and good governance (Lofstedt, 2004:237-260). The Better Regulation initiatives have been criticised especially for the poor quality of its Regulatory Impact Analyses (RIAs) (Lee and Kirkpatrick, 2004; Mather and Vibert, 2005; Torriti, 2007:239-276). Critics also blamed the Commission for conducting too many RIAs at first (Ambler, Chittenden and Shamutkova, 2003, 2004; Ambler, Chittenden and Hwang, 2005). Much has changed since then, however. In November 2004 European Commission President Barroso came to office with an administration which was "right-centre and free-market oriented, in the Anglo-Saxon model", and which was therefore able to regain the momentum for regulatory reform (Lofstedt, 2006:3).

One of the striking features of the new regulatory vision is that external stakeholder participation is obligatory: policy-makers are formally required to involve, engage, and consult stakeholders. This is a drastic change in how regulators operate, and it underlines the importance of the research done for this book. So many fundamental changes, so the author contends, have necessitated a fresh theoretical approach. Traditional views on the relationship between the regulators and the regulated should be cross-examined, and if these views are no longer sustainable, revision is in order.

Adrienne Héritier argues that the new modes of governance promoted by the Commission "are guided by the principles of voluntarism (non-binding targets and the use of soft law), subsidiarity (measures are decided by member states), and inclusion (the actors concerned participate in governance)" (Héritier, 2002:187). The new policy instruments of governance are wide-ranging: from consultations, codes of conduct, eco-labels, and scorecards, to benchmarking, best practices, high-level fora, voluntary agreements, and co-regulation (Zito *et al.*, 2003:509-511). In addition, regulatory reform implies simplification of existing law (through consolidation, codification, and repeal) and a reduction of administrative costs

59 OECD Working Party on Regulatory Management and Reform (4.05.2007) Third special session (Paris). OECD country reviews on regulatory reform at http://www.oecd.org/countrylist/0,3349,en_2649_201185_1794487_1_1_1_1,00.html (2007).

("cutting red tape"). Pursuant to the reform, EU and national politicians announced targeted reductions in administrative costs of between 20 and 25 percent (Wiener, 2006:49-56; Better Regulation website, 2007). Commission officials have emphasised the importance of simplification and cost reduction, arguing that Europe's competitiveness depends upon such regulatory reforms. A 2005 Communication drew a connection between less bureaucracy and more growth (CEC, 2005e).

Improving the quality and transparency of regulatory oversight and analyses (*viz.* Regulatory Impact Assessments) has been a key theme of recent governance debate. Suggestions span the gamut from a Directive requiring assessment of the net benefits of regulation, to creation of a strong centralised regulatory EU oversight body to evaluate the worth of regulatory proposals (Hahn and Litan, 2005:473-508). In 2004 Claudio Radaelli conducted research for DG Enterprise on indicators of regulatory quality, and the following year gleaned further insight by sitting on an expert panel along with the Better Regulation Executive (a UK body) and the National Audit Office in the UK. His view is that the role of Better Regulation "in regulatory politics and its impact on the legitimacy of regulatory governance is bound to increase" (Radaelli and De Francesco, 2007). In particular, Radaelli considers the Regulatory Impact Assessment (RIA)[60] to be the cornerstone of "better regulation" and "good regulatory governance". On the other hand, he stresses that, due to multiple approaches and actors' differing preferences, "impact assessment differs markedly throughout the EU"[61] (Radaelli, 2005:1-25). Radaelli's work is a good example of the importance to the author of primary research – both the personal participation and the review of policy papers – to understanding the challenges that national and international regulators face.

Daniel Naurin discusses the EU's "democratic deficit" and calls for greater "transparency" in the Union's policy-making processes (Naurin, 2008). Naurin empirically tested this nostrum of deliberative democratic theorists, that greater transparency will transform the political

60 The Regulatory "Impact Assessment identifies the likely positive and negative impacts of proposed policy actions, enabling informed political judgements to be made about the proposal and identifying trade-offs in achieving competing objectives. It also permits to complete the application of the subsidiarity and proportionality protocol annexed to the Amsterdam Treaty". Over the last few years the Commission has already developed several special impact assessment instruments and methods: Business Impact Assessment; Regulatory Impact Assessment; Sustainability Impact Assessment; thus, prior appraisals, in order to take account of such Treaty objectives as sustainable development, environmental protection, and health, had to identify the relevant variables *ad hoc*. The new Impact Assessments brought all existing procedures under one roof, and will be required for each new proposal. However, the Commission considers Impact Assessments as "an aid to decision-making, not a substitute for political judgement. [...] An impact assessment will not necessarily generate clear-cut conclusions or recommendations. It does, however, provide an important input by informing decision-makers of the consequences of policy choices". The "new impact assessment method integrates all sectoral assessments concerning direct and indirect impacts of a proposed measure into one global instrument, hence moving away from the existing situation of a number of partial and sectoral assessments. It provides a common set of basic questions, minimum analytical standards and a common reporting format" (CEC, 2002l, CEC, 2002n).

61 For inconsistent implementation, see also the table "Overview of measures in the area of Better Regulation and Impact Assessment" in Wiener (2006).

processes of the European Union from market-style bargaining (*a.k.a.* "horse trading") to public-spirited deliberation. The results were both disappointing and encouraging: the impact of transparency was found to be overrated, although to the extent that it did make an impact, it affected lobbyists' behaviour even behind closed doors. Stakeholder participation is already a form of transparency, and the principles of the Commission's new governance initiative, of which stakeholder consultation is an integral part, go part way toward reaching Naurin's transparency goals. On the other hand, as the evidence in this book shows, few of those now entitled to participate in the new governance are actually doing so. It is a real question whether anyone but those stakeholders most intensely affected by the regulatory process (business above all) will bestir themselves to take note of the stream of information now emerging from the Commission's new consultative and participatory processes. It may well be that the democratic deficit is actually an "apathy surplus" amongst the general public, which no amount of transparency can overcome.

2.1.5 Independent Regulatory Agencies: solution or dilemma?

Quite clearly, the power of policy stakeholders and policy communities to either prevent or control policy change was, in the past, subject to severe constraints by Member State governments and by other exogenous forces.[62] In many instances policy stakeholders were responding-to rather than creating policy change. However, trends that began in the late 1970s, such as globalization and its consequent exposure of Europe to heightened competition, or the progressive integration of the Single Market, have forced European governments to abandon traditional modes of governance. Majone has analysed in great detail the transition of the "interventionist state" (or "positive state") into the "regulatory state". In the past, state power consisted mostly of taxing and spending; the regulatory mode has enhanced the state's rule-making powers (Majone 1997:139-167; 2005). Majone claims that the EU institutions have become the very regulators of the "new regulatory state" (Majone, 2001:263-277). With the establishment of the Single Market "the traditional roles and methods of regulation and control were breaking down under the pressure of powerful technological, economic and ideological forces, and were dismantled or radically transformed" (Majone, 1997:143). Often referred to as "deregulation", it could more accurately be seen as "re-regulation at a different level of governance" (Majone, 1997:143).

The liberalisation of utilities (*viz.* telecommunications, energy, water, transportation) necessitated a reform of national administrative structures (Peters, 2002:263-277). This reform was made viable by the establishment across Europe of independent national regulatory agencies with powers to implement and enforce sundry sector-specific regulatory regimes made in Brussels. For instance, the agency for telecommunications in Germany is RegTP (Regulierungsbehörde für Telecommunication und Post, 1996); in France it is ART (Autorité de Régulation des Télécommunications, 1996). In Britain the corresponding regulatory

62 This applies to European and national policy. See for example Richardson (1994b).

agency (the Office of Communications, or Ofcom) had been set up by the Telecommunications Act as early as 1984, making the UK a pioneer in telecoms liberalisation.[63]

Of the five institutional designs for utility regulation identified by Dominik Böllhoff – *viz.* the ministry, the administrative agency, the competition authority, industry self-regulation, and the Independent Regulatory Authority (IRA), sometimes called the National Regulatory Authority (NRA) (Böllhoff, 2002:241-245) – the last one is the solution most discussed amongst scholars (Mark Thatcher, 1999b, 2001b, 2002b, 2005b; Robert Baldwin and Martin Cave, 1999). Debate has raged in recent years over whether to erect a pan-European regulatory agency, and if so, whether it should just superintend the national IRAs or take exclusive responsibility for implementation and enforcement as a "European" telecommunications regulator (Thatcher, 2001b:315). An alternative to such an agency would be "bottom-up" coordination between national IRAs. The latter would be helped by a formalisation of the methods of coordination, yielding a "network" type of European regulation (Coen and Doyle, 1999:83-106), and would vindicate the principle of subsidiarity that figures prominently (at least in theory) in the Commission's European Governance White Paper of 2001. The difficulties of coordination, of allocation of responsibilities, and of rendering decisional processes transparent, however, continue to pose serious challenges to the IRA concept.

Mark Thatcher examined the regulatory regime – the institutional, procedural and constitutional aspects of economic regulation – that has been set up over the utilities (Thatcher, 1997b), and especially over telecommunications (Thatcher, 1999a). A "regulatory state" hypothesis emerged on the reform's effects on the relationship between stakeholders and regulators and on stakeholders' participation in regulatory politics (Thatcher, 2002a:859-872). In Thatcher's view, the independent regulatory agencies (IRAs), which are an essential element of the "regulatory state" model, have opened up their decision-making processes – and now stand in contrast with the closed processes of the EU's main institutions before the delegation of regulatory power (Thatcher, 2002b:945-972). His more recent research concludes that IRAs are not only legally separate from the national general government, but also embody real organisational autonomy in policy-making and implementation, constituting a "third force" of actors independent of elected politicians (Thatcher, 2005a). Thus the institutional design of IRAs points away from the traditional assumptions and practices of lobbying (such as trading votes for favours), and indeed reduces the opportunities for lobbying.

With the emergence of Brussels as the prime locus of regulatory authority in general (and the ICT sector in particular), certain dilemmas had to be faced that were novel in the governing experience of the EU institutions. On the one hand, Brussels as usual lacks the power to implement its own directives. It has neither the right to tax nor material means of coercion; both of these fundamental powers of government remaining exclusively with the

63 Ofcom was reformed in January 2004. The legacy regulators that have been merged into the Office of Communications are Oftel (Office of Telecommunications), BSC (Broadcasting Standards Commission), ITC (Independent Television Commission), RA (Radiocommunications Agency), Radio Authority, ACTs (Advisory Committees on Telecommunications), Spectrum Auctions and SMAG (Spectrum Management Advisory Group).

Member States. Implementation was therefore delegated to the Member States of necessity. However, the novel development of the privatisation of utilities entailed novel problems of implementation. In addition to the EU's well-known problems – like the national variation in the legal and institutional landscape, and the "strong tension between the creation of a single European market through centralised EU-level legislation and its decentralised implementation by national-level authorities" (Thatcher and Coen, 2008:806), – there arose the peculiar difficulty that utilities had long enjoyed a legally privileged position in the national economy. Regulatory authorities organised at National Level, where their decisions would have the force of law, yet independently of national governments and the political temptations they lie under, appeared to be the best solution available. Thus, the IRA was invented. It was both a response to the special conditions of utility privatisation and regulation, and a "chapter" in the ongoing search for a solution to the general problems of EU governance:

> EU legislation is frequently broad and difficult to implement, and conditions in national markets vary, so the same rules must be applied differently to achieve a similar objective ... the sheer variety of national institutions responsible for implementing EU legislation makes consistency across member states very difficult ... [c]onsequently, there is a real risk of conflict between the principles of a single market – notably equality of treatment among firms and ending barriers to entry – and its administration by a multiplicity of member states. (Thatcher and Coen, 2008:807)

The coordination problems that arose between the multitude of newly enfranchised IRAs was "solved" as well as it ever will be, given the EU's hybrid nature, by the setting-up of the European Regulators Group by Commission Decision (2002/627/EC) to encourage "cooperation and coordination between national regulatory authorities and the Commission, in order to promote the development of the internal market for electronic communications networks and services" (BEREC website, 2012). This has been superseded as of January 2010 by the Body of European Regulators for Electronic Communications (BEREC) (for more about BEREC see Section 7.2.3 below).

2.2 THE PROCESSES OF POLICY MAKING

The following Section reviews the scholarship which supports the Stakeholder Action Matrix and the Policy Influence-Timing Model. Sub-section 2.2.1 summarises some classical views of the EU policy process, while Sub-section 2.2.2 presents the Stages Heuristic – a theorisation that divides the policy process into temporal segments.

According to Paul Sabatier, "The process of public policy-making includes the manner in which problems get conceptualised and brought to government for solution; governmental institutions formulate alternatives and select policy solutions; and those solutions get implemented, evaluated, and revised" (Sabatier, 1999b:3). All of this involves a complex set of interacting elements over time, especially:

1. *Actors*: Usually hundreds of actors from groups of private and public stakeholders (companies, NGO, consumer groups, *etc.*) and governmental organs are involved at different policy stages and levels of government. Each of these actors and classes of actors has different values/interests, perceptions of the situation, and policy preferences (Sabatier, 1999b:3-4).

2. *Multiple governance levels*: Developing new regulations or revising existing regulations involves different levels of government – local, regional, national, European, and international (Sabatier, 1999b:3-4).

3. *Time factors and policy stages*: The process, from the emergence of a problem through to the drafting of a new regulation, its implementation and evaluation, takes time. Time is always an important factor, although the time spans that Sabatier and Jenkins-Smith (1993c:3) suggest (a decade or more) are perhaps not applicable to a fast-moving arena like ICT policy.[64]

4. *Policy debates*: In the course of legislative hearings, litigation, and proposed administrative regulations the actors normally have very technical disputes over the severity of the problem, its causes, and the probable impacts of alternative policy solutions.

5. *Economic interests*: "Policy disputes seldom resemble polite academic debates" (Sabatier, 1999b:4). They revolve around large amounts of money that are to be spent or saved through the implementation and enhancement (or not) of independent regulatory agencies, licence fees, administrative charges, *etc.*

6. *External factors (sub-systems)*: Policy-making may be shaped indirectly. Public perceptions, values, attitudes, feelings, emotions, and other behaviours may play an important role. These can definitely influence the information – decision – action – feedback stages of decision-making (Greene, 1993:7, 10).

2.2.1 EU decisional processes: the classical view

Most of the scholarly work on the EU focusses on the formal processes of decision-making at the European level (Beate Kohler-Koch and Rainer Eising, 1999; Hussein Kassim 1994, Guy Peters, 2001, 2002). Institutionalists concern themselves with the more formal, observable building-blocks of government and view public institutions as the centres of decision-making (Elinor Ostrom, 1999, 2007; Douglass North, 1990, 2005). In their view, organisations are created by groups of people, and governance arrangements attempt to coordinate their collective actions (North, 2005; Ostrom, 2007:239-264). By contrast, behaviouralists are "scholars consumed with what people actually do, interpret public policy as the result of

64 It took less than seven years for the EU Telecommunications Liberalisation directives and the new Regulatory Framework for electronic services and networks to be transposed into national law (1 January 1998 and 24 July 2003, respectively).

the interaction of powerful forces, some of which may be far removed from the halls of government" (Gerston, 1997:5).

As Hix has pointed out, traditional international-relations approaches to analysing the EU have revolved around the issue of the degree of integration: "since its birth in the 1950s ... the EC [EU] has mainly been studied as an example of supranational integration of, or intergovernmental co-operation between, (previously) sovereign nation-states" (Hix, 1994:1). Much has been written about the complexity of the EU's supranational institutions (the Commission, the European Court of Justice, Parliament) and about the impact of the intergovernmental Council of Ministers on EU policy (Garrett and Tsebelis, 2001:357-390; Falkner, 2002:98-119; Bromley, 2001:1-26; Cram, Dinan and Nugent, 1999:3-19, Sandholtz and Sweet, 1998:1-26). Previous scholarly work has also concerned itself with "improving" the formal institutions of European decision-making, and in doing so has neglected the importance of informal institutions, such as the EU's now-famous "culture of consensus", and of the private sector. In response, a broader conception of governance that extends beyond the formal rules of the state to include various kinds of informal social influence and control has been developed (Baldwin and Cave, 1999:2; Majone, 2005).

The long-established tradition of studying political action involving external interests in national politics has been supplemented of late by a trend toward analysing business interests (as one of those informal social influences) in transnational settings. The studies addressing this development at the European Level are by now well established (Greenwood, 2000a:241). Most are based on narrowly drawn case studies of the formation of advocacy coalitions on such issues as air-pollution (Sabatier, 1993:13-40), offshore energy (Jenkins-Smith and Clair, 1993:149-176), water policy-making (Richardson, 1996a:139-167), and environmental policy (Richardson, 1996b).

Sabatier and Mazmanian have complained, however, that many of these case studies, done in the 1980s, "become so immersed in the detail of programme implementation that they lose sight of the macro-level and political variables that structure the entire process" (Sabatier and Mazmanian, 1981:3). To date, no serious attempt has been made to explain the outcomes of business stakeholder influence, either purely theoretically or through modelling. Justin Greenwood and Jeremy Richardson did make a first attempt, but their "collections of case studies" from scholars merely challenge traditional views about EU policy-making without providing a new approach. Perhaps the theoretical development lag is owing to the conventional assumption that external stakeholders are not serious factors in policy-making; or perhaps established scholars have simply neglected the mounting evidence for commercial-sector involvement.

This book shows that policy-making is no longer a simple question of intergovernmentalism *versus* supranationalism. Both the scholarly literature and the popular press discuss the outcomes of intergovernmental conferences like the European Councils (or "Summits") in terms of national interests. EU policies, however, are no longer mere culminations of intergovernmental bargaining, appearances to the contrary notwithstanding. As some scholars already recognise, a wide range of non-governmental actors are involved at all levels of a complex process that Tsebelis has described in terms of "nested games" (Tsebelis, 1990). This book recognises the complexity and instability of stakeholders and their "games", and makes certain assumptions to accommodate that, in order to develop a model that addresses questions left unanswered (*cf.* Section 1.4.1).

2.2.2 The Stages Heuristic: the temporal approach

One of the most influential frameworks for understanding the policy process has been the Stages Heuristic.[65] It divides the policy process into a series of "stages", – the typical ones include: agenda setting, policy formulation and legitimation, implementation, and evaluation – and internal causative factors affecting the myriad stages of sundry policy process have been analysed in great detail.

Harold D. Lasswell articulated the first formal conception of policy science in 1951. He insisted on a multidisciplinary approach, and emphasised the interactive effects among the different processual stages. The policy stages he described and defined included: intelligence, recommendation, prescription, invocation, application, appraisal, and termination. His conception of a delineated, sequential policy process was much admired and, as stated above, many authors have availed themselves of his framework, explicitly or implicitly (Lasswell, 1951).

Charles Jones' *An Introduction to the Study of Public Policy* (1977) and James Anderson's *Public Policy Making* (1979) were among the first "public policy" volumes. Both works, leaning heavily on Lasswell (1951), distinguish as stages of the policy process: problem identification, agenda setting, adoption, implementation, and policy evaluation. Both cast these stages within a broader social environment characterised by political institutions, political opinion, political culture, and other constraints on decisions. Each stage involved distinct policy actors, time-periods, and institutions.

In 1983 Brewer and deLeon published *The Foundations of Policy Analysis*, which laid out in great detail (with rationales) certain interesting stages of the policy process. These works and their advocacy of the Stages Heuristic redirected research by an entire generation of noted policy scholars, who turned to the study of stages instead of specific issue areas. "The stages approach tends to focus on political processes within political institutions, emphasising political realities more than political formalities and concentrating on the behaviour of the participants in the process" (Jones, 1977:3). The assumption is that what actually happens inside political institutions will form predictable behavioural patterns even without formalisation. Legal and historical factors and the formal institutions they produced are not excluded, but are supplemented by social, economic, and psychological analyses in the attempt to understand actual decision-making more fully (Jones, 1977:2-3 *et passim*). The Stages approach focusses on how political institutions really work, the main emphasis being on broadly generalising about the behaviour of a given institution; although how it works on specific policy issues may also be treated. Typical questions include: "How is this function achieved?" and "How does the behaviour of specific actors contribute to the function of the institution?" (Jones, 1977:4).

65 The terms "stages approach" and "(institutional) process approaches" are used synonymously in the literature.

In 1988 DeLeon came out with *Advice and Consent*, which compared the relative strengths and weaknesses of the whole method of segmenting the policy stages, insofar as it affected the policy science research agenda. He clearly identified the downside to the Stages Heuristic: distinguishing specific stages focusses scholars on one stage at a time, to the neglect of the process as a whole. Too many researchers ended up viewing the process as a sharply differentiated set of activities, portraying a disjointed, episodic process, whereas the reality was a more ongoing, continuous one. Above all, the heuristic imposes an artificial linearity on the operations and politics of a process that actually consists of a nexus of feedback actions or recursive loops; *e.g.* any evaluation of the policy formulation may loop back to agenda setting rather than onward to the next (formal) step of implementation; whilst policy formulation and agenda-setting often feed back and forth on each other (deLeon, 1988).

In the following decade the Stages Heuristic was subjected to even more severe criticism, mainly from Sabatier and Jenkins-Smith (1993a, 1993b, 1999), who claimed that stages (their term for policy "process") are after all only a heurism the reliability of which is limited. It was useful for stimulating empirical research in the 1970s and early 1980s, but since then has outlived its usefulness and needs to be replaced or substantially revised. Sabatier and Jenkins-Smith complained that the heuristic fails to explain the evolution of policy, identifying no governing causes that drive the process within and across stages.[66] The assumption that there is a single policy process about a single legislative proposal oversimplifies a "cycle" that quite often consists of multiple, interacting cycles involving multiple policy proposals and draft laws on multiple levels of governance. They conclude that the "Stages Heuristic suffers from descriptive inaccuracy" (Nakaruma, 1977), and a great deal of recent empirical study finds that deviations are quite frequent; especially, evaluations of existing programmes often affect agenda setting in unpredictable ways. Scholars like Nakamura echo this criticism, pointing out that proposed sequences of stages are often descriptively inaccurate, and that interactions take place between non-consecutive stages (Nakamura, 1997:142-154).

Another criticism is that the heuristic has a built-in legalistic, top-down bias, resulting in a tendency to neglect external players and to restrict the view of policy to specific legislation; and that it may be inapplicable entirely when the theorised dominant player does not exist. One might add to Sabatier and Jenkins-Smith's criticisms that the influence of multiple *private* stakeholders within the policy process is also widely neglected.

66 Input into the technical aspects of policy debates can play an important role in policy evolution, often involving a heterogeneous mix of stakeholders providing expert input at different stages of the policy process. For example, the "European Cookie Law" (Directive 2002/58 on Privacy and Electronic Communications), which came into effect on 26 May 2011, amended existing privacy legislation, requiring websites to obtain informed consent from visitors before storing or retrieving any information on a computer or Internet browser. Article 5(3) of the Directive, which is "technologically neutral" (*i.e.* leaves it up to the regulatee to invent a practical solution) , sparked a long and complex debate throughout the whole policy process about how this law might be enforced (esp. on websites hosted outside the EU); what the technical options were; and how it would impact functionality. Allocation of this debate to one specific stage in the policy process would have been impossible, as agreeing the Cookie Law's content was an unpredictable, iterative process between regulators, service providers and technical experts.

Sabatier and Jenkins-Smith admit the model does have the "heuristic" value of dividing a complex and variegated policy process into manageable analytic units. The re-conceptualisation accomplished by the heuristic has also enabled a useful treatment of certain topics within the Institutionalist framework, such as policy impact, which implicate the capacity of governmental institutions to achieve policy objectives. Finally, the conception of a process of policy-making operating across diverse governmental institutions has provided an advantageous alternative to the institution-bound approach of traditional political science, which overemphasised the features of particular institutions.

DeLeon himself acknowledges that Sabatier and Jenkins-Smith "do not necessarily undercut the legitimacy or viability of the policy process approach" (deLeon, 1999:26). He defends the "traditional policy sciences" by arguing that Sabatier and Jenkins-Smith's Advocacy Coalitions Framework is "depressingly inadequate when both ends and means [of the policy process] are uncertain or undetermined" (deLeon, 1997).

The author seconds deLeon's view that the Stages Heuristic continues to enhance our understanding of a policy process, and therefore has its place in political science. For this reason this approach was leveraged to develop the Policy Influence-Timing Model in Chapter One. Moreover, scholars generally have paid little or no attention to the most urgent question of practitioners and policy stakeholders *external* to the EU institutions: *At which point [*viz. *stage] in the policy process will my input count the most?* The Policy Influence-Timing Model gives the answer.

2.3 MULTI-LEVEL STAKEHOLDER PARTICIPATION AND ADVOCACY COALITIONS

The scholarship on business influence over EU policy suggests that business activities at the European Level are trending toward greater coordination and political sophistication. However, these data are being presented as is, without analysing actual or systematising possible forms of stakeholder influence. Current scholars share the author's view that studies of EU interest intermediation still lacks systematic analysis of *types* of influence, *i.e.* the conditions under which private interests actually exert influence. The author has concluded that influence accrues to external stakeholders to the extent that they form "advocacy coalitions" composed of actors who recognise each other as having similar interests (Michalowitz, 2007:132-151). Accordingly, this book analyses not only how external stakeholders participate in the decision-making process, but also in what forms and when they are most efficient in influencing it.

This Section reviews the scholarship that formed the basis for the Stakeholder Action Matrix. Sub-section 2.3.1 considers the complex relationship of regulators and external ICT policy stakeholders in the EU multi-level governance system. Sub-section 2.3.2 reviews policy networks and communities, followed by Sub-section 2.3.3, which introduces the interest-based approaches to policy influence that constitute the foundations of the Advocacy Coalition Typology of stakeholders contained in this book.

2.3.1 The regulators and policy stakeholders: a complex relationship

Ever more studies have been published in recent years that explicitly concern the structure and role of the EU institutions and their mutual interaction. Some concern the formation and enforcement of European law (Moussis, 2001); others focus on the EU institutions, particularly their roles in policy-making (Nugent, 1994, 1999, 2000; Richardson, 1994, 1996, 2001). These roles are defined by the Treaty of the European Union (TEU) and have been studied in great detail. This book does not engage in the debate over institutional reform or the supposed weaknesses of the TEU, but merely addresses the EU as it actually is. Its scope is limited to charting the influence of external stakeholders over the ICT policy process.

The EU's policy-making system extends far beyond economic policy, unlike other regional supranational arrangements. Its quasi-federal nature; the extreme and unusual openness of its decisional processes to external stakeholders, in comparison to other multinational regimes; the considerable weight of so many national governments, all create an unpredictable, multi-level policy-making environment (Richardson, 2001a:5; Peters, 2001:77-94; Peters and Wright, 2001: 155-178). A multiplicity of actors is involved: the Member State governments; representatives of regional and local authorities; the EU institutions and other European bodies and agencies; and a host of other stakeholders of varying size and importance, each with its own interest (Mazey and Richardson, 1993; Greenwood and Aspinwall, 1997:1-30; Aspinwall, 1997:196-213). Individuals, groups and associations both public and private compete for influence. As decisions do not normally result from the action of a single actor or institution, parties must search for allies and form coalitions. Faced with such a labyrinthine policy process, the analyst hoping to find his way out of it alive must seek some simplifying "thread of Ariadne". This book furnishes such a thread in the form of the Advocacy Coalition Typology presented in Chapter One and elaborated in Chapter Five.

Neill Nugent has made a significant contribution to the EU governance debate, and sees the EU as a system becoming ever more multi-layered and interconnected as between policy actors. The EU shoulders a broader policy responsibility and has developed a more complex institutional structure than is found in other international bodies. It has progressed far beyond the essentially intergovernmental nature of many international organisations to incorporate into its structure and operation many "supranational" characteristics (Nugent, 1994:329-431).

Policy-making is served by a relatively small bureaucracy; the European Commission is not a large institution, contrary to popular misconceptions.[67] It lacks adequate resources to prepare the number of legislative proposals that the Council of Ministers frequently requests, creating a high dependency on outside sources of information and expertise. Many

67 The Commission currently employs approximately 25,000 European civil servants including also administrative officials, experts, translators, interpreters and secretarial staff. This is fewer than the number of staff employed by a typical medium-sized city council in Europe. For example, Surrey County Council (UK) employs in total about 23,000 staff to service its one million residents. Britain's Home Office currently employs twice as many people as the Commission: almost 70,000 staff located across England and Wales. In total, the civil service in the UK employs more than 550,000 staff in 150 government departments, executive agencies, and non-departmental public organisations (Home Office website, 2007).

"Commission officials" are in fact seconded national officials or private experts on 3-5 year contracts.[68] The Commission relies heavily on other external actors, including national governments, firms and interest groups (Thatcher, 2001a; van Schendelen, 1994; Coen, 1998). Openness to contact from outside is important, as confirmed by the Commission's own statement of its policy on contact with outside interests: "The Commission has always been an institution open to outside input. The Commission believes this process to be fundamental to the development of its policies. This dialogue has proved invaluable to both the Commission and to interested outside parties. Commission officials acknowledge the need for such outside input and welcome it" (CEC, 1992).

Laura Cram has studied European policy actors and how they collaborate, with a special focus on the "IT sector". She notes that representatives from ICT firms are an omnipresent force in the EU's ICT policy process. Their contributions vary widely in manner and degree: as individuals, as actors on committees, in consultation groups, or as group members in industry federations and national and European standards bodies (Cram, 1995:23-37). This private-sector involvement did not come about without some effort by the Commission. Major ICT firms were attracted by the incentives of research programmes which were initiated by the Commission to support its policy objectives of research and innovation. Cram notes that DG Information Society "now enjoys a rather symbiotic relationship with the industry, which is involved at almost every stage of policy deliberation in the area" (Cram, 1997:75). "Several officials in [legacy] DG XIII[69] have, for example, commented that they are in such close contact with industrial representatives from the IT sector that they could hardly consider this lobbying – there is an ongoing process of consultation between industry and the policy-maker" (Cram, 1995:23). It is widely acknowledged that the Commission actively influences the level of participation by interest groups, their style of lobbying, and the quality of their access to the EU institutions. As Broscheid and Coen conclude, by "accepting that the Commission actively influences lobbying, we observe that the greatest level of lobbying activity clusters around the regulatory policy domains of the Commission" (Broscheid and Coen, 2007:361).

There is also increasing evidence that European interests-representation has become more diversified and specialised. Mark Aspinwall points out that, more than ever, European interest groups are protagonists, seeking to influence policy rather than simply monitoring it. Interest groups target specific issues, sometimes only *ad hoc* and for a limited time (Aspinwall, 1997:198). Investigating the logic behind apparently *ad hoc* lobbying behaviour has been Pieter Bouwen's research programme. He devised a theoretical framework to explain the easy access of business interests to political actors. He finds in addition to

68 In 1997, DGXIII [Directorate General Telecommunications, Information Market and Exploitation of Research], Unit A1 (Telecommunications Regulation), which was responsible for preparing the regulatory package for the "Telecommunications Liberalisation", employed just 35 staff. Approximately 50% were Commission functionaries; 30% were seconded from national telecommunications operators; 10% worked as technical, legal and economic experts; and 10% worked as contractors/support staff (Rossmeissl, 1997).

69 DG XIII was the former Directorate-General for Telecommunications, Information Industries and Innovation; now DG Information Society.

action by individual companys a further recourse to third-party representation by lobbyists or industry associations (Bouwen, 2001). Baldwin notes that a common theme of interest-group theorists is to "see regulatory developments as the products of relationships between different groups and between such groups and the state" (Baldwin and Cave, 1999:21). The general thesis that policy-making is dominated by stakeholders in "an ongoing process of consultation" is what inspired the refinement –initially suggested by the author's participant observation of stakeholders at consultative events – which is his Industry Governance Theory, the theory that the process is actually dominated by one group of stakeholders in particular.

Mark Thatcher's comparative study of the European telecommunications landscape over the last 30 years (Thatcher, 1999b) propounds a robust theory about the influence over public-sector management and government decision-making of national institutions and policy actors, including politicians, industrial interest groups, consumer representatives, and trade union interests. Thatcher uses the European telecoms industry as a "test environment" in which to study the operation and impact of various industrial policies. He contends that dissimilar institutional features (legal systems, state competition agencies, civil service structures) lead to dissimilar patterns of policy formulation in different countries. To prove this theory, Thatcher undertook a historical comparison between four countries – Britain, France, Germany and Italy – and their process of decision-making in the substantive EU regulation of telecommunications, as to the types of policy participants, their spheres of action, and their degrees of autonomy and relationships to the central government. He discovered that the Commission and the Member State governments acted as partners. The only major conflicts between them concerned constitutional rather than substantive issues (Thatcher, 2001a:558-583). One has to wonder what is the cause of this striking harmony, given so many differences of detail? Something knitted them together, and it was not their national diversities.

Thatcher has also argued that "EC [EU] regulation favoured certain factors within domestic arenas and disadvantaged others" (Thatcher, 2005a:112). The reform in telecommunications, for example, fits with governments' reform strategies and the interest of incumbent telecoms operators in international alliances; while the representatives of labour found their position weakened by EU regulation. He stresses that the winners had been involved in the Europeanisation process pro-actively: governments were pivotal to the making of EU regulations, and postal services' and telecommunications operators' (PTOs') managements lobbied at the European Level while enjoying close relationships with their Member State governments. Thatcher concludes that certain Member State governments and big business interests control EU integration – a hypothesis that finds corroboration in the research in this book (Thatcher, 2005a:102-127).

Given that the Commission has become more open in the last ten years, and given its slender resources yet pressing need to fully understand national and sectoral problems, it is eager to forge symbiotic relationships with EU-wide interest groups. An effective working relationship requires the latter to be well informed, to represent their interests accurately, and to understand the rules of the EU policy-making game (Philip and Gray, 1996:xvii). Yet even as stakeholders become more embedded in the policy process, mere participation in stakeholder political activities does not always guarantee policy influence. The relative influence of the actors who participate in shaping the European Information Society project varies significantly. Differences in organisational structure, permanent staff deployed, budgeted resources, diversity of interests, and "enforcement" powers (especially informal powers of influence and financial contribution) may be huge (Chadwick, 2006:220-221). Jeremy Richardson stresses that even if an actor is successful at one institutional site, its "deals" may become unstuck at another, due to the multitude of different channels of influence or "pressure-points" rival lobbyists may exploit. He sees in this inherently disjointed policy process a problem for the "joined-up governance" (*i.e.* closer collaboration between stakeholders and government officials) of the European Union (Mazey and Richardson, 2001a:217-238).

Understanding the influence of stakeholders in the EU policy process and the "symbiotic" relationship between stakeholders and the regulator really calls for an exact empirical investigation of who these external stakeholders are and what they have done to influence ICT regulations and standards. Hitherto this has been lacking in scholarly studies. This book contains a Survey administered by the author to actual European ICT policy stakeholders and an eCommunications Framework case study in order to fill this gap in the scholarship.

2.3.2 Policy networks and communities

In the 1980s another branch of research – called policy network theory (*a.k.a.* "policy communities", "issue networks", or the "policy universe") – was pioneered to describe more informal and heterogeneous sets of relationships between multiple actors in certain policy fields. In 1992 Benson defined a policy network as:

> a cluster or complex of organisations connected to each other by resource dependencies and distinguished from other clusters or complexes by breaks in the structure of resource dependencies (Benson, 1992:148).

Network analysts argue that within a policy domain/subsystem, organisations with an interest in a given policy area develop patterns of resource exchange by which they seek to enhance their influence over policy events (Laumann and Knoke, 1987a). Negotiations are seen as an everyday and ubiquitous feature of political life. In this process members of policy domains continually negotiate between themselves to become the elite, while trying to participate in collective decision-making for the policy subsystem as a whole (Laumann and Knoke, 1987a:12).

For scholars like Stephen Brooks, "the policy community approach has become the dominant paradigm in the study of interest groups" (1994:2). He notes it is rather an approach than a model, as no single body of formal propositions about interest group behaviour, state-stakeholder relations, policy change, *etc.* has been developed. The reasons for its popularity, he claims, are that it is empirically accurate; that it avoids the pitfalls of wider generalisation; and that it does not apply a class-based approach to interest groups and their influence (Brooks, 1994:2-3).

Charles Raab also stresses the importance of policy networks. He "sees networks as being based on personal relationships between known and trusted individuals who share beliefs and a common culture" (McPherson, 1988:5). Whilst acknowledging the importance of actors, he argues in a later revision based on new research into policy networks that a network model calls for structures as well (Raab, 2001:551-556). The importance of structure is confirmed by David Knoke's studies of networks, which have investigated how network theory can unify topics as diverse as corporate governance, business management, and public policy-making. He found business networks that have led to continual transformations of organisational structures and processes. Network analysis encompasses a wide range of phenomena under the rubric of "collective action" within organisations, from work-team relations to fora facilitating members to "voice their opinion and exert some control" (Knoke, 1990a:5). Knoke has also investigated types of inter-organisational relations such as Industry Standards Groups; Action Sets;[70] research and development consortia; as well as strategic business alliances like cartels, joint ventures, and cooperatives. Having concluded that "explanations of the structure of alliance networks within an organisational field are underdeveloped" (Knoke, 2001:140), he has turned to analysing data from the Global Information Sector (GIS) Project, which has revealed the importance of strategic alliance networks and co-operation in the ICT sector.[71]

Investigating informal collective action as well, Knoke concludes, "Individuals choose their involvements in collective action organisations on the basis of their rational cost-benefit calculations, their desire to conform to group norms, and their affective ties to the collectivity. The understanding of the individual choice process is essential to explain how an organisation constrains its members' behaviours and how these behaviours shape the system's functioning" (Knoke, 1990a:44). Another important observation of Knoke is that mutual trust is needed to regulate and sustain long-term collaboration in partnership between autonomous and otherwise rival corporations. Indeed, other factors bind together individual actors into a community besides common interests and common beliefs, and trust is one of the main ones. Trust is considered an intervening factor in the alliance-formation process (Knoke, 2001:150-156).

The sharedness of beliefs and their contribution to the stability of policy communities is emphasised by Grant Jordan, who sees policy communities as:

> a special type of stable network, which has advantages in encouraging bargaining in policy resolution. In this language the policy network is a statement of shared interests in a policy problem: a policy community exists where there are effective shared 'community' views on the problem. Where there are no such shared views no community exists. (Jordan, 1999:327)

---

70 "A short-lived organizational coalition whose members coordinate their efforts to influence public policy-making. It's cohesion is vulnerable to disintegration by the greater willingness of some participants to strike compromises with opponents" (Knoke, 2001:124).

71 The author has not investigated formal strategic alliances, based on contractual relations; rather he has concentrated on informal collective action of business organisations.

The policy community as a concept needs further clarification to explicate the assumptions that relationships between stakeholders are lasting and that they wish to participate in the policy process directly. Rhodes repeatedly states that "policy communities are networks characterised by stability of relationships, continuity of a highly restrictive membership and vertical interdependence based upon shared delivery responsibilities" (Rhodes, 1985:15; Rhodes, 1990:240; Rhodes and Marsh, 1992:182). Martin Smith faults the excessive attention given the role of groups and the nature of the interactions between groups and the state, and the neglect of the nature of the state itself. He concludes, "Policy networks increase autonomy by creating mechanisms of infrastructural power and by sealing off sectors of policy from wider interests within government and society" (Smith, 1994:53). Smith confirms that policy networks are structured and stable relationships that empower state actors and interest groups to obtain and maintain control over policy areas (Smith, 1994:53). The ICT industry's dominance of the ICT policy domain exemplifies such a "sealed-off" policy community; while their belief system, forming the basis of Advocacy Coalition Type Three (see Section 2.3.3 below), constitutes the "effective shared 'community' views" that according to Jordan define a policy community.

Manuel Castells even talks of *The Rise of the Network Society* (2000) and the "network enterprise". Castells argues that the technological revolution; globalisation of economies; changes in the conduct of business (decentralisation, closer relationships with other firms, management restyling, real-time delivery); state intervention deregulating selected markets; and new communication channels, all are reshaping society. The new "source of productivity lies in the technology of knowledge generation, information processing and communication" (Castells, 2000:16-18). Castells' overarching conclusion about these trends is that the Information Society's new processes are increasingly organised around networks. According to Castells, networks are open structures, able to expand without limit; they can always integrate new "nodes" provided these are capable of communicating within the network. "A network-based social structure is a highly dynamic, open system, susceptible to innovation" (Castells, 1996:470). In his most recent work, Castells propounds a networked "Communication Theory of Power" that spans corporate communication, financial, "cultural-industrial", technological and political networks, all operating at multiple-levels, of which the Internet is an important enabler (Castells, 2009).

The same forces shaping the Information Society as a whole are equally shaping its policy processes. An integral part of this trend is Europeanisation, which in Europe is driving the above-noted changes, especially deregulation and pan-European networking as by the European Commission's Trans-European Networks programme. Maria Green Cowles has provided the following definition of Europeanisation, which stresses the importance of policy networks: "We define Europeanization as the emergence and development at the European level of distinct structures of governance, that is, of political, legal, and social institutions associated with political problem-solving that formalize interactions among the actors, and of policy networks specializing in the creation of authoritative European rules" (Cowles, Caporaso and Risse, 2001:3). Claudio Radaelli points out that the Europeanisation of public policy may take diverse forms and affect actors, resources, and policy instruments (Radaelli, 2003:36); however, the emergence of new, cross-national policy networks and communities is considered a key development of Europeanisation (Featherstone, 2003:20). European research and development programmes are one example of how Europeanisation works in practice. The network idea – that bringing different actors together can foment innovation and stimulate scientific and economic development – is one of the foundations of EU R&D. EU-funded programmes "force" companies and other stakeholders to collaborate and network with each other, as a condition of receiving subsidies and other funding.[72] Many of these programmes support or lead to new regulatory initiatives, thus providing a platform for discussion and evaluation of Information Society policies and standards. These developments impinging upon the ICT sector have given rise to another policy community so distinctive that the author has given it the term "Project groups", *alias* Advocacy Coalition Type Four (see Section 1.5.3 above).

Although Paul Sabatier believes that the policy domain framework "meets the criteria [for being a good framework] fairly well, and much of the empirical work is quite impressive" (1999a:11), critics have argued rightly enough that merely to demonstrate that networks exist does little to explain anything. Dowding, for example, argues that "the policy community literature is an interesting way of organising pluralist thought, but it cannot be expected to give explanations of policy outcomes. [...] Describing some policy communities as 'open' and others as 'closed' tells us about the nature of networks of group and state actors; but this description does not explain why these different sorts of policy community exist" (Dowding, 1995:136-158). A theory of power is needed, according to Dowding. Although the author propounds no formal theory of power in this book, the discovery of Industry Governance in the ICT (and likely in other) industrial sectors indicates one place where researchers might look in their quest for such a theory, and, on a high level of abstraction, what kind of power is in play to create the communities that exist, and the outcome of their struggles for influence.

The interest-based approach presented and analysed in the following Section is also intended to address some of the inherent weaknesses of the rather too unstructured policy network theory.

2.3.3 Interest-based approaches: advocacy coalitions and epistemic communities

For many years Sabatier and Jenkins-Smith worked on studies (1988, 1993, 1999) with affinities to the policy network theory, which pointed to the existence of organisations and networks, and which also fit into the framework of an interest-based approach. Instead of speaking generically of "interest groups", these authors spotlighted the existence of "advocacy coalitions", "epistemic communities" , and "discourse coalitions". These are networks of actors bound together by a common policy project based on shared principal beliefs. "Actors

72 See Framework Programmes for Research and Development, and the EUREKA (European Research Coordination Agency) programme to support RTD on the basis of establishing joined ventures between firms of more than one country.

are acting together, not because they expect material advantages, but because their value-orientations and world-views command or oblige them to do so" (Braun, 1999:17).[73]

Advocacy Coalition Framework (ACF)

The Advocacy Coalition Framework (ACF) is the "conceptual framework" originally developed by Paul Sabatier and Hank Jenkins-Smith as an alternative to the Stages Heuristic in their attempt to explain environmental policy processes in the US. Attracting growing interest among European scholars, the ACF involves mapping the belief systems of policy elites and analysing the conditions under which policy-oriented learning across advocacy coalitions occurs. Their framework focusses on the mutual interaction of advocacy coalitions within a given policy subsystem.

Advocacy coalitions comprise individual and collective, public and private actors operating at multiple levels of governance. They aim to influence government and other institutions in an instrumentally rational fashion by circulating amongst multiple venues in an intergovernmental system. In addition to sharing policy goals, Sabatier asserts that advocacy coalitions are held together by a common belief system consisting of three structural characteristics: (1) a deep normative core that defines "a person's underlying personal philosophy"; (2) a policy-oriented core which defines "fundamental policy positions concerning the basic strategies for achieving core values within the subsystem"; and (3) a set of secondary elements comprising a multitude of so-called "causal beliefs", or beliefs about how to bring about results in the real world, after having found the information necessary to implement the policy core (Sabatier, 1993:30-31).

The ACF defines policy change as a function both of competition between advocacy coalitions within the same subsystem, and of events causing changes outside the subsystem (*e.g.* system-wide governing coalitions or socio-economic conditions) (Sabatier and Jenkins-Smith, 1993c:5-6). At least four basic premises inform their understanding of policy processes: (1) that policy change can require a time span of a decade or more; (2) that change is primarily influenced by "policy subsystems" (defined as "interactions of actors from different institutions who follow and seek to influence governmental decisions in a policy area"); (3) that these subsystems include an intergovernmental dimension and involve all levels of government; and (4) that public policy and belief systems may be conceptualised in the same way, *i.e.* as a set of prioritised values and causal assumptions (Sabatier, 1993:16-17).

The ACF has been current for thirty years now. It has stimulated much interest amongst the countries of the OECD,[74] and has undergone considerable revision since its

73 By claiming that business organisations form such a coalition, the author denies that the neglect of material incentives forms an essential trait of the advocacy coalition. However, the author contends to the contrary that for business, at least, "material advantages" must always play an important motivational role. Even the most patient business organisations expect an eventual return, in one form or another, on their investment in these activities (*e.g.* competitive advantages, cost savings). But this does not preclude or mutually repel shared "value-orientations" or "world-views".

74 Sabatier quite usefully identified empirical applications of the ACF in thirty-four cases, which are listed in Sabatier and Jenkins-Smith, 1999:126.

original publication in the early 1980s: "The ACF has become a much more integrated framework and/or theory for understanding long-term policy change in modern societies" (Sabatier, 1999a:266). The ACF's great strength for this book is its synthesis of bottom-up and top-down approaches to the theory of policy formulation and implementation. It is generally applicable, though originally developed in the context of the American energy- and environmental policy subsystem. The criteria that define a good framework are also met: the terms are clearly defined; the concept is consistent; it has causal drivers (Sabatier's core values and external perturbations); and it is broad in its application. Constructive criticism has come from Schlager, who faults the ACF for focussing exclusively on coalition beliefs, neglecting coalition behaviour; consequently, it does not sufficiently take co-ordinated behaviour into account (Schlager, 1995:243-270).

The Stakeholder Action Matrix propounded in Chapter One incorporates the Advocacy Coalition Framework, aggregating large numbers of actors into a manageable number of policy community types, while accounting for the "driving factor" of basic policy position or coalition beliefs. This reduces the great diversity of actors to a small set of units that can be applied in various scholarly and practical contexts to various ends.[75] Sabatier himself suggested (in the chapter titled "Directions for Further Research") that "collective action and coordination problems with coalitions, and the conditions under which they can be overcome, would be an excellent opportunity to develop and test" (Sabatier and Jenkins-Smith, 1999:153). This book addresses some of these problems by investigating how members of these coalitions take action to achieve their common goals at all levels of government.

Epistemic Communities

The concept of the epistemic community[76] was originally formulated by Peter Haas, but was refined by Paul Sabatier in a special issue of *International Organization* in 1992. Peter Haas himself formally defined it for the first time as follows:

> An epistemic community is a network of professionals with recognised expertise and competence in a particular domain and an authoritative claim to policy-relevant knowledge within that domain. Although an epistemic community may consist of professionals from a variety of disciplines and backgrounds, they have (1) a shared set of normative and principled beliefs, which provide a value-based rationale for the social action of community members; (2) shared causal beliefs, which are derived from their analysis of practices leading or contributing to a central set of problems in

75 For this reason the Survey presented in Chapter Six aims to show evidence that "coalition beliefs" have an impact on ICT policy decision-making. If the Survey respondents had opined that beliefs play no role, they would not have been posited as "driving factors".

76 This kind of transnational network is called "epistemic" after the branch of philosophy traditionally known as epistemology. Meaning the "theory of knowledge", the word originated from the Greek *episteme* (knowledge) and *logos* (word/speech). It deals with the nature, origin and scope of knowledge. Historically, it has been one of the most investigated and most contested of all philosophical subjects. Much of this debate has focused on analysing the nature and variety of knowledge, and how knowledge relates to similar notions such as truth and belief, and it often concerns the justification for knowledge claims.

> their domain and which then serve as the basis for elucidating the multiple linkages between possible policy actions and desired outcomes; (3) shared notions of validity – that is, intersubjective, internally defined criteria for weighing and validating knowledge in the domain of their expertise; and (4) a common policy enterprise – that is, a set of common practices associated with a set of problems to which their professional competence is directed, presumably out of the conviction that human welfare will be enhanced as a consequence. (Haas, 1997:3)

Haas sees reason in this process of policy co-ordination *via* epistemic communities. In his view, the situation in which policy-makers find themselves leads almost naturally to the use of experts of various kinds.[77]

In practice, national governments may call upon epistemic communities to help achieve coordination of international policies or form intergovernmental organisations aiming for regulatory co-operation. Epistemic communities may be national or transnational. The success of international policy coordination depends largely on the institutions comprising the decisional processes of the countries involved. Regularly consultation with epistemic communities influences even the way national policy-makers conceive their policy objectives. Transnational epistemic communities operating across the EU may have become even more influential, as their "causal beliefs" and "policy preferences" may have been represented to the gamut of national policy-makers who have sought their advice.

Haas points out that "uncertainty" at the international level drives policy-makers toward epistemic communities (Haas, 1997:3). He argues that "in international policy co-ordination, the forms of uncertainty that tend to stimulate demands for information are those which arise from the strong dependence of states on each other's policy choices for success in obtaining goals and those which involve multiple and only partly estimable consequences of action" (Haas, 1992:3-4). He continues that these uncertainties to which decision-makers are exposed are the "result of the increasingly complex and technical nature of the issues on the international agenda" (Haas, 1997:12). This includes monetary, macroeconomic, technological, and social issues. Uncertainty is a very important element, as it motivates decision-makers to consult epistemic communities especially when unexpected events or crises occur. This process may even be driven not by real-world events but by scientific reports that make their way into the news and capture the attention of the public. Forced to take action, decision-makers seeking informational certainty will defer to experts able to provide credible technical advice (Haas, 1997:14-16).

Haas distinguishes epistemic communities from the broader scientific community and from all individuals in the same discipline or profession, by the fact that epistemic communities aim at a goal they believe in. Although scientific communities and individuals may hold causal

77 The concepts of "experts" and "expertise" are contested within the discipline of epistemology under the general heading of "expert knowledge". Although some philosophers – notably beginning with Socrates – have undermined claims to expert knowledge, this must lie beyond the scope of this book, except to note that members of epistemic communities, including the one featured here, are convinced of their own knowledgeable superiority and that the European Commission evidently agrees in consulting them especially in its regulatory processes.

beliefs or policy orientations in common (*e.g.* professional codes of conduct and ethics) and may to some degree share a consensual knowledge base (*e.g.* professional experience), they do not have the "normative commitments" of an epistemic community. Nevertheless, specific interest groups within a discipline or profession (*e.g.* one established to evaluate technical standards or interoperability for a new product) may sometimes be classified as epistemic communities. To be properly included in Haas' definition, a "knowledge-based group" must share both normative and causative beliefs, as well as a common policy enterprise (Haas, 1997:16-20; see also Figure 1.1 in Appendix One: "Distinguishing between stakeholders and actors").

An epistemic community is distinguished from an advocacy coalition, in that it involves scientific expertise as an essential dimension of community and action. In constructing the Advocacy Coalition Typology presented in Section 1.5.3, the author did not intend to suggest that advocacy coalitions (or their types) exclude other structures of collective action. Indeed, he claims that Advocacy Coalition Type Four is an epistemic community at the same time, because their "value-based rationale for social action" includes the shared normative belief that technology is the most powerful means available to humanity to solve even its social problems. The "central set of problems" in the domain of regulation of ICTs is to advance the interoperability and technological convergence of solutions. Their "shared notions of validity" feature the individual's ability to contribute substantially to the solution of these central problems and to the social betterment which technological developments are supposed to create. Finally, their "common policy enterprise" is to accelerate technological advances by creating a regulatory framework conducive to this end, eliminating the political, legal and even commercial (*viz.* profit-motivated) barriers to the social realisation of the technological advances that have already happened.

Adler and Haas identify four mechanisms whereby epistemic communities exert influence. The first is *policy innovation*: epistemic communities outline the policy issue, that is, define the scope of the problem, the policy objectives, and the forum where the problem is to be solved; define national interests; and set standards and develop regulations. The second is *policy diffusion*, whereby transnational links are used to disseminate the views of the epistemic community. This may be achieved by communication with scientific bodies and other international organisations, at international conferences or exhibitions, and *via* publications and other methods of exchanging knowledge and information. Acceptance of their ideas Europe-wide or internationally may then be exploited to pressurise EU Member State governments. The third mechanism is *policy selection*, where decision makers approach selected epistemic communities for advice and support, in hopes that the recommendations and advice of "experts" will legitimate their policy choices. The fourth is *policy persistence*, the credibility and authority of an epistemic community which determines how long its influence will be sustained. To uphold this, it must itself sustain an ongoing consensus of goals, beliefs, and ideas over a significant time-frame. Epistemic communities can significantly contribute to policy evolution as a process of learning, and this can be crucial to understanding how policy-making and the quality of output improves over time (Haas and Adler, 1997:375-387).

Advocacy Coalition Type Four often gets called in by the European Commission to provide advice on complex technological-regulatory issues. This gives "Project groups" the power and opportunity to be "selected" to "innovate" policy solutions. The Seventh Research Framework Programme even has an online Register for Experts to make themselves known and available to give the Commission advice. The Commission started this up in its "Call addressed to individuals for the establishment of a database of prospective independent experts to assist the Commission's services [*i.e.* DGs] for tasks in connection with the Seventh RTD Framework Programme" (CEC, 2006hh).

Sabatier argues that within a subsystem "actors can be aggregated into a number of advocacy coalitions composed of people from various organisations who share a set of normative and causal beliefs and who often act in concert" (Sabatier, 1988:133). He demonstrates that an advocacy coalition may include actors from a variety of positions and functions, from interest group leaders to elected officials, who share a "belief system" – defined as a set of causal assumptions, problem perceptions, and basic values (Sabatier, 1988:133). But in addition, clear coordination of these activities must be evident over time. For Sabatier shared beliefs are the principal "glue" of politics.

One of Sabatier's hypotheses seems especially relevant to recent developments in the EU, that "[p]olicy-oriented learning across belief systems is most likely where there exists a forum which is (a) prestigious enough to force professionals from different coalitions to participate and (b) dominated by professional norms" (Sabatier, 1988:156). The European Commission seems to be moving towards institutionalising structures which bring together groups of policy actors, be they called epistemic communities, advocacy coalitions, or diverse policy communities. Already by 1988 Sabatier had observed that these structures "force debate between professionals with diverse belief systems, during which their views get aired before peers. Under such conditions, the ambition for professional credibility and the norms of scientific debate will bring about a rigorous cross-examination of methodological (and epistemological) assumptions, to the gradual elimination of the more improbable causal assertions and the invalidation of the more questionable data. Thus, a convergence of views probably happens over time concerning the nature of the problem and the consequences of various policy alternatives" (Sabatier, 1988:156).

Again, policy-makers seem intent on securing agreements and stability. They recognise that this process must involve all types of stakeholders in the given policy domain; for example, representatives of important companies; industry associations; consumer groups; international organisations; local or national governments; and participants in task forces, working groups, and other initiatives. Peter Haas and his collaborators emphasise the growing importance that experts play in policy making, above all at a supranational or international level, and the wider influence that their shared beliefs attain thereby (Haas, 1992).

A study published by the European University Institute in Florence investigated the role of experts in the creation of the European Monetary Union (EMU) by analysing the work of the Delors Committee which drafted the EMU blueprint. It was concluded that the Committee and its experts "operated as the definition of an epistemic community suggests" (Verdun, 1996). The Member States needed a body of experts who could legitimate their policy choice of a Single EMU, and used their collective knowledge and advice of experts to buttress their own decisions and subsequent acts.

Peter Cowhey maintains that in the telecommunications field epistemic communities have played an important role in framing the policy context and influencing the decisions of States. As summed up by Adler and Haas, "Without the influence of an epistemic community of engineers concerned about the design and international coordination of telecommunications equipment and standards, the regime would not have moved in the direction of multilateral agreements" (1992:377).

We expect to see two (apparently) contradictory trends emerging. *Firstly*, the desirability of epistemic communities that can construct complex transnational coalitions of actors will force all policy stakeholders to become more focussed on European Level. Other policy actors, such as Chambers of Commerce, ISPs or cable operators, and standards institutes, will follow the example of large industry organisations, seeking to create and participate in a multi-layered European policy system of transnational coalitions. *Secondly*, the "politics of uncertainty" and need for professional competence will drive Member States and interest groups to try to coordinate their European strategies with each other, in order to avoid unpleasantly surprising each other in Council, and to "compare notes" on highly technical issues. National regulators already coordinate their activities through a number of pan-European policy organisations, such as the European Regulators Group, the European Spectrum Policy Group, and the Committee of Permanent Representatives of the Member States (COREPER). This is also the view of Richardson, who is outstanding for having applied the concept of epistemic communities to concrete cases (1996a:30).

Advocates of the epistemic communities concept, however, have been notably cautious in claiming explanatory power. Haas notes that "the extent to which state behaviour reflects the preferences of these networks remains strongly conditioned by the distribution of power internationally" (Haas, 1992:7). It is essential to note that epistemic communities are also "constrained by the need for policy makers, at both EU and national levels, to involve other kinds of actors, particularly conventional interest groups", as well as the committees, councils, and task forces whose primary purpose is to advise the Commission in its decisional processes (Richardson, 1996c:43).

Epistemic communities may even be rivals in some cases; for example, EU standards institutes and private standards organisations may share the same belief system but not necessarily the same objectives on every policy initiative. Epistemic communities may get caught up in interest-group politics. Industry associations may vary in size and structure from a few hundreds of members organised at National Level to tens of thousands organised on European Level with access to a global network of resources. As Sabatier noted, advocacy coalitions also vary in terms of their members' backgrounds and economic and political positions. Obviously, all these factors can influence the duration and complexity of the decisional processes within coalitions. Consensus building may also depend on such externalities as the maturity of the market which the new law is intended to regulate.

Expert Networks

A concept closely related to advocacy coalitions and epistemic communities is the "expert network". Experts, of course, support policy-makers in making their decisions; often they are the ones who work out a manageable and well defined set of alternatives, from which decision-makers can make yes/no choices. Expert advice for policy-choice (EAP) may be given in various ways, to various audiences, and at various stages of policy formation. Many expert groups participate in these stages. Each expert community provides a sort of quality control of the knowledge in a special domain. This may be effected by peer review or by the use of other recognised methods such as professional licensing. Professionals trained in dealing with the problems of private-sector clients can put such experience to use in policy advising. The advantage of such people is that they have concerned themselves with practical not merely abstract knowledge. Consequently, technical and legal professionals participate regularly in parliamentary hearings, committee hearings, and other policy fora. Duncan MacRae stresses that it is essential for these expert policy advisors to interact with the consumers of their advice, *viz.* officials, leaders and organisations (MacRae and Whittington, 1997).

Expert policy advisors can make many other contributions besides recommending a course of action to a final decision-maker. Advisors can provide background guidance without making policy recommendations; give preparatory advice by describing problem conditions, or modelling the problem; give indirect advice through journalists or other analysts; and develop the foundations for policy analysis (MacRae and Whittington, 1997).

Many authors have examined how new technologies have altered the way opinions are discussed and formed. Bechmann concluded that the Information Society "changes the very sources of wealth-creation and the governing factors in production. Labour and capital, the central variables of the industrial society, are replaced by information and knowledge as the main variables in the new emerging society" (2000:44).

One approach to the economics of technology and how this impacts the socio-technical process of negotiation is the Actor-Network Theory (ANT). ANT provides a language to describe how, where, and to what extent technology influences human behaviour (Monteiro, 2001:71-83). The author acknowledges that technology has an impact on social and political interactions and negotiations, but does not investigate this further in this book, as he believes technological choices themselves are more often than not driven by purely technical considerations that bear only a tangential relation to the political.

2.4 THE NEED FOR NEW THEORISATION

The foregoing review has found obvious gaps in the scholarship investigating how policy stakeholders shape EU industrial regulation in general and ICT regulation in particular. Neither a mere review of the existing scholarship, nor the deductive inferences that might have derived from it, could have sufficed to develop all of the concepts presented in this book, particularly about stakeholder influence on ICT regulatory processes, or how business organisations leverage their influence by resorting to multiple channels of influence and multiple collaborative alliances. The Aarhus Convention of 1998 and the European Governance White Paper of 2001 stimulated a Europe-wide debate over stakeholder participation in public policy. This led to a sea change in the ways that the European regulator and the Member States engaged with business organisations and other private stakeholders.

Even the vastest body of scholarship on this subject, if published before 2000, would be obsolescent, hence the necessity of an empirical approach cannot be gainsaid.

As for generalisations that might help one understand this new shape of EU policy-making, it is true that theories abound which might be brought to bear on business influence in general, as witness Claire Cutler (1999; 2002), Wyn Grant (1993; 2000), Wolfgang Streeck and Philippe Schmitter (1985; 1991), Susan Strange (1988; 1996), and Doris Fuchs (2004; 2005). But with the notable exceptions of Justin Greenwood (2000a; 2000b; 2001a), Jeremy Richardson (1993; 1996; 2001), and Laura Cram (1995; 1997), little attempt has been made to clarify how the private sector is involved specifically in ICT policy and regulation. Certainly no model specific to ICT policy has so far been created that comprehensively takes external influences into account.

Much of the scholarship concentrates on broad-based interest group representation, as witness Greenwood *et al.* (1994; 1995; 1997; 2000; 2001), Mazey and Richardson (1996; 2001), Van Schendelen (1994; 1998), Pedler (1994, 1996), Coen (1997; 1998; 2003; 2007; 2009), and Knill (2001). The scholarship on lobbying strategy consists of series of case studies; little effort has been made to join them up or link them to broader theory, or to accumulate evidence on specific topics of universal interest (Baumgartner and Leech, 1998). The case studies of practitioners involved in policy-making are almost the only empirical studies on the decisional processes of European ICT policy. Even the most basic terminology – like "Information Society", "collaboration", and "ICT" – is subject to a wide range of interpretations, and while many scholars formulate rigorous definitions for their own purposes, there is not much consistency of usage (*cf.* Zacher, 2000:53-59).

The main lesson is that the EU's policy-making processes, and business collaboration in them, are complex and diverse, making reliable generalisation very difficult (Greenwood, Grote and Ronit, 1994). Hence it was deemed necessary to undertake a detailed empirical investigation, which in the event included a questionnaire Survey, a multi-level case study, and a comprehensive review of policy papers and regulations.

Much scholarship seems to confirm the popular perception that business influence on European policy is complex and can only be understood by "insiders". It is assumed that detailed insight into the vast number of stakeholders involved in EU policy making, even for a defined policy area such as ICT policy, is impossible. Case studies and surveys may be useful, but must remain incomplete. No attempt is made to categorise external stakeholder types and mentalities in order to simplify – and so improve – understanding of stakeholder influence over EU policy in general or ICT policy in particular. While many of the "ingredients" for developing models already exist, little actual model-developing has taken place. Besides, no single theoretical framework meant to be universally applicable, however authoritative, can disregard the specifics of the policy domain in question and still fully explain its decisional processes.

While the author found that policy processes in the abstract have been extensively studied (see Section 2.2 above), and the factor of *time* is widely acknowledged as important, insufficient work has been done to investigate how time affects stakeholders who are trying to have an impact on EU policy. This book neither views EU policy-making *sub specie aeternitatis* (*i.e.* in some timeless form) nor takes "snapshots" of it; the method, rather, has been to regard the policy cycle as a whole made up of temporal parts. This approach has afforded novel insights into the detailed structure of policy-making at European Level.

No scholar has brought all of these elements together at once; the conclusion is inescapable, then: further research into business influence on the EU's governance of the ICT sector is called for, leading to a new framework capable of modelling, over the policy cycle as a whole, the interactions of all actor collectives, both individual organisations and groups, in a multi-level policy-making system. Existing models are too generic to be fully explanatory under the exceptional policy-making circumstances inside the EU, and the Commission in particular. The theory and models developed by the author and presented in Chapter One accomplishes this by synthesising elements of several theoretical perspectives.

CHAPTER 3

METHODOLOGY

This Chapter on methodology is divided into seven Sections. Section 3.1 presents the logical orientation of this book, which is "abductive" in the words of Charles Sanders Peirce, rather than either purely inductive or purely deductive. Section 3.2 describes how triangulation was built into all data-gathering methods, which contributed to the overall reliability of the data, while Section 3.3 explains the basic methodological approach, Grounded Theory. Section 3.4 and 3.5 describe the methods used to collect secondary and primary data, respectively. Section 3.6 outlines the methods used to design the case study. Section 3.7 presents how to construct a robust model, while Section 3.8 outlines the criteria used to assess the Stakeholder Action Matrix, and discusses the assumptions underlying it.

3.1 METHODS OF LOGIC

The following section defines some theoretical concepts deployed in this book. It may be of particular interest to scholars, as it was discovered that Peirce's logical methods amount to a form of triangulation which the author calls "logic triangulation".

3.1.1 Abduction, abductive induction, and probabilistic deduction

The logic of social scientific inquiry has traditionally been considered as either deductive or inductive, or a combination of both. Induction is an approach in which generalities are inferred from particular observations. Deduction infers particular consequences on the basis of assumed general theories. If a scientist had evidence that a certain religious minority, for example, tends to favour a specific political viewpoint, then extrapolates this to the hypothesis that all religious minorities tend to favour the same political view, and proceeds to test this against further evidence, this would be an inductive approach. With a deductive approach, the same scientist would start with the hypothesis that religious affiliation influenced political viewpoints and then begin observations to prove or disprove this hypothesis.

The theory and models presented in this book, however, were the result of a different form of logical inference, called "abductive"[78] logic in the terminology of the American

78 These words, deriving from Latin, meant literally *de-duct-ion* = "from-lead-ing" [leading one *from* general truth *to* particular truth], *in-duct-ion* = "onto-lead-ing" [leading *onto* general truth from more particular truths] (in-duct-ion)", and "off-lead-ing" [leading general truth *off* of an incomplete set of particular truths]. In fact, in Classical antiquity induction was commonly confounded with abduction. It was Peirce who first rigorously distinguished them.

philosopher of Pragmatism Charles Sanders Peirce. This is a type of logical inference distinct from either inductive or deductive logic, although Peirce used it in conjunction with these other two. Once the theory and models had "occurred" to the author abductively, he was then positioned to use both inductive and deductive logic to test the abductive inference, probing its truth and accuracy. It is well known in Philosophy of Science circles that neither inductive nor deductive logic, nor both together, can provide a sufficient explanation for how theoretical ideas originate.

A classic example of how the human mind transcends the trammels of both inductive and deductive logic is seen by comparing human grandmasters of chess with chess-playing computers. The computers are obliged by their strictly deductive logical structure to consider and eliminate billions upon billions of manifestly absurd chess moves in order to find the infinitesimally small number that are even potentially "winning" moves; whereas, the human grandmaster can go directly to the same moves after considering no more than one hundred or so possibilities, simply because the human brain is not limited by inductive or deductive logical structures.

The ancient Greek philosopher Aristotle was the first to codify inductive and deductive logic, using the concept of the *syllogism* as a template (Ross, 1928). The deductive syllogism had the form of two premises, one being taken for universally true and the other being an assertion about particulars, on the basis of which one conclusion – a truth not already contained in the premises – was deemed certain, thus:

Premise 1: There exists a class of beings B of all of which attribute A is true

Premise 2: There exists an individual or sub-class C belonging to B

Conclusion: Therefore, A is also true of C

A concrete example, drawn from the world of ICT, would be:

Premise 1: All computers use electricity

Premise 2: IBM Thinkpads are computers

Conclusion: Therefore, Thinkpads use electricity

Of course, the reliability of deductive logic (in the real world – outside of mathematical reasoning where no messy facts exist to contradict one's assumptions) depends on the reliability of the premise taken to be universally true.

The form of logic that, unlike deduction, does not depend on the universal truth of either of the premises is called induction, which is an argument from probability; the archetypal form of which may be given thus:

Premise 1: There exists a class of beings B of which attribute A is true with probability p/q (as determined by experiment)

Premise 2: There exists an individual or sub-class C belonging to B

Conclusion: Therefore, A is true of C with probability p/q

A concrete example of an inductive syllogism would be:

Premise 1: 100% of computers use electricity (determined by common sense!)

Premise 2: IBM Thinkpads are computers

Conclusion: Therefore, 100% of IBM Thinkpads use electricity

Induction is often confused with another form of reasoning which is actually more like (though not exactly the same as) abductive reasoning (about which more below). This form is an uncertain method of reaching universal truths, as two concrete examples of contrasting reliability illustrate:

Example A.:

Premise 1: IBM Thinkpads are computers

Premise 2: IBM Thinkpads use Intel Processors

Conclusion: Therefore, all computers use Intel Processors

Example B.:

Premise 1: IBM Thinkpads are computers

Premise 2: IBM Thinkpads use electricity

Conclusion: Therefore all computers use electricity

Abduction is a third kind of logic distinct from deduction or induction, which although less well known than either, actually forms the basis for most of the social and even natural scientific reasoning that leads on to testable hypotheses. The Stakeholder Action Matrix and the Industry Governance Theory presented herein were results of *abductive inference* of the kind first rigorously expounded by American philosopher and logician Charles Sanders Peirce (1839-1914). Abduction has often been characterised as *inference to the best explanation*: "*Abduction* … is a form of inference that goes from data describing something to a hypothesis that best explains or accounts for the data" (Josephson, 1994:5). Abductive logic typically starts from a set of accepted facts – which seem to the researcher to be not obviously related to one another by any explicit logical connexions – and infers the most likely (or best) explanation to explain them all. Abduction is not the hypothesis itself, but rather the inferential process that leads to the hypothesis as its end result. After an hypothesis "occurs" to the theorist (or modeller) abductively, then he may turn to inductive and/or deductive logic to help test and probe its truth and accuracy.

Although Peirce and his logical investigations may not be as well known to the social science community as they deserve to be, there can be little doubt of the rigour or the great value of his insights for the social scientist of today. "From the early 1860's until [Peirce's] death his output in logic was voluminous and extraordinarily varied. One of his logical systems [*N.B.*: just *one*] became the basis for Ernst Schroeder's great three-volume treatise on logic, the *Vorlesungen über die Algebra der Logik*, and Peirce became widely regarded as the greatest logician of his day. By all who are familiar with his work he is considered one of the greatest logicians who ever lived" (Stanford University Encyclopaedia of Philosophy website – "Charles Sanders Peirce").

Abductive reasoning has proved its value not only on paper, but even when put to the "acid test" of computer logic developed in the laboratory and tested in practice. Important discoveries about abductive logic have been made whilst designing, building, testing and analysing "expert" automation for medical diagnosis, in applied mathematics, and other tasks upon which abduction is the only feasible method of tackling the problem. These discoveries have demonstrated that abductive inference, even though it lies mostly outside the *formal* framework of mathematical logic and probability, can be described precisely enough for programming computers which achieve practically good performances (Josephson, 1994).

If abductive reasoning could be reduced to an archetypal syllogism, it would look something like this:

Premise 1: There exists a collection of data D (or observations or facts or "givens");

Premise 2: Hypothesis H_0, if true, would explain D – *and* no alternative hypotheses H_i explain D as well as (better than) H_0;

Conclusion: Therefore, H_0 is probably true.

The probativity of a conclusion depends on the corroboration of multiple criteria, to wit:

1. How convincingly H_0, considered in isolation, explains D [absolute convincingness].
2. By how much H_0 excels H_i as an explanation of D [relative convincingness].
3. How exhaustively the universe of H_i was probed for (better) alternative explanations [exhaustion of alternatives].
4. How well H_0 fares when tested by the following "pragmatic" criteria [pragmatic limitations of the search for truth]:
   (a) The cost/benefit ratio of H_0 being false *vs.* H_0 being true.
   (b) The urgency of reaching a conclusion, weighed against the likely fruitfulness of waiting for further evidence or for undreamt-of alternative explanations, as well as against the feasibility of seeking these out at the given time (Josephson, 1994:5).

These last criteria, however incongruous in an "academic" setting, where truth is supposed to be pursued for its own sake regardless of "cost", make part and parcel of Peirce's philosophical account of truth as being the yield of the search for truth. Truth cannot *knowably* transcend the limitations of our search for it. The father of philosophical Pragmatism, Peirce propounded unique criteria by which the truth of propositions was to be judged in general. "When [Peirce] said that the whole meaning of a (clear) conception consists in the entire set of its practical consequences, he had in mind that a meaningful conception must have some sort of experimental 'cash value', must somehow be capable of being related to some sort of collection of possible empirical observations under specifiable conditions [...] his views are quite close to those of, say, Einstein, who held that the whole meaning of a physical concept is determined by an exact method of measuring it" (Stanford Encyclopaedia of Philosophy website – "Charles Sanders Peirce":7). As for abductive inference, it is best explained in Peirce's own words:

> Deduction is necessary inference; but if it is applied to probability, then, while remaining in itself necessary, it concludes a probability. That gives the doctrine of chances. Induction is a totally different sort of inquiry, proceeding, by means of experiment, to obtain an answer to a previously propounded question. It has two species: the extensive, where the question is how much, and the comprehensive, or abductive, where the question is to be answered by yes or no (or else is merely susceptible of a vague answer). Abduction is distinguished from abductive induction in not being, properly speaking, experimental, that is, it makes its observations without reference to any previously propounded question, but, on the contrary, itself starts a question, or problematically propounded hypothesis, to explain a surprising observation. (Charles Sanders Peirce, 1902)

In the same memoir, Peirce illustrated the relationships between abduction, abductive induction, and "probable" (or probabilistic) deduction. *When confronted with the unknown, abduction is the primordial inference to be made*, and induction and deduction come in by consequence of the abduction, to test it against other facts and to reduce it under the rigour of mathematical logic to whatever extent proves possible. This Peirce calls a "mixed" argument. It is noteworthy that what Piece is referring to amounts to what might be called *logic triangulation* in the methodology of triangulation.

Here is Peirce's own example of a mixed argument:

> Suppose, then, that, being seated in a street car, I remark a man opposite to me whose appearance and behaviour unite characters which I am surprised to find together in the same person. I ask myself, How can this be? Suppose I find this problematic reply: Perhaps he is an ex-priest. He is the very image of such a person; he presents an icon of an ex-priest. Here is an iconic argument, or abduction of it. Secondly, it now occurs to me that if he is an ex-priest, he should be tonsured; and in order to test this, I say something to him calculated to make him take off his hat. He does so, and I find that he is indeed tonsured. Here at last is an indication that my theory is correct. I can now say that he is presumably an ex-priest [the abductive induction], although it would be inaccurate to say that there is any definite [*i.e.* numerically expressible] probability that he is so, since I do not know how often I might find a man tonsured who was not an ex-priest, though evidently far oftener than he would be one. The supposition is, however, now supported by an inductive [*sic*] induction, a weak form of symptomatic or indexical argument. It stands on a widely different basis from that on which it stood before my little experiment. Before, it rested on the flimsy support of similarity, or agreement in 'flavor'. Now, facts have been constrained to yield confirmation to it by bearing out a prediction based upon it. Belief in the theory rests now on factual reaction to the theory. Thirdly, while the man's hat is off, I read in the crown of it a name that has been pasted into it. I have no doubt whatever that it is the man's name. I do not go into the question of how I come to be so confident of that. As long as I have no doubt, it matters not how doubt came to be destroyed. I get out of the car, and go to call upon the chancellor

of the diocese; and that he will tell me the truth I equally believe implicitly. I ask the chancellor, 'Who is Michael Wo-Ling Ptah-Hotep Jerolomon?' [...] He replies, 'He is an ex-priest'. 'Is he the only man of that name?' 'No, there are, or may be, fifteen. Fourteen of them reside in this town and are ex-priests. The fifteenth went, twenty years ago, to High Thibet, and has never been heard of since.' [...] So, it might conceivably have been an accident that the man was tonsured, but now that the name Michael Wu-Ling Ptah-Hotep Jerolomon signifies for me a probability of more than fourteen to one of being an ex-priest, I must think that the probability on that ground alone is over fourteen to one that he is an ex-priest [the probable deduction] [...] fourthly, combining the arguments into one mixed argument, and considering, what is logically relevant, that I have no serious stake in the question, I am satisfied to consider the mixed argument as proof ...". (Peirce, 1902)

3.1.2 Application of Peirce's logic

The conclusions presented in this book follow from a mixed argument consisting of abduction, abductive induction, and (to the extent possible) probabilistic deduction, in that same order as Peirce used in his illustration, so that the structure of the reasoning process that led to the Industry Governance Theory exactly matches (in the abstract) Peirce's reasoning about the ex-priest. "[Instead of testing an existing hypothesis,] abduction ... starts a ... hypothesis to explain a surprising observation" as Peirce put it. The surprising observation that originated the abductive train of reasoning that led to the author's Industry Governance Theory was made as a *stagière* with DGXIII-A1 (Telecoms Regulation Unit) of the European Commission. Contrary to all prior expectation, the author found that industry was heavily involved in regulatory policy. This contradicted two of the author's expectations in particular: (1) that Commission functionaries undertook all or most of the fact-finding and analysis needed for regulating the ICT (or any other) market; and (2) that, if public employees lacked the specialist knowledge certain situations called for, the Commission delegated the work to "neutral" third parties, especially academics. Instead, the author eyewitnessed secondees from industry doing much of the background work which the Commission relied on when deciding fundamental regulatory issues. Of course, the Commission took care to define and in that sense limit the roles and responsibilities of industry secondees; thus, there was no question of industry "taking over" the Commission or even "capturing" it in the classic sense in the political science literature of corrupting the regulatory process to private benefit. Nonetheless, the author witnessed how much the Commission relied on information and skills brought in by the secondees, and that this reliance did influence what was considered technically (and thus politically) "doable" inside the DG XIII. This gave the industry something like a "veto" of regulatory policy, rather than the power to command and control the Commission's internal process. The importance of industry secondees to the Commission is evident in the trouble the Commission has taken to formalise its relations with secondees and formulate its internal governance of them, as in Decision C(2008)6866 "laying down rules on the secondment to the Commission of national experts and national experts in professional training". The Commission acknowledges how much it will "benefit from the high level of their professional knowledge and experience, in particular in areas where such expertise is not readily available" (CEC, 2008b). It even has a portion of its budget allocated just for "buying outside expertise".

His eyes opened, the author began to notice other things: in all of the main venues of the ICT policy process industry participants outnumbered all other stakeholders and/or dominated the proceedings:

(1) *European Commission Staffing*: Out of the 35 staff members of DG XIII-A1, for example, only about 50% were Commission functionaries, all of 30% were seconded from national telecoms operators, and the rest were independent contractors. As a *stagière* the author was unable to tell, without specifically enquiring, who were public functionaries and who were seconded industry staff, so seamlessly had industry already merged with the Commission.

(2) *Outsourcing of studies and feasibility pilots*: the Telecoms Regulation Unit was involved in at least six studies during the author's *Stage*, all of which were outsourced to technical experts in industry. Occasionally other experts were involved, *e.g.* private consulting company KPMG, a major advisor to the ICT industry, also carried out in 1996 on behalf of DGXIII-A1 a pivotal study titled "Public Policy Issues Arising from Telecommunications and Audiovisual Convergency", *Report for the European Commission,* which served as the basis for the Commission's ICT Convergence Green Paper COM(97/623/EC). The author also witnessed first-hand as a *stagière* how the lack of technical expertise in the Commission could yield the surprising situation that, when tendering telecoms liberalisation studies, DGXIII-A1 had to call upon industry experts themselves to do all the evaluation of the tender proposals received from industry!

(3) *Stakeholder consultations and workshops held by intergovernmental organisations*: The author eyewitnessed, for example, the ITU Radio Spectrum Management Workshop held in 1996, where he noted the industry participants, mostly technical experts, defining the policy agenda – which has been identified above as the Issue Emergence policy-process "stage" – through the lively debate they carried on with governmental representatives (from NATO and the Commission). The debate the author heard was about the provision of "universal" services, and how reasonable it would be to require operators to provide universal access to fixed telephone lines for all citizens, even those living in remote areas, *e.g.* Lappland. The intergovernmental organisation (ITU) staff did not drive the debate, but merely facilitated (by chairing) it, while the industry participants did nearly all the debating and actually defined essentially all of the issues.

It appeared to the author that industry dominance was complete. "It's industry that regulates the Commission, not the other way around" was the thought that kept springing to mind. The observable state of affairs presented the "icon" of Industry Governance, as Peirce would have said. Subsequent observation and reflection confirmed this conjecture as the best explanation; as all conceivable alternative theories – *e.g.* that the public functionaries "oversee" industry staff in some ultimate sense that keeps plenary control of output in "public" hands, or that the author's observations had been atypical – became discredited, falsified by the research that makes up this book.

Take for instance the alternative hypothesis that so many secondees were invited into the DGs, not because the Commission needed their expertise, because merely so that the Commission could buy expertise on the cheap, insofar as secondees, like contractors and other temporary staff, do not involve all of the overhead expense of pensions, health care *etc.* of permanent employees. Yet the most cursory observation sufficed to falsify this hypothesis. For six months the author shared an office with telecoms industry experts seconded from Member State telecommunications providers and government agencies (*viz.* in the UK, Spain, France, the Netherlands and Denmark), who advised and supported the Telecoms Regulation Unit in the development of policy papers. The assigned duties witnessed by the author included drafting, for example, the Commission's Decision COM(96)608 on "Assessment Criteria for National Schemes for the Costing and Financing of Universal Service in Telecommunications and Guidelines for the Member States on Operation of such Schemes" (CEC, 1996g) and its Recommmendation on "Interconnection in the liberalised telecommunications market" (CEC, 1998b (adopted 29 July 1998)).[79] The Commission relied on industry experts at least as much as on any functionary, implying that Commission staff could not have done the work by themselves, for lack of both sufficient experience of performing complex yet commercially viable calculations, or insight enough into a soon-to-be-liberalised market to formulate the regulatory guidance contained in its own policy papers without external help. Moreover, collaboration with industry experts made likelier that industry would accept the commercial accuracy of mobile-telephonic roaming prices to be capped under the policy in this paper. The author was able to observe these experts' daily routine and when they attended meetings, as well as to peek in on their work output. After leaving the Commission at the end of his *Stage* the author stayed in touch with some of them and learnt that, after their secondments, some continued to be invited to meetings with the Commission and other stakeholders in Brussels, an unlikely high status for a temporary contractor. All of this more than sufficiently supports the inference that the Commission does not accept secondees from industry just because it has an interest in "cheap qualified" labour, but genuinely lacks and needs their expertise.

Expert secondees mostly work for incumbent State-owned telecoms monopolies (albeit in transition to private ownership). The author became intrigued by the question of how far these incumbents themselves wielded influence over which experts to second to the Commission. Could it be the member-State governments determined who is seconded? Thus, the author toyed with another alternative theory, that "industry governance" was really just another chapter of the now-familiar intergovernmentalism, which fully explained the shared control of the ICT regulatory regime. However, this theory too was soon overturned by plainly observable facts. In retrospect, the ICT market had not been liberalised as of 1996, the year of my *Stage*; so that operators such as Vodafone or Orange either did not exist yet or were too small to matter. Once the transition to private ownership was complete and the ICT market liberalised by 1998, government control of secondments was not even a conceivable

79 This Recommendation formed the template for future Recommendations in this field, the latest of which is *Commission Recommendation Part 1 – Interconnection Pricing* of 20.03.2000. This document presents "best current practice" interconnections charges and is intended to provide guidance to the National Regulatory Authorities (NRAs).

possibility, yet secondments from industry continued as usual. But even before this, during the transition itself, the State-owned telecoms incumbents were themselves in dire need of *commercially* viable technical expertise, and were as dependent on the (private) "industry" as the Commission. After making these theory-comparative observations, exhausting all the alternatives the author could think of – including the theory that his observations constituted an atypical sample (refuted by the sheer volume of observations made in so many venues over so many years), – he found that the Industry Governance Theory was the only one left standing.

Repeated observations of these surprising facts – that the regulators were dependent upon the regulated ICT industry for both factual expertise and ideas, and that this reliance had become critical and pervasive enough to empower industry to "govern" the EU's and UK's ICT regulatory policy processes, – precipitated his inference to the Industry Governance Theory. (The Four-Level Model and Advocacy Coalition Typology, and the Policy Influence-Timing Model as well, were abductively inferred from similar observations of the same events in the same venues.) Industry Governance was then tested inductively by a focussed case study, a policy paper review, and by a statistical Survey, with the purpose of finding empirical data that might confirm or disconfirm the abductions. The results amply warranted the abductive induction that the author's (abducted) theory was confirmed. The Survey also presented numerical data justifying a probabilistic deduction that big business wields *measurably* disproportionate power over the EU's policy processes, which, as well as refining, also confirmed the core of the Industry Governance Theory. Deductive inference from certain theories already to be found in the literature was resorted-to only in parts; other, more generic (*i.e.* not industry-specific) theories and models which the author neglected, but from which he might have reached by deduction the same conclusions actually reached by abduction, did not figure in the train of reasoning leading to the theories and models in this book.

Since the Industry Governance Theory, the Four-Level Model and Advocacy Coalition Typology, and the Policy Influence-Timing Model were all arrived at by abductive reasoning, it follows that their probativity may be judged by the four criteria mentioned above: absolute convincingness, relative convincingness, exhaustion of alternatives, and the pragmatic limitations of the search for truth. The explanations contained in this book satisfy each one of these criteria.

The theory and models together constitute the best joint-explanation for the vast number of observations personally experienced by the author over fourteen years of participant observation (see below), and none of the data subsequently gathered for this book ever counter-instanced any one of them. The theory-*cum*-typology-*cum*-models thus convincingly explain all observations, as this book will demonstrate. And no other theories known to the author explain this plenitude of observations even as well, let alone better.

The author does acknowledge that a deductive element was involved in arriving at his inchoative Stakeholder Action Matrix, insofar as he took cognisance of the well-known "multi-level governance" nature of policy processes in the EU. Everywhere in Europe, applicable law is to be drawn from national, Community and international sources. Nevertheless, to adapt the multi-level notion to *private stakeholder participation* (not a function of the

State) constituted a leap into the dark, as little theorisation or empirical research covered this new phenomenon of *external* (and mostly informal) stakeholder participation. Nothing guaranteed that these private stakeholders participated on more than one Level when seeking to influence EU regulation.

The author's more than fourteen years' participant observation meets Peirce's pragmatic criteria under heading four especially well. The cost if the theories or models should be false is quite low. The author's reasoning has already passed the test of peer-review and open-ended debate in Academe, as this book's content formed the basis of a doctoral dissertation. The publication of this book will put his theories before the wider audience of practitioners, who themselves constitute a very low-cost verification process. Moreover, the benefits in case the theory and models presented herein are true are far higher, as they not only advance scientific knowledge, but should help practitioners deal with the real-world rigours of the EU's policy processes. What is best of all is that, however urgent it may or may not be to reach a conclusion, the likelihood is very low of finding contrary evidence given the sheer length of time of the author's participant observations. In a practical sense there is little feasible way of seeking out "special data" unavailable to other researchers in venues other than the ones the author has already participated in.

3.1.3 Logic triangulation

The Industry Governance Theory is an abbreviation for what might more precisely be termed the *Industry-Associative* Governance Theory, which the author arrived at largely through the reasoning process that Peirce called "abduction" and "abductive induction" (see Section 3.1.1 and 3.1.2 directly above). The scholarship review presented in the previous Chapter was designed to round out the author's inference to the Industry-Associative Governance Theory with corroboration taken from other scholars by deductive reasoning. Scholars of global political economy, of law and politics, and of international relations have developed theories that dovetail with the Industry-Associative Governance Theory. Anyone deducing conclusions from their insights might have arrived at substantially the same Theory. Purely theoretical considerations, then, in their own way verify the results independently attained by the author, who arrived at substantially the same theory by empirical methods.

In the next Section the matter of "triangulation" will be explored. It will be explained how scholars of methodology recognise four types: data-, method-, theory-, and investigator-triangulation. But a fifth type not yet recognised by other scholars should be called *logic* triangulation, and that is what is here claimed for the multiple reasoning processes that have been brought to bear on the author's data.[80]

3.2 METHODS OF TRIANGULATION AND THE RELIABILITY OF DATA

This section explains how methods of "triangulation" can assist researchers to probe and to demonstrate the validity and reliability of their data and of the inferences that they draw

80 It is the author's contention that what Peirce called a "mixed" argument (see Section 2.1.1 above) is just another word for logic triangulation.

therefrom. The first Sub-section introduces the concept of triangulation, which has been applied not only in social science but also in the professions, such as auditing (where it is called the "three-way match"). Sub-section 3.2.2 explains data triangulation. Sub-section 3.2.3 describes the different types of methodological triangulation, as identified by Denzin (also called "mixed strategies"). The last Sub-section, 3.2.4 mentions methods of triangulation not deployed herein, namely theory triangulation and investigator triangulation.

3.2.1 The concept of triangulation

Triangulation is a term borrowed into the social sciences from astronomy, navigation and surveying. Astronomers, for instance, used to reckon the distance from the earth to a fixed star by observing it from two different points on the earth, of known distance from each other, then using trigonometry to compute from the angles of observation the lengths of the sides of a notional triangle linking the star to the two observation points. In social science the term indicates, according to Cohen and Manion (1986:254), the "attempt to map out, or explain more fully, the richness and complexity of human behavior by studying it from more than one standpoint [as the same star may be observed from two different 'standpoints' on the earth]". O'Donoghue and Punch (2003:78) define it as a "method of cross-checking data from multiple sources to search for regularities in the research data".

Because the same patterns of decisive industry influence, coalition typicality and timing of influence were everywhere observed, the resulting clarity with which the theory and models in this book were evidenced persuaded the author to dispense with the tedium of *explicit* comparisons or "triangulations" of data. Moreover, as expounded below in Section 3.3, the method of *saturation* entailed by Grounded Theory is itself perhaps the ultimate triangulation. This book has therefore not "demonstrated" its triangulation, such that attention is called to the act of triangulation as proof that it happened. This Section, however, will serve as the central reference-point for the *implicit* presence throughout the book of this method, explicating the varieties of triangulation that are hereinbelow operative in practice.

The data-gathering methods deployed for this book contain so many and so conspicuous *built-in* acts of triangulation as to render superfluous "show" triangulations. Moreover, the sheer multiplicity of data-gathering acts, such as stakeholder events attended, rendered it unfeasible to triangulate all discrete observations explicitly, and idle to triangulate a mere sample of them, as their overlap was so manifest. The sundry methods deployed in the research for this book, outlined in this Chapter, empowered the author to explore EU ICT policy from simultaneous multiple perspectives, theoretical as well as empirical. This in itself is triangulation.

Few doubts about whether the author's data-gathering methods entailed built-in triangulations can survive confrontation with the facts of his research plan. The phenomena being observed in the field involved always the same actor groups, sometimes even exactly the same individual actors – with certainty in many cases, with high probability in others. Fourteen years' participant observation certainly involved the same actors in some stakeholder events witnessed. Most of the respondents to the questionnaire Survey were chosen either from mailing lists of the participants in these same events, or from the business cards and participant lists collected when personally attending. The probability is overwhelming that the author was observing the behaviour of substantially the same stakeholders while using both methods (participant observation and sample survey). Part One of the case study of the 2006 Review consisted of a review of every single response that the European Commission received from its own consultation; thus, it is certain that all of the stakeholders who actively participated were observed by the author. Part Two was focussed on one UK event drawn from the population of events in which the author was a participant observer; it included the very same stakeholders, of which the author was an eyewitness. In addition, to triangulate with the case study, the author reviewed the records of other stakeholder-participatory events, the preliminary findings of which had been selected from the total population of policy papers reviewed for the Regulatory Compliance Matrix. The same population of stakeholders were found once again.

Denzin (1978), whose book *The Research Act* outlines the main elements of dealing with multi-method research, defined triangulation as a way of approaching difficult or uncertain research "by using what I have termed multiple strategies of field research … in order to overcome the problems that stem from studies relying upon a single theory, single method, single set of data and single investigator" (1978:291). Denzin affirms that triangulation may be used not just between methods and data, but even between investigators and theories. This book has made extensive use of data- and method triangulation, while making little use of theory triangulation and none of researcher triangulation. The multiple data sources that the author availed himself of crossed a time span of fourteen years, took place in many countries of Europe, and ranged over many actors and actor types. The multiple methods included participant observation, policy paper review, case study, and questionnaire survey. A fifth type of triangulation, overlooked by Denzin, was used for this book, which as noted above may be called *logic* triangulation. The author's logic triangulation is discussed in depth above (Section 3.1.3).

3.2.2 Data triangulation

Under this rubric Denzin identifies three sub-categories: (1) time triangulation, which cross-checks whether the phenomenon in question is purely ephemeral; (2) space triangulation, which cross-checks whether it is merely local; and (3) person triangulation (Denzin, 1978:295-297). The latter method combines (1) and (2) with other traits to cross-check if a behavioural phenomenon is confined to certain social classes or other personal and/ or organisational types. This book has relied on data triangulation extensively in all three senses, especially (3).

Time triangulation was performed in that the author was a participant observer in ICT regulatory stakeholder events spanning a fourteen year period of time from 1996 to 2010, during which European ICT regulation underwent profound changes. The responses to the questionnaire Survey, however, fell within roughly the same timeframe (the year 2004). The 2006 Review case study encompassed (notwithstanding the title) a single thread of regulatory developments spanning the time between September 2005 and December 2008; thus, the whole "life cycle" of the policy initiative in question. Finally, even though the policy-paper review undertaken for Part One of the case study focussed on a narrow window of time, the Regulatory Compliance Matrix policy-paper review (whence it sprang) spans 20 years of policy output, when the European Commission repeatedly spearheaded multiple overhauls of its ICT regulatory regime.

Denzin's second sub-category, *space triangulation*, was implicitly relied-on in that data was gathered on stakeholder activity across a wide geographical field encompassing large swathes of the European continent and beyond. The author's participant observation covered stakeholder events at many different venues in five countries: Belgium, France, Switzerland, the UK and the USA. Moreover, the questionnaire Survey was sent to respondents from fifteen EU countries. The case study involved stakeholders not only from the UK but also from across the EU. The policy paper review, on the other hand, was confined to the European Commission in Brussels and its Single Market jurisdiction.

Person triangulation, the third sub-category, was relied on in all three of the social contexts Denzin identifies, (a) aggregate, (b) interactive and (c) collective.

(a) In the *aggregate* individual behaviour is considered in isolation from its spontaneous or institutionalised social contexts and then (if there is more than one individual) summed up or "aggregated". In this sense, the questionnaire Survey aggregated the answers of a population of individual respondents chosen precisely for the diversity of their social contexts, and thus for their non-representativeness of any one context: age, organisational rank and responsibility, professional experience, and industry-subsectoral situation were all different. This deliberate diversity constitutes implicit triangulation. Another method of data-gathering, participant observation, built-in triangulations by exposing the author to a very wide range of persons differing from one another not only in the ways just mentioned, but also in gender, social origin, walk of life (*i.e.* those outside the ICT industry, such as representatives of consumer organisations and NATO), and in other ways perhaps too numerous to relate. It is a striking result of this triangulation that the author never observed any of these personal variables to affect the uniformity of data observed, and thus to falsify any of the theorisations that sprang from them. They affected neither the "mentality" of the Advocacy Coalition Types nor the dominance of industry. For this reason, too, "show" triangulation was felt unnecessary, such was the manifest uniformity of the data. The policy paper review, being desk research, did not feature aggregate triangulation. And the case study focussed on personal interaction and/ or organisation, not on aggregations of individuals.

(b) The *interactive* (or coordinated) is Denzin's second personal triangulation context, where individual behaviour as such is still studied but only within a social context, yet intimate enough for individual identity to remain observable, as in small groups like families or committees. The author's own participant observations were undertaken in just such social settings – personal meetings, roundtable discussions, workshops, presentations, conferences, focus groups and other fora where individual behaviour is conditioned by small-group interactions.

Finally, (c) the *collective* is the last person triangulation context, where the person is subsumed under hierarchical organisation, and individual identity is submerged by corporate identity. Here the "observational unit is an organisation, a group, a community, or even an entire society" (Denzin, 1978:296). The several policy paper reviews that the author undertook gave detailed insight into the behaviour of the Commission, certain organisations created by and/or answerable to the Commission, and the fora set up by the Commission for use by stakeholder organisations. In addition, this review also included the findings of commissioned reports and of numerous consultations actually held by the Commission and by other regulatory bodies. These documents detailed the behaviour of the participating organisations as such. Even the author's participant observation gave some insight into organisational behaviour, in that some of the stakeholders were present at events to represent their organisations' views rather than express their own.

3.2.3 Methodological triangulation

Under this rubric Denzin distinguishes two types of triangulation: (1) *within-method* and (2) *between-method* (Denzin, 1978:301-304). Within-method triangulation requires that the same method is used on multiple dimensions of the same phenomena, that is, things capable of being measured on several different scales or against multiple "yardsticks". Data are gathered on the same phenomenon, but on different occasions; or else the researcher "employs multiple strategies within the research method to examine the data" (Denzin, 1978:301). Between-method triangulation studies the same object using a range of differing methods.

Within-method triangulation was relied on for this book; for instance, in the form of "control questions" in the questionnaire Survey. Respondents were asked several different ways about their level of "satisfaction" with the EU regulatory regime; *viz.*, how satisfied they were with: EU regulators (Question 3); specified EU policy initiatives (Question 5); and specified EU policy outputs (Question 11). Within-method triangulation also happened by virtue of the author's participation in so many stakeholder events at different times, but sometimes at essentially the same time. The sheer number of events constituted a population of observed behaviours that in principle could have been subjected to statistical testing. This was done only informally, because multiple observation yielded such a consistent "picture" (or "iconic" argument in Peirce's lingo) from which generalities could be inferred. Some or all of that data might well have presented an inconsistent picture or one that contradicted the author's Industry Governance Theory, in which case explicit triangulation would have been appropriate. Within-method triangulation between the policy paper review for the Regulatory Compliance Matrix and the more focussed policy paper review for Part One of the case study was also relied on. The focussed review yielded more in-depth data about organisational behaviour that might well have contradicted the picture given by the broader but less deep review.

Between-method or *cross-methods* triangulation between all data-gathering methods used for this book was conspicuously relied on. All of the methods were brought to bear not only on the same class of behavioural phenomena, but even on the same concrete data-points. As noted above, the probability is virtually certain that some Survey respondents were the same people the author observed as a participant in stakeholder events – given the methods used to select respondents. The same reasoning applies to the relation between participant observation and policy paper review: many of the same organisations (or their representatives) figured in both data-gathering efforts. These efforts were so comprehensive that the probability of overlap between concrete data sets studied by all methods is very high, even if the author did not actually calculate its numerical value. It follows that these different methods were brought to bear on the same experiences and constituted built-in, multiple acts of triangulation.

3.2.4 Other modes of triangulation not used herein

This book did not rely on Denzin's methods under the rubric of *theory triangulation*, which would have required that alternative or competing theories are used to try and explain the same phenomenon (Denzin, 1978:297-301). As all three empirical outputs – the theory and model(s) – are complementary rather than substitutional, and one could still "survive" even if another were to be falsified, theory triangulation as such was never deployed.

Denzin's last rubric, *investigator triangulation*, requires that more than one researcher/author examines the same or some of the same data (Denzin, 1978:297). It might be argued that other scholars have in fact come to similar conclusions as the author, but this ought to be characterised more as independent corroboration than triangulation, as it was serendipitous rather than planned. On the other hand, the Survey could be considered a substitute for a triangulation of the author (and his participant observations) with other "investigators" and researchers, namely the Survey respondents. Participant observation risks being too subjective; all observations are interpreted through the eyes of one participant; hence the Survey's open-ended questions constituted triangulation of a sort, whereby certain issues arising from the events observed by the author were addressed by other participants in their own words. Their viewpoints were thus "cross-checked" or triangulated against the author's. It is noteworthy that the Survey results revealed no substantial disagreements over the issues in question.

It is evident that a wide variety of empirical methods were relied-on in researching this book, which tested the reliability of the resulting data, as theorised by Webb:

> When a hypothesis can survive the confrontation of a series of complementary methods of testing, it contains a degree of validity unattainable by one tested within the more constricted framework of a single method. (Webb *et al.*, 1966:174).

Douglas, who calls methodological triangulation "mixed strategies", argues that researchers should start with a minimum of methodological control and with as much natural interaction as possible (Douglas, 1976). One of the advantages of using triangulation or mixed strategies is to "overcome any problems of a bias" (Burgess, 1984:146). By applying these methods redundantly, the author was able to develop theory and models based on reliable and bias-free data. This is one of the most important foundations of scientific research and practical guidance.

3.3 GROUNDED THEORY

The author discovered Grounded Theory as a formal, codified method after his participant observation and most of his other research had largely been completed. It transpired, however, that he had in fact applied most of the elements of this methodology all along, even while still a *stagière* and when first becoming interested in participating in stakeholder meetings; in effect, the author rediscovered Grounded Theory independently on a practical level.

Grounded Theory is a qualitative research method originated by Barney Glaser and Anselm Strauss, and published in their seminal book *The Discovery of Grounded Theory* (1967). According to Goulding, "Grounded theory, in contrast to theory obtained by logico-deductive methods, is theory grounded in data which have been systematically obtained through 'social' research [...] The main thrust of this movement was to bridge the gap between theoretically 'uninformed' empirical research and empirically 'uninformed' theory by grounding theory in data" (2002:41). Glaser and Strauss, who were not trained logicians, originally understood their approach as inductive; however, later theorists who refined their method realised that Grounded Theory is essentially *abductive* in its methods (Reichertz, 2007:214 *et passim*; Charmaz, 2006). It is widely acknowledged in logician circles that Grounded Theorists have yet to fully fathom the contribution of Peirce (Locke, 2007:566).

Although it cannot be considered abduction *per se*, Grounded Theory facilitates abductive inferences in preference to either deduction from assumed premises or inductive testing of ready-made hypotheses. It does so by the ways it gathers and handles data, a procedure that may be analysed in four sequential stages (though in practice these "stages" inevitably run together): (1) *Incidental Comparison*, (2) *Categorical Comparison*, (3) *Self-Closure*, and (4) *Write-up*.

3.3.1 Incidental Comparison

The first stage, Incidental Comparison is in turn analysable in three sub-stages or steps: *Coding*, *Comparing Incidents*, and *Memoing*. Coding, as Glaser and Strauss called it (1967) – (other Grounded Theorists call it Naming, *e.g.* Locke, 2001), – is a process by which the researcher, having observed in the field multiple "incidents" of a social phenomenon, sorts through his records of particular observations to analyse their mutual similarities and differences, attempting to categorise each incident in terms of its *social meanings* to the observer and to the observee, rather than in terms of mechanistic causes (Locke, 2001:47). Expressing "in shorthand" the meaning of the incident, coding is a conceptualising label spontaneously thought up by the researcher on the spot or whilst reviewing his field notes.[81] This is an iterative process, meaning that the researcher may go back into the field to gather data many times before reaching the data- or theory "saturation" point, where further data merely reinforce the foregone theorising without abducing any new insights.

Neither Peirce nor Glaser and Strauss were able to specify any deduction-like procedure for thinking up the coding (*viz.* iconic argument) that best fits the phenomenon. It would seem some automatic process of the brain. One may hazard the guess that the coder is assimilating what he observes *to his own previous experience*. It is essential all the same that

81 Peirce's illustration of abductive reasoning featured just this sort of coding, in effect; except he called it an "iconic argument", the word icon deriving from the Greek εικων, which meant image. The odd-looking man in the street car struck Peirce as the "spitting image" of an ex-priest, and perhaps the word icon expresses more vividly than coding what Glaser and Strauss meant.

he takes precaution against subsuming his observations under any foreknown *theory*, either his or others'.

*Coding (*or *categorisation)* requires the researcher to seek by trial and error to group discrete incidents together intelligibly in what Glaser and Strauss called categories, or explanatory pigeonholes, in *The Discovery of Grounded Theory*, Part I (1967:23). Coding is the act of recording in writing, either on the spot or subsequently upon review, not a description of the incident itself – (although that too is to be recorded) – but rather what the participants said about its social meaning to themselves *and/or* whatever may strike the researcher as constituting its broader or more "theoretical" meaning (Locke, 2001:47).

To this end researchers are expected to "check at the door" all preconceived theories and foregone conclusions, and let the data speak for themselves. According to Karen Locke, Grounded Theory relies on a phenomenological technique known as *bracketing*, whereby we self-consciously "surface and examine our biases and pre-existing theoretical commitments specifically so that we can 'bracket' them out" (2001:46); *i.e.* neutralise their influence over us, not by repressing them or pushing them out of mind, but rather through acute self-awareness.

It is noteworthy that the researcher's own opinions must not ground all social meanings in question; careful note must be taken of the observees' opinions, especially the language in which they express them. Glaser and Strauss (1967) insisted that two types of coding were distinguishable: (1) categories constructed out of the researcher's own lingo, and (2) categories derived from the observees' spontaneous wording. It is the latter that often creates theoretical puzzles, while the meta-commentary categorisations that resolve them spring from abstractions expressed in the researcher's lingo (Locke, 2001:50).

This aspect of Grounded Theory made an essential part of the research underlying this book. The author did not merely note the Commission's self-criticisms or its self-disciplined resolve to reform its regulatory procedures by involving stakeholders in future proceedings, but also problematised it by pointing out that the Commission took this course of action from a position of weakness (*viz.* lack of technical expertise) not strength. It was quite interesting that the Commission, in touting its Better Regulation initiative, could not avoid problematising its own previous performance. For the author this was the kernel of puzzlement and the genesis of his research efforts. It was a puzzle solved on his own terms with the Industry Governance concept, one the Commission itself never used.[82]

Grounded Theorists advise the researcher, in this beginning stage, to assign multiple meanings to any given incident, viewing it from as many angles as possible and judging which one "works" best. Here Grounded Theory displays its origins in the American philosophy of Pragmatism, by defining Truth as whatever "works out" in practice (over the

82 The Industry Governance theory, of course, was confined by the bounds of the author's research to the ICT industry and does not cover all industries subject to the Commission's regulatory powers. On the other hand, the Commission's Better Regulation agenda included all of the policy domains within its jurisdiction. The mismatch is one that can and ought to be resolved by future research that investigates whether the Industry Governance theory applies as well to these other domains (at least those in which industry is involved).

long run) – working-out surpassing mere predictivity to encompass also "sense-making". The more possible meanings the researcher brainstorms for each phenomenon or incident at first observation, the likelier he will find the *best* categorisation, having exhausted the alternatives. This, by the bye, is exactly what Peirce's conditional criteria of abductive inference call for.

Although willing to approach his research without theoretical preconceptions, the author had actually undergone a different but equivalent experience years before reaching that point. In the very beginning, when he was still a *stagière* with the Commission, the author had entertained the naïve view that public functionaries developed essentially all of the Commission's policies. This view was immediately contradicted by the reality observed all around; the author was forced to abandon the "theoretical" assumptions brought to his *Stage*.

As illustration, consider how the Advocacy Coalition Typology evolved. Right from the beginning of his participant observation, the author was perceiving patterns emerging from the "chaos" of events. He was already wondering "where stakeholders were coming from" – not just geographically and organisationally but also motivationally. He began mentally to sort the attendees into "boxes" or categories, which eventually evolved into the Advocacy Coalition Typology.

Comparing incidents is the next step in Incidental Comparison, after all or much of the coding has been developed. The coding is then used to compare incidents to each other both retrospectively and as they emerge. This the author did both during and immediately after participation, habitually comparing and contrasting stakeholders' interactive behaviours, especially noting evidence of belief systems. Stakeholders expressed their opinions quite assertively, engaging one another in often heated debates. Again and again they were heard to express ideas, implicit goals and impediments to goals, in both similar and contrasting words. The Advocacy Coalition Typology gradually solidified amidst the whirl of events. For example, the Public Sector and NGO Type, which included consumer groups and labour unions, focussed on threats *to themselves* – such as to health or to the environment or to employment – and demanded protections of various kinds from the government. In stark contrast, the Industry Type was preoccupied with practical implementation of the government's regulatory regime and with profitability (*viz.* cost/benefit of regulation). Other participants seemed not to have a "self-interested" agenda as such, but thought mainly about the technical (including human/organisational) impediments to achieving the other participants' agendas – and about how to get funding from government bodies in order to tackle them. Yet despite these manifest differences, all participants were stakeholders in one outcome of the same regulatory process.

Thus, fieldwork consisted of finding out whether a certain behavioural pattern observed in certain individuals or groups (*i.e.* beliefs, common interests) was applicable to all stakeholders, such that the pattern could be said to represent a stakeholder Type. To this end, the author would read the informational material distributed before events, and after events the minutes and the list of participants. Once the [four] Types of participant groups had been identified,[83] the author tried classifying (*i.e.* coding) subsequently observed stakeholders under these Types. Once the author found the "fit" to be exact, he proceeded thereafter systematically to apply these categories whenever he attended stakeholder meetings. He continually compared the behaviour of these Types as further details of the common thread of a belief system emerged that "coded for" those stakeholders, who could then be subsumed definitively under one category. Thus the author refined the characteristics of each Type in light of both prior and posterior observation.

Take for example the Project-groups Type. The first thing the author noticed about them in stakeholder meetings was their technical knowledgeability and their hunger for funding from the Commission. Only later, after passing over from mere observation to active participation in Commission-funded projects did the author eyewitness how such Project groups, once funded, attacked the technical problems defined by the funded programme. It was only amid this activity and the author's participation in it that this Type revealed to him its fundamental belief system: (a) a focus on technology for its own sake rather than politics; (b) a faith in technology as a solvent of social problems; and (c) scepticism of politicians who demanded more than it was technically possible to deliver.

Observation is a passive role whereby only what is visible on the surface comes to light. By also actively participating in the Framework Programme and responding in person to the Commission's calls for consultation, the author positioned himself to understand the hidden depths of this particular Type. By a like methodology the other Types of stakeholders were approached and their depths plumbed as well. The author then found it possible to use the same coding when reviewing and counting the stakeholders identified in consultation reports as having responded to the Commission's "calls for input" and its invitation to participate in consultation processes, which included meetings and written reports. This constituted abductive induction, a form of hypothesis-testing that validated the codes. At this point the author realised he had an "infrastructure" in place to compare the coded Types and their divergent belief systems with each other, but also with other theoretical categories such as the four Levels of governance. This "mixed argument" (in Peirce's words) is what enabled the synthesis of the Four-Level Model with the Advocacy Coalition Typology, yielding the Stakeholder Action Matrix.

After the researcher has finished constructing some of his theoretical vocabulary, this can be used to attach to an unmanageable myriad of observed and recorded incidents manageably few common names which have sprung from the data and not from prior conjecture. He can also test what meaning he thinks he perceives in these common names by testing them against further observations which are now guided by meanings "endogenous" to the research. The coding can be "fine-tuned" in light of the results of guided observation, and methodical

83 The first three were identified rather easily: public-sector and non-profit organisations; industry associations; and those interested in funding and technical aspects. A fourth Type – "individual advocates" – was identified last, as its members were affiliated with no organisation or project, and thus their behaviour was not conditioned like the other Types by institutional or "structural" determinants in that sense. They were conspicuous by their personal interest in the consultation, but otherwise were observed to believe in common only that "highly competitive market environment requires some protection of those outside the industry" and "technology advances society".

note can be taken of both similarities and differences between both categories and incidents (Locke, 2001:48-9).

Memoing is the last step of Incidential Comparison. It is the habit and practice of noting down categories, meanings, guesses, hunches, perceptions *etc.*, right when they occur to the researcher and are still fresh in mind. It is important that these insights are put down in writing, as writing confronts the researcher with an objectification of his thought processes, forcing him where necessary to articulate his theorisations with greater precision.

The author followed the methods of Grounded Theory rather closely throughout his fourteen years' participant observation of stakeholder meetings. It was possible to confirm the categorisation that became the Advocacy Coalition Typology, while it was still immature, because the "protocol" of stakeholder events required participants before voicing their opinion to introduce themselves by name and organisation. The author was thus able to observe and memo which representatives of which organisations advocated what. This was supplemented by the "information packs" received before most events which listed registered participants, and the minutes distributed after the event by the organisers. The author kept systematic records of participants at both the events participated in and those discovered through policy paper review – comparing subsequent observations of stakeholders to the tentative categories and the tentative categories to each other. These "observations upon observations" were also recorded memo-style. For example, after every event held by the Commission, each participant was matched against the author's tentative categories, looking for evidence to confirm or refute the categorisation. For example, in the beginning the author had tentatively sub-categorised "manufacturers" under "Commercial organisations", as distinct from "telecoms operators" which were categorised under "Industry associations". Subsequent observation, however, convinced the author that these participants thought sufficiently alike and acted sufficiently in concert with each other to justify grouping them together. This led to Advocacy Coalition Type Three (Industry-focussed Associations). Thus, the author arrived at his final Typology in just the way that Glaser and Strauss describe.

The author created an audit log of all the events attended and stakeholders met; took minutes during all stakeholder events and subsequent meetings with selected stakeholders; filed away his personal notes, the event agendas, and the handouts and minutes that were distributed; and then used this information for research – to take but one example, by consulting the Stakeholder Directory that the author personally compiled to verify that his Typology was exhaustive (see Appendix Six). In cases where clarification was required, the author discussed matters with the event organisers.

3.3.2 Categorical Comparison

The second stage of Grounded Theory is *Categorical Comparison*, when the activity of comparison changes. As Locke explains it, "[During this stage researchers] spend less time comparing data incidents to each other and more time comparing data incidents to the drafted conceptual category [or code], thinking about all of the elements that might make [the category] up – its properties and dimensions", the better to find aspects that need "tweaking"

(Locke, 2001:51). In short, the researcher rises above comparing discrete, concrete social incidents to each other, in order to compare not only (1) further social incidents to his coding of them (so far), but also (2) comparing his codes to each other. Doing (1) accomplishes one of two things: (a) to confirm that existing codes and their theorised characteristics suffice, as is, to subsume the new data-point; or if not (a), then (b) to occasion further elaboration of codes. Doing (b) in turn may mean either (i) thinking up another code, in case the existing repertory explains too little, or (ii) elaborating the characteristics of existing codes to bring fuzzy aspects into sharper focus.

Comparing the several codes to each other is done to the end of abductively inferring an overarching explanatory framework that *makes sense of their observed co-incidence* in the underlying social situation (Locke, 2001:51-52). In particular, the researcher is to compare the characteristics of the several categorisations, to see if any ("iconic") common threads run through some, or most, or all of them. This is facilitated by comparing new observations to the whole scheme of coding, not to just one code in isolation. Diagramming the conceivable relationships between codes and their characteristics is another common strategy for constructing and clarifying a framework that can fit all of the theorised categorisations into it (Locke, 2001:52).

This is precisely what the author did to arrive at the end-product of his research, the Stakeholder Action Matrix arising from the Four-Level Model and the Advocacy Coalition Typology. Once four Levels of governance had been identified from observation and prior scholarship, the author "projected" the Advocacy Coalition Typology onto the whole multi-level governance structure, with the Levels of governance arrayed vertically and the typology horizontally; yielding sixteen distinct Advocacy Coalition Types in theory. This was at first based on mere conjecture, which left "holes" in the Matrix where hard evidence should have been. The author then understood what more to look for, and proceeded to find out enough evidence to confirm or falsify the conjecture – especially through the Survey, and in particular Question 2 (see Section 6.4.1 below). Thus, the Survey, in addition to being a statistical sampling, constituted what Glaser and Strauss call "theoretical sampling" as the preferred method of testing one's theoretical gambits. Years of laborious "coding" soon stood vindicated.

3.3.3 Self-Closure

The third stage of Grounded Theory is called *Self-Closure*, because the method contains within itself the means of bringing itself to an end. The researcher continues to gather data in the field (or laboratory) until the point is reached when he begins to notice that the extra data is adding no further value to the coding. Grounded Theorists usually call this *theory saturation* (*e.g.* Locke, 2001:53), although it may also be called "data redundancy". At the point of "saturation" further data merely corroborate what prior data have already evidenced, *i.e.* the categorical coding or basic theoretical apparatus of the research. It is worth emphasising that the saturation-criterion does not consist in the (lack of) strikingness of the data considered in isolation, but in whether they exert any more influence on the development of the coding or theoretical apparatus. If development of further theoretical insights is no longer happening or expected, no reason exists to continue gathering data, and this phase of the research may be ended. Grounded Theorists expect to gather data to saturation, an aspect of Grounded Theory methodology evidently designed to substitute for statistically controlled sampling in qualitative research settings where no statistical control is feasible.

The data-gathering carried out by the author exceeded the criterion of saturation in most instances, carrying the process to the point of *supererogation* and *completion.* In his archival research, his Survey, and his case study the author was careful to record essentially everything. The appendices attest to this with exhaustive compilations like his Regulatory Compliance Matrix. The policy paper review that grounded this Matrix reviewed *all* of the Commission's policy output at the relevant level of detail. Likewise, the participant observation memoing recorded essentially all stakeholders who participated in all events attended by the author, and the resulting Stakeholder Directory in Appendix Six includes not only these stakeholders but all others whom the author was able to identify by all other means. For the case study the author observed every step of the European Commission's policy-making process in its 2006 eCommunications Framework Review.[84] The Roadmap for the EU Regulatory Framework Review (Table 7.3), the tabulated result of this (and of all other data-gathering methods therein involved), presents a data-complete panorama of stakeholder influences operative throughout this process. These data grounded the inference and the development of the Policy Influence-Timing Model presented in Chapter One. In pursuing data-repletion the author may not have adhered to Grounded Theory methodology "to the letter", but his methods nonetheless entailed saturation.

3.3.4 Write-up

Write-up, the last stage, is straightforward. A researcher at this stage has in his "coded data, a series of memos, and a theory" all the essential ingredients of finished research (Glaser and Strauss, 1967:113). This book is the write-up of everything done in the more than fourteen years of research of ICT regulation, its processes and its participants.

3.4 METHODS OF COLLECTING SECONDARY DATA

Both qualitative and quantitative methods were necessary for the developing theory and models focussed on external stakeholder influence on ICT regulation, as the author's preliminary research had found too little evidence of any kind about this phenomenon to falsify theories or construct models. The necessary data-collection was carried out in three overlapping stages, as set forth in this and following Sections (Section 3.4 through 3.6): (1) secondary data-collection; (2) primary data-collection, and (3) a case study. Section 3.4 describes in detail the methods deployed to gather data from secondary sources. Firstly, comprehensive desk research into the theoretical scholarship was undertaken. Next, an

84 In the case of his participant-observation research, extensive observation records were kept; nevertheless not every event attended was memorialised in a document in every detail. In some instances, the author had to supplement his memos with personal memories of these events in order to draw inferences and conclusions. In most cases, however, the extant written records triggered and refreshed his memories; that is, he has seldom had to rely on unaided memory alone.

archival review was conducted to gather as much data as possible about the content of the EU's regulation of ICT. This covered but was not limited to the applicable regulations and publications produced by the European Commission.

3.4.1 The scholarship review

The first stage of secondary research encompassed a theoretical literature review, including books, periodicals, and collections of essays, and scholarly debate on the subject of policy processes and stakeholder influence. Investigated were opinions of researchers and scholars about the process of ICT policy-making in the EU, including theoretical concerns and problems, characteristics of EU ICT policy, and how the policy process has changed in recent years.

The review concentrated on recent publications (*i.e.* within the last twenty years), due to the sheer voluminousness of the topic, from policy-making and governance in the EU to the far-reaching changes in policy processes, and on to the novel involvement of non-institutional stakeholders. ICT policy is such a fast-moving area that even ten-year-old publications often seem obsolete. Adding to this dilemma are the recent EU enlargements (EU25 in May 2004 and EU27 in January 2007); the regulatory reform for "better regulation and lawmaking"; the formation of new regulatory bodies and task forces; and the perpetual formation of new interest groups. For this reason, much of the author's research into key contemporary debates about the role and influence of external stakeholders on EU ICT policy has had to be empirical.

The results of this review, that is, the scholarship supporting the author's theorisation, have been presented in Chapter Two, above. These are themselves theories – a scholarship review is a review of theory, not data – which the author modified or expanded as suited his purposes and the data he found. In general, scholars propound theories of general applicability couched in nebulous terms at a high level of abstraction. Without modification and adaptation to the facts and circumstances of ICT policy making, such theories would not have been immediately useful. Some of the theories, such as Sociological Institutionalism and Institutional Rational Choice, although reviewed at some point and applicable in the abstract, were nonetheless excluded from Chapter Two as adding little value to this book.

3.4.2 Archival analysis

European ICT policy and regulation could not have been understood solely by reviewing the scholarship; primary research was required in the publications of the European Commission (*viz.* Green and White Papers, Communications, studies, presentations, statistics, project results, legislation, EU policy initiatives, and action plans), and in the publications of major actors involved in the policy processes. Information collected from stakeholder workshops, European conferences, and other EU-related events was also mined. This desk research also covered the views of opinion leaders expressed in speeches, presentations and press releases.

The author compiled an electronic repository of policy papers, documents about current European regulations and standards, and other relevant documents. He found these official documents by searching the "Europa" and "Eur-Lex" websites. A telecoms solicitor based in

London who had worked for Ofcom and the European Commission also provided a structured list of telecoms regulations used by her law firm. This formed a core which the author was able to extend to encompass all ICT regulations, yielding the Regulatory Compliance Matrix. It contained the classification (refined as required) applied to the official documents the author had been reviewing at the same time.

Firstly, the data collected from the policy paper review provided a holistic overview of the European Information Society and its legal and regulatory framework, as presented in Chapter Four. This data was then compiled into the Regulatory Compliance Matrix, included in Appendix Five, which lists all relevant EU and global ICT regulations and standards, and gives examples of UK ICT law.

Secondly, this general policy paper review laid an important foundation for the author's description of the sundry channels of stakeholder participation treated in greater detail in Section 5.2 below.

Thirdly, this review served as a "matrix" from which sprang Part One of the case study in Chapter Seven on participation in the 2006 Review at the European Level, which had to rely on the content of policy papers, consultations and other updated information published by the European Commission *via* its "Europa" website, *via* mailing lists, and *via* FP newsletters. Thus, part of the case study was dependent upon this prior archival analysis.

3.5 METHODS OF COLLECTING PRIMARY DATA

The primary research included a Survey and fourteen years of participant observation. Sub-section 3.5.1 describes the selection of the Survey respondents, and the design and distribution of the Survey questionnaire. The participant observation Sub-section 3.5.2 below outlines how the author gained access to valuable data through interlocution, attendance of presentations and participation in stakeholder events.

3.5.1 Questionnaire Survey

The Survey on Stakeholder Participation in Information and Communication Technologies (ICT) Policies, Regulations and Standards (hereinafter called the "Survey") surveyed by questionnaire a sample of industry experts and non-governmental organisations. The overall aim of this primary research was to collect attitudinal and background information on stakeholders actively participating in policy-making and standards-setting processes, particularly to learn more about their main initiatives and how they tried to influence decisions. Chapter Six, "The Survey and Analysis of Results", and the Survey Report (see Appendix Four) are the result of this primary research.

Statistical methodology and the selection of samples of ICT stakeholders across Europe formed the basis of the representative results. The target group consisted of industry-, regulatory and standards experts from business organisations, NGOs, government agencies, and regulators, as well as researchers and scholars from universities. Respondents were identified from the following data sources: the approximately 150 business cards given to the author by fellow participants at numerous stakeholder events; mailing lists from two major industry associations (the European Electronic Messaging Association and the European

Expert Network), whose membership was known to be active in policy consultations or in European Commission programmes; and publicists who, having published articles in European journals and electronic newsletters like *CORDIS*, could be ascertained to be experts on ICT regulatory and standards issues. The rationale for using these sources was that respondents had to have the necessary technical expertise, be participating in stakeholder events, and be familiar with EU ICT policy. Hence the best population of such prospective respondents who were also accessible to the author consisted of fellow participants in events like the ones the author had attended. The sample was well distributed across countries (by population size), age groups, and business sectors, justifying the conclusion that this Survey is representative in its socio-demographic characteristics. The response rate of 45% was sufficient for making statistical interferences about the population of ICT stakeholders in general.[85]

The Survey sampled "stakeholders", but this category (and the sample) included officials working in the public sectors of the Member States, who also had a "stake" in the outcome of regulation at the European Level. On the other hand, the sample excluded any person who worked for the *European* regulator. EU *fonctionnaires* could not have been objective about their own work; including them might have skewed the overall results. Nevertheless, a series of face-to-face, semi-structured interviews were held with leading associational, regulatory and standards-setting actors at European Level; *viz.* key staff in the European Commission, mainly from DG Information Society and DG Enterprise; the European standards institute (CEN); industry associations (ICC, CBI, EEMA); and international organisations (the EU representation to the UN, ITU, OECD). The objective of all of these interviews was to understand the interviewees' responsibilities for key EU policy outputs, such as major policy White and Green Papers and Communications, and whether and how they had collaborated with external stakeholders to achieve them. The semi-structured format allowed the flexibility for further inquiry into the interviewee's specialism and specific involvement with stakeholders. The interview questions were formulated with a view to supplementing the information already gleaned from the massive review of EU policy papers and Framework Programme documents. Specifically, the author wanted more insight into the details of the processes – stakeholder consultations, Framework Programme involvement, and R&D activities – that had contributed to these major policy documents.

The data from the interviews and from the archival review "triangulated" with each other inasmuch as both datasets independently verified that external stakeholders played an important role in the shaping of policy outputs. Both interview- and Survey questions were designed to elicit information on stakeholder input into EU regulatory processes, which was expected to evidence its volume and intensity not only at the European Level but also on multiple other Levels of governance. The kind of information solicited directly bore on

85 For a parametric test to be valid, a sample size of at least 30 is generally accepted as sufficient, which is much smaller than the number of data which were obtained (McClave, Benson and Sincich, 1997). The sample of 202 completed questionnaires is a representative sample size for the population size in question; therefore, the statistical findings ought to be reliable and valid. The statistical analysis, in connexion with the case study and other secondary research conducted, is adequate for testing the research hypotheses.

the falsification (or verification) of the Industry Governance Theory, which claims massive stakeholder involvement in the policy processes in question. The selection of interviewees as well as Survey respondents was undertaken in accordance with the definitions of key ICT stakeholders in Chapter Five, "Key Actors and their Channels of Participation".

The Survey was sent out before the watershed of 1 April 2004, when the ten new Members from Eastern Europe joined the EU. The date yielded thus focussed on the EU15.[86] Stakeholders from the new Member States had to familiarise themselves with EU ICT regulations and with forms of participation new to them, and the national regulators were as of April 2004 still in the process of amending and adopting the new modes of regulation. As negotiated before accession, some new Member States were given additional time for adopting certain elements of the complex regulatory frameworks. Because of these complications, it was deemed most fitting to cover the EU15 only. Resource limitations, too, would have made it extremely time-consuming to widen an already rather wide-ranging survey.

The designing of the questionnaire relied on a number of mutually triangulating sources of expert advice: (a) an elaboration session reviewing the Survey's methodology with the author's doctoral supervisor and with Professor Ray Lee, an expert in survey methodology at Royal Holloway; (b) advice from the National Statistics Office of the United Kingdom; (c) the author's methodology and content review of selected social science, consumer- and technical surveys; (d) familiarisation with relevant scholarship on survey design and execution, including Dillman and Salant (1994); Dillman (2000); and Blaxter, Hughes and Tight (2001); (e) face-to-face meetings with *fonctionnaires*[87] of the European Commission and CEN to identify and refine the Survey questions;[88] (f) previous personal participation in

86 The EU15 countries: Austria, Belgium, Denmark, Finland, France, Germany, Greece, Ireland, Italy, Luxembourg, Netherlands, Portugal, Spain, Sweden, United Kingdom.
The EU25 countries: EU15 + Cyprus, Czech Republic, Estonia, Hungary, Latvia, Lithuania, Malta, Poland, Slovakia, Slovenia.
The EU27 countries: EU25 + Romania and Bulgaria.

87 European functionaries are officials who work for the EU institutions.

88 Individual meetings were set up with the following individuals for clarification of the survey content and to discuss opportunities for stakeholder participation in EU ICT policy and standards-setting initiatives. Due to the sensitivity of the interviewees and confidential content of these interviews, where Commission *fonctionnaires* gave sometimes brutally candid insight into regulatory strategy and policy stakeholder participation, the author found it afforded him far better access and candour to eschew the use of recording devices.
- Cunningham, George (April 2003): Head of EU Delegation, EU Office, Meeting, New York.
- Mastrogiacomo, Giovanni (April 2003): Industry Policy & Economic Development, EU Office, Meeting, New York.
- Büscher, Reinhard (4.5.2003): EC DG Enterprise, D/4, Head of Unit "ICT industries & services", Meeting, Brussels.
- Zimmerman, Rainer (4.5.2003): EC DG Information Society, C/1, Head of Unit "electronic components", Meeting, Brussels.
- Ketchel, John (8.5.2003): CEN (European Committee for Standardization) Director, Meeting, Brussels.
- Mela, Chrissa (8.5.2003): EC DG Information Society, A/3, Information Resource Centre,

stakeholder activities at the National, European, and Global Levels to gain better insight and understanding of stakeholder interactions;[89] and (g) a pilot study involving ten experts in ICT regulations and standards, who critiqued the questionnaire's content and layout.

The Survey was conducted between April and September 2004, using two distribution channels: (a) *Postal mailing of a hard copy questionnaire* – these were sent to 150 selected individuals whom the author had met personally at workshops and/or specialists who had been speakers at regulatory/standards events; *viz.* the *Comité Européen de Normalisation* (CEN), *a.k.a.* European Committee for Standardisation workshop; the Information Society Technologies (IST) conference in Helsinki; launch events and information days of the EU's Fifth and Sixth Framework Programmes (FP); InfoSecurity Europe conference. The solicitation included a cover letter, brief instructions for completing the questionnaire, a privacy statement, and the questionnaire with a return envelope. Also (b) *Targeted emails with an electronic questionnaire attached* – approximately 450 individuals were approached, with approval, through three Europe-wide e-mailing lists: (i) a Framework Programme mailing list for eCommunications services and infrastructures, (ii) a European standards body mailing list, and (iii) a European e-business and security association mailing list. A total of 224 questionnaires were returned, of which 202 were selected and assessed for the Survey. The 22 questionnaires left-over were rejected either because they were less than 50% completed, or because the respondents came from countries outside the EU15. Answers to open-ended questions, however, were accepted from all respondents.

Information Officer, Meeting, Brussels.
- Bucher, Anne (9.5.2003): EC DG Information Society, A/1, Head of Unit "eEurope and IS Strategy", Meeting, Brussels.
- Hallentie, Timo (9.5.2003): EC DG Information Society, Scientific Officer, "IST Programme", Meeting, Brussels.
- Broster, David (9.5.2003): EC DG Information Society, D/6, Head of Unit "eTEN", Meeting, Brussels.
- Comyn, Gerard (9.5.2003): EC DG Information Society, A/2, Head of Unit "Strategies for IST Research", Brussels.
- Anselman, Norbert (9.5.2003): DG Enterprise, G/2, Head of Unit "Standardisation", Brussels.

89 Examples include:
- Event: "eContent Information Day", DTI Conference Centre, 7.02.2003.
- Event: "FP6 IST Information Day", Institute of Mechanical Engineers, Westminster, 11.02.2003.
- Event: "Towards a global dependability and security framework- IST workshop", DTI Conference Centre, 27.02.2003.
- EU Information Day: "eAwareness for Europe – Information Security Awareness and the Role of Local Government", endorsed by OECD, Socitm (Society of Information Technology Management), RAND Europe, IAAC (Information Assurance Advisory Council), SOLACE (Society of Local Advisory) and Intellect (UK trade body for the UK based IT, telecommunications and electronics industry), London, 2.06.2003.
- CEN/ISSS Workshop on Data Protection and Privacy (CEN/ISSS WS/DPP) (9.07.2003), CEN Premises, Rue de Stassart 36, Brussels.
- Conference: ITU Telecom World 2003: 12 - 14.10.2003, Geneva, Switzerland.
- Response to the Consultation for the European Governance White Paper COM(2001/428 final), March 2002.

The Survey participants were invited in the questionnaire to provide comments and whatever personal views they cared to submit. The resulting qualitative data exhibited a polarisation between the extremes of either enthusiasm or disaffected anger. Clearly this is not an unbiased sample of opinion; self-selection bias is manifest in such a polarisation. Therefore, an alternative, less unreliable method to gather qualitative data was required. This was supplied both by the author's own participant observation and by the case study presented in Chapter Seven, which was partly based on that participant observation.

3.5.2 Participant observation

For many years, from 1996 to 2010 (and beyond), the author personally participated in a very large number and variety of stakeholder activities (for one researcher), while conducting, in the same time-frame, in-depth, face-to-face interviews with a divers set of political actors chosen by the author. The rather enormous dataset that had already emerged in the first years formed the core and springboard for the author's subsequent doctoral research. When in the course of this undertaking he learned that most companies consider their political "influencing strategies" to be confidential information, and that some of his research questions were of a sensitive nature, the author realised that the survey method on its own would likely prove inefficient. Thus, he made the decision to continue attending stakeholder events as frequently as before and to interview strategically placed acquaintances made at these events; having already experienced how this was a more engaging approach to the persons who had the information needed. Not only would the new data triangulate with the Survey due to respondent population overlap, it would also help open up the monolithic "black box" of the business firm – called an Anonymous Society (abbreviated S.A.) on the Continent because of the opacity of the "corporate veil" behind which the actors within it are shielded from public scrutiny – so as to get on the inside where insider information would be accessible. The author in this way came to learn of many of the approaches adopted by company actors for pro-actively participating in the policy process. The data thereby discovered included not only information on organisational strategies but also on a range of stakeholder activities both individual (*e.g.* participation in EU "expert calls") and collective (*e.g.* membership of Europe-wide associations).

The problem encountered by many social scientists who overrely on survey methods, statistical measures and necessarily "linear" experimentation, is that these inadequately capture the subjective elements of social life (Burgess, 1984:79). The method of *participant observation* has proved indispensable: the theory and models in this book presupposed a profound understanding of stakeholders and their belief systems; the (undocumented) interactions between them and between Types of them; and their ulterior motives and hidden agendas. It is indeed a method often applied in conjunction with other social science methods. Jorgensen asserts that participant observation methods deepen and enrich the case study method. "Case studies conducted by way of participant observation attempt to describe comprehensively and exhaustively a phenomenon in terms of a research problem" (1989:19). Part Two of the case study, "Participation at National Level – The 2006 Review in the UK", drew on the author's rather large "database" compiled through participant observation. As noted in the previous Section on Grounded Theory, participant observation is considered the ideal position for a researcher for purposes of Grounding (Charmaz, 2006:21).

According to Burgess, the participant observation method "involves the researcher in taking a particular role within a culture in order to examine at first hand a social situation from a participant's point of view" (1984:98). To be successful, the participant observer must as a rule avoid "perturbing" the behaviour of the persons whom he is trying to observe in their "naïve" candour; he must not attract undue attention if he wants to capture his observees speaking and acting spontaneously. Yet he cannot in most social situations do nothing but passively look on with notebook in hand and escape notice as an outsider; to be accepted as "ordinary", he must take on an active role in the business afoot in the social scene observed. This obliges him, according to Burgess, to engage in both "role taking" and "role making" (1984:98); *viz.*, not just taking up "roles" (routinised social performances) already in being, but even creating his own in the necessary and appropriate circumstances. At a minimum, the participant observer must be a role-taker, accepting the part assigned to him by others. The role-making observer goes a step beyond this and actively develops relationships (Burgess, 1984:92-96; Delbridge *et al.*, 1994:50-52) in order to gain acceptance; to win trust; and to develop co-operation, rapport and friendship (Jorgensen, 1989:69-81).

As David Waddington points out, "[r]esearch settings inevitably vary in the extent to which they are open or closed off to public scrutiny" (1994:108). The author would add that settings also vary in the *ways* in which they may be open or closed off. Most stakeholder events would appear to fall squarely on the "open" end of the spectrum. Appearances can be deceiving, however. It is true that the author rarely encountered positive barriers to entry at most of the events he attended for over fourteen years. On the other hand, it is rare even for scholars, let alone the press or the public at large, to actually scrutinise these events. Furthermore, the culture of consensus cultivated by EU regulators and the consensus-building of stakeholder associations ambitious for influence meant that quite often sharply clashing viewpoints got reconciled in published outputs like policy papers and other official publications. Getting past such a subtle, deeply embedded form of gatekeeping likewise commended participant observation. Thus, participant observation – its insider vantage-point and its *entrée* past gatekeepers – was practically the only method for pursuing data sufficient to characterise accurately the policy-making behaviour of stakeholders. The author therefore took an active role within stakeholder-consultative processes, which enabled examination of those social situations at first hand from a stakeholder's viewpoint.

Amidst attending all the diverse stakeholder activities presented in this book, the author maintained a disinterested stance toward all policies, and avoided joining in with the self-interests of regulators, businesses, and other stakeholders. Disinterestedness was achieved by focussing on the collection of evidence, and by refraining from participation in purely politically motivated or interest-driven debates.

Participant observers frequently have difficulties blending seamlessly into their milieu in order not to disturb with their presence the spontaneous and candid behaviour of the other parties. This is a recurring problem for anthropologists who endeavour to study their own societies, as witness Burgess's discussion of the difficulties (1984:15-16). The author did not have the same difficulties because the events participated-in invited public participation. His presence passed unnoticed, and what he observed was never disturbed by his observing it. With a high degree of probability what he observed was authentic and accurate.

By its detractors participant observation is reputed to be an uncontrollably biased, one-sided data-gathering method. Robert Yin, a major methodologist, asserts that participant observation does not yield reliable, comprehensive and unbiased data "due to [the] investigator's manipulation of events" (1994:80), and may only serve in a supporting role to narrow methods like the case study (1994:). This may be true of the sort of participant observation that is only briefly engaged-in for purposes of constructing a case study. However, a project of participant observation may extend over quite a long duration of time and breadth of location, especially if engaged in for its own sake and not as a chore. Becker, a noted critic of participant observation (*cf.* 1958:652), nonetheless concludes, "Because [the long-term participant] observes *over a long time*, he finds it hard to ignore the mass of information supporting an appropriate hypothesis he may neither have expected or desired ..." (1970:52 [emphasis added]). Under these circumstances participant observation may rise to the comprehensiveness and reliability of other methods, and will always yield denser and richer data than sample surveying, however statistically valid. The search for the ideal dataset that is representative yet "untainted" by any deliberate selection of the researcher is another method entirely. Survey methods may be statistically controlled, while participant observation is not; nevertheless, participant observation can approach or even exceed the representative accuracy of surveys, inasmuch as selection biases are the more cancelled-out the longer and more intensive is the participation. Grounded Theorists have concluded likewise, expressing the matter somewhat differently (and slightly more to the point) with the concept of *saturation*: "Whereas statistical sampling ends when the researcher has collected data from all available elements in the predetermined sample, inductive and contingent non-probability sampling ends [ideally] when the 'saturation point' is reached. That point is normally determined by the discovery that additional interviews [or participant observations] are yielding so little new information [that] more interviews would be a waste of time" (Hood, 2007:161). Although Grounded Theorists distinguish between data-saturation and theory-saturation (Hood, 2007:161-162), the distinction detracts nothing from the force of the author's argument.

Anselm Strauss, the co-discoverer of Grounded Theory, lays down that to achieve saturation, the Grounded participant observer's attendance ought to be diverse, broad-based and long-lasting (Strauss and Corbin, 1994). The author's participation as an observer in ICT industry events lasted for over fourteen years and comprised more than 100 events, including ICT stakeholder meetings, ICT conferences, and EU-focussed presentations – a participant observation schedule that was indeed diverse, broad-based and long-lasting. It was diverse because participation encompassed events hosted by a wide variety of organisations operating at all Levels of ICT governance (see Table 7.1 below). It was broad-based because it covered not only lectures and other purely academic presentations attended by "traditional" researchers, but also events hosted by participants in the industry, by industry associations and by the regulators. It was long-lasting because it covered the period from when the author worked as a s*tagière* for the European Commission (1996) through when he was involved in EU projects with PricewaterhouseCoopers (1998-2002), and only ended in 2012. It can hardly be gainsaid that such a manifold record of participation has achieved data saturation *at least* equivalent to statistically controlled representativeness.

By the same token, whatever biases might be inherent in a unique observer may be controlled or at least made visible to others by explicating in advance of participation what questions are to be answered; *viz.* the participant poses the questions to be investigated. Moreover, an observer who like the author begins participating with no agenda except curiosity is likely to be less biased than many scholars of methodology give him credit for. All of the foregoing considerations point to participant observation as the best method this author could have chosen for doing the research underlying this book. The author is hardly the first researcher to understand the merits of participant observation; as Delbridge and Kirkpatrick have concluded:

> [P]articipant observation was the most appropriate choice of methodology to deal with research which aims to understand complex social relations and organizational processes. Furthermore, we strongly refute the notion that this choice was in any way purely ad hoc or unscientific. We have also demonstrated that participant observation is not a 'soft' option. While we acknowledge that there are problems of both a theoretical and practical nature – in particular those of reflexivity and the minimization and understanding of bias – we firmly believe that participant observation has an important role to play in the task of understanding social phenomena. (Delbridge and Kirkpatrick, 1994:59)

The author's participant observation took place within a threefold format: firstly, he personally attended seminars and presentations by scholars researching the Information Society and its regulation, who had either first-hand experience with ICT regulators or were leading academics in the field of ICT regulation.[90] Secondly, he personally attended various consultation events, such as workshops, presentations and conferences with policy experts and stakeholders, so as to engage himself in the debates and glean further insights into the views of stakeholders. Many of these key personnel are "opinion leaders" who have been responsible for shaping policy outputs decisively.[91] Thirdly, he had around 40 face-to-face meetings and interviews with stakeholders and regulators on all Levels.[92] The Table in Section 7.1 provides a detailed overview of the scope of the author's participant observation.

---

90 Examples include: Manuel Castells, presentation on 18 March 2004; Mark Thatcher, lecture spring 2003; Ian Walden, lecture 2003.

91 Examples include: Fabio Colasanti, Director General for "Information Society" since 2002, conference on 12 November 2003; Jim Dougal, Head of the European Commission Representation in the UK from 2002-2004, conference on 28 April 2004; Erkki Liikanen, Commissioner for DG Enterprise and Information Society from 1999-2004, conference on 12 October 2003; Romano Prodi, President of the European Commission from 1999-2004, presentation on 19 January 2004.

92 Examples include: Anne Bucher, European Commission Head of Unit for eEurope and IS Strategy/ Brussels; Marie Farrell, Policy Manager at the International Chamber of Commerce/Paris; Gilbert Germain, European Public Affairs Practice Leader at PricewaterhouseCoopers/PwC.

Participant observation is not confined to participation in various kinds of events, direct observation, and discussions and interaction with participants. It also covers informal face-to-face interviews (sometimes called "buttonholing"); secondary observation of events (*e.g.* anecdotes and hearsay from informants); experiential perceptions of the observer, *esp.* perceptions of non-verbal behavioural cues ("body-language"); structural and organisational information from the event itself, *e.g.* agenda, list of participants, backgrounds of presenters and key organisers; and analyses of outputs by the observed stakeholder group, such as minutes, presentations and work papers (Delbridge and Kirkpatrick, 1994:43).

To gain the best access to as many stakeholder-participatory events as was feasible to attend, the author subscribed to various electronic mailings lists[93] and newsletters[94] that published event announcements and descriptions. But he also discovered that these subscriptions steered him to further participant information through press releases, calls for tenders and consultations, reports and studies *etc.*, which he would not likely have found on his own. Section 7.1, "Schedule of participant observation", describes in greater detail which events the author selected for participation in, what role he took up or made for himself, and how he documented his observations and participation.

An example of the author's participant observation may suffice to bring everything together in the reader's mind. Since the European Parliament enacted the eCommunications Framework Directive in December 2009, the author has participated in a number of events and conferences dealing with the transposition of this Directive into UK national law, focussing in particular on ePrivacy regulation, and the revision of the existing Data Protection Directive 95/46/EC. On 25 January 2012 the European Commission unveiled its draft European Data Protection Regulation 2012/11/EC "On the protection of individuals with regard to the processing of personal data and on the free movement of such data", which will supersede the Data Protection Directive 95/46/EC. In many of these stakeholder events, attorneys from major law firms took the stage; *e.g.* Quentin Archer from Hogan Lovells International LLP; Rosemary Jay from Pinsent Masons LLP; Bridget Treacy from Hunton & Williams LLP, and Phillip Rees from McGuire Woods LLP; often joined by representatives of national regulatory authorities; *e.g.* Christopher Graham, the UK Information Commissioner; David Smith, the Deputy UK Information Commissioner; Emma Martins, the Data Protection Officer from Jersey. Most of these events were facilitated by industry associations, *esp.* Intellect UK, BCS and ISACA. In addition to such events, which were concerned with compliance and review, regulators have also delegated staff to advise business on certain elements of privacy like how to comply with EU Cookie Law; *e.g.* Senior Guidance Manager Dave Evans from the ICO.

---

93 Examples include: Information Society Newsroom Update Weekly (DG Information Society], Enterprise & Industry e-Newsletter (DG Enterprise], EU News and Funding (Enterprise Europe Network in London], DigiCult - NEWS from the European Commission on cultural heritage, digital libraries & digital preservation research (DG Information Society], Singleimage Workshop: Finance in FP7.

94 Examples include: CORDIS Newsletter, RTDinfo.

Shortcomings in the data protection regulations were detected, probably due to the fact that certain non-EU stakeholders might not have been sufficiently involved in the consultations. An example of such an unrepresented stakeholder is the Sedona Conference on Cross-Border Discovery and Data Privacy, a US-based industry association "dedicated to the advanced study of law and policy in the areas of antitrust, complex litigation, and intellectual property rights". Its members – law firms, eDiscovery service providers, and US government officials – tried to resolve conflicts that had arisen between EU data protection law and demands to transfer personal information to the US for litigation purposes (Conference – "The 3rd Annual Conference on Cross-Border Discovery & Data Privacy", 22-23 June 2011).

It should be noted that even at this post-implementation stage of the regulatory cycle, the industry had become dominant in identifying and resolving these shortcomings of the EU regime. This evidences that industry governs beyond the implementation stage; it is thus proved to be involved, often in a predominating way, at each and every point of the policy cycle.

3.6 THE CASE STUDY

For pragmatic reasons it is important to match a research strategy to the nature of the investigation involved and the kind of research questions posed. The case study is one such strategy. Fritz Scharpf suggests that the insights gleaned from good case studies have a depth and persuasiveness that social scientists should not lightly dismiss in their quest for the elusive goal of generalisable empirical regularities and universal "scientific laws". A good case study requires that the researcher is diligent in data collection and already has an experience-based understanding of how things may happen (Scharpf, 1997). For the research presented in this book a case study of stakeholder participation in the eCommunications Framework Review 2006 was chosen, and its results evaluated against an analytical framework that allowed theoretical revision.

Robert Yin, perhaps the foremost authority on case study methods, distinguishes five main research strategies: "experiment, survey, archival analysis, history or case study" (Yin, 1994:13). He notes that each of these strategies may serve the purposes of explanatory, descriptive, or exploratory research (Yin, 1994:1-16). Yin does not preclude the possibility of applying multiple strategies in particular instances to generate better results. The criteria supposed to inform the eventual choice between the five strategies include: the kind of research question asked; the amount of control the researcher has over the constituent events; and the time frame that is the main focus (whether contemporary or historical) (Yin, 1994:4). Last but not least, issues of reliability and validity have to be addressed.

Which of these strategies befitted the present book? Actually, the research project which formed its basis embraced not just the case study, but every one of Yin's research strategies except experiment, which was not feasible under the circumstances and given the kind of data the author was interested in (which included data of a historically contingent nature). Thus, the methodological difficulties of choosing between them all were avoided.

Robert Yin also identified six distinct sources of case study data: archival records, documents, direct observation, participant observation, interviews and material artefacts; all of which were drawn upon for the research supporting this book except material artefacts.

The quality of case studies increases substantially if data about the same phenomena can be gathered from two or more sources, and/or if a gapless "chain of evidence" can be developed within the case study, *i.e.* explicit links, transparent to the reader, made between the questions asked, the data collected, and the conclusions drawn (Yin, 2003:83ff). The case study presented in this book has followed Yin's methodological reasoning and recommendations.

The logical approach taken to data thus produced was inductive, in that theories and models were inferred from the observation of empirical reality (Hussey, 1997:13). This applies especially to the Four-Level Model, inducted from a particular instance (embodied in the Case Study below), which claims that general patterns are to be discerned in the decisional processes actually observed.

A research design is a hypothetical chain of inference relating the data to be collected back to the initial question by way of answer. As suggested by Robert Yin (1994:18 *et passim*), the articulation of a theory determines in part how a case study design is supposed to operationalise and explicate it. Design quality depends critically on the validity of data and the reliability (*i.e.* repeatability) of results[95].

The design of the case study in Chapter Seven was aligned to the theory and models through the following chain of inference. First, telecommunications regulation in general and the eCommunications Framework in particular were reviewed over a period of 20 years. Secondly, stakeholder participation in the 2006 eCommunications Framework Review was examined in national (*viz.* UK), European, and international terms. The 2006 Review was treated as a typical instance of the eCommunications Framework, which was considered a typical instance of ICT regulation in general – that which the theory and models are concerned with.[96] Third and lastly, the findings of the study were summarised, and formed one of the pillars of the Industry Governance Theory. The case study thus helped to fill-in gaps in the "picture" of the relative dimensions of stakeholder involvement, especially respecting the consultative interactions between stakeholders and the European and national regulators in the policy process.

Case studies encapsulate processes that in their entirety are too vast for the understanding of researchers. To understand the totality of industry predominance in contemporary regulatory processes would require a knowledge of all the facts of every regulatory proceeding having taken place at all Levels of governance. Such a body of knowledge cannot be captured within the confines of any one or even very many scholarly works. Case studies are intended to allow the individual researcher to substitute a few samples for the whole population.

---

95 "Reliability is concerned with the findings of the research. The findings can be said to be reliable if you or anyone else repeated the research and obtained the same results." [...] "Validity is concerned with the extent to which the research findings accurately represent what is happening in a situation; in other words, whether the data collected is a true picture of what is being studied." (Hussey and Hussey, 1997: 173).

96 This chain of inferences exemplifies what Nachmias and Nachmias meant by their words, "[T]he research design defines the domain of generalizability; that is, whether the obtained interpretations can be generalized to a larger population or to different situations" (Nachmias and Nachmias, 1976:29).

In selecting the first case to study (Part One: Participation at European Level – the 2006 Review process), the author was attracted to one of the more recent policy initiatives at the European Level – the "Regulatory framework for electronic communications infrastructure and associated services" or 2006 eCommunications Framework Review, launched by the Commission in Communication COM(2002/21/EC) – because it was the most comprehensive (being a "framework"); had the greatest impact on industry and consumers; and thus might be expected to generate the highest level of stakeholder involvement. Once this choice had been made, pursuit of its ramifications followed.

Four Levels of governance having been identified, it was necessary to look for evidence of industry predominance on Levels additional to the European, if a theory of *industry governance* overall was to be sustained. The United Kingdom was chosen for Part Two of the case study as a ramification of the eCommunications Framework , in order to evidence industry involvement at National Level; because of the abundance of and ease of access to information, and because the author had many opportunities to participate personally in stakeholder activities with BERR and Ofcom, the UK national regulatory agencies.

The last part of the study (the Supplement) – the ramification at Global Level of the eCommunications Framework – was undertaken because stakeholder activity at a Level beyond the European had been previously identified, and the existence of this Level called for empirical exploration as well. But the author was faced with a peculiar difficulty at this Level, as the eCommunications Framework, being a European law, is not binding at Global Level. Therefore, a specific regulatory ramification already addressed by the Framework – data protection in general and unsolicited email ("spam") in particular – was selected because no wider policy initiative related to the Framework was available at Global Level. Furthermore, international organisations adopting policy positions, because they lack the enforcement powers of national and European regulatory authorities; usually put out nothing more binding than guidelines and recommendations. Hence, one could expect that stakeholders might behave differently, *e.g.* be less motivated to participate, where their interests are exposed to a significantly lesser degree of risk.

A ramification study on Sub-national Level was never undertaken, because it would have demanded access to the inside of an ICT business organisation in order to eyewitness processes related to some wider policy or standards-setting exigency. The author was unable to gain access in sufficient depth to the insider dynamics operating between various classes of stakeholders within a large business organisation; *viz.* technical specialists, compliance department, sales department, and board of directors. The Survey reported in Chapter Six was designed to compensate for this lack of insider access. Although it polled individuals rather than organisations, all the respondents were insiders themselves, and their aggregated responses may reasonably be assumed to give some insight into the policy process on Sub-national Level.

3.7 CONSTRUCTING A MODEL

The "atomic" ingredients of theoretical concepts must be related to each other in structured ways that simplify the burden of theorising. There are different ways of looking at these simplifications of reality known as "conceptual frameworks". Conceptual frameworks identify the variable factors and relationships between actors (for example) that account for certain recurring phenomena. According to Elinor Ostrom, conceptual frameworks span the gamut from a modest set of variables to an elaborate paradigm. Frameworks "attempt to identify the universal elements that any theory relevant to the same kind of phenomena would need to include, and therefore can be used to compare theories". Researchers can use the elements identified by the chosen framework to determine what questions ought to be addressed in their analyses (Ostrom, 1999:39-40).

Compared to a framework, a fully specified theory has more information content, in the sense that more questions have to been answered, and all will have to be answered empirically. As suggested by Sabatier, a theory provides a more focussed set of logically rigorous relationships. Typically, a theory assigns values to at least some of the variables that constitute it. Alternative theories can be consistent with the same framework (Sabatier, 1999b:6). Theories must be built in part on assumptions, and the choice of these assumptions partly determines the theory's success at explaining complex phenomena (Friedman, 1953). Compared to frameworks, the criteria for evaluating theories are well known and accepted. Ostrom points out that "theories are evaluated for their capacity to generate predictions supported by empirical evidence and to provide coherent explanations for observed regularities" (Ostrom, 1999:64). The question remains, if theories reach the goals of science so well, why are frameworks needed for scientific research? Frameworks can provide "stability" to overarching research programmes by defining questions, variables and highlighting a paradigm, which then can be refined in theories. As more theories are developed within a framework, this framework will attract more research interest.

A model is a simplification of reality that tries to represent a well-defined situation. It is usually much narrower in scope, and much more precise in its assumptions, than the underlying theory (let alone framework). When one models a process, such as the decision-making process of the European Council, one reduces it in conception to the minimum number of elements logically necessary to account for what the modeller theorises is going on in reality. Thus, to render reality theoretically manageable, simplifying assumptions are made, *e.g.* about who the principal actors are; what their motivations are; what they know about themselves and other actors; what each actor is likely to do in order to achieve his goal; and how actors interact with each other (Pierce, 1994:3). Theories assert universal truths, whereas models purport merely to give hypothetical instantiations of theory; therefore, models are best fitted to explain particular cases or limited sets of cases – unlike theories, which are supposed to be of general applicability.

As suggested by Karl Popper, the development of a scientific theory or model should start with the identification of a scientific problem, followed by observation and recordation of data or measurements of the phenomena involved in the problem. One may then correlate these recorded observations, and try to guess (or abduct) generalisations or theories that "explain" all of them. The quality of the theory (and thus the progress of science) lies in the evolution of its problem. In the Popperian philosophy of science, the formulation of hypotheses is an affair of minor importance; what matters is whether hypotheses are able to survive attempts at empirical falsification. Theory is considered a tentative solution.

Knowledge grows through elimination of errors and critical discussion of theory, so that a better understanding of problems may be gained. There is a feedback loop whereby new problems are revealed calling for more universal solutions and theories (Popper, 1994:155-159). The growing number of often conflicting theories can be seen as a challenge for researchers. "Simplification" and "elimination", as suggested by Popper, introduces a sort of "Darwinism" into the practice of social science, whereby selection through "the survival of the fittest [theory]" will cull the throng of theories down to manageable numbers.

This discussion of model construction is rounded out by the following Section, which presents a list of rules widely recognised as helping to formulate and evaluate a good model. The author used these criteria to assess the Stakeholder Action Matrix and the supporting Policy-Influence Timing Model presented in Chapter One. Ticking off the "criteria for good models" is one way to assess whether and how these models fare against objective criteria.

To show that duplication of effort has been avoided, the following Section will also present and critically analyse the policy-process models in the existing literature. The shortcomings of these models justified the making of a new one, the one presented in this book.

3.8 METHODS OF ASSESSING MODELS

Sub-section 3.8.1 summarises the scholarly criteria used in formulating and evaluating models. In Sub-section 3.8.2 , the limitations of existing models of the policy process are identified. Sub-section 3.8.3 outlines the four basic assumptions that underlie the Stakeholder Action Matrix, and form its foundations.

3.8.1 Criteria for a good model

Every framework has its strengths and limitations; however, there are a number of criteria that may help us assess the value of theories and models. It is widely recognised in the field of political science that the following rules avail in formulating and evaluating a good model (*cf.* Sabatier, 1999b:8; King, Keohane and Verba, 1994: 99-113; Lave and March, 1997:59-73):

1. It must meet the "criteria of a scientific theory, that is, its concepts and propositions must be clear and internally consistent"; it must be falsifiable[97]; be based on carefully selected dependent variables; maximise correctness; and it must identify clearly probable causal drivers (Sabatier, 1999b:8).
2. It must be the subject of recent conceptual development and/or empirical testing, so that it is not obsolete.
3. It must be a positive theory that also seeks to explain as much of the phenomenon under study as possible (Sabatier, 1999b:8). Both scholars and practitioners are more

97 Karl Popper (1968, 1994) is most closely identified with the idea of falsifiability. In his view, a fundamental asymmetry exists between confirming a theory (verification) and disconfirming it (falsification); therefore, a hypothesis or theory ought to be designed such that it will be feasible to prove it false.

interested in the occurrence of an event than in non-occurrence, and more in the big picture than in isolated details.

4. It must address an important set of factors that will engage political scientists looking at different aspects of policy-making – *e.g.* conflicting values and interests, information flows, institutional arrangements (Sabatier, 1999b:8).
5. At a minimum it should provide "a descriptive language that helps us to discover whether or not we are talking about the same thing and thus to compare assumptions, hypotheses, and findings across the variety of complex and unique cases that we are studying" (Scharpf, 1997:30).
6. The model should be economical in its elements and its assumptions; the leaner and less cluttered the model, the more likely it is to be taken up by modellers.[98]
7. Models are customarily evaluated by their "productiveness" or predictive power. Many scholars argue that productiveness is the main criterion by which a model should be judged (Pierce,1994:4-5). How well do they explain known outcomes? Do they successfully predict what has not yet happened but is known or suspected to be going to happen in the foreseeable future? According to Anthony Downs, "[t] heoretical models should be tested primarily by the accuracy of their predictions rather than by the reality of their assumptions" (1957:2).
8. A good theory must have the potential for "contributing to a better world by helping policy activists understand the policy (or other) process, by indicating the variety of guidance instruments available to them, and perhaps most of all, by showing how individuals with solid information can make a difference over time" (Sabatier and Jenkins-Smith, 1993a:231).

The author is sympathetic to the view that economy (or logical parsimony) is essential to the success of a model, but would also suggest that too many modellers have reduced their models to so few elements that falsification or criticism is difficult if not impossible. Not only is it difficult to falsify simplistic or tautological models, but hardly any predictions can be derived from so few elements. Like horoscopes, their predictions are vague and their outcomes are optimistic. Despite this, horoscopes are still consumed and scholars still develop models that can be discussed theoretically (if inconclusively), but have limited practical use. To take the author's own model for an example, it would have been insufficient merely to categorise stakeholder belief systems in the abstract, leaving the reader to guess who these stakeholders are.

This critique suggests one further criterion for the design and evaluation of models – their adaptability to specific policy situations, *e.g.* one stage in the policy process; or to specific environments, *e.g.* at the regional or national or European level; or to different policy sectors. The author's research results lead him to argue that most models and theories that could be deployed as explanations simultaneously in the agricultural, pharmaceutical and ICT sectors would be of limited use to the actors involved. This is because the dynamics

98 Roy Pierce uses the term "parsimony" to refer to the principle of Ockham's Razor, stressing the importance of presenting the core of a "complex world" (Pierce, 1994:4).

shaping regulation in these sectors are importantly and practically different. Europe's agricultural policy, for example, is founded on heavy subsidies, and often influenced by social agendas and traditional "lobbyists". By contrast, ICT policy follows the economic agenda of liberalisation, with participation by a greater diversity of stakeholders.

A "good" model is not enough, however. It must be useful not only to the social scientists who theorise from it but also to the practicing actors whose behaviour it is supposed to explain. A truly satisfactory model must be useful not only to those who have developed it, but also to those who are "captured" in it. This means that policy stakeholders should be able to "profit" by the model when dealing with each other or the regulator. This may be realised through a broadened understanding of the possible pathways of interaction; of one's own and other actors' behaviours; and of the best timing for accomplishing given objectives.

3.8.2 Limitations and contributions of existing models

Many who study, teach or practice in the field of European politics and regulation have grown ever more dissatisfied with the overvaluation of the supranational EU institutions in the policy process. Most scholars denounce the EU's democratic deficit, but when they turn to analyse the EU policy process, their main focus is on the decisional process within these supranational institutions.

Both the denunciation and the supranational tunnel-vision entail serious logical and empirical deficiencies. Firstly, most scholars simply ignore the variety of external input that policy makers take in at the European level. As demonstrated in this book, EU policy makers must weigh-in the interests of all policy stakeholders, not just those of the Member-States as such; the existing national and international legislation, regulations and standards; the diverse socio-economic classes and social interest groups ("civil-society"); as well as diverse organisations at multiple levels of governance. Secondly, the complexity and technicality of EU governance necessitates an element that might be considered "undemocratic", but which may be inevitable in a real-world decisional process. The Swiss model of direct democracy, with 7.4 million citizen-participants, could not possibly be applicable to the European Union, with 494 million citizens (in the EU27).

The dominant contemporary theory of policy-making, the Stages Heuristic of Jones (1977), Anderson (1979) and others, should be enhanced and used in conjunction with the Advocacy Coalition Model defined by Sabatier and Jenkins-Smith (1993a; 1993b) so as to give a rounded view of the policy world in both "space" and time. This book furnishes strong evidence – based on recent policy-process models, and on the Survey and case study in this book – that the ICT policy process:

1. consists of a continuous and interactive process among different stages, which implies series of feedback-driven actions and recursive policy cycles, as witness the regular Reviews of the eCommunications Framework
2. creates policy outputs that favour synergetic policy packages, that amend regulations as part of a wider policy programme, or that establish new regulations that will complement existing regulations

3. involves distinct policy actor types, which include regulators, civil-society organisations and State or quasi-State institutions, *e.g.* IRAs and standards institutes that support implementation; and
4. leads to the formation of groups of stakeholders (*viz.* epistemic communities/ advocacy coalitions) on multiple Levels who pursue similar interests, and who interact with each other on the same and on different levels.

3.8.3 Assumptions of the Stakeholder Action Matrix

It is widely recognised that, more than institutional research, interactionist policy research is dependent on empirical data, which must be collected specifically for each policy-interaction case (Scharpf, 1997). It was for this reason that so much empirical research was conducted for this book. This eventuated in the construction of a comprehensive model of stakeholder interaction, the Stakeholder Action Matrix presented in Chapter One.

The following theoretical assumptions underlie the design of this Matrix, as it features actors and actor constellations, both collective and cooperative. First, as much scholarship suggests, it is assumed that "epistemic communities" and "advocacy coalitions" really exist and apply to the author's *explanandum* (Richardson, 1996a:33). Sabatier acknowledged that his research often featured a high number of actors (from 50 to 100) in a policy subsystem. He admitted that the advocacy coalition is an abstract construct, but insisted it enabled the analyst to classify sundry actors to produce a more systematic understanding of a complex reality (Nahrath, 1999:41-58). For Schlager advocacy coalitions are dominated by corporate groups (*e.g.* business organisations), who as such are confronted with the classic dilemma of collective action, the reconciliation of conflicting interests (Schlager, 1995:245ff). The author's desk research presented in Chapter Two convinced him that the Advocacy Coalition concept was the most useful for the Stakeholder Action Matrix, as he had already observed as a participant that actors/stakeholders organise themselves politically as communities of interest.

Having identified within this model those stakeholders who are most involved in the policy process and whose choices ultimately determine the final outcome (see Chapter Five), the question arose of the stability of their preferences and hence coalitions. The characteristic perceptions and preferences of actors may be relatively stable (as assumed in rational-choice theories), and may reflect the values and objectives of the organisation they represent. Like Paul Sabatier, the author rejects the view that "actors are primarily motivated by short-term self-interest and thus that coalitions of convenience of highly varying composition will dominate policy making over time" (Sabatier, 1993:27). It is assumed, then, that coalition stability results not only from stable preferences and beliefs in general, but also from the stable economic and organisational interests and hence preferences of stakeholders. Indeed, this may well be one of the secrets to the predominance of business influence in ICT-sector governance.

It is also assumed that the concept of policy actors is not limited to individuals but embraces collectives or individuals who act collectively; *viz.* corporate entities, public interest groups, industry (or trade) associations, professional associations, labour unions, government organisations and committees. With the exceptions noted in the Stakeholder Action Matrix itself, individual actors matter only insofar as they act in behalf of their organisations (*cf.* Laumann & Knoke, 1987b:9); indeed, even collective actors have been aggregated into "clusters" (Sub-national, National, European and Global) and into Advocacy Coalition Types "composed of people from various governmental and private organisations who share a set of normative and causal beliefs and who often act in concert" (Sabatier, 1993c:18).

Sabatier assumes "policy brokers" are generally responsible for mediating conflicts between coalitions (Sabatier, 1993:18-19); however, the author assumes, to the contrary, that in fact mediation is often achieved not by other (third-party) actors, but by framing institutions such as conferences and consultation processes.[99] While it is acknowledged that government is a universal mediator in theory, the author assumes that government is not in practice universally trusted, hence no third-party actor can always mediate all stakeholder interests. The new information arising from institutional and external dynamics is also apt to move advocacy coalitions to revise their preferences or alter or modulate their strategies.

The Stakeholder Action Matrix also assumes that interactions in decisional processes follow logical patterns. Chapter Two expounded some concepts and models purporting to explain the interactions between policy actors. Actors may carry-on collective action in the form of "policy networks"; on the basis of convergent cost-benefit calculations, which pursue common political projects based on common preferences; and because of beliefs (normative and causative) and interests (see Section 2.3.2 above). Another concept is the "epistemic community", which is said to influence regulators through the innovation, diffusion, selection, and persistence of its policy ideas (see Section 2.3.3 above). The scholarship review and the case study both suggest that "aggressive" lobbying has mostly been replaced by stakeholders offering expert advice and by policy-makers seeking their support to legitimate policy choices, an arrangement known as "expert networks" (see the discussion of expert networks in Section 2.3.2 above).

Furthermore, following Sabatier, the Stakeholder Action Matrix assumes that belief systems may exert even more influence over behaviour than individual or organisational interests. Beliefs are more verifiable and stable than interests; yet as Sabatier points out, self-interests and organisational interests still need to be identified, because belief systems incorporate and define these interests. The belief systems of the actors featured in the Matrix were identified and verified in superabundant detail through more than fourteen years' participant observation, as well as through the Survey – (another instance by the bye of how triangulation was built into the author's data-gathering methods).

Finally, it is assumed that EU and Member-State institutions behave rationally and are open to ideas from stakeholders, *i.e.* they actually follow their own "open governance principles". EU institutions are important, but are not the focus. Private influencers external to the EU institutions are the main focus; hence, *proof* that EU institutions behave rationally *etc.* lies beyond the scope of this book.

99 *Cf.* Survey Question 4: "How does your organisation participate in policy-, regulatory and standards-setting activities at the EU level?"

PART III

Core Findings: Regulatory Governance and Policy Influence

I have come to the conclusions that politics [and governance] are too serious a matter to be left to the politicians.
(Charles de Gaulle, 1890-1970)

CHAPTER 4

THE LEGAL AND REGULATORY FRAMEWORK OF THE EUROPEAN INFORMATION SOCIETY

The eCommunications Framework is closely related to the vast domain of e-Business regulation, which covers computer fraud and cyber crime; intellectual property law; liability for online transactions and services; and online contracts (Lloyd, 2000a, 2000b). Today e-Business affects nearly every aspect of our lives. We use electronic banking services, access information stored in online databases, and place orders that depend on electronic transmission *via* public communication networks. The development of a satisfactory regulatory framework for eCommunications is a matter of critical importance for e-Business suppliers and consumers who without legal certainty could not assess the nature and extent of their risks and liabilities well enough to make suitable arrangements; inhibiting investment in new ICT.

"Traditionally, all forms of communication have been subject to some form of official control" (Lloyd, 2000b:29), a generalisation which applies, for example, to the printing press, the telephone, and the postal service. But existing regulation is being challenged by the rapid evolution of new forms of communication technologies, which constitute a core element of e-Business. Various scholarly attempts have been made to define the legal and regulatory framework for the Information Society; however, too often the focus has been on the United States (Wendy Currie, 2000), or on one narrow corner of the Information Society, such as data protection, information security or the regulatory framework (Ian Walden, 2001).

This Chapter looks at the legal and regulatory framework of the Information Society *as a whole* and *in Europe*. It sets the stage for investigation of stakeholder influence on ICT regulation by exploring the content and boundaries of the Information Society and its technology. Moreover, by "staking out" the relevant policy domains, a foundation is laid for the identification of the stake-holders who are attempting to shape the content of these domains (a matter investigated in Chapter Five). Only if the *ICT* policy domain is clearly distinguished from other, closely related industrial sectors likewise subject to EU regulation can a model specific to the ICT sector of the European economy be developed. The goal is for the generalities inferred from these data to be true and accurate, and distinct from the different generalities that might be applicable elsewhere.

The first part of this Chapter (Sections 4.1 through 4.2) provides background on the main policy initiatives at the European and Global Levels. This is a largely historical overview that spans the era of telecommunications liberalisation (1984-2006) and includes the inauguration of the European Information Society.

In the second part (Sections 4.3 and 4.4) the EU's strategic vision as embodied in the objectives set by the European Council are reviewed. Following this is a review of how the European Union Treaties have empowered the supranational institutions to enact and implement telecommunications policy; ICT research and development; competition policy, which lays down the principles for an open market economy; and targeted programmes to improve infrastructure and collaboration in R&D. This information then enables the abstraction of the relevant policy frameworks, regulations, and standards of the services and networks of European information and communication technology. Sub-section 4.4.5 describes some of the platforms and vehicles that the European Commission has designed to implement the Council's strategic objectives; to review regulation; and to improve ICT services and networks in close collaboration with certain policy stakeholders.

The third part (Sections 4.5 and 4.6) reviews the relevant regulatory frameworks for ICT that EU legislation has enabled. It maps the regulatory domains of interest to ICT policy stakeholders by identifying the main regulations, related technical standards, and frameworks and guidelines. The third part also addresses standards, which help business organisations implement "technology-neutral" regulatory requirements; also analysing government- and industry-driven standards-setting to explain the different approaches to the creation of new standards by.

The last part of this Chapter, Section 4.7, presents the results of the foregoing analyses in the form of a matrix, which the author has named the Regulatory Compliance Matrix. Having defined and analysed the legal framework of the Information Society, the next Chapter looks at the "stakeholders" who have rights and liabilities in these policy domains and are therefore involved in shaping their content.

4.1 THE EUROPEAN INFORMATION SOCIETY: INITIATIVES AT THE EUROPEAN LEVEL

The Commission has developed a pan-European vision for the role of ICT policy in promoting the growth of the European economy. It behoves one, then, to become thoroughly familiar with this vision if one would investigate and understand the ICT policy process in any depth. This will enable one to pinpoint the key issues of regulatory policy which in practice require buy-in and input from stakeholders. A brief historical overview will also help to identify repeating patterns of agenda-setting as well as preferred platforms for policy formulation and implementation. It may also help identify the "key" stakeholders, those who have a ongoing interest in ICT regulation.

The first cycle of European Community telecommunications policy was initiated in 1984, with the establishment of a common regulatory framework. The second cycle was launched in 1987, and culminated in the liberalisation of all telecommunications networks and services in the Single Market by 1 January 1998. Not long afterwards it was realised that the rapid pace of technological change, convergence issues, and the repercussions of liberalisation had outrun existing policy, necessitating a single, adaptable framework overarching the entire realm of electronic technologies. This was enacted and took effect in (nearly) all Member States as of July 2003. The high concept of this third cycle of regulation transcended telecommunications to encompass even broadcasting (with the exception of content); was focussed more on the emerging needs of e-Commerce; and in particular, integrated the regulation of information security.

The European Commission's 1993 White Paper on "Growth, competitiveness and employment" marks the beginning of this new, comprehensive policy on ICT which became known as the European Information Society. The Commission identified the transition to an Information Society as the master-key to economic growth, competitiveness, job creation, and a continually improving standard of living and quality of life in Europe's future (CEC, 1993). A High-Level Expert Group (HLEG) was set up under the chairmanship of Martin Bangemann to follow up this "visionary" policy document. The HLEG's remit was to furnish the Commission with advice from Europe's most knowledgeable experts about how best, in the context of the Information Society, to achieve its strategic goals of job creation, social solidarity, equality of opportunity and access, and the conservation of European cultural diversity. In 1995 the Commission created the Information Society Forum (ISF), consisting of 128 members, as a permanent advisory body.[100] The ISF was to "provide the opportunity for representatives from a variety of different groups, including the social partners, to contribute to open debate and reflection on the challenges of the Information Society including the social and societal aspects, as well as to raise the level of public awareness"[101] (Information Society Forum website, 2007). Ever since, the ISF has been working on the implementing framework of the Information Society, and has indicated to the Commission which projects deserve priority within this framework.

In May 1994 the HLEG published its first report on "Europe and the Global Information Society" (also known as the Bangemann Report), which analysed the social aspects of the Information Society. The Report proposed "an Action Plan of concrete initiatives based on a partnership between the private and public sector to carry Europe forward into the Information Society" (CEC, 1994a:4). It stressed that "the enormous potential for new services relating to production, consumption, culture and leisure activities would create large numbers of new jobs" only if the public and private sectors collaborate (CEC, 1993:23). The Report also explored what role the EU might play in bringing about favourable conditions for both the technological and the social regulation of a European Information Society. Before the Bangemann Report, material and technical challenges had dominated the debate over the Information Society, along with the question of which regulatory environment was most conducive economically to the widespread deployment of ICT technology. The impact on society of implementing technological change and the issues arising from the consequent

100 The appointed members were drawn from business, user- and consumer organisations, research institutions, representatives from regional and local authorities, as well as non-governmental organisations such as employers associations and trade unions.

101 Mission of the Forum, defined in the Conclusions of the EU/Central-Eastern European Countries (CEEC) Forum in 1997.

social transformation added further complexity to the regulatory challenge (Ducatel, Webster and Herrmann, 2000:9).

The EU's first Information Society Action Plan, titled "Europe's Way to the Information Society", was published in 1994 by the Commission. The main objectives were to accelerate full liberalisation of telecommunications infrastructure and services; "to strengthen and reorient ICT research programmes; and to incorporate the new Information Society dimension into all relevant Community policies" (CEC, 1994d:7).

The HLEG presented its first Interim Report in January 1996. While the HLEG was solely responsible for this Report, around 20 private and public organisations also submitted written comments, even though, at this time, public consultation was much less developed than it would later become (CEC, 1996a). The ISF published its first Annual Report only five months later (Information Society Forum, 1996), which put forward similar recommendations to the HLEG's. Other European and national expert advisory groups were set up at this time to formulate their own policy recommendations; various EU policy papers were published;[102] and more independent studies were commissioned by the European Commission.[103]

Later in 1996 the Commission published a Green Paper titled "Living and Working in the Information Society: People First" in order to stimulate broader awareness and discussion of the social issues raised by the Information Society. The Green Paper broached issues touching the responsibilities of national, regional and local authorities, and of civil society. The Commission strove throughout 1996 to elicit public comment on the Green Paper and on the HLEG and ISF Reports (CEC, 1996d).

In April 1997 the HLEG presented another Report titled "Building the European Information Society for us all" (CEC, 1997a). This Report expounded on the High-Level Group's own collective thoughts, opinions and beliefs, based on the public comments that had lately been rendered on the social dimension of the Information Society. Taking the debate a step further, the HLEG proposed a policy framework that would take into account the gamut of opportunities and challenges presented by the Information Society. In the process the Group outlined a number of core recommendations which have subsequently influenced policy development in such domains as e-Learning, e-Commerce, e-Government, telework and employment, globalisation, cohesion policy and social inclusion, and transparency and democracy. It then defined the Information Society as follows:

---

102 Examples include: COM(1996/359) "Standardization and the Global Information Society: The European Approach", Communication from the Commission to the Council and the European Parliament, 24 July 1996 (European Commission: Brussels); COM(96/395) "The Information Society: From Corfu to Dublin – the new emerging priorities", Communication from the Commission to the Council, the European Parliament, the Economic and Social Committee and the Committee of Regions, 24 July 1996 (European Commission: Brussels);
COM(96/392) on "Regulatory transparency in the internal market for Information Society services", Communication from the Commission to the European Parliament, the Council and the Economic and Social Committee, 30 August 1996 (European Commission: Brussels).

103 Examples include: the KPMG Study (September 1996) "Public Policy Issues Arising from Telecommunications and Audiovisual Convergence"; the Andersen-IENM Study (1996) "Strategic Developments for the European Publishing Industry towards the Year 2000".

> The Information Society is the society currently being put into place, where low-cost information and data storage and transmission technologies are in general use. This generalisation of information and data use is being accompanied by organisational, commercial, social and legal innovations that will profoundly change life both in the world of work and in society generally. (CEC, 1997a:16)

On the heels of the Bangemann initiatives the Member States launched their own series of national Information Society "strategies". Most of these initiatives shared a common format: expert groups were set up to produce policy statements and initiate action programmes. The detailed process was managed differently, however. Whereas external bodies of experts advised policy-making executives at European Level, on the National Level external bodies of advisors were appointed by public officials (*e.g.* Sweden), or else empanelled on committees under direct ministerial control (*e.g.* Denmark, Finland, the Netherlands), and tasked with formulating policy (Ducatel, Webster and Herrmann, 2000:6). This shows that the channels of stakeholder influence may differ from country to country, and between the National and European Levels; a fact which complicates attempts by stakeholders to design an overall strategy for influencing ICT policy.

By 1999 it had become clear that EU Information Society policy required stakeholder input if the EU was to reach anything specific policy-wise that would answer to the new policy context. By then, the Information Society was no longer a policy vision but ever more a reality. The mushrooming of the Internet, an economy ever less manufactory and ever more knowledge-based, and the advent of mobile communications were the most obvious indicators.

The Commission's Communication COM(99/687/final), titled "eEurope – An Information Society for all", which was welcomed by the European Council of Lisbon on 24 March 2000, set a new strategic goal for the EU for the coming decade: "to become the most competitive and dynamic knowledge-based economy in the world, capable of sustainable economic growth with more and better jobs and greater social cohesion" (Europa website – Lisbon Strategy, 2006). The Lisbon Strategy has in particular emphasised that Europe's "businesses and citizens must have access to inexpensive, world-class communications infrastructure and a wide range of services" (CEC, 2000:3). To achieve this goal, the European Council asked the Commission to elaborate an eEurope 2002 Action Plan (CEC, 2001c), which "was endorsed at the Feira European Council in June 2000 as part of the decade-long Lisbon Strategy of economic, social and environmental renewal" (Barani, 2004:6). The implementation of the Action Plan was to be monitored by benchmarking national progress toward reaching its set goals.[104] eEurope 2002 was later complemented by the eEurope+ initiative (embracing the East European accession candidates) which set out eleven "action areas" in which a total of 64 "targets" were to be achieved by the Member States before the end of 2002.

104 eEurope annual Benchmarking Report: COM(2002)62 on "Impacts and Priorities" of 5 February 2002 provided intermediate measurements for the benchmarking of eEurope, which is based on a schedule of 23 sector-specific indicators endorsed by the European Council in November 2002. The accompanying 'Commission Staff Working Papers' provided a commentary on progress toward each of the 64 targets.

In June 2002 the Seville European Council approved COM(2002)263, the eEurope 2005 Action Plan superseding eEurope 2002. The new Plan focussed on a limited number of key priorities where government was supposed to be well-positioned to give the impetus: modernisation of public services; completion of a favourable regulatory environment for e-Business; and a secure-made broadband infrastructure. Eventually, this series of eEurope Action Plans evolved into the new i2010[105] (European Information Society 2010) strategy, an initiative launched by Commissioner Viviane Reding at the Seville European Council in June 2002. This builds "towards an integrated approach to Information Society and audiovisual media policies in the EU" (Europa website – European Information Society 2010, 2006). To support this initiative, in June 2006 the Commission set up a Task Force on ICT Sector Competitiveness and ICT Uptake, which became the main ICT-related initiative (CEC, 2006l). The Task Force's mandate was to identify major obstacles to Europe's competitiveness in and uptake of ICTs, and to help mobilise the European ICT sector and recommend specific policy responses to the i2010 initiative targets. The members of this Task Force included telecoms incumbents, new market entrants (consisting of both large and medium-sized firms), SMEs, Chambers of Commerce, investors, consumer groups, trade unions, and academia[106] (CEC, 2007m).

Fast, interactive and low-cost international telecommunication is perhaps the most radical feature of the new technology. The Commission has argued that ICT positively facilitates access to information and knowledge; yet also acknowledges that the spread of ICT, and the stepped-up globalisation it is causing, poses a social policy challenge for Europe. Rather than conceiving globalisation as a threat before which society must submit, the new strategy demands that policy-makers are pro-active in seeking to leverage the benefits of globalisation for all of society. At the Global Level, too, international organisations have been taking initiatives that address issues arising from the advent of a global Information Society. These will be investigated in the following Section.

4.2 THE GLOBAL INFORMATION SOCIETY: INITIATIVES AT THE GLOBAL LEVEL

The Internet and other associated communication systems are inherently global in nature. The Commission has sought to integrate into the European ICT policy framework a minimal set of universal rules that have been developed at the Global Level. In order to meet this goal, the Commission has been working with multilateral organisations, including the International Telecommunications Union (ITU), the Organisation for Economic Co-operation

105 The letter *i* stands for a single European *i*nformation space; for *i*nnovation and *i*nvestment in research; and for *i*nclusion, better public services, and quality of life.

106 For the full report of the ICT Task Force, a list of members and details of working arrangements, see ICT Task Force website at http://ec.europa.eu/enterprise/ict/taskforce.htm (accessed September 2007).

and Development (OECD), the World Intellectual Property Organisation (WIPO),[107] and the World Trade Organisation (WTO). The initiatives of global organisations and participants are analysed in more detail in Chapter Five, but key developments include especially the following. The Commission has closely collaborated with ITU in fighting spam ("spam initiative"), and with the OECD to promote Internet security, as evidenced by its holding workshops and formulating voluntary guidelines on the topic. The Commission has also proposed a European Patent that merges the EU design registration system with the international registration system of WIPO. The Commission's discussions with WTO have focussed on the removal of barriers to free trade in data encryption technology, in opposition to the US government and its intelligence services.

When the G-7 held their Summit at Naples in July 1994, the Heads of State emphasised the desirability of developing an Information Society worldwide, and agreed to send their concerned ministers to a follow-up meeting, held in Brussels on 25-26 February 1995 at the invitation of the European Commission. This Information Society Conference, at which every G-7 country plus the EU itself was represented at ministerial level, held discussions on infrastructure development and access; essential software applications; issues of regulation and competition law; and the social and cultural dimensions. The Conference did not exclude private-sector representatives from each G-7 country, who demonstrated some of the benefits and capabilities of information technology (CEC, 1995a; CEC, 1999b; Europa website – ISPO, 2006).

Certain principles concerning the global Information Society were agreed by G-7 countries shortly after their 1995 Summit. Before that, in December 1994 thirty-four democratic leaders at the Summit of the Americas had adopted a declaration of global information infrastructure principles. Concurrently, an industry coalition representing the industrialised nations, consisting of the American Information Technology Industry Council (ITIC), the European Association of Manufacturers of Business Machines (EUROBIT), and the Japanese Electronic Industry Development Association (JEIDA) adopted a raft of recommendations. The group condensed its views into a paper delivered to the February 1995 Information Society Summit of the G-7. Following this summit, in May 1995 the G-7 Roundtable of Industrialists met to discuss issues arising from the Information Society. All this indicates that global industry was endeavouring to collaborate with the governments of the most developed countries to shape ICT policy direction on the Global Level. One year later, OECD published guidelines on the rights of information access and use, which covered privacy, data protection, data security and intellectual property rights. The strategic policy decisions made at these summits bore consequences for the global Information Society, as these ministers and industry participants represented the "Great Powers" of the world of ICT. Certain common themes ran through the diverse declarations of principles adopted by the leadership of the Summit of the Americas, G-7 nations, OECD, and the ITI-EUROBIT-JEIDA

107 WIPO is a specialised agency of the UN established by the EIPO Convention of 1967. It promotes international protection of intellectual property and fosters co-operation on copyright, trademarks, industrial design, and patents between the 179 member states (World Intellectual Property Organisation website, 2006).

coalition and the Roundtable of Industrialists, namely trade liberalisation, interoperability between software and hardware, and information security.

4.3 EUROPE'S VISION: EU POLICY OBJECTIVES

The EU's strategic objectives for ICT policy are formally set by the European Council, which convenes the Heads of State of the Member States, their Ministers of Foreign Affairs, and the President of the Commission. To understand these objectives and how they arose from the overall policy vision of the EU, it is necessary to overview the European Council's strategic guidelines, declarations, and resolutions.

The Lisbon European Council in March 2000 launched an initiative to prepare the EU for the challenges of the twenty-first century. The Lisbon Council's Agenda 2010 ("the Lisbon Agenda") set a 2010 deadline for the EU Member States to achieve "higher growth, more and better jobs and greater social inclusion. Information and communication technologies (ICTs) were identified as playing a key role in achieving them" (CEC, 2004j:3). The Spring Brussels Council in March 2004 reiterated the key role of ICTs (CEC, 2004d; Council of the European Union, 2005a); as did a subsequent report (the "Kok Report") of the High-Level Group on the Lisbon Strategy (High-Level Group, 2004), which the 2004 Brussels Council had asked the Commission to set up.[108] The Report identified several problem areas needing attention, especially concerning economic integration and social cohesion across the EU and its Member States; including the brain drain threat; hidden barriers to free movement of (ICT) services; the quality of the legal framework and its potentially deadening effect on entrepreneurship; and possible social dysfunctions as in the labour market. The implicit worry underlying these and other such European Level initiatives was that the poorer, technologically more backward Member States might be "left behind" if Single Market integration were to be incomplete, leading to a "two-speed Europe" in ICTs. The Commission presented its strategic objectives for 2005-2009 to the Spring Brussels European Council of 2005 (CEC, 2005d; CEC, 2005h; CEC, 2005m), which also discussed the mid-term review of the Lisbon Strategy.

Addressing the shortcomings and delays in the implementation of the Lisbon Strategy, the Council called for urgent action to re-focus on the priorities of growth, employment, and competitiveness. It appealed to all concerned stakeholders – parliaments, regional and local bodies, social partners, and civil society – to take a pro-active part in attaining its objectives. The European Economic and Social Committee was urged to join the economic and social committees of Member States and other partner organisations in setting up "an interactive network of civil society initiatives" to advance the Strategy (Council, 2005:3). All of this

108 In April 2004 EU President Prodi announced the launch of the Group, which carried out its work from May to October 2006. The Group's remit was to formulate proposals about how to renew the Lisbon strategy, and about how to enhance its actual implementation. The Group, which met six times, was chaired by Mr Wim Kok, former Prime Minister of the Netherlands, and comprised 13 leading independent figures representing the main stakeholder groups (trade unions, business, political authorities, academics, consumers). The final report of 1 November 2004 helped the Commission in preparing proposals for the mid-term review of the Lisbon strategy, included in its spring report to the European Council in March 2005 (CEC Press Release, 2004a).

urgency and appeal was fundamentally driven by the worry that the US and Japan would dominate the future of the ICT industry, leaving Europe only the scraps.

The Council identified the following elements as key to successful implementation: a genuine dialogue between those directly involved in the knowledge-based society in both the public and private sectors; maintaining the investment rate in R&D at 3% of GDP;[109] incentivising private investment in projects crucial for competitiveness, which will help close the "technology gap" (to which the 7th Framework Programme is supposed to lend fresh impetus); Member States' initiatives to support innovative SMEs and promote joint research and partnerships for innovation; new EU initiatives, *e.g.* creation of a European Research Council, a Community Competitiveness and Innovation Programme, a European Technology Institute, the i2010 initiative for ICT research and innovation; the extension by the European Investment Bank of its Structured Finance Facilities to R&D projects; and other "flanking" measures, *e.g.* supporting measures for eco-innovation and eco-technology (Council of the European Union, 2005a). The 2006 Brussels European Council tried to give further political impetus to the relaunched Lisbon Strategy by mobilising all relevant national and Community resources and by establishing a new governance mode based on public-private partnership and policy-goal "ownership". The Council decreed that this was to be achieved through a new Inter-Institutional Agreement; an Integrated Guidelines package for the several National Reform Programmes (NRP) (CEC, 2006n); an enhanced and consolidated fiscal programme (*a.k.a.* the Stability and Growth Pact); and the EU's spending plans for 2007-2013 (covering FP7 and public-private partnerships) (Council of the European Union, 2006). The Lisbon Agenda shows that even at the highest, strategic policy level, industry was perceived as a crucial element for achieving policy objectives, and that is why it was invited to contribute its expertise to the formulation and implementation of high-level ICT policy.

At the Brussels Economic and Financial Affairs (Ecofin) Council in November 2006, the Member State finance ministers described as "encouraging" the overall progress toward meeting the Lisbon objectives, but urged that more is to be done particularly in fostering private R&D investment (CEC, 2006e:5). Since 2002 the European Councils (of Heads of State), alluding to the overall EU objective of "becoming the world's most competitive economy by 2010", have identified more investment in RTD as one of the key challenges. As of autumn 2006 each Member State must report on the implementation of their National Reform Programme under the Lisbon Strategy, setting out political commitments and priority areas for national economic reform.[110]

109 The objective of increasing European research spending to 3% of gross domestic product (GDP) by 2010 is still a long way off. In 2005 the figure was just 1.93%, compared to 2.6% in the United States and 3.2% in Japan. Following revision of the Lisbon Strategy in 2005, all Member States have now established targets for RTD expenditure, tailored to their specific situations, in their National Reform Programmes. Were these to be met, by 2010 RTD intensity in the EU would amount to 2.6% of GDP (CEC, 2002o, CEC, 2007h).

110 Member States' autumn 2006 reports on the implementation of their National Reform Programmes are available at: Lisbon Strategy website http://ec.europa.eu/growthandjobs/key/nrp2006_en.htm (accessed December 2006).

The Lisbon Council of 2000 not only set the policy agenda for a decade, it had also introduced the new term "Knowledge Society", which incorporated the elements of the Information Society plus "every aspect of the contemporary economy where knowledge is at the heart of value added, from high-tech manufacturing and ICTs through knowledge-intensive services to the overtly creative industries such as the media and architecture" (High-Level Group, 2004:20). To bring about this new Knowledge Economy and Society as well as a fundamental re-engineering of business processes to be built on ICTs, the Lisbon Strategy and the High-Level Group on the Lisbon Strategy defined the following long-term ICT-policy objectives:

1. *The Information Society*: defining a regulatory framework for eCommunications; encouraging the spread of ICTs; creating conditions for e-Commerce; supporting European leadership in mobile communications technologies;
2. *Research and Technological Development (RTD)*: setting up of a European Research Area of research and innovation; boosting spending on RTD to 3% of annual GDP; making Europe more attractive for its best brains; promoting new technologies, and
3. *Education and Human Capital*: halving the number of early school leavers; adapting education and training systems for the knowledge society; fostering lifelong learning for all; promoting and facilitating mobility. (High-Level Group, 2004:20)

The European Commission had drawn up the Lisbon Strategy in order to ensure that "Europe's businesses, governments and citizens continue to play a leading role in shaping and participating in the global knowledge- and information-based economy" (CEC, 2006f). The assumption behind this general policy objective was that Europe could not benefit fully from the sustainable growth, the productivity, competitiveness and new jobs, and the social progress potential in ICTs if too many Europeans are left behind. Accordingly, the Commission has been endeavouring to stimulate developments that will enable all Europeans to participate equally in the Information Society, especially by supporting research into new ICTs.

The Commission published COM(2004/747/EC), its Communication on "Challenges for the European Information Society beyond 2005", to launch a broad policy debate on the European Information Society after indicating the main developments which European-level policy might facilitate, including: content and services, "eInclusion", public services, skills and work, interoperability of technologies and services, trust in e-Commerce, and ICT industry policy.

The European Commission, DG Information Society in particular,[111] have settled on the following methods for achieving the Lisbon objectives:

111 Information Society Directorate General ("DG") Mission Statement: "The Information Society DG of the European Commission is charged with ensuring that Europe's citizens, governments and businesses continue to play a leading role in shaping and participating in the global information society. The DG is driven by the European Commission's eEurope action plan and has specific responsibility for increasing the understanding, development and uptake of information and communication technologies and their applications within the European Union.
It does this by stimulating research into the development of new information and communication

1. Stimulating research into the development and deployment of new information and communication technologies
2. Establishing and maintaining a framework of regulation and standards designed to generate competition
3. Stimulating the development of applications and content, and
4. Encouraging and enabling European businesses, public services and citizens to cooperate and participate in European initiatives that will enable them to gain greater benefit from the Information Society. (Europa website – European Information Society, 2006)

Nevertheless, the complex nature of regulating the Information Society has inexorably drawn other European Commission DGs into the drafting of policy recommendations and implementation supporting measures (*viz.* DG Enterprise, DG Competition, DG Research, DG Internal Market, DG Employment and Social Affairs). But this has obliged ICT stakeholders who wish to influence the EU's ICT regulation to take pains to monitor the Commission as a whole and not just (despite its name) DG Information Society.

4.4 LEGAL BASES

This Section reviews how the Treaties of the European Union (TEU) have laid down the basic legal authority on which the regulation of ICT and related policies rest. This is followed by a more detailed analysis of the specific regulatory domains that Information Society policies and standards may cover. There is a core set of laws which applies to all business organisations; *viz.* corporate governance, and contract and competition law; information security and data protection rights; copyright, and related rights in the Information Society; and electronic commerce regulations. A subsidiary set applies only to electronic communications service-providers and manufacturers, or organisations that use these services. This covers communications and infrastructure regulations; digital content and media; and policies with implications for the ICT industry, such as certain environmental policies.

4.4.1 Treaties establishing the European Union

The treaties establishing the European Union are effectively its basic constitutional texts. Four founding Treaties have laid the foundation for European integration: the Treaty of Paris (1952), establishing the European Coal and Steel Community (ECSC); the Euratom Treaty (1957) establishing the European Atomic Energy Community (EAEC); the Treaty of Rome (1957), establishing the European Economic Community (EEC); and the Treaty on European Union (1993), often referred to as the Maastricht Treaty. The mechanism relied on to liberalise the telecommunications sector was already embedded in the Treaty of Rome,

---

technologies; establishing and maintaining a framework of regulation and standards designed to generate competition; and stimulating the development of applications and content while supporting initiatives that encourage and enable all European citizens to benefit from, and participate in the information society."

Article 90 (now Article 86 of the consolidated Treaty).[112] Moreover, the Treaty of Rome had already set the political direction for the internal market and harmonisation in Article 100a (now Article 95 of the consolidated Treaty). The Maastricht Treaty created an even broader framework, especially in the domain of telecommunications, in Title XV on Trans-European Networks.

Institutional reforms brought significant changes over a long time, introducing new regulatory responsibilities for the supranational institutions and organs established by the Merger Treaty (Brussels, 1967); the Single European Act (Luxembourg and The Hague, 1987); the Treaty of Amsterdam (1997) amending and consolidating the EU Treaties; and the Treaty of Nice (2003). The following Section identifies the main policy competences established by the Treaties on which Information Society policy and initiatives rest (Europa website – Summaries of EU Legislation, 2012).

4.4.2 European telecommunications policy

European telecommunications policy was initiated in 1987 by the Commission's Green Paper on "the Development of the Common Market for Telecommunications Services and Equipment" (CEC, 1987a). This Paper ultimately led to the liberalisation of the telecommunications sector. It set three main goals, all of which are as valid today as ever: (1) *liberalisation* of the monopolised segments of the telecoms market; (2) *harmonisation* of the variegated national rules and standards then in force over the sector; and (3) strict application of the EU's *competition rules* to prevent anti-competitive collusion in the newly liberalised market segments, or the formation and abuse of dominant market positions. The drive toward liberalisation culminated on 1 January 1998, when all telecommunications networks and services in all Member States were officially liberalised. The importance of competitive liberalisation becomes clear once it is understood that the EU is in competition with other economic blocs and regions of the world. Regulators must deregulate; failure to do so invites "corporate flight", whereby companies relocate their activities to regions that have more liberal and competitive telecommunications regimes (Vogel, 1997:169-193).

The legal basis for the mandatory liberalisation decreed by EU telecoms policy may be found in Article 95 (on Internal Market Harmonisation, part of the "accompanying measures"), Articles 81 and 82 (on Competition), and Articles 47 and 55 (on the Right of Establishment and Services) of the Treaty of the European Union (TEU or Maastricht Treaty").

4.4.3 Information and communication technologies

The EU's authority to regulate and help fund (*i.e.* promote) the ICT industry springs from TEU Title XVIII on Research and Technological Development, of which Article 163(1) states, "The Community shall have the objective of strengthening the scientific and

112 Article 86 endows the Commission with power to address appropriate directives or decisions to Member States on "public undertakings and undertakings to which Member States grant special or exclusive rights", and to enforce the rules contained in the Treaty, in particular rules on competition for "undertakings entrusted with the operation of services of general economic interest or having the character of a revenue-producing monopoly".

technological bases of Community industry and encouraging it to become more competitive at international level, while promoting all the research activities deemed necessary by virtue of other chapters of this Treaty". Article 163 encourages "undertakings, including small and medium-sized undertakings, research centres and universities in their research and technological development activities of high quality". Co-operation, market integration, common standards, and the sweeping-aside of fiscal and legal obstacles to pan-European collaboration is considered the main factor driving research and deployment of new technology; thus, TEU authorises funding of demonstration projects such as Framework Programmes and related EU-sponsored research projects.

4.4.4 European competition policy

The TEU posits competition as essential to an open-market economy, leading to lower prices, higher quality, and expanded customer choice. Competition also fosters technological innovation. But these eventualities depend on fair play on the part of both businesses and governments. The Treaties have given the European Commission wider powers to implement and enforce EU-wide rules on fair trade in goods and services.

Article 4 of the TEU spotlights the importance of competition by stating that EU law must be made "in accordance with the principles of an open market economy with free competition". Articles 81-89 of the TEU define the "Rules on Competition" for private and public undertakings and Member State aid to private enterprises. Article 81 of the TEU prohibits agreements, decisions and restrictions "of competition within the common market, and in particular those which: (a) directly or indirectly fix purchase or selling prices [...]; (b) limit or control production, markets, technical development, or investment; (c) share markets or sources of supply; [and] (d) apply dissimilar conditions to equivalent transactions with other trading partners, thereby placing them at a competitive disadvantage". Article 82 of the TEU further forbids "any abuse by one or more undertakings of a dominant position within the common market".

The strict application of the principles laid down in Articles 81 and 82 has always been a matter of great interest both to the EU regulator and to ICT stakeholders. Moreover, Article 85 empowers the Commission (in the person of DG Competition) to "investigate cases of suspected infringement of these principles, propose appropriate measures to bring it to an end and to authorise Member States to take measures". Pursuant to these mandates, the regulatory authorities of the Member States have set up investigative bodies to hear complaints from all competition policy stakeholders. The UK's Ofcom even publishes a record of its investigations of the issues raised by complaints, the responses of the parties concerned, and Ofcom's decisions (Thompson, 2003; Kilgour, 2003). This empowers stakeholders to influence ICT regulation not only *ex ante*, by participating in the policy process, but also *ex post*, by bringing specific competition complaints (Ofcom, 2005).

Article 157 of the TEU (Title XVI on Industry) stipulates, "The Community and Member States shall ensure that the conditions necessary for the competitiveness of the Community's industry exist". It also calls for Member States to take positive action to guarantee "open and competitive markets", including making "structural changes"; "encouraging an environment favourable to initiative and to the development of undertakings"; and fostering an industrial policy of "innovation, research, and technological development".

4.4.5 EU programmes to improve infrastructure and collaboration in RTD

Research and development programmes targeting ICTs were first undertaken in 1984 through the ESPRIT Programme (European Strategic Programme for Research & Development in Information Technology). Soon afterwards, in 1986, specialised programmes followed to spur innovation through applying "telematics" to issues of transportation, health care, and distance education. [113]

Articles 154, 155 and 156 of the TEU mandated the construction of Trans-European Networks (TEN) in transportation, energy, and telecommunications. This led to the founding of the European Information Super-Highway. Article 155 stressed the importance of measures "to ensure the interoperability of the networks, in particular in the field of technical standardisation", and called for guidelines setting the priorities and objectives of these Trans-European Networks, and for supporting projects of common interest, particularly through pioneering, pilot programmes and feasibility studies, and loan guarantees and interest-rate subsidies.

On the basic-research level, the TEU empowered the Commission to set up the Community Research and Development Information Service (CORDIS), a "technology marketplace" for collaboration between stakeholders on research projects within the Framework Programmes. CORDIS reviews developments in all aspects of EU research and innovation, as well as disseminating results and advertising requests for collaboration. Collaboration requests have been issued in the areas of financial support, joint venture agreements, private-public

113 Within the EU RTD Framework programmes, there were several programmes relating to ICT that contributed to developing Europe's digital and later broadband telecommunications infrastructure. Examples include:
RACE (Research & Development in Advanced Communications Technologies for Europe): EU programme (1985-1995) that contributed to the introduction of Integrated Broadband Communications (IBC) and Integrated Services Digital Networks (ISDN).
ACTS (Advanced Communications Technologies and Services): FP4 programme (1994-1998): "to develop advanced communication systems and services for economic development and social cohesion in Europe, taking account of the rapid evolution in technologies, the changing regulatory situation and opportunities for development of advanced trans-European networks and services" (Decision number 1110/94/EC of the EP and of the Council of 26 April 1994). The specific objectives of ACTS were to support the development of "interactive digital multimedia services; photonic technologies; high-speed networking; mobility and personal communication networks; intelligence in networks and services; [and] quality, security and safety of communication systems and services".
ESPRIT (European Strategic Programme for Research and Development in Information Technology): FP4 programme (1984-1998) that covered long-term research, software technologies, technologies for components and subsystems, multimedia systems and focussed industry research.
TELEMATICS: FP4 programme (1984-1998) that focussed at sector-specific applications of ICT, such as administration, transport, research, education and training, libraries, healthcare, environment, disabled and elderly people, and languages.
TEN-TELECOMS: Investment stimulation action of the Maastricht Treaty to stimulate the large scale deployment of Trans-European telecommunication Networks.

partnerships, licence agreements, marketing arrangements, development support, information exchange, and training (Europe website – CORDIS, 2006). These examples show that the European regulator is involved not only in drafting and implementing policies, but also in pro-actively engaging ICT stakeholders in their implementation and following-up with funding and support for the development of new technologies.

4.5 POLICY FRAMEWORKS, REGULATIONS, AND STANDARDS

One of the overriding social goals of EU policy is the equality of all European citizens. In terms of the Information Society, this means evenly distributing the benefits of ICTs throughout the Union. However, the sectoral convergence of telecommunications, IT, and broadcasting is reshaping the communications market and making obsolete the classical division of regulatory functions between these sectors. In order to establish a more efficient regulatory regime, the Commission pitched an "umbrella" legal framework that overarches not only communications infrastructure (Internet access and broadband networks) but also novel, related services such as e-Commerce; fixed, mobile, terrestrial (mobile and fixed), and satellite telecommunications; digital television; radio spectra; and technical standardisation. The principles decreed to undergird this forward-looking framework were that pan-European regulation must in future: (1) "be based on clearly defined policy objectives"; (2) "be the minimum necessary to meet those objectives"; (3) "enhance legal certainty in a dynamic market"; (4) be technology-neutral; and (5) be enforced as close as possible to the regulated activities (CEC, 1999c:v *ff.*; CEC, 2000d).[114] The last point (5) invokes the subsidiarity principle, which mandates that, at the very lowest level, companies should first "self-regulate" by implementing internal regulatory compliance policies and procedures monitored by their respective Member State, only upon the failure of which are the official regulatory bodies (*viz.* IRAs) on the National Level to intervene; with the whole scheme being coordinated at the European Level.

Found amongst the author's comprehensive review of EU Information Society policy and standards documents drafted between 1994 and 2012 were not only workaday policies, regulations and programmes, but also high-level strategic initiatives. These included eEurope and the FP5/FP6 Information Society Technology (IST) programmes, which address major economic and social challenges associated with the implementation of regulations and standards in the telecoms sector. The following Section summarises the relevant European Information Society regulations, categorising the main types of regulation in preference to exhaustively listing policies and activities. An exhaustive list, however, is included in Appendix Five to this book.

114 The Commission received over 200 responses to its consultation between 15 February 2000 and 15 April 2000, including from governments, regulatory authorities, industry associations, consumer and user bodies, market players and commercial organisations, consultancies, research institutions, and universities. (A list of respondents is attached to the Communication.) In addition, over 550 people attended a two-day public hearing held by the Commission on 25 and 26 January 2000 (CEC, 1999c; CEC, 2000d).

4.5.1 Corporate governance, and contract- and competition law

The recent spate of corporate-finance scandals in the US (*e.g.* Enron and the subsequent collapse of its financial auditor, Arthur Andersen) and in Europe have underscored the necessity of corporate-governance regulation, especially focussing on financial reporting and statutory audit. The goal of such regulation should be to rebuild stakeholders' and employees' trust in corporate business and reporting practices.

European corporate-governance regulation is influenced by the standards set by international organisations such as the Organisation for Economic Co-operation and Development (OECD),[115] the US Securities and Exchange Commission (SEC),[116] as well as Member State initiatives. The UK has a long history of being at the forefront of innovating corporate governance procedures and practices (Lannoo and Khachaturyan, 2004:41). It has led other European countries and the EU regulator to meet emergent challenges in the development of corporate governance measures.[117] In the latest development, the UK has attempted to concentrate responsibility by shifting the corporate-governance focus from impersonal internal-control structures onto the effectiveness of persons in senior management and corporate boardrooms, including non-executive directors, senior independent directors, and companies' main committees.[118]

115 To develop a set of corporate governance standards and guidelines, OECD established the Ad-Hoc Task Force on Corporate Governance to develop non-binding principles that embody the views of Member States on this issue. This was the first initiative by an inter-governmental organisation to develop the core elements of a good corporate governance regime. High priority was given to the interests of shareholders, who put their trust in corporations to employ their invested funds wisely. The OECD Principles highlight the importance of companies implementing a corporate governance framework to ensure that timely and accurate disclosure is made of all material matters regarding the company, which implies the ultimate responsibility of the board to steer (OECD, 1999b).

116 The most important legislative initiative of the SEC in recent years was the Sarbanes-Oxley Act of 2002 (Senate and House of Representatives of the United States of America, 2002).

117 A detailed analysis of several UK corporate governance reports, in particular the Cadbury Report on "Financial Aspects of Corporate Governance" (December 1992), the Rutteman Guidance (December 1994), the Greenbury Report (July 1995), the Hamel Report on "Corporate Governance" (June 1998), the Turnbull Report on "Internal Control: Guidance for Directors on the Combined Code" (September 1999), and the Higgs Report (January 2003) revealed that the UK has been able to influence US corporate-governance regulation (Sarbanes-Oxley Act 2002 on "Corporate Responsibility"). In return, through SOA the US has been influencing and accelerating the development of an EU-wide corporate-governance regulatory regime. "The Commission has expressed serious concerns over the [US] measures put forward, in particular the unnecessary outreach effects of the SOA for EU companies and EU auditors" (CEC, 2003h:9). EU-based corporations that have US parent companies or subsidiaries listed on a US stock exchange (regulated by the Securities and Exchange Commission) need to comply with the Sarbanes-Oxley Act 2002. The Commission has therefore had to reconsider EU priorities for the overhaul of EU corporate governance, initiated by the Commission's 1996 Green Paper (COM 1996/338) on "The Role, Position and Liability of the Statutory Auditor within the European Union" and laid down in Council Directive 84/253/EC "the 8th Directive".

118 In April 2002 Gordon Brown, the UK Chancellor of the Exchequer, and Patricia Hewitt, Secretary of State for Trade and Industry, appointed Derek Higgs to chair an independent commission to review the effectiveness and responsibilities of non-executive directors. The Higgs Review, published in January 2003, suggested revisions to the Combined Code that incorporated the Review's recommen-

The European Commission decided to respond to the increasing loss of public trust in audit functions and to the increasing influence of overseas (especially US) regulations following the financial reporting scandals at the beginning of the 21st century. The Winter Report was commissioned by the Commission to confront the fallout over recent corporate scandals, and address the improvement of corporate governance in the EU. It catalysed a range of policy initiatives in this area (Winter, 2002).[119] For example, in September 2003 the Commission released Communication COM(2003)236 on "Reinforcing the statutory audit in the EU" and Action Plan COM(2003)284 on "Modernising Company Law and Enhancing Corporate Governance in the European Union". On 28 September 2005 the European Parliament adopted Directive 2006/43/EC on the "statutory audit of annual accounts and consolidated accounts, amending Council Directives 78/660/EEC and 83/349/EEC and repealing Council Directive 84/253/EEC". Like the Sarbanes-Oxley Act, this modernised corporate governance and audit framework is applicable even to non-EU auditing firms conducting audits for companies listed on stock-exchanges in the EU. It is a prime example of the increasing number of national and regional regulations having global repercussions. To win over all concerned stakeholders and investors, the European Commission has held regular meetings, particularly with EU finance ministers, the SEC, and key decision makers in the US Congress.

Other general regulatory regimes with impact on business organisations include consumer protection, *e.g.* Commission Communication COM(2002)208 on "Consumer Policy Strategy 2002-2006"; contract law, *e.g.* Directive 2002/65/EC on "distance marketing of financial services" for online contracts/distance contracts; competition law, *esp.* the protection of new market entrants from unfair trade practices by established companies; and commercial dispute resolution/ settlement procedures, *e.g.* Commission Recommendation REC(2001)310 on "Principles for out-of-court bodies involved in the consensual resolution of computer disputes". The OECD works on codes of ethical conduct and practice for corporations. It has also published *Guidelines for Consumer Protection in The Context of Electronic Commerce* (2001), which advise businesses, governments and consumers on ethical advertising and marketing; sales methods and transactions; provision of services; data and payment security; and redress and dispute resolution.

---

dations. Following consultation on the proposed changes, the Financial Reporting Council (FRC), which is responsible for the Combined Code, revised the Code. Professor Laura Tyson, Dean of the London Business School, was also asked to lead a 32-member task force into looking at how companies might enhance board effectiveness by drawing on broader pools of talent with varied and complementary skills and experience (Higgs, 2003; Tyson, 2003; Financial Reporting Council, 2006; Financial Reporting Council website, 2007).

119 One motive for the report was to "co-ordinate and strengthen efforts undertaken by and within Member States to improve corporate governance". The immediate objectives of the Winter Group were to improve shareholder protection and to restore confidence in the system, which had been shaken by the scandals. However, the Winter Group also focussed on improving efficiency and the competitiveness of EU firms, so as to facilitate the development of the Single Market and empower growing cross-border investment.

4.5.2 Information security and data protection rights

Both the Commission and the private sector consider information security and privacy protection an important factor in the uptake of the Internet and e-Business; thus, information security and privacy policy has become an important item on the Information Society agenda. The EU is concerned to find suitable solutions to the legal and technological challenges posed by user authentication, network integrity, personal confidentiality and data protection, and network security (Europa website – eEurope 2005 TRUST, 2006).

To enhance trust and confidence in the Internet, information security has been identified as a high priority for the Commission and for business organisations. Commission Communication COM(1997)503 on "Ensuring Security and Trust in Electronic Communication – Towards a European Framework for Digital Signatures and Encryption" outlines the EU strategy, subsequently implemented by Directive 1999/93/EC on "A Community Framework for Electronic Signatures". This initiative was supported by cybercrime regulation, *e.g.* Commission Communications COM(2000)890 on "Creating a Safer Information Society by Improving the Security of Information Infrastructures and Combating Computer-related Crime", and COM(2001)198 on "Network and Information Security: proposal for a European Policy Approach". In addition, the Decision on "Liberalising the intra-Community trade of encryption products"[120] now guarantees that hardware and software tools for encryption are available across the EU (Council, 1999c). Commission Communication COM(2006)251 on a "Strategy for a secure Information Society" spotlighted the need to strike the right balance between freedom of technological innovation, self-regulation, and State regulatory measures. The Commission sought to address and resolve these security challenges by taking a stakeholder-participatory approach that would involve the private sector (CEC 2006r).

The creation of the European Network and Information Security Agency (ENISA) shows that ICT security has been identified as a top priority. Set up in 2004 by EU Regulation 2004/460/EC, it has been fully operational since September 2005. The agency's remit is to facilitate co-operation and information exchange on issues of network and information security. ENISA also serves as an informal "think tank" for Member States and EU organs seeking advice on matters related to network and information security (CEC, 2003a; CEC, 2004g; ENISA website, 2006).

The importance of information security for the uptake of electronic communication services has been widely recognised at the Global Level, as witness UNCITRAL's "Uniform Rules on Electronic Signatures" (1998) and OECD's "Guidelines for the Security of Networks and Information Systems: Towards a culture of security" (2002). Appropriate legislation has also been enacted by all EU Member States. To supplement governmental security regulation, business organisations have also developed codes of conduct for e-Business, and trust seals for websites; and have, moreover, adopted both international and local information security

120 This may be seen as an answer to US encryption regulations, *esp.* the "Revised Encryption Regulations" (July 2000), which allowed the export of any encryption product to the members of the European Union and other European and Pacific Rim allies without a license. Under this new US regulation US exporters no longer had to undergo a 30-day technical review for shipments to any of these countries.

standards such as BS7799/ ISO 17799:2005 (a.k.a. ISO/IEC 27001), which was developed by the British Standards Institution and rolled out globally by the International Standards Organisation. Research conducted by the Gartner Group, an industry research company, highlights the importance of information security. Web security standards and products are often seen as a crucial factor in developing business partnerships that use Internet technology (Wagner, 2003:1).

After information security, data protection is the second major concern in establishing public trust in information technologies. Directives 1995/46/EC on the "Protection of individuals with regard to the processing of personal data and on the free movement of such data" and 1997/66/EC on "Processing of personal data and the protection of privacy in the telecommunications sector" have been replaced by the new Framework Directive (2002/58/EC) on the "Processing of personal data and protection of privacy in the electronic communication sector". That data protection has become a core element of the new Framework Directive clearly evidences the importance given to the issue by the European Commission.

According to the European Committee for Standardisation, "Within Europe matters of data protection and privacy have been handled through legislative means, and it has been broadly assumed that such legal measures were adequate to ensure effective protection. Outside Europe, there is greater reliance on self-regulation, and on the internal policies that such practices require" (CEN/ISSS, 2002). This state of affairs is clearly in flux, as key actors like the United States enact sectoral data-protection laws, *e.g.* in the finance and medical sectors. This book, however, will not dwell on sector-specific regulation, lest the focus on stakeholders and their actions be lost. To bridge the gaps created by diverse jurisdictions and sector-specific regulations, the Data Protection Working Party, established as the independent EU Advisory Body on Data Protection and Privacy by Directive 95/46/EC Article 29, has developed a number of recommendations and opinions on specific issues. Examples are Recommendation 3(99)3/final on the "Preservation of traffic data by Internet Service Providers for law enforcement purposes" and Opinion (2000)5009/final on "Certain data protection aspects of electronic commerce". Transfer to third countries outside the EU is addressed by European Parliament Resolution (2000)0177 on "Safe Harbour Privacy Principles", which were developed in close co-operation with the US Department of Commerce.

At the Global Level, the OECD has published Guidelines on the "Protection of privacy and transborder flows of personal data" (OECD, 2002a). But in addition, the OECD also helps in the implementation of its Guidelines by furnishing inventories of technical solutions. For example, its Working Party on Information Security and Privacy issued DSTI/ICCP/REG(98)12/FINAL on "Inventory of Instruments and Mechanisms contributing to the Implementation and Enforcement of OECD Privacy Guidelines on Global Networks".

4.5.3 Copyright and related rights in the Information Society

As R&D leads to marketable ideas that need legal protection, intellectual property law is another pillar of ICT policy. Without intellectual property rights, R&D would suffer enormously and investment in it might even cease. Security and data protection are mainly consumer and user issues, whereas copyright in particular protects producers of software, databases, and content for services in the Information Society. At the European Level, copyright is protected by Directive 2004/48/EC on the "Enforcement of intellectual property rights"; Directive 2001/29/EC on the "Harmonisation of certain aspects of copyright and related rights in the Information Society"; and Directive 2001/84/EC on the "Resale rights for the benefit of the author of an original work".

Computer programmes were protected under a copyright regime by Directive 1991/250/EC on the "Legal protection of computer programmes", now superseded by Directive 2009/24/EC. This protects inventors against unauthorised copying as well as translation, adaptation or other alterations of the programme; and against a programme's unauthorised distribution to the public.

On 6 July 2005 the European Parliament by an overwhelming majority of 648 to 14 rejected the Council's common position to implement Directive 2002/92/EC on the "Patentability of computer-implemented inventions". This rejection involved the difference between patents and copyright in the rigour with which their respective intellectual property regimes exclude competitors. The patentability of computer programmes would overly restrict other market players in advancing their technology; whereas copyright is limited to applications, which is less anti-competitive. The net result of this rejection is that the patent offices of those Member States which recognise the patentability of computer software may continue to issue patents for computer-implemented inventions, with no harmonisation at European Level, and the European Patent Office remains confined to co-ordinating the acquisition of national patents. The key to agreement over the Community Patent now lies somewhere in hands of the Council (Ferrero-Waldner, 2007). Although one might suppose that stakeholders everywhere have similar interests, when it comes to restrictions on personal freedom by intellectual property law, harmonisation cannot always be achieved.

In 2006 the European Council issued Regulation No 1891/2006 on "Community designs" allowing a form of registration which merges the EU's "design registration system" with the international registration system of WIPO. This enabled companies to file only one application to obtain protection of a design both in the EU and in countries signatories of the Geneva Act of the Hague Agreement on international registration of industrial designs (CEC, 2006g). Additionally, Directive 2003/793/EC approves the Community's accession to the Protocol of the WIPO (defined in the Madrid Agreement) on trademarks. This reveals a Commission strategy, in the field of intellectual property and related rights, to protect European inventors internationally, even at the cost of relinquishing into international hands its own authority to regulate.

Other rights that protect databases have been created by Directive 1996/9/EC on the "Legal protection of databases", and rights that protect semiconductor designs by Council Decision 1994/828/EC on the "Extension of legal protection of typographies of semiconductor products to persons from certain territories".

4.5.4 Electronic commerce

The legal framework is critical to the long-term success of e-Commerce. Commerce transacted electronically must be enforceable with certainty and predictability, and the free "movement" (or remote availability) of electronic services must not be legally interfered with. The EU approach has been to try and strike a balance between the need for regulation of e-Commerce and the risk of over-regulating, which might impede its growth. EU legislation completing the internal market for e-Commerce focusses on the essentials, such as the unimpeded provision of electronic services throughout the EU, and providing legal certainty to customers and businesses engaging in e-Commerce.

The Distance Selling Directive 97/7/EC protects consumers who shop by phone or mail-order, or *via* the Internet or digital TV. Protection includes written confirmation of an order, a seven-working-days' right of withdrawal, and provisions against credit card fraud. The e-Commerce Directive 2000/31/EC on "Certain legal aspects of Information Society services, in particular electronic commerce, in the internal market" provides additional protections against cybercrime. The previously discussed Distance Contracts Directive 2002/65/EC and Copyright Directive 2001/29/EC round out the EU's e-Commerce legislation.

As taxation is considered by Member States to be within their exclusive competence, taxation of e-Commerce is regulated at European Level only by one Communication and one Regulation. The Communication is COM(1998)374 on "e-Commerce and indirect taxation", which provides guidelines "to ensure that taxation is certain, simple and neutral in order to avoid any distortion of the market and to promote the growth of electronic commerce". The Commission's objective is to clarify, adapt, and simplify the existing tax systems, while endeavouring to exclude any new taxes on the provision of these services, including *via* the Internet. Council Regulation 2002/792/EC, temporarily amending Regulation 1992/218/EC on "Administrative cooperation in the field of indirect taxation [VAT] as regards additional measures regarding electronic commerce" introduces additional measures necessary for the registering of foreign e-service traders for VAT purposes and for distributing the VAT receipts to the Member States where the services were actually used. The new regulation removed a significant competitive handicap by mandating that EU exporters to markets outside the EU no longer have to collect VAT from their overseas customers. As the European Union lacks taxation powers of its own and authority over the tax policies of its Member States, any arrangements involving taxation of international trade may only be temporary.

The Commission has introduced measures encouraging self-regulation complementary to EU legislation in a number of industrial sectors. The Commission believes that self-regulation initiatives could facilitate commerce in electronic services and products, while obviating the need for mandatory public instruments, and conserving the flexibility that the market requires. For example, to replace lawsuits with a cheaper, faster mode of dispute resolution, the Commission has been recommending codes of conduct and/or ADR mechanisms (CEC, 2002i). The Safer Internet Action Plan (Council Decision 276/1999/EC) calls on Internet service providers to voluntarily suppress illegal content (*viz.* child pornography, illegal obscenity, defamation, hate speech, unsolicited commercial communications, and copyright infringement) and other content, whether legal or not, considered harmful to minors.

To assist it in evaluating self-regulatory models and codes of conduct for Internet content and services, the Commission has funded research projects into Internet self-regulation, such as the Safer Internet Action Plan. The latter's objective was to gather information on the role self-regulation might play in the protection of minors, consumer protection, data protection and privacy, and network and data security.[121] Its Communication COM(2002)152 on "Promoting safer use of the Internet by combating illegal and harmful content on global networks"; Council Decision 2002/864/EC on "Promoting safer use of the Internet" (initiating the Safer Internet Work Programme 2004); and Council Decision 2005/854/EC on "Establishing a multi-annual Community programme on promoting safer use of the Internet and new online technologies", all re-emphasised the desirability of self-regulation and reliance on codes of conduct.[122] In June 2005 the Commission initiated the Safer Internet Forum, a discussion forum for industry representatives, child welfare organisations, regulatory authorities, and policy makers to exchange experience and knowledge.

The Safer Internet Forum continues to support national co-regulation or self-regulation options, and to encourage industry self-regulation (Europa website – Safer Internet Forum, 2007). Research conducted for the Safer Internet Action Plan found that nowadays many commercial organisations use web-seals (accreditations), web-certificates (trustmarks), third-party ratings, codes of conduct, and other mechanisms to encourage the uptake of e-Commerce and to boost business and consumer confidence in the Internet.

---

121 An example of self-regulation projects/studies funded by the European Commission is: Oxford University Centre for Socio-Legal Studies, Programme in Comparative Media Law & Policy (30.04.2004) "Self-Regulation of Digital Media Converging on the Internet: Industry Codes of Conduct in Sectoral Analysis". Report for the European Commission, Oxford. Website: http://www.selfregulation.info (accessed May 2007).

122 For example, Decision No 276/1999/EC "Adopting a multi-annual Community action plan on promoting safer use of the Internet by combating illegal and harmful content on global networks" Contains the following on page 7:

"1.2. Encouraging self-regulation and codes of conduct

- For the industry to contribute effectively to restricting the flow of illegal and harmful content, it is also important to encourage enterprises to develop a self-regulatory framework through cooperation between them and the other parties concerned. The self-regulatory mechanism should provide a high level of protection and address questions of traceability.
- In view of the transnational nature of communications networks, the effectiveness of self-regulation measures will be strengthened, at European Union level, by coordination of national initiatives between the bodies responsible for their implementation.
- Under this action line, guidelines at the European level will be developed for codes of conduct, to build consensus for their application and support their implementation.
- This action will be carried out through a call for tender to select organisations that can assist self-regulatory bodies in developing and implementing codes of conduct. In connection with the establishment of codes of conduct, a system of visible 'quality-site labels' will be encouraged to assist users in identifying Internet service providers that adhere to codes of conduct. Measures will be taken carefully to monitor progress.
- This will be done in close coordination with the promotion of common guidelines for the implementation, at national level, of a self-regulation framework as advocated by the Council recommendation on protection of minors and human dignity."

(CEC, 1999e:7).

Business associations, such as the International Chamber of Commerce, especially welcome self-regulation. ICC recommends that legislatures and regulatory bodies consider self-regulatory mechanisms as compelling alternatives to legislation, mandatory auditing, or business restrictions. e-Business is simply business that is conducted using any of the applications that rely on the Internet, such as e-mail, web services, electronic data interchange, instant messaging, file transfer protocol (FTP), or e-shopping carts (ICC, 2003). Thus, the same rules apply as in classical business, so that the same self-regulation that facilitates classical business is seen as equally facilitating electronic business.

4.5.5 Communications and infrastructure

Integration into the Single Market and liberalisation of goods and services have been the overriding goals which EU telecommunications policy has always served. In 2000 the Commission proposed a package of new legislation to enhance competition, particularly at the local-loop level (Council, 2000g), so as to adapt EU legislation to telecommunications, information technology, and mass-media "convergence"; opening the door to competition even at household level. It also introduced more general adaptability into the framework, enabling it to evolve with the ICT marketplace. The framework notably defined rights and obligations for all market suppliers, be they telephone companies, cable operators, or other service providers.

The new regulatory eCommunications Framework consists of five harmonisation Directives adopted in 2002 for implementation by the Member States by 24 July 2003 (Europa website – eCommunications Framework, 2006).

Firstly, Directive 2002/21/EC on "A common regulatory framework for electronic communications infrastructure and associated services" (*a.k.a.* the Framework Directive) imposes obligations on Member States to regulate services provided *via* electronic communications networks. It also defines the remit of IRAs and establishes protocols for harmonising the application of the regulatory framework throughout the EU.

Secondly, Directive 2002/19/EC on "Access to, and interconnection of, electronic communications networks and associated facilities" (*a.k.a.* the Access Directive) establishes rights and obligations of operators seeking interconnection, and lays down objectives and procedures for national regulatory authorities.

Thirdly, Directive 2002/20/EC on the "Authorisation of electronic communications networks and services" (*a.k.a.* the Authorisation Directive) harmonises and simplifies "authorisation rules and conditions in order to facilitate their provision throughout the Community". A notable innovation is the substitution of general authorisation for individual licences.

Fourthly, Directive 2002/22/EC on "Universal service and users' rights relating to electronic communications networks and services" (*a.k.a.* the Universal Service Directive) defines the "minimum set of services of specified quality to which all end-users have access, at an affordable price in the light of specific national conditions, without distorting competition". This includes an obligation to provide "certain mandatory services such as the retail provision of leased lines".

Fifthly and finally, Directive 2002/58/EC on the "Processing of personal data and protection of privacy in the electronic communications sector" (*a.k.a.* the ePrivacy Directive) repealed Directive 97/66/EC on "The processing of personal data and the protection of privacy in the telecommunications sector" and supplemented Directive 95/46/EC on "The protection of individuals with regard to the processing of personal data and the free movement of such data". The new legislation was brought-in in order to govern the gamut of issues arising from the electronic communications subsector, including confidentiality of communications; data retention, for auditing and other purposes; preservation of connection data by the Member States for police surveillance purposes; unsolicited electronic messages ("spam"); "cookies", or hidden information exchanged between an Internet server and a web browser; and the entry of personal data in public directories.

This new telecommunications regime is supported by important flanking policies and initiatives for eCommunications. In June 2002 the Commission published Communication COM(2002)301 titled "Towards the Full Roll-Out of Third Generation Mobile Communications", which analysed the financial, technical, commercial, and regulatory challenges associated with the roll-out of third-generation mobile services, *a.k.a.* 3G or Universal Mobile Telecommunications Services (UMTS). The Communication set a practical agenda of support for the deployment of 3G in hopes of empowering the EU to be on the leading edge of technological progress, as recommended by the eEurope 2005 Action Plan. Other flanking eCommunication initiatives removed obstacles to mobile broadband services (CEC, 2004e; CEC, 2004h).

On the debit side, some new Commission policies have caused discomfort among network operators and service providers, such as the one that dictated the prices for international "roaming" which operators could charge European citizens travelling within the European Union. Consumers enjoyed lower prices for both making and receiving calls, and better transparency of roaming charges (CEC, 2006t; Europa website – New Roaming Regulation, 2006). The Commission held two consultations on this issue. The first, on 20 February 2006, focussed on international roaming and received fifty-one responses. This initiative was broadly welcomed by ministries, NRAs, consumer and user associations, and some smaller mobile operators. Operators associations and most operators, both incumbents and entrants, were opposed to regulatory intervention, stressing the effectiveness of competition within roaming markets (CEC, 2006a; Europa website – New Roaming Regulation, 2006). The second consultation introduced a concrete regulatory proposal – "pegging" retail roaming prices to the customer's "home prices" for comparable domestic retail services, meaning that the customer would not pay for receiving a call while travelling in another EU country – to which forty-nine responses were received. Most commercial organisations were against any form of regulation, whereas six commercial operators, the European Regulatory Group, and the ten responding Member States favoured wholesale market regulation (CEC, 2006k, Europa website – New Roaming Consultation, 2007). The Commission concluded that "there is ... little evidence that the market alone is working" (CEC, 2006bb:10), and argued that, despite industry claims that the wholesale market is becoming more competitive, the evidence suggested that in too many cases, whatever savings may be being made at wholesale level are not being passed through to the consumer at retail level. The Commission concluded that roaming prices for consumers are not transparent, readily comprehensible or aligned with domestic prices (CEC, 2006bb). The Commission found that industry had taken considerable time to respond to threats of regulation. Encouraged by the Member States, consumer groups, and the ERG (which has been superseded by BEREC as of 2010), the Commission has introduced a new Regulation on roaming that was approved by the European Parliament and the Council of Ministers in 2007. It decreed that prices shall not exceed €0.49 per minute for making calls and €0.24 per minute for receiving calls, excluding VAT (CEC, 2007l). This has been complemented by Regulation 531/2012 on "Roaming on public mobile communications networks within the Union", which extended retail roaming tariffs to SMS messages and data. It reduced the maximum retail charges for calls even further – to €0.29 per minute for any call made and €0.08 per minute for any call received from 1 July 2012 on. From 1 July 2014 this "price fixing" will become even more stringent, reducing prices to €0.19 and €0.05, respectively. This regime will remain in force until 30 June 2017. This exemplifies how the symbiosis of the industry with the European regulator is generally but not always favourable to industry. Consumers, however, clearly benefit from these lower prices.

The European Union has also set a policy and implemented a legal framework for developing satellite navigation applications. The most ambitious project is to build a global navigation satellite system (GNSS), consisting of GALILEO for space applications (comprising 30 satellites) and Egnos, a system that complements and improves the performance of the Global Positioning System over Europe, both of which will provide a set of positioning, navigation and timing services (CEC, 2006ee; CEC, 2006ff; Galileo website, 2006). GALILEO and its spin-offs are expected to create a huge market in equipment and services for the private sector; whence private sector involvement in the GALILEO programme has been considered key to a commercial orientation, with a view to the generation of revenues, efficient management and financing.[123]

4.5.6 Digital content and media

The Commission has maintained that boosting the eCommunications sector also entails boosting content and services. Accordingly, it has drafted and adopted digital content regulations to facilitate companies' and consumers' access to information. Audiovisual regulations mandate the freedom of "all comers" to provide services in the public interest. This book will not analyse media regulation in detail, but for completeness's sake it is made part of this general regulatory overview. The main audiovisual and media regulatory proposals are contained in Communication COM(2006)646final on the "Television without

123 GALILEO is a joint initiative of the European Commission (Directorate Energy and Transport) and the European Space Agency (ESA). Following a mandate from the Council of Ministers of the European Union (Council Regulation No 976/2002 of 21 May 2002 "setting up the Galileo Joint Undertaking"), the European Commission took impotent legislative initiatives to establish a Joint Undertaking. This constituted a single management structure for the development phase and mobilised public and private funds. Private sector involvement in the GALILEO programme is considered by the Commission as the key for a commercial orientation with the view to the generation of revenues, efficient management and financing.

Frontiers Directive" mandating the free movement of broadcasting services throughout the EU; and in Council Recommendation 2006/952/EC on "The protection of minors and human dignity" providing guidelines for national legislation to outlaw harmful content transmitted through electronic media. The mandatory Television without Frontiers Directive is complemented by voluntary "soft law" initiatives codifying conduct in the distribution of audiovisual content over electronic networks; *viz.* the European Charter for the Development and the Take-up of Film Online (2006) (CEC, 2006d); the Media Literacy initiative; and Council Recommendation 2005/865/EC on "Film heritage and the competitiveness of related industrial activities".

The public sector at both European and National Levels collects, produces, reproduces, and disseminates a gamut of information in the social, economic, geographical, touristic, business, statistical, educational, and other domains. The Public Sector Information Directive 2003/98/EC is designed to facilitate companies' access to the public sector, adding "information" to the public sector's valuable resources. The Lund Principles and the European Action Plan on Digitalisation additionally sets an action agenda for the European Commission, helped by the Member States, which ranges from the bottom-up involvement of cultural institutions (for instance in determining cases of best practice) to top-down public policy initiatives. The technology of media is just one aspect of the Information Society; content is its "lifeblood". The initiatives above require that this wide range of information is digitalised and made available to European citizens.

4.5.7 ICT-Specific Environmental Regulation ("Green IT")

The spillover from certain policy areas, such as environmental policy, to industrial policy in general and ICT policy in particular is plainly observable. The debate on global warming (see Kyoto agreement); on the reduction of energy consumption and rubbish; and on improved technologies for the sorting and recycling of environmental and economically important waste material (*e.g.* plastic polymers, automotive shredder residues, electrical and electronic equipment), has had an impact on ICT policy. The importance of environment policy is also supported by various projects funded under the 6th and 7th Framework Programme.[124]

Directive 2002/96/EC on "Waste Electrical and Electronic Equipment (WEEE)" aims to minimise the impacts of electrical and electronic equipment on the environment by designing products *ab ovo* with recycling in mind and by encouraging reuse, recycling, treatment, and recovery of WEEE. The Directive places responsibility for financing most of these goals on "producers", which includes manufacturers, sellers and resellers of own-brand equipment, and importers and exporters of electrical and electronic equipment into the EU.[125] Private

124 The "Work Programme 2007: Cooperation – Theme 6 Environment" covers 41 areas, structured under the following five categories: (1) Climate, change, pollution, and risks; (2) Sustainable management of resources; (3) Environmental technologies; (4) Earth observation and assessment tools for sustainable development; and (5) Horizontal actions. (CEC (2006gg); European Commission Environment website (2007)).

125 The WEEE Directive applies to a wide range of categories of electrical and electronic equipment, and therefore has implications for manufacturers, service providers and users. The fol-

households are allowed to return WEEE without charge. Alongside this is the related Directive 2002/95/EC on "Restrictions of the use of certain Hazardous Substances in electrical and electronic equipment" (RoHS), which seeks to reduce the environmental impact of WEEE by restricting the use of certain hazardous substances during manufacture.

The industry has responded to these new regulatory requirements with different forms of collaboration, for example the European Recycling Platform (ERP). This is intended to develop and operate for its members a common, cost-effective "waste management procurement platform" (ERP website, 2012). This is a good example of how regulations can instantiate industry collaboration and even drive innovation. Founded by four international manufacturers of electronic consumer and business products (Braun/ Gillette Company, Electrolux Group, HP and Sony), the ERP has brought more than 800 members together, including multinationals, retailers, distributors and SMEs (ERP website, 2012).

4.5.8 Implementation: policy initiatives and action plans

One main EU objective is to keep Europe's businesses, governments, and citizens in the lead in shaping the global knowledge- and information-based economy. To this end, the EU has developed a range of publicly funded programmes and initiatives featuring the following vehicles: stimulating R&D of new ICTs; facilitating the development of applications, services, and content; and strengthening the international competitiveness of European businesses by encouraging joint research co-operation. This Section presents the EU's main R&D projects and programmes, which are open to bidding by all stakeholders in the Information Society.

EU funding for technology companies and academic institutions is formatted in consecutive four-year programmes. These Framework Programmes (FPs), as they are called, for research and technology development[126] are designed to encourage technology uptake and to support the EU's ICT policy objectives.[127]

FPs are the EU's main means of supporting leading-edge RTD. The budget has increased steadily with each new FP, and the EU has focused on ICT as a top priority. The Fourth FP (FP4), lasting from 1994 to 1998, allocated more than a quarter of its total budget to ICT programmes; *e.g.* IT, telematics, and advanced communication technologies and services (ACTS). While FP4 focussed on technology, the thematic programmes of FP5 (1998-2002) reflected the social elements of the Information Society policy agenda. The Commission allocated funding for ICT systems and services for citizens; for new methods of

lowing ten product categories which should be taken into account are listed in Annex IB of the Directive: (1) Large household appliances; (2) Small household appliances; (3) IT & telecommunications equipment; (4) Consumer equipment; (5) Lighting equipment; (6) Electrical and electronic tools; (7) Toys leisure and sports equipment; (8) Medical devices; (9) Monitoring and control instruments; and (10) Automatic dispensers.

126 The European Commission in its policy papers uses the term "Research and Technological Development" (RTD). In this book, the more generic term Research and Development (R&D) will be used throughout.

127 The Framework Programmes were as follows (Framework Programmes website, 2006; 2007): FP4 (1994-1998, budget of €13 billion); FP5 (1998-2002, budget of €15 billion); FP6 (2003-2006, budget of €19 billion); and FP7 (2007-2013, budget of €53.3 billion).

work and electronic commerce; for multimedia content and tools; and for socially essential technologies and infrastructure, *e.g.* the "User-friendly Information Society" programme. The overarching goal was to involve more European citizens in using ICTs, boosting the rate of economic growth and creating new jobs in Europe. Another main objective of FP5-funded programmes was to stimulate the innovativeness of European industry, to enhance their global competitiveness, and to support the Community policy of sustainable development (*e.g.* the "Competitive and sustainable growth" programme). FP6 (2003-2006) prioritised research on the Information Society and the eEurope Action Plan. The projects featured medium- and long-term R&D on the next generation of technologies, which integrate computers and communications networks into the everyday environment, *e.g.* the "Information Society Technologies" (IST) programme.

The IST Programme encompassed most ICT research activities between 1999 and 2006. It constitutes the "second pillar" of the eEurope Action Plan, which provided funding for research into user-friendly technologies and applications. Taking more than 30% of the FP budget,[128] the IST programme was the largest priority theme in FP6. Clearly, the IST programme was conceived as being at the heart of building a knowledge-based society; it addresses such Information Society issues as security and privacy, education and training, e-Government, and e-Health. The thematic priority of IST contributes directly to realising the European policy goals for the Information Society agreed at the Lisbon Council of 2000, the Stockholm Council of 2001, and the Seville Council of 2002, and as reflected in the eEurope Action Plan. A number of related, non-FP programmes supported FP6, including eTEN, eContent Plus, the Safer Internet Action Plan, and the preparatory action for security research (see Section 5.2.4 below). The focus of eTEN today, for example, is the practical realisation of online services like e-Government (*e.g.* e-Procurement), e-Health, e-Learning, "eInclusion" (*i.e.* services for the elderly and disabled), and eTrust and security services for SMEs (Europa website – eTEN, 2006).

The Commission stresses that the current FP7, spanning 2007-2013, "provides new impetus to increase Europe's growth and competitiveness. The programme places greater emphasis than in the past on research that is relevant to the needs of European industry, to help it compete internationally, and to develop its role as a world leader in certain sectors" (Framework Programmes Website – FP7, 2007). FP7 is deployed in four thematic sub-programmes: "Cooperation", to promote European leadership in key technologies through the cooperation of industry with diverse research institutions; "Ideas", to consolidate the excellence of Europe's science base by stimulating European-level competition; "People", to open up career prospects and mobility ("free movement") for researchers; and "Capacities", to amplify Europe's R&D capacities (CEC, 2005b). The largest single portion of the FP7 budget was allocated to ICTs: €9.11bn, or 17% of the total budget of €53.3bn (Anonymous, 2007a:1-3).

The Commission stresses that FP7 was planned based on a process of consultation with stakeholders that took more than twelve months, from 30 July to 15 October 2004. The

128 Allocated budget: € 3.6bn under FP5 and € 3.625bn under FP6 (Framework Programmes website, 2006).

Commission solicited a consultation to allow all interested individuals and organisations to submit comments that address which thematic domains for transnational collaborative research the FP7 ought to support. A total of 1,824 responses were received, of which approximately half came from individuals and half from organisations. Interestingly, the most organisation responses came from industry associations (26.7%, or 246 in total), closely followed by universities (25.4%, or 234 in total).[129] These figures show that industry not only seeks EU funding but is also involved in setting the programmatic agenda of the funding in the first place. The Commission based its proposal for FP7 on these results; on other written contributions and position papers submitted to the Commission; and on the outcomes of related workshops and other events relating to specific fields of research.

Further input came in February 2006, when an expert panel led by Dr Erkki Ormala, Vice President of Technology Policy at Nokia Corporation, prepared a report evaluating the previous five years (1999-2003) of the R&D Framework Programmes. The panel made important recommendations, which included more industry participation, especially by SMEs; streamlined and simplified administration; and more emphasis on radical innovation and risk-taking (Ormala, 2005:22ff). The Commission also consulted extensively with scientific associations and other umbrella bodies, both political and technical, to hear their views and the views of the Community at large about FP7. Most of these recommendations were incorporated into FP7, making it radically different in design from previous Framework Programmes.

A review of this design reveals that the Commission was aware of problems with previous programmes, especially too complex funding schemes, excessive amounts of paperwork, bureaucratic delay, and lack of consortium autonomy. Participants in FPs and policy stakeholders have for years been criticising its excessively bureaucratic processes, which often repelled smaller organisations especially.[130] The Commission endeavoured to address these issues in FP7; for example, operations and financing were reviewed so as to simplify application to and participation in the Programme; and a "sounding board" was established, staffed by representatives of small companies and research teams – groups that face the highest hurdles to participation (CEC, 2005b).

It will be FP7's implementation and management, however, that will prove whether the Commission can deliver. More than previous programmes, FP7 will be sharply focussed on R&D, answering the needs specifically of European industry by way of European Technology Platforms and the new "Joint Technology Initiatives" (JTIs). These projects, particularly the

---

129 For individual and organisational responses, the highest number of responses came from within universities/higher education (33.9%, 618 in total), followed by research institutes (22.1%, 403 responses), industry associations (17.1%, 311 responses), governmental bodies (8.9%, 163 responses), commercial organisations (6.3%, 114 responses), and others (11.8%, 215 responses).
Contributions were received from a variety of countries, with the highest numbers coming from the UK (15.1%), Germany (13.1%), the Netherlands (11.5%), France (8.4%) and Spain (8.3%) (CEC, 2004f; CEC, 2005c).

130 For further information about views on EU-funded programmes, refer to the Survey Report in Appendix Four, especially Question 5 ("What is your opinion of publicly funded programmes?") and section D ("How could participation in ICT regulation and standards-setting be improved?").

European Technology Platforms, will be defined through dialogue with industry and situated in research fields of major European public interest. The new public-private partnerships (PPPs) are given legal personhood under EU law. Moreover, international co-operation has been fully integrated into all four thematic sub-programmes, authorising projects to sign up international partners. FP7 also features a "Risk-Sharing Finance Facility" to encourage private investment by facilitating access to European Investment Bank (EIB) loans in the case of large research projects (Europa website – CORDIS FP7, 2006).

The importance of security, accessibility, usability and exploitability – with the objective of enhancing interoperability and enrichment – of European digital content is embodied in two Web-focussed programmes: "eContent plus" (2005-2008) supports the production, distribution, and use of European digital content, and promotes linguistic and cultural diversity and content transmitted over global networks (Europa website – eContent Plus, 2006). The "Safer Internet" initiative (followed by "Safer Internet Plus" in the 2005-2008 period) dealt with illegal and harmful content. The scope of Safer Internet Plus encompasses the latest online technologies, *viz.* "mobile and broadband content, online games, peer-to-peer file transfer, and all forms of real-time communications" (CEC, 2005l; Europa website – Safer Internet Plus, 2006).

The Commission has developed strategies for combatting high-tech crime and cybercrime, covering privacy violations (illegal collection, storage, modification, disclosure or dissemination of personal data); content-related offences (publishing child pornography or defamatory statements online); intellectual property offences; and unauthorised access to IT systems ("hacking, computer sabotage and distribution of viruses, computer espionage, computer forgery, and computer fraud") (CEC, 2000e:13; CEC, 2005f).

The European Commission considers the "eEurope" initiative essential for giving new impetus to the Information Society at the highest political level. It builds on existing policies at European and National Levels, strengthening and supplementing them where necessary (CEC, 1999d; CEC, 2000h). Following on eEurope 2002, the eEurope Action Plan 2005, which was launched at the Seville Council in June 2002, covered eleven "action lines" regrouped around three priorities: (1) a cheaper, faster and more secure Internet; (2) more investment in people and skills; and (3) encouragement of all Europeans to use the Internet. The Action Plan declared as its aims to provide a "favourable environment for private investment" and for the creation of new jobs; to modernise public services; and to foster a dynamic environment for e-Business through widespread availability of broadband access at competitive prices and within a secure information infrastructure (CEC. 2002g:3ff.).

The three European Standardisation Organisations (ESOs)[131], namely CEN, CENELEC and ETSI, responded to the eEurope initiative by jointly preparing for the European Commission a Rolling Action Plan to take account of the new priorities identified in eEurope 2005 (CEN Management Centre *et al.*, 2001). This was updated in July 2002 in collaboration

131 The three ESOs recognised by the European Commission and the European Free Trade Association (EFTA) share responsibility within Europe for creating standards; each has responsibility in its own designated technical area: The European Committee for Standardisation (CEN) in areas other than the electrotechnical and telecommunications field; the European Committee for Electrotechnical Standardisation (CENELEC) in the electrotechnical field; and the European Telecommunications Standards Institute (ETSI) in telecommunications, broadcasting, and certain aspects of information technology.

with the ICT Standards Board (ICTSB) (CEN Management Centre *et al.*, 2002). The updated Plan set up a three year work programme to deliver the standards needed to support "the widespread availability and use of broadband networks throughout the Union by 2005 and the development of Internet Protocol IPv6 … and the security of networks and information, eGovernment, eLearning, eHealth and eBusiness" (Council, 2002:17).

After the eEurope 2005 Action Plan ended, the Commission launched a follow-up initiative titled "i2010 – A European Information Society for growth and employment", which set out the ICT sector's envisioned contribution to a renewed Lisbon Strategy of stimulating growth, competitiveness and employment. The Commission's view is that the Information Society is moving from the "pilot phase" to "wide deployment", as ICT matures and globalises. Three "pillars" have been identified as undergirding these policy objectives: (1) a Single European Information Space offering affordable and secure high-bandwidth communication, rich and diverse content, and digital services; (2) world-class performance in ICT research and innovation; and (3) an Information Society that is inclusive, provides high quality public services, and promotes a high quality of life (CEC, 2005g:5ff.). The eCommunications Framework falls under the first pillar, and specific objectives have been set out in the i2010 Initiative (CEC, 2005g; Europa website – European Information Society 2010, 2006). Funding for i2010 was mobilised through the Commission's eTEN programme, which had been designed *inter alia* to aid the development and deployment of public electronic services.

To achieve the i2010 targets, the Commission nominated a steering group, who in turn started up a forum for strategic discussions, for the exchange of experiences, for monitoring the progress of the cross-sectoral implementation of e-initiatives, and for addressing any other problems encountered (Council, 2003). Stakeholders have consistently got involved, even in this steering and monitoring stage of the policy process, through benchmarking[132] and exchanging best practices. This should help adjustments to the current i2010 Action Plan filter through all the more in due course.

The Commission believes that the liberalisation of telecommunications is the key driver of a wider dissemination and uptake of ICTs. Digital mobile communications is a salient example of how ICT research and development can be furthered by the mode of ICT regulation. European GSM technology, launched in the early 1990s, was developed and tested within the EU research projects of the Framework Programmes. The fast uptake of the GSM standard was accelerated by the full liberalisation of the telecoms market in 1996. "By mid-2001 there were close to 260 million GSM users in the EU" (Europa website – European Information Society, 2006). Now GSM has become established as a worldwide standard used in 130 countries (Europa website – Summaries of EU Legislation, 2012). This shows that European research and development programmes can succeed in launching innovative products and services.

The author has discovered that EU funding is an important enabler of stakeholder collaboration, bringing together industry and research organisations with common interests.

132 Whereby national statistical institutes (NSIs) and Eurostat would be invited to cross-check the Commission's survey data, and to distribute their findings to the European Council's Working Party on Information Society Services prior to official release of the (checked) surveys.

European R&D programmes lead to collaboration for more than the limited project period; often they bring stakeholders with different skills and resources together into long-term partnerships. This insight helped to enlist EU projects participants to take the Survey presented in Chapter Six.

4.6 EUROPEAN ICT STANDARDS

With the explosive growth of ICT industries, especially the growing convergence of information and telecommunications technologies since the early 1990s, compatibility standards have risen in prominence (Schmidt and Werle, 1998). Standards are especially important for supporting the implementation of regulatory requirements. Users can access global networks allowing them to share databases and documents as well as communicate with each other. Consequently, standards-setting has been transformed from an internal affair of companies into a matter of co-operation (and competition) between interdependent players (Besen and Farrell, 1994:117-131). Today the European Standards Organisations, Member States' standardisation bodies, and private consortia all define standards. Additional standards initiatives may arise from agreements on specifications; from public-private workshops; or from any other form of consensus building.

This Section explains how international standards-setting processes have been emerging, emphasising the governance-related questions that remain unresolved to date; *e.g.* Who decides international standards? and How do they influence the standards-setting process in Europe? Note in the following that two mainstream standardisation types may be distinguished: (1) institutional standards and (2) industry standards.

4.6.1 Risk management and control frameworks

Non-technical international standards emerged first from the internal governance of multinational companies operating world-wide. There are a number of corporate governance frameworks that assist business (and other) organisations to implement their regulatory compliance obligations more effectively and consistently.[133] Governance frameworks and guidance establish a common terminology; provide standards against which organisations can assess their control and compliance systems; and give guidance in deciding how to improve them.

Examples include the COSO Internal Control- and COSO Enterprise Risk Management Frameworks, developed by the Committee of Sponsoring Organizations (COSO) of the Treadway Commission (an American private-sector consortium); the Control Objectives for Information and Related Technology (CobiT), developed by the IT Governance Institute of the

133 Implementation of compliance with regulation and laws often involves significant uncertainty and costs for industry. Based on empirical evidence (*e.g.* from Sarbanes-Oxley corporate-governance regulation, and the eCommunications Framework) the precise costs are difficult to predict, while the implementing measures and guidance in the early stages of new regulation are considered by policy stakeholders to be insufficient. For assistance and guidance the industry has three opportunities: either they (1) produce guidance individually; (2) work in collaboration and develop guidelines that often evolve into industry best practices; or (3) leverage existing frameworks like those presented in this Section.

Information Systems Audit and Control Association (ISACA); the Capability Maturity Model Integration (CMMI), developed by the Software Engineering Institute; ISO 17799:2005 for Information Security Management and ISO/IEC 20000-1:2005 for IT Service Management, developed by the International Organization for Standardization; and the IT Infrastructure Library (ITIL), developed by the UK Office of Government Commerce. Although specific standards such as ITIL and ISO 17799:2005 apply to specific subject-matters, they can nonetheless be "mapped up" to more general frameworks, such as COSO and CobiT, thus forming a hierarchy of guidance materials. COSO and CobiT have the major advantages of being globally accepted and promoted as open standards available to all organisations (Williams, 2006:26-28).

These frameworks are in turn supported by more generic project-management methodologies; *e.g.* Projects in Controlled Environments (PRINCE), developed by the UK's Central Computer and Telecommunications Agency (CCTA) to become a UK government standard for IT project management; PRINCE2, which is now a *de facto* standard for project management in the UK (revised by the Office of Government Commerce); and the Project Management Body of Knowledge (PMBOK), developed by the Project Management Institute. Moreover, ISO 10006:2003 ("Quality Management Systems – Guidelines for quality management in projects") provides guidance for projects of varying complexity and in different environments (Office of Government Commerce – PRINCE2 website, 2007; ISO website, 2007; Project Management Institute website, 2007).

Most governance and internal-control[134] frameworks have been developed through the collaboration of "independent institutes", professional associations, and industry. Strong evidence suggests that industry is involved not only in shaping regulations, but also in defining compliance frameworks. For example, COSO was originally an independent private sector initiative set up in 1985 under the sponsorship of the National Commission on Fraudulent Financial Reporting.[135] While the COSO framework was originally developed in the USA,[136] it is nowadays applied globally. Even more organisations were involved in

134 "Internal control is broadly defined as a process, effected by an organisation's board of directors, management or other personnel, designed to provide reasonable assurance regarding the achievement of objectives in the following categories: (1) Effectiveness and efficiency of operations; (2) Reliability of financial reporting, and (3) Compliance with applicable laws and regulations" (COSO website, 2007). The IT Governance Institute defines *controls* as "the policies, procedures, practices and organisational structures designed to provide reasonable assurance that business objectives will be achieved, and that undesired events will be prevented, or detected and corrected" (CobiT website, 2007).

135 Members of the Project Advisory Council to the Committee of Sponsoring Organisations (COSO) are: PricewaterhouseCoopers (principal contributor), General Motors, Motorola, Du Pont de Nemours & Company, Protection Life Corporation, Moss Adams LLP, Protiviti Inc., World Bank, North Carolina State University, Bringham Young University. The Oversight has the Institute of Management Accountants, the Institute of Internal Auditors, Financial Executives International, American Accounting Association and the American Institute of Certified Public Accountants. (COSO(2004) *Enterprise Risk Management Framework*, page i).

136 In 1995 the Canadian Institute of Chartered Accountants (CICA) developed a similar control framework, the Guidance on Control (GoCo). CICA website at http://www.cica.ca (accessed February

developing the control objectives, management guidelines, and maturity models of CobiT version 4.0 – a total of 116 individuals representing business organisations, professional firms, and universities are mentioned as contributors.[137]

Owing to global corporate-governance and financial-controls regulation (*viz.* the Sarbanes-Oxley Act; the Basel II Accord; the Market in Financial Instruments Directive) and to the increasing number of new regulations at all Levels, compliance frameworks have been widely used by organisations in recent years. The latest trend is to align and "map" (*i.e.* cross-reference) multiple partly-overlapping frameworks. For example, the IT Governance Institute has produced a framework for integrating (so far as possible) diverse guidance documents produced both by international standards organisations and by private organisations. The initial set of CobiT 4.0 mapping documents cover ISO/IEC 17799, PMBOK, CMM, ITIL and PRINCE2.[138] Private and professional organisations often create *de facto* standards by promoting frameworks and guidance that help implement regulatory compliance. The more widely these frameworks are used, the more likely it is that the regulator, or bodies that work closely with the regulator, will endorse their use for implementing compliance.[139]

4.6.2 Multi-level interactions in the creation of standards

In May 1985 the Council adopted the New Approach to technical harmonisation, which although it made pan-European standards the cynosure of policy action and debate, was also purposely designed to operate on multiple Levels of governance, particularly in respecting the principle of subsidiarity.[140] The New Approach confines the Commission and Council to specifying only the "essential [standards] requirements", in terms of health, safety, and environmental and consumer protection, which products sold in the EU must meet. It then delegates the task of developing the technical standards in detail ("technical specifications") to the National and Sub-national members of three *private*, non-profit European Standards Organisations (ESOs): the European Committee for Standardisation or *Comité Européen*

2007).

137 This includes members of the Board of Trustees, ITGI Committee, CobiT Steering Committee and expert developers and reviewers. (IT Governance Institute (2005) *CobiT 4.0: Control Objectives, Management Guidelines, Maturity Models*, (ITGI: Rolling Meadows).

138 IT Governance Institute (2005) *CobiT Mapping: Overview of International IT Guidance*, 2nd Edition (ITGI: Rolling Meadows). Mapping documents have been produced for "ISO/IEC 17799:2005", "ITIL", "Prince2", "CMM" (Capability Maturity Model), "PMBOK" (Project Management Body of Knowledge), "COSO ERM", "TOGAF" and "CMMI".

139 For example, in April 2005 the European Commission selected CobiT, ISO 17799 and the IT Baseline Protection Manual (developed by the Federal Office for Information Security BSI) as the "three internationally accepted standards to be used to provide information security and control over its agricultural paying agencies" (Commission Regulation No 465/2005, adopted on 22 March 2005). The US Securities and Exchange Commission (SEC) and Public Company Accounting Oversight Board (PCAOB) specifically identified and endorsed the COSO Framework as the *de facto* standard for internal controls in promulgating its first round of rules under section 404 (Internal Controls).

140 Under the old approach, directives contained a high degree of detail on technical product specifications. The completion of technical work would require as long as a decade, or more.

de Normalisation (CEN), the European Committee for Electro-technical Standardisation or *Comité Européen de Normalisation Eléctronique* (CENELEC), and the European Telecommunication Standards Institute (ETSI).

The close collaboration between these organisations under the New Approach has also raised the quality and impact of their work. In 1990 the Commission published a Green Paper on "The future development of European standardisation" (CEC, 1990c). Amongst its proposals was that ESOs should pro-actively expand civil society (particularly consumers' and consumer organisations') participation in every stage of the standards-setting processes, even if most of them are organised at the National and Sub-national Levels. Another proposal was to set up groups of stakeholder experts pro-actively to define new work items, including the revision of standards considered too lax. Yet another was to give (not only pan-European) stakeholder organisations observer status (but no vote) on technical committees and working groups with power to comment on proposals. In addition, all Member States have national standards institutes, and the Green Paper proposed to empower these institutes' delegations to the EU standards institutes to vote on proposed EU-wide standards.[141] This shows that the New Approach invites collaboration between public and private organisations on multiple Levels from the Sub-national right up to the European.

The Commission is charged with initiating standardisation on behalf of the EU. Examples of initiation include drawing up the agendas for ESOs to develop standards supporting Single Market services; reduced barriers to trade in services (CEC, 2003l); and electronic invoicing.[142] With the support of the Member States, the responsible Directorate General of the European Commission, having identified a specific need for a standard, mandates CEN, CENELEC and/or ETSI to work with the industry concerned to develop the standards they require. The standards institutes delegate technical committees and working groups to engage with all affected stakeholders, especially industry fora and consortia, and consumer associations, even those organised on the National and Sub-national Levels. The Commission facilitates the process by sponsoring workshops to promote the benefits of standards[143] and to raise awareness about ongoing policy initiatives. Open consultations where all stakeholders have an opportunity to voice their concerns are the preferred vehicle for collecting feedback on standards-setting.

The New Approach, begun in 1985, has politically determined that consumer participation in the policy process is a necessary precondition for the acceptability and expansion of pan-European standardisation, and it remains a fact that most consumer organisations are organised at a Level of governance no higher than the National. To answer the New

141 A complete list of all national standardisation bodies and their websites are provided in Appendix Six (Stakeholder Directory of ICT Policy and Standards-Setting).

142 Directive 2001/115/EC on "electronic invoicing": "Common standards should enhance the interoperability of e-invoicing systems, by overcoming at least some of the practical difficulties involved in sharing electronic files between companies and complying with Member States' [different] book-keeping rules".

143 Examples: EC Workshop on European standardisation for services on 9 March 2004, organised by DG Enterprise, Jean-Paul Mingasson.

Approach, the Association pour la Normalisation Européenne pour les Consommateurs (ANEC) *a.k.a.* the European Association for the Co-ordinaion of Consumer Representation in Standardisation, was set up by national consumer bodies from the Member States of both the EU and the European Free Trade Association (EFTA) to coordinate policy action so as to involve consumer representatives in standardisation processes. ANEC has become a member of several European standardisation bodies, including CEN and CENELEC, and is financially supported by the European Commission. As a member of these European standards bodies, ANEC is accepted onto their technical boards and general assemblies, and can even play a role on their administrative boards (ANEC website, 2003).

The Commission also recognises the importance of voluntary standards, many of which are created on the Sub-national Level (*esp.* inside business organisations), especially in sectors like services which have never had legally binding standards (*e.g.* Internet usage policies; codes of company ethics; private whistle-blowing policies; employees' manuals; and consumer complaint policies). In its Communication COM(2003)747final on "The competitiveness of business-related services and their contribution to the performance of European enterprises", the Commission states that it "will promote the setting up of voluntary standards led by the services providers, in the same way as for manufactured products". Even voluntary standards are considered to improve market efficiency and price transparency, and to empower service providers and manufacturers to achieve economies of scale that lead to better competition. At the same time the Commission argues, in the same Communication, that "an 'over-standardisation' process or the emergence of many different non-compatible standards across the different EU countries would lead to negative effects" (2003:26).

More and more standards around the world are being shaped by international standards development organisations (Mattli, 2001:328). Stakeholders consider it crucial that international standards are adopted where possible, and that memberships of these international organisations are open to the concerned national standards bodies of all countries.[144] Besides the International Organization for Standardization (ISO), other international standards-setting organisations include the International Electrotechnical Commission (IEC), the International Telecommunications Union (ITU), and the Organisation for Economic Co-operation and Development (OECD). "The ISO, IEC and ITU ... account for over 85 percent of all current international standards, and each year they collectively issue upwards of 1000 new or revised standards" (David and Shurmer, 1996:792).

The EU's New Approach has in fact already affected international standards organisations. CEN and ISO on the one hand, and CENELEC and IEC on the other, have forged reciprocity agreements with each other, codified in the Vienna and Dresden agreements, respectively. The EU and the USA differ substantially on the desirability of migrating the New Approach to the Global Level. The EU's view is that international standards should be set by standards bodies that allow representation of stakeholders globally, whereas the Americans insist that standards, although international, may be created by private companies and should win global acceptance through actual industry use (Mattli, 2001:330).

144 Defined by the International Standards Organisation.

Many reformers hold the view that international standards organisations, in particular the ISO and IEC, ought to open up their own processes to stakeholder participation in ways similar to the European example (Mattli, 2001:330). The current processes reflect mainly the interests of the industry and not all major societary players. Formulating and adopting "guiding principles of openness and transparency" would lay a stronger foundation for the political acceptability of international standardisation (Mattli, 2001:331).

Of all stakeholder participations, consumer participation is the least integrated on multiple Levels of governance. "[T]he only group … allowed to represent consumer interests at the [Global] level is Consumers International (CI), an umbrella organization representing over 200 independent consumer organizations from almost 100 countries" (Mattli, 2001:331). Because CI representatives are barred from serving inside international standards bodies in any controlling capacity such as technical management and policy formulation, and indeed, because CI is short of fiscal means even for posting observers on every significant international standards-setting committee, consumers generally lack real influence over standards.

One development that has raised the legal and political profile of standards is the widespread adoption by industrial nations of the Standards Code of the Tokyo Round of the General Agreement on Tariffs and Trade (GATT), also known as the Agreement on Technical Barriers to Trade ("TBT Agreement") (WTO, 1994) – itself a refined, expanded version of the Standards Code adopted at the Uruguay Round in 1994. National regulatory differences can raise significant technical barriers to trade. Moreover, according to a 1999 OECD study, "up to 80% of [international] trade (equivalent to around US$4 trillion annually) is affected by standards or associated technical regulations" (OECD, 1999c).

The TBT Agreement obligation to adapt new regulations to international standards extends also to pre-existing ones. A signatory may ask another signatory to justify any regulation that the other is "preparing, adopting, or applying", and such justification "must include an explanation for any decision not to use international standards" (GATT TBT Agreement, Article 2.5).

When signatories develop new standards or regulations that "depart from extant international standards or when international standards do not exist and when the new measure 'may have a significant effect on trade of other parties', signatories are required to go through a notice-and-comment period [which is open to international comment] before the [new] standard or regulation takes effect" (Mattli, 2001:329). "Advance notice of the proposed measure has to be given to the … WTO secretariat, and interested parties must have enough time to comment" (Mattli, 2001:329). A Code of Good Practice supports this process in Annex 3, Substantive Provision for "the preparation, adoption and application of standards" (WTO, 1994). This Code "describes rules for openness, transparency, notification of work in progress, utilization of international standards, and consideration of comments received" (Mattli, 2001:343). It is "addressed to all standards bodies – international, [globally] regional, and national, whether public or private" (Mattli, 2001:343). Articles 2.5, 2.9 and 2.10 provide that failure to use international standards is liable to be found to constitute an "unnecessary" obstacle to international trade (WTO, 1994).

4.6.3 Public-private interactions: the rising influence of private stakeholders

In the mid-1990s the Commission preached, and still often quotes today, that *technological neutrality* is the "gold standard" by which an industry regulatory regime ought to be measured. Technological neutrality means that regulators must not address norms to any particular technology *per se*, lest the speed of technological development and the comparative slowness of the policy process causes regulation to lag permanently behind (and renders the Single Market poorly governed or even ungovernable). Accordingly, Europe strives to keep its regulations as "technology-neutral" as possible. Certain EU Directives authorise the Commission to compile and publish reference works of generally recognised standards which support the authorising Directive. Consequently, as Ian Walden noted, a Member State's laws must presume compliance with EU Directives when a product from another Member State is compliant with the standards compiled by the Commission. Walden notes, however, that technology is not neutral, arguing that ICTs are fundamentally altering the technical landscape, creating unique issues that policy-makers must be prepared to address (Walden, 2001:546).

Another overarching principle is pan-European technical harmonisation. An important step toward harmonising the European ICT market, "promoting the interconnection and interoperability of national networks as well as access to such networks" (TEU, Article 154 [ex 129b]), is to develop minimum standards applicable throughout the Single Market. Stakeholders, particularly ICT companies, have an interest in such harmonisation, and consequently are eager to partake in standards-setting.

The shape-shifting governance arrangements that have arisen to formulate, disseminate and implement standards have drawn the attention of scholars. Some have noted how these arrangements alternate as to the public and private actors engaged, depending on the nature of the market externalities to be addressed: "varying combinations of private and public governance according to the respective interests and competencies of the two spheres, and varying levels of governance – national, regional, or global – according to the scope of the problem and the capacity of institutions" (Abbott and Snidal, 2001:345). This shows that standards-setting can knit together stakeholders on various Levels of governance who might not otherwise interact. In fact, in addition to the official standards organisations at the National Level, many private consortia and fora have lately been set up which complement and compete with the incumbent national and international organisations. Studies have discovered that the frequency and intensity of jurisdictional conflicts remain low (Werle, 2001:392-419), indicating that organisations operating on multiple governance Levels have succeeded in achieving co-ordination and consensus over standards.

Ian Walden even argues that with the liberalisation of the telecoms market, "the number of participants in the standard-setting process has risen dramatically, while the effective role of governments has diminished significantly" (Walden and Angle, 2001:347). The twin questions of the extent of government withdrawal from the governance of telecommunications and the wider ICT sector, and of the new role industry associations play, make up an essential part of this book. The most salient issues are: (1) which venues firms select for co-operation in standards-setting (see also Austin and Milner, 2001:411-431); and (2) whether and why private standards organisations contribute positively to the increased need for ICT standardisation.

Almost 350 private industry consortia are working on informal ICT standards (CEC, 2003b:26). Standards co-operation ranges organisationally from *ad hoc* committees to formal business associations that manage the collective affairs of their member firms. These groups are so many fora where technical experts may meet, debate, and choose between alternative proposals. Industry standards consortia in particular prevent the emergence of multiple incompatible solutions. Organisations like the ISF create new standards out of good practices, to cover new technologies like personal digital assistants (PDAs), wireless networking, and forensics. Strong evidence suggests that "since the 1990s, no one has launched any major new IT product without ensuring support from either the major industry players, the standard bodies or both" (Enticknap, 2004:30).

The need for co-operation and product design integration even between competitors is obvious. In April 2004 Microsoft settled a bitter legal dispute with Sun Microsystems over the latter's Web-standard Java. Microsoft paid Sun more than £850 million to resolve antitrust and patent issues. A sharing agreement has permitted Microsoft to continue to support Java in its Internet Explorer web browser, and both companies even made Microsoft's rival web-service architectures – Java Enterprise Edition and .net – interoperable with Java (Mohamed, 2004:12). Moreover, in 2007 "the European Court of First Instance[145] (CFI) upheld the European Commission's 2004 decision to fine Microsoft £497 million for anti-competitive practices. The CFI found Microsoft culpable of abusing its market dominance for bundling the Windows operating system with its Media Player", and also for having refused "to share interoperability information with its competitors" (Saran, 2007:10). The decision was welcomed by many industry analysts for having forced Microsoft to submit to the principles of open standards and interoperability. Some analysts also argued that this could solve current problems with active [global] directories run on other operating systems which have to "communicate" with Microsoft Exchange email servers (Saran, 2007:10).

Companies that develop technologies containing underlying protocols that then become the industry standard may gain significant market power. Examples of successful such standards are Flash/Flew (Macromedia), MS Windows platform (Microsoft), Bluetooth (the Bluetooth Special Interest Group),[146] Linux (IBM), and .net (Microsoft). It may be argued that industry is essential to the setting of standards that will assist the development of new technologies. On the other hand, it is questionable whether standards ought to be commercially exploited by companies lucky enough to have them widely accepted. The

145 Now called the General Court, it is the lower division of the Court of Justice of the European Union (of which the European Court of Justice is the upper division or appeals tribunal).

146 Bluetooth is an open wireless technology standard for exchanging data over short distances from fixed and mobile devices. It was developed by telecoms vendor Ericsson in 1994, and the Bluetooth Special Interest Group which Ericsson set-up to manage the development of further specifications now has more than 16,000 telecommunications, computing, networking and consumer-electronics member companies (Bluetooth SIG website, 2012).

unregulated proliferation of standards might also lead to the "balkanisation" of the European market, or might promote conflict between official standards deriving from standards institutes and industry-made standards.

Sometimes information-security and interoperability issues, and the urgent need for technical harmonisation, may lead to *ad hoc* industry consortia.[147] Radio Frequency Identification (RFID) is one example of an industry standard forged through many challenges and complexities involving multiple stakeholders agreeing a single standard in the process of standardisation. RFID is an automatic identification protocol that relies on data stored and remotely retrieved using devices called RFID tags or transponders. RFID is used mainly in the business supply chain to track and identify such items as products, shipping crates, and livestock, but analysts believe it will be used more and more to track consumer goods, and gather customer information and location data. Another example of the complexity of the process of diverse stakeholders agreeing a single RFID standard is found in the retail sector, where manufacturers, wholesalers, distributors and retailers must all arrive at the same solution that will work throughout the logistics chain. Yet agreement was reached nonetheless, showing how strong is the motivation toward multi-level co-operation, especially in the absence of vertical integration of the market.

As consumer privacy has become a concern, so RFID advocates, suppliers, and users have forged a set of best-practice guidelines on how firms ought to use the consumer information they gather *via* RFID. The guidance covers data collection, data security, and consumer notification (Mohamed, 2006:8). Standards are rarely developed in isolation, and the RFID standard was built upon existing standards.[148]

The "line between public and private standards-setting, however, is often blurred. Some public standards bodies are dominated by private actors"[149] (CEN Technical Committee website, 2006). Private standards organisations often enhance their institutional legitimacy by mimicking public bodies in their devices and procedures. The increasing fusion and interdependence between the public and private sectors in the setting of standards makes way for industry to play once more a predominant role in multi-level governance processes.

147 Examples of standard industry consortia are: The Big Four accountancy firms and US-based insurance giant AIG International develop a cyber-risk standard model that can be used by companies in all industries (Huber, 2004: 10).
The Wi-Fi Alliance (more than 300 members from more than 20 countries) launched the WiFi Protected Access (WPA) security protocol. Mayor industry players such as Alvarion and Intel develop WiMAX (WiMAX Forum website, 2003).

148 Examples of RFID-supporting standards are: JTC 1/SC 31 automatic identification and data capture techniques; ISO TC 104 /SC 4 identification and communication; ISO/TC204 Transport information and control systems; CEN TC 278 road transport and traffic telematics; ETSI EN 300 440-2 Version 1.1.1 (2001-09) electromagnetic compatibility and radio-spectrum matters (ERM); ERO SRD-CEPT/ERC 70-03 Recommendation relating to the use of Short Range Devices (SRD); Universal Postal Union S25-1G data constructs for the communication of information on postal items, batches and receptacles (RFID standards website, 2007).

149 Good examples are the CEN technical workshops, which are often dominated by business organisations.

Business furthers its own goal of market integration by harmonising standards, to the benefit of themselves and consumers likewise.

4.7 CONCLUSION: A REGULATORY COMPLIANCE MATRIX

The following *Regulatory Compliance Matrix* (Figure 4.1) is a compendious inventory of all regulations currently in force and applicable to the Information and Communications Technology (ICT) industry and to ICT governance issues. No inventory can ever be 100% complete, due to the quickness of changes, but the Regulatory Compliance Matrix at least maps, concisely but comprehensively, the principal domains of legislation, regulation and norms, and their content, and matches them to ancillary standards, frameworks and other guidance, as presented below. It is a template from which may spring a summation of all of the regulatory compliance goals that a business organisation would need to consider – a 'synoptic manifest' that makes all of these goals and the ongoing progress in meeting them visible to the whole organisation simultaneously. The key areas covered by the Matrix are:

1. Corporate governance, finance, accounting and contract law
2. Consumer protection and employment law
3. Information security
4. Data protection and privacy rights
5. Copyright and related rights
6. Electronic commerce

and specific ICT laws, regulations and norms; such as for

1. The Information Society
2. the Internet
3. telecommunications
4. digital media and content
5. radio services and equipment
6. audiovisual services
7. environmental ("Green IT")
8. other ICT-specific norms

This Matrix is doubly important because, after assembling all the compliance domains that interest companies, it helps identify their possible channels of policy participation, as presented in the next Chapter (Five). If ICT regulation had been one-dimensional and simple, involving nothing more than telecommunications expertise (let us say), then the Commission would not have been forced to rely on stakeholders' technical input – an input they had seldom needed before the liberalisation of the ICT market – to help manage this ramifying regulatory domain. By exhibiting the sheer complexity of ICT regulation, the Matrix shows how such a vast domain demands enormous technical expertise – more than the Commission could possibly have mustered – and not only that, but also social and economic "local" knowledge held by the non-expert stakeholders personally affected by an industry that touches and ties together virtually all the people of Europe. The only (collective) actor who can be said to span the entirety of this technical and social nexus is "the industry" itself – meaning the nodal firms who intermediate the far-flung supply- and demand sides of the market and thus the whole "ICT universe". This already shows the practical inevitability of Industry Governance.

The Regulatory Compliance Matrix may also serve as a template for future research into stakeholder participation in other regulatory domains of similar complexity, by illustrating how mapping out a policy domain's legal and (formally) normative system greatly helps the researcher to fully fathom it.

Depending on the *type of organisation* (*e.g.* profit or non-profit; eCommunications network provider or network user) and on the *type of business* (*e.g.* online sales, digital content provider), organisations are bound to comply with certain specific regulations. The Regulatory Compliance Matrix in Appendix Five provides a detailed list of international guidelines and EU regulations, together with some examples of UK national regulations. The author compiled this compendious list of regulations and standards over a period of several years. It is based on his work experience with the European Commission,[150] and with two Big Four professional audit firms in Regulatory Compliance Audit and Advisory Services. The regulatory categories are aligned with the standard ones used in law journals (Archer and Goldman, 2006) and by the European Commission. The Matrix has been scrutinised by more than 20 professionals and scholars in the area of ICT law, audit, and technical advisory services, and revisions have been made accordingly. The author therefore concludes that this Matrix constitutes an accurate "snapshot" of the domain of current ICT regulations and standards.

The Regulatory Compliance Matrix contains four fields: (1) general regulations, which apply to business organisations in general; (2) general standards, including compliance frameworks, audit programmes, widely adopted technologies, and standards that support the implementation of general regulations; (3) ICT regulations, which apply specifically to the ICT industry or to business in general insofar as it uses these technologies; and (4) ICT standards developed by standards organisations and the industry in order to support specific ICT solutions and to comply with specific ICT regulations.

150 *Stage* with the Commission's Directorate General "Directorate General Telecommunications, Information Market and Exploitation of Research", unit A1 "Telecoms Regulation', 1996 (the year before the European Telecommunications Market was liberalised). Active involvement in FP4/FP5/FP6 EU studies (*e.g.* "Market study on Telecommunications, Multimedia, Integrated Applications & Information Services until 2010", published in 1997 by DGXIII-A1); pilot programmes (*e.g.* "EuroTrust PKI Project", 1998, under the European Trusted Services Programme); and services (*e.g.* "FP5 electronic Certification Service Provision", 1999-2002).
Since 1998, the author was actively involved in more than 15 EU funded studies and "pilot services" in the ICT field. This required an ongoing communication process with stakeholder groups and European and national regulators.

Figure 4.1: The Regulatory Compliance Matrix

	LAWS, REGULATIONS and NORMS	STANDARDS, FRAMEWORKS and GUIDANCE
A. GENERAL	**1. Business regulation (corporate governance, finance, accounting, contract law)** *e.g.* 8th Company Law Directive, SOx, Anti-bribery and corruption law, public procurement, contract law, Value Added Tax **2. Consumer protection and employment law** *e.g.* Distance marketing, distance selling and alternative dispute resolution, Working Time Directive **3. Information security** *e.g.* Electronic signatures, network security, cybercrime **4. Data protection and privacy rights** *e.g.* EU DP Directive, data retention, Safe Harbour Principles **5. Copyright and related rights** *e.g.* Intellectual property rights, patents, trade marks and design, hardware, software **6. Electronic commerce** *e.g.* payment systems, global anti-Spam initiatives	• **Compliance frameworks defined by industry** *e.g.* COSO Enterprise Risk Management Framework, Cobit, Incoterms • **Standards defined by European/ national standardisation institutes** e.g. CEN, EESSI, ETSI, ITSEC, ITU • **Standards defined by international organisations** *e.g.* ISO, ITU, OECD guidelines • **Third party attestations** *e.g.* SAS70 (US), FIT 1/94 (UK), IAS 6 (Int.) • **Targeted industry initiatives** *e.g.* payment systems, trusted services • **Guidance issued by regulatory agencies** *e.g.* DP Working Party, IRAs, specialized agencies such as trade mark/ patent registration offices • **Technical standards defined by industry and industry associations** e.g. software standards for documents, images, videos and music, Internet software and web technology, operating systems, databases

B. ICT SPECIFIC		
	1. The Information Society *e.g.* The New Regulatory Framework for eCommunications services, telecoms licences, Trans-European Networks **2. Internet regulation and activities** *e.g.* Safer Internet use **3. Telecommunications regulation** *e.g.* Wireless policy, access and interconnection, satellites **4. Digital media and content** *e.g.* Digital interactive TV, digital content, protection of minors **5. Radio services and equipment** *e.g.* Radio interference, compatibility, equipment **6. Audiovisual services** *e.g.* Audiovisual media services **7. Environmental ("Green IT")** *e.g.* Waste electrical and electronic equipment, energy efficiency, other green IT regulation, climate change **8. Other ICT-specific norms** *e.g.* Wireless, fixed line, data storage and power management	• **Communication and Infrastructure Standards** *e.g.* for fixed line lines, mobile standards, (UMTS, GPRS, GSM), wireless applications (WAP, WiFi, WiMAX) authentication Dial-in User Service, VPN, encryption, eComm and Internet standards • **IT Platforms Protocols** e.g. ICT/IP • **Digital media and content** • *e.g.* MPEG, FTH technology, IPTV, VOD, VGA • **Industry standards for Operating Systems** *e.g.* Microsoft Win/XP OS, UNIX, SUN, Apple Macintosh • **Industry standards for software** *e.g.* JPEG, PDF, .xls, .ppt, .doc, Real Player, Flash, Java Scripts • **Publicly funded research** *e.g.* FP7 conducting "proof of concept" pilots, developing industry recommendations /draft guidance • **Other ICT-specific guidance** *e.g.* Internet Protocols (IPv6) and World Wide Web, other open standards • **Technical standards defined by industry and industry associations** *e.g.* Bluetooth, RFID

The Matrix shows that ICT regulations and standards do not only affect conventional stakeholders, such as telecoms operators, Internet service providers and IT equipment suppliers. Some regulations, such as those covering data protection, information security, copyright and e-Business, affect nearly all stakeholders. Hence stakeholders on all Levels ought to be involved in policy-making and standards-setting processes. The Matrix presented above identifies and categorises not only those ICT regulations and standards which are of primary interest to this book; it provides a structured system for understanding everything comprised in regulation of ICT, and how standards support that. No similar attempt has been made to overview how the Information Society may be defined from a legal and regulatory perspective.

Similar frameworks might be compiled for other highly regulated sectors, such as finance or pharmaceutics, or for other regions or countries. For instance, two such matrices, one for the United States and one for Japan, might be compiled so as to compare the regulatory frameworks in these countries, identify regulatory gaps or assess structural weaknesses in regulation. The results might be usefully applied to the OECD Regulatory Reform Index, or to a critique of the regulatory approach of the European regulator or regulators in other regions or countries. Industry associations as well as the OECD's Directorate for Science, Technology and Industry (STI) might adopt this or develop a similar matrix, to summarise and assess regulations for the annual OECD Economic Outlook publications, which focus on regulatory reforms. However, such matter falls outside the scope of this book.

This Regulatory Compliance Matrix will enable the author in the next stage of this book to identify, classify and analyse the key stakeholders involved in shaping this framework. The combined value of this and the following Chapters consists in helping us better understand the whole policy-process.

CHAPTER 5

STAKEHOLDERS AND THEIR CHANNELS OF PARTICIPATION

Various scholars have attempted to describe the influence of business organisations and associations on the Information Society policy agenda (Marsden, 2000; Cram, 1995). However, no attempt has been made to categorise such policy stakeholders and check whether any patterns can be found in their behaviour and beliefs. This Chapter makes that attempt – first, systematically to identify the key stakeholders in the ICT policy sector and their policy objectives, then, to inquire by what channels they seek to influence the ICT policy process in their own favour. This inquiry is a key step in the analysis needed to construct the Stakeholder Action Matrix. To understand multi-level stakeholder influence thoroughly, we need to know the key actors, both individual and corporate, who "hold" a "stake" in regulatory outcomes and whose choices ultimately determine that outcome. And we need to know their channels of participation in order to conclude that sufficient means of stakeholder influence now exist outside the classical forms of lobbying, laying an adequate foundation for verifying this book's Industry Governance Theory.

This Chapter consists of two Sections. Section 5.1 identifies the key "actors", meaning not only the stakeholders but also the regulatory authorities, at all Levels: Sub-national, National, European, and Global. The categorisation of the stakeholders at all four Levels was found to exhibit the same typology: (1) Individual advocates; (2) Public-sector and non-profit organisations; (3) Industry-focussed associations; and (4) Project groups. Some of these stakeholders and their initiatives are dealt with in other Chapters. Additional information on the behaviour and characteristics of the stakeholders, such as their perceptions and preferences, has been presented in the scholarly review in Chapter Two (Sections 2.3.2 and 2.3.3).

The author has identified more than 600 stakeholders involved in shaping ICT policies, regulations or standards at various Levels. Given this vast number, only the most influential can be presented in this Chapter. Appendix Six lists other key stakeholders, with website references for further information. While this Stakeholder Directory provides an synopsis at the European and Global Levels, it is not exhaustive for Member States. Nevertheless, it is the most comprehensive stakeholder directory to date and thus the best starting point for identifying key actors whose involvement in the policy process may be expected.

Section 5.2 introduces the sundry channels of stakeholder participation, from the consultative process through participation in technical committees, to engagement in direct lobbying, funded framework programmes, and other vehicles. Other channels of stakeholder participation have also been described and analysed elsewhere in this book.

5.1 KEY STAKEHOLDERS

It is often difficult for policy stakeholders, scholars and even EU officials interested in the EU's policy processes to identify non-institutional specialists, who, by playing a key role in policy decision-making, conserve the democratic nature of the EU and its institutional output. For example, the consultation process the European Commission undertakes when forming strategies for European ICT R&D provides employment for thousands of stakeholders, technical experts and lobbyists (*a.k.a.* "public affairs practitioners"). Of course, many companies and other organisations have set up representations in Brussels and in Member State capitals to deal efficiently with the Commission's Directorates and EU-funded research programmes, and with sundry legislatures and judiciaries. But businesses do not always influence EU policy so directly. They may leverage the experience and networks of other stakeholders – in particular, through their own membership of national, European, and international *industry associations*.

For present purposes, industry associations bear the most important influence over, hence are the most useful sources of information about regulatory actors and policy-making interactions. Businesses and other stakeholders and regulatory actors all rely on the procedural rules and strategic aims of these associations in order to collaborate successfully. This view is also supported by rational-choice theorists and policy researchers. Policy research deals mainly with collective and corporate actors – political parties, labour unions, government ministries, and international organisations – not with individuals acting on their own account. These composite actors are not only constituted by their defined objectives, they also depend on rules of procedure for their cohesion and practical operation. Corporate and collective actors "exist" only to the extent that the individuals acting within and for them succeed in coordinating their preferences. In practice this is only possible within a defined frame of reference constituted by organisational rules (Scharpf, 1997:39ff).

On the other hand, it is also widely acknowledged that institutionally unattached individuals such as journalists, analysts, researchers and others play important roles in the formation, dissemination and evaluation of policy ideas and policy proposals (Sabatier, 1993:24; Heclo, 1978). In most cases these individuals do operate from some existing platform or network, but often disseminate their own views. But this need not always be the case; for example, a political leader who *sua sponte* as it were raises concerns about competitiveness in the broadband market may be speaking for his party; a scholar may be articulating the views of a well-defined school of thought; a journalist may be reflecting the stance of his periodical. But this is not a prerequisite of individual policy influence.

5.1.1 Stakeholders and advocates

The number of both individuals and organisations seeking to influence the decisional processes of ICT policy is growing. In the interest of thoroughness, the key stakeholders have been categorised on four Levels of governance which they seek to influence, as noted in Chapter One:[151]

1. *Sub-national Level*: businesses, professional advisors, and interest- or pressure groups organised nationally and transnationally in Europe
2. *National Level*: national associations operating at National Level, and Member State governments and regulators who represent national and regional interests
3. *European Level*: European industry associations and cross-sectoral business groups, whether independent or affiliated with EU institutions, as well as European standards institutes, EU regulatory authorities, and EU funded organisations
4. *Global Level*: global industry associations, international governmental summit conferences, and intergovernmental organisations that set global policy agendas and launch targeted global initiatives

The author has characterised or typified these actors systematically, as to their motives and modes of action, into Advocacy Coalition Types. The reader is advised that the Advocacy Coalition Type differs both theoretically and ontologically from the concrete advocacy coalitions analysed by Sabatier (1993a; 1993b). His advocacy coalition is an actual ensemble of persons who can be identified and even interviewed. An Advocacy Coalition *Type*, by contrast, is a higher-order abstraction constructed by the author in order to simplify a complex policy world full of multiple competing advocacy coalitions.

As the word implies, such a "Type" groups together many real advocacy coalitions which, just because they are plural, must differ with each other over something (or else they would have merged or never hived apart). A "golden thread" nevertheless runs through their petty differences and binds them together respecting the "big questions". This thread constitutes a hardcore belief system that endures in the teeth of secondary differences, and is distinctive enough from the hardcore belief systems of others, that it stands out as a Type.

Stakeholder categorisation was based on empirical research, which included the author's participation in stakeholder activities and a review of policy papers, consultation responses and official journals published by the EU institutions. The detailed results of this research effort are presented in Appendix Six. Four Types of advocacy coalitions involving stakeholders were identified as interacting both with other stakeholders and with non-stakeholding actors at all four Levels of governance:

151 When developing the Stakeholder Action Matrix, the author distinguished between (1) four levels of stakeholder influence, which determine the vertical structure of the model, (2) four horizontal advocacy coalitions that spread across all four levels of stakeholder influence and only hung together through a belief system, and (3) the sixteen (possible) advocacy coalitions that round out the Stakeholder Action Matrix theoretically.

1. *Type One: Individual advocates* – including prominent businessmen and politicians, and other opinion leaders, lobbyists, and press and media personalities.
2. *Type Two: Public-sector and non-profit organisations* – governments (from lower Levels) and organisations with links to government, consumer associations, trade unions and public interest NGOs.
3. *Type Three: Industry-focused associations* – sectoral and cross-sectoral industry associations, and organisations linked to government bodies.
4. *Type Four: Project groups* – both institutional and non-institutional actors who participate in publicly (and sometimes privately) sponsored and funded projects, programmes and research initiatives.

5.1.2 Arbitrators and mediators

Additionally, another category of actors who do not form advocacy coalitions has been noted: that of *arbitrators and mediators*, including regulators. These are supposed to mediate between stakeholders who would be advocating otherwise irreconcilable interests. The arbitrating or mediating actors on any given Level have not been included in the Advocacy Coalition Typology *at that Level*, as the role of arbitration or mediation is incompatible with stakeholding and advocating.

Moreover, policy actors may be divided into stakeholders and non-stakeholders only in theory. It is an empirical question whether any actors actually exist who hold no stake at all in policy process outcomes. Stakeholders at National Level, for example, are identifiable by their demand for arbitration/mediation of their competing interests by persons authorised to do so (more or less impartially and disinterestedly) by national governments. Those vested with such authority are presumed to be non-stakeholding actors. It follows in theory that they make no part of any Advocacy Coalition – *ex officio* because they are charged, often by law, with arbitrating and mediating between adversarial stakeholders, and *ex hypothesi* because the author assumes that they fulfil their charge faithfully. Of course, arbitrators and mediators probably do not always act impartially, and empirical investigation may discover that they have connived with one or more advocacy coalitions.

On any given Level, those who mediate between stakeholders must be excluded from that Level's Advocacy Coalition Types; only that Level's stakeholders do any "advocating" as such. It is especially noteworthy that all of the EU institutions (the European Commission, for example) are excluded at the European Level. However, arbitrators and mediators on one Level can and perhaps inevitably do turn into interested advocates on higher Levels who seek arbitration or mediation by authorities higher than themselves. Indeed, this is one reason for distinguishing several Levels. For example, local and regional officials and governments, who arbitrate and mediate at the Sub-national Level, become stakeholders and advocates in search of coalition partners at higher Levels, including but not limited to the National one. (This is *prima facie* evidence, by the bye, of interaction between [National] Level actors and the "public-sector and non-governmental organisations" of Advocacy Coalition Type Two.)

5.1.3 ICT policy stakeholders at Sub-national Level

A primary goal of certain stakeholders at the Sub-national Level is to form "platforms" with stakeholders having similar commercial and professional interests. Business actors do this because their overriding objective is to secure the formulation of regulations supportive of their technical and commercial needs. It may be argued that business organisations, like non-profit organisations, operate at the National, European, and Global Levels; therefore, to theorise a Sub-national Level adds an unnecessary layer to an already complex structure. Nevertheless, weighty considerations argue in favour of a Sub-national Level when developing a stakeholder model.

Firstly, most private persons and organisations ordinarily make decisions at a Level subordinate to national and supranational political authority. It is important to identify these persons and organisations and the key decision makers within them ("corporate actors"), and their specific involvement in the policy process. Analysing their views and intentions in particular, and their policy trend, makes it easier to predict the reasoning that they will urge as key influencers during the policy consultation stage.

Business organisations involved in the ICT policy process may be telecommunications and network operators, Internet service providers (ISPs), equipment and infrastructure suppliers, software developers and vendors (covering applications, operating systems, and databases), and professional firms (systems integrators, legal firms, *etc.*). As all business organisations use ICT, it is also important to understand the views of ICT-using businesses (not otherwise involved in the industry) and their likely requests for regulatory changes. Empirical evidence suggests that at the Issue emergence and/or Initiation Phases of the policy or regulatory cycle, even individual advocates can succeed at influencing business decisions within an industry sector, and/or decisions by local or regional governments – sometimes even above this Level. Top management, including executive directors or board members and industry specialists, may then be quoted in influential professional publications; lobbyists and think tanks may succeed in influencing regulators or the public; journalists may gather and disseminate information about events and issues, stimulating a wider public debate.

The second reason for including a Sub-national Level in the Four-Level Model is that sub-national private organisations develop and implement operational policies, procedures, codes of conduct, and other forms of internal rules and guidelines,[152] which in nearly every legal system they are contractually bound to comply with. This self-regulation may be a response to regulatory requirements, but it may also fill a regulatory gap. For example, most organisations have implemented an Internet and email misuse policy to define and bar inappropriate uses of Internet technology by employees. On the one hand, these policies may be designed to meet regulatory requirements related to content, copyright, and downloading of files; on the other hand, as self-regulations they also support business needs, such as

152 Examples are: Operational policies: compliance policy, Internet and email usage policy, IT security policy, data protection and privacy policy; Procedures: complains handling, backup procedures; disaster recovery and emergency procedure; Codes of conduct: corporate and social responsibility, energy conservation, customer care "promises", ethical and environmental codes; and Rules and guidelines: online sales guidelines, health and safety guidelines.

confidentiality of messages, IT security, businesslike use of corporate email systems, and network performance.

A third reason is that business organisations, in particular, differ from other organisations in the way they make decisions. By contrast with industry associations, businesses themselves are typically hierarchical organisations under the control of their owners directly, or of managers representing the owners or beneficiaries who hold jointly the "stock"; *e.g.* publicly listed companies overseen by a board of directors elected by shareholders. Generally, international business organisations take decisions through a central process dominated by a leadership within a defined governance structure. The individual self-interests of the decision-makers are supposed to be set aside in the employment relationship with the company (March and Simon, 1958). Thus, individual employees may only be "stakeholders" in policy processes insofar as they act in behalf of their organisation.

Fourthly, it is a striking fact that most policy ideas adopted and implemented at higher Levels actually originate at Sub-national Level. Decision-making and solution-finding within private organisations, especially large international business organisations, mirrors similar processes of interaction observed inside public organisations. For example, business organisations define corporate governance practices and processes (internal policies), and this generates policy ideas that influence the wider regulatory environment in which they operate (external policies). Thus "governance" is carried on within hierarchies at a Level lower than the hierarchy constituted by national government.

Fifthly, many private organisations and corporate actors interact with the European regulator directly. Over 250 companies and 270 consultancies have permanent representative offices in Brussels so as to offer their services and liase in policy matters with the EU; British and American corporations appearing to dominate the lobbying culture (Philip and Gray, 1996:xix). The Commission for its part leverages this close involvement and encourages especially business organisations to provide (for example) experts independent of itself to help evaluate its own proposals, and to monitor and review its projects (Europa website – Framework Programme Experts, 2007; Europa website – Safer Internet Plus Call for Independent Experts, 2007). Business organisations are thus involved in all stages even of the public funding process, from formulation through execution to retrospective assessment.

Sub-national Level – Types One through Four

Nor is the Sub-national Level defective; it contains all four Advocacy Coalition Types outlined above. Advocacy Coalition Type One, for example, includes the senior and middle management of private organisations in addition to journalists, politicians, other opinion leaders, academics, and members of think tanks.

Contrary to what one might expect from the foregoing discussion of mediators *vs.* advocates, the Sub-national Level also harbours stakeholders belonging to Advocacy Coalition Type Two, Public-sector and non-profit organisations, even though at this Level the "public sector" is supposed to consist of mediators not stakeholding advocates. Yet local or regional governments, for example, may for "activist" reasons deny to businesses needed action on specific regulatory requirements, such as waste-management services, planning permissions, or licences. Not only representatives of regional consumer associations but also trade-union members who are employees of business organisations may demand consumer protection or health and safety measures. This evidences that regulatory pressures may arise from the "bottom up", so that one needs not leave the Sub-national Level in order to see interaction with members of Advocacy Coalition Type Two.

Small and medium-sized companies, in particular, who have less developed European or international networks, cooperate through local business contacts, business organisations, and professional associations, all of them stakeholders who constitute Advocacy Coalition Type Three. And Chambers of Commerce and Industry represent businesses at all levels, including at regional and municipal levels.

Local and regional governments also sponsor programmes and initiatives employing the Project groups who constitute Advocacy Coalition Type Four. These help stimulate collaboration and innovation in industry, often in tandem with other local organisations. Examples of local or regional development programmes include: "Flanders in action: A socio-economic stimulus for Flanders" (Belgium); and the Regional Development Agencies (RDAs) in England, *e.g.* in the West or East Midlands. These are partly financed by the EU's Structural Funds, organised into the European Regional Development Fund (ERDF), the Cohesion Fund, the European Social Fund (ESF), and the European Grouping of Territorial Co-operation (EGTC) (Europa website – EU Portal, 2006). Participants in these Project groups on Sub-national Level often collaborate above their Level, forming collaborative relationships with partners and regulators on National and European Levels (Europa website – EU Portal, 2006).

Encouraged by the creation of the EU Committee of the Regions (CoR) in 1994, the number of representations of Sub-national regional governments in Brussels has grown apace. Each Member State has formed its own regional delegation, consisting of regional political leaders – *e.g.* members of regional or federal parliaments and assemblies – who commend regional issues to the CoR (Europa website – Committee of the Regions, 2007).

5.1.3 ICT policy stakeholders at National Level

Although representing mainly national and ethnically regional interests, and enforcing regulations at the National Level, most national policy actors see the need for a "Brussels presence", either to develop relationships with other members of the pan-European groups to which they belong, or to have more access to the EU institutions for funding. Additionally, the prestige from such a presence enjoyed in the home country over other organisations is an intangible incentive. Actors on the National Level interact with stakeholders of all Types. Most "national policy actors" in Brussels, primarily larger business organisations, come from the UK, Germany and France (Philip and Gray, 1996:xix).

National Level – Type One

National governments acknowledge the importance of ongoing dialogue with individuals (Advocacy Coalition Type One) who are business and civil society leaders. For example, the British government announced in its Budget Report 2006 the establishment of an International Business Advisory Council as a platform encouraging UK business investment globally. The government pre-selected twelve members for the Council, among whom were Bill Gates of Microsoft Corporation and Meg Whitman of eBay (Healey, 2006:68). These leaders were invited to work closely with the government to vet laws and other UK state interventions for their foreign-investment friendliness.

Business leaders aside, individuals or small groups may potentially influence the national policy direction, among them national politicians, lobbyists, journalists for national newspapers, or committees set up to make recommendations or investigate affairs. Their opinions may even influence policy at the European Level. In this the media play an especially important role. Broadcasters and the print press facilitate their own influence when they report events or publicise statements by individuals holding key institutional positions; thereby they influence indirectly the opinions of elites, the mass public, and politicians. This evidences that members of Advocacy Coalition Type One (Individual advocates) exist on the National Level.

National Level – Type Two

Member State governments' ministries, and national scientific organisations also interact with European regulators. These actors of Coalition Type Two represent national government interests directly at the next higher, European Level. Every EU Member State has set up national regulatory authorities (NRAs) and independent regulatory authorities (IRAs), the former by national government initiative, the latter in consequence of European regulation (notwithstanding having been set up at National Level). The first IRAs were the eCommunications regulators; the UK's Ofcom for example. The second wave of IRAs were the data protection and privacy regulators that enforced EU data protection law at the National Level; the UK's Information Commissioner Office (ICO) for example.[153] These members of Advocacy Coalition Type Two (Public-sector and non-profit organisations) are quite active on European Level. Indeed, as noted in Chapter Two, Section 2.1.4 titled "The new mode of governance in Europe", the delegation of powers to IRAs has contributed to creating a new mode of governance. IRAs have both regulatory powers and regulatory discretion; they advise policy makers at all Levels, and forge networks to exchange policy ideas with other key actors. Their importance as *both* mediators and stakeholders has been widely acknowledged both by scholars and by the European Commission (New Modes of Governance Project website, 2007).

National Level – Type Three

Despite the fact that so many industry associations exist at the European Level, many of them – members of Advocacy Coalition Type Three – are also organised at Member State level. Associations are normally defined as "bottom-up" organisations designed to serve the preferences of their members. Not only are leaders expected to be accountable, directly or indirectly, to the membership, but members' preferences, when expressed, are supposed to override those of the leadership. Examples of national industry associations are, in the

153 For a complete list of all EU15 IRAs, see Appendix Six: Level 2: Public-sector and non-profit organisations, "Regulators in Europe - eCommunications" and "Regulators in Europe – Data Protection/Privacy".

UK for example: the British Chambers of Commerce (BCC), the Confederation of British Industry (CBI), the Internet Service Provider Association UK (ISPA UK), and the UK Telecoms Services Association.[154] These associations interact with policy-makers at the National Level, typically by aggregating the views of their members, and advocating in their behalf before national regulatory authorities and government ministries.

All EU Member States have established national standards bodies, which mediate or at least facilitate consensus building mainly between business interests. Although not stakeholders or advocates themselves (at National Level), they do often constitute the principal fora where stakeholders congregate to do their advocating. In the UK these include the British Standards Institution (BSI) and the British Electrotechnical Committee (BEC).[155] The national standards bodies develop national and international[156] norms and standards; provide training; offer product-testing services; and certify management systems and products. Most national standards institutes in Europe are fully independent of their national governments. They focus on working closely with stakeholders to develop consensus on standards that meet market exigencies. These activities call for both industry and standards experts to contribute their skills and experience to the processes of standardisation. The chairmen and board members of most national standards institutes have either held senior management positions in their industry, or at least have strong ties to it, a fact which ensures that commercial interests (*e.g.* the cost implications of new standards) are taken into consideration.[157] Hence they belong with Advocacy Coalition Type Three.

National Level – Type Four

Various Project groups – members of Advocacy Coalition Type Four – act and interact at the National Level, where numerous well-funded programmes and initiatives are available. Business organisations, universities and research institutions receive public support for

154 For a compendious list of EU15 industry associations, see Appendix Six: Level 2: industry-focussed associations.

155 For a complete list of EU15 standards institutes, see Appendix Six: Level 2: Standards Institutes – National Standardisation Bodies.

156 The British Standards Institute stresses that the BSI Group operates in 86 markets worldwide. It manages UK interaction with the standards bodies of Europe and the International Organisation for Standardisation. It also serves as secretariat to over 200 European and international committees (British Standards Institute website, 2007).
DIN, the German national standards body, estimates that 90% of the standards work now carried out is international in nature (Deutsches Institut für Normung website, 2007).
AFNOR, the French standardisation institute estimates that 80% of its work relates to European and International standardisation (Association française de normalisation website, 2007).

157 For example, the BSI Chairman (Sir David John) is currently also Chairman of Premier Oil plc and Balfour Beatty plc. The Chief Executive, Director and four Non-Executive Directors all held senior management positions in the industry before joining BSI. The CEO and Executive Director of DIN (Prof. Dieter Ameling) has close ties with the steel industry. More than 60% of the Presidential Board Members and Technical Directors have worked for international companies in the past. The Director General of AFNOR (Olivier Peyrat), his Executive Committee and most of the Administrative Board members have close links to industry associations and consumer associations.

investment in R&D through programmes sponsored by the Member States. The results of studies, pilot projects, and funding for new technologies not only determine future funds allocation, but are also used to justify policy decisions and initiatives.

The Commission's Green Paper COM(2007)161 on "The European Research Area: New Perspectives" concluded that national R&D programmes and initiatives over the past decade have evolved toward richer and more coherent, but also more complex policy mixes (CEC, 2007f). Member States are increasingly taking a multi-annual, strategic approach to R&D, thereby offering a more stable and predictable, inherently long-term environment like the Framework Programmes at the European Level. The UK, for example, with its "Science and Innovation Investment Framework 2004-2014", is tackling research and its broader innovation aspects in an integrated manner (CEC, 2007h). As the Survey results showed, participants in national and European publicly funded programmes are using their involvement to develop their networks; to get involved in regulatory and standards initiatives at an early stage; and to influence policy and standards.

Following the revision of the Lisbon Strategy in 2005, all Member States now have established targets for R&D expenditure in their National Reform Programmes which, were they to be met, would by 2010 result in an EU-wide R&D intensity of 2.6% of GDP (CEC, 2006x). The establishment of R&D public-private partnerships (PPPs) is intended to help achieve these investment objectives and to create new dynamics for knowledge circulation. The UK, for example, has launched networking and clustering schemes ("Knowledge Transfer Networks"), and established national technology platforms after the pattern of the EU's Innovation Platforms. PPPs also increasingly inform research activities by taking account of the strategic needs of the economy while simultaneously incentivising businesses to become more active in the policy process (CEC, 2007h). This expansion of R&D funding is inevitably driving an expansion of the number and influence of stakeholders who enter the policy process through their involvement in National-level research projects.

Conferences and exhibitions, sponsored both publicly and privately, are another important platform upon which for stakeholders of Type Four to exchange ideas and views, providing the opportunity to "network", *i.e.* discuss technical challenges and agree blueprint solutions (*viz.* launching new standards to improve interoperability between products, orjoining together for funding for further research). Appendix Six provides details about these national conferences, as well as about similar events at the European and Global Levels.

5.1.4 ICT policy stakeholders at European Level

European Level – Type One

At European Level, Advocacy Coalition Type One – Individual advocates – consists of individuals acting in their own capacity, such as lobbyists who, representing major stakeholders, through their own individual charisma shape governmental policy and public opinion; press and media personalities with pan-European coverage through CNN Europe, RTL, Reuters, *etc.*; and prominent businessmen, *viz.* "oligarchs", venture capitalists and entrepreneurs. Even if individual makers of Europe-wide opinion (*e.g.* media tycoons, individual politicians) are not deliberately engaged in the policy process, they often influence it indirectly. The fact that the views of such individuals are broadcast all over Europe is evidence enough of interaction between the European Level and Advocacy Coalition Type One.

European Level – Type Two

Advocacy Coalition Type Two at European Level includes governments and political leaders who represent their respective national interests in Brussels, including both Member State Ambassadors to the EU representing their countries' interests, and national politicians participating in Ministerial conferences. Also represented in this coalition type are NGOs and other private but non-profit associations of pan-European reach; *e.g.* the European University Association, Euro-CASE (the European Council of Applied Sciences, Technologies and Engineering), the European Trade Union Confederation (ETUC), the European Consumers Organisation (BEUC). The proliferation of Europe-wide public-interest associations in recent years, and their efforts to influence EU policy through their own publicised conferences and through deliberate input into EU decisional processes, suffices to establish the existence of interactions between advocates of Coalition Type Two and other stakeholders and mediators at the European Level. All of these stakeholders profess a common concern for the many Europeans who are likely to become marginalised by the advent and the intrinsic development of the Information Society.

European Level – Type Three

Very many Advocacy Type Three stakeholders focus their activities on the European Level above all. A vast number of industry-focussed associations and fora exist at this Level. Some of them are fully independent, others are closely linked with the EU institutions. Advocates of Coalition Type Three interact on the European Level first and foremost by participating in publicised meetings and workshops of their own, which often host Commission staff members. In most cases, participation requires invitation or membership; and this long-term commitment by participating organisations tightens the bonds between them. Often long-term financial commitment is entailed, implying an expectation of achieving clearly defined objectives through their activities. These are the stakeholders who most often respond to invitations to attend policy events hosted by the EU institutions, as the case study in Chapter Seven evidences (see Section 7.3 below). The author has sub-categorised these associations and fora as follows:

1. *Sectoral European industry associations*, which are independent of regulators and fully committed to serving the interests of their members. Many of them have representation at the National Level as well. Examples include the European IT Roundtable, EUROSPACE (the Association of European Space Industry), the European Public Telecommunications Network Operators' Association (ETNO), the European Telecommunications Services Association (ETSA), the European Telecommunications Satellite Association (EUTELSAT), the European Internet Service Providers Association (EuroISPA), and the European Competitive Telecommunications Association (ECTA).

2. *Cross-sectoral European industry associations*, which ply a wider trade than ICT issues; for example, the European Round Table of Industrialists (ERT), and the Association of European Chambers of Commerce and Industry (EUROCHAMBERS), both of which are primarily interested in representing the interests of multiple industries; also, the Union of Industrial Employers Confederations of Europe (UNICE) and the European Tech Investment Forum (ETIF).
3. *EU-linked organisations*, which have strong ties with, including being sponsored by the European supranational organs; the stakeholders and direct beneficiaries of which, however, are primarily businesses.[158] Prime examples include the European Space Agency (ESA), the European Network and Information Security Agency (ENISA), and the European Registry of Internet Domain Names (EURid).

Representatives of industry associations often participate on the committees of pan-European regulatory groups (by invitation) or in workshops hosted by the European standards institutes; which sufficiently evidences the interaction of Type Three advocates with both stakeholders and the non-stakeholding actors of the European Level.

European Level – Type Four

Advocacy Coalition Type Four consists of Project groups who participate in EU-funded research programmes and initiatives. These include, for example, the EU Framework programmes (FPs), targeted EU Research Projects – *e.g.* Pan-European Laboratory for Next-generation Networks and Services (PANLAB), – or the European Network for Market-oriented Research and Development (EUREKA). Further details about these fora are provided below in Section 5.2.4 ("Funded programmes and initiatives") of this Chapter. Prospective and ongoing Project groups with similar interests meet for networking at pan-European conferences such as the Infosecurity Europe, Mobile Enterprise, the Internet World, the European Wireless Conference, or the annual Cable Congress. All these venues of interaction prove that advocates of this Coalition Type are very much engaged with actors on the European Level.

European Level – Arbitrators and Mediators

In addition, at European Level there exist "arbitrators and mediators" who offer platforms for stakeholder participation designed to mediate their conflicting interests. These may be divided into two sub-categories: (1) policy-consultative bodies set up by the Commission or Council, and (2) tributary activities facilitated by the standards institutes.

The EU institutions have established several permanent bodies to advise them on ICT and other regulatory issues. The first sub-category of European-Level arbitrators and mediators include:

158 For a compendious list of sector-specific European industry associations, cross-sectoral industry associations and European organisations with links to European institutions, see Appendix Six: Level 3: industry-focussed associations.

1. The Independent Regulatory Authorities, established by European Regulations, which include the Article 29 Data Protection Working Party, the European Regulators Group (ERG) which has been superseded by the Body of European Regulators for Electronic Communications (BEREC), and the Radio Spectrum Policy Group (RSPG).
2. Official EU committees and councils (*a.k.a.* "comitology") which assist the Commission in developing, adopting and implementing the proposals and measures necessary to carry out its responsibilities.
3. Certain publicly funded scientific institutes that have been established by the EU to manage R&D at the European Level.
4. Sundry private organisations mediating at the Sub-national Level which maintain strong links to EU institutions.[159] Some of these bodies and their involvement with European-level stakeholder activities are examined below in the eCommunications Review case study.

The second sub-category of European-Level arbitrators and mediators comprises European standards institutes. These are important because it is estimated that as many as 350 industry consortia are working on informal ICT standards (CEC, 2003b:26). The official European standards institutes are the *Comité Européen de Normatisation* (CEN) or European Committee for Standardisation, the *Comité Européen de Normalisation Électrotechnique* (CENELEC) or European Committee for Electronic Standardisation, and the European Telecommunications Standards Institute (ETSI). The Information Society Standardisation System (CEN-ISSS) and the European Workshop for Open Systems (EWOS), established within the CEN/CENELEC framework, support the work of the standards institutes by focussing on specific Internet standards such as encryption. Furthermore, there are some European standards institutes which have no direct connection with the EU institutions, and have been set up by independent private or public-private organisations, or by government-approved third-party licensors.[160] The importance of standardisation in the EU leapt dramatically after the European Council adopted in May 1985 its New Approach to technical harmonisation which delegated detailed technical standards development to CEN, CENELEC and ETSI (see Section 4.6.2 above). The New Approach enhanced the quality and importance of the output of these standards institutes.

In consequence the Commission published a Green Paper COM(90/456/EC) on "The future development of European standardisation" (CEC, 1990c). Among its proposals was encouragement of more consumer participation at every stage of the standards-setting process. "Expert groups" were also to be set up and empowered to propose new work items, including the revision of standards considered too lax. Their observer status on technical

159 For a compendious list of European committees and councils, European scientific organisations, and European organisations with strong links to the EU institutions, see Appendix Six: Level 3: Public-sector and non-profit organisations.

160 For examples of European standards organisations with EU links *versus* European standards organisations with no EU links, see Appendix Six: Level 3: industry-focussed associations.

committees was to enable these expert groups to comment but not vote. In mid-1997 CEN created the European Committee for Standardisation/Information Society Standardisation System (CEN/ISSS) to supply standardisation services and products specifically for Europe's Information Society. CEN/ISSS Workshops are less formal than CEN Technical Committees, and thus are designed to find a quicker, more market-driven approach to eliminating technical barriers. Sundry stakeholders have been invited to participate in its working groups, including vendors, service providers, manufacturers, consumers and regulators. These working groups are assisted by focus groups assembled on demand by the European Commission, and CEN organises public consultations and subsequently provides recommendations on future standardisation work based on the feedback received (CEN/ISSS website, 2006).

5.1.5 ICT policy stakeholders at Global Level

The Internet and eCommunication services are by nature global, which necessitates that a minimal set of universal rules are created at the Global Level. Accordingly, the Commission has been coordinating initiatives with such multilateral organisations as the UN, OECD, the ITU, and the WTO. It has also been dialoguing with individual countries, including the USA, Japan, various accession candidates, and the non-EU countries of the Mediterranean. The EU is constrained in its freedom to trade or not to trade goods and services with third countries by certain international agreements, such as those made under the auspices of the WTO and OECD. It follows that the lobbying of these Global-Level organisations, even by private stakeholders, could well influence the Union's ICT policy decisively.

Global Level – Type One

Advocacy Coalition Type One on Global Level may include retired UN General Secretaries, Nobel Peace Prize winners, multinational corporate tycoons (*e.g.* Bill Gates, who sponsored "PCs for Public Schools"), or rich businessmen who, becoming philanthropists, support global IT projects (*e.g.* Larry Ellison, who donated software to the Federal government that empowered it to build and run a national identification database). The Advocacy Coalition Typology predicts that their behaviour and beliefs are very similar to Advocacy Coalition Type One at European Level (see both Sections 5.1.3 and 1.5.3 above), however their personal backgrounds might differ.

Global Level – Type Two

Advocacy Coalition Type Two – Public-sector and non-profit organisations – includes nation-states participating in global fora such as the WTO or OECD or UN/ITU, as well as non-profit/ non-governmental organisations such as the WIPO or the World Science Forum (WSF).

Global Level – Type Three

Advocacy Coalition Type Three – Industry-focused associations – includes BIAC, the Business and Industry Advisory Committee to the OECD, the Global Dialogue on eCommerce (GBDe), the International Telecommunications Satellite Organisation (INTELSAT), the International

Chamber of Commerce (ICC), GSM Association (GSMA), and the Anti-Phishing Working Group (APWG).

Global Level – Type Four

Advocacy Coalition Type Four – Project groups – participate in such fora as the Internet Engineering Task Force (IETF), the Internet Protocol (version 6) Forum, the World Wide Web Consortium (W3C), as well as numerous global conferences, including the World Congress on Information Technology, CeBit and the IPTV World Forum.

Advocacy Coalition Type Four often attracts technological "geeks" who hardly concern themselves with politics, but who are looking instead for a technological solution to the world's problems. Their enthusiasm is infectious and draws followers who may widen the agenda; this is what enables them to build advocacy coalitions in the first place, and makes them so formidable an Advocacy Coalition Type. When it comes to technology, they may be perceived as innovators or early adopters who love "gadgets". For example, they are typically the first to adopt new ICT solutions in their organisation, while everyone else is still apprehensive.

5.2 CHANNELS OF PARTICIPATION AND THEIR BENEFITS

Before examining the channels by which business organisations and other stakeholders participate in the EU policy process, the question why these stakeholders ever decide to allocate scarce private resources to such activities in the first place will be discussed briefly. In sum, the author has been led to conclude that the EU's regulatory-reform and economic-policy objectives, with the Lisbon Agenda at its centre, require European and national regulators to adopt business-friendly regulations, and that this may end up favouring business organisations over non-profit organisations.

Businesses which participate actively in EU ICT-policy decisional processes stand to gain a number of lucrative advantages. According to Germain (2003) and Leandri (2003), their early and/or active involvement may:

1. yield timelier knowledge of policy proposals interesting to business; of the current and future legal and regulatory framework; and of their potential impact on themselves
2. supply them more information about grassroots support for policy proposals
3. afford opportunities to influence desired standardisation or harmonisation proposals while these can still be influenced
4. establish long-term working relationships with lawmakers and regulatory agencies
5. enable the spotting of future regulatory trends and warning signals.

Participating in the EU policy process may also help companies identify and exploit business opportunities, such as new market opportunities for their goods or services; or avoid demands that they adapt to national practices or standards in other Member States. If companies fail to influence the regulator, they may suffer competitive disadvantages and even losses (van Schendelen, 1994b:5).

All major policy decisions in the European Union are taken by the assembled Ministers of the Member States, normally after consulting or co-deciding with the European Parliament. But the Commission's role "as the proposer of action at the Community level and as well the implementer of the policies decided by Ministers means that it is important for many organisations across the whole range of activities to have close contact with the Commission, to be fully informed what is being considered and to provide their own input to the process" (Philip and Gray, 1996:28). The author has discovered (once again) that no Commission proposals come "out of the blue"; on the contrary, they nearly always attempt to reflect the wishes and concerns of the Member States, the sub-national regions, industry and consumer organisations, professional associations, businesses, and citizens generally. The Commission is thus the most interesting European institution for stakeholders who wish to influence ICT policy. The following six Sections describe the six main vehicles the author was able to identify, which stakeholders use to influence the ICT policy agenda.

5.2.1 The consultation process at European Level

Since 1992 the number of legislative proposals initiated by the Commission has dropped radically, while resort to Green Papers and Discussion Papers has increased (Philip and Gray, 1996:xviii). The Green Papers process allows interest groups through consultation to articulate their views and concerns over a longer time-frame, which affords them more influence over EU policy. In the past the Commission consulted in its policy processes only those organisations and associations which were registered in its Directory of Interest Groups. Such organisations gained exclusive access to valuable information. Old-fashioned lobbying was seen as the key to success in shaping regulations, and "those who lobby a directorate or department consistently over time are commonly consulted in advance by those handling the policy initiatives for which it is responsible" (Anonymous, 1999a:168).

Changes to this traditional approach have accelerated since 2000. The outcome of the European governance debate, as well as the Commission's own Communication COM(2002)704 "Towards a reinforced culture of consultation and dialogue – General principles and minimum standards for consultation of interested parties by the Commission" (CEC, 2002s), have made it mandatory for the Commission to be pro-active in consulting interested parties "outside the loop", and to follow certain minimum consultation standards. This is in line with the EU's original constitutional framework, which required that "the Commission should [...] consult widely before proposing legislation and, whenever appropriate, publish consultation documents" (Treaty of Amsterdam, 1997). But it is also important for pragmatic reasons that all or many more stakeholders in the policy process are consulted and treated adequately and equitably. The Commission has emphasised the need to "reduce the risk of the policy-makers just listening to one side of the argument or of particular groups getting privileged access on the basis of sectoral interests or nationality" (CEC, 2001d:17).

Best practice in consultation is supposed to serve the twofold purpose of improving the quality of the policy process and of encouraging the participation of interested parties and the public. Today, the "consultation mechanisms form part of the activities of EU institutions throughout the whole legislative process, from policy-shaping prior to a Commission proposal to final adoption of a measure by the legislature and implementation" (CEC, 2002s:4). Consultation allows the stakeholders who have been presented in this Chapter to provide their input. The case study in Chapter Seven analyses in greater detail the outcomes, participants, and timelines of the consultation processes carried out at both European and (UK) National Levels pursuant to the 2006 eCommunications Review.

5.2.2 Task forces and High-Level Groups

When new policy issues arise that call for an immediate response, a task-force approach is often resorted to. In the Commission's view these policy development instruments have already proven successful in such policy domains as maritime, automotive and pharmaceutical affairs. The operational set-up always follows the same scheme: industry associations and other private stakeholders identify the issues, discuss them in working groups, and present their findings in reports to the Commission. One example – a brainchild of the 2005 Lisbon Programme and its new industrial policy initiative (CEC, 2005i; see also CEC, 2005n and CEC, 2005o) – was the launch in January 2006 of a multi-stakeholder Task Force on ICT Sector Competitiveness and ICT Uptake (the "ICT Task Force"), the objectives of which were to identify the main obstacles hindering Europe's competitiveness in and uptake of ICT; to recommend how to overcome these obstacles; and to complement i2010, the Commission's ICT-related initiative, with coordinated consultative output and encouragement of stakeholder engagement (CEC, 2006h; ICT Task Force website, 2007). The ICT Task Force was jointly managed by DG Enterprise and DG Information Society & Media, with the support of other Commission departments according to interest and need. It featured innovative fora for engagingstakeholders and mediators.

The Task Force itself consisted of seventeen CEOs from industry organisations but just eight non-industry stakeholders from academia, trade unions, Chambers of Commerce, and consumer associations, and trade associations,[161] which was held to constitute an adequate spectrum of stakeholder representation (CEC, 2006i). Twenty-five "Sherpas", or deputies with ombudsman responsibilities, were assigned to assist in the settlement of disputes between Task Force participants, and to attend its further consultations to mediate conflicts.

161 ICT industry members included: Mandriva, Alcatel, Cegid, STMicroelectronics, Sun Microsystems, Microsoft Corporation, Cisco Systems, Siemens Communications, Tele2, IBM, Intel, IONA Technologies, BT Group, Philips Consumer Electronics, Deutsche Telecom, Nokia Corporation, SAP; and the other stakeholders were: EUROCHAMBERS, European Private Equity & Venture Capital Association (EVCA), INSEAD University, PREST (Manchester Business School), European Association of Craft, Small and Medium-Sized Enterprises (UEAPME), European Consumer Association (BEUC), European Metalworkers' Federation (EMF), and UNI-Europa (a trade union).
The group of industry associations that channelled information to and from their members to help validate the views emerging from the working groups consisted of: Business Software Alliance (BSA), European Competitive Telecommunications Association (ECTA), European ICT Association (EICTA), European Software Association, European Semiconductor Industry Association (ESIA), European Telecommunications Network Operators Association (ETNO), and ObjectWeb. (CEC, 2006i).

Finally, the Task Force set up six working groups[162] to address the main issues identified by the Task Force. While the Task Force membership was fixed for its duration, the six working groups were open to all, *i.e.* to stakeholders not members of the Task Force. With more than 200 permanent members and *ad hoc* participants, then, the ICT Task Force may be seen as powerful stakeholder representation, as well as powerful evidence of Industry Governance. At the end of 2006 each working group presented a topic paper, which was incorporated into the Task Force's final report. The report identified the main obstacles in the way of a European knowledge-based economy; made concrete recommendations; and called upon the Commission and the Member States to take all steps needed to eliminate these obstacles hindering Europe's competitiveness (EU ICT Task Force, 2006). According to the ICT Task Force website, its key aim of creating "a more favourable environment for business in the EU" must be an ongoing one, and continues to this day (Europa website – Enterprise and Industry, 2012)

Another instrument favoured by the Commission for forging consensus on strategic policy issues is the "High-Level Group" comprising both Member State representatives and stakeholders. These groups discuss strategic policy issues within the framework of a specific policy initiative; give input and advice on possible improvements and adjustments of policy actions; offer a forum for stakeholders to exchange experiences and views on issues – with the Commission Services involved, – all leading to the development and implementation of a policy strategy.

High-Level Groups are set up to attain a specific policy objective and their tenure is limited. For example, in March 2006 the Commission Decision 2006/215/EC launched the i2010 High-Level Group in pursuance of its Lisbon Agenda and of the strategically important i2010 Initiative (CEC, 2006c). This was an advisory "expert" group comprising Member State officials specialising in ICT policy – the Ministers and Deputy Ministers or Secretaries of State for ICT, communications, technology and innovation, science, and/or e-Government. Meeting up to three times a year, it was open to observers from accession candidates and European Economic Area (EEA) member countries. The Commission intended this process to "strengthen dialogue with stakeholders and work with Member States to address ICT issues these [*sic*], notably through the open method of co-ordination" (CEC, 2005g:12).

Although High-Level Groups comprise only selected officials and experts, they are nonetheless highly influential in setting the policy agenda. The i2010 High-Level Group in particular was asked to review the effectiveness of the i2010 Initiative strategy; use benchmarking to monitor its implementation and policy evolution; and provide the Commission with guidance and expertise on any matter relating to the strategy. The Group's first discussion paper on "The Challenges of Convergence" identified fifteen concrete challenges, stimulating debate that called for the Commission's consideration (i2010

162 The working-groups were: WG1 ICT Uptake (32 permanent members + 7 *ad hoc* participants); WG2 IPR for competitiveness and innovation (45 permanent members + 7 *ad hoc* participants); WG3 Innovation in R&D, manufacturing and services (36 permanent members + 7 *ad hoc* participants); WG4 SMEs and entrepreneurship (33 permanent members); WG5 Skills and employability (24 permanent members); WG6 Achieving a Single Market (32 permanent members) (CEC, 2006l).

High-Level Group, 2006a). Other examples of High-Level Groups that have shaped ICT regulation in similar ways include the Information Society High-Level Expert Group under the chairmanship of Martin Bangemann (see Section 4.1 above), and the High-Level Group on the Lisbon Strategy, which was chaired by Wim Kok (see Section 4.3 above).

5.2.3 Direct lobbying

Since 1987 the EU has sought to emulate the democratic principles of the Member States by increasing the authority and powers of the European Parliament (EP) (Garrett and Tsebelis, 2000:9-38). Given its newfound vital role in approving European legislation and setting the EU budget, attempts to lobby the EP may be expected to become more frequent in the future. Interested parties will likely either directly approach individual MEPs or try indirectly to influence their decisions. (In the past, industry groups have usually appealed to the European Court of Justice as a last resort, to influence the policy process when other approaches proved unsuccessful.)

Direct lobbying has its limitations. Lobbyists, Commission staff, MEPs, and senior public services officials have come under pressure to become more transparent and accountable in their dealings with each other and with the public. Whereas in the US lobbying is regulated by law under the Foreign Agents Registry Act (1938) and the Federal Regulation of Lobbying Act (1946), the European approach differs somewhat (Anonymous, 2001:6). In contrast to the US, the Commission has created an open register of lobbyists in hopes of achieving greater transparency. This voluntary database, known as CONECCS for "Consultation, the European Commission and Civil Society",[163] compiles information on European "civil society organisations" and their interplay with the EU. In addition, the Council of Ministers and the Commission maintain registers of accredited lobbying companies who are allowed fairly open access to both institutions (Anonymous, 2001:9). In 1992 the EU adopted a voluntary code of conduct for profit-making lobbying organisations such as public affairs firms, business consultancies and law firms (Philip and Gray, 1996:xxi). Moreover, in July 1998 the EP required MEPs to declare all major gifts in kind or "services" received from interest groups, including administrative or research support. These measures try to control and channel stakeholder pressure, in particular from dominant business organisations or lobbying groups. This is needed because the consultative process depends on "multi-stakeholder" input to remain impartial – which has not always been guaranteed in the past.

One development with impact on direct lobbying has been the Commission's Green Paper COM(2006)194 of 3 May 2006 on the "European Transparency Initiative" (CEC, 2006q), which has sparked a debate over transparency in the three modules for dealing with external influence: (1) registration of lobbyists,[164] (2) the Commission's minimum standards for

163 230 interest groups have registered for the policy area "Enterprise", 133 for "Internal Market" and 57 for "Information Society" (Europa website – Civic Society, 2007).

164 In the European Transparency Initiative Green Paper COM(2006)194, lobbying was defined as "activities carried out with the objective of influencing the policy formulation and decision-making process of the European institutions. The Commission explicitly underlines the legitimate and useful role of lobbying activities in a democratic system" (page 5).

consultation, and (3) the disclosure of information about the beneficiaries of EU funds under shared management. The Commission consulted widely on this Green Paper: an overview of the more than 160 responses received was published in Commission Staff Working Document SEC(2007)360. On the same day the Commission adopted a Communication COM(2007)127 titled "Follow-up to the Green Paper 'European Transparency Initiative' " (CEC, 2007e), which set out the next steps the Commission would take. The Green Paper called for sound relations with lobbyists through their registration and their adherence to a code of conduct. "Public affairs consultancies, corporate lobby units ('in-house representatives'), NGOs, think-tanks, trade associations and law firms" were "encouraged to join the register and offered the opportunity to indicate to which [expertise] category they belonged" (CEC, 2007e:3). Applicants for the register automatically "have to subscribe to a code of conduct, which would be enforced credibly and transparently" (CEC, 2006q:8). A monitoring scheme and "sanctions … in the event of incorrect registration and/or breach of the code of conduct" were also implemented (CEC, 2007e:3). On 27 May 2008 the Commission published the final draft of its Communication COM(2008)323 on "The European Transparency Initiative: A framework for relations with interest representatives (Register and Code of Conduct)" (CEC, 2008a). Accompanying measures have been implemented, such as making available an informational register of public consultations on the "Your Voice in Europe" website. The Commission also relaunched online its register of interest representatives (now called the Transparency Register) on 23 June 2008.[165]

It is important to note here that the nature of lobbying has changed over the past 20 years. According to David Coen, "[T]he timing, take up, and the style of [lobbying] activity have altered as EU procedural rules have changed and EU interests and functionaries learnt to trust one another" (Coen, 2007b:9). Today the Commission enforces a "high level of transparency" to ensure that the Union is "open to public scrutiny and accountable for its work" (CEC, 2006q:2). Many lobbyists have endorsed measures like codes of conduct, consultation standards, and voluntary registration. This shows that even classical lobbying is moving away from adversarial, zero-sum advocacy in the direction of a consensus-building style of public consultation which seeks policy solutions which enhance the welfare of all stakeholders.

5.2.4 Funded programmes and initiatives

The Green Paper COM(2007)161 on "The European Research Area: New Perspectives" concluded that national R&D programmes and initiatives over the past decade have evolved toward richer and more coherent, but also more complex policy mixes (CEC, 2007f). Member States are increasingly taking a multi-annual, strategic approach to R&D, creating a more

165 On 11 August 2009 2,123 interest representatives were registered, consisting of 125 professional consultancies/law firms, 1,175 in-house lobbyists and trade associations, 597 NGOs and think tanks, and 226 "other" organisations; of which 1,004 were registered with DG "Enterprise", 1,038 with "Internal Market", and 642 with DG "Information Society" (Europa website – Civic Society, 2009). (Note that lobbyists may register in multiple policy areas.) On 23.6.2008 the Commission had re-launched its online register of interest representatives at http://ec.europa.eu/civil_society/index_en.htm.

stable and predictable research environment that is inherently long-term like the Framework Programmes at European Level. The UK, for example, with its Science and Innovation Investment Framework 2004-2014 is tackling research and its broader innovation aspects in an integrated manner (CEC, 2007h). As the Survey results have shown, participants in national and European publicly funded programmes have been using their involvement therein to expand their networking, to get involved in regulatory policy and standards initiatives at an earlier stage, and thus to influence policy output.

Other important vehicles of stakeholder participation are programmes and initiatives of the EU. As elaborated in Chapter Four, in Section 4.3 on "Europe's vision: EU policy objectives", the European Council has put research, innovation and competitiveness high on its agenda ever since the launch of the Lisbon Strategy. Europe-wide programmes and initiatives are considered key to the Strategy's successful implementation. Chapter Four inventoried some of the important programmes established by the EU Treaties to enhance infrastructure and collaboration on R&D, including ESPRIT, RACE, ACTS, TEN and CORDIS. Also covered were the recent policy initiatives and action plans under the Framework Programmes, such as the telematics programmes (FP5), the eEurope Action Plan (FP6), and the IST programme (FP6).

On 1 January 2007 the Seventh Framework Programme (2007-2013) was launched and diverse European initiatives were introduced in support. Under FP7 the European Commission set up the first Europe-wide public-private partnerships (PPPs), the so-called "Joint Technology Initiatives" (JTIs).[166] Funded through the pooling of capital from the private sector, Member States, and the EU, JTIs are intended to create an integrated European Research Area (ERA) driven by industry needs and focussed on clear, joint, pan-European technological and economic objectives.

These programmes and initiatives offer industry and other stakeholders a good opportunity to influence the policy agenda. In particular, ICT-rich e-Government initiatives offer stakeholders and the general public opportunities to participate and directly influence public bureaucracies and their policy decisions (Chadwick and May, 2003:271-300). At the 2007 business summit in Brussels, Mr Potočnik, European Commissioner for Science and Research, was sustained by all panellists in saying that the new instruments will facilitate competitiveness and mobility between research disciplines (Anonymous, 2007c:11; European Business Summit, 2007; European Business Summit website, 2007).

Shortly afterwards, the Commission published a Green Paper on "the European Research Area" (CEC, 2007q), which sparked a broad debate about how to approach creating a fruitful ERA while addressing the needs of business, the scientific community, and the public. The Commission not only requested active participation in this initiative, it relied on broad stakeholder input to build consensus about how to make ERA a success. Two of its six high concepts stressed the importance of industry to that success, stating that "excellent research

166 JTIs are legal entities which are proposed as a new way of realising public-private partnerships in relevant industrial research and development fields at the European level. They are supported by Article 171 of the Treaty on European Union: "The Community may set up joint undertakings or any other structure necessary for the efficient execution of Community research, technological development and demonstration programmes".

institutions are engaged in effective public-private cooperation and partnerships", and that "effective knowledge-sharing between public research and industry" is brought about by them. Stakeholders were empowered *via* an online consultation to engage in this debate and to express their views on overall priorities for ERA (CEC, 2007f; Europa website – European Research Area, 2007).

European policy-makers have become geared-up to consult not only industry but also the scientific community, affording scientists opportunities to share their concerns and knowledge. However, consulting under time pressure with an ever larger number of experts, on issues of ever growing complexity, has become ever more difficult. To the end of easing this burden, several registered scientific organisations have been set up at European Level to provide pools of technical research talent.[167]

In 2008 a new research initiative was launched: the European Institute of Innovation and Technology (EIT), intended to integrate scientific research with innovation in higher education, research and business. Integrated public-private networks knitting together universities, research organisations, and businesses are to benefit industry by facilitating access to the results of publicly funded research (Council of the European Union, 2008; Europa website – European Institute of Innovation and Technology, 2008). Business organisations, by forming PPPs that involve the public sector as a partner in funding and participating in scientific research, have an opportunity to influence the research agenda. This often conduces to flanking policies that support their research initiatives, and thus one more mechanism for influencing public policy at an early stage of the cycle. Private input into the research agenda helps to make EU-funded research more results-oriented and commercialisable. By contrast, past research culture produced projects that typically died after the public funding ran out, without adding value to the EU economy.

5.2.5 Committees

It is widely recognised that the so-called "comitology", or committees set up by the EU institutions to provide policy input, furnish an important venue for European governance. Committees "seem to be omnipotent at every stage in the decision-making process of the Union" (Christiansen and Kirchner, 2000:1). They make a critical contribution to the effectiveness of EU policy-making, providing essential arenas for specialised problem-solving and bargaining between interested actors. Committees "shape policy and play a significant role in contributing to the formulation and adoption of binding rules" (Schaefer, 1996:21). Van Schendelen estimates that the comitology as a whole counts at least 50,000 representatives from the Member States,[168] divided more or less equally between the public and private sectors (van Schendelen, 1998:5).

---

167 See Appendix Seven for a compendious list of European scientific organisations.

168 The European Commission's Comitology Register has since April 2008 furnished the public with "background information and documents relating to the work of these committees". As of August 2012 304 committees were listed in the Register and more than 22,700 related documents had been published. (Europa website – Comitology Register, 2012).

Comitology was a system of joint or "fused" control of the Commission's enforcement and implementation of EU law by committees of personnel appointed by the Member State Executives, usually the permanent bureaucracies. According to the Eurofound website, "comitology enable[d] the Member States to influence decision-making even when powers have been delegated to the Commission" (Eurofound – Comitology website, 2012). The Lisbon Treaty formally abolished comitology, rendering the Commission autonomous of Member State governments, and a European Parliament ordinance will soon replace it with a Delegated Acts regime whereby the Commission's implementation will be controlled solely through European Parliamentary oversight (*a.k.a.* "scrutiny"). Comitology is nonetheless briefly discussed here because it may still govern some EU laws which were enacted before the Lisbon Treaty came into force (Europa website - Comitology, 2012).

Four types of comitology committees may be distinguished: (1) *advisory committees* "give their opinions to the Commission, which must try to take account of them"; (2) *management committees* "intervene when implementing measures relate[d] to the management of programmes and when they have budgetary implications"; (3) *regulatory committees* "are responsible when the implementing measures relate to legislation applicable in the whole of the European Union"; (4) and *regulatory committees with scrutiny* "must allow the Council and the European Parliament to carry out a check prior to the adoption of measures of general scope designed to amend non-essential elements of a basic instrument adopted by codecision" (Europa website - Comitology, 2012). There are four comitology codes of procedure: for advisory committees, for management committees, for regulatory committees, and for common commercial policy committees.

The Council Decision on "procedures for the exercise of implementing powers conferred on the Commission (the Comitology Decision)" of 28 June 1999 decreed that certain committees, made up of national and/or European officials, were to be responsible for assisting the Commission in implementing its Directives (Council Decision, 1999b; see also Docksey and Williams, 1994:117-145). Under the procedures applicable to these committees, the Commission Services submitted draft implementing measures, and the committees delivered their opinions on these draft measures before the Commission adopted them (Council Decision, 1999b). Even though the Member States delegated to the Commission their power to implement regulations, they took care to maintain overall control, and comitology became their instrument of choice (Christiansen and Kirchner, 2000:4).

At its peak there were about 1,200 committees, subcommittees, and working parties working within the institutions of the European Communities (CEC, 2001a:142; CEC, 2007a). Examples of committees created under Community law with influence over ICT policy implementation include:

1. Scientific and Technical Research Committee (CREST)
2. European Research and Development Committee (CERD)
3. Scientific and Technical Committee (CST)
4. European Co-operation in the Field of Scientific and Technical Research (COST)

5. Advisory Committee of the Joint Research Centre (JRC)
6. Committee for the implementation of a multi-annual Community programme to make digital content in Europe more accessible, usable and exploitable (eContentPlus)
7. Committee for the implementation of a multi-annual Community programme on promoting safer use of the Internet and new online technologies (Safer Internet Plus)
8. Communications Committee (CoCom), established by the Framework Directive (2002/21/EC)
9. Radio Spectrum Committee (RSC), established by Radio Spectrum Decision (676/2002/EC), and the
10. FP7 ICT Committee, the programme committee for the execution of the specific programme "Cooperation", which implemented the Seventh Framework Programme (2007-2013) of the European Community for research, technological development and demonstration activities.

Such committees typically consist of representatives of the Member States and are chaired by a representative of the European Commission or other EU institutions. Recent developments in EU legislation include a tendency toward textual open-endedness, that is, leaving the law half-defined and in need of additional clarification and implementation measures, which may entail external expert input on specific matters (CEC, 2002t).

Yet the current comitology regulations decree that they are open only to the staffs of EU institutions and Member State representatives and national regulatory bodies, with external stakeholders allowed to attend only by invitation. Businesses must therefore "target" the national and European official members of these committees in order to persuade them to present concerns and recommendations on their behalf. The author found only very limited involvement by private stakeholders in any of these committees, whether expert committees during the policy-development stage, or working parties during the policy-decision stage, or advisory committees during the policy-implementation stage.[169]

Increasingly, comitology committees have been coming under much criticism precisely for their non-transparency and inaccessibility to stakeholders (other than Member State officials); scholars have questioned both comitology's effectiveness and its democratic legitimacy (Rhinard, 2002:185-210). Even the UK House of Lords has professed puzzlement, complaining that "who sits on them, when they meet, how they work and what they decide, is something of a mystery, except to insiders, assiduous Brussels watchers and a few academics and students" (House of Lords Select Committee on European Communities, 1999).

5.2.6 Global ICT fora

International intergovernmental organisations are in the legal sense ultimately creatures of treaty. The participation of sovereign countries in international organisations is voluntary, and the enforcement of any decisions they make even on States parties can be more difficult than at the National or European Level (Schiavone, 1997:3-5). The most influential of the international organisations are as follows.

169 For a typology of committees in the EC policy process, see Schaefer (1996).

United Nations (UN)

The international forum most interesting to stakeholders is the United Nations and its more than 30 affiliated organizations, known together as the UN system. These specialised agencies support a number of global initiatives, the most relevant of which for this study is – (besides the ITU) – the UN Commission on International Trade Law (UNCITRAL).[170] Although private businesses and their industry associations cannot be members of the UN, the EU represents the interests of European industry, having observer status at the UN and maintaining relations with several UN organs and specialised agencies. The most important platform for ICT stakeholder participation at Global Level has been the UN-sponsored World Summit on the Information Society (WSIS) (United Nations General Assembly, 2002). The WSIS in 2006 spawned a number of initiatives, such as the Global Alliance for ICT and Development (GAID), the UN Internet Governance Forum, and the ICT for Development Platform. While membership of the UN and of most of its specialised agencies is restricted to sovereigns, these initiatives in particular were designed to engage private and other Sub-national stakeholders in the UN policy dialogue and to open up opportunities for them to shape ICT policy at Global Level; evidencing a main thesis of this book, that even "traditional governmental organisations" pro-actively seek advice from businesses to help shape their ICT policies and strategy.

The second half of the second WSIS summit, held in Tunis on 16-18 November 2005, concluded with the "Tunis Agenda for the Information Society", which recognised the importance of stakeholder participation, especially in consultation, decision-making, and promotion and implementation of Internet governance in general; as well as in measures for combatting cybercrime, security threats, and "spam in particular". It encouraged both private-sector participation in the policy process and also PPPs in its implementation (WSIS, 2005).

The evidence continues to accumulate that the United Nations, particularly the UN Commission for Science and Technology for Development (CSTD), will become more accessible to business organisations in the foreseeable future. On 26 April 2007 the UN Economic and Social Council (ECOSOC) sanctioned the participation of businesses and NGOs at the 10th CSTD session, an intergovernmental meeting held in Geneva on 25 May 2007. Business organisations, once accredited to the WSIS, were permitted to participate in sessions of the 10th CSTD on an exceptional basis, without prejudice to the established rules of procedure (UNESCO, 2007a and 2007b). Paragraphs 14 to 17 of ECOSOC Resolution 2006/46 laid down that civil society, in particular the business sector, and first and foremost SMEs and industry associations receiving accreditation from the WSIS, should be mobilised so as to ensure their meaningful and effective participation in future events (UNESCO, 2006).

The 10th session of the CSTD in fact gave international ICT businesses like Nokia, Orange, Oracle, and Sun Microsystems the opportunity to present their views on taxation, spectrum management, deregulation, interoperability, research funding, and other ICT-related issues. The conference concluded with the adoption by consensus of a Draft Decision and

170 For further examples of UN bodies, as well as well-established special interest groups and conferences that facilitate and promote further integration of ICT and trade, see Appendix Seven: Level 4: Public-sector and non-profit organisations.

Draft Resolution, for submission to the ECOSOC. This declared that ICT has "a vital role in development, but [that] massive investments and the involvement of the private sector" are also needed (UNESCO, 2007c:10). This suggests that the influence of private stakeholders has impacted the development philosophy of the conference (UN Commission of Science and Technology for Development, 2007a, 2007b; United Nations, 2007).

International Telecommunications Union (ITU)

The ITU, founded in 1865, is the oldest of all intergovernmental organisations.[171] It is divided into three core sectors: radiocommunications (R), telecommunications standardisation (TS), and telecommunications development (TD), providing a platform for both governments and the private sector to collaborate on the coordination of international telecommunications networks and services. ITU is the most active global organisation in ICT regulation and standardisation, hosting every month an average of 20-30 workshops and conferences covering topics ranging from radio spectrum regulation through interconnection and network issues to satellite technology. Sector Members (non-governmental stakeholders) may actively participate in these meetings, at which both official decision-makers and potential commercial partners engage in discussions that may eventuate in commercial, financial or technical opportunities, and joint ventures. As participation in most meetings is open to all ITU members, many international ICT businesses have joined the ITU (Schiavone, 1997:178-180). Advisory groups and consensus-building assemblies facilitate the representatives of States Parties, Sector Members, and regulators to participate in the setting of priorities and the formulation of strategies[172] (ITU Members website, 2007). The ITU's most important event is its annual World Conference on International Telecommunications. The ITU monitors the development of the ICT industry and facilitates co-operation between other global organisations; consequently, it has become a major driver of ICT initiatives (ITU Events website, 2007). For example, it played a leading role in the preparation and organisation of the WSIS. The ITU also organises other multi-stakeholder initiatives, such as the annual "ITU Telecom" global conference.

---

171 ITU membership includes 191 Member States, over 600 Sector Members (membership includes 27 UK based organisations, such as BBC, BT plc, Cable & Wireless plc, Ericsson UK, Hutchison 3G UK Ltd, Inmarsat Ltd, Lucent Technologies UK Ltd, Nokia UK Ltd, Nortel Networks, O2, Orange, SES Satellite (Gibraltar) Ltd, Vodafone Group Services Ltd, VT Communications Ltd), Regional and other International Organizations, Regional Telecommunication Organizations, Intergovernmental Organizations Operating Satellite Systems, 140 Associates (participants in study groups) and over 180 Regulators (the UK is represented by Ofcom). (International Telecommunications Union members website, accessed June 2007).

172 ITU membership includes 191 Member States, over 600 Sector Members (including 27 UK based organisations, such as BBC, BT plc, Cable & Wireless plc, Ericsson UK, Hutchison 3G UK Ltd, Inmarsat Ltd, Lucent Technologies UK Ltd, Nokia UK Ltd, Nortel Networks, O2, Orange, SES Satellite (Gibraltar) Ltd, Vodafone Group Services Ltd, VT Communications Ltd), regional and other international organisations, regional telecommunication organisations, intergovernmental organisations operating satellite systems, 140 Associates (participants in study groups), and over 180 Regulators (the UK is represented by Ofcom).

Organisation for Economic Co-operation and Development (OECD)

The OECD's Directorate for Science, Technology and Industry (STI) is another intergovernmental organisation at Global Level that welcomes the input of private stakeholders. It provides Member State governments with analytical bases for policy formulation and with advice on the scientific, technological and industrial situation. The STI claims to provide "a forum for governments, business, civil society and academia for constructive dialogue on how best to design and implement policies to sustain growth in knowledge-based economies" (OECD, 2006; OECD website – STI department, 2007). The OECD hosts events, working groups, and a series of specialist committees such as the Industry Committee, the Committee on International Investment and Multinational Enterprise, and the Trade Committee. If no suitable bodies exist on a specific issue, the OECD may establish an *Ad Hoc* Task Force, such as the *Ad Hoc* Group on the Steering and Funding of Research Institutions. Any number of OECD committees may get involved in the preparation of OECD guidelines and recommendations for the benefit of all kinds of organisations on all Levels of governance. In providing these services the OECD welcomes input from non-OECD countries, the IMF and World Bank, business organisations, trade unions, and other interested parties (OECD, 1999b). The OECD disseminates the results of its policy consultations and other activities in the form of "outlooks" and "scorecards", industry and market reports, best practices guides, guidelines, statistical surveys, and case studies and databases.[173]

The OECD's global guidance has assisted governments, businesses and consumers in doing business online; in conserving privacy when storing personal data electronically and preventing unauthorised disclosure of it; in formulating codes of company conduct; and in compliance with data protection regulation.[174] The OECD has also published sundry reports covering matters as diverse as checklists for the development of anti-spam regulations; law

173 Key publications (categorised) include: (1) *Outlooks and scorecards*: the annual "OECD Science, Technology and Industry Outlook", a comprehensive review of key trends in science, technology and innovation policy, and includes statistics on R&D funding, patents, research projects and other indicators of innovative performance; the annual "Reports on Consumer Policy"; "OECD Communications Outlook" (2005); "OECD Information Technology Outlook" (2006); the annual "OECD Science, Technology and Industry Scoreboard", which presents internationally comparable data on the knowledge-based economy. (2) *Reports* (more than 500): *e.g.* "OECD Principles and Guidelines for Access to Research Data from Public Funding" (2007), "Classifying ICT Services" (2007); "Seizing the Benefits of ICT in a Digital Economy" (2003). (3) *Best practices*: *e.g.* "Report of the OECD Task Force on Spam: Anti-Spam Toolkit of Recommended Policies and Measures" (2006); "OECD Recommendation on Cross-Border Co-operation in the Enforcement of Laws against Spam" (2006); "Guide to Measuring the Information Society" (2005). (4) *Guidelines*: *e.g.* "OECD Guidelines for the Security of Information Systems and Networks: towards a culture of security" (2002); "OECD Guidelines on the Protection of Privacy and Transborder Flows of Personal Data" (2004); "Privacy Online: OECD Guidance on Policy and Practice" (2004); "OECD Guidelines for Consumer Protection in the Context of Electronic Commerce" (1999). (5) *Statistical surveys*: *e.g.* "OECD Statistics Catalogue" (2006); "OECD Input-Output tables" (2006); "Compendium of Patent Statistics" (2006); "OECD Broadband Statistics" (2006). (6) *Case studies*: *e.g.* "e-Commerce Business Impacts Project: Italy, banking" (2001). (7) *Databases*: *e.g.* "OECD Telecommunications Database" (2003).

174 For details of OECD on this topic, see the Regulatory Compliance Matrix.

enforcement; identification of culpable parties; handling of complaints; gathering of evidence; setting of regulatory priorities; determining fines, sanctions and remedies; and many other issues related to spam (in this instance).[175]

OECD principles are not legally binding unless actually adopted by Member States; they are nevertheless always very influential. OECD works closely with the European Commission[176] to raise awareness about ICT issues – a "partnership" reflected in senior Commission representatives' regular attendance at OECD workshops (Liikanen, 2004).

Business organisations have no significant direct input in OECD proceedings; however, they do get to influence OECD proceedings through the Business and Industry Advisory Committee (BIAC), an organisation independent of but officially recognised by the OECD. Its member organisations include national Chambers of Commerce, employer's confederations and industry confederations – a fact which highlights the importance to individual businesses of membership of industry associations. Its 34 standing committees and task forces mirror all policy issues covered by the OECD, providing members with information on OECD policies and their implications for business and industry (Business and Industry Advisory Committee website, 2006).

World Trade Organisation (WTO)

The World Trade Organisation is the main international body addressing norms to its Member States on matters of trade in goods produced by private businesses. One of the main achievements in the ICT sector is the WTO General Agreement on Trade in Services (GATS) in telecommunications, which has encouraged competition in the global telecoms market. Since only states or customs unions can become members of the WTO, the views of industry and commerce have to be presented by Member-State representatives. The EU, which is defined in trade terms as "a customs union with a single external trade policy and tariff" (World Trade Organisation website, 2007), is a WTO member in its own right; the European Commission represents EU interests at WTO meetings. While trade policy negotiations officially take place at Member-State level only, advice from business organisations, consumers and NGOs is taken into account during negotiations (World Trade Organisation website, 2007).

International Chamber of Commerce (ICC)

The main *private* organisation representing business interests on the Global Level is the International Chamber of Commerce (ICC), which comprises industry experts and business leaders in addition to companies, industry associations and national Chambers of Commerce. According to its Factsheet, the ICC "has unrivalled authority in making rules that govern the conduct of business across borders. Although these rules (such as Incoterms and the

175 For details of OECD on this topic, see the Regulatory Compliance Matrix.

176 Supplementary Protocol No. 1 to the Convention on the OECD provides that "the Commission of the European Communities shall take part in the work of the Organisation. The European Commission thus takes part in the meetings of the Council of the OECD and in the work of all the other bodies of the Organisation".

Uniform Customs and Practice for Documentary Credits) are voluntary, they are observed in countless thousands of transactions every day and have become part of the fabric of international trade" (ICC, 2012). The ICC hosts a specialist group on ICT matters, the ICC Commission on e-Business, IT and Telecoms (EBITT), whose appointees have expertise on the public policy aspects of ICTs. They develop business strategies, policies and procedures concerning ICTs and e-Commerce for other ICC members (e-Business, IT and Telecoms website, 2006). Using a consensual decisional process, EBITT addresses such varied matters as telecom liberalisation, trade-related matters, information and network security, consumer confidence in e-transactions, data protection and privacy, cybercrime, and business law. As the author learned from interviews conducted in the course of his own research, the ICC is deeply involved in developing self-regulatory rules and best practices at Global Level across the gamut; including, in the ICT field for example, digital tools like Internet applications to help companies negotiate contracts online. These feature built-in security coding in addition to model contract clauses and the so-called INCOterms (International Commercial terms), or standard ICC terms of trade (Astrup, 2003; ICC, 2002b).

Secondarily, the ICC constitutes an advocacy interface between its members and concerned governments and intergovernmental organisations (ICC, 2003). It seeks to influence national governments through its network of national committees. Evidently, the ICC has been successful in representing "business views" to governments and global organisations. To take but one example gleaned from the author's own interviews, at the 2003 WSIS, EBITT presented a "Compendium on ICT and e-Business policy and practice" which furnished ICC recommendations to ICT policy-makers[177] (Farrell, 2003).

At the Global Level, the ICC's International Secretariat has links to many intergovernmental organisations. Representatives of the OECD's STI, for example, confirmed in an interview that the ICC is that Directorate's main interface with business organisations (Dryden, 2003). ICC representatives participate heavily in international conferences, and annually present its members' views on policy issues to the G-8, and on copyright and trade law to the WIPO and UNCITRAL, amongst others (ICC, 2003:4-6). The ICC also advises the WTO on investment and trade liberalisation matters. The ICC uses the media and other public fora to influence governments concerning the multi-lateral trade negotiations carried on by the WTO. For example, the ICC conveys business support for further trade liberalisation through newspaper articles and press interviews in addition to policy recommendations provided directly to the WTO (*e.g.* ICC recommendations for the Doha Agenda, May 2004; Qatar ministerial conference, June 2001). The evidence suggests that the ICC is a powerful international association, notwithstanding that national Chambers of Commerce enjoy a more numerous membership.

177 Marina Farrell presented together with Ayesha Hassan (Senior Policy Manager) ICC's policy statements and responses to specific ICT and e-business policy initiatives at the WSIS, which covered *e.g.* Broadband Deployment, Storage of traffic data for law enforcement purposes and the impact of Internet content regulations.

5.3 CONCLUSIONS: KEY LESSONS LEARNED

The findings presented in this Chapter support the conclusion that the EU institutions neither view ICT regulation as merely a correction of market failure, nor conceive the European regulator as having sole control over changes to the regulatory environment; rather, the EU actually takes on board the recommendations of diverse stakeholders operating at multiple Levels. This, in turn, supports the further conclusion that the EU's ICT policy process is actually based on the public interest, at least elite pluralism, and on certain deliberative democratic principles such as transparency.

The findings presented in this Chapter – combined with the findings presented in Chapter Four culminating in the Regulatory Compliance Matrix – support the Stakeholder Action Matrix presented in Section 1.5.4 above, evidencing the involvement of ICT stakeholders on all Levels of governance so far identified. The Chapter conclusions may be itemised as follows.

Firstly, the empirical evidence presented in this Chapter shows that stakeholders are operative and exert influence on all Levels of governance. To bring structure to the investigation of this complex process and to enable better theorisation, the author has grouped the stakeholders into four empirically tested Advocacy Coalition Types: (1) Individual advocates, (2) Public-sector and non-profit organisations, (3) Industry-focussed associations, and (4) Project groups.

Secondly, Information Society "policy ownership" is no longer considered exclusively national. Considering the number of stakeholders at the European Level, and that around 80% of all regulations and standards in Europe bear an EU stamp (Hix, 2005:4), policy ownership is now vested in the EU institutions. This "forces" stakeholders to operate on multiple Levels of governance, and indeed, this is confirmed by the finding that the same Advocacy Coalition Types are operative on multiple Levels.

Thirdly, due to the globalised nature of ICT, international organisations have increasingly influenced the European regulator by providing guidelines and recommendations, and by creating new fora and initiatives to collect and digest stakeholder input at the Global Level. Nevertheless, the relative influence and power of international organisations varies significantly, depending on their organisational structure, available budgets, and number of staff employed (Chadwick, 2006:220-121). Hence, international organisations often try to increase their influence by stretching their responsibilities, or by adopting enhanced policy agendas. For example, the ITU was competing to become the dominant driver of the Information Society agenda when it organised the World Summits on the Information Society in 2003 and 2005 (Chadwick, 2006:221).

Industry, and in particular large business organisations that operate globally, have recognised the importance of these changes, and that European regulation must fit within the international framework for "governing" ICT now under construction globally, and have adjusted their regulatory strategies accordingly. International organisations, although generally closed to private stakeholders, have begun to consult some of the biggest of the latter. Those European ICT stakeholders who have had an opportunity to participate in global fora and initiatives have thereby been empowered to influence EU regulation, at least indirectly. This being so, other stakeholders ignore the Global Level at their peril.

Moreover, the evidence in this Chapter supports the Policy Influence-Timing Model as presented in Section 1.4 above. In mapping the multiple channels of influence used by stakeholders to influence the policy process, the existence of channels enabling influence at the earliest stages of the EU policy process – issue emergence and policy formulation – has been established.

A number of conclusions follow concerning the EU regulatory regime. *Firstly*, regulating a dynamic market driven by innovation, technological advances and fierce competition necessitates expert input and wide consultation of diverse interest groups. As shown in this Chapter, industry is involved in all stages of policy making – from even before agenda-setting to retrospective review.

Secondly, broad consultation has almost certainly increased the input of smaller voices from all Levels, leading to a higher degree of democratic legitimacy and to a fresh impetus in the policy process. These developments represent a clear change to the Commission's technocratic style, and to the "lobbying culture" that in most observers' view dominated European politics before 1990. The more transparent style of consultation has created many opportunities for broader stakeholder participation in making European ICT policy at all stages of the policy process. Even so, because of their tighter financial situation and sparser staffing, small organisations, if they would influence policy effectively, must adopt a different approach to large organisations. The factors distinguishing large organisations, such as deep knowledge in specific regulatory domains and more personal contacts with the officials who make policy and implementing regulations, are beyond small organisations' reach. Therefore, small organisations are well advised to join industry associations and Chambers of Commerce, where their individual views can be gathered and "batched" by the associations' officers, who are better connected.

In sum, this Chapter has shown that in order to push the Information Society project forward to success the Commission stands in need of essential support from industry. The fact is that the Commission's formal empowerment and legal entitlement to push the EU agenda forward is untrammelled on only one front, to wit, market liberalisation (including market integration and competition). This means that often other policy dimensions such as civil society promotion and protection are at least *relatively* neglected by the work of the Commission. Hence industry is widely seen as the perennial winner of any competition for influence over European ICT policy and regulation. The next Chapter presents in depth the views of this all-important stakeholder group concerning issues of participation in the European ICT regulatory processes.

CHAPTER 6

THE SURVEY AND ANALYSIS OF RESULTS

This Chapter presents a quantitative analysis of the data collected from 202 respondents, who participated in the Survey on Stakeholder Participation in Information and Communication Technologies (ICT) Policies, Regulations and Standards administered between April and September 2004. Some descriptive results, such as means and percentages of yes/no answers, are contained in the Survey Report and Data Sheets in Appendix Four.[178] No recent survey known to the author has the scope of this Survey, and its results may be supposed accurate insofar as Advocacy Coalition Types and their beliefs are stable and long-lasting; as the author witnessed first-hand over fourteen years of participant observation.

This Survey was designed to test the theory that stakeholders, particularly large businesses, are involved in regulatory processes on all Levels of governance, by seeking evidence of any aspect of this phenomenon. Although it is true that all stakeholders may not have access to every venue, the variety of channels nevertheless offers plenty of opportunities for all stakeholders to participate. The Survey was also designed to find out which channels stakeholders do in fact use to participate, and to generate quantitative data evidencing this. Finally, the Survey was designed to explore which of the several Advocacy Coalition Types the respondents fall into.

The original goal was to collect current quantitative data attesting to active stakeholder participation in the policy and standards-setting processes; to investigate the views of stakeholders; and to learn more about the forms of their interaction with the regulator (*i.e.* the European Commission), and how they seek to influence its decisions. This Survey included questions about the following issues:

1. how organisations perceive ICT regulations and standards
2. how stakeholders participate in decision-making processes and influence regulations
3. what the stakeholders' regulatory objectives are; and
4. how the European regulator and European standards-setting bodies might improve their decision-making processes.

178 A summary of the answers to open-ended questions, which were posed in order to glean qualitative insights into the views and concerns of stakeholders involved in the policy process, is included in Appendix Eight of the original publication of this survey (Reinke, 2009).

One other purpose of the Survey was to test specific aspects that the author may have found in the questionnaire responses (or in the scholarly literature) that suggests a relationship exists between organisational size and participation in stakeholder activities. For this purpose, organisational size may be taken as the *independent variable* and participation the *dependent variable*.

Starting with this general null hypothesis – *no significant variance was found between various organisations and their characteristics concerning (aspects of) their participation in the regulatory process* – ensured that a cautious and critical approach was adopted when conducting statistical tests on the data (Hussey, 1997:126).

The Methodology Chapter (Three) described the overall Survey strategy and the methods of collecting primary and secondary data. It also described the development of the Survey questionnaire, the selection of the sample size, and the distribution of the questionnaire to the targeted group of respondents.

6.1 STATISTICAL METHODS

This Section summarises the main statistical methods used to analyse the raw data received from the Survey. A result was defined as significant if it is unlikely to have occurred by chance, given that the null hypothesis is not false. The author used a confidence level of 95%, which corresponds to a p-value/significance level of 0.05. The smaller the p-value, the more significant the result is said to be. So a test that yields a p-value less than 0.05 is considered significant (*i.e.* the null hypothesis is rejected).

Variance was defined as the mean of the squared deviations. The variance used every single data item, but yields an answer in squared units. To avoid this the units were de-squared by taking the square root of the variances. This result is known as the *standard deviation*; the wider the distribution spread over the dimension studied, the larger the standard deviation. A *normal distribution* is one particular probability distribution often found to describe accurately enough a random distribution of values for a variable of a population. The frequency curve of such a normally distributed population, known as a normal curve, has a symmetrical "bell" shape.

The following statistical methods were used to analyse the Survey raw data:

- *Arithmetic mean* ($\bar{x}$): the standard arithmetic "average" of a frequency distribution, often simply called the *mean* (sum divided by the number of cases).
- *Median:* value above and below which half of the cases fall; also referred to as the 50th percentile.
- *Pearson's (2-sided) chi-square test* (χ^2): statistical procedure that tests a null hypothesis that the relative frequencies of occurrence of observed events follow a specified frequency distribution. This test is also used to test if 2 variables are independent or not, based on frequency counts.
- *Analysis of Variance (ANOVA)*: procedure that tests if there is a significant difference in the mean value of a particular quantity across different sub-groups of the data (e.g.

male/female, France/UK/Germany, *etc.*). The null hypothesis is that no difference exists in the population. It can also test for interaction effects between different groupings (*e.g.* gender with country).

- *Standard deviation* (sd): the square root of the variance, by definition. Smaller deviations imply that there is a higher degree of consensus between the responses.
- *Levene test*: procedure to test the homogeneity of variances of different groupings. The null hypothesis is that the variances of the different groupings are equal. This is useful for testing that data is appropriate for ANOVA, which assumes equal variances of underlying groupings of the (statistical) population.
- *Pearson correlation coefficient* (r): a measure of the linear relationship between two variables x and y. A positive value implies the variables are positively related, *i.e.* an increase in one variable usually implies an increase in the other variable. A negative value implies a negative or inverse relationship.
- *Linear Regression Analysis* (R^2): estimates which coefficients of a linear equation involving one or more independent variables best predict the value of the dependent variable. The R^2 value tells us how well the model fits the data, specifically how much of the variance in the dependent variable is described by the model.

6.2 METHOD OF QUANTITATIVE ANALYSIS OF SURVEY RESULTS

In order to make the opinions of the respondents comparable, various numerical indices were used to gauge their answers to most of the questions; for example, the answer-values for Question 2 were: "very strong involvement" = 100; "strong involvement" = 75; "involvement" = 50; "passive involvement" = 25; and "non-involvement" = 0. The method of comparing different groups was thus by comparing the mean answer-value indices within each group. The confidence interval of the following data is very nearly +/-6.8%, based on the return of 202 out of 450 questionnaires, and assuming a total population "out there" of 10,000 participant stakeholders (Creative Research Systems website, 2009). This is probably a low estimate.

The respondent organisations were grouped into three size ratings: "large" organisations = at least 500 employees; "medium-sized" organisations = 50 to 499 employees, and "small" organisations = 1 to 49 employees. The author also grouped organisations according to whether they were "for-profit" (commercial) or "non-profit". The latter included government organisations, universities, and NGOs.

For the quantitative data analysis the author focussed on those Survey questions which he believed were the most informative for answering the research question and which provided valuable data for supporting the theory and models. As the amount of data gathered through the Survey was quite large, it was necessary to focus in on the data that best explained stakeholder activities and behaviours. Consequently, some questions were excluded from the assessment, *e.g.* the "warm-up" question (Question 1), or questions where insufficient answers (less than 50% response rate) were received, *e.g.* Question 12 about the eCommunications Framework.

Supporting documentation includes the Data Sheets in Appendix Four (Survey Report) which contain the cumulative Survey results.[179]

The statistical analysis classified the respondents' answers along two dimensions: (1) organisational type, and (2) organisational size, looking for significant differences in the answers of different classes of respondent. If for-profit organisations are generally more driven by commercial interests, while non-profits exhibit interests in other matters and dependency on government funding, the author was interested to find out whether a different pattern would emerge in the answers of these two types of Survey respondent.

However, some limitations had to apply to the analysis and comparison of the respondents' answers according to organisational size. As the following table shows, hardly any "large" non-profit organisations took the Survey; thus, the author was obliged to restrict the analysis to for-profit organisations when comparing organisations of different sizes.

Table 6.1: Distribution of sizes of organisations

Size of Organisation	Profit	Non-profit
Small	21%	15%
Medium	26%	13%
Large	16%	N/A [2%]
Total	66%	34%

These results are based on Question 13.

6.3 DEMOGRAPHIC ANALYSIS

6.3.1 Analysis of Survey respondents

Business Sector

66% of the respondents worked for "business & industry" (blue chip companies/ICT manufacturers, software developers, network operators, telephony incumbents, technical solution providers, *etc.*); 13% for "administration and government" (City Councils, member-State government ministries, standards bodies, international organisations, *etc.*); 9% for universities (researchers, scholars); and 12% for NGOs (R&D centres, consumer associations, *etc.*).

The sample to whom questionnaires were sent was split approximately 50/50 between profit and non-profit organisations. However, the response data show that for-profit organisations returned many more questionnaires *per capita* than non-profits: for-profits were 66% of all respondents while non-profits were 34%. Figure 6.1 graphs response to the Survey by sector.

179 For statisticians and others who are interested in the SPSS tables that were generated for the statistical tests, these are presented in Appendix Seven (Results – SPSS Quantitative Data Analysis) of the original publication of this survey (Reinke, 2009).

Figure 6.1: Sector of Respondents

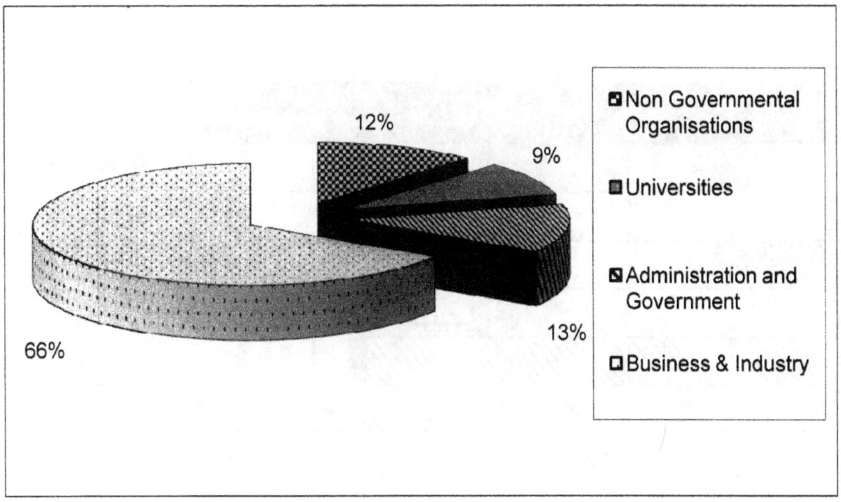

Profile of the Organisations

39% of the respondents belonged to "small" organisations (<49 employees), 24% to "medium" (50-499 employees), and 37% to "large" (>500 employees). No attempt was made to distinguish *relative* size compared to other organisations of the same type, as this would have complicated the Survey with an excessive load of assumptions. Over half (64%) reported having a European and international focus, while only 13% described themselves as "local and regional" players; 23% saw themselves as "national" players.

Most of them were headquartered in a Member State of the European Union (89%), while 7% were headquartered in the US. In the sample, American multinationals constituted the strongest influencer of European policy and standards outside the EU. All of the US-based respondents were "businesses". Looking at business organisations only, 9% were headquartered in the US. The figure below graphs the respondents' organisations' number of employees across all business sectors.

Figure 6.2: Number of Employees

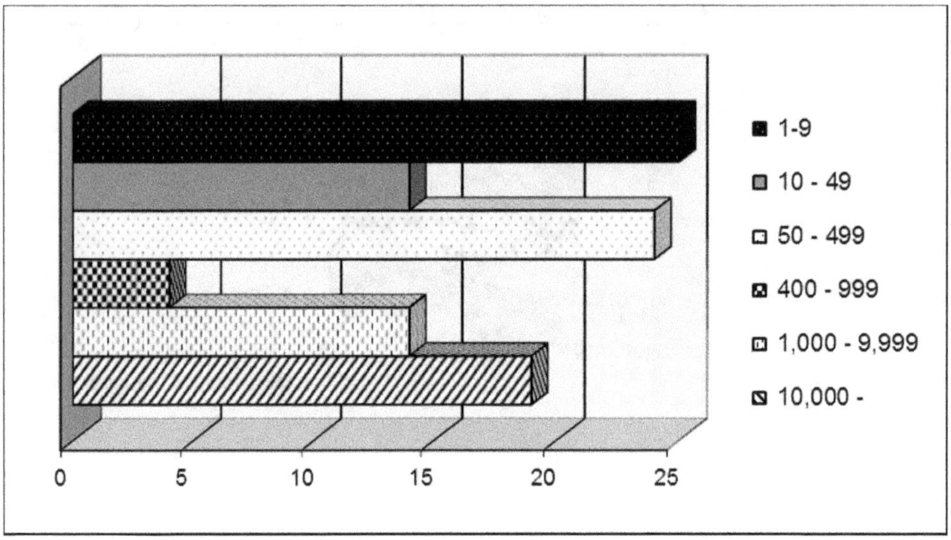

Profile of the Respondents

According to the Survey results, 96% of respondents "like to have responsibility" and 76% preferred to make business decisions instead of private decisions [or personal]. Therefore it may be concluded that the respondents were "active decision-makers". The author knew when selecting the sample that most respondents had played an active role in policy and standards-setting processes. The fact that most respondents like having responsibility hints that they are directly or indirectly involved in decision-making processes. Their commitment to decision-making is high, despite the fact that 64% believe that they endure more stress when they have to make decisions. Only 3% of the respondents were younger than 30, and 7% were older than 60. The results hint that the policy process is in fact open to all stakeholders if, as the data show, it is open to all age groups; so that seniority is not a limiting factor. The figure below graphs the respondents by age-group.

Figure 6.3: Age Groups [180]

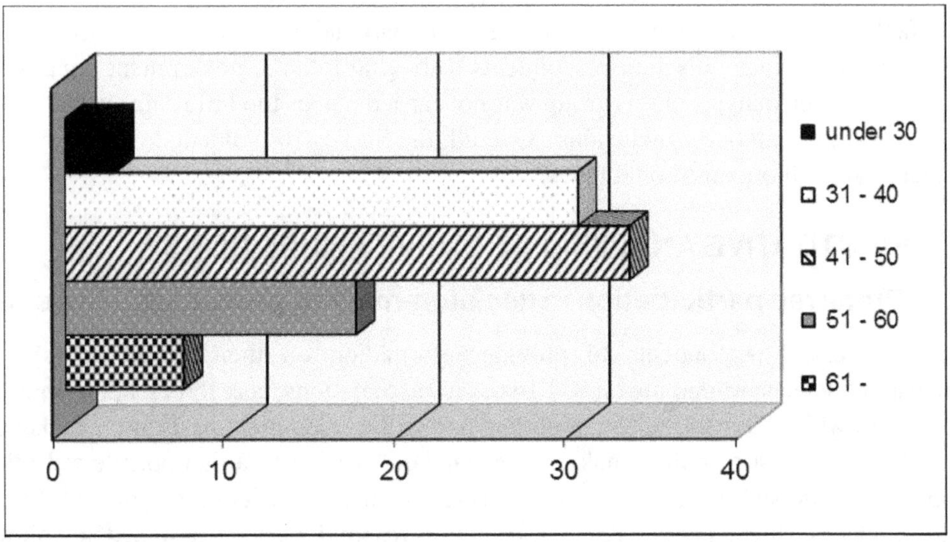

Geographic Distribution

As one might expect, most of the respondents came from the largest EU Member States: France, Germany, Italy, Spain, and the United Kingdom. It should be noted that Spain was under-represented, with only 5% of replies compared to 12-15% for the other big EU States. Belgium, with its many European and international organisations, reflected a European view more than a national one, accounting for 14% of the total respondents. 202 returned questionnaires from all 15 EU Member States were analysed for this Survey; thus, the respondent population is shown to be rather evenly distributed and represents all peoples of the EU15.

6.3.2 Size *versus* for-profit or non-profit organisation

Statistical tests revealed no significant difference between medium and non-medium organisations. Of the small organisations, 58.3% were for-profit organisations and 41.7% were non-profit organisations (see SPSS Table 1 in Reinke, 2009).[181] This difference was not statistically significant. The Survey results gave no reason to believe that small organisations are more likely to be for-profit organisations (p-value of 2-sided Chi-Square Test is 0.086, SPSS Table 2); if anything, the results showed the opposite.

For medium organisations, 66.7% were for-profit organisations and 33.3% were non-profit organisations (SPSS Table 3). Again this was not statistically significant (p-value of 2-sided Chi-Square Test is 0.874, SPSS Table 4).

180 As can be seen from this chart, the age groups are fairly normally distributed.

181 All SPSS tables mentioned in this Chapters are published in Appendix Seven of the original publication of this survey (Reinke, 2009).

Of large organisations 88.9% were for-profit and 11.1% non-profit organisations. This did constitute a significant difference (p-value of 2-sided Chi-Square Test is 0.001, SPSS Table 5), due to the fact that only a few international government organisations exist (SPSS Table 6). Since only four respondents belonging to large government organisations responded, further analysis of this group was not carried out, as too little data existed to allow statistically representative conclusions. Overall, the Survey respondents were fairly evenly distributed over all organisational types.

6.4 QUANTITATIVE ANALYSIS OF SURVEY QUESTIONS

6.4.1 Preferred participation in decision-making processes (Question2)

Question 2 asked respondents to provide information on their organisations' active participation in decision-making on ICT issues *via* associations, task forces, and committees; the results of which have formed an important part of the evidentiary basis of the Stakeholder Action Matrix. A list of policy-making and standards-setting fora that operate at National, European, and Global Levels was provided, in order to make it easier for respondents to gauge which Level was which. For each of their responses respondents were assigned the following additive numerical involvement-indices, where the word "involvement" indicates the depth of stakeholder participation. If a respondent reported on Question 2 that his organisation engaged in "active participation in policy advice", then there was assigned an index of 100 (very strong involvement); if "responses to consultations", then 75 (strong involvement); if "hosting of events", then 50 (involvement); if "participation in workshops", then 25 (passive involvement); and if "no involvement", then 0. If several of these activities were reported at once, then the indices were added together, up to a maximum of 100.

Only a descriptive analysis of the statistical means for all organisations was performed. It is evident from Figure 6.4 that, with the sole exception that Framework Programmes were preferred at European Level, organisations generally preferred industry associations to all other channels of participation (on the same Level) in regulation and standards debates. 78% reported having participated in national industry associations and 50% having contributed to issues *via* European industry associations. Approximately 30% reported having been involved in the activities of such international industry associations and interest groups as the Internet Security Forum, the WiFi-Alliance, the International Telecommunications Union, and the International Chamber of Commerce (ICC). The Survey data highlight the fact that European Programmes and Initiatives are widely participated-in (74% positive), which, in conjunction with other Survey data – such as Question 6(e) below, that 65% of organisations "participate in funded programmes" in order to "influence the policy-making process/ standards development" – supports the inference that such Programmes and Initiatives are widely considered an effective way to influence the EU's decision-making on ICT issues. Even though the work of OECD and UN organisations is highly valued (see Question 3), participation is the lowest in these international organisations, for the obvious reason that these particular organisations are less open to private (non-sovereign) stakeholders. For example, Chapter Five detailed how the OECD requires non-sovereign stakeholders who wish to voice their opinions to the OECD to join the International Chamber of Commerce

(ICC) or else – by invitation only – the Business and Industry Advisory Committee (BIAC). The following diagram allows comparison of respondents' "active participation".

Figure 6.4: Preferred channels of policy participation

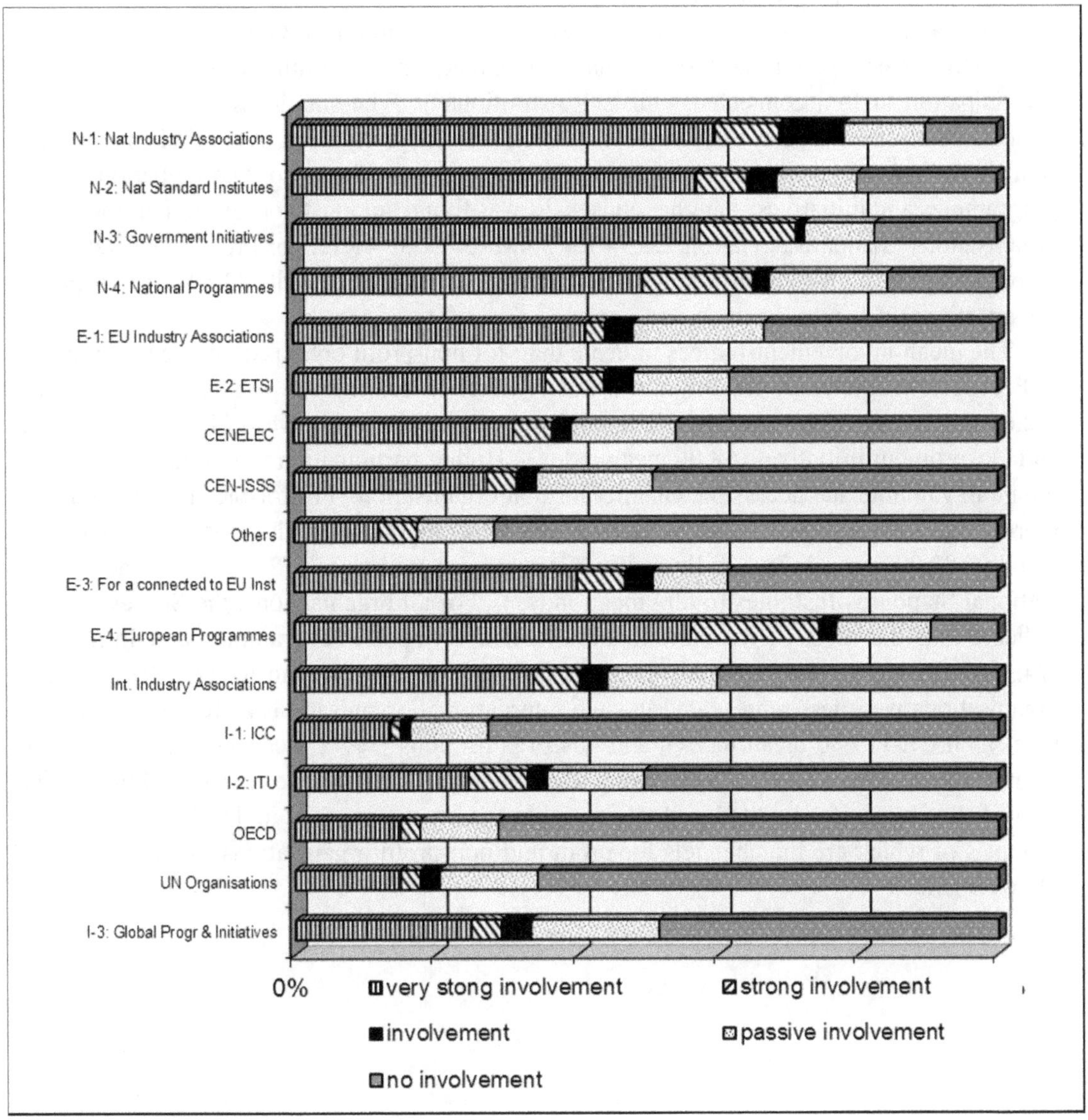

Question 2: "What is your organisation's active participation in the decision-making on ICT issues via associations, task forces, and committees?"

In this response to Question 2 about the "active participation of your organisation in the decision-making process" a significant difference was found.[182] For-profit organisations reported an average involvement-index of 80 in National Industry Associations, higher than the reported average involvement-index therein of non-profit organisations, which was 61.11 (p-value = 0.001; SPSS Table 7 and 8).

The standard deviations of the responses of all organisations to Question 2 are between 35.05 (for "participation in the International Chamber of Commerce") and 45.7 (for "participation in fora connected with EU institutions"). The smallness of this difference indicates that the degree of consensus on participation is pretty even over all channels, as a smaller deviation indicates more consensus amongst respondents. For "participation in EU programmes and initiatives" a higher consensus was found amongst non-profit than for-profit organisations (standard deviation: 22.98 for non-profits; 39.45 for for-profit organisations), who also had a higher mean involvement-index (70.53 for for-profit, 82.69 for non-profit organisations).

The mean involvement-indices indicate that, for non-profit organisations, representation in European Programmes and Initiatives was reported to be the most participated-in activity (82.69 mean index), followed by National Programmes and Initiatives (74.07 mean index) and Government Initiatives (68.00 mean index). Higher participation is assumed to indicate the more valuable and accessible channel for that organisation. For for-profit organisations, representation in National Industry Associations was reported to be the most participated-in activity (80.00 mean index), followed by Government Initiatives (72.37 mean index), and National Standards Institutes (69.09 mean index). For all organisations, the Survey results indicate that the most active participation was in European Programmes and Initiatives (74.39 mean index) and National Industry Associations (74.13 mean index). Respondent organisations were less represented in such international organisations as ICC (18.15 mean index), OECD (19.86 mean index), and UN organisations (21.91 mean index). As tabular format was deemed best for summarising a very complex dataset, the corresponding results of the other sub-questions under Question 2 have been summarised in Table 6.1 to form a synopsis of which are the channels for-profit and non-profit organisations use at all Levels of governance.

182 ANOVA was performed between profit and non-profit organisations for the mean response to Question 2. (If the ANOVA (p-value) is greater than 0.05, then we know that no significant difference exists at 95% confidence level.)

Table 6.2: Mean responses and standard deviation of responses for profit & non-profit

Question	Mean involvement index of profit organisations	Mean involvement index of non-profit organisations	Significance level of difference (ANOVA)	Standard deviation of indices (for all organisations)	Standard deviation for profit/non-profit organisations
L2 – National industry associations	80.00	61.11	*) 0.001	36.15	Profit 33.62 N-Profit 38.44
L2 – National standards institutes	69.09	37.00	*).000	45.08	Profit 42.29 N-Profit 43.52
L2 – Government initiatives	72.27	68.00	.532	39.94	Profit 39.69 N-Profit 40.73
L2 – National programmes and initiatives	63.07	74.07	.090	39.32	Profit 40.47 N-Profit 36.00
L3 – European industry associations	60.09	27.17	*) .000	44.87	Profit 45.22 N-Profit 34.89
L3 – a) ETSI	59.31	19.31	*) .000	44.64	Profit 43.08 N-Profit 34.89
L3 – b) CENELEC	49.03	19.31	*) .000	44.38	Profit 45.14 N-Profit 34.89
L3 – c) CEN ISSS	40.77	23.86	*) .028	42.89	Profit 44.93 N-Profit 35.34
L3 – Fora connected with EU Institutions	45.28	60.22	.068	**45.70**	Profit 46.56 N-Profit 42.22
L3 – European programmes and initiatives	70.54	82.69	*) .041	35.46	Profit 39.45 N-Profit 22.28

Question	Mean involvement index of profit organisations	Mean involvement index of non-profit organisations	Significance level of difference (ANOVA)	Standard deviation of indices (for all organisations)	Standard deviation for profit/non-profit organisations
L4 – International associations a) Internet Security Forum	51.39	28.26	*) .003	44.40	Profit 45.19 N-Profit 38.22
L4 – b) ICC	18.13	18.18	.994	**35.05**	Profit 35.56 N-Profit 34.35
L4 – a) ITU	35.78	35.23	.943	42.73	Profit 43.16 N-Profit 42.22
L4 – b) OECD	18.63	22.73	.537	36.66	Profit 36.17 N-Profit 38.06
L4 – c) UN organisations	19.61	27.27	.248	36.66	Profit 34.58 N-Profit 41.00
L4 –Global programmes and initiatives	35.61	34.09	.841	41.80	Profit 42.44 N-Profit 40.74

Question 2: "What is your organisation's active participation in the decision-making on ICT issues via associations, task forces and committees?"

*) Significant Difference (ANOVA < 0.5)
Note: L2 = National Level; L3 = European Level; L4 = International [Global] Level
Standard deviations have been rounded to two decimal places.

Next, the author contrasted large with small (but not medium) business organisations, comparing the mean involvement indices derived from the answers to Question 2 of small and large business organisations (SPSS Table 10). Medium business organisations were left out for contrast's sake. Interestingly, the standard deviation of the indices of large organisations' answers to the sub-question about active participation in National Industry Associations was very small (5.81), indicating a very high level of consensus on this issue. By contrast, for small businesses the standard deviation was very much larger (40.43), indicating much less consensus on the value of active participation in these associations. This is probably because membership of associations can be costly, and not only in terms of membership fees. Typically, members of industry associations, in order to extract the maximum value from membership, must send experts to attend association events. Large businesses, although not necessarily employing more experts *per capita*, are more likely to have experts "to spare", in the sense that costs for one expert are a smaller percentage of total staff costs.

The statistical significance of the differences between the standard deviations (indicating level of consensus) of small- and large-firm respondents was also reported for National Industry Associations, in the Levene Statistic = 202.244, with p-value < 0.001, which is "significant" (SPSS Table 12). The author also found statistically significant the differences in level of consensus on participation between small and large firms who were involved in National Standards Institutes (for the p-values refer to the table below), Government Initiatives, European Industry Associations, ETSI, CENELEC, the Internet Security Forum, the ITU, and Global Programmes and Initiatives. However, for these latter channels of participation, the difference in consensus level was slighter. This is easily explained by the fact that the small firms' level of consensus tends to remain low for most channels of involvement, whereas the large firms' level of consensus can vary rather drastically from channel to channel. At the very highest (Global) Level of governance, however, small firms show a higher level of consensus about involvement than large ones; but this would most likely be due to small firms' coming to a high consensus to *forgo* involvement, which is much more expensive than involvements closer to home.

For "participation in global programmes", a very small mean involvement-index for small business organisations (8.93 mean index) was noticed compared to multinational firms (59.72 index). The level of consensus on (non-)involvement amongst small firms (26.54 standard deviation) was also higher than normal on this issue. Although not as stark, the same contrast between big and small firms shows up in the answers to the other sub-questions about involvement on the Global Level; except that both sizes of firms show rather low levels of involvement in the affairs of the UN and OECD (which screen private involvement).

The foregoing analyses paint a highly consistent picture, whence it follows that bigger firms may be expected to exert even more influence at the Global Level compared with small firms, than at lower Levels of governance (where they also exert more influence); the grand inference being that large firms dominate the Industry Governance phenomenon. It is remarkable that small firms continue to participate at all in stakeholder activities – on all Levels of governance, – and *a fortiori* remarkable that they participate as much as they do.

Table 6.3: Mean responses and standard deviation of responses for large & small organisations

Question	Mean involvement index of profit organisations	Mean involvement index of non-profit organisations	Significance level of difference (ANOVA)	Standard deviation of indices (for all organisations)	Standard deviation for profit/non-profit organisations
L2 – Industry associations	98.61	62.50	*) 0.000	34.57	*) large 5.8, small 40.43
L2 – National standards institutes	93.06	35.94	*) 0.000	43.57	*) large 23.61 small 41.12
L2 Government initiatives	83.33	59.38	*) 0.009	38.52	*) large 31.62 small 42.00
L2 National programmes and initiatives	66.67	58.33	0.401	41.75	*) large 43.09 small 40.53
L3 European industry associations	82.35	57.81	*) 0.016	41.81	*) large 35.64 small 44.65
L3 a) ETSI	84.72	46.42	*) 0.000	40.45	*) large 31.78 small 40.66
L3 b) CENELEC	65.28	35.71	*) 0.010	46.02	*) large 44.83 small 42.72
L3 c) CEN ISSS	51.11	33.93	0.131	45.06	large 47.59 small 40.38
L3 Fora connected with EU institutes	54.16	38.33	0.176	47.13	large 47.25 small 46.30
L3 European programmes and initiatives	76.38	65.63	0.249	38.21	large 36.32 small 40.04

Question	Mean involvement index of profit organisations	Mean involvement index of non-profit organisations	Significance level of difference (ANOVA)	Standard deviation of indices (for all organisations)	Standard deviation for profit/non-profit organisations
L4 International industry associations a) Internet Security Forum	77.78	28.33	*) 0.000	47.13	*) large 39.54 small 41.38
L4 b) ICC	28.17	10.71	0.063	39.39	*) large 44.92 small 28.41
L4 a) ITU	48.61	25.00	*) 0.036	44.98	*) large 45.88 small 40.83
L4 b) OECD	23.61	16.07	0.448	39.06	*) large 41.81 small 35.50
L4 UN organisations	20.83	17.86	0.734	34.35	*) large 34.07 small 35.26
L4 Global programmes and initiatives	59.72	8.93	*) 0.000	44.99	*) large 44.03 small 26.54

Question 2: "What is your organisation's active participation in the decision-making on ICT issues *via* associations, task forces, and committees?"

*) Significant difference (ANOVA < 0.5)

6.4.2 Analysis of responses to stock assertions

The questionnaire presented a series of stock assertions on which respondents were invited to comment. To ensure that their responses revealed at least a tendency, the "no opinion" option was suppressed.

Opinions on EU ICT regulation and standards-setting (Question 11)

This question looked at different aspects of regulation and standards-setting, the better to understand organisations' motives for participating in the policy process. Of all stock assertions, the assertion that "EU regulation and Europe-wide applicable standards strengthen the EU ICT industry in the world" garnered the most agreement: 83% either strongly agreed or agreed. Also garnering strong support were the assertions that "EU regulation and standards are industry-orientated" (70% strongly agreed or agreed) and that "only large multinational organisations can really influence regulations" (68% strongly agreed or agreed).

The assertion garnering the least agreement was that "their organisation/company has been successful in influencing EU regulation/standards": only 32% strongly agreed or agreed. Hardly more agreement (33% strongly agreed or agreed) met the assertion that "EU ICT regulation is forcing European industry to adopt many detailed norms and regulations that we don't want and need".

To assess how much respondent stakeholders valued technologies strongly supported by EU regulatory and standards initiatives, some specific questions on GSM and UMTS were asked. 71% of the respondents agreed or strongly agreed that "the European mobile market (GSM) has been a success story (as compared to the US) because of EU telecoms regulation and liberalisation", yet only 36% strongly agreed or agreed that "UMTS (third generation of mobile phones) will be as successful as GSM". The best explanation for these seemingly contradictory data is that Europe-wide regulation can be a "double-edged sword", but in the paradoxical sense that too much success may bring-on a comeuppance. The GSM standard proved a remarkable success at just the time market liberalisation was also introduced by the Commission. The upstart telecoms operators spawned by these developments and their profit opportunities seemed a bottomless source of tax revenue to Member State governments, which proceeded to raise licence fees to such high levels that most observers now anticipate far lower profits under the new UMTS standard.

The following is a more detailed analysis of these responses. To facilitate this analysis a level-of-agreement index was assigned to respondents' answers: "strongly agree" was assigned an index of 100; "agree" an index of 66; "disagree" an index of 33; and "strongly disagree" an index of 0. This indexing enabled the author to compare the level of support given to each stock assertion by the whole population of respondents.

To start with an overview, the mean level-of-agreement indices for the whole population of respondents are presented in the following figure. These were calculated on the basis of the whole gamut of responses, from "strongly agree" to "strongly disagree". Note that an index higher than 50 means more agreement than disagreement on average, while less than 50 means more disagreement.

Figure 6.5: Opinions about EU ICT regulation and standards

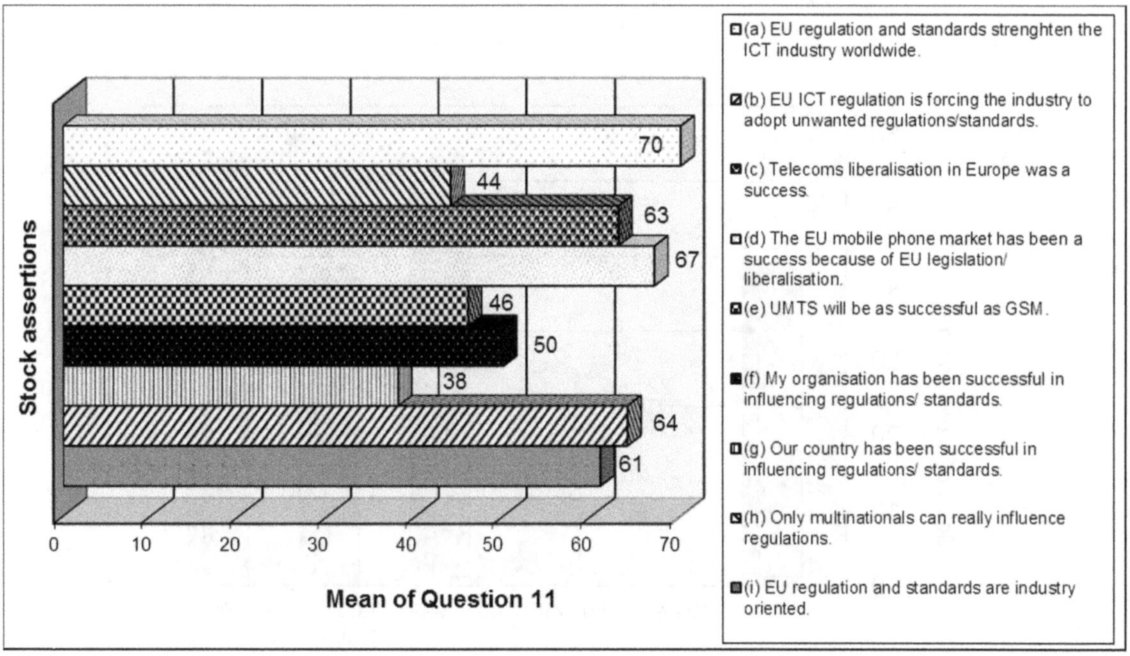

Question 11: "The following are some opinions about EU ICT regulations and standards-setting. To what extent do you agree or disagree with the following statements?"

"My organisation/company has been successful in influencing EU regulations/ standards" (Question 11f)

On the one hand, no statistically significant difference was found between the index means of for-profit (mean index = 38.89, SPSS Table 14) and non-profit organisations (34.44) in answers to the question of whether one's own organisation had successfully influenced EU regulations and standards (Question 11f). On the other hand, a small but significant positive correlation was found between the organisation's size and its perception of its own influence on EU regulations and standards (Pearsons Correlation coefficient = 0.178, with p-value = 0.019, SPSS Table 13).

For for-profit organisations this correlation was slightly stronger (Pearsons Correlation coefficient = 0.287, with a p-value = 0.001, SPSS Table 14). This implies that size matters less for non-profit organisations' self-perception. The following figure graphs the correlation between (for-profit) organisational size and perceived mean influence (SPSS Table 15).

It seems anomalous that the smallest business organisations reported such a high level of success in influencing policy outcomes. This could be explained if this category were found to include many individual advocates who achieved success due to personal factors, such as expertise or contractual nexus.

Figure 6.6: Opinion of own success at influencing EU policy (by business size)

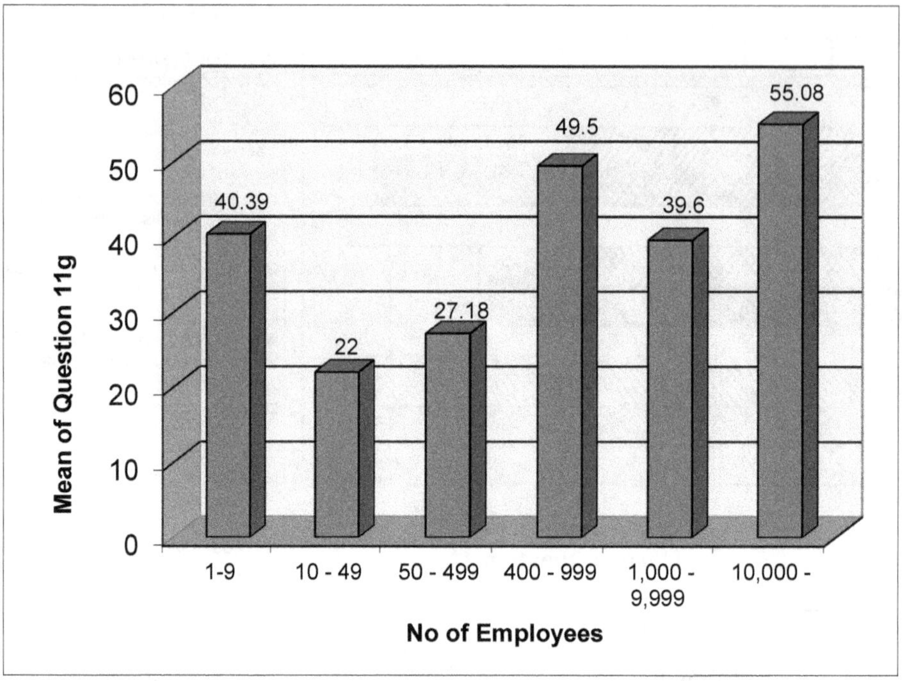

Question 11: "The following are some opinions about EU ICT regulation and standards-setting. To what extent do you agree or disagree with the following statements?"

"Only large multinational organisations can really influence regulations" (Question 11h)

The perception that "only large multinational organisations can really influence regulations" (Question 11h) is the more widespread, the smaller the business organisation. A significant negative correlation was found between the size of the business organisation and this response (Pearsons Correlation coefficient = –0.192, with a p-value = 0.035, SPSS Table 17). It was also found that the larger the responding business organisation, the less widespread was the perception that large business organisations wield all the real power over ICT regulation. The smallest for-profit organisations were found to be the most "paranoid" about the influence of large organisations. However, when "non-profits" where factored into the analysis – which included Member-State but not Commission functionaries, – the same negative correlation was not found to be significant (p-value of 0.086, SPSS Table 16); suggesting perhaps that the perception of big business influence was conditioned by the perception of smaller businesses of their own vulnerability to the "predations" of big business. Nevertheless, the fact remains that a majority of every category of respondents (including non-profits[183]) did answer that big business influence predominated.

The following figure graphs this correlation for for-profit organisations (SPSS Table 18):

Figure 6.7: Perception that business size matters (by business size)

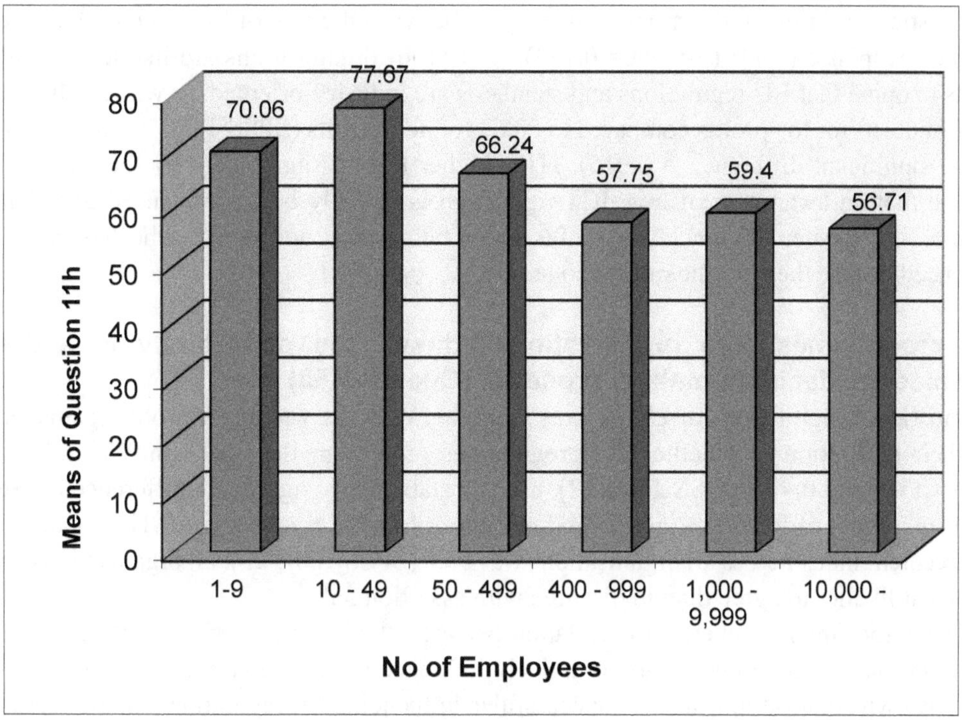

Question 11: "The following are some opinions about EU ICT regulation and standards-setting. To what extent do you agree or disagree with the following statements?"

A significant negative correlation was found between sub-Questions 11h ("only large multinational organisations can really influence regulation") and 11f ("my organisation/ company has been successful in influencing EU regulations/standards"): the Pearson Correlation coefficient was –0.336, with p-value < 0.001 (SPPS Table 19). This means that smaller firms have a tendency to estimate the influence of multinational organisations as greater than the multinationals themselves estimate it. This explains also why smaller firms and individuals often criticise the perceived disproportional influence over policy of larger organisations compared to smaller.

These data give a fairly consistent picture: respondents generally believed "the other guy" (in the shape of "large multinational organisations") has more influence than themselves. It is

183 64% of non-profit organisations on average answered in the affirmative to Question 11h, according to the author's Survey's raw dataset.

remarkable that most respondents nonetheless showed interest and willingness to participate in the policy process. The level of hostility to regulation was low, while a broad consensus held that EU regulations and standards boosted the standing of all European firms in the world.

"EU regulations and standards are industry-oriented" (Question 11i)

No statistically significant correlation was found between the size of for-profit organisations and their response to 11i (p-value= 0.133). For-profit organisations are likelier than non-profits to opine that EU regulations and standards are industry-oriented, as witness the mean index of 66.13 for for-profits compared to 58.63 for non-profits (SPSS Table 21, with p-value for the significant difference = 0.015). This higher level of agreement by for-profits may indicate that an awareness of how ICT regulation is actually being influenced goes hand-in-hand with greater influence: for-profits know better than non-profits who has the most influence because they are the ones who have it!

"EU programmes give organisations/industry the opportunity to actively influence the decision-making process" (Question 5a)

No statistically significant correlation was found between the size of for-profit organisations and their perception of whether EU programmes give them the opportunity to influence policy (p-value = 0.475, SPSS Table 22), nor any statistically significant difference between the mean indices of for-profit (60.12) and non-profit (55.42) organisations. The mean level-of-agreement index across all organisations was 58.6 (SPSS Table 23); all organisations were somewhat likelier to agree than to disagree with assertion 5a.

The author then checked for correlation between stock assertion 5a ("EU programmes give organisations the opportunity to actively influence the decision-making process") and 11f ("My own organisation has been successful in influencing EU regulations and standards"). A statistically significant correlation (Pearson Correlation = 0.295, with a p-value < 0.001, SPSS Table 24) was indeed found between these questions, which confirms the author's expectation of correlative positive responses to these questions. The positive correlation found here is another example of the data-triangulation that was built into most data-gathering methods used in the research for this book.

"Not everybody has the same opportunity to participate in EU programmes and participate in shaping the regulatory framework for EU ICT policy and standards" (Question 5f)

There was a small but significant negative correlation (Pearson Correlation = –0.198, with a p-value = 0.025, SPSS Table 25) between for-profit organisations' size and their opinion of how much opportunity they had to participate in EU programmes. No significant difference was found between mean indices of for-profit (61.03, SPSS Table 26) and non-profit organisations (66.18).

As expected, a significant correlation was found between agreement with assertion 5f and agreement with assertion 11h that "only large multinational organisations can really influence regulations", which also constitutes validation by triangulation of the consistency of the data (p-value < 0.001, SPSS Table 28). These questions are related to the differences in the perceived fairness of participation in the policy process across different organisations.

"Our country has been successful in influencing EU regulations/standards" (Question 11g)

This question tried to identify which Member States the Survey respondents perceived as having been most successful in influencing EU regulations and standards. The Survey ignored Luxembourg in this analysis, as only 2 responses were received from this country. Statistically significant differences in mean level-of-agreement indices were found between the answers received from respondents from Spain and Germany (p-value = 0.004); between those from Spain and the UK (p-value < 0.001); and between those from France and the UK (p-value = 0.015).

Table 6.4: Significance of differences at influencing EU policy (by country)

Countries with significant difference	P-value	Mean responses
Germany - Spain	0.003	59.47 – 24.75
UK - Spain	<0.001	66.10 – 24.75
UK - France	0.015	66.10 – 40.33

These results are based on Question 11.

Figure 6.8 below graphs the perception of organisations in the EU15 countries as to whether their home countries had successfully influenced EU regulations and standards (SPSS Table 29). In general, the Nordic countries, which host ICT industries with dominating market power, perceived themselves as having greater influence over the EU's ICT regulatory regime. Germany and Sweden in particular boast companies like Siemens, T-Mobile, Bluetooth Consortium, and Ericsson, and these two are the self-reportedly most influential Member States.

Figure 6.8: Success of own country at influencing EU policy (by country)

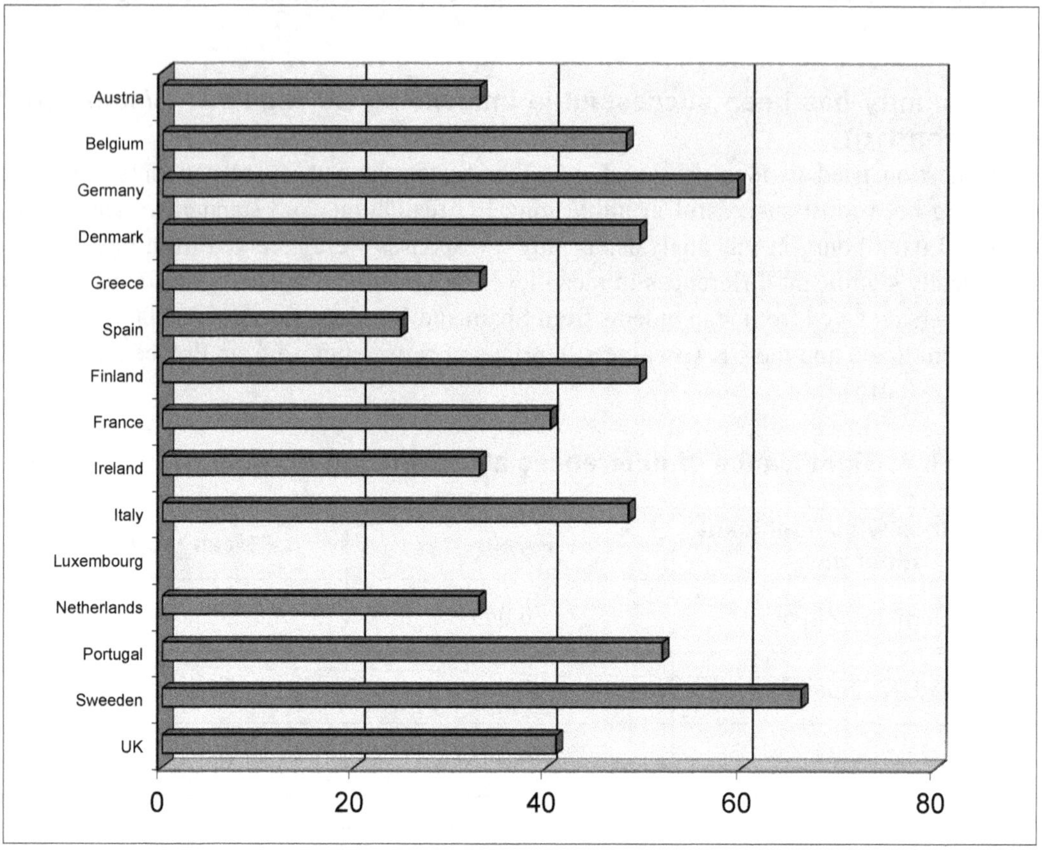

Question 11: "The following are some opinions about EU ICT regulation and standards-setting. To what extent do you agree or disagree with the following statements?"

"Our organisation participates in funded programmes for the following reasons" (Question 6)

Respondents were asked to think of the motives that actually drove them to be involved in Funded Programmes, and how important it was for their organisation to participate in these Programmes. The Survey revealed that stakeholders' main motives for involvement were (a) "to secure funding for Research and Development, and for new product/service development" and (f) "to find partners with the same interest in knowledge exchange and network building", followed by (g) "to understand regulations and standards and to get involved at a very early stage". Question 6g tried to sound the interest of organisations in improving their own compliance (and possibly influencing the regulator as well).

Quite arrestingly, the respondents proved least interested in the most obviously commercial motives: (b) "to generate revenue" or (c) "to make profits". It is remarkable that, even though "revenue" and "profits" were explicitly offered as possible motives, so few organisations (even for-profits) expressed interest in such commercial objectives. The following figure graphs the mean level-of-agreement indices for each of the motives given under this question.

Figure 6.9: Reasons for participating in funded programmes

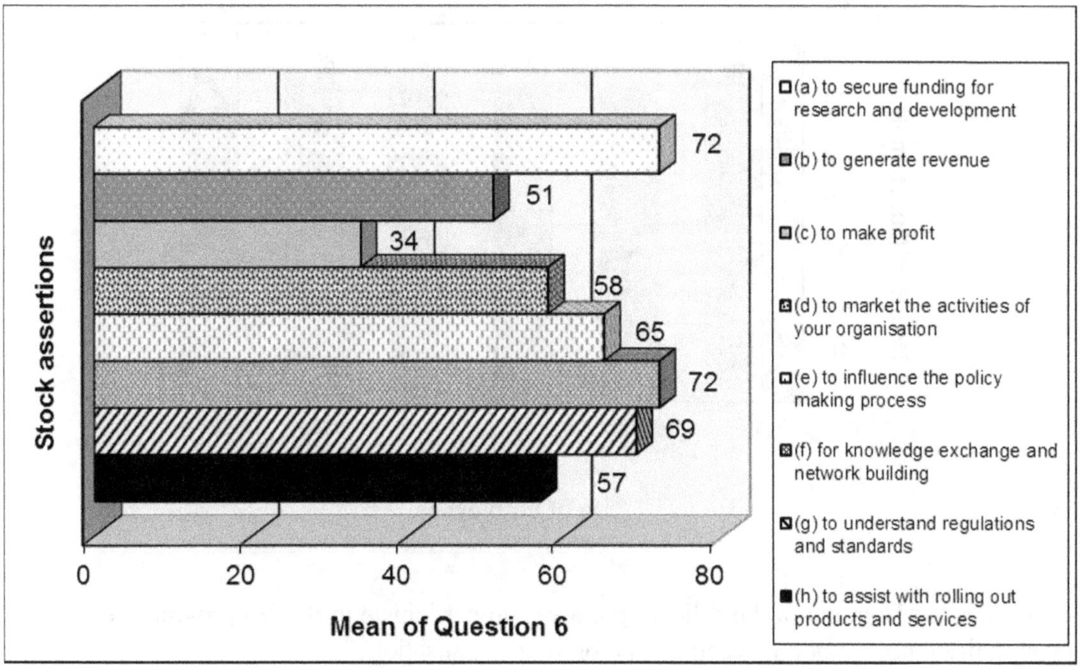

Question 6: "Thinking of the following reasons to participate in funded programmes, could you indicate how important each one is for your organisation?"

The author further analysed motive (e) "to influence the policy-making process and standards development". The SPSS analysis showed a statistically significant difference (p-value < 0.001) between the mean level-of-agreement indices of for-profit (69.80) and non-profit organisations (54.10, SPSS Table 30). On the other hand, no significant correlation was found between size of organisation and motive (e). The following figure graphs the tendency for larger organisations to believe that funded programmes are important for their influence over the policy process.

Figure 6.10: Motive for participating in funded programmes: to influence EU policy (by business size)

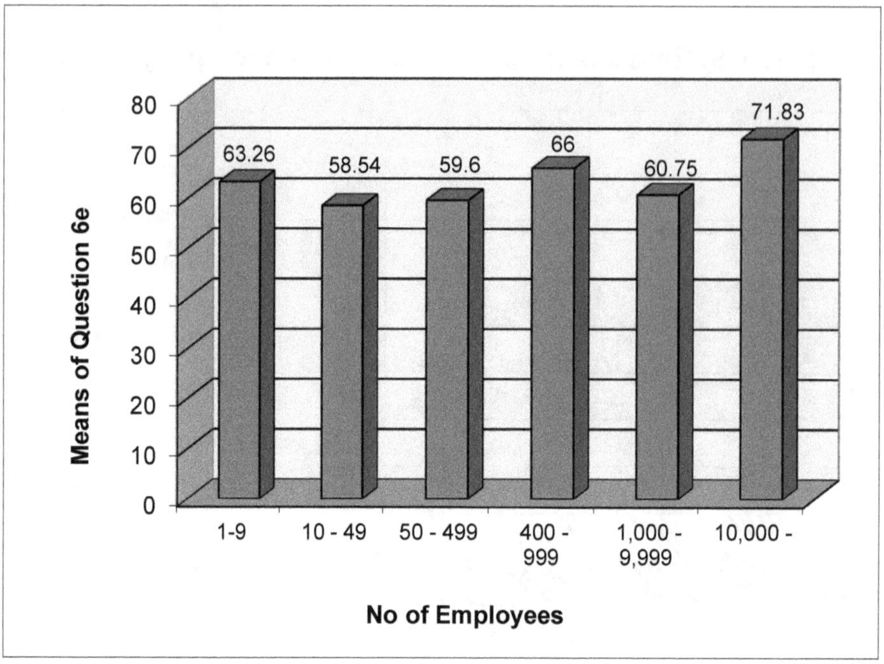

Question 6: "Thinking of the following reasons to participate in funded programmes, could you indicate how important each one is for your organisation?"

"Some stakeholders feel that regulation has a negligible impact on their organisation, others believe it has a very big impact. Which comes closest to you?" (Question 7):

The author tried to assess the impact of ICT regulations and standards on the respondents' organisations by asking them whether they perceived the impact to be "very big" (index = 100), "big" (index = 66), "small" (index = 33), or "not at all" (index = 0).[184] The results showed a significant difference (p-value = 0.001) in the mean size-indices of the answers to this question. For-profit organisations rated the impact of regulations on them (mean index of 68.27, SPSS Table 32) as higher than non-profit organisations did (mean index of 55.81). As for a correlation between their responses to Question 7 and for-profit organisations' size, a statistically significant linear relationship was found (p-value = 0.008). Larger firms tended more than smaller ones to believe that regulations had more of an impact on themselves than on smaller firms, but the difference was slight (SPSS Table 33). One may infer from this

184 Question 8 asked "In which Compliance, Regulation and Industry Standards areas is your organisation specifically interested?". The answers to this question are presented in the Survey Report, Appendix Four.

statistic that larger firms are more motivated than smaller firms to get involved in the policy process, because they wish to influence matters that affect them more.

"To keep myself and my organisation updated on regulatory developments, I use the following sources of information" (Question 10)

Respondents were given a choice of three possible answers: "usually" (frequency-index = 100), "sometimes" (index = 50) and "never" (index = 0). To find out on which Level of governance – Sub-national, National or European – organisations predominately communicated in order to keep themselves informed about regulations and standards, the author ran several statistical tests on Question 10. The amount of direct communication by for-profit organisations with local authorities, the national regulator, other national governmental institutions, and the EU institutions was analysed. The author found that the larger the organisation, the more active it was in directly communicating with Sub-national, National, and European information sources. The figure below graphs this linear relationship (SPSS Table 34).

Figure 6.11: Information sources, part 1 (by business size)

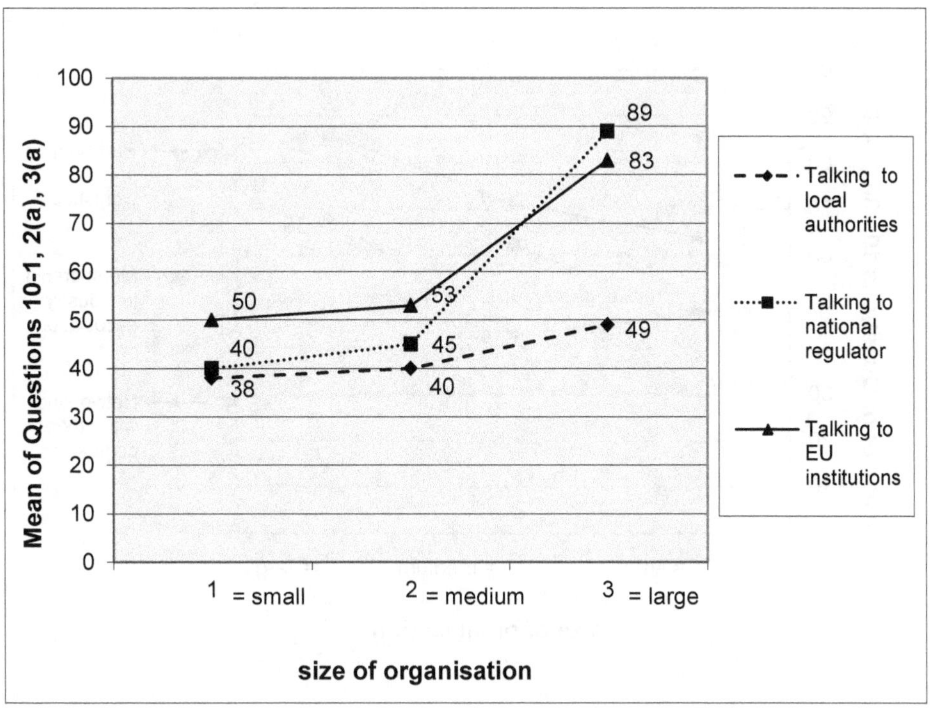

Question 10: "How do you keep yourself and your organisation informed (sources of information)?"

A similar trend was observed for sundry activities, such as participating in EU workshops, membership of industry associations, and networking with other companies. Larger organisations reported being significantly more active in participating in EU workshops and committees, obtaining information through membership of industry associations, and communicating with other companies in order to obtain information on regulatory developments. In particular, the very high peak of 89 for the mean frequency-index of "large" for-profit organisations in relation to the answer "talking to national regulator" might be explainable by the fact that the national incumbent telcos have transferred their original very close relationships with their host governments to the new Independent Regulatory Authorities. A correlative inference might be drawn that for-profit SMEs trust the EU regulator more than their own national regulators, possibly just because of their close relations with large national incumbents. On the other hand, this may be a statistical artefact of the circumstance that individuals involved in EU Programmes had no classification of their own but were lumped together with the smallest organisations (1-9). Such individuals would then be expected to have better contacts with EU institutions.

Figure 6.12: Information sources, part 3 (by business size)

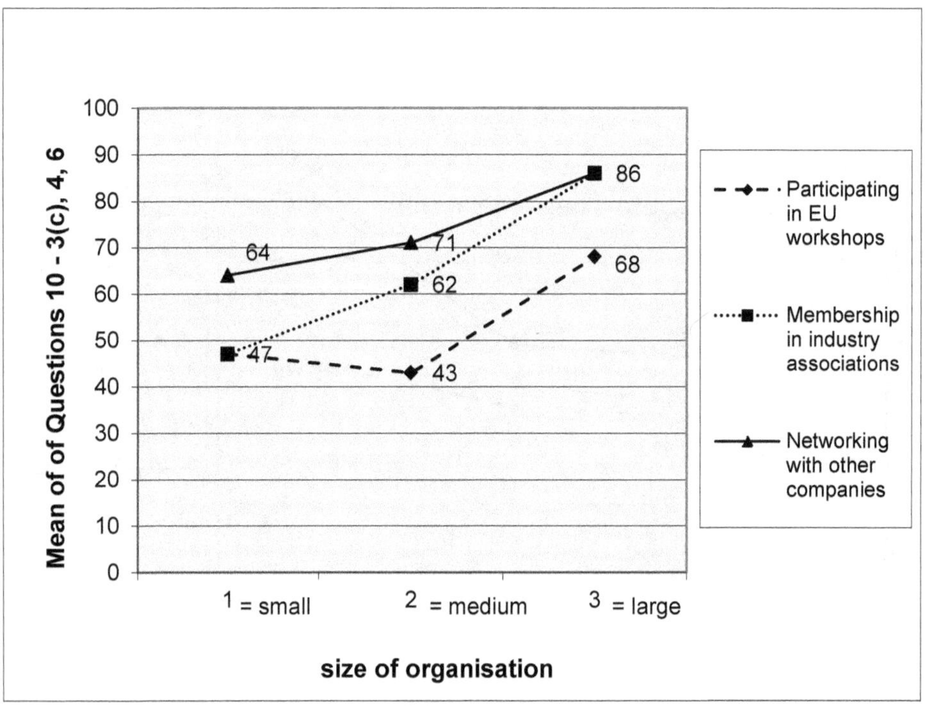

Question 10: "How do you keep yourself and your organisation informed (sources of information)?"

The results graphed in Figure 6.12 clearly show that large business organisations participate in more information-gathering activities than SMEs. These data triangulate with the data presented in Table 6.2 ("L2 – Industry associations" and "L3 – European industry associations" and "L4 – International industry associations"). Both datasets tell us that large firms are more involved in industry associations than SMEs.

Figure 6.13 gives an overview of the mean indices of organisations' information sources by country (see SPSS Table 35 for details).

Figure 6.13: Information sources, part 3 (by country)

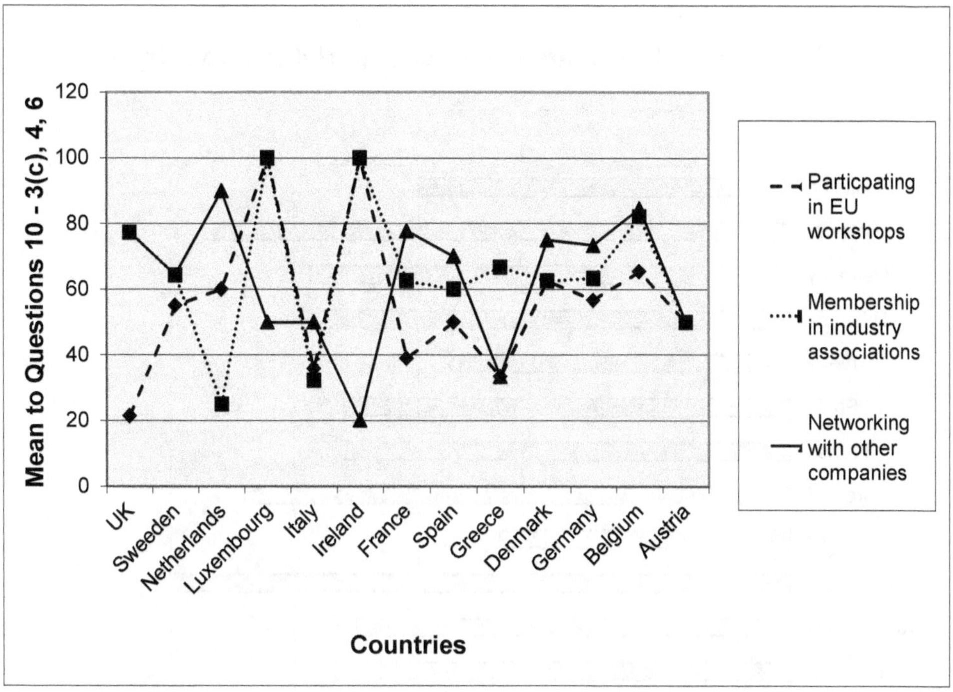

Question 10: "How do you keep yourself and your organisation informed (sources of information)?"

The question of organisation size suggested the question whether respondent stakeholders in larger countries were more involved in pro-actively gathering information through EU workshops, industry associations, and other business networking activities? Analysis showed that there was no correlation between country size and the level of involvement by organisations based in that country.

However, for-profit organisations from Belgium (mean frequency-index of 65.38) reported significantly more gathering of information through EU Workshops and Committees than organisations from Sweden (21.43). For-profit organisations from the UK (mean index of 77.27) and Belgium (82.14) reported significantly higher use of Industry Associations at all Levels of governance than organisations from Italy (32.14) or the Netherlands (25.00).

It was also noted that for-profit organisations from Belgium (mean frequency-index of 84.62) reported significantly more Networking with other companies than did for-profit organisations from Greece (33.33) or Italy (50.00). The p-values of these differences were 0.005 and 0.001, respectively.

As the next Figure (6.14) shows, if these indices for each country are summed, the result is that organisations based in Belgium and Luxembourg are revealed to be the most pro-active in gathering relevant information than anywhere else in Europe, almost surely due to proximity.

Figure 6.14: Information sources, part 4 (by country)

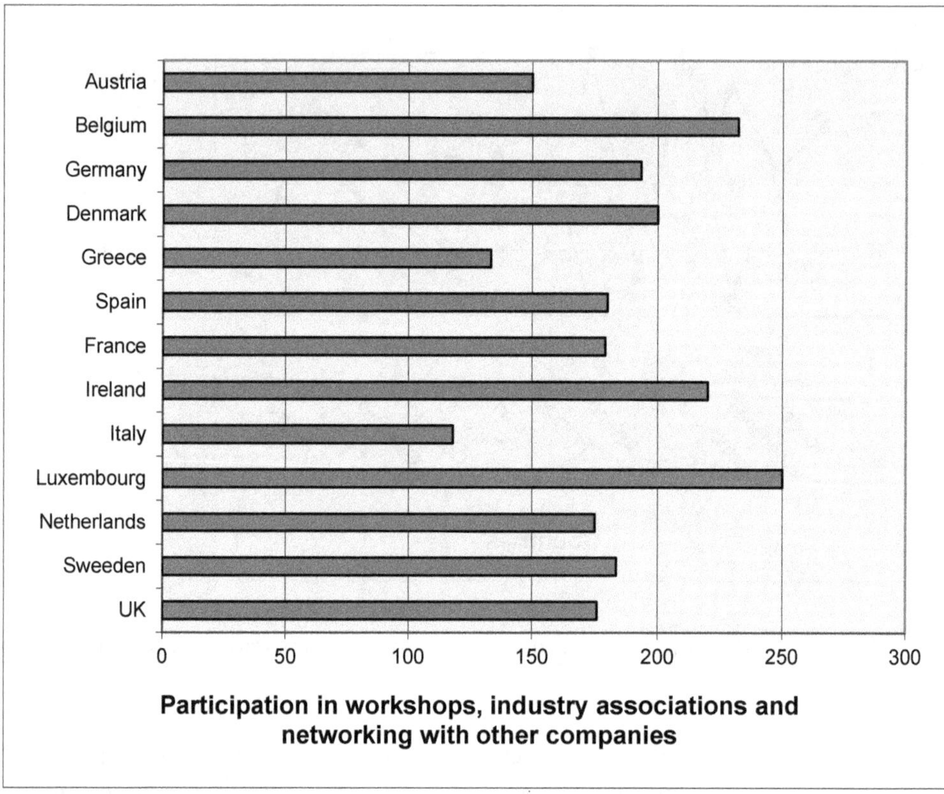

Question 10: "How do you keep yourself and your organisation informed (sources of information)?"

6.4.3 Forms of participation in the EU policy process (Question 4)

After analysing who the main participants were and which facilities they used to keep themselves informed about regulatory developments, the author enquired into their channels of participation in the policy process. First he looked at the participation forms of all organisations. The most commonly reported channel was "participating in conferences and workshops" (response rate of 88% of all participants), followed by "participation in consultations" (74%) and "expert hearings and evaluations" (67%). By contrast, "service contracts" (24%) and participation in "European committees" (33%) were the least commonly reported channels of participation in policy processes at the European Level.

These data are remarkable for revealing a stark contrast between the frequency of respondents' reported actual participation in various channels and the frequency of the European policy scholarship's investigation of these channels. The channel most frequently investigated by scholars is comitology, whereas this was reported to be one of the least frequently used channels by actual participants. It is inferred that, for external stakeholders at least, comitology is scarcely accessible or they would be making more frequent use of it.

Figure 6.15: Channels of participation (all organisations)

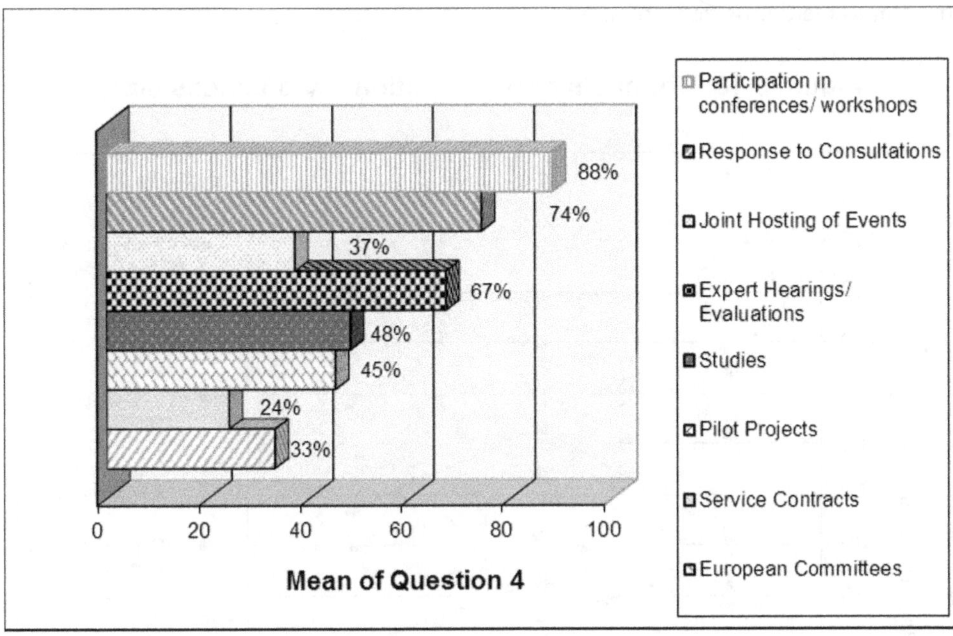

Question 4: "How does your organisation participate in policy, regulatory and standards-setting activities at the EU Level?"

The author then analysed participation in these channels by for-profit *versus* non-profit organisations. Statistically significant differences in the response rates of for-profit and non-profit organisations were found for the channels of "sending experts to hearings" (p-value = 0.001) and of "continued involvement in committees" (p-value = 0.008, SPSS Table 37). 75% of for-profit organisations reported sending experts to hearings or participating in evaluations, while the corresponding value for non-profit organisations was just 50% (SPSS Table 36). 39% of for-profit organisations indicated continued involvement in committees, but for non-profit organisations it was just 21%. As staff of the EU institutions did not participate in this Survey, the response rate for non-profit organisations' participation in comitology might look excessively low, but in fact this is another indication that, apart from political actors, comitology is less accessible to the public.

A second analysis of channels of participation considered organisational size. Significantly more large firms (93%, SPSS Table 38 with p-value = 0.007) than medium-sized firms (63%) reported sending experts to hearings or participating in evaluations. As well, a significantly larger proportion (67%) of multinationals than small (p-value = 0.03, 37%) and medium firms (p-value = 0.001, 25%) reported continued involvement in committees. Although large firms use these channels more frequently, in some cases medium-sized companies excelled them. In particular, medium-sized firms seemed to be more active in such government-funded programmes as "conducting studies", "participation in pilot projects", and "service contracts". This may be explainable on the supposition that many of the projects under these programmes may not be large enough to bear the larger overhead of large firms in comparison to medium-sized firms.

Figure 6.16: Channels of participation (by business size)

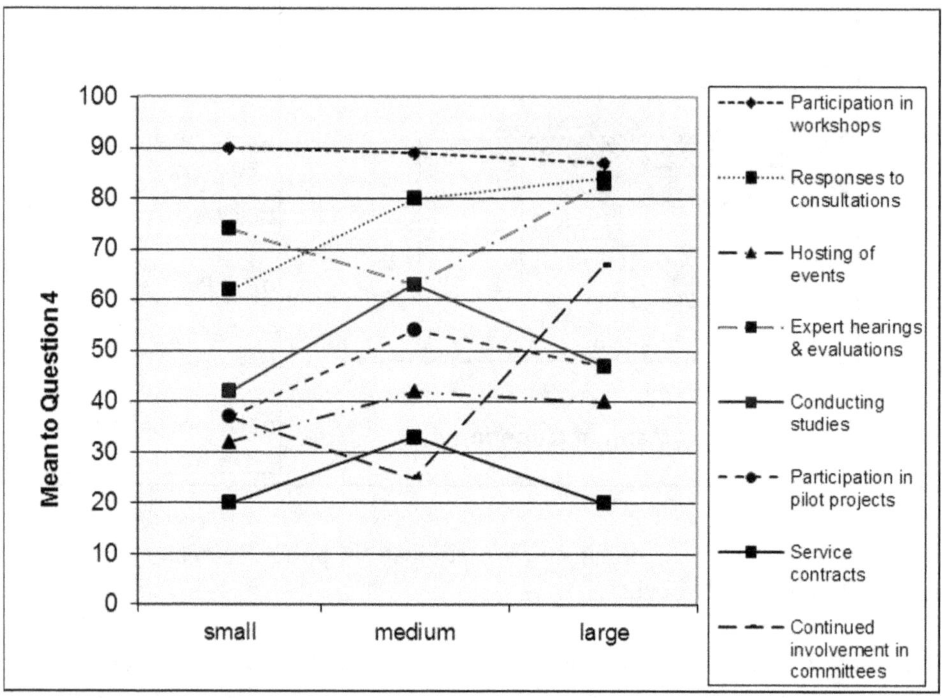

Question 4: "How does your organisation participate in policy, regulatory and standards-setting activities at the EU Level?"

6.4.4 Degree of satisfaction with one's own and other stakeholders' participation (Question 3)

Finally, the author was interested to find out how satisfied were respondents and their organisations with the participation of diverse stakeholders in the policy and standards-setting processes. The respondents were to choose between four answers to each sub-Question: "strongly satisfied" (satisfaction-index = 100), "satisfied" (index = 66), "dissatisfied" (index = 33), and "strongly dissatisfied" (index = 0). Non-profit organisations (mean satisfaction-index = 58.87) were significantly more satisfied with their own participation (p-value = 0.037, SPSS Table 40) in policy and standards-setting processes than for-profit organisations were (mean index = 51.14, SPSS Table 41). Non-profit organisations were also more satisfied (mean index = 46.96) with the activities of government in the policy process than for-profit organisations were (mean index = 39.48). The difference was statistically significant (p-value = 0.048). Interestingly, for-profit and non-profit organisations were both more satisfied with the regulator, standards institutes, guidelines and recommendations on the European and/or Global Levels than with the politicians and governments of their own countries on the National Level. From this it was concluded that, as previously inferred, stakeholders participate less at Global Level not because they do not value the work of international organisations, but because of such other factors as "less accessibility", especially for SMEs. Figure 6.17 graphs stakeholder satisfaction with National, European, and Global Levels of policy processes and outcomes.

Figure 6.17: Satisfaction with other policy actors

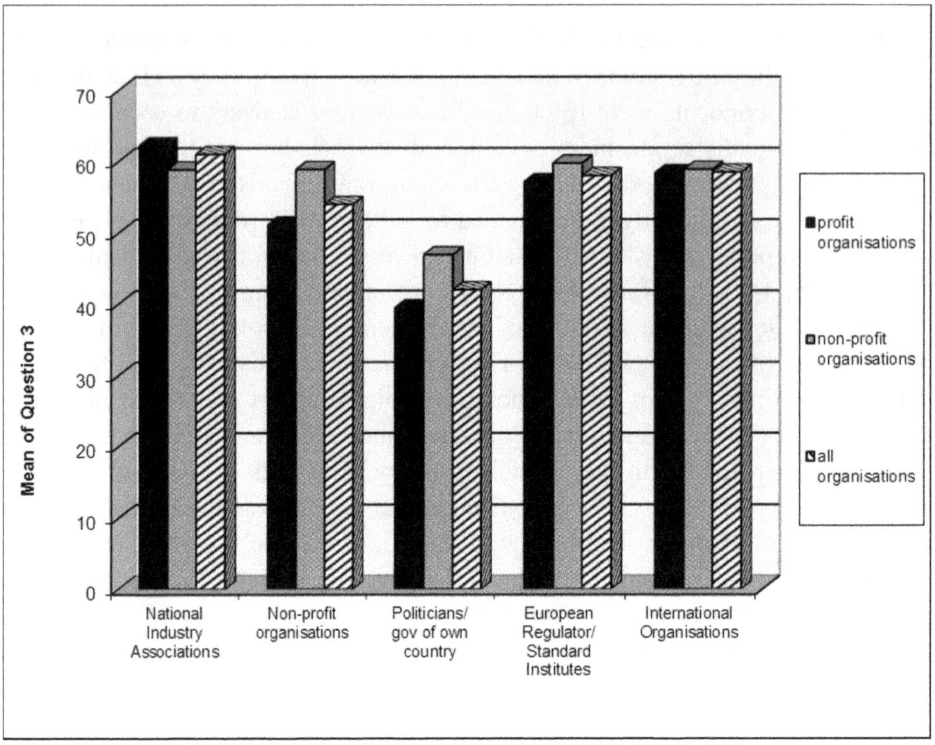

Question 3: "How satisfied is your organisation with the activities of these stakeholders [listed in Question 2] in the policy and standards-setting process?"

The author wondered if a correlation existed between satisfaction with stakeholder activities and active participation in these activities. Statistically significant positive correlations were found (correlation = 0.196, p-value = 0.015, SPSS Table 42) between all organisations' involvement with National Industry Associations (Question 2 N-1) and their degree of satisfaction with Industry Associations (Question 3), as well as between such involvement and the degree of satisfaction with European regulatory and standards institutes (correlation = 0.190, p-value = 0.02). This indicates that satisfaction with National Industry Associations increases in tandem with participation in them.

On the other hand, a negative correlation was found between participation in pan-European Industry Associations and satisfaction with International Organisations (correlation = -0.193, p-value = 0.03), implying that something about increased engagement with Pan-European Industry Associations leads to greater dissatisfaction with International Organisations. It may be that Pan-European Industry Associations are themselves a type of international organisation, so that other international organisations seem less appealing the more experience of participation one has with pan-European associations. The latter deal more effectively with matters of most concern to European organisations.

And yet, significant positive correlations were found between participation in UN organisations and satisfaction with both National Industry Associations (correlation = 0.211, p-value = 0.015) and International Organisations (correlation = 0.224, p-value = 0.012, SPSS Table 42). A statistically significant positive correlation was also found between the participation of organisations in the ITU and their satisfaction with National Industry Associations (correlation = 0.347, p-value < 0.001). This corroborates the general inference of a positive correlation between participation and satisfaction.

6.5 SYNOPSIS OF FINDINGS CONCERNING LARGE-BUSINESS PARTICIPATION

The following findings, gleaned from divers parts of the Survey and here collated, indicate very strongly that, overall, the bigger the business, the more active its participation in the regulatory process. In the following, small and medium-sized businesses have been grouped under the conventional rubric of "SMEs".

1. Large business organisations show a higher level of consensus about the worth of active participation in National Industry Associations than SMEs (Question 2, SPSS Table 10).
2. Large firms are much likelier than SMEs to participate in National Industry Associations, National Standards Institutes, Governmental Initiatives, European Industry Associations, ETSI, CENELEC, Internet security associations, ITU, and Global Programmes and Initiatives (Question 2, SPSS Table 12).
3. Large and multinational firms are likelier than SMEs to participate in Global Programmes and Initiatives (Question 2, SPSS Table 10 and Table 12).
4. Business organisation size correlates with their being perceived as successful at influencing EU regulations and standards. Large business organisations believe that they are more successful in shaping regulations and standards (Question 11f, SPSS Table 13 and 14).
5. A significant negative correlation was found between size and agreement with the assertion in Question 11h that "only large multinational organisations can really influence regulation". This means that SMEs are likelier to believe that only multinationals can influence regulation (Question 11h, SPSS Table 13 and SPSS Table 14).
6. Large business organisations are likelier than SMEs to believe that regulation has an impact on themselves (Question 7, SPSS Table 33). This may (in part) explain why larger business organisations are more actively involved in policy processes.
7. Large organisations are likelier than SMEs to contact Sub-national, National, and European information sources (Question 10, SPSS Table 34).
8. Large organisations reported participating more actively in EU Workshops and Committees than SMEs, obtaining information through membership of industry associations, and networking with other companies (Question 10, SPSS Table 34).

9. Significantly more large firms than SMEs send experts to hearings and evaluations, and more large firms than SMEs reported continuing involvement in committees (Question 4, SPSS Table 38).

6.6 CONCLUSIONS: TRENDS IN THE RESPONSES OF THE SURVEY RESPONDENTS

In this Chapter the author has categorised and summarised the results of the quantitative data analysis. The Survey questionnaire response data have yielded enough empirical evidence to confirm the Industry Governance Theory – that not only business, but large businesses in particular dominate the policy process. Most respondents agreed that "EU regulations and standards are industry-oriented", from which it may be inferred that industry influence over EU regulations and standards is more powerful than the influence of other stakeholders – in the opinion of those very other stakeholders. But most respondents also agreed that "EU programmes give organisations the opportunity to actively influence the decision-making process" (Question 5a). And most of those who agreed with either of these stock assertions agreed with the other as well. The inference may be drawn from this that stakeholders realise they have had the same opportunities to participate as business, and that the greater influence of businesses stems from their greater participation. One may infer, however, that participation follows resources. It is surely not coincidental that the most pervasive participant, big business, is also the one with the most resources. This was perhaps indirectly attested in the data from Question 2, where the enormous difference in level of consensus for participation in industry associations between the largest and the smallest businesses may best be explained as owing to a corresponding difference in resources for participation.

But greater resources alone cannot explain why business shows higher participation in policy processes; there have to be motives for participating at all. One of these was discovered in the answers to Question 7, wherein for-profit organisations expressed more belief than non-profit organisations that "regulation has a higher impact" on themselves. This implies that industry would give high priority to influencing policy processes that will in turn influence themselves and their future market behaviour. Other observations, such as the rich vein of data yielded by the author's participant observation, corroborate this conclusion. This justifies the inference of an *Industry* Governance Theory, by showing *why* this is likely, in contrast to possible alternatives such as a *Consumer* Governance theory or a *Labour* Governance theory.

The other main motive for industry's greater participation rates in the policy process was revealed by Question 3, the answers to which showed that non-profit organisations are more satisfied with the activities of government in the policy and standards-setting processes than for-profit organisations. Industry scrutinise the "outputs" more, because they are more regulated than other stakeholders, and so bear higher costs of compliance with regulations. (It may also be that some of the respondents classified as "non-profit", being in government themselves, were self-satisfied.) From this higher dissatisfaction of industry one may infer a cause of the phenomenon of "industry governance" as the main driver changing the way the marketplace is regulated.

Once the data from the divers parts of the Survey are collated for a synoptic comparison (Section 6.5) of "large" (for-profit) organisations as the author has defined them (>500 employees) with other for-profit organisations, large businesses stand out from both small and medium-sized businesses. The predominance of large businesses within the industry governance mode is superabundantly supported by the Survey findings. It should surprise no one, then, if this extra measure of participation pays off in the coin of extra influence over the processes being participated-in.

For-profit organisations send significantly more experts to hearings and are more involved on committees than non-profit organisations (Question 4, SPSS Table 36). It ought to be clarified that the attendance of industry experts is demanded by regulators; their attendance is not something that industry "pushes" on the consultative process. The data confirm that the technical expertise of business in particular is in great demand at consultative hearings and committees – not only desired but required by the regulator. This goes to the motives of the regulators themselves in not objecting as much as they might to industry's predominating influence. For its part, industry has invested enormous sums in its technical wizardry and would be unhappy to see it "ridden-over roughshod" in the making of ICT regulation.

Finally, the Survey constitutes a rich dataset attesting to the sundry channels of stakeholder influence that have been identified in theory as either having been made available by regulators or else created by the stakeholders themselves. It should be no surprise by now that industry associations also dominate all of these channels.

One of the surprises was how slightly for-profit organisations prefer dealing with their profit-motivated peers in industry associations over dealing with government and standards institutes. The Survey (Question 2) showed that for-profit organisations participate most actively, and are involved in the following organisations (in order of greatest involvement): Industry Associations (mean frequency-index = 80.00), Government Initiatives (mean index = 72.37), and National Standards Institutes (mean index = 69.09). This suggests that for-profits highly value government initiatives – possibly because they help industry to an early understanding of upcoming regulations and how they will likely impact products, services and markets. Business organisations seek intelligence about their competitors, but also about the prospective policy environment in which they must bring their products and services to market.

This inference is corroborated by the data from Question 6, where the motives most commonly reported (by all organisations, for-profits included) for participating in EU Publicly Funded Programmes were "to secure funding for Research and Development, and for new product/service development", "to find partners with the same interest for knowledge exchange and network building", and "to understand regulations and standards and to get involved at a very early stage". Contrary to conventional expectation, for-profit organisations do not participate in these programmes for short-term profit; the Question included "profits" as one of the possible motives, yet this was one of the least frequently cited motives, even by businesses. For-profits are primarily interested in amassing knowledge for its long-term strategic value. This may explain why the European Commission could have envisioned forging symbiotic relationships with profit-making concerns possessing deep technical knowledge. Commission-sponsored programmes create reciprocating advantages capable of motivating companies to enter into such relationships with their own regulator, instead of "hoarding" knowledge in an adversarial relationship. The industry is revealed to harbour not just short-term commercial objectives, but also long-term strategic visions about integrating forthcoming regulations and standards into their prospective new products and services. Such vision would be prerequisite to the capacity to govern; thus, the data attest that industry does not lack this capacity.

This conclusion is reinforced by data from Question 3. Organisations more "satisfied with their involvement" in National Industry Associations are also more satisfied with European Standards Institutes and the European regulator. Thus, organisations which are "satisfied with" (at a minimum willing to continue undertaking) collective action in policy matters are likelier to wage a successful relationship with the European regulator. This supports the Industry Governance Theory in finding that the "industry" as a whole does harbour organisations capable of partnering with the regulator in making policy.

Indeed, it may well be that active participation in policy-making is good for business, as the answers to Questions 3 and 2, when tested for statistical correlation, exhibited significant positive linkage between organisations' index for participation in the ITU and their index for satisfaction with National Industry Associations. It would seem that involvement on several Levels of governance simultaneously may generate synergies that lead to a more successful engagement with the regulatory environment as a whole. The Stakeholder Action Matrix would be affirmed insofar as involvement on all Levels may be inferred from the fact that it "pays" for industry to operate on multiple Levels of governance.

The data also yield some empirical evidence of the involvement of all stakeholder Advocacy Coalition Types on all four of the Levels of ICT governance theorised in the Stakeholder Action Matrix. This confirms that the model is not mere conjecture, but a living reality consisting of real actors trying to meet their own individual objectives by promoting those of their Advocacy Coalition Type.

The Survey did not succeed in determining conclusively how stakeholder participation broke down into the Advocacy Coalition Types used in the Stakeholder Action Matrix. The Survey methodology proved insufficient to this purpose. In particular, the SPSS software could not handle the relevant comparisons; *e.g.* a respondent who works for a business organisation might well have the mentality of Type Three (Industry-focused associations) or Type Four (Project groups), depending on whether that respondent worked in upper management or lower in the hierarchy as a technical expert.

Another thing the Survey has not evidenced is the "logic of time" in the matter of influencing the policy process. As a process is a structure of time, this dimension of regulatory politics is explored through the case study in the next Chapter, which theorises the level of influence of (external) stakeholders throughout the policy-process lifecycle. The Survey's defects have thus been compensated by this case study of the eCommunications Framework, which illustrates the importance of the timing requisite for effective influence over this process.

CHAPTER 7

A CASE STUDY: THE e-COMMUNICATIONS FRAMEWORK

This Chapter presents a complex case study the core of which is in Part One. Part Two and the Supplement concern its ramification at the National Level and a satellite case at Global Level, respectively. It features stakeholder involvement in the latest round of ICT regulatory revisions, and in a concomitant move to regulate unsolicited email ("spam") at Global Level. The case study demonstrates the emergence of a new kind of regulatory governance, in which the views and concerns of industry predominate *de facto* even over traditional political authority.

In the past, regulators were accustomed to acting in the manner of monarchs, but times have changed. The technical complexity of ICT in particular, and the speed with which the market is evolving, have outstripped the capacity of bureaucratic functionaries to command and control. Accordingly, the EU supranational institutions have resolved to approach regulation in a new way, by relying crucially on the knowledge and expertise of private stakeholders. Inevitably, the regulator became dependent on these various stakeholders in order to make progress in regulatory reform. In this state of affairs, business and industry are ascendant: the regulator depends the most on them because they are collectively the most knowledgeable. But they are also collectively the most highly motivated, having more at stake, and more directly, than do other stakeholders, which also explains why they are now predominant. Here in essence is the Industry Governance Theory, which the case study in this Chapter lays the empirical foundation for. But in addition, it supports the Policy Influence-Timing Model, providing a major part of its empirical foundation, as set forth in Table 7.3: "Roadmap for the EU Regulatory Framework Review", below.

7.1 SCHEDULE OF PARTICIPANT OBSERVATION

As detailed in Section 3.5.2 of Chapter Three, the author personally participated in industry and stakeholder events multiple times per year for many years. These included conferences open to the general public; stakeholder meetings for individuals and representatives of organisations who were interested in one particular policy area; and personal meetings and interviews, both formal and informal, initiated by the author with both stakeholders and regulators on all Levels of governance. As presented in the Timeline below, these participant observations spanned a long stretch of time – from 1996 to 2010, and beyond. These years of personal participation form the matrix from which this case study sprang.

Table 7.1: Timeline – Research phases and participant observation (examples only)

Timeline of participation →

	1996	2002	2005	2010
Phases	*Pre-research*	*Early research*	*Culminating research*	*Post-research*
Participant observation (Examples)	➢ *Stage* with the European Commission, Telecoms Regulation (DGXIII, A1) ➢ ONP Committee, Telecoms Council, ITU Workshop, *etc.* Brussels ➢ Participation in EU FP projects FP projects (*e.g.* European Trusted Services) ➢ The Forum for Electronic Business events ➢ IST Conference, Helsinki	➢ Response to the "European Governance White Paper" consultation ➢ FP6/IST events with DTI, London ➢ CEN events and meetings, Brussels ➢ European Commission meetings, Brussels ➢ EU Delegation to the UN meetings, NY ➢ ITU Telecom World 2003, Geneva ➢ OECD meetings in Paris ➢ ICC meetings, Paris ➢ London Chamber of Commerce event ➢ CBI meeting, London	➢ DTI/ BERR stakeholder meetings, London ➢ various UK conferences and events, *e.g.* - Regulator and expert presentations - Policy and stakeholder consultations - Trade fairs and other networking events - Subject Matter (including legal) training sessions	➢ Industry Association events, *e.g.* - Intellect (ICT industry association), UK - British Computer Society, UK - Information Systems Audit and Control Association, London chapter.

In the first, pre-research phase of participation, spanning 1996 to 2001, the author engaged in "scattershot" participation, where he attended not only in preferred events, but in any and all that were available and accessible. In the second, early-research phase, spanning 2002 to 2005, the author made the necessary effort to procure *entrée* to events that had been less accessible during the first phase, particularly on the Global Level. During the third, culminating phase, spanning 2006 to 2009, the author focussed on events at National Level, *i.e.* UK stakeholder meetings organised by regulators or by industry associations. This participation gave insight into how even stakeholder gatherings on the Sub-national and National Levels have empowered industry to exert agenda-setting and policy-content influence over EU regulators, not just British national regulators.

The author systematically put his participant observations on record in field notes from the beginning, and documented nearly all of the events attended. There were so many that, for the reader's convenience, Table 7.2 is provided to synopsise them categorically, giving examples of each category.

Table 7.2: Examples of Participant Observation from 1996 to 2012

<table>
<tr><th>Categories of participation</th><th>Examples of participations and of observes</th></tr>
<tr><td colspan="2">Global Level</td></tr>
<tr><td>Events with international organisations</td><td>• "Internet World 2002" Conference in London (11-12.6.2003)
• "ITU Telecom World 2003" Conference in Geneva (12-14.10.2003)</td></tr>
<tr><td>Personal meetings with representatives of international organisations</td><td>• OECD meetings in Paris: Hilary Carroll, Information Officer; Anne Carblanc, Information Security and Privacy; John Dryden, Deputy Director of Directorate Science, Technology and Industry; Dimitry Ypsilanti, Telecoms and Information Services Policy (11 & 12.12.03, Paris)
• International Chamber of Commerce (ICC) meetings: Jonas Astrup, Policy Manager for Commercial Law and Practice, Jurisdiction and Applicable Law in e-Commerce; Marie Farrell, Policy Manager for e-Business, IT and Telecoms (Data Protection) (12.12.03)
• EU Delegation to the UN meetings in New York: George Cunningham, Head of EU Delegation (April 2003)</td></tr>
<tr><td colspan="2">European Level</td></tr>
<tr><td>Events with the European Commission</td><td>• Open Network Provision (ONP) Committee (Brussels, 1996)
• Information Society Technologies Conference (Helsinki, 22.-24.11.1999)
• "FP6 IST Information Day", DTI event (London, 11.2.2003)
• "Technology-enhanced learning & access to cultural heritage – IST workshop", DTI event (London, 25.2.2003)
• "Towards a global dependability and security framework – IST workshop" (London, 27.2.2003)</td></tr>
<tr><td>Personal meetings with European Commission functionaries</td><td>• various meetings with the European Commission, Brussels (see Section 3.5.1)</td></tr>
<tr><td>Personal meetings with European Standards institutes</td><td>• European Committee for Standardization (CEN) meeting: John Ketchel, Director CEN (Brussels, 8.5.2003).</td></tr>
<tr><td>Other events at European Level</td><td>• CEN Data Protection event (Brussels, 3.5.2003)</td></tr>
<tr><td>Industry and industry association events</td><td>• EEMA events (The Forum for electronic business, now called The European association for e-identity and security)</td></tr>
<tr><td colspan="2">National Level</td></tr>
<tr><td>Events with National Regulators</td><td>• BERR events (London, 7.3.206, 11.5.2006 and 27.7.2006).</td></tr>
</table>

Categories of participation	Examples of participations and of observes
Conferences on National Level	• Confederation of Business Industries (London, 12.10.2004) • eContent Information Day with DTI (London, 7.2.2003)
Industry and industry association events	• Intellect UK stakeholder meetings (various): Information Sharing and Security & Privacy group (London, 2004-2012) • Information Systems Audit and Control Association (London, 2004-2012) • British Computer Society (London, 2004-2012)
Sub-national Level	
Events on Sub-national Level	• London Chamber of Commerce and Industry (London, 25.02.2004) • The Communications Industry and e-Commerce Forum (London, 12.11.2003)

In search of deeper understanding of issues of concern to ICT stakeholders and regulators, and of the ways they collaborated to address these challenges, the author not only attended stakeholder and ICT policy-related meetings, committees, conferences and workshops as an observer, but also, during the pre-research and early-research phases of his participant observation project, undertook tasks that stakeholders and "lobbyists" typically perform. In particular, the author: –

1. contributed to consultation processes through personal responses to White Papers[185]
2. played a role in several EU funded studies, EU Service Pilots, and Service contracts[186]

185 Response to the "European Governance White Paper" consultation (COM(2001/428 final) drafted for EEMA (The forum for electronic business), March 2002.

186 Examples include:
European Commission, Cabinet Bangemann (1996) "Status Report on the Development of the Information Society in Europe", Brussels.
European Commission, DG XIII-A1 (1996) "Market study on Telecommunications, Multimedia, Integrated Applications & Information Services until 2010", Brussels.
European Commission, DG XIII-A1 (September 1996) "The Market Development of the Internet and the Implications of the Telecommunications Sector", Brussels.
European Commission, Advanced Communications Technologies and Services (ACTS) Programme (1996) "TEN-34 Research Project for Open Network Provision and Leased Lines", provided by DANTE (Delivery of Advanced Network Technology to Europe), Brussels.
European Commission, DG XIII (1998) "European Trusted Services I: EuroTrust Public Key Infrastructure Project", pilot programme, provided by PricewaterhouseCoopers (London), Baltimore Technologies (Dublin) and EdelWeb (Paris). CORDIS website at http://cordis.europa.eu/infosec/src/study7.htm (accessed January 2007).
European Commission, DG XIII (1999-2002) "Fifth Framework Programme Certification Service Provider (FP5-CSP)", Brussels/ London, provided by PricewaterhouseCoopers (London), GlobalSign (Brussels) and Zergo (Basingstoke).

3. personally responded to calls for experts for evaluation and consultancy assignments, and developed a network of contacts with companies and organisations who regularly contribute to EU studies and to the R&D Framework Programme; and
4. informally but regularly "chatted up" functionaries and expert advisors in DG Information Society[187], DG Enterprise[188], and other DGs responsible for ICT policy.[189]

Appendix Six contains a compendious Directory of more than 600 stakeholders engaged in shaping policies, regulations and standards on all Levels of governance. In addition, Appendix Two: "Participant Observation: Interlocutors, Presentations and Events" comprehensively lists (a) the face-to-face meetings and interviews conducted; (b) presentations witnessed; and (c) stakeholder events attended.

From the records of participation already in hand there emerged the kernel around which this formal case study was elaborated. Each of the events participated-in effectually amounted to a case study in miniature, whence the whole participation constitutes in effect a population of inchoative case studies. From this population the author selected one event to be studied in depth – the 2006 Review of the eCommunications Framework, – to provide insight into stakeholder activities on different Levels of governance; to the end that the reader may understand more fully the nature of what the author discovered in the other events he participated in. The case examined here in depth relied on the same methods of participant observation and archival review used in the rest of the research that makes up this book.

Part One of the study actually involved comprehensive review of all EU consultation Papers, Reports, and stakeholder responses from the 2006 Review; rather than personal attendance in meetings. In this the author leveraged his experience of years of participation on European Level. By contrast, Part Two relied entirely on the author's direct, personal participation in events to do with the Review, hosted by the UK Department of Trade and

187 Examples of relevant policy units of DG Information Society: Audiovisual, Media, Internet (Directorate A); Electronic Communications Policy (Directorate B); Lisbon Strategy and Policy for the Information Society (Directorate C); Network and Communication Technologies (Directorate D); Content (Directorate E); Emerging Technologies and Infrastructures (Directorate F); Components and Systems (Directorate G); and ICT for Citizens and Businesses (Directorate H).

188 DG Enterprise was created by a merger of the former DGs for small and medium-sized enterprises (SME2), industry and the innovation directorate. DG Enterprise refocusses industry policy on entrepreneurship and on creating an environment supporting innovation. Its goal is to supply policy fostering the competitiveness of enterprises that will revitalise Europe through creating a knowledge-based economy in Europe. Examples of relevant policy units of DG Enterprise: Regulatory Policy (Directorate C); Standardisation (Unit C-2); Technology for innovation/ICT industries and e-business (Unit D-4).

189 DG Competition: Telecommunications and post, information society coordination (Unit C-1); Information industries, Internet and consumer electronics (Unit C-3); State Aid II – Telecommunications and Media (Unit H-3).
DG Internal Market: Better Regulation Cycles: Legal Aspects (Unit B-3); Copyright and Knowledge-based Economy (Unit D-1); Company Law, Corporate Governance and Financial Crime (Unit F-2).

Industry (DTI).[190] The case study Supplement covers events not directly observed, but which also left a "paper trail" to understand which the author's participation experience was an indispensable aid. All the stakeholder events previously attended in a certain sense "triangulated" the secondary materials the author was obliged to use for this phase of the case study.

7.2 BACKGROUND TO THE CASE STUDY

7.2.1 The Electronics Communication Framework

As of 25 July 2003 the EU's eCommunications Framework comprehends the regulation of all infrastructure that transmits communications electronically, whether the content be voice or data, by fixed or wireless media, or through circuit-switched or Internet-based means; together with the associated services. The Framework consists of five EU directives laying down certain principles and procedures for regulating the provision of electronic communications products and services. Chapter Four of this book has already presented this regulatory framework in some detail (see Section 4.5.5 above).

The overriding mid- to long-term goal of the new Framework is to substitute regulation *at European Level* by market forces for regulation by legal command and bureaucratic control, in line with the Commission's strategic focus on Single Market integration. It is also hoped that this may reduce the number of legal regulations imposed on, and compliance costs borne by the industry. The Framework initiated a transformation of the EU regulatory regime to *ex post* control under general competition law. The Commission intended to bring about not only a predictable and stable regulatory environment capable of promoting innovation, investment and competition, but also one that "provides a set of rules that are simple, aimed at deregulation, technology-neutral and sufficiently flexible to deal with fast-changing markets in the electronic communications sector" (Europa website – eCommunications Framework, 2006). These market virtues are also considered the best means of ensuring that users are protected and their needs met – the ulterior purpose of governmental regulation, after all (Europa website – eCommunications Framework, 2006).

Despite the "economic" nature of the new regulation, the eCommunications Framework does not purport to abolish *ex ante* regulation altogether, but merely to delegate it to the new National Regulatory Authorities (NRAs) at National Level. NRA regulatory decisions are, however, to be subject to a review mechanism at the European Level – known as the "Article 7 procedure" – which is intended to safeguard the Single Market by promoting the consistency of *ex ante* regulation across the EU. To further consolidate this goal, the Commission in 2009 issued Regulation (EC) No 1211/2009 (25 November) setting up the Body of European Regulators for Electronic Communications (BEREC) to interface between the Commission and NRAs, and to serve in the capacity of both a standards institute and a harmonisation forum for the latter, promoting coordination and co-operation across Member

190 The Department was renamed in 2009 and is now the Department for Business, Innovation and Skills (BIS). Before that, from 2007-2009 it was known as the Department of Business Enterprise and Regulatory Reform (BERR), was merged with the Department for Innovation,, Universities and Skills and subsumed under the new BIS framework.

State regulatory regimes. Although BEREC does consult private stakeholders, actual participation in its workshops is open only to regulators. The Framework does not deal with content services, which are subject to other rules at European Level, but it does empower NRAs to take action against uncompetitive markets in situations where content services are bundled-in with eCommunication services.

The justifications of the Framework's market liberalisation rest on two main pillars. The first is that the convergence of digital technologies must be reckoned with. The Framework is meant to be technology-neutral: telecommunications, the Internet and broadcasting are no longer to be considered separate kinds of transmission. Technological trends identified in 1999 (CEC, 1999c) are still in evidence today. In the coming years, today's "circuit-switched", voice-based, single-service telecom networks will be progressively replaced by Next Generation Networks (NGN), which are "packet-based" and multi-service; until eventually the Internet Protocol (IP) becomes all-pervasive. Clearly, from the viewpoint of economy of regulatory means, technology-dependent regulation would have required many more regular (and expensive) reviews, and could not have provided the macro-level regulatory stability needed to meet higher policy objectives. The welter of novel technologies cannot possibly be understood by the Commission alone, who *nolens volens* are obliged to consult industry experts in networks, computer programming, transmission media and many other esoteric matters.

The second pillar justifying the eCommunications Framework is its grounding in the overarching competition purposes of the EU customs union. The Framework has been designed to facilitate the move toward truly competitive markets featuring enhanced cross-border competition. One of the main principles of the Framework is that sector-specific regulation of the market power of dominant companies may be rolled back as soon as markets become sustainably competitive. Competition between network operators may in the meantime be reinforced, as by "unbundling the local loop" – freeing up for the competitive delivery of services that last mile of copper wire connecting homes to telephone exchanges, – or as by obligating mobile operators to offer "number portability" to customers who change to another operator. All this enhances consumers' bargaining power in dealing with suppliers (CEC, 2006g; CEC, 2006aa).

7.2.2 The policy cycle of telecoms regulation

Historically, the European telecommunications sector has been dominated by *régies*, or publicly owned monopolies, because it was generally assumed that telecommunications services merely expanded upon postal services, the State monopoly of which no one thought to question.[191] These cozy arrangements could not survive integration to the Single Market, and the dynamism that this introduced into the telecommunications market in particular. Politicians and industry experts alike hold market integration and technological convergence

191 Most postal and telegraph services across Europe had been made over into state-owned monopolies by the mid- to late 19th century, a state of affairs that seems likely to have continued indefinitely but for the outside intervention of the EU.

responsible for the privatisation that sparked open competition in the Member States' telecommunications and media markets.

The first cycle of the new EU telecoms policy was launched in 1984, supported by input from a wide range of stakeholders. The European standards institutes were called upon by the Commission to develop new standards that would address the issues of interoperability so often posed by national standards that diverged so widely. Network operators and service providers were invited to participate in publicly funded technology-development programmes at European Level. Market analysts, researchers, and professional firms participated in EU market- and industry-specific studies, gathering data to inform the development of policies more attuned to industry and consumer needs.[192] Stakeholders suddenly had an opportunity to influence ICT policy by getting involved in the preliminary empirical studies and pilot programmes being launched under the EU aegis.[193]

The second cycle of the new Europe-wide telecommunications policy got under way in 1987, and was timetabled to culminate by 1 January 1998 in the liberalisation of all Member States' markets for telecommunications networks, equipment and services. The Maastricht Treaty (or TEU) added a new legal dimension to European integration in the telecommunication sector in Title XV on "Trans-European Networks", specifically Articles 154, 155 and 156. These articles declared that the EU "must aim to promote the development of Trans-European Networks [TEN]" that would remove the national barriers to pan-European telecommunications operations, services and equipment.

Certain quasi-constitutional legal instruments enabled liberalisation of the EU telecommunications sector; in particular, the Commission's power, derived from Article 86(3) of the TEU, to quash any special or exclusive rights to produce telecommunications equipment or provide services conferred by Member States on national public enterprises. Also weighing in were measures such as the Harmonising Directives, based on Articles 95 and 86 of TEU, and the Open Network Provision (ONP) Directive mandating open access to all publicly available telecommunications networks and services, by whomever owned. The Commission's Infrastructure Green Papers, COM(94/440EC) and COM(95/158/EC), emphasised the urgency, in a globally competitive environment, of implementing the existing ONP Directive and of developing another directive on interconnection (CEC, 1994f). Together with the Licensing Directive, which provided for the vetting of new entrants into the market, these measures made up the "1998 package" of legislation that paved the way for a pan-European telecommunications market.

All interested parties in the telecommunications sector were invited in the consultations on Parts I and II of the Infrastructure Green Paper to comment not only on issues and proposals specific to infrastructure liberalisation, but more generally on the overall regulatory approach that the Commission was proposing in order to ease transition toward a fully liberalised

192 In the era of State-ownership "regulation" was unnecessary in that the State controlled the "industry" through direct management of the *regie*; thus, the State's needs were by definition always met.

193 Examples are Telecommunications/eCommunications studies and feasibility programmes ("pilots") funded under the eTEN programme (former TEN-TELECOMS), Information Society Project Office (ISPO), PROMISE, the Community Research and Development Information Services (CORDIS) and the Framework Programmes.

telecoms environment. As part of the consultation a series of hearings was held, which began with a Round Table for the Chairmen of Network Operators on 10 February 1995, at which 54 fixed, mobile and alternative infrastructure companies were represented; followed by a General Consultation Meeting on 20-21 February 1995, attended by 125 organisations; a Meeting with the Trade Unions on 14 March 1995; and a Meeting with the *Ad Hoc* High-Level Committee of National Regulatory Authorities on 16 March 1995. Eight written contributions were submitted by national regulatory authorities, 33 by industry associations, and 67 by service and network providers (CEC, 1995c; Europa website – Green Papers, 2006). It is evident from this roster of participants that a wide range of private stakeholders participated in the consultation, and that the industry had a big input into it.

Accelerating ICT convergence and rapidly changing technologies persuaded the Commission to create a single, "coherent", but evolvable framework for regulating electronic communications. This prompted the third cycle in the development of a Europe-wide telecommunications policy, commencing on 10 November 1999 when the Commission published a Communication titled "Towards a new framework for electronic communications infrastructure and associated services – the 1999 communications review" (CEC, 1999c). The Commission first reviewed the existing telecommunications regulatory framework pursuant to its obligations under Article 8 of Directive 90/387/EEC of 28 June 1999 on the "Establishment of the internal market for telecommunications services through the implementation of open network provision" (CEC, 1990a). The 1999 Review synthesised the results of diverse Commission-commissioned reports and studies, as well as public consultation results which had fed back into the review process and were taken into account by the Commission in formulating its Position. Stakeholders could have participated in consultations on the Convergence Green Paper, the Radio Spectrum Green Paper, and more than sixteen other studies commissioned especially for the 1999 Review (CEC, 1999c),[194] and covering areas as diverse as convergence between fixed and mobile networks and services, interconnection, and licensing.

Interested parties were given until 15 February 2000 to comment on the policy proposals outlined in the 1999 Telecommunications Review. Many industry stakeholders did in fact respond to the invitation to comment, testifying to their interest and also to their probable influence. Of the 225 named stakeholders who responded, 42 or 19% of them came from governments, regulatory authorities, and other public authorities; 42 or 19% from industry associations; 28 or 12% from consumer and user groups; 94 or 41.5% from individual commercial organisations; ten or 4% were individuals or consultancies; three or 1.5% were research institutions and universities; and six or 3% were other associations. The Annexe of the 1999 Communications Review consultation report lists all respondents in this consultation (CEC, 2000d).

The results of the consultation were presented in COM(1999)539, the "Communication of the 1999 Communications Review", which set forth the policy objectives that a large majority of respondents favoured, while also presenting critical and divergent views from the minority. All of this feedback was used in drafting the six Directives and one Decision

194 *Cf.* Annexe I – List of current studies linked to the 1999 Review: CEC, 1999c:56.

that made up the new regulatory framework for telecommunications of June 2000. The Communication integrated elements of other policy objectives drawn from the eEurope Strategy and the Lisbon European Council, *e.g.* a "low-cost competitive communications infrastructure" (Council of the European Union, 2000). The Member States were obligated to implement the legislative package by 25 July 2003, with the exception of the Data Protection Directive which was to be implemented by 31 October 2003.

A glance at telecommunications policy over the last decades shows that the policy process is cyclical. The first cycle, launched in 1984, was superseded in 1996 by the "1998 regulatory package" (named after the transposition deadline). The policy of this cycle was in turn reviewed in 1999, and got superseded in 2000 by the "2003 package", which was reviewed in 2006, leading to the launch of a third cycle. This latest review became the case study presented directly below.

7.2.3 Fora for the perpetual participation of stakeholders

Up to this point, the author has looked at stakeholders and their participation at a high level of abstraction, without describing what in particular their participation consists in. But that the reader may witness for himself that these are real acts of real people, we briefly but in some detail consider instances of actual fora that exist for no other purpose but to communicate stakeholder views. After that we will proceed to the case study.

Fora provided by public officials

Under the 1998 Regulatory Framework as amended by the eCommunications Framework of 2003 a total of five working groups and committees were set up at European Level to assist the Commission in developing the eCommunications internal market and in monitoring the consistent application of regulations enacted pursuant to the Framework. These were:

1. the European Regulators Group (ERG) for electronic communications networks and services (CEC, 2002q; CEC, 2004i; European Regulators Group website, 2006)
2. the Radio Spectrum Policy Group (RSPG) (CEC, 2002p; CEC, 2002r; Radio Spectrum Policy Group website, 2006)
3. the "Article 29 Working Party", or Working Party on the Protection of Individuals with regard to the Processing of Personal Data (CEC, 1995b; CEC, 1997b; CEC, 2002e)
4. the Communications Committee (CoCom), subsuming the previous Open Network Provision Committee and Licensing Committee, which were instituted under the 1998 regulatory package for telecommunications[195] (CEC, 2002d); and
5. the Radio Spectrum Committee (RSC)[196] (CEC, 2002r).

195 The Communications Committee was established by the Framework Directive 2002/21/EC (Article 22 and Recital 34). The CoCom "assists the Commission in carrying out its executive powers under the New Regulatory Framework and the Regulation on the .eu Top Level Domain" (Communication & Information Resource Centre Administrator website, 2008).

196 The Radio Spectrum Committee was established under the Radio Spectrum Decision 676/2002/EC: "The RSC assists the Commission in the development and adoption of technical implementing

All of these bodies have always been dominated by regulators and public-sector officials. Both the ERG (since 2010 renamed BEREC) and the RSPG are designed to furnish vehicles for coordination and co-operation between NRAs and the Commission. Both working groups are required to consult with stakeholders on market-, technological and regulatory developments; however, participation in their meetings is for regulators only, seemingly ruling out stakeholder influence.

Taking the European Regulators Group (ERG) for an example, it was set up in 2002 as an independent advisory group to debate and advise on eCommunications regulation (superseded by BEREC in 2010). It comprised the NRA Heads of 33 countries, interfacing between them and the Commission, and was charged with operating in so transparent a way as to allow both service providers and end-users to provide their recommendations and feedback. Its overriding goal was "to ensure the consistent application of the regulatory framework in all Member States, with the Commission having the responsibility to keep the European Parliament informed on the Group's activities on an annual basis" (CEC, 2002a). The ERG took into consideration the "objectives given to NRAs in Article 8 of the Framework Directive (2002/21/EC) of promoting competition, contributing to the development of the internal market and promoting the interests of EU citizens". Its Expert Working Groups (*viz.*, the Mobile Market WG, the Fixed Network WG, the End User WG) and its project teams were responsible for drafting reports that subsequently were ratified (or not) by the NRA Heads at plenary meetings. The ERG's output was published in the form of common positions, opinions, best practices, (annual) reports, benchmark studies, work programmes, and minutes of meetings.

The ERG Chairman presented this output at European conferences and regular meetings with industry associations – (among them the ECTA, ETNO, INTUG, ECCA, and GSM Association), – discussing industry views on key issues and regulatory developments. Stakeholders might also express their views through frequent ERG-hosted public consultations, the contributions to which were then made available to all whom it might concern. Interestingly, it was also the case that stakeholders at National Level could influence the ERG *indirectly* by influencing their national IRAs (*via* consultations for example); a circumstance which will become particularly noteworthy in the context of Part Two of this case study (wherein Ofcom facilitated stakeholder meetings for the eCommunications Framework Review).

In November 2006, due to the serious concerns of many stakeholders about the implementation of eCommunications regulations in the Member States, the Commission formally requested advice from the ERG on how best to bring consistency to the regulation of electronic communications in Europe's internal market. The Commission acknowledged that an economic regulatory regime like the Framework may have to be adapted to national circumstances, but at the same time noted with concern the competitive distortions that might arise if like remedies were not applied to like situations across Europe. Following this occurrence, the Commission considered the option of relying in future on the ERG and

measures aimed at ensuring harmonised conditions for the availability and efficient use of radio spectrum, as well as the availability of information related to the use of radio spectrum."

IRAs for more consistency in the internal market. However, it was proposed that, to bring this off, the ERG would have to be transformed from an advisory body into a permanent, independent body responsible for harmonising regulation of all electronic communications networks and markets in the EU (Reding, 2006a). This "enhanced ERG" came into being in 2010 per Regulation (EC) No 1211/2009 "establishing the Body of European Regulators for Electronic Communications (BEREC) and the Office".

Fora provided by private industry associations

This example shows that European regulatory bodies provide industry with access to the policy process, and national bodies with an alternative platform to represent national stakeholder interests. The Survey in Chapter Six evidenced that industry associations are the preferred vehicle for businesses to convey their views to the authorities. To round out the "picture" of stakeholder involvement with regulatory bodies, the author has selected for further analysis two pan-European industry associations – the European Internet Services Providers Association (EuroISPA) and the European Competitive Telecommunications Association (ECTA) – which function as private policy fora where industry stakeholders may articulate their views to regulators.

With approximately 850 members, EuroISPA is the largest association of ISPs in the world. It collaborates with the European Commission and with other stakeholders to establish an efficient framework for the evolution of eCommunications in the EU. EuroISPA regularly, pro-actively participates in public consultations, industry events and conferences, EU workshops and roundtables, and publishes a newsletter disseminating its views. The association also interacts with regulators at the National, European and Global Levels, as witness its participation in the public hearings in ERG's consultation on "Significant Market Power Remedies" in 2006; in the European Parliament [Political] Group Hearing on "Data Retention" in 2005, convened by ALDE (the political group Alliance of Liberals and Democrats for Europe); in the OECD Forum Session on "Emerging spam issues" in 2005; and in the EP Citizens' Rights Committee Hearing on a "Safer Internet" in 2004. EuroISPA's wide-ranging interaction with regulators and its facilitation of consensus-building exemplifies the value of industry associations, especially for smaller service providers who cannot afford engagement on their own. A common position taken by 850 ISPs is much more powerful than 850 individual views presented in onesies and twosies, and this explains why EuroISPA has been so successful in gaining direct access to regulators.

Even more impactfully, EuroISPA endeavours to influence the policy agenda by issuing joint statements on important matters with other industry associations, *viz.* the European Public Telecommunications Network Operators' Association (ETNO),[197] the European Competitive Telecommunications Association (ECTA), the European Cable Communications

197 ETNO represents 40 of Europe's largest and most established telecoms groups. It has an established Regulatory Policy Working Group that closely monitors the implementation of the eCommunications Framework and promotes an investment-friendly and harmonised regulatory environment (European Public Telecommunications Network Operator's Association website, 2006).

Association (ECCA),[198] and GSM Europe (GSME).[199] When the major industry associations in the provision of electronic communication services express common views jointly, these are difficult for the regulator to ignore (Anonymous, 2006a; EuroISPA website, 2006).

EuroISPA believes the fundamental principles of the 2002 Regulatory Framework remain as valid today as when first implemented, hence it is wary of frequent, radical overhauls of the regulatory regime because of how they may impact its members; as businesses need legal certainty and stability to stay profitable. To express these concerns (but also as a routine matter of addressing developments directly affecting its membership), EuroISPA responded in detail to the eCommunications Review (EuroISPA, 2006).

Another private industry association pro-actively engaged in regulatory policy development is the ECTA, with 150 corporate members, including both individual service providers, operators and suppliers, and national industry associations. ECTA offers them opportunities to participate in conferences, seminars, networking events, briefings, and executive meetings. An in-house Regulatory Forum coordinates its collaboration with the European Commission. The Forum meets three or four times a year to agree priorities for the industry and discuss emerging issues. Another means of collecting senior-level telecoms executives' input and of formulating industry consensus are the ECTA Telecoms Executive Roundtables, where panels of discussants meet to explore high-profile current issues, to wage conceptual leadership, to exchange experiences, and to engage in networking.

The ECTA has very successfully influenced a number of consultations over the Regulatory Framework, including the 2006 Review and the ERG consultation on Remedies in January 2006. Its input was so highly valued that the Commission expressly cited it, saying that the data it provided "tends to support the claims made by the European Competitive Telecommunications Association (ECTA) in their response to the Call for Input" (CEC, 2006y:9). The ECTA was trying to evidence that Member States which had implemented the EU regulatory framework in an "effective and pro-competitive manner" had attracted the most private investment, a finding also corroborated by the OECD Regulatory Reform Index for the telecoms sector. The reader should note that the ECTA, the OECD and the Commission have all agreed to justify regulatory policy not on the basis of consumer benefit but of investment climate. Indeed, the Commission actually "evangelises" the Members States (as it were) to adopt this supply-side orientation, its Staff Working Document "on the Review of the EU Regulatory Framework for electronic communications networks and services" (SEC(2006) 816) recommending that they and the NRAs implement a business-supportive environment

198 ECCA seeks "to foster co-operation between cable operators and to promote and represent the interests of its members at the European level." It has 35 member organisations in 20 different countries across Europe. The association has a Regulatory Forum, which organises the Regulatory Committee (European Cable Communications Association website, 2006).

199 GSME is the European industry association for mobile phone operators. It represents around 147 operators in 50 countries/areas in Europe. GSME operates a Regulatory Working Group designed to track the eCommunications Framework and to deliver a consensus to European regulators on legislative issues and initiatives. The Working Group publishes position papers and holds face-to-face meetings with policy makers (GSM Europe website, 2006).

where investment can flourish. This proves, as well as anything could, the predominance of industry interests and viewpoint at the European Level of governance.

The ECTA also presented its views on "key convergence issues" at the OECD Roundtable in June 2005; at the Conference of Postal and Telecommunications Administrations (CEPT) held in April 2005 on the theme of "Effective regulatory regimes and impact on investments in the telecoms sector"; and at the Centre for European Policy Studies (CEPS) workshop held in September 2005 on the theme of "Promoting investment through competition" (European Competitive Telecommunications Association website, 2006). The ECTA holds an Annual Regulatory Conference to which Commission officials, national regulators, postal and telecommunications ministers, and the chief legal counsels of telecoms service operators are invited. The list of attendees of the 2005 ECTA Conference, which reads like a Who's Who of European officialdom, suggests that ECTA interacts effectively with the most influential European policy-makers.[200] The latest Annual ECTA Regulatory Conference (28 November 2011) and the special conference on the theme of "Ultra-Fast Broadband: Policy & Practice" (21 May 2012) took place in Brussels and were attended by high-profile speakers from the Commission and Member States, indicating continuing influence at the highest political levels (ECTA website, 2012).

7.3 CASE STUDY – PART ONE: PARTICIPATION AT EUROPEAN LEVEL – THE 2006 REVIEW PROCESS

In 1999 the European Commission defined five fundamental principles of Better Regulation that were to inform all of its future regulatory frameworks:

1. "Regulation should be based on the clearly defined policy objectives" of a) "fostering economic growth and competitiveness thereby promoting employment" and b) providing public goods where market forces alone fail to deliver them.
2. "Regulation should be kept to the minimum necessary to meet those policy objectives".
3. Regulation should strike the right balance between adaptability and legal certainty.
4. "Regulation should aim to be technologically neutral", or if non-neutral, should be justified on objectively justifiable grounds.
5. "Regulation may be agreed globally, regionally or nationally, but should be enforced as closely as is practicable to the activities being regulated" (CEC, 1999c:12-13; CEC, 2006aa:34).

To monitor enforcement of these principles, and to keep pace with new market developments and technological changes, the eCommunications Regulatory Framework

200 At the ECTA 7th Annual Regulatory Conference (29th November – 1st December 2005) speakers included Stephen Carter (Chief Executive, Ofcom), Kip Meek (OFCOM, 2006 chair of the European Regulators Group), Peter Scott (European Commission/DG Information Society, Head of Unit B1 - Policy Development and responsible for the 2006 Review), Peter Rodford (European Commission/ Information Society, Head of Unit B2 – Implementation of the Regulatory Framework) and Robert Pepper (Senior Managing Director, Cisco, formerly FCC).

provides for a regular "review" of the existing regime, especially as to its market-liberalising performance. Before launching the 2006 Review of the Framework, the Commission consulted with the concerned Member-State ministries at two high-level meetings in September 2005, with follow-up meetings in March 2006. This proves that the Commission does not draft proposals in isolation, but holds thorough consultations with Member State officials before even launching a new regulatory initiative.

Not content with consulting just the Member States, the Commission also held at European Level preliminary comitology meetings with the Communications Committee and Radio Spectrum Committee, while continuing discussions with the European Regulators Group, Radio Spectrum Policy Group, eEurope Advisory Group, and the Article 29 Working Party. Finally, the Commission consulted the results of more than 40 eCommunications studies and surveys commissioned to external consultants and conducted between 2000 and 2005, and 15 Commission Staff Working Documents and assessments published since June 2002. Private stakeholders were given an opportunity to provide feedback in 13 preliminary consultations, and to participate in more than 14 workshops organised by the Commission and open to the public, all beginning in March 2004.[201]

The Commission's first formal review of the legal instruments that define the Framework took place in 2006. This constitutes the subject-matter of this case study. Besides its five constituent Directives, the list of markets susceptible to *exante* regulation was reviewed in Recommendation C(2007) 5406 rev1 on "susceptible markets under the current Directives" (CEC, 2007p).[202] The 2006 Review was intended to conduct "a thorough examination of the framework's principles and implementation, especially to remove any bottlenecks delaying the provision of faster, more innovative and competitive services" (Europa website – eCommunications Framework Review, 2006).

The Review proper was launched at the end of November 2005 with a preliminary Call for Input (CEC, 2005a) that allowed stakeholders to air in advance their views on possible changes. At the EU Telecommunications Council held on 1 December 2005 the concerned Ministers represented the interests of their respective national regulators and stakeholders

201 The Annexe of SEC(2006)817 Commission Staff Working Document provides a detailed list of consultation, expertise and information sources used by the Commission for the eCommunications Framework Review 2006. See also Europa website – Documentation.

202 The Commission argues that the main reason for regulating the eCommunications markets is that these markets, which were originally dominated by state-owned monopolies, are still subject to structural problems in competition. In its draft of a new Recommendation the Commission has considered reducing the current list of 18 (7 retail and 11 wholesale) specific eCommunications markets that are deemed susceptible to *ex ante* regulation. The Commission believes that competition is already effective in six of these markets, and therefore steps may be taken to further deregulate the telecommunications industry. In the 2006 Review consultation the Commission requested stakeholder input on whether two further markets might be removed from the list of markets susceptible to regulation: the "wholesale market for access and call origination on public mobile telephone networks" and "the market for broadcasting transmission services." Retail telephone texting (SMS) as part of "mobile call termination" will be subject to EU regulation for the first time. Neelie Kroes, Commissioner for Competition, stressed that "the Commission's aim is less, but more effective, regulation" (CEC, 2006m; Reding, 2006a).

in the upcoming Review (CEC, 2005a; Europa website – eCommunications Framework Review, 2006). The preliminary Call for Input was closed on 31 January 2006 and, as with most consultations, the contributions were published on the Internet (unless confidentiality had been requested). Of the 155 *named* public and private stakeholders who responded to the Call,[203] 24 or 15.5% of the total number of respondents came from government, regulatory authorities and other public authorities; 40 or 26% came from industry associations; 5 or 3% from consumer and user bodies; 76 or 49% from individual commercial organisations (of which 51 or 33% of the whole were from telecoms network and Internet service providers, and 25 or 16% of the whole from manufacturers); 6 or 4% were individuals or consultancies; 2 or 1.5% were from research institutions and universities; and 1 or approximately 1.5% was classified as "other associations" (Europa website – eCommunications Framework Review Results, 2006). With more than three-quarters of the responses originating with individual business organisations or industry associations, it may be inferred as self-evident that this stakeholder group had the strongest interest in, and likely had the most influence over the pending main consultation as well.

On 24 January 2006 the Commission held a one-day public workshop in Brussels, open to all interested parties, on the eCommunications Framework Review and on its Recommendation on relevant markets susceptible to *ex ante* regulation. 440 experts from industry and trade associations participated, debating and addressing open questions posed by the Commission. With Mr Fabio Colasanti, Director General of DG Information Society and Media, and Mr Philip Lowe, Director General of DG Competition, also in attendance, stakeholders had an opportunity to express their observations and concerns to the Commission's highest administrative level.

It is worth noting that such consultations do not take place in isolation, but in coordination with other measures involving collaboration between the Commission and stakeholders; for example, this workshop followed up the Commission's publication of its 11th Report (CEC, 2006p) on implementation of the Framework. It described the current regulatory state of affairs, presenting economic data on the ICT market; market developments in mobile and fixed services; broadband services; and consumer interests. Together with the consultations and stakeholder meetings, these Annual Reports are considered to be a vehicle for the European Commission to gather together data and findings that may contribute to the ongoing review of the Framework.

On 29 June 2006 the Commission published the formal Communication that launched the public consultation on the future of the regulatory framework for electronic communications (CEC, 2006s). 204 public and private bodies submitted comments on the five already existing eCommunications Framework Directives. An analysis by respondent category showed that 27 or 13% of all responses received were from governments, regulatory authorities and other public authorities; 65 or 32% from industry associations; 9 or 4.5% from consumer associations; 91 or 44.6% were from individual commercial organisations (of which 80 or 39% of the whole were from telecom network and Internet service providers, and 11

203 N.B.: Omitted from these statistics are those who requested confidentiality.

or 5.5% of the whole from manufacturers); and 12 or 6% from individuals, consultancies, research institutions, universities and other associations (Europa website – eCommunications Framework Review responses, 2007; Europa website – eCommunications Framework Review on relevant markets, 2007). Again, more than three-fourths of the respondents were from individual commercial organisations or industry associations, demonstrating, by their active participation, a continuing interest in the consultation and policy process. Comparison with the results of the 2005 Call for Input shows the percentage of participants from industry associations, telecom networks, and Internet service providers had risen slightly, indicating, if anything, an increased interest by the regulatees directly affected by possible regulatory changes.

Two Staff Working Documents were published on the same day to launch the consultation. The first, the "Proposed Changes" Working Document, explained the major proposed changes to the eCommunications Framework's approach to spectrum management, and toward reduction of the NRAs' procedural burden of constantly reviewing which markets are susceptible to *ex ante* regulation; as well as other changes designed to consolidate the Single Market, protect consumer interests, enhance security, and get rid the EU of outdated provisions. This document also addressed the concerns of stakeholders, from disabled users to operators with significant market power (CEC, 2006y). This is evidence that the Commission takes care to verify that they have articulated stakeholders' *actual* concerns before moving them onto the policy agenda.

The second Working Document was the Commission's own Regulatory Impact Assessment, which presented its cost-benefit analysis of the proposed regulations (CEC, 2006aa). The Commission estimated and analysed the regulatory implications; recommending options for revising the Regulatory Framework and providing justification for the "Proposed Changes" Communication. It was emphasised that these proposals were to wait upon an intensive consultation process. This process will be analysed in depth directly below.

There followed on 13 July 2006 a public presentation of the changes contemplated in the eCommunications Framework to diverse stakeholders, whose concerns and questions the Commission officially addressed. The presentation was open to all parties interested in the Regulatory Framework, evidencing that the Commission seeks to make itself more accessible to stakeholders by hosting events like this; an inference reinforced by the fact that stakeholders were allowed to interact directly with the key Commission functionaries responsible for drafting the policy proposals (CEC, 2005a; CEC, 2006cc; CEC, 2006dd).

The consultation was closed on 27 October 2006; however, the results of the 2006 Review provided stimuli for new activities, which are now presented. The responses received in the 2006 Review consultation were published on the eCommunications Framework website in November 2006. In November 2007 the Commission published COM(2007)697rev1, a second Communication that reported on the 2006 Review consultation and on the proposed regulatory package of reforms to the existing Framework.[204] It summarised the grounds

204 The package adopted by the European Commission included: Directive COM(2007)697rev1 amending the Framework Directive (2002/21/EC), the Access and Interconnection Directive (2002/19/EC) and the Authorisation Directive (2002/20/EC); Directive COM(2007)698 amending the Universal Service Directive (2002/22/EC) and Data Protection and Privacy Directive (2002/58/EC); Regula-

and objectives of this proposal by proclaiming that "to enhance investment, innovation and consumer benefits in electronic communications, Europe needs a coherent regulatory framework for the digital economy that is future-proof, market-oriented, and exploits the advantages brought by the completion of the internal market" (CEC, 2007j:1). The follow-up Impact Assessment SEC(2007)1472 that accompanied this second Communication provides further evidence that the overarching theme was economic effects (although consumer rights were not altogether neglected), supported by the objectives of Better Regulation[205] (CEC, 2007b).

This second Communication marked the last step in the 2006 Review process preparatory to submitting to the European Council a formal legislative proposal revising the eCommunications Regulatory Framework. This initiated negotiation of the revised Directives over the following 12-18 months (2007-08). Once this stage was reached, business and other stakeholders ceased to have much input into the shape of the regulations. Although the proposal was discussed in European Parliament committees under the Co-decision Procedure, with but few exceptions (such as parliamentary expert hearings) external stakeholders were excluded.

The practice of the EP, supposedly the most democratic EU institution, presents a striking contrast with that of the Commission, reputedly so aloof and unapproachable. It might even be argued that, by adopting the principles of the New Governance, the Commission has done more than any other EU institution to roll back the "democratic deficit".

It is conceded that in the final stages of the legislative process the EU Telecoms Council did issue a routine press release after each of its (closed) meetings (Europa website – Council of the European Union: Transport, Telecommunications and Energy, 2007). In general, however, after a Council reaches political agreement on a legislative text, and its Common Position is published in the L-series of the Official Journal of the European Communities, no stakeholder input or even influence is permitted or desired. The European Parliament's Communications Committee may also have invited interested parties to a debriefing session giving a general overview of discussions within the Committee, and all EP documents finally adopted, including the Preparatory Reports drafted by the Rapporteurs and discussed in EP committees, were published on the Legislative Observatory's website (European Parliament

---

tion COM(2007)699rev2 establishing the European Electronic Communications Market Authority; COM(2007)696rev1 "Report on the outcome of the Review of the EU regulatory framework for electronic communications networks and services in accordance with Directive 2002/21/EC and Summary of the 2007 Reform Proposal"; Recommendation C(2007)5406rev1 on "Relevant product and services markets within the electronic communications sector", and SEC(2007)1483 explanatory note; Impact Assessment SEC(2007)1472; and COM(2007)yyy on "Reaping the full benefits of the digital divide in Europe: A common approach to the use the spectrum released by the digital switchover" (Europa website – eCommunications Framework Review proposal).

205 The Impact Assessment SEC(2007)1472 identifies three main themes which are "(1) Better regulation by ensuring competition, investment and regulation, and spectrum management; (2) the Completion of the Single Market in eCommunications by enabling regulatory consistency and effectiveness; and (3) Connecting with citizens through improving users' rights, consumer protection, privacy and security".

website – Legislative Observatory, 2007). This did provide some transparency, presumably contributing to Parliament's accountability to the electorate, but it involved no direct participation of external stakeholders, unlike the Commission's consultative procedure. Indeed, Article 23(1) of the eCommunications Framework Directive of 2002 not only compels the Commission to exchange information with external policy stakeholders, it even mentions specific private and public stakeholder groups that are to be kept informed[206] (CEC, 2002d).

The EP held its first reading on 24 September 2008; its second on 6 May 2009; and the third on 24 November 2009, when the two new Directives (2009/140/EC) and (2009/136/EC), and the 1211/2009 Regulation establishing BEREC, were formally adopted. The Council of Ministers (*i.e.* Heads of State) and the European Parliament agreed the reform package on 24 November 2009, entailing that the Member States must have transposed the new Framework by 25 May 2011 (Europa website – eCommunications Framework Review, 2006; European Parliament website – eCommunications Framework, 2008; UK DTI website – eCommunications Review, 2006). The new Framework consolidates the original five constituent Directives into two, which are informally known as the "Framework" and "Privacy" Directives. A summary of the stages comprising the 2006 Review is presented below. The table also shows how stakeholder involvement and influence typically wax and wane over time.

Table 7.3: Roadmap for the EU Regulatory Framework Review

Activities for the eCommunications Framework Review and Implementation	Indicative Timetable	Stakeholder involvement
The European Commission commissioned eCommunications studies and surveys from external consultants, launched consultations, and organised open workshops for stakeholders.	2000 - 2005	Yes (active)/ studies & surveys
Press Release: First review of susceptible markets in new Regulatory Framework.	02/07/2004	No
The Commission discussed the review with Member States' Ministries, the Communications Committee (Cocom), and the Radio Spectrum Committee.	September 2005	No
Preliminary Call for Input on the forthcoming Review of the "EU Regulatory Framework for electronic communications and services" (25 November 2005).	25/11/2005 – 31/01/2006	Yes (active)/ consultation

206 Article 23 (Exchange of Information) of the Framework Directive (2002)21 requires:
"1. The Commission shall provide all relevant information to the Communications Committee on the outcome of regular consultations with the representatives of network operators, service providers, users, consumers, manufacturers and trade unions, as well as third countries and international organisations.
2. The Communications Committee shall, taking account of the Community's electronic communications policy, foster the exchange of information between the Member States and between the Member States and the Commission on the situation and the development of regulatory activities regarding electronic communications networks and services".

Activities for the eCommunications Framework Review and Implementation	Indicative Timetable	Stakeholder involvement
Ministers at the EU Telecommunications Council discuss the Review.	01/12/2005	No
Workshop with Commission senior staff (Brussels).	24/01/2006	Yes (active)/ workshop
Commission published COM(2006)28final on "Market Reviews under the EU Regulatory Framework – Consolidating the internal market for electronic communications".	06/02/2006	No
Commission published COM(2006)68 - "European Electronic Communications Regulation and Markets Report 2005" (11th Implementation Report).	20/02/2006	N/A
Debriefing session between the Communications Committee and interested parties.	23/03/2006	Yes (passive)/ debrief
Publication of contributions to Call of Input on Europa's Information Society website.	March 2006	Yes (passive)/ responses published
Debriefing session between the Communications Committee and interested parties.	08/06/2006	Yes (passive)/ debrief
Communication COM(2006)336 "on the Review of the EU Regulatory Framework" Staff Working Documents SEC(2006)816 "Proposed Changes" and SEC(2006)817 "Impact Assessment".	29/06/2006	No
Launch of public consultation by Communication COM(2006)334 on the "Review of EU Regulatory Framework for eCommunications Networks and Services".	29/06/2006 – 27/10/2006	Yes (active)/ consultation
Draft Commission Recommendation C(2007)5406 on "Relevant Product and Service Markets within the eCommunications sector susceptible to *ex ante* regulation in accordance with Directive 2002/21/EC". Commission Staff Working Document SEC(2006)837draft of Recommendation "on Relevant Product and Service Markets within the eCommunication Sector".	29/06/2006	No
Launch of public consultation on the Commission's Recommendation "on Relevant Product and Service Markets within the eCommunications Sector".	29/06/2006 - 27/10/2006	Yes (active)/ consultation
Public presentation over 2 days by the European Commission (Brussels).	13/07/2006	Yes (active)/ workshop
Public workshop hosted by the European Commission and broadcast live over the Internet (Brussels).	10/10/2006	Yes (active)/ workshop
Debriefing session between the Communications Committee and interested parties.	12/10/2006	Yes (passive)/ debrief
Publication of contributions to public consultation on the Review of the EU Regulatory Framework (available on Europa website).	23/11/2006	Yes (passive)/ responses published

Activities for the eCommunications Framework Review and Implementation	Indicative Timetable	Stakeholder involvement
Consultation of the European Regulators Group (ERG) by the European Commission to ensure consistency of Regulation on eCommunications in Europe's internal market. Further consultations took place following this initial briefing.	30/11/2006 - 27/02/2007	Yes (active)/ indirect influence via ERG through NRAs
Decision C(2006)6364 on a "List of standards and/or specifications for electronic communications networks, services and associated facilities and services, replacing all previous versions".	11/12/2006	Yes (active)/ indirect influence via ESOs
Debriefing session between the Communications Committee and interested parties.	25/01/2007	Yes (passive)/ debrief
Communication COM(2007)155 on "Europe Electronic Communications Regulation and Markets 2006" (12th Implementation Report).	29/03/2007	N/A
Debriefing session between the Communications Committee and interested parties.	4/04/2007	Yes (passive)/ debrief
EP committees and Council working groups discuss the new Regulatory Framework (German and Portuguese Presidencies).	1st– 3rd Quarter 2007	No
The European and Social Committee (EESC), representing civil society, and the Committee of the Regions, representing local and regional authorities, provide their opinions to the Council, the Commission and the European Parliament.	3rd Quarter 2007 - 4th Quarter 2007	Yes (active)/ indirect influence via EESC and Committee of the Regions
Second Communication COM(2007)697rev1 reporting on the public consultation on the functioning of the new Regulatory Framework.	13/11/2007	Yes (passive)/ results of consultation
Directive COM(2007)698 amending universal services and user's rights and concerning the processing of personal data and protection. Draft legislative proposals for European Parliament and Council Directives modifying the Regulatory Framework (Co-Decision Procedure).	13/11/2007	No
Regulation COM(2007)699 issued by the European Parliament and Council setting up the European Electronic Communications Market Authority.[207]	13/11/2007	No
Staff Working Document SEC(2007)1473 summary "Impact Assessment" issued.	13/11/2007	No
EP appoints lead Committees and Rapporteurs to advance the proposal; meetings timetabled; detailed discussions in EP Committee on Industry, Research and Energy (ITRE) and EP Committee on Internal Market and Consumer Protection (IMCO).	1st Quarter 2008	No
Preliminary debate in European Parliament on new eCommunications Framework, followed by public hearing.	4/02/2008	Yes (active)/ indirect influence via public hearings
EU Telecommunications Council publishes general approach and progress report.	12/6/2008	No

Activities for the eCommunications Framework Review and Implementation	Indicative Timetable	Stakeholder involvement
1st Reading in European Parliament adopting 126 amendments to consolidated Framework Directive and 155 amendments to consolidated Privacy Directive.	24/9/2008	No
Meetings of Council Working Groups.	3rd Quarter 2008	No
Amendment by Commission of proposed consolidated Framework Directive, *i.e.* for electronic communications networks and services, Access and Interconnection Directive, and Authorisation Directive (COM(2008)724-2007/0247(COD). (The EP adopted 126 amendments to the proposal at its first reading on 24 September 2008.)	6/11/2008	No
Amendment by Commission of proposed for a Universal Services Directive, Data Protection Directive, and Regulation (EC) No 2006/2004 on consumer protection cooperation (COM(2008)723-2007/0248(COD). (The EP adopted 155 amendments to the proposal at first reading on 24 September 2008.)	6/11/2008	No
Amendment by Commission of proposed Regulation establishing the European Electronic Communications Market Authority *i.e.* (EEMA) COM(2008)720-2007/0249(COD).	6/11/2008	No
EU Telecommunications Council publishes its Common Position.	16/2/2009	No
2nd Reading in European Parliament adopting the Council's "Common Position". Approval with Amendments.	6/5/2009	No
Opinion of the European Commission issued.	30/7/2009	No
Agreement and adoption in the Council of Ministers. Proposal rejected by EP triggering Conciliation between EP and Commission.	30/7/2009	No
First Conciliation Committee meeting to agree joint text. An agreement on the EU telecoms reform was reached by the EP and the Council of Ministers.	04/11/2009	No
3rd Reading in European Parliament. Adoption of the Amendments to the two Directives that consolidated the original five, and of the one new Regulation. [208]	24/11/2009	No
Publication of Council Common Position in the Official Journal. Publication of legal texts in the L series of the Official Journal (Official Journal L 337 of 18.12.2009).	18/12/2009	No
Transposition of the Revised Framework in EU Member States (18 months after adoption in Council). [209]	25/05/2011	No

7.4 CASE STUDY – PART TWO: PARTICIPATION AT NATIONAL LEVEL – THE 2006 REVIEW IN THE UK

The 2002 "regulatory package" of European directives on electronic communications had been implemented in the UK through the Electronic Communications Act of 2003, setting up the Office of Communications (Ofcom).[210] Ofcom is an IRA "wholly independent of the UK Government and reports to Parliament rather than ministers" (BERR website, 2007).

While most Member States responded on their own behalf to the EU's Regulatory Framework Review, leaving national stakeholders on their own recognisance, the UK government rather uniquely synthesised into a "UK response" (in lieu of a response of its own) the input solicited from individual stakeholders in workshops facilitated by several of the UK's specialised regulatory agencies. These agencies, namely the Department of Trade and Industry (DTI) and Ofcom,[211] then reconciled the diversity of stakeholder views expressed in the tributary workshops. The government's preparations for the 2006 Review were open to all interested parties, and DTI and Ofcom jointly conducted the stakeholder meetings to seek consensus, after which participants with outstanding issues specific to themselves might contact the Review team on an *ad hoc* basis.

This evidences that Member State governments sometimes even co-opt business organisations to represent national interests in Brussels, in lieu of getting directly involved. It may be that industry is more trusted in Brussels than are the Member States' governments. If so, this would be because industry consistently supports, and indeed constitutes the most

207 The proposed "European Electronic Communications Market Authority" is the "enhanced ERG" with extended competencies, which was eventually set up as BEREC.

208 Directive (2009/140/EC) of 25 November 2009 "amending Directives (2002/21/EC) on a common regulatory framework for electronic communications networks and services, (2002/19/EC) on access to, and the interconnection of, electronic communications networks and associated facilities, and (2002/20/EC) on the authorisation of electronic communications networks and services". Directive (2009/136/EC) of 25 November 2009 "amending Directive (2002/22/EC) on universal services and users' rights relating to electronic communications networks and services, Directive (2002/58/EC) concerning the processing of personal data and the protection of privacy in the electronic communications sector and Regulation (EC) No (2006/2004) on corporation between national authorities responsible for the enforcement if consumer protection laws".

Regulation (EC) No 1211/2009 of 25 November 2009 "establishing the Body of European Regulators for Electronic Communications (BEREC) and the Office".

209 For the latest developments on the eCommunications Framework Review, refer to the Europa website at http://ec.europa.eu/prelex/detail_dossier_real.cfm?CL=en&DosId=196418#400925

210 Ofcom brought together five previously separate regulators: the Broadcast Standards Commission, the Independent Television Commission, Office of Telecommunications (Oftel), the Radio Authority and the Radiocommunications Agency.

211 Claire Hobson (DTI, Head UK Telecoms Policy) and Nigel Hickson (DTI, Head European ICT Policy) had responsibility for the coordination. Ofcom provided support in preparing the 2006 Review response, namely Tom Kiedrowski (Ofcom, Policy Manager within the Strategy and Market Developments Group) and Jim Niblett (Ofcom, Director International Telecoms Regulation & Co-ordination). (DTI website – ICT Policy, 2006; DTI website – Telecoms, 2006; Ofcom website, 2006).

vital actor for the EU's Single Market agenda, whereas governments are more interested in bargaining over the spoils of the EU budget. Industry seeks an instrumental influence over regulation to construct a regulatory environment conducive to business success, whereas Member State governments may be suspected of seeking power for its own sake, heedless of the better outcome.

DTI and Ofcom held four public consultation meetings in the first six months of preparing the so-called Government Response, all of which the author attended. An introductory stakeholder meeting was held on 22 December 2005 to share preliminary thoughts on the scope and priorities of the 2006 Review. A second meeting on 3 February 2006 walked stakeholders through the views of the UK Government then emerging in response to the Commission's Call for Input (CEC, 2006s), and updated them on how these views had been developing. In a third meeting of 7 March 2006 stakeholders discussed and agreed the final draft of their input. The fourth meeting of 27 July 2006 instructed stakeholders on the main proposals of COM(2006)334, in the Call for Input together with the associated Staff Working Papers; *viz.* the Proposed Changes and the Impact Assessment. Stakeholders were also encouraged to review the Commission's plan for changes to its previous Recommendation on Relevant [*i.e.* "regulation-susceptible"] Markets.[212]

The final UK Government Consultation Response was submitted to the Commission on 27 October 2006. BERR (DTI's successor, 2007-2009) held a follow-up stakeholder meeting on 19 November 2007, four days after the Commission published its proposals for modifying the eCommunications Framework. The importance of these modifications for businesses, consumers, and the UK economy was explained in presentations by BERR and Ofcom, and then in a speech by Stephen Timms, the UK's Minister of State for e-Commerce and Competitiveness. These facts prove that the UK Government fully supported the new participatory governance, and welcomed the BERR-Ofcom stakeholder meetings (Hobson, 2007; Niblett, 2007; Timms, 2007).

All subsequent stakeholder meetings followed a common pattern: (1) an update on the latest EU developments deriving from the 2006 Review; (2) presentations by officials from BERR and Ofcom outlining key points of concern to UK stakeholders; and (3) stakeholder discussions and agreement of an Action Plan pending the next meeting.

As a participant observer in these stakeholder meetings at both National and European Levels, the author witnessed that, even though the participants in the UK meetings represented many diverse interests, from telecoms operators to consumer groups, fewer industry association representatives attended these meetings than attended those held by the Commission. This is an interesting discovery which suggests that the industry prefers acting through industry associations *when participating at European Level. Individual* business organisations frequent national more than European stakeholder events (*cf.* Section 6.4.1, Question 2, above); however, the expense of accessing the European Level makes it more economical to channel input through membership of industry associations. Most

212 Minutes of UK stakeholder meeting (DTI Conference Centre, Victoria Street, London). Presentations are available on the DTI website – eCommunications Review minutes.

national industry associations are part of a powerful, wider European network, with direct representation in Brussels and contacts inside the EU institutions (*cf.* Chapter Five).

A review of the content of the UK Response, which according to his eyewitness observation reflects the input of UK stakeholders faithfully enough, convinced the author that it contained no obvious differences from the concerns raised at the European Level by stakeholder groups. Considering the essentially Europe-wide scope of the telecommunications industry, and that many participants in the 2006 Review represent global business organisations, this is no surprise.[213]

During the UK stakeholder meeting of 7 March 2006, most of the 57 participants were either industry associations (11 participants or 19%) or else commercial organisations (29 participants or 51%, of which 18 or 32% were telecoms operators/ISPs, 7 or 12% telecoms manufacturers, and 4 or 7% professional firms/consultancies). Next were governmental and regulatory bodies (13 or 23%) and individuals (4 or 7%). The 64 participants who attended the stakeholder meeting of 27 July 2006 included industry associations (9 participants or 14%), commercial organisations (36 participants or 56%, of which 21 or 33% were telecoms operators/ISPs, 7 or 11% manufacturers, and 8 or 13% professional firms/consultancies), followed by governmental and regulatory bodies (8 or 13%), individuals/universities (4 or 6%) and consumer associations (7 or 11%). These data show that stakeholder participation at National Level in the UK, as at European Level, is dominated by business interests, who comprised 70 percent of participants. This suggests that business influence over the UK regulator is equally predominating. In this, what we might call "industry governance" at the National Level (at least in the UK) reflects what is to be observed at the European Level.

7.5 CASE STUDY – SUPPLEMENT: GLOBAL PARTICIPATION

The Global Level differs from the other Levels of governance in the Four-Level Model, in that it lacks a unitary Executive with coercive powers; thus, one cannot expect the same amount of regulatory activity. Initiatives occur more haphazardly and tend to be more narrowly focussed. Moreover, the global agenda must happen to chime with national and supranational (*viz.* EU) agendas first, before any truly "global" initiative becomes possible. It therefore behoved the author to choose a case to study where this had happened, and the Information Society agenda was one such case. One aspect of the EU Regulatory Framework of particular concern to industry and users of eCommunictions services outside EU jurisdiction was the prohibition against spam.[214] Although the EU policy process does not

---

213 Examples of "global players" that attended UK stakeholder meetings were: NTL, Yahoo, Wanadoo, Verizon, T-Mobile, Vodafone, Cable & Wireless, Nortel, BT (operators); and Motorola, Ericsson and Nokia (manufacturers).

214 Definition of spam: "the abuse of electronic messaging systems to send unsolicited bulk messages, which are generally undesired" (The Anti-Abuse Project website, 2008). The content of spam often causes harm *via* viruses, illegal prescription drug solicitations, financial scams, instant messaging attacks (spam), and so on. Spam is more widely used for indiscriminate volume emails rather than badly targeted marketing.

formally require the involvement of actors and stakeholders beyond EU jurisdiction,[215] spam was a good example of how European industry influences the EU policy agenda, through its influence on international initiatives which impact EU policy.

The evidence of the spam initiatives suggested that regulation had not been successful in reducing it. Spam had increased in the teeth of multiple prohibitive regulatory initiatives at both National and European Levels. National and EU regulators, then, were forced to look for a solution at the Global Level, and therefore one not based on command-and-control state coercion. The initiatives identified by the author were primarily attempts at technological fixes, such as blocking or scanning unsolicited emails by ISPs, the anti-spam toolkit (an OECD initiative), and self-regulatory measures by service providers. All of these solutions depended on the technical capacity and good will of the industry; thus, industry influence over policy output predominated even on the Global Level.

Despite the lack of a formal requirement for consultation at the Global Level, the research done for this book suggests the international arena is wide open to stakeholder input. Although less evidence exists than at National or European Levels, the Supplement presents some evidence that the ICT industry has an important impact on both policy input and policy output.

One issue that has attracted much attention from both regulators and stakeholders, as closely related to privacy, is the matter of unsolicited commercial emails (UCE), sometimes known as "spam". Spam has been defined as any bulk, unsolicited, marketing "e-mail sent *without* the consent of the addressee and without any attempt at targeting recipients who are likely to be interested in its contents" (DTI website, 2006). The concept of "unsolicited commercial electronic email" itself covers not only SMTP-based e-mail, but also SMS, MMS and "any form of electronic communication for which the simultaneous participation of the sender and the recipient is not required" (CEC, 2004c:5).

Spam is widely recognised as one of the most significant electronic communications issues facing the Internet today. By July 2004 it accounted for more than 65% of all global e-mail traffic – an amazing increase of 23% over February 2003 (Brightmail[216] website, 2006). As of 2011 the figure was up to 75% (Symantec website, 2012). "This costs global businesses an estimated €10bn a year in lost productivity" (Thomas, 2003:28) – which explains the industry's interest in tackling the issue. Spam is a problem for many reasons: it clogs up the email inboxes of individual and corporate subscribers; slows down Internet connections; provokes annoyance by wasting time and resources; reduces productivity; causes bulk-volume handling problems for ISPs; and heightens the risks of malicious content spreading from computer to computer. Individuals and business organisations worldwide have expressed ever more concern over spam, and have requested regulators to take action to help them reduce it. As all stakeholders are affected by spam, there is a strong interest by all in solving this problem.

215 Therefore, this part of the case study forms a Supplement only.

216 Cybersecurity specialist Symantec acquired Brightmail in March 2004. The market for cybersecurity software and solutions is very dynamic for providers offering tools for blocking spam and viruses. This reflects the constant evolution of new cyber-attack methods.

On the policy input side, industry has been integral to any international solution to spam. For example, industry input was considerable during the thematic "Countering spam" meeting of the ITU's WSIS, which took place in Geneva on 7-9 July 2004. In the associated workshops, public and private stakeholders were invited to define the scope of the problem; discuss technical solutions; increase awareness among users; and plan bilateral co-operation (ITU SPAM website, 2008). A direct result of this WSIS meeting was the launch of a "cybersecurity" initiative, called the WSIS Action Line C5. In annual meetings since then, industry has been invited to give input that would meet this agenda (ITU Cybersecurity website, 2006). In April 2005, within the framework of its "Countering spam" project, ITU conducted its Survey on Anti-Spam Legislation worldwide. In June 2005 it organised a WSIS thematic conference on Cybersecurity that included a dedicated "Countering spam" day. The conference was open to all UN members, international organisations, ITU Sector Members, and WSIS-accredited NGOs and businesses (ITU website – Cybersecurity and SPAM, 2006).

In 2007 a High-Level Expert Group (HLEG) on Cybersecurity was launched under the aegis of the ITU's Action Line C5 initiative, consisting of major industry players in this field amongst other "privileged" expert stakeholders (ITU HLEG, 2008). Such experts are the top specialists in their fields; number less than one hundred; and have supreme authority when shaping the high strategy of policy-makers. The remit of the HLEG was to propose long-term strategies to combat cybercrime and promote measures for cybersecurity. The HLEG identified five pillars of security online, which were (1) legal measures; (2) technical and procedural measures; (3) organisational restructuring; (4) capacity building; and (5) greater international co-operation. This broad agenda indicated that multiple-stakeholder input would be needed to solve problems.

Besides the ITU/UN, only one other policy actor has had any real impact in terms of co-ordinating efforts to combat spam and cybercrime. This is the OECD, which has produced a plethora of guidelines and reports on data protection and privacy, laying an online security foundation for organisations operating globally. These global guidelines, built upon existing national and supranational regulations, may assist governments, businesses and consumers in doing business online; storing personal data, while preventing its unauthorised disclosure; formulating codes of conduct; and complying with data protection regulation (OECD website – STI directorate, 2007).

However, guidance was not enough to solve the spam problem. International organisations also initiated projects to reduce spam. For example, the OECD set up a Task Force on Spam, which on 10 March 2005 hosted an open-forum session on "Emerging spam issues" that drew-in business organisations (*e.g.* Oracle, Microsoft, VISA Europe, MessageLabs), industry associations (*e.g.* Euro ISPA), and regulators (*e.g.* FTA). It was clearly recognised by regulators at all Levels that without the involvement of industry no solution was possible. The OECD Task Force even developed an "anti-spam toolkit", an instrument to help industry, regulators and governments improve their anti-spam policies and devices. The OECD also published sundry reports covering matters as diverse as checklists for the development of anti-spam regulations; law enforcement; identification of culpable parties; handling of complaints; gathering of evidence; setting of regulatory priorities; determining fines, sanctions and remedies; and other issues related to spam (OECD website – Anti-SPAM toolkit, 2006; OECD website – SPAM task force, 2006).

Industry also played an important role in implementing policy output. Industry promoted a variety of measures and initiatives which implement anti-spam (self-)regulation and technical standards. The OECD believes that "to appropriately deal with spam on the Internet the generally applicable anti-spam laws in countries should be coupled with self-regulatory initiatives undertaken by private sector players" (OECD website – SPAM task force, 2006). Businesses and industry associations sought to promote self-regulation and technical solutions for handling unsolicited commercial e-mail by launching initiatives such as EuroISPA's "Combating Spam"; the Anti-Spam Technical Alliance (ASTA), a collaboration of leading Internet Providers; and the Anti-Phishing Working Group, a global pan-industrial and law enforcement association (Robert, 2005; Nash, 2004; ASTA, 2004; Anti-Phishing Group website, 2006).

Another of the many examples of private anti-spam implementing initiatives was the Spamhaus Project, which aimed to "provide dependable realtime anti-spam protection for Internet networks" (Spamhaus Project website, 2007). Founded in 1998, the Spamhaus Project is an international non-profit initiative sponsored by twenty-two international business organisations and run by a team of twenty-five investigators and forensics specialists located in nine countries. What was particularly interesting for stakeholders wishing to beef up the regulation of spam was that the Spamhaus Project cooperates with law enforcement agencies to pursue spammers worldwide, and lobbies governments for more effective anti-spam legislation (Spamhaus Project website, 2007).

Sometimes the industry takes the initiative in contributing to a solution. Interestingly, the UK Parliament's All Party Internet Group's visit to Washington, DC in 2003 was sponsored by Microsoft and MessageLabs (All Party Parliamentary Communications Group website, 2007). Shortly after the US visit, the UK's Internet Telephony Service Provider's Association (ITSPA) published its Code of Practice to raise residential customers' awareness of and confidence in the fledging VoIP industry. This proves business organisations have a genuine interest in resolving such issues cooperatively with regulators, and that, as in this case, the industry often tries to keep one step ahead by introducing self-regulatory schemes.

These data show how the spam affair united regulators and stakeholders cross-sectorally and cross-nationally. The consensus was that the coordinated efforts of all interested stakeholders were needed to enable their diverse efforts to succeed. Many other anti-spam initiatives were launched at all Levels of governance, most of them offering stakeholder participation.

However, *Industry Governance* does not apply at the Global Level in the same way as at National or European Levels, as the policy cycles are shorter and the initiatives have less impact on business organisations. In contrast with the European Level, policy initiatives at the Global Level can come from any quarter and still succeed. This makes it less likely for industry (or any other single actor) to predominate at this Level; hence, the Industry Governance Theory must be qualified to that extent. To take but one example of how the public sector has contested industry predominance, in January 2004 the UK led a global initiative in conjunction with European regulators to reduce spam, called "Secure your server". The

Office of Fair Trading (OFT), DTI, and the Information Commissioner's Office (ICO) signed a Memorandum of Understanding (MoU) with the US Federal Trade Commission (FTC), the Australian Communications Authority (ACA) and the Australian Competition and Consumer Commission (ACCC) to provide mutual assistance in enforcing anti-spam laws. The MoU, which was extended to 27 countries, allowed enforcement authorities to work together to apprehend spammers (Ofcom website – Spam, 2006).

This evidences that industry dominance is much shakier at the Global Level, but this is precisely because all attempts at initiating universal policies are also liable to fall apart on a Level of governance where no overarching sovereign power exists to give permanence to policy choices. Equally importantly, international governing organisations are less inclined in the first place to depend on private stakeholders alone, because their members are typically sovereign states who insist on their own influence predominating. Industry thus has less opportunity to bring its influence to bear on policy inputs and outcomes, and this would hold true even if industry stakeholders are as motivated to participate at Global Level as they evidently are at National and European Levels.

7.6 CONCLUSIONS

This case study has helped close certain gaps, and answer certain questions thus far outstanding, for which the data collected through participant observation, the Survey, the policy paper review, and other methods had proved inadequate. The following conclusions have been broken down according to their relevance to the several different Parts of the case study.

Part One: Participation in the EU. The policy paper review undertaken especially for this Part of the case study and presented in Section 7.2 laid a broad empirical foundation supporting not only the Industry Governance Theory but also the Policy Influence-Timing Model. It was demonstrated that the EU's principles of Better Regulation led to a consultative process, and as the evidence of the 2006 Review shows, around three-fourths of the respondents were from industry or industry associations. Industry Governance is clearly attested at European Level. Part One also confirmed the Policy Influence-Timing Model, manifested in Table 7.3 "Roadmap for the EU Regulatory Framework Review". This table provides a detailed overview – based both on the same policy paper review and on the author's participant observation – of how stakeholder influence peaked at the beginning of the 2006 Review, declining thereafter over time.

Part Two: Participation at National Level. The data gathered especially for this Part of the case study was based on participant observation, to the point of data-saturation. It also supports the Industry Governance Theory. As demonstrated by the breakdown of participants in Section 7.4, industry predominated numerically over all other attendees in all stakeholder meetings (without exception) hosted by DTI and Ofcom which the author eyewitnessed.[217]

217 On the other hand, the dominance of industry associations as such was less significant here than at the European Level. This confirms a result from the Survey that business preference is to contact European regulators directly.

Supplement: Global participation. The data gathered especially for this Part of the case study from heterogeneous documentary archives constitute in effect a "family" of vignettes providing some evidence of the importance of industry on the Global Level. Although less evidence exists than at National or European Levels, the evidence that *was* found shows, not only that industry is visible in policy-making processes, but also that some aspects of policy-making at the Global Level of governance may depend, if anything, even more on the industry, both to "enforce" international guidances that are inherently less enforceable than they would be at lower Levels of governance, and to implement the purely technical solutions that are sometimes the only realistic alternative left to policy-makers.

PART IV

Applications Theoretical and Practical

Courage is what it takes to stand up and speak;
courage is also what it takes to sit down and listen.
(Winston Churchill, 1874-1965)

CHAPTER 8

CONCLUDING PRACTITIONER GUIDANCE: A REGULATORY COMPLIANCE TOOLKIT

Once new EU regulations have been transposed into national law, the question remaining for businesses is, How can an effective regulatory compliance programme be designed and sustained? Most organisations with regulatory liability have adopted regulatory compliance strategies as a structured approach to meeting their legal duty to control and perfect their compliance programme. Essential to any effective programme is a clear roadmap to the destination, and that in turn requires an efficient means of identifying exactly which regulatory "destinations" the roadmap ought to be leading the organisation to. This Chapter gives practical guidance on how to run a cost-effective compliance programme, from conducting a non-compliance risk assessment to drawing a roadmap to the next level of compliance maturity.

This Chapter will also situate the Regulatory Compliance Matrix presented above in the broader context of the compliance programmes of business organisations, to which it makes a major contribution in terms of operational efficiency savings and risk reduction. Amid this, it will be well to introduce the rest of the compliance programme panoply: Risks and Controls Matrices (RCMs), Compliance Maturity Models, and their graphic synopses – the "Heatmap", which sums up the RCM by estimating and plotting the degree of risk, and the "Roadmap", which sums up the Maturity Model by mapping actions to timings.

8.1 THE GENERAL LACK OF EFFICIENT ORGANISATION

In times of constantly new imposed corporate governance regulation, and relentless innovation and rapid convergence between information and communication technologies (ICTs), the regulations that businesses must comply with are becoming increasingly complex and fast-changing. To keep up with developments, governments have been forced to fundamentally redesign their regulatory frameworks, the new watchword being *better* regulation that stresses transparency and partnership rather than adversarial relations between regulator and regulatee. In addition, the regulatory environment continues to move beyond national confines, exposing businesses, wherever incorporated, to ever more supranational regulatory demands – *e.g.* from both DG Information Society[218] and the Federal Communication

218 DG Information Society or "DG Infso" is a Directorate-General of the European Commission. It supports innovation and competitiveness through ICT research and development and defines and implements the EU's regulatory framework for ICT policy.

Commission. Businesses need to "comply creatively" by developing their own in-house governance mechanisms, yet there remains a dearth of creative solutions. This Section proposes a helpful approach.

Until now, the problem has been that many regulatees have approached regulatory compliance *ad hoc* without a robust, holistic approach that is integrated into the organisation's system of governance. In particular, instead of batching operationally related regulations to be addressed together and at once, businesses typically structure their approach legalistically, grouping compliance measures around legislative rubrics like "Sarbanes-Oxley" or "Information Security and Privacy". This imposes cost-inefficiencies due to duplication of time and effort, as legal regimes inevitably "overlap".

Regulatory compliance is something that keeps risk and compliance managers awake at night, especially in highly regulated industries like utilities, financial services or pharmaceuticals. Thus, the methods outlined here have been tried and tested before, by medium-sized and larger corporations, in multiple governance contexts. It has been found that managing compliance can eat up vast resources, especially the most valuable and expensive (*viz.* managerial and/or expert) man-hours. This must be avoided "at all costs", and it is the purpose of this Chapter to explain how best to do just that.

8.2 WHO BENEFITS MOST?

The following approach works well for all organisations, but it is especially useful for:

1. highly regulated industries whose compliance costs are correspondingly substantial
2. joint ventures who need to hold down costs by avoiding duplication of effort
3. multinationals with global operations and many (often diverse) business units/entities who need to streamline the governance of compliance across multiple jurisdictions; and
4. conglomerates resulting from mergers and/or acquisitions, who need to reap the benefits of synergies from harmonised operations across all holdings by centralising compliance efforts.

It is an approach that also serves small- and medium-sized (SME) enterprises especially well, who cannot afford in-house legal counsel. However, in this context, the concept must be bespoke made as a "lite" version. The Regulatory Compliance Matrix may or may not be applicable in the public sector – as government agencies are nowadays required to be accountable to oversight bodies, – depending on whether or not they have crafted their own in-house equivalent.

This comprehensive approach to compliance programmes bears some resemblance to the way many SEC registrants responded to the requirements of Sarbanes-Oxley, by demanding a focussed, enterprise-wide initial investment, and realising efficiency gains in the long run.

8.3 KEY COMPLIANCE CHALLENGES: THE FOUR PILLARS

ICT organisations and IT departments are under increasing pressure to achieve full regulatory compliance, and face expanding liability for failure to do so. The key challenges that arise from this fast-moving situation may be divided between four pillars: Governance, People, Controls, and Technology.

Governance

Senior management must always "own", and *take the lead in sponsoring* the company's compliance programme (and so be held accountable for it). "The buck" of ultimate responsibility always stops at the most senior managerial level. It will be up to senior management to initiate the prerequisite company-wide assessment of non-compliance risks from which the basic compliance strategy will be forged. In particular, the risk of legal liability, given the heightened pressure from regulatory authorities to comply, and the risk of reputational loss (*e.g.* through catastrophic information security breaches) must be minimised as soon as practicable. These risks are not confined to the company's own liabilities and damage and their "local" consequences, but may even spiral into a reaction by the regulator, who may impose costly new industry-wide regulations. Senior management are in some ways quite dependent on and vulnerable to middle management. Every company has routine monitoring procedures in place requiring reporting to higher levels – but this makes these reporters gatekeepers of the flow of information upwards. Company directors must take care to check up on the honesty of this gatekeeping by means of independent auditors (internal or external) who test the systems in place, probing for control failures. Both monitoring and auditing are therefore essential to a successful compliance programme. The dimensions of the Governance compliance pillar are:

G1:	Senior Management sponsorship
G2:	Responsibilities and Accountability
G3:	Strategy
G4:	Risk Assessment
G5:	Monitoring
G6:	Quality Reviews and Audits (QR&A)

People

All company personnel must be made aware and trained to participate pro-actively in the overall compliance effort. Each affected employee's role and responsibilities – (and nearly all will be affected) – must be precisely defined beforehand, with particular attention given to (a) the *scope of vigilance,* (b) *warning signals,* (c) *reporting functions* and (d) *escalation procedures*, in which training will count the most. Although the company cannot train third parties or make them aware, it is essential that company personnel become pro-actively engaged in external events involving other stakeholders, by which they learn of (and communicate back) upcoming regulatory changes, best practices of industry peers, and common problems with regulation. The dimensions of the People compliance pillar are:

P1: Training and Awareness
P2: Stakeholder Activities
P3: Ethics and Compliance

Control through Policies and Processes

Before all else, senior management must "send a message" firmly committing themselves to the company-wide goal of perfected compliance. Only then does it make sense to proceed to the next level and design specific policies, procedures and processes, which, once designed, must be implemented with particular attention to their operational effectiveness as tested, reviewed and improved periodically on schedule. The ever-changing regulatory environment demands an approach that leaves room for generational evolution and interoperability of controls. The management of third-party compliance has been necessitated by the trend toward outsourcing/ offshoring of data collection and storage in third countries (outside the EU), and/or handling of data by third parties. This has drastically altered nearly every company's risk landscape, appetite, calculation and analysis (particularly in having widened the scope for fraud). The dimensions of the Control compliance pillar are:

C1: Policy ("Compliance Statement")
C2: Procedures and Processes
C3: Methodology
C4: Incident-Response Plans
C5: Third-Party Compliance Management
C6: Systems Support

Technology

In the interest of cutting costs, it behoves the company to automate as many of the above functions as possible. The degree of automation will depend on the company size and the corresponding economies of scale. Larger organisations have the advantage of being able to rely much more on integrated GRC (governance, risk management and compliance) software packages with capability to handle the demands of multiple stakeholders and multiple regulatory liabilities. With or without automation, small companies can take advantage of methodological tools like those presented in this book, which are quite affordable for companies of every size and help manage the entire compliance programme through all its phases. The dimensions of the Technology compliance pillar are:

T1: Automated Tools (Software Applications)
T2: Methodological Tools (Process and Content Management)
T3: Analysis and Business Intelligence

8.4 THE ADVANTAGES OF THIS APPROACH

Business organisations and their IT departments are under increasing pressure to comply with all applicable regulations and face expanding liability for not doing so. As budgets become tighter, as regulations change faster, and as fines for non-compliance get tougher, smarter, more cost-effective approaches to regulatory compliance are needed. Most organisations with regulatory liability have adopted compliance strategies that provide sustainable structures and routines for meeting the necessity to control and perfect the organisation's compliance efforts. The key benefits of using a robust regulatory compliance approach – enabling the organisation to represent to regulators that they have taken all appropriate measures, – may be summarized as follows:

1. A well-structured and -executed compliance programme enhances the identification of regulatory gaps; – *i.e.* nescience of regulatory requirements or of non-compliance with known requirements – which may lead to fines and/or reputational losses.
2. It improves efficiency to deploy simple approaches and tools that facilitate identifying applicable regulations and cost-efficient compliance solutions.
3. An approach that can bring compliance controls to bear on batches of regulations instead of piecemeal reduces costs significantly. The wider view allows a reduction – if not elimination – of duplication of the effort of testing as well as reporting.
4. A clearly structured programme defines responsibilities precisely and holds accountable the key individuals involved in the process, making it more likely that the organisation will meet its compliance objectives.

8.5 THE PHASES OF REGULATORY COMPLIANCE PROGRAMMES

This Section features a key element of this general solution, the Regulatory Compliance Matrix. From this Matrix the roadmap to perfected compliance will spring. Additionally highlighted will be the many other ways that a holistic synopsis of the regulations applicable to one organisation contributes to its compliance effort, including scoping the programme with precision; streamlining internal governance structures; and identifying regulatory stakeholders whose collaboration may help shape the regulatory process itself in ways that benefit the organisation.

This Section is divided into four Sub-sections, representing the core *Phases* of constructing and executing a compliance programme. Sub-section 8.5.1 presents the Regulatory Compliance Matrix ("the Matrix"). Sub-section 8.5.2 describes the design of a regulatory Risk & Controls Matrix (RCM), starting with a risk assessment and ending with recommendations for management. Sub-section 8.5.3 outlines a bespoke Compliance Maturity Model that synergises with the Matrix to measure progress toward perfected compliance. Sub-section 8.5.4 describes the use of the tools of heatmaps and roadmaps to address compliance issues.

8.5.1 Phase 1: Regulatory Compliance Matrix

The *Regulatory Compliance Matrix* is a novel solution that like an encyclopaedia gathers together all of the overlapping requirements of widely scattered regulatory enactments, arranging them into convenient categories. It assists with the identification of applicable laws, regulations and norms, as well as relevant standards, frameworks and guidance; furnishing senior management a strategic panorama of all *generally* applicable regulations, from which they can pick out those applicable to *their own* organisation. This integration of liabilities helps minimise the register of compliance controls, quickly creating efficiencies that significantly reduce the costs of compliance. But the Matrix also maps applicable laws and regulations onto specific solutions like industry standards and other such guidance. These innovations lay the foundation for a sustainable, cost-effective, corporate-wide compliance programme that may then be focussed on compliance areas of the highest risk with the deployment of the Maturity Model presented herein. The Maturity Models developed to date, by contrast, have focussed narrowly on regulatory "domains", a perspective lacking the pivotal information only a Regulatory Compliance Matrix can supply.

The Matrix synergises with the organisation's governance structures by enabling managers to comprehend at one glance – and right from the start – the gamut of their regulatory obligations. Management is empowered to avoid wasteful duplication of effort due to *ad hoc* reactivity; to adapt more quickly to further regulatory demands as they emerge; and to navigate the complexity of disparate compliance requirements and solutions. The Matrix has been presented in all its detail in Chapter Four. (N.B.: This is the Matrix for the Information and Communication Technology (ICT) industry.)

The Matrix also adds something valuable to any effort at compliance by identifying the mutual similarities and identities of similar regulations, "killing two birds with one stone". It thus serves two purposes at once: it (1) "batches" similar regulations for unified, cost-optimal compliance, and (2) steers the compliance/ risk practitioner more surely toward "shelter" from the regulatory and commercial risks of non-compliance.

8.5.2 Phase 2: Risks and Controls Matrix

Once the applicable regulations and corresponding guidance have been identified through the Matrix, these results may be used to develop in stages the organisation's Risks & Controls Matrix (RCM). Stage 1 identifies the risks. Stage 2 formulates controls, activities and reporting requirements. Stage 3 undertakes an effectiveness review. Stage 4 puts out recommendations on how to mitigate and manage compliance risks.

Stage 1. Conduct a risk assessment

The first step is to identify and assess the risks. One must distinguish "inherent" from "residual" risk: *inherent risk* is the risk that the organisation would incur losses if it implemented no controls (*i.e.* the gross risk or "pre-controls" risk). *Residual risk* is whatever risk remains after controls have been implemented (*i.e.* the net risk or "post-controls" risk). Risk is to be understood as likelihood of loss multiplied by impact or severity of loss. Residual risk can only be further mitigated by (usually expensive) improvements in the technical efficiency of controls; thus, the organisation's "risk appetite" must determine its willingness to spend money on making such improvements (assuming they are possible). If the organisation's appetite is low, then it is well advised to document its residual risks and subject them to monitoring, review and (if possible) improved control. General and specific regulatory risks are to be identified, and their criticality (high/ medium/ low) estimated. Guidance on risk management is contained in ISO 31000:2009 and ISO/IEC 31010:2009,[219] which defines risk management as "coordinated activities to direct and control an organization with regard to risk" (ISO 31000, 2009:2), and risk assessment as the "overall process of risk identification, risk analysis and risk evaluation" (ISO 31000, 2009:4).

Some general risks include:

1. *Consequences of negligence/unawareness*: management remains unaware of all of the applicable industry regulations.
2. *Liability for non-compliance*: the organisation fails fully to comply with all applicable regulations on all Levels of regulatory governance, and is exposed to legal liability.
3. *Effects of untrained key personnel*: Those who might have prevented breaches of compliance are insufficiently trained to meet the organisation's regulatory obligations.
4. *Reputational damage*: Customers injured or affronted by management negligence withdraw their custom and spread word of their dissatisfaction.

Some specific risks of regulatory compliance with data handling laws may, for example, include:

1. Installed data protection controls shielding information systems that hold sensitive data and personal information from unauthorised access are insufficient to protect the data held.[220]
2. A public authority in receipt of a valid FOI request does not respond by the [twentieth] working day after receiving the request for information.[221]
3. The personal data held was not acquired for a "specified and lawful purpose",[222] and/ or the data subject did not give consent.
4. Personal data is "transferred to a country or territory outside the European Economic Area" without the data subject's knowledge.[223]

---

219 ISO 31000:2009 "Risk management -- Principles and guidelines" provides principles and generic guidelines on risk management. The key components of the ISO 31000 standards are risk registers ("records of information about identified risks"), accountability, risk management process (risk assessment, risk identification, risk analysis, risk evaluation, risk treatment, [risk] monitoring and review), risk management framework, integration and terminology.
ISO/IEC 31010:2009 "Risk management – Risk assessment techniques" supporting ISO 31000 through guidance on selection and application of systematic techniques for risk assessment.

220 Bundesdatenschutzgesetz [(German) Federal Data Protection Act] 1990 (amended 1994), Annexe, §1.

221 UK Freedom of Information Act 2000, Article 10(1).

222 UK Data Protection Act 1998, Schedule 1, Principle 2.

223 UK Data Protection Act 1998, Schedule 1, Principle 8.

A wide array of literature on risk management exists, often featuring detailed case studies of it and demonstrating its benefits to organisations in both the public and private sectors (*e.g.* Hopkins, 2012).

Stage 2. Define control activities and reporting requirements

To address these risks, specific control activities must be defined, for which existing guidance and standards may be consulted. In addition, it is important to define reporting requirements, including their format, frequency (*viz.* ongoing/ daily/ weekly/ monthly/ yearly). Last but not least, it must be specified who is to monitor these controls. COSO is a good example of a useful internal control framework which has been applied in many different contexts to the enhancement of corporate governance (Root, 2000). Over the past ten years, this framework has become the industry *de facto* standard for enterprise risk management (ERM) (see Steinberger, 2011).

Stage 3. Review controls' effectiveness

The effectiveness of the controls that have been crafted ought to be tested for effectiveness immediately upon installation. For example, to test whether the Data Protection Policy has been communicated to staff at least annually and is being followed, the auditor may take the following two steps:

1. *Test for design effectiveness*: For example, the reviewer (or auditor) of data protection compliance must check the Data Protection Policy and supporting documentation to see if it includes the basic elements expected of such a policy, such as a statement of purpose, definition of staff responsibilities, rules for disclosure and transfer of data subjects' personal information, and for processing subject access requests, together with the contact details of the organisation's Data Protection Officer.
2. *Test for implementation*; *i.e.* is the control *operationally* effective? For example, a control which, although drafted, only exists stored on the Compliance Officer's PC, so that no one else is aware of it, is clearly of limited use. Through discussions with management it may be determined where "ownership" of the policy lies, and whether it has been communicated to staff and included in training and awareness courses. As with any audit, a random sample of data subjects must be selected out of the organisation's computer system for determining, for example, the extent to which the policy on subject access requests is known and has been followed.

Stage 4. Recommendations for improvement

The auditor must first of all document his findings (for example, any control weaknesses), then make recommendations for compliance improvement. Such recommendations usually stem from a combination of auditors' experience and judgement, industry best practices – typically found out by interacting with peers and learning about their controls environment

– and through best practice guides produced by regulators,[224] standards institutes,[225] and industry associations.[226] The following table illustrates how the findings and other reportable information might be presented to the head of audit for compilation along with the results of other relevant audits. Risk and Compliance Matrices (RCM) have also come into use recently, but these are still confined to mapping compliance within just one legal domain at a time, such as Sarbanes-Oxley (SOX).

224 Information Commissioner's Office of the UK provides a range of guidance; for example, "A Quick 'How to Comply' Checklist" (ICO, V2.0 27/05/08); "CCTV Systems and the Data Protection Act 1998" (ICO website, 2012); "Privacy and Electronic Communications Regulations" (ICO website, 2012); and "Good Practice Note – Checklist for handling requests for personal information (subject access requests)" (ICO website, 2012).

225 CEN/ISSS Data Protection and Privacy Workshop has developed tools to assist [organisations] in complying with their data protection and privacy obligations and monitoring their data protection compliance. (CEN/ISSS, 2008-2009 Work Programme, 14 March 2009).

226 *E.g.*, Intellect UK, Data Protection and Data Security Guidelines for Offshoring and Outsourcing, Second Edition (November 2010); Intellect UK, 'A checklist to achieve data protection compliance' (2001).

Table 8.1: The Risks and Controls Matrix (RCM) - Examples

	0. Regulatory Compliance Matrix		1. Risk Assessment	2. Controls and reporting		3. Controls effectiveness	4. Recommend-ations
Ref	**Regulation**	**Existing Guidance**	**Risk and Criticality (High/ Medium/ Low)**	**Control Specification**	**Reporting frequency**	**Actual Designing and Implementation**	**Findings**
1	Data Protection Directive	Generally Accepted Privacy Principles (GAPP)	*High* - The data privacy controls in place around information systems holding sensitive data and personal information are insufficient to protect.	The Information Security policy takes into consideration Data Protection obligations in relation to the use and adequate retention of personal and sensitive personal data.	Monthly	*Test design-effectiveness* – (1) Obtain a copy of the Information Security policy, and check that data protection obligations have been taken into account. (2) Validate that these are consistent with obligations on use and retention.	[To be completed]
2	UK Data Protection Act 1998	Generally Accepted Privacy Principles (GAPP)	*High* - The data controller doesn't respond within 40 days of receiving notice in writing from a person requesting the data controller to cease or not begin processing his personal data.	A weekly information security report or subject access request (SAR) report flags up close deadlines so that regular alert messages are sent to the data controller a few days before the deadline.	Quarterly	*Test operational effectiveness* – (1) Obtain a sample of relevant reports/ alert emails. (2) Request system or other evidence that show that the response deadlines have been met.	[To be completed]
3	Data Protection Directive/ Data Retention Directive 2006/24/EC	Data Retention Policy (in-house)	*Medium* – Personal data is kept longer than necessary. Electronic communications (incl. traffic & communication data) is not retained in line with the Data Retention directive. Retention periods for other documents are ignored.	Policies and procedures are put in place to expire retention of personal information within the system and of other data that should be destroyed/ deleted.	Annually	*Test operational effectiveness* – (1) After discussion with management, obtain the relevant policies covering expiry of retention of personal information. (2) validate that the policies are being followed by surveying a sample of records/ documents.	[To be completed]

8.5.3 Phase 3: Regulatory Compliance Maturity Model

Professional advisory firms and Governance, Risk and Compliance (GRC) Departments have been using various kinds and qualities of Maturity Model for many years. Governments also employ the concept, as witness the Cabinet Office and the National Health Service of Her Majesty's Government, both of whom recently published their own bespoke models; *viz.* CESG, "Guide to IA Self-Assessment using the HMG IA Maturity Model and Assessment Framework" (14 April 2011),[227] and NHS Infrastructure Maturity Model (NIMM) (NHS website, 2012). Industry researchers and business associations develop their own Maturity Models to support their members' needs; examples include Gartner's *IT Management Process Maturity Model*, and ISACA's *COBIT Maturity Model* (Gartner Group, 2005).

The ongoing and current state of a compliance campaign is usually presented to senior management in a Maturity Model, which estimates how far the organisation has progressed in meeting its regulatory control objectives. The fusion of a Maturity Model and a Regulatory Compliance Matrix would furnish them with a multi-dimensional benchmark gauging not only the host organisation's compliance progress, but also the comparative progress of peers in the same industry, and even comparative compliance between industry sectors. The Matrix-Model fusion presented herein estimates progress through five levels of compliance.

Level 1 Nascent – compliance is the reactive state of first-blush awareness in which the organisation, in trying to come to grips with fulfilling its regulatory obligations, has yet to make headway.

Level 2 Initiative – compliance sees the organisation's efforts still lacking consistency and formal documentation, yet making some real progress in laying an internal governance foundation for managing its own compliance efforts.

Level 3 Established – compliance involves the organisation in designing and documenting comprehensively its compliance policies and procedures, while implementation is yet incomplete.

Level 4 Perfected – compliance shows the organisation has fully implemented its policies and procedures, yet inefficiencies in the design and operation of compliance persist and cause some problems.

Level 5 Perfected – compliance requires that the organisation's processes have been optimised and its employees have adapted to the new order; thenceforward only ongoing monitoring is needed for smooth operation.

The following diagram summarises the types of variables that define a generic Maturity Model over the four pillars presented above: – governance, people, controls, and technology.

227 N.B.: CESG is the UK's "National Technical Authority for Information Assurance" (CESG website, 2012).

Figure 8.1: The Regulatory Compliance Maturity Model

	LEVEL 1: Nascent	LEVEL 2: Initiative	LEVEL 3: Established	LEVEL 4: Advanced	LEVEL 5: Perfected
Governance	This includes degree of maturity for Senior Management sponsorship, Responsibilities and Accountability, Strategy, Risk Assessment, Monitoring and Quality Reviews & Audits.				
People	This includes degree of maturity for Training and Awareness, Stakeholder Activities and Ethics and Compliance.				
Control through Policy and Processes	This includes degree of maturity for Policy, Procedures and Processes, Methodology, Incident Response Plans, Third-Party Compliance Management and Systems Support.				
Technology	This includes degree of maturity for automated tools, Methodological Tools, and Analysis & Business Intelligence.				

The benefits of a Model-Matrix fusion include (1) reduction of costs through the synergy effects of avoiding duplication of effort; (2) fast identification of compliance gaps; and (3) the manifestation of organisation-wide goals or 'destinations', which at a minimum entails internal governance efficiencies, such as a single organisation-wide framework for internal compliance reporting. In economic terms, a Model-Matrix fusion goes far toward achieving Pareto-optimality in compliance, whereby pursuing a higher degree of overall compliance does not compromise the compliance already achieved. In practical terms, a Model-Matrix fusion will ease the pressures on CIOs, COOs and other professionals with key regulatory responsibilities.

8.5.4 Phase 4: Heatmaps and Roadmaps

Part of any effective strategy are ways and means of digesting large volumes of information in a format that abstracts from incomprehensible detail, providing those responsible with a high-level, executive overview of the whole situation. Heatmaps and roadmaps are such tools that present data graphically, enabling senior management to take-in at a glance their current compliance status and/or the pathway to higher compliance levels. Both tools facilitate prioritising executive actions and taking decisions on the next steps in budget planning, resource allocation and schedule development.

A Risk Assessment Heatmap plots the likelihood of a risk happening against the severity of its impact, giving a global measure of the magnitude of risk. The two dimensions plotted yield a vector for each category of risk which may itself be used, in turn, to construct a Residual Risk Heatmap that plots magnitude of risk against the maturity of the organisation's effort to contain it. This empowers management to decide summarily which steps to take next to achieve the next level of compliance maturity. Figure 8.2 illustrates how a heatmap can represent risk intuitively by plotting inherent risk (= impact or severity of loss × likelihood of occurrence) against current maturity of risk-controls.

Figure 8.2: The Risk Assessment Heatmap

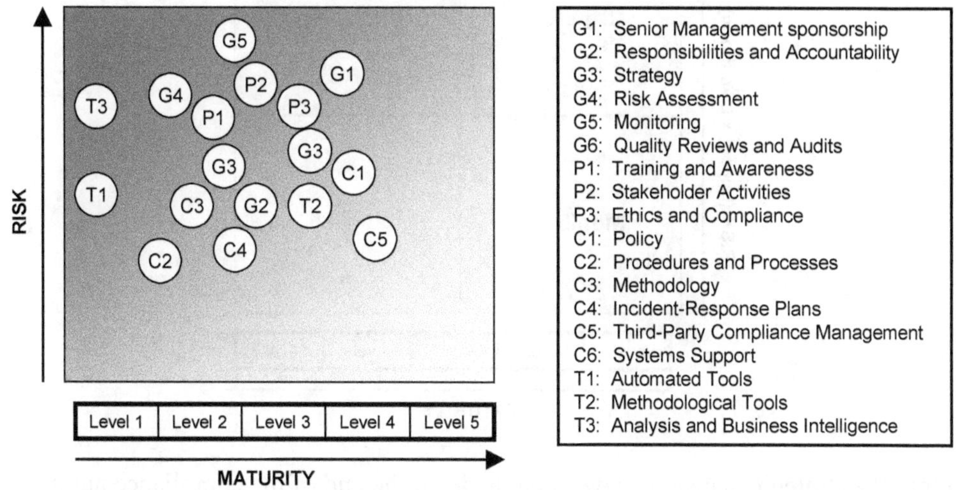

The issues plotted on the heatmap, depending on where in it they fall, may be classified in accordance with one of four "quadrants" in an Action Quadrant Diagram: The *Ignore* quadrant contains low-risk, high-maturity issues; the *Monitor* quadrant contains low-risk but low-maturity issues; the *Important* quadrant contains high-risk yet high-maturity issues; the *Urgent* quadrant contains both high-risk and low-maturity issues. Thus Diagram, drawn up by the Chief Compliance Officer, may be presented to upper management, who can then apply their risk appetite to the classified issues to indicate a plan of action. Thus, a heatmap is a strategic tool useful for clarifying an overview of the organisation's current risk and compliance situation.

Figure 8.3: Action Quadrant Diagram

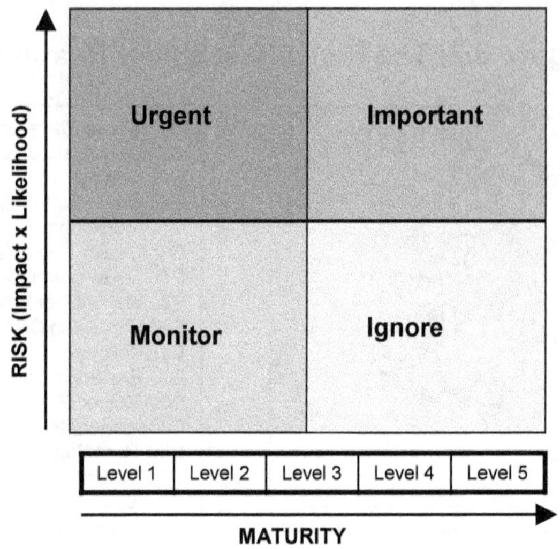

Once the strategic decisions have been made, at the end of the compliance audit and risk assessment, another tool may be applied to their tactical execution. This is the "roadmap" to higher maturity to be drafted and executed by the Chief Compliance Officer. It maps all specific actions that have been agreed in order to bring the organisation's compliance to (the desired) maturity. Roadmaps plot actions with their "milestones" (or sub-goals, such as reports, check-points/sign-offs or completion of specific project "deliverables") against an agreed timeline.

Figure 8.4: The Roadmap

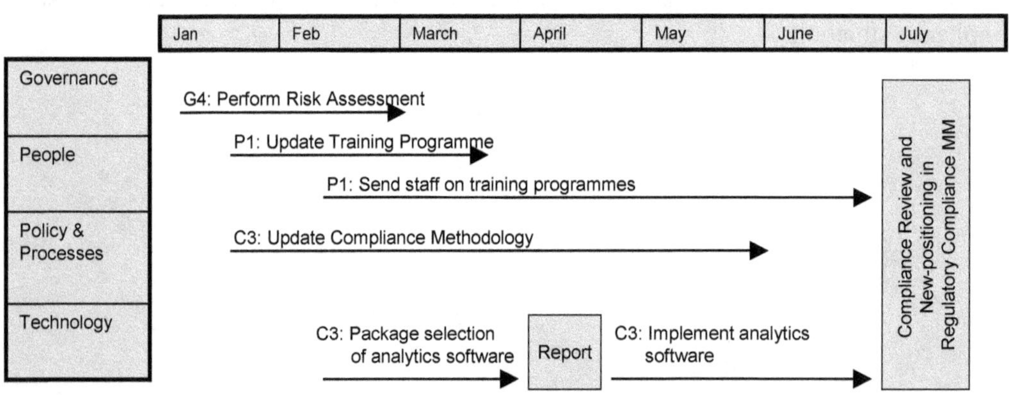

8.6 CONCLUSION

As with the regulatory policy-making process, which has been shown to be industry-governed, industry also must initiate the design and implementation of clearly structured regulatory compliance programmes. This Chapter has presented a number of processes and tools that businesses may use to improve compliance effectiveness, minimise costs, and lay the foundation for robust programmes. To summarise this chapter, in order to move to compliance maturity, the Compliance Department and upper management must together devise a high-level master plan, to include the phases of (1) scoping, (2) risks and controls assessment, (3) compliance-status evaluation, and (4) tactical planning.

First Phase: The regulations which are applicable to the organisation must be identified. The *Regulatory Compliance Matrix* quickens identification, while also mapping them to frameworks, standards and guidance which may aid development of the risk controls necessary to fulfil the organisation's obligations.

Second Phase: The specific controls must be taken from the Compliance Matrix or else designed in house. These may then be compiled into the organisation's own *Risks and Controls Matrix*, a tool which has been widely used, for example, in Sarbanes-Oxley compliance reviews.

Third Phase: The organisation's current maturity of compliance must be estimated. The *Regulatory Compliance Maturity Model* provides benchmarks to this end regarding each specific (set of) regulations or regulatory domain. This enables construction of the *heatmaps* that enable preparation of an effective tactical plan of execution.

Fourth Phase: A structured approach to addressing insufficient or non-compliance must be drawn up. The *roadmap*, which consists of specific control actions to be implemented and their corresponding timelines, furnishes an action plan for advancing the current compliance state.

Application of this Regulatory Compliance Toolkit should greatly enhance the organisational efficiency of regulatory compliance programmes, cutting resource costs (in particular personnel costs – in-house staff, consultants, contractors) whilst simultaneously speeding up the process of meeting regulatory objectives. The deepest benefits of this toolkit, however, may be captured only if senior management buy-in for the long term not one-off. Thus, maintenance of the compliance programme is a necessity: risks and controls must be periodically monitored and their effectiveness reported. As a normative inventory, the Regulatory Compliance Matrix must be updated at least annually and sometimes oftener, while the Regulatory Compliance Maturity Model is the benchmark against which compliance effectiveness or weakness is to be measured through a regular course of compliance reviews. When convenient, this may be supplemented by creating or updating Heatmaps and Roadmaps. Applied consistently, and provided it is fully integrated into ordinary business operations, this regulatory compliance toolkit can lead to long-term cost savings.

CHAPTER 9

REFLECTIONS ON INDUSTRY GOVERNANCE

This Chapter draws the ultimate lessons contained in this book based on the findings of the author's fourteen-year participant observation of business influence over ICT regulation and standards-setting. On the empirical side we have investigated changes in ICT policy – and the role of policy stakeholders' discourse in changing it – at the multiple Levels of the overall EU policy process. We have also made contributions to the theoretical understanding of the complexity of EU policy-making, and have shown how external stakeholders shape EU regulatory outcomes.

The overarching lesson to be drawn is that, although the EU institutions may retain a formal "last word" over which policy initiatives are proposed, adopted and implemented, business organisations have become the driving force in the pivotal, formative agenda-setting and consultation Phases of the public policy-making process. Since this process is wide open to all stakeholders, it is evident that industry is predominating mostly because of the participatory default of other stakeholders.

More particular lessons are drawn in this Chapter from key general themes, which cut across the scholarship and policy-paper reviews, the case study, and the Survey results. Section 9.1 provides an outline of the general lessons that can be learned about the New Governance in Europe, and stakeholder influence therein. Section 9.2 presents an originating narrative consisting of the author's personal reflections on how his research evolved, the challenges he faced, and how he plans to continue research in this domain. Section 9.3 summarises the main contributions of this book for practitioners and scholarship.

9.1 NEW GOVERNANCE IN EUROPE AND STAKEHOLDER INFLUENCE

In democratic states national regulation results from a decisional process that includes the ratification of new regulations by national parliaments elected by the people. However, the nature of the EU institutions and the objectives set by the Treaty of the European Union have put European policy output in the regulation of ICT markets upon a uniformly liberal economic footing. Such a policy bias, together with the empirical findings presented herein, has led to the general conclusion that the ICT policy process has become governed largely by the industry (see Chapter Seven). This conclusion was reached after weighing-in three factors that have been primarily responsible for the New Governance in Europe:

1. changes by European and National regulators to their principles of good governance, including stakeholder consultation and participation, the creation of new independent regulatory authorities, and the empowerment of the European standardisation institutes;
2. new market dynamics stemming from the liberalisation of the utility markets, which have stimulated technological advances and the convergence of telecommunications, broadcasting and IT; and
3. the emergence of new service providers, who demand freer competition, the removal of market distortions, and better access to markets.

The new Industry Governance Theory maintains that ICT regulation is not primarily created by legislators who demand something to satisfy their hunger for re-election or career advancement. It is rather part and parcel of a wider, more economical (or "thrifty") regulation that is intended to support the liberal goals of competition, economic growth and job creation. Economical regulation lies at the heart of the Industry Governance Theory. In the *milieu* of these new goals business interests naturally come to the forefront of decision-making. This reasoning is corroborated by the EU's own policy papers as well as by Mark Thatcher's Regulatory State model. Furthermore, both the EU and the Member States have attached the highest importance to, and invested great expectations in the new Regulatory Impact Assessment procedure, made mandatory in order to prioritise the economic and business implications of any new regulation.

The EU's Information Society policy agenda itself sufficiently justifies the conclusion that ICT regulation is shaped by business organisations and in the following ways conforms to economical-policy principles, as the Industry Governance Theory would predict.

1. The Information Society is a liberalising project set up to dismantle monopolies in infrastructure, products and services, and to create a competitive and open marketplace.
2. The new eCommunications regulatory regime aims to knit together and then to harmonise legally the otherwise fragmented European ICT sector, through common rules and standards as well as through the freedoms of movement.
3. The EU has established a number of regulatory mechanisms (*e.g.* IRAs) the purpose of which is to stimulate competition and prevent the abuse of dominant market positions[228] by monopolist and/or incumbent operators.

The Information Society initiative was launched by the 1993 Delors White Paper on "Growth, competitiveness and employment" and the 1994 Bangemann Report on "Europe

228 One of the challenges that regulators and IRAs face is to strike the right balance between sector-specific regulations, the provision of basic services to all users (the universal services concept) and competition rules. "Dominant market position" is defined in Article 82 of the EU Treaty and identifies certain activities, such as imposing unfair trading conditions, as establishing an abuse of the dominant position within the Common Market.

and the global Information Society". These two White Papers were crucial to winning broad support from all stakeholders for the proposition that the ICT sector is supremely important to "economic growth, competitiveness, job creation and improvements in the quality of life for all Europeans" (CEC, 1993). These White Papers, together with the Treaty of the European Union, laid the necessary political and legal foundation for deregulating all ICT sectors, but especially those exclusively served by state-owned enterprises or anti-competitively overregulated (*e.g.* consumer telecommunications equipment). The 2002 eCommunications Framework Directive further entrenched the EU's market-oriented approach by mandating the sector's privatisation and liberalisation. The 2006 eCommunications Framework Review then enabled policy stakeholders to participate in revisionary regulatory decisions through consultation, a strategy that helped cement political agreement over the Information Society agenda.

The evidence presented in this book has confirmed the theory presented in Chapter One, that the making of ICT regulations and standards in Europe has become critically dependent on business (and potentially other private) stakeholders, to the point that these have become the real governors. The new governors are not pure technocrats, either. It is true that, on the technocratic side, an increasing access of business to the Commission's technical committees has been observed (Mazey and Richardson, 1993; Schaefer, 1996; Christiansen, 2000); yet on the visionary side as well the growing importance of business leaders and their ideas, both commercial and political, to the "grand strategy" of European public policy has also been noted (Marina Cowles, 1995, 2001). Industry Governance is therefore a vision of society (*viz.* the Information Society) that has been conceived and is being pursued by the industry, and in which the Commission plays a chiefly supporting role.

The Advocacy Coalition Typology and its inventory of hardcore belief systems sufficiently reveals the visionary quality of industry governance and the place of its grand strategy in the overall "ecology" of the Types. All of the Types involved in the making of European ICT policy embody the vision of the Information Society, notwithstanding how their emphases may differ. Type One ("Individual advocates") advocate that the public interest comes first, and that technology is in fact in the public interest; hence regulation must be moderate. Type Two ("Public-sector and non-profit organisations") advocate that "little people" (employees, consumers, SMEs, people in remote parts of Europe) deserve protection and must be included in the new Society. Type Three ("Industry-focussed associations"), constituting the industry, advocate that the future absolutely depends on the dynamism of European business, and regulation must never inhibit that. Type Four ("Project groups") advocate that technology can solve problems that government by regulatory command will never be able to solve. The Advocacy Coalition Types and their belief systems complement each other, and together they constitute that on which the Commission has merely pasted the label "Information Society".

It has been remarked that the high concept "Information Society" is susceptible to different and even competing interpretations. Hence the momentous misfit between two of its principal visions. "The gulf between the two principal competing visions of the global Information Society – the social [represented by civil society] and the economic [represented primarily by business organisations] – is either likely to weaken policy or to be resolved by the ascendancy of one vision over the other" (Chadwick, 2006:227). Chadwick conjectures that "the economic vision is likely to prove dominant" (Chadwick, 2006:227) – a conjecture that has now been confirmed by the immediately foregoing Chapters of this book.

The examples of the 2006 Review (see Sections 7.3 through 7.4) and the Roaming regulation (see Section 4.5.5) show that, without a regulatory framework, the free market may not always deliver economic growth and global competitiveness. It may be questioned whether the Single Market and the Lisbon Agenda, despite huge fiscal outlays, have fulfilled their promise of creating new jobs and stimulating investment in R&D. The sky is not sunny for everybody. Trade unions, the mass media, and even some politicians argue that the investments in new technologies and initiatives specified in the Information Society agenda, along with the entailed globalisation, have resulted in job losses rather than gains for some. They claim, moreover, that the difficulties many telecommunications operators and Internet firms faced in the early 21st century, leading to so many liquidations, mergers and acquisitions, have created knock-on unemployment in many other industries, too.[229] These developments have brought about a reduction of European ICT market players and, inevitably, job losses even within the industry. Moreover, e-Commerce – from e-finance to e-Learning to e-Health – threatens to replace traditional jobs in the service sectors by empowering new market players to compete with them in offering the same (or better) services. Finally, jobs in ICT services are too often outsourced offshore.

On the other hand, an improved regulatory environment may well be more conducive even to the social ends embodied in the Single Market and the Lisbon Agenda. This home truth was cited in the 2000 White Paper on European Governance; followed up by the Action Plan for better lawmaking, which aimed at legislating less but better (CEC 2002k). At the same time the "European Convention on the future of the Union" recommended to the European Council that simplifying and rigorously implementing existing EU legislation, in preference to adopting new legislation, would liberate the power of European business to generate the economic growth undergirding job creation (European Convention website, 2008).

The Lisbon Agenda goal of boosting European research spending to 3% of GDP by 2010 remains a long way off as of 2012.[230] Critics of the Agenda also bring up the detrimental impact of other policies imposed on the market in pursuance of its "social agenda". Policies intended to stimulate investment and competition are widely assumed to have succeeded. However, quantitative measurement of their impact in boosting innovation, productivity and economic growth has proved difficult, as the ICT sector is interconnected with other sectors. For example, the uptake of third-generation broadband, mobile, wireless Internet services depends on the employment of these technologies by the retail, financial-services, and other sectors.

229 The literature often mentions the "dot-com bubble", which means the speculative stock-market bubble between 1995 and 2001. The "bursting of the bubble" led to falling stock prices, loss of confidence in eCommerce/online markets, and unemployment in the "new industries sector".

230 The European Commission found that average R&D spending in the EU was equivalent to 1.85% of GDP in the five years before 2010, and no significant growth was noted over this time (Cordis website, 2012). For the EU27 R&D spending was 2.00% in 2010, well below Japan (3.45%) and the United States (2.79%) (Eurostat websites, 2012).

The weak points and deficiencies of the Lisbon Agenda should not lead policy stakeholders, however, to reject supporting the effort to create a regulatory environment conducive to the growth of an industry with such powerful and far-reaching effects on Europe's economic future. Policy-making in the modern world is increasingly characterised by complexity and uncertainty (Haas, 1992:1-54), a view shared by many scholars (Richardson, 2001; Sabatier, 1993; McCormick, 2001). The European regulator is ever more challenged by this policy-making environment, and has little real choice but to seek help wherever help is to be found. Hence the New Governance agenda, which has opened up many more opportunities for stakeholders to get involved – right now – in shaping European ICT regulation.

Let the critics debate the legitimacy and democratic *bona fides* of the European Union; the direct involvement of policy stakeholders in issue emergence and initiative, agenda-setting, and policy-reshaping through participant consultations is much more directly, powerfully democratic than relegating these powers to "representatives" who are very imperfectly so, and purblind to boot because national boundaries obscure the broader European economic reality. Any excuse for neglecting participation in the ICT policy decisional process is an opportunity missed for business organisations and other policy stakeholders. No further demonstration of this is needed than the author's own participant observation: he managed to gain access to an enormous range of stakeholder activities and events, even though he belonged to no "exclusive club" or "policy elite". This evidence alone is conclusive that the policy process no longer takes place "behind closed doors", but is now wide-open to the smallest stakeholders.

The question of which actors influence policy formation is central to political science, and the study of public policy implicates the impact of stakeholders. An observed increase in active involvement especially by commercial organisations has raised alarms that a European policy-making process assumed to be classically hierarchical and idealised as disinterested is being exposed to bias from self-interested partisans. It is high time to cross-examine the alarmists in light of the theory and empirical evidence presented in this book – even if other stakeholders continue to "put in a non-appearance". Business participation mitigates some of the negative consequences of regulation, and thereby contributes to economic development for European society as a whole.

9.2 ADVICE TO PRACTITIONERS IN THIS FIELD

This Section summarises the main lessons that can be learned regarding not just business influence on the making of ICT regulation, but also the best ways to comply with them once they become implemented. This book has presented channels of effective influence at Sub-national, National, European and Global Level. Three specific conclusions may be drawn from this evidence.

1. The principles of New Governance and Better [ICT] Regulation developed and now adopted by the Commission will furnish even more opportunities in future for stakeholder participation in the policy process.
2. The predomination of large business organisations in the ICT policy process, even in the teeth of the Commission's outreach to non-business and smaller business

organisations, indicates that not all policy stakeholders have fully absorbed the new opportunities for participation in EU regulation and standards-setting; which implies that they stand in need of guidance.

3. Business organisations that lack a regulatory *compliance* strategy are more likely to miss these new opportunities and find themselves increasingly marginalised in the policy process.

9.2.1 Enforcing the principles of good governance of ICT regulation

European regulators have reached the point where Better Regulation has become a top priority for both regulators and business organisations. All policy stakeholders have opportunities actively to participate in shaping legislation; hence they share responsibility for its quality, either through participation or in default thereof. New methods of participation like Regulatory Impact Assessments only work if business organisations disclose information about business concerns (such as compliance costs) not only to legislators and independent regulatory authorities but also to other policy stakeholders. The potential benefits can only be realised if businesses are willing to conduct internal cost-benefit assessments whenever European and national regulators fail to carry out their own due diligence. The outcomes of these assessments need to be shared between businesses, regulators *and other stakeholders*.

The European Commission which came to power in November 2004 was resolute in setting a Better Regulation agenda, which was welcomed by the industry. Policy stakeholders have long been lobbying for a "less is better" regulatory approach, to reduce business's compliance burden. The evidence of the initiatives and regulations discussed in this book show that these Better Regulation procedural objectives need to be pursued at both EU and National Levels. The Commission's White Paper "on European Governance" and the results of the White Paper consultation underline how essential to policy-making are regulatory impact assessments, policy coordination, and comprehensive consultation procedures. The author has eyewitnessed a growing understanding throughout Europe that legislation is made effective through the willing participation of key stakeholders, ranging from technical experts and lawyers to researchers, business management, the public sector and NGOs.[231]

However desirable stakeholders' input may be in the abstract, in practice the degree of their influence is contingent upon many independent factors. The Survey in Chapter Six revealed that large business organisations' influence predominates over the policy agenda at all Levels. It also revealed that companies who can afford to maintain "representations" nearby the headquarters of EU institutions participate significantly more in shaping policy. This more active involvement may also be explained by the belief of large business organisations

231 This was also a key finding of the report by the UK Better Regulations Task Force launched at the UK Presidency Better Regulation Conference in September 2005. Subsequently, the UK launched a "Better Regulation Executive" office to reduce and remove unnecessary regulation athwart the public, private and voluntary sectors. All stakeholders were invited to submit their ideas for reducing or simplifying regulation. Moreover, a new Impact Assessment procedure is in place to query all new regulation whether it is necessary and will be executed with minimal burdensomeness. This Impact Assessment must be employed by all policy-makers from November 2007, and public consultations are an integral part of its procedures. Impact Assessments need to be published, analysed and presented together with policy options (Better Regulation Executive website, 2007).

that regulation actually impacts their organisation.[232] On the other hand, the Survey also suggests that the value of organisational size and nearness to the regulator is overestimated by smaller business organisations.[233]

The author was led not only to theoretical conclusions, but to practical insights and recommendations as well. Theorisation ought not to be pursued for its own sake, as abstract knowledge, but also for its utility in the task of making policy-making more efficient, thus contributing to the improvement of society. The following are recommendations which actors participating in ICT policy-shaping processes may find highly useful and fitting.

Active participation in national and European industry associations, as well as in European research programmes, is probably the single most useful step that businesses both large and small can take. Policy activism not only provides better opportunities for business to understand regulations and standards and how to comply with them (having gotten involved at a sufficiently early stage to have helped shape them), but also conduces to greater industry satisfaction with the output of European regulatory authorities and standards institutes.

The Survey results imply that the Commission could do even more to promote its Better Regulation agenda and support stakeholder participation throughout the EU policy process.[234] Desiderata identified by Survey respondents included:

1. a clearer definition of responsibilities in the policy process;
2. greater care taken by the regulator to set achievable policy objectives;
3. funding for smaller stakeholders and their industry associations; and
4. a deeper understanding and appreciation by stakeholders of the international dimension of EU standards and regulations.

Where regulation of the ICT industry and markets is called for, it is concluded that the following four Better Regulation principles ought to be followed by regulators at all times:

- ICT regulation should be kept technologically neutral, be driven by market needs, and stimulate competition. Not only favourable market conditions but also an appropriate regulatory framework helps sustain investment in ICTs.[235]
- Regulators need to avoid overregulation, which is seen by businesses and even by some regulators as a hindrance to trade, economic growth and prosperity. By heaping financial, regulatory and operational burdens onto business, overregulation

232 *Cf.* Survey Question 7: "Some stakeholders feel that regulation has a negligible impact on their organisation, others believe it has a very big impact. Which comes closest to your believe?".

233 *Cf.* Survey Question 11h: "Only large multinational organisations can really influence regulations".

234 *Cf.* Survey Question 3: "How could involvement in the policy and standards-setting process be improved?"

235 This view is widely shared by the industry, business associations (*e.g.* the International Chamber of Commerce), and academia.

inevitably hinders the adoption of new technologies and creation of new services by businesses; hampering economic development. Of course, the regulator must guarantee the provision of the "universal services" defined in Directive 2002/22/EC, namely, the availability of network access to all consumers at reasonable and affordable rates and all of the related benefits that follow from this.

- Regulators must minimise the additional costs to businesses of implementing and complying with new regulations. The cost implications for business should be taken into account even in the drafting stage; an objective that has been pursued so far through Regulatory Impact Assessments. Fines, especially for first-time non-compliance, ought to be moderate and rarely or never endanger the organisation's solvency and existence, and thus the jobs and third parties who depend on it. The regulator should endeavour to provide easier, more cost-effective sanctions for non-compliance than court proceedings. One suggested approach would be to expand alternative dispute resolution (ADR) facilities (possibly online), and/or to make reasonable attempts at leveraging the internal policies of companies (*e.g.* consumer satisfaction policy).
- Despite all the efforts of Brussels to achieve its Better Regulation agenda, the Survey revealed that numerous ICT stakeholders still believe too many EU regulations lack simplicity and precision. Granted, the sheer number and variety of market players providing eCommunications services (*viz.* content providers, hosts of email, web and backup-centre services, Internet service providers, network providers) is a challenge for "simple regulation". The Internet is a global medium and service providers are operating in a borderless global marketplace. Even so, this complexity obligates the regulator all the more to define precisely the terms and conditions used in, the jurisdictional scope of, and the markets governed under a given regulation. The regulator ought to consider emulating the proceedings of standards institutes, which have succeeded in defining technical and operational requirements with the requisite clarity.

9.2.2 Effective participation in EU ICT regulations and standards

Formulating and taking a course of action demands a commitment of resources. Since resources are always limited and typically oversubscribed, it is a lengthy and complex process to get a problem-solving course of action formulated and legitimated as policy. Stakeholders can support such a process, offering up their own prepared consensus and their experience about the need for and content of a given regulation. Single stakeholders are unlikely to be able to determine outcomes unilaterally, and this book has revealed the all-importance of collaboration amongst all actors. In real-world interactions, however, it is often the case that one actor or actor-collective takes the lead in pursuing a policy outcome favourable to itself, while all others follow up the rear. And larger business organisations are of course better positioned than any others to take-on a leadership role.

The consistent message that emerges from this book is the need for the involvement of stakeholders – whether in the form of individuals, organisations or associations – in regulatory and standards-setting processes. In the past, democratically elected representatives decided industrial policy. Needed now are the best practices for enabling that policy dialogue and policy participation which will facilitate a wider consensus on compliance in the implementation Phase. A key role for EU institutions in the transition toward the Information Society is to strike a balance between the formal decision-maker's leadership and participation by all stakeholders.

Policy-making and -implementation are collective acts. *Models that theorise stakeholder involvement must also be practically useful to those very stakeholders in the process of problem-solving in a collective setting.* Clearly, the EU has an ongoing and very "productive" policy process, given the enormous volume of ICT policy, regulations and standards. Equally clearly, there must exist a vast range of actors, epistemic communities, policy institutions, and idea-makers from which so much policy output could have emerged. It follows that no single model can hope to explain everything that happens.

As EU policy is often sectoral or sub-sectoral, a "universal" model that would explain EU policy-making in general, including its interactions with regional and national policy-making, must have less explanatory power than a model focussed on EU industrial policy. Many reasons argue the desirability of a policy model specific to the ICT industry:

- Stakeholders, interests, and belief systems differ from sector to sector of the European economy.
- The ICT policy process itself is exceptionally complex, requiring specialised technical, economic, and regulatory experience and expertise.
- EU politics is prone to changing its own systemic decisional rules. Evidence of this constant change include cyclic regulatory process reform and the development of such new EU regulatory institutions as the European Research Council or the European Regulatory Group for Electronic Communications Networks and Services. These conflicting dynamics call for an approach to modelling that is quite specific as to time and place.

The innovative value of the Stakeholder Action Matrix lies in its endeavour to be thus specific by understanding external stakeholders, their belief systems, and their ways and means of policy participation, in the conviction that this will progress our theoretical insight into EU decisional processes. As a bonus, this same specific model of ICT policy-making may also support stakeholders seeking the most effective practical way to influence the ICT regulator. The focus on stakeholders, as both individual and collective actors, enables us to survey the gamut of actor types, relationships and behaviours and discern stable patterns therein. External stakeholders are engaged in a multiplicity of activities, some of which are taking place in several arenas simultaneously. The author witnessed the proliferation of policy networks operating at once at National, European and Global Levels. Stakeholders were observed to work transnationally, collaborating with other policy actors so as to choose which resources to mobilise at any given juncture (whence the author derived the concept of Advocacy Coalition Types).

Diverse actors and actor-relationships may emerge on different occasions; in this sense the policy process is episodic and cyclical, leading to different actions at different points in the process manifold. Hence the practical as well as theoretical value of the Policy Influence-Timing Model, which gives indications of the processual stages at which stakeholders may enjoy maximal influence, because the regulator is most receptive to stakeholder input.

Based on the two models presented in this book, combined, the author has reached three key conclusions. The first is that *timing is the most powerful element in wielding the influence to shape regulations*. Once a policy proposal is beyond the consultation stage, influencing its content is very difficult and in very many cases impossible. The entire policy process, from issue emergence through to policy review after the fact of implementation, takes a very long time. Companies wishing to influence policy must constantly monitor not only EU institutions, but also other stakeholders and indeed the underlying market situation. *Successful participation demands that business stakeholders engage in policy debates at the earliest feasible stage.*

The second key conclusion is that stakeholders have neglected to realise their capacity to influence the regulator *in indirect ways*. This fact recommends *forms of participation which are likelier to influence other stakeholders' opinions* (indirect influence) no less than the European regulator's (direct influence). Depending on the degree of self-interestedness in a new regulation or standard, policy stakeholders may (for instance) participate in the EU's Framework Programmes *via* studies, pilots ("proof of concept"), and services contracts – the results of which are bound to influence (even to determine) the regulator's policy preferences one way or another. The Survey results proved that it is highly popular with stakeholders to participate in European, national and/or international consultations; in public workshops and conferences; and above all in industry associations whose purpose is to forge consensus in advance, in order to present a united front to the regulator. The Survey showed that *collaboration between stakeholders with common objectives increases their success rate*.

The third key conclusion is that the modes of collaboration amongst stakeholders and between stakeholders and the regulator, have not been as effective as they could be. This suggests *the necessity of continually submitting the collaborative relationship to revision and improvement.* Better co-operation between business organisations, governments, and other key stakeholders[236] is needed on R&D, Internet security, and other issues critical for ICT. This book has presented evidence that the Lisbon Strategy can be achieved only through public-private partnership. It is widely acknowledged that Internet security threats demand a response broader than government regulation alone. The results of the case study hereinabove suggest that the European regulator will fail to control spamming (for instance) without global co-operation, consumer education, technical solutions, and active private-sector participation in all of these processes; in addition to industry self-regulatory initiatives.

A further consideration in favour of increased industry participation in regulatory policy is the fact that *inconsistent laws, regulations and guidelines in diverse regions have proved obstructive to the conduct of business*. Clearly, better co-ordination between

236 The survey conducted for this research lists academia and non-governmental organisations as "other" key stakeholders.

industry, governing bodies, and international organisations is needed in addressing policy inconsistencies and their consequences. This may be achieved by encouraging not only intergovernmental bargaining and consensus building, but also clear public consultation processes and the universal transparency that allows continuous information flows and regulatory updates between the public and private sectors.

9.2.3 Adoption of a regulatory compliance strategy

This book has shown that regulatory compliance is becoming increasingly important. Governments worldwide are putting companies under ever more scrutiny as corporate failures and fraud have proved the need for better regulation. Businesses are being challenged more than ever to comply strictly with all applicable internal (Sub-national), National, European and Global norms: – legislation, guidelines, technical standards, codes of conduct, and corporate policies, contractual terms and by-laws. Understanding and complying with the "minefield of regulation" can be a difficult and expensive task, especially for smaller organisations.

Changes set in motion by European and national regulators; market conditions; emerging technologies and factors endogenous to the industry, as described in Chapter One under the Industry Governance Theory, demand that policy stakeholders choose a new approach to regulation. *Businesses and other stakeholders are well advised to adopt regulatory compliance strategies and implement regulatory compliance programmes* as presented in Chapter Eight. This more than anything else they can do will support them in monitoring, analysing, influencing and complying with emerging regulatory measures. The eCommunications Framework and the recent adoption of corporate-governance regulations by regulators worldwide exemplify the need for business organisations to redefine more precisely how they respond to new regulations. Regulatory compliance must become part of senior management's agenda, as it opens the door to many new opportunities and challenges. A combination of business processes, trained staff, and infrastructure and supporting technologies is indispensable to establishing an effective framework for dealing with regulatory demands and issues. Compliance needs to be seamless and transparent inside organisations before cost savings and effective implementation can be realised.

In order to hold down the costs of compliance and ensure that regulation supports business objectives, it is also advisable that business organisations and other policy stakeholders apply an approach that consists of the following elementary steps:

1. *Risk analysis and compliance assessment by business of weaknesses or gaps in the current regulation or regulatory framework.* Regulatory compliance weaknesses can be related to general or industry-specific regulation, as outlined in the Regulations-Standards Compliance Matrix.
2. *Design and implementation of a regulatory compliance strategy* (or programme) and supporting internal control processes to arrange for minimal interruptions while adapting to new or changed regulations.
3. *Continuous monitoring of the organisation's compliance* with legal obligations.

4. Pro-active efforts to influence and even initiate the public policy agenda and the development of regulations, and to influence the development of new, and improvement of existing regulations and industry standards, using the manifold channels of influence available at each of several stages of the policy process.

The implementation of a regulatory compliance strategy and programme can be achieved by banding together with other stakeholders – in particular through networking and the formation of advocacy coalitions – and by encouraging the more widespread implementation of regulatory compliance strategies by other stakeholders. The Section titled "Risk management and control frameworks" in Chapter Four has presented several governance and compliance frameworks, such as the COSO Internal Control Framework or CobiT, which may assist organisations in designing and implementing a comprehensive approach to regulation, while Chapter Eight has provided step-by-step guidance in how to manage compliance programmes.

9.3 ORIGIN AND DESTINY OF THIS BOOK

9.3.1 The past: origination narrative

The author's interest in ICT regulation sprang from his participation, during and after working for the European Commission, in the initiatives and activities of its Framework Programme, which promoted the European Information Society. There was not then and, to date, there has never been any structured and easily digestible master documentation of ICT legislation wherein interested parties could find out all EU norms currently applicable to themselves. The information that stakeholders needed was scattered throughout multiple websites of several Directorates General of the Commission and beyond. The author was puzzled why both the Commission and the major stakeholders would leave the regulatory regime disjointed and in an uncategorised state, and wondered how public policy fit into the wider concept of the Information Society, which was said to be transforming all sectors of the economy with as much impact as the advent of electricity and petroleum *circa* 1900. The author began systematically to attend EU ICT policy stakeholder events and EU funded research projects on his own as a "participant observer". It was then that he conceived an ambition to define and compendiously summarise in matrix format the entire content of the European Union regulatory regime for ICT. This ambition eventuated in the Regulatory Compliance Matrix presented in Chapter Four.

After participating for several years, the author had accumulated such a large database that he was able to perform data-mining and -matching. This gave a comprehensive overview of the stakeholders who were participating in these events, whereupon it was noticed that some stakeholders participated more consistently in the ICT policy process than others. Did this pattern persist at the other Levels of governance besides the European one? This convinced the author to undertake further research allowing him to participate personally in other stakeholder events, such as at the National and Global Levels.

Changes in European and national regulatory regimes, market- and technology developments, and the emergence of new industries and services have changed the way regulation is shaped. This was reflected in the repeated observation, made during subsequent attendance at events at multiple Levels of ICT governance, of an emerging tendency toward a new form of governance in Europe, namely *governance by industry* as opposed to *governance by the State*. This insight was reflected in another repeated observation, that certain groups of stakeholders were encountered at all Levels. Should the multi-layered character of decision-making be seen as a general feature of European policy governance, or symptomatic only of ICT policy?

It was this empirical research – derived from participant observation, from a pan-European survey, and from a review of key scholarship – which formed the evidentiary basis of the *Industry Governance Theory*, a theory revolving in the author's mind ever since working for the Commission. Subsequent doctoral research, which included a comprehensive policy paper review and a case study, revealed that optimal timing – near the beginning of the policy cycle – is critical for industry (and other external stakeholders) to succeed in influencing regulation at any Level. This finding was theorised in the *Policy Influence-Timing Model* presented above.

Additional research was conducted to identify who dictates the changes of pace and direction in EU ICT policy. This suggested the question of whether some actors may be – wittingly or unwittingly – excluded from this policy process. Having previously identifying the active players, the author was led to the questions: What use did they make of such networks or platforms as committees, working groups, alliances, industry associations, and research programmes? And, on which Level(s) of governance, whether Sub-national (*viz.* private, regional), National, European, Global or others, did they operate? Continuing research discovered that groups of stakeholders organised themselves for greater impact into "advocacy coalitions", and that certain types of advocacy coalitions were found operating on all Levels. These findings were developed at length into the Four-Level Model and the Advocacy Coalition Typology, which the author combined successfully into the Stakeholder Action Matrix presented above.

9.3.2 The future: reflections and ideas

The author's personal reflections are thoroughly positive concerning both his approach and the results achieved. Not only when working at the European Commission and later as a doctoral researcher at Royal Holloway, University of London and the London School of Economics, but also during his subsequent professional career in assurance and advisory services, the author has participated and continues to participate personally in multitudes of stakeholder consultation events, observing behaviour and developments that often mismatch conventional perceptions about regulators and their interactions with stakeholders.

As a *stagière* with the European Commission's Telecoms Regulation Unit in 1996, the author was astonished that out of 35 staff only about 50% were Commission functionaries, and that of the remaining 50%, around 30% were seconded from national telecommunications operators, while 10% were external technical, legal and economic experts, and 10% were contractors or support staff (Rossmeissl, 1997). Under Cor Berben's leadership, this small team of experts drafted the whole legal framework[237] for creating, out of a vast congeries of fragmented markets, a single telecommunications market for equipment and services, which ultimately (at that time) comprised about 370 million consumers and a total of around 16 million enterprises. It formed "the largest economic entity in the world" (CEC, 1996d:32). Although the EU Telecommunications Council, the European Council and the European Parliament were responsible for debating and ratifying this regulatory package, Cor Berben's team drafted the legal text; prepared the speaking notes and "defence points" for Commissioner Martin Bangemann, who presented the drafts to the Telecommunications Council; liased with the translation department; amended the legal text as the policy process required; and monitored the latest developments in the Member States and in other regions, *e.g.* the Federal Communications Commission in the US. Yet Cor Berben had many other responsibilities at the same time, such as chairing the Open Network Provision Committee (ONP Committee) and liasing with contractors who were preparing sundry studies and feasibility projects on other topics. The working environment was comparable to multinational corporations like Microsoft or SAP more than to the textbook stereotype of large bureaucratic organisations employing only civil servants who produce lots of paperwork, without much interaction with others apart from other public institutions.

The author's stint as a *stagière* at the Commission included many other experiences that convinced him that the Commission is not just the executive body of the European Union. In reality it seemed to be the *primum mobilum* of EU legislation. One evening, after the translation department had closed, the author was called upon to translate from English into German a few paragraphs of Martin Bangemann's Defensive Points for the ONP Framework, which had been prepared by the staff of DG XIII Unit A1 ("Telecoms Regulation") for presentation at the EU Telecommunications Council of 21 March 1996. It suddenly struck the author as odd that the Commission, which is conventionally depicted as nothing more than a body of "agents" of their Member State principals, providing administrative support to an all-powerful European Council of Member State representatives, should be *defending* a Position against critics within the Council, as if the Commission were equal to the Council. But upon reflection the author realised that a Council of Ministers of [fifteen] States, without the Commission's guidance, might well have argued endlessly in circles about practically any substantive issue. The European Parliament, too, is essentially clueless about legislation

237 The 1998 Regulatory Package, which the Telecommunications Regulation Unit drafted and reviewed, included at this time Directive 97/13/EC on "A common framework for general authorisations and individual licences in the field of telecommunications services" (Licensing Directive); Directive 97/51/EC "Amending Council Directives 90/387/EEC and 92/44/EEC for the purpose of adaptation to a competitive environment in telecommunications" (Open Network Provision Directive); Directive 97/33/EC on "Interconnection in telecommunications with regard to ensuring universal service and interoperability through the application of the principles of open network provision (ONP)"; Directive 98/61/EC "Amending Directive 97/33/EC with regard to operator number portability and carrier pre-selection"; Directive 98/10/EC on "The application of open network provision (ONP) to voice telephony and on universal service for telecommunications in a competitive environment"; and various accompanying legal regulation, such as the Commission Recommendations of 15 October 1997 on "Interconnection in a liberalised market" and Commission Recommendation of 24 November 1999 on "Leased Lines Interconnection Pricing in a liberalised telecommunications market" (Europa website - 1998 Regulatory Package, 2008).

so specialised that even policy experts often struggle to understand it, and nearly always follows the Council's lead in the end anyway. It is the Commission, then, who wields the real power in the EU. It not only "interfaces" with policy stakeholders, but it even mediates between different interests within the EU institutions, while defending its own output before them all.

And yet the author's research has proved conclusively that *the Commission itself depends on the telecommunications industry* for the expertise and critical resources needed to do all of the above. It follows that, if the European Parliament depends on the Council, the Council on the Commission, and if the Commission in its turn depends just as abjectly on industry experience and expertise, then truly *Industry Governs*.

Putting all the pieces of the puzzle together was a different story. Discovering and presenting sufficient evidence of the growing influence of business organisations over EU ICT regulations and standards was not so difficult, as multiple sources of evidence both in the scholarship of others and in the author's own empirical research could be found. However, developing robust models that lent support to the basic theorisation was challenging. The initial insights of a *stagière* could be of interest to both practitioners and scholars faced with a complex and bewildering policy-making process; much depended on how much success (or the reverse) they were having in understanding and negotiating that process. The author noticed early on that the same relatively few stakeholders were participating in nearly all the events, and realised that these who engaged deeply did know their way through the labyrinth, while those who never tried were lost and had to accept whatever came out of the labyrinth as binding on themselves. Scholars too seemed to be overwhelmed by the empirical reality of such a complex organism, and with but a few exceptions confined themselves to vacuous generalities about "institutions" without making any attempt to understand the powerful external forces impinging on them.

Regulation is a dynamic process, and ongoing research was indispensable for keeping abreast of it so as to achieve the objectives of this book. After working out the theories and models featured hereinabove, continuing developments like the 2006 Review of the eCommunications Framework demanded close monitoring of events and constant updating of the affected Sections of this book and its appendices. For some aspects of ICT regulation and standardisation, reliance on the scant number of recent official publications was the only recourse; and most scholarship on EU policy focusses on the regulator and on formal institutions, ignoring stakeholder participation or at best treating it as secondary. These circumstances exacted of the author supernumerary empirical research efforts; hence the comprehensive policy paper review and the continuing personal participation in a legion of stakeholder activities and events.

The Review, which began in mid-2004, is now complete; the European Parliament passed the final amendments of the revised Regulatory Framework at its 3rd reading on 24 November 2009; however, implementation of the revised framework was only completed in 2011. The past two years of the implementation saw intensified bargaining between Member State governments represented by their ministers of telecommunications and industry, the EU regulatory authorities, and key stakeholder groups who identified major objections to certain aspects of the new package; which complicated the policy process with additional consultations.

9.4 ONCE AND FUTURE CONTRIBUTIONS TO THE FIELD

It has been argued that there is little meeting of the minds between theorists/modellers and policy practitioners. On the one hand, policy makers live in a world of time-pressure, power play, conflict, influence, bargaining, and concession. They may view new ideas, even those originating with business actors, as a threat to the stability of the positions and approaches that they have developed over the years (Greene, 1993:8). On the other hand, policy stakeholders may consider conventional theoretical models overbroad in scope and too abstract to be useful. Accordingly, one of the objectives of this book was to develop concepts that could bridge this disconnect. A policy process that many scholars have dismissed as "too complex" or "undemocratic", and which business stakeholders and the wider civil society have declared themselves dissatisfied with, due to its opacity and unaccountability – this is the challenge the author took up in writing this book. He has ended up controverting these widespread assumptions, bringing simplification and clarity to an inaccessible domain for scholars, and a discernible way through for those who must engage themselves with it. The author's ulterior ambition has always been to find a solution that would be both useful to practitioners, and would demystify at least a few of the conundrums that theorists have struggled with in vain. His faith has been that the best answer to the one would be also the best answer to the other – a faith which has been vindicated.

9.4.1 Main contributions – relevant for practitioners and scholars

The yield of all these efforts should interest practitioners, students and scholars of EU policy and business influence, policy stakeholders, business organisations, and regulators. The main contributions of this book may be summarised as follows: –

(1) *Industry Governance* – The author found out early on that few scholars had even attempted to describe or analyse in depth the ways in which the private sector is involved in ICT policy and regulation. The matter had been investigated only *in general terms*. By investigating at the level of *individual* stakeholders and concrete instances of their involvement in ICT policy, the author found superabundant evidence identifying business as the main driver of trends in regulatory policy and standardisation. On the basis of these findings a new theory, the Industry Governance Theory was developed. The Theory challenges the populist view that the EU's decisional processes are non-transparent and run a democratic deficit. Stakeholder participatory proceedings are transparency itself, and if industry does govern, it is more because of uninterest and indeed apathy on the part of so many other actual and potential stakeholders.

(2) *The Stakeholder Action Matrix* – This model contributes synoptical clarification and typological simplification to the debate over European integration and multi-level governance. By integrating the sundry Levels of governance and Types of stakeholders into

a single model, the author corroborated the neo-functionalist view[238] that the power of nation-states is declining, at least in Europe, whilst influential new actors are emerging, some of whom operate at all policy-making Levels. The Stakeholder Action Matrix treats European integration not as a theoretical speculation, but as the empirical reality that it is, impacting policy at all Levels.

(3) *The Advocacy Coalition Typology* – Although some scholars have inquired into the influence of individual organisations over the Information Society policy agenda, no attempt had been made before this book to systematise these influencers, or to investigate whether patterns could be detected in the behaviour and/or interests of whole categories of influencers. This book may be considered a major contribution to analysing advocacy coalitions, and might be used as a springboard to investigating stakeholder influence in other industries. Deploying this theoretical framework enabled the author to categorise ICT stakeholders into Advocacy Coalition Types, vastly simplifying our understanding of stakeholder motivations. At the same time, he has also provided empirical evidence rounding out existing but narrowly focussed case studies of advocacy coalitions, so as to confirm the validity of the concept. Common belief systems are important to the creation and sustainable functioning of industry associations – a major factor in shaping ICT regulation and standards, as we have seen. But they also undergird other coalition building by stakeholders, even those that cross the Sub-national, National, European and Global Levels of policy-making, as evidenced above in Section 5.1. It is a fact that, in fourteen years of participant observation in stakeholder events and consultations, these Types were everywhere seen to be remarkably stable, and their underlying belief systems never underwent any evolution.

(4) *The Policy Influence-Timing Model* – This model adds the value of a dynamic time dimension to a phenomenon that has usually been approached as consisting of discrete episodes (or stages) to be studied in isolation, or else as a nebulous "process" which is nonetheless left temporally featureless. Although based on the Stages Heuristic, which does divide "processes" up into (notionally) temporal parts, the Policy Influence-Timing Model contributes a unique, general truth – that stakeholder influence waxes and wanes, and consequently that it is necessary to *time* one's attempts at policy influence.

(5) *The Regulatory Compliance Matrix* – Vast swaths of ICT governance and regulation are confusing to many practitioners and scholars. The Regulatory Compliance Matrix developed for this book helps clarify the whole field of ICT regulation by laying out the principal domains of both general and specific ICT legislation, regulations and norms together with pertinent, supporting standards, frameworks and guidance. Applied consistently over

238 Neo-functionalism asserts that the importance of nation-states declines as EU integration expands. It considers that the power of supranational institutions and interest groups are the driving factor behind EU integration (Haas, 2004). Its theoretical approach features the concept of "positive spillover", the mechanism that regional integration within one economic sector will create incentives for integration in interrelated sectors, a process which can "creep onwards" indefinitely. Spillover can take place on Sub-national as well on National and European Levels.

time and updated on a regular basis, the Matrix should furnish a stable monitoring and assessment mechanism for ICT stakeholders wishing to determine which regulations and laws will likely affect them.

(6) *Regulatory Compliance Practitioner Toolkit* –Organisations have been obliged to design and execute Regulatory Compliance Programmes in order to keep the risks of non-compliance with a complex regulatory regime within manageable bounds. To assist practitioners in this, an overview of the most practical tools used by businesses, and the professional service firms that advise them, was included in this book. Featured are risk identification and assessment tools, Risks and Controls Matrices, Heatmaps and Roadmaps. Additionally, a concise and *ready-to-use* Regulatory Compliance Maturity Model has been provided. Maturity models are not a theoretical abstraction but a tool tried and tested by many private and public organisations.

This book has contributed a scientific theory, practical models and a typology, all of which can assist practitioners and researchers who wish to look further into stakeholder participation in policy processes in fields beyond ICT governance. In contributing these novelties, the author looks forward to becoming part of fruitful and stimulating future debates on policy-making and policy output.

9.4.1 The author's contribution to the world of Better Regulation

It is often affirmed that the completion of a publication is just the beginning of a long journey. The author's journey began fourteen years ago but is far from being over. A pathway to further investigations inspired by this book may lie in analysing stakeholder influence in other industry sectors, such as financial services or pharmaceuticals. If the Industry Governance Theory has identified a phenomenon widely operative across industrial sectors, some traditional views on European public policy may no longer be viable unless revised to reflect the changes wrought by the new mode of governance in Europe.

From everything presented herein it is clear that every subject of EU regulation struggles to comply with the many, varied, and complex regulations, and must struggle no less than regulators themselves to keep track of new technologies and new market developments. The root of success is "better regulation" in the first place. To this end, the author will continue to engender thought leadership and to share practical results, the better to contribute to this important policy and regulatory field.

The author's experience in regulatory compliance, business assurance and theorisation, as well as the contacts he has forged with the regulators, industry associations, and stakeholders, could greatly help businesses in developing their compliance frameworks.

To accomplish this, continuing research and interaction with the relevant policy actors is of prime importance. Updates of the Regulatory Compliance Matrix should furnish a highly useful overview of ICT law and regulation to practitioners and scholars, and probably even to regulators themselves. Although the Regulatory Compliance Matrix is peculiar to the ICT sector, similar frameworks could be compiled for other highly regulated sectors, or for other regions or countries beyond Europe.

To sum up the objectives the author has derived from the intensive labours expended on this book, the he intends in the years to come to promote Better Regulation and to develop better programmes of governance and ICT regulatory compliance. This especially involves encouraging stakeholders to take more initiative and to make use of the channels for participation that have been created by the New Governance, and by being signposted herein, made more accessible. This book should assist both the author and others in the same line of work to render practical advice to stakeholders who are just now getting involved. All who are involved already, both practitioners and academic specialists, may thereby stimulate debate and promote the new regulatory agenda.

This book, having analysed business stakeholder influence over ICT policy and recommended ways of constructing regulatory compliance programmes, has given insight into the EU policy process. Although the author ventures to assert that his Policy Influence-Timing Model and Stakeholder Action Matrix are sustainable for many years to come, the fact remains that laws, regulations, norms, and stakeholders are all in constant flux. It is therefore essential to employ an empirical and practical approach to researching both European ICT policy and methods of effective compliance, otherwise both practitioners and scholars may fall behind policy developments and find themselves in the same position the regulator was once in – obliged to play catch-up owing to the emergence of new markets, to unforeseen changes in the economy, and to rapidly evolving technologies.

BIBLIOGRAPHY

BIBLIOGRAPHY

This bibliography covers books and collections of essays, publications of institutions and organisations, speeches, presentations press material and statements made at conference.

Abbott, Kenneth; Snidal, Duncan (2001) "International standards and international governance", *Journal of European Public Policy (Special Issue: Governance and International Standards Setting)*, Vol. 8, No. 3 (Taylor & Francis Ltd.: London), pp. 345-370.

Adler, Emanuel; Haas, Peter M. (1992) "Conclusion: epistemic communities, world order, and the creation of a reflective research program"; *International Organization*, Vol. 46, No. 01 (Cambridge Journals), page 367-390.

AFNOR (Association française de normalisation) website (2007) at http://www.afnor.org (accessed June 2007).

All Party Internet Group (APIG) website (2006) at http://www.apig.org.uk (accessed September 2006).

All Party Parliamentary Communications Group (apComms) website (2007) at http://www.apcomms.org.uk/ (accessed July 2007).

Ambler, Tim; Chittenden, Francis; Shamutkova, Monika (2003) *Do Regulators Play by the Rules?* (British Chamber of Commerce: London).

Ambler, Tim; Chittenden, Francis; Shamutkova, Monika (2004) *How much Regulation is Gold Plate? A study of UK Elaboration of EU Directives* (British Chamber of Commerce: London).

Ambler, Tim; Chittenden, Francis; Hwang, Chanyeong (2005) *Is EU Regulation Good for us?* (British Chamber of Commerce: London).

ANCE ("The European consumer voice in standardisation") website (2003) at http://www.anec.org (accessed June 2003).

Anderson, C. Leigh; Dobel, Patrick (2002) "Progress and the Promise of Public Policy", in Anderson, C. Leigh; Looney, Janet W., eds. *Making Progress: Essays in Progress and Public Policy* (Lexington Books: Lanham MD, USA), pp. 3-28.

Andersen-IENM (1996) "Strategic Developments for the European Publishing Industry towards the Year 2000" (commissioned by the European Commission: Brussels).

Anderson, James Elliot (1979) *Public Policy-Making* (Praeger: New York).

Anonymous (1996) *European Public Affairs Directory 1999* (Landmarks: Brussels).

Anonymous (1997) *Dictionary of Government and Politics*, 2nd edition (Peter Collin Publishing Ltd.: Teddington, UK).

Anonymous (1999a) "Consultation, Concealment or Confusion? EURIM uncovers the current Practices and Principles in forming European IT Policy, and recommends more transparent consultation processes", *Information Technology & Public Policy: The Journal of the Parliamentary Information Technology Committee*, Vol. 17, No. 3 (July) (Green Shires Group).

Anonymous (1999b) *The Directory of 9300 Trade and Professional Associations in the EU* (Euroconfidential S.A.: Genval, Belgium).

Anonymous (2001) *Lobbying in the European Union: Explanatory guide and contacts*, 2nd edition (Euroconfidential S.A.: Genval, Belgium).

Anonymous (2004a) *European Union Law*, 4th edition (Cavendish Publishing: London).

Anonymous (2004b) "More calls for spam co-operation", *Computer Business Review* (March), p. 10.

Anonymous (2005) "The Internet is a global medium and should not be in the control of one nation", *Information Age*, November (Newbury), p. 13.

Anonymous (2006a) "Commission publishes three new reports on telecoms regulation", *CORDIS focus Newsletter*, No. 270 (September), p. 4 (European Commission: Luxembourg).

Anonymous (2006b) "EuroISPA Secretariat's Column", *EuroISPA Newsletter*, No. 14, Spring 2006, p. 4 (EuroISPA: Brussels).

Anonymous (2007a) "FP7 takes off", *CORDIS focus Newsletter*, No. 274 (January), pp. 1-3 (European Commission: Luxembourg).

Anonymous (2007b) "Potočnik on competitiveness instruments: same aim, different angle", *CORDIS focus Newsletter*, No. 277 (April), p. 11 (European Commission: Luxembourg).

Anonymous (2007c) "Research high on agenda at Spring European Council", *CORDIS focus Newsletter*, No. 277 (April), p. 4 (European Commission: Luxembourg).

Anti-Phishing Working Group website (2006) at http://www.antiphishing.org/ (accessed July 2006).

Apgar, Mahlon (1998) "The Alternative Workplace: Changing Where and How People Work", *Harvard Business Review*, May/June, pp. 121-136.

Archer, Quentin; Goldman, Oli (2006) "E.C. Computing, Telecommunications and Related Measures", New Section: Tables of Measures, Issue 2 (Sweet & Maxwell: London).

Aspinwall, Mark (1997) "Collective attraction – the new political game in Brussels", in Greenwood, Justin; Aspinwall, Mark, eds. *Collective action in the European Union: interests and the new politics of associability* (Routledge: London), pp. 196-213.

ASTA (2004) "Anti-Spam Technical Alliance: Technology and Policy Proposal" *Document*, 22 June 2004 (ASTA: published on website).

Astrup, Jonas (2003) Policy Manager, Commercial Law and Practice, Jurisdiction and Applicable Law in E-Commerce, *Personal interview* on 12.12.2003 at ICC (Paris).

Austin, Marc; Milner, Helen (2001) "Strategies of European standardization." *Journal of European Public Policy (Special Issue: Governance and International Standards Setting)*, Vol. 8, No. 3 (Taylor & Francis Ltd.: London), pp 411-431.

Baldwin, Robert (1995) *Rules and Government* (Oxford University Press: Oxford).

Baldwin, Robert; McCrudden, Christopher, eds. (1987) *Regulation and Public Law* (Weidenfeld & Nicholson).

Baldwin, Robert; Scott, Colin; Hood, Christopher (1998) *A reader on regulation* (Oxford University Press: Oxford).

Baldwin, Robert; Cave, Martin (1999) *Understanding regulation: theory, strategy, and practice* (Oxford University Press: Oxford).

Baldwin, Robert; Hood, Christopher, Rothstein, Henry (2001) *The Government of Risk: Understanding Risk Regulation Regimes* (Oxford University Press: Oxford).

Barani, Bernard (2004) "Satellite communications: the contribution of the 5th framework programme and future perspectives". International Journal of Satellite Communications and Networking, Vol. 22 (Brussels).

Bartle, Ian (2005) *Globalisation and EU policy-making: The neo-liberal transformation of telecommunications and electricity* (Manchester University Press: Manchester/New York).

Bassett, Paul (Office of Government Commerce) and Dingwall, Colin (Department for Constitutional Affairs) (29 March 2006): Intellect "DP/FOI Seminar" (Intellect: Intellect Conference Suite, Russell Square, London).

Baumgartner, Frank; Leech, Beth (1998) *Basic Interests* (Princeton University Press: Princeton).

Bechmann, Gotthard (2000) "Concepts of Information Society and Social Function of Information", in Banse, Gerhard; Langenbach, Christian; Machleidt, Peter, eds. *Towards the Information Society – The Case of Central and Eastern European Countries* (Springer-Verlag: Berlin/New York), p. 37-52.

Becker, Howard S. (1958), "Problems of inference and proof in participant observation", *American Sociological Review*, 23:652-660.

Becker, Howard (1970), Sociological Work: Method and Substance (Aldine: Chicago).

Beetham, David; Lord, Christopher (1998) "Legitimacy and the European Union", in Weale, Albert; Nentwich, Michael, eds. *Political Theory and the European Union* (Routledge: London), p. 15-33.

Bell, Daniel (1976) *The Coming of Post-industrial Society: A venture in Social Forecasting* (Basic Books: New York).

Benson, John K. (1992) "A Framework for Policy Analysis", in Rogers, D.; Whitten, D., eds. *International Coordination* (Iowa State University Press: Ames), pp. 137-176.

Benz, Arthur; Eberlain, Burkard (1996) *Regions in European Governance: The Logic of Multi-Level Interaction*, European University Institute Working Paper, RSC No. 98/31 (Robert Schuman Centre: San Domenico, Italy).

BEREC website (2012) at http://www.erg.eu.int/ (accessed August 2012).

BERR (July 2007a) "Next Steps on Regulatory Reform." (HM Government: London).

BERR (2007b) (Department for Business Enterprise and Regulatory Reform) "Next Steps on Regulatory Reform." July 2007 (HM Government: London).

BERR (Department for Business, Enterprise and Regulatory Reform) website (2007) at http://www.berr.gov.uk (accessed August 2007).

BER (Better Regulation Executive) website (2007) at http://www.cabinetoffice.gov.uk/regulation/ and http://www.betterregulation.gov.uk/ (accessed August 2007).

Besen, Stanley; Farrell, Joseph (1994) "Choosing how to compete: strategies and tactics in standardization", *Journal of Economic Perspectives*, No. 8, pp. 117-131.

Better Regulation Executive (2007) *Regulation and Business Advice: A Report by the Better Regulation Executive* (BERR: London).

Better Regulation Executive website (2007) at http://www.cabinet-office.gov.uk/regulation/ (accessed May 2007).

Better Regulation website (2007) at http://ec.europa.eu/governance/better_regulation/index_en.htm (accessed May 2007).

BIAC (Business and Industry Advisory Committee) website (2006) at http://www.biac.org (accessed May 2006).

Black, Julia (1996) "Constitutionalising Self-Regulation", *Modern Law Review*, Vol. 59, No. 1, pp. 24-55.

Blaxter, Loraine; Hughes, Christina; Tight, Malcolm (2001) *How to research* (Open University Press: Buckingham/Philadelphia).

Bluetooth SIG website (2012) at http://www.bluetooth.org (accessed August 2012).

Böllhoff, Dominik (2002) "The New Regulatory Regime: The Institutional Design of Telecommunications Regulation at the National Level", in Héritier, Adrienne, ed. *Common Goods: Reinventing European and International Governance,* Governance in Europe series (Rowman Littlefield: Oxford), pp 235-261.

Bosch, Gerhard; Webster, Juliet; Weissbach, Hans-Jürgen (2000) "New Organizational Forms in the Information Society", in Ducatel, Ken; Webster, Ken; Herrmann, Werner, eds. *The Information Society in Europe: Work and Life in an Age of Globalisation* (Rowman & Littlefield Publishers: Lanham MA, USA), pp. 99-118.

Bouwen, Pieter (2001) "Corporate Lobbying in the European Union: Towards a Theory of Access", *European University Institute (EUI)*, No. 2001/5 (EUI: Florence, Italy).

Braun, Dietmar (1999) "Interests or Ideas? An Overview of Ideational Concepts in Public Policy Research", in Braun, Dietmar; Busch, Andreas, eds. *Public Policy and Political Ideas* (Edward Elgar Publishing Ltd.: Cheltenham, UK), pp. 11-29.

Brewer, Gary; deLeon, Peter (1983) *The Foundations of Policy Analysis* (Brooks Cole: Monterey CA, USA).

Brightmail website (2006) (filter Software Company, acquired by Symanyec) at http://www.brightmail.com (accessed August 2006).

British Standards Institute(BSI) website (2007) at http://www.bsi-global.com (accessed June 2007).

Bromley, Simon (2001) "Governance and the European Union", in Bromley, Simon, ed. *Governing the European Union* (SAGE: Thousand Oaks CA, USA/London), page 1-26.

Brooks, Stephen (1994) "Policy Communities and the Social Science", in Brooks, Stephen; Gagnon, Alain-G., eds. *The Political Influence of Ideas: Policy Communities and the Social Sciences* (Praeger Publishers: Westport CT, USA/London), page 1-12.

Broscheid, Andreas; Coen, David (2007) "Lobbying activity creation in the EU: empirically exploring the nature of the policy good", *Journal of European Public Policy*, Vol. 14, No. 3 (Routledge: London), pp. 346-365.

Burgess, Robert (1984) *In the Field: An Introduction to Field Research* (Georg Allen & Unwin: London).

Burns, Tom; Baumgartner, Thomas; DeVille, Philippe (1986) *Man, Decisions, Society: The Theory of Actor-System Dynamics for Social Scientists* (Routledge).

Business Link website (2007) at http://www.businesslink.gov.uk (accessed August 2007).

Cabinet Office (2002) "Regulatory Reform: The Government's Action Plan", with forward by the Prime Minister Tony Blair, February 2002 (Her Majesty's Stationery Office: London).

Cabinet Office & Better Regulation Executive (2007a) "A Code of Practice for Regulators: A Consultation" *Consultation on the Regulators' Compliance Code and the scope of the Code and the Principles of Good Regulation*, May 2007 (Her Majesty's Stationery Office: London).

Cabinet Office & Better Regulation Executive (2007b) *Consultation on the Draft Regulatory Enforcement and Sanctions Bill: Implementing the Hampton Vision*, May 2007.

Caporaso, James A.; Wittenbrinck, Joerg (2006) "The new modes of governance and political authority in Europe", *Journal of European Public Policy*, Vol. 13, No. 4, (June) , (Routledge), pp. 471-480.

Castells, Manuel (1996) "The Information Age: Economy, Society and Culture", in Castells, Manuel, ed. *The Rise of the Network Society*, 1st edition (Blackwell Publishers: Oxford).

Castells, Manuel (2000) *The Rise of the Network Society*, 2nd edition (Blackwell Publishers: Oxford).

Castells, Manuel (2004): "Politics and power in the network society." *Presentation* on 18 March 2004, LSE Miliband Lecture, London.

Castells, Manual (2009) *Communication Power* (Oxford University Press: New York).

Castillo, José Candela (2001) "Rapport sur l'application du droit communautaire par les États members et sur le contrôle de celle-ci par la Commision, contenant des recommendations en vue de les améliorer du point de vue de la gouvernance démocratique européenne", *Report*, 25 July 2001 (European Commission, Secretariat: Brussels).

Cave, Martin (2000) "How far can deregulation of telecommunications go?", in Marsden, Christopher T., ed. *Regulating the global information society* (Routledge: London), pp. 93-107.

Cawson, Alan; Morgan, Kevin; Webber, Douglas; Holmes, Peter (1990) *Hostile Brothers: Competition and Closure in the European Electronics Industry* (Clarendon Press: Oxford).

CEC (1983): Directive (83/189/EEC) "A procedure for the provision of information in the field of technical standards and regulations", 28 March 1983 (European Commission: Brussels).

CEC (1987a): (87/290/EEC) "Towards a Dynamic European Economy: Green Paper on the Development of the Common Market for Telecommunications Services and Equipment", *Green Paper*, adopted 30 June 1987 (European Commission: Brussels).

CEC (1987b): Directive (87/372/EEC) "the frequency bands to be reserved for the coordinated introduction of public pan-European cellular digital land-based mobile communications in the Community" (European Commission: Brussels).

CEC (1988): Directive (88/182/EEC) amending Directive (83/189/EEC), 22 March 1988 (European Commission: Brussels).

CEC (1990a): Directive (90/387/EEC) on "the establishment of the internal market for telecommunications services through the implementation of open network provision", as amended by Directive (97/51/EC) of the European Parliament and of the Council, 29 October 1997, OJ L 295 (European Commission: Brussels).

CEC (1990b): COM (90/388/EC) of 28 June 1990 "on competition in the markets for telecommunications services" (European Commission: Brussels).

CEC (1990c): COM(90/456/EC) "The development of European standardisation: Action for a faster technological integration in Europe", *Green Paper,* 8 October 1990 (European Commission: Brussels).

CEC (1990d): Directive (90/544/EEC) on "the frequency bands designated for the coordinated introduction of pan-European land-based public radio paging in the Community" (European Commission: Brussels).

CEC (1991): Directive (91/287/EEC) on "the frequency bands to be reserved for the coordinated introduction of public pan-European cellular digital land-based mobile communications in the Community" (European Commission: Brussels).

CEC (1992): COM(1992)2272 "An Open and Structured Dialogue between the Commission and Special Interest Groups", Sec (92)2272 (European Commission: Brussels).

CEC (1993): COM(1993)700 "White Paper on growth, competitiveness and employment: The challenges and ways forward into the 21st century", *White Paper*, 5 October 1993 (European Commission: Brussels).

CEC (1994a) "Europe and the Global Information Society: Recommendations to the European Council", also known as "Bangemann Report", published in May 1994 (High-Level Expert Group: Brussels).

CEC (1994b): Directive (94/10/EC) "materially amending for the second time Directive (83/189/EEC), adopted", 23 March 1994 (European Commission: Brussels).

CEC (1994c): COM(94/145/EC) "Towards the Personal Communication Environment: Green Paper on a common approach in the field of mobile and personal Communications in the European Union", Green Paper adopted April 1994 (European Commission: Brussels).

CEC (1994d): COM(1994)347 "Europe's Way to the Information Society – An Action Plan", 19 July 1994 (European Commission: Brussels).

CEC (1994e): (94/440/EC) on the "liberalisation of telecommunications infrastructure and cable television networks. Part 1: principle and timeline", Green Paper adopted on 25 October 1994 (European Commission: Brussels).

CEC (1994f): (94/682/EC) on the "liberalisation of telecommunications infrastructures and cable television networks. Part 2: A common approach to the provision of infrastructure for telecommunications in the European Union", *Green Paper,* adopted on 25 January 1995 (European Commission: Brussels).

CEC (1995a) "Conclusions of G-7 summit 'Information Society Conference'", DOC/95/2 (European Commission: Brussels).

CEC (1995b): Directive (95/46/EC) on "the protection of individuals with regard to the processing of personal data and on the free movement of such data", 24 October 1995 (European Commission: Brussels).

CEC (1995c): (95/158/EC) Green Paper on "the liberalisation of telecommunications infrastructure and cable television networks", *Consultation*, adopted on 3 May 1995 (European Commission: Brussels).

CEC (1996a): COM(January 1996) "Building the European Information Society for us all. – First reflections of the High Level Group of Experts", *Interim Report* (European Commission: Brussels).

CEC (1996b): COM(1996)338 "The Role, Position and Liability of the Statutory Auditor within the European Union", Green Paper (European Commission: Brussels).

CEC (1996c): COM(1996)359 "Standardization and the Global Information Society: The European Approach", Communication from the Commission to the Council and the European Parliament, 24 July 1996 (European Commission: Brussels).

CEC (1996d): COM(1996)389 "Green Paper - Living in the Information Society: People First", Draft 22/07/96, DG Employment, Industrial Relations and Social Affairs, *Green Paper* (European Commission: Brussels).

CEC (1996e): COM(1996)392 concerning "regulatory transparency in the internal market for information society services", Communication from the Commission to the European Parliament, the Council and the Economic and Social Committee, 30 August 1996 (European Commission: Brussels).

CEC (1996f): COM(1996)395 "The Information Society: From Corfu to Dublin - The new emerging priorities", Communication from the Commission to the Council, the European Parliament, the Economic and Social Committee and the Committee of Regions, 24 July 1996 (European Commission: Brussels).

CEC (1996g): COM(96)608 on "Assessment Criteria for National Schemes for the Costing and Financing of Universal Service in Telecommunications and Guidelines for the Member States on Operation of such Schemes" (European Commission, Brussels).

CEC (1997a): COM(April 1997) "Building the European information society for us all." Final policy report of the high-level expert group, prepared by Soete, Luc- Chairman of the HLEG, April 1997 (Directorate-General for Employment, Industrial Relations and Social Affairs, Unit V/B/4: Brussels).

CEC (1997b): Directive (97/66/EC) concerning "the processing of personal data and the protection of privacy in the telecommunications sector" (European Commission: Brussels).

CEC (1997c): COM(97/623/EC) on "the Convergence of the Telecommunications, Media and Information Technology Sector, and the Implications for Regulation: Towards an Information Society Approach", *Green Paper*, adopted on 03.12.97 (European Commission: Brussels).

CEC (1998a): (98/596/EC) on "radio spectrum policy in the context of European Community policies such as telecommunications, broadcasting, transport, and R&D" *Green Paper* (European Commission: Brussels).

CEC (1998b): Recommendation 98/511/EC on "Interconnection in the liberalised telecommunications market" (European Commission: Brussels).

CEC (1999a) *The European Commission web-directory of interest groups* (European Commission: Brussels).

CEC (1999b) "The G-8 Global Information Society Pilot Project", final report (Brussels).

CEC (1999c): (99/539/EC) "Towards a new framework for Electronic Communications infrastructure and associated services – The 1999 Communications Review", *Commission Communication*, 10 Nov 1999 (European Commission: Brussels).

CEC (1999d): COM(1999)687final) "eEurope: An Information Society For All", Communication on a Commission Initiative for the Special European Council of Lisbon, 23 and 24 March 2000 (European Commission: Brussels).

CEC (1999e): Decision No 276/1999/EC "Adopting a multi-annual Community action plan on promoting safer use of the Internet by combating illegal and harmful content on global networks", 25 January 1999 (European Commission, Brussels).

CEC (2000a) "The Commission and non-governmental organisations: building a stronger partnership", *Commission Discussion Paper*, presented by President Prodi & Vice-President Kinnock (European Commission: Brussels).

CEC (2000b): COM(2000)154 "Strategic objectives 2000-05", February 2000 (European Commission, Brussels).

CEC (2000c): Resolution (2000)0177: "European Parliament Resolution: Safe Harbour Privacy Principles", developed by the U.S. Department of Governance in consultation with the European Commission (Brussels).

CEC (2000d): COM(2000)239 "The results of the public consultation on the 1999 Communications Review and Orientations for the new Regulatory Framework", 26 April 2000, *Commission Communication* (European Commission: Brussels).

CEC (2000e): COM(2000)890 on "Creating a safer Information Society by improving the Security of Information Infrastructures and Combating Computer-related Crime" (European Commission: Brussels).

CEC (2000f): SEC (2000)1547/7 "Work Programme: White Paper on European Governance - Enhancing democracy in the European Union", *Commission staff working document*, 11 October 2000 (European Commission, Brussels).

CEC (2000g): Regulation (2887/2000/EC) on "unbundled access to the local loop", *Official Journal*, published 30 December 2000 (European Commission: Brussels).

CEC (2000h): COM(June 2000) "eEurope 2002 - An Information Society For All: Action Plan prepared by the Council and the European Commission for the Feira European Council, 19-20 June", 14.6.2000 (European Commission: Brussels).

CEC, (2001a) *EURO-GUIDE: Yearbook of the institutions of the European Union and the other European organisations*, 18th edition, forward Guy Verhofstadt (Editions Delta: Brussels).

CEC (2001b): Directive (2001/115/EC) of 20 December 2001 "amending Directive (77/388/EEC) with a view to simplifying, modernising and harmonising the conditions laid down for invoicing in respect of value added tax ("electronic invoicing"), 20 December 2001 (European Commission: Brussels).

CEC (2001c): COM(2001)140final) "eEurope 2002: Impact and Priorities", *A Communication to the Spring European Council in Stockholm*, 23-24 March 2001, adopted 13 March 2001 (European Commission: Brussels).

CEC (2001d): COM(2001)428final) "European Governance White Paper", 25 July 2001 (European Commission: Brussels).

CEC (2002a) "Commission creates Radio Spectrum Policy Group and European Regulators Group", *European Commission Press Release*, IP/02/1171, published on 29 July 2002 (Brussels).

CEC (2002b) *EURO Lobbying: Directory of European Union Trade and Professional Associations*, 7th edition (Editions Delta: Brussels).

CEC (2002c): COM(2002) "Safer Internet Action Plan", *Work Programme 2003-2004* (European Commission: Brussels).

CEC (2002d) Directive (2002/21/EC) on "A common regulatory framework for electronic communications infrastructure and associated services" (the Framework Directive), (European Commission: Brussels).

CEC (2002e) Directive (2002/58/EC) "procession of personal data and protection of privacy in the electronic communications sector (Directive on privacy and electronic communications)", 31 July 2002 (European Commission: Brussels).

CEC (2002f): COM(2002)62 on "Impacts and Priorities", *eEurope Benchmarking Report*, 5 February 2002 (European Commission: Brussels).

CEC (2002g): Directive (2002/77/EC) on "competition in the markets for electronic communications services" (European Commission: Brussels).

CEC (2002h): COM(2002)152 "Adopting a multiannual Community action plan on promoting safer use of the Internet by combating illegal and harmful content on global networks.", 22 March 2002 (European Commission, Brussels).

CEC (2002i): COM(2002)196 "Green Paper on Alternative Dispute Resolution in civil and commercial law", 19 April 2002 (European Commission, Brussels).

CEC (2002j) COM(2002)263 "eEurope 2005: An information society for all", *An Action Plan presented in view of the Seville European Council*, 21/22 June 2002 (European Commission: Brussels).

CEC (2002k) COM(2002)275 "European Governance: Better lawmaking", 5 June 2002 (European Commission, Brussels).

CEC (2002l) COM(2002)276 "Impact Assessment" (European Commission: Brussels).

CEC (2002m) COM(2002)277 "Consultation Document: Towards a reinforced culture of consultation and dialogue-proposal for general principles and minimum standards for consultation of interested parties by the Commission" (European Commission: Brussels).

CEC (2002n): COM(2002)278 "Action plan: Simplifying and improving the regulatory environment", 5 June 2002 (European Commission, Brussels).

CEC (2002o): COM(2002)499 "More Research for Europe: Towards 3% GDP", published 11 September 2002 (European Commission, Brussels).

CEC (2002p): Decision (2002/622/EC) on "establishing a Radio Spectrum Policy Group", 27 July 2002 (European Commission, Brussels).

CEC (2002q): Decision (2002/627/EC) "establishing the European Regulators Group for Electronic Communications Networks and Services" (European Commission: Brussels).

CEC (2002r): Decision (2002/676/EC) on "a regulatory framework for radio spectrum policy in the European Community (Radio Spectrum Decision)", 7 March 2002 (European Commission, Brussels).

CEC (2002s): CEC COM(2002)704 "Towards a reinforced culture of consultation and dialogue - General principles and minimum standards for consultation of interested parties by the Commission", 11 December 2002 (European Commission, Brussels).

CEC (2002t): COM(2002)719 "Council Decision amending Decision 1999/468/EC laying down the procedures for the exercise of implementing powers conferred on the Commission", Proposal for a Council Decision, 2002/0298 (CNS), 11 November 2002 (European Council, Brussels).

CEC (2002u) "European Governance: Preparatory Work for the White Paper" (European Commission, Luxembourg).

CEC (2003a) "European Commission proposes creation of Network Security Agency to boost Cyber Security in Europe." *Press Release*, IP/03/208, 10 February 2003 (European Commission: Brussels).

CEC (2003b) "Harmonisation of technical standards", *Cordis – RTD Results*, No. 44, September 2003 (European Commission: Brussels).

CEC (2003c) *"IST – A thematic priority for Research and Development under the Specific Programme "Integrating and strengthening the European Research Area in the Community Sixth Framework Programme"*, 2003-2004 work programme (European Commission: Brussels).

CEC (2003d) "Report from the Commission on European Governance", *European Commission Reports* (Office for Official Publications of the European Communities: Luxembourg).

CEC (2003e) "World Summit to set out strategic vision for a global information society." *Press Release*, IP/03/1673 (European Commission, Brussels).

CEC (2003f): COM(2003)71 "Updating and simplifying the Communities' *acquis*", 11 February 1003, including Commission Staff Working Document SEC(2003)165 (European Commission, Brussels).

CEC (2003g): Directive (2003/98/EC) on "the re-use of public sector information", 17 November 2006 (European Commission: Brussels).

CEC (2003h): COM(2003)236 "Reinforcing the statutory audit in the EU", Communication (European Commission: Brussels).

CEC (2003i): COM(2003)284 "Modernising Company Law and Enhancing Corporate Governance in the European Union: A Plan to Move Forward", *A Working Document of DG Internal Market* (European Commission: Brussels).

CEC (2003j): Recommendation (2003/497/EC) "Commission Recommendation On Relevant Product and Service Markets within the electronic communications sector susceptible to ex ante regulation in accordance with Directive (2002/21/EC) of the European Parliament and of the Council on a common regulatory framework for electronic communication networks and services" (European Commission: Brussels).

CEC (2003k): Decision (2003/548/EC) on "the minimum set of leased lines with harmonised characteristics and associated standards referred to in Article 18 of the Universal Service Directive" (European Commission: Brussels).

CEC (2003l): COM(2003)747final "The competitiveness of business-related services and their contribution to the performance of European enterprises", 04 December 2003 (European Commissions, Brussels).

CEC (2004a) "President Prodi and Mr Wim Kok announce the establishment of the High-level Group on the Lisbon Strategy", *European Commission Press Release*, IP/04/518. 22 April 2004 (Brussels).

CEC (2004b) "Summit reaches consensus on Information Society plan of action." Based on Information from the World Summit on the Information Society, *Cordis Focus*, No. 236, 12 January 2004 (European Commission: Brussels).

CEC (2004c): COM(2004)28 on "unsolicited commercial communications or SPAM", 22 January 2004 (European Commission: Brussels).

CEC (2004d): COM(2004)29 "Report from the Commission to the Spring European Council. Delivering Lisbon. Reforms for an Enlarged Union", 20 February 2004 (European Commission: Brussels).

CEC (2004e): COM(2004)61 on "Connecting Europe at high speed: recent developments in the sector of electronic communications", 3 February 2004 (European Commission: Brussels).

CEC (2004f): COM(2004)353 "Analysis of the Stakeholder Consultation on Science and Technology, the key to Europe's future: Guidelines for future European policy to support research", 10 December 2004, DG Research (European Commission: Brussels).

CEC (2004g): Regulation (EC) No 460/2004 "Establishing the European Network and Information Security Agency", 10 March 2004 (European Commission: Brussels).

CEC (2004h): COM(2004)477 on "Mobile broadband services", 30 June 2004 (European Commission: Brussels).

CEC 2004i): Decision (2004/641/EC) "amending Decision (2002/627/EC) establishing the European Regulators Group for Electronic Communications Networks and Services" (European Commission: Brussels).

CEC (2004j): COM(2004)757 on "Challenges for the European Information Society beyond 2005", 19 November 2004 (European Commission: Brussels).

CEC (2005a) "Call for Input on the forthcoming review of the EU regulatory framework for electronic communications and services, including review of the Recommendation on relevant markets", 25 November 2005 (DG Information Society: Brussels).

CEC (2005b) "EU Research – Building Knowledge Europe: The EU's new Research Framework Programme 2007-2013." *Memo*/05/114 (European Commission: Brussels).

CEC (2005c) "Responses to the Consultation on Research Themes in FP7", 16 March 2005 (European Commission: Brussels).

CEC (2005d): COM(2005)24 "Working together for growth and jobs – A new start for the Lisbon strategy", *Communication to the Spring European Council*, from President Barroso in agreement with Vice-President Verheugen, 2 February 2005 (European Commission: Belgium).

CEC (2005e) COM(2005)97 final "Better regulation for growth and jobs in the European Union.", 16 March 2005 (European Commission: Brussels).
CEC (2005f): Decision (2005/222/JHA) on "attacks against information systems", 24 February 2005 (European Commission: Brussels).
CEC (2005g): COM(2005)229 "i2010 – A European Information Society for growth and employment", 1 June 2005 (European Commission: Brussels).
CEC (2005h): COM(2005)330 "Common Actions for Growth and Employment: The Community Lisbon Programme", Communication from the Commission to the Council and the European Parliament, 20 July 2005, (European Commission: Brussels).
CEC (2005i): COM(2005)474 on "Implementing the Community Lisbon Programme: A Policy Framework to Strengthen EU Manufacturing – towards a more integrated approach for Industrial Policy", 5 October 2005 (European Commission: Brussels).
CEC (2005j): COM(2005)646final "Proposal of the Commission to update the 1989 'TV without Frontiers' Directive to keep pace with rapid developments in Europe's audiovisual sector (Audiovisual Media Services Directive: Towards a modern framework for audiovisual content)", proposed by the Commission 13 December 2005 (European Commission: Brussels).
CEC (2005k): SEC(2005)791 "Impact Assessment Guidelines", 15 June 2005 (European Commission, Brussels).
CEC (2005l): Decision (2005/854/EC) on "establishing a multiannual Community Programme on promoting safer use of the Internet and new online technologies", 11 May 2005 (European Commission: Brussels).
CEC (2005m): SEC(2005)981 on "Common Actions for Growth and Employment: The Community Lisbon Programme", Commission Staff Working Document (European Commission: Brussels).
CEC (2005n): SEC(2005)1215 on "Annex to the Communication of the Commission on Implementing the Community Lisbon Programme: A Policy Framework to Strengthen EU Manufacturing – towards a more integrated approach for Industrial Policy", 5 October 2005, *Commission Staff Working Paper* (European Commission: Brussels).
CEC (2005o): SEC(2005)1216 on "European Industry: A Sectoral Overview", 5 October 2005, *Commission Staff Working Paper* (European Commission: Brussels).
CEC (2006a) "Call for comments: Regulation of international roaming charges (1st phase: 20 February - 22 March 2006)", 20 February 2006 (European Commission: Brussels).
CEC (2006b) "Commission calls on Member States to contribute to the European digital library." *Press Release* IP/06/1124 (European Commission: Brussels).
CEC (2006c): Decision (Draft, 2006) on "setting up a high level expert group advising the European Commission on the implementation and the development of the i2010 strategy" (European Commission: Brussels).
CEC (2006d) "European Charter for the development and the take-up of film online", 23 May 2006 (European Commission: Brussels).
CEC (2006e) "Finance ministers welcome progress on Lisbon objectives." *Cordis focus*, No. 273, December 2006, p. 5 (Office for Official Publications of the European Communities: Luxembourg), page 5.

CEC (2006f) *Improving Lives – Creating Opportunities for the Future,* DG Information Society & Media Brochure, incl. Mission Statement (European Commission: Brussels).

CEC (2006g) "Industrial property: Commission welcomes Parliament support on proposals linking EU design registration system with WIPO international system", *European Commission Press Release*, 18 May 2006 (Brussels).

CEC (2006h) "Meeting with ICT industry trade associations in Brussels on 17/1/2006." *Minutes*, 18 January 2006 (European Commission: Brussels).

CEC (2006i) "Membership of ICT Task Force." *Document* (European Commission: Brussels).

CEC (2006j) "The Review 2006 of the EU's regulatory framework for electronic communications: Frequently Asked Questions." *Memo* 06/257, 29 June 2006 (European Commission: Brussels).

CEC (2006k) "Second phase public consultation on a proposal for a regulation on mobile roaming services in the Single Market", *Press Release*, 3 April 2006 (European Commission: Brussels) .

CEC (2006l) "Task-Force on ICT sector competitiveness and ICT uptake: Coordinators of Working Groups." *Document*, 6 July 2006 (European Commission: Brussels).

CEC (2006m) "Telecoms: Commission tables plans to boost competition among telecoms operators and build a single market for services that use radio spectrum", *European Commission Press Release*, IP/06/874, 29 June 2006 (Brussels).

CEC (2006n): COM(2006)30 on "Communication from the Commission to the Spring European Council: Time to Move up a Gear – The new partnership for growth and jobs", 25 January 2006 (European Commission: Brussels).

CEC (2006o): Directive (2006/43/EC) on "statutory audit of annual accounts and consolidated accounts", adopted by the European Parliament on the 28 September 2005 (European Commission: Brussels).

CEC (2006p): COM(2006)68 "European Electronic Communications Regulation and Markets 2005 - The 11th Implementation Report", 20 February 2006 (European Commission: Brussels).

CEC (2006q): COM(2006)194 "Green Paper: European Transparency Initiative", 3 May 2006 (European Commission, Brussels).

CEC (2006r): COM(2006)251 "A strategy for a Secure Information Society: Dialogue, partnership and empowerment" (European Commission, Brussels).

CEC (2006s): COM(2006)334final on "the Review of the EU Regulatory Framework for electronic communications networks and services", *Consultation Paper*, 29 June 2006 (European Commission: Brussels).

CEC (2006t): (2006/382/EC) "Proposal for a Regulation on roaming on public mobile networks within the Community and amending Directive (2002/21/EC) on a common regulatory framework for electronic communications networks and services", 12 July 2006 (European Commission: Brussels).

CEC (2006u): COM(2006)629 "Commission Legislative and Work Programme 2007", adopted 24 October 2006 (European Commission: Brussels).

CEC (2006v): COM(2006)689 "A strategic review of Better Regulation in the European Union" (European Commission: Brussels).

CEC (2006w) COM(2006)691 on "Measuring administrative costs and reducing administrative burdens in the European Union" (European Commission: Brussels).

CEC (2006x) COM(2006)816 "Communication from the Commission to the Spring European Council: Implementing the renewed Lisbon strategy for Growth and Jobs – A year of delivery", Annex "Macro-economic, micro-economic and employment issues", published 12 December 2006 (European Commission: Brussels).

CEC (2006y): SEC(2006)816 "Commissions Staff Working Document – Proposed Changes", 28 June 2006 (European Commission: Brussels).

CEC (2006z): COM(2006)817 "Commission Staff Working Paper: Impact Assessment", 28 June 2006 (European Commission: Brussels).

CEC (2006aa): SEC(2006)817 "Commissions Staff Working Document – Impact Assessment', 28 June 2006 (European Commission: Brussels).

CEC (2006bb): SEC(2006)925 "Commission Staff Working Paper - Impact Assessment on Policy Options in relation to a Commission Proposal for a regulation on Roaming on Public Networks within the Community", 12 July 2006 (European Commission: Brussels).

CEC (2006cc): SEC(2006)837 "Relevant Product and Service Markets within the electronic communication sector susceptible to ex ante regulation in accordance with Directive 2002/21/EC of the European Parliament and of the Council on a common regulatory framework for electronic communication networks and services" (Brussels).

CEC (2006dd) "Review of the EU regulatory framework for electronic communications networks and services", *Public Presentation*, 13 July 2006 (Brussels).

CEC (2006ee): Green Paper COM(2006) on "Satellite Navigation Applications" (European Commission: Brussels).

CEC (2006ff): Regulation (1943/2006/EC) "amending the Statutes of the Galileo Joint Undertaking annexed to Council Regulation (EC) No 876/2002" (Brussels).

CEC (2006gg): COM(2006)6839 "Work Programme 2007: Cooperation – Theme 6 Environment (including Climate Change)" (European Commission, Brussels).

CEC (2006hh): Commission Notice (2006/C 205/16) "Call addressed to individuals for the establishment of a database of prospective independent experts to assist the Commission's services for tasks in connection with the Seventh RTD Framework Programme" (European Commission, Brussels).

CEC (2007a) "Comitology Committees assisting the European Commission", *List of committees by policy sector*, published in May 2007 (European Commission: Brussels).

CEC (2007b) "Commission proposes a single European Telecoms Market for 500 million consumers", *Press Release*, IP/07/1677, published 13 November 2007 (Brussels).

CEC (2007c) COM(2007)yyy on "Reaping the full benefits of the digital divide in Europe: A common approach to the use the spectrum released by the digital switchover", *Communication* (European Commission: Brussels).

CEC (2007d) "Together since 1957: the rise of research in the EU policy agenda", *Cordis focus*, issue no 279, (Office for Official Publications of the European Communities: Luxembourg), page 1-3.

CEC (2007e) "Follow-up to the Green Paper European Transparency Initiative", SEC(2007)360, 21 March 2007 (European Commission: Brussels).

CEC (2007f): COM(2007)161 "The European Research Area: New Perspectives", *Green Paper*, 4 April 2007, SEC(2007)412 (European Commission, Brussels).

CEC (2007g): COM(2007)374 "Mid-term review of industrial policy: A contribution to the EU's Growth and Jobs Strategy", 04 July 2007 (European Commission: Brussels).

CEC (2007h): SEC(2007)412/2 "Commission Staff Working Document - Accompanying the Green Paper: The European Research Area: New Perspectives COM(2007)161", 4 April 2007 (European Commission: Brussels).

CEC (2007i) COM(2007)696rev1 "Report on the outcome of the Review of the EU regulatory framework for electronic communications networks and services in accordance with Directive (2002/21/EC) and Summary of the 2007 Reform Proposal" (European Commission: Brussels).

CEC (2007j) Directive COM(2007)697rev1 "amending the Framework Directives (2002/21/EC), the Access and Interconnection Directive (2002/19/EC) and the Authorisation Directive (2002/20/EC)" (European Commission: Brussels).

CEC (2007k) Regulation COM(2007)699rev2 "establishing the European Electronic Communications Market Authority" (European Commission: Brussels).

CEC (2007l): Regulation (717/2007/EC) of the European Parliament and of the Council of 27 June 2007 on "roaming on public mobile telephone networks within the Community and amending Directive 2002/21/EC" (European Commission: Brussels).

CEC (2007m): SEC(2007)917 Commission Staff working document on 374 "Mid-term review of industrial policy: A contribution to the EU's Growth and Jobs Strategy", 04 July 2007 (European Commission: Brussels).

CEC (2007n): SEC(2007)926 Information note from the President of the Commission on "Better Regulation and enhanced Impact Assessment", 19 June 2007 (European Commission: Brussels).

CEC (2007o): SEC(2007)1472 "Commission Staff Working Paper - Impact Assessment for COM(2007)697, COM(2007)698, COM(2007)699" (European Commission: Brussels).

CEC (2007p): Recommendation C(2007)5406rev1 on "relevant product and services markets within the electronic communications sector and SEC(2007)1483 explanatory note" (European Commission: Brussels).

CEC (2007q) Green Paper COM(2007) 161 final "The European Research Area: New Perspectives", {SEC(2007) 412}, 4 April 2007 (European Commission, Brussels).

CEC (2008a) Communication COM(2008)323 "European Transparency Initiative A framework for relations with interest representatives (Register and Code of Conduct)" (European Commission, Brussels).

CEC (2008b) Decision C(2008)6866 "laying down rules on the secondment to the Commission of national experts and national experts in professional training" (European Commission, Brussels).

CEC (2009a) COM(2009)277final on "Internet governance: the next steps" (European Commission: Brussels).

CEC (2009a) "Agreement on EU Telecoms Reform paves way for stronger consumer rights, an open internet, a single European telecoms market and high-speed internet connections for all citizens." *Memo*/09/491 (European Commission: Brussels).

CEN Management Centre, CENELEC Secretariat and ETSI Secretariat (2001) "The contribution of European standardization to the eEurope Initiative: A Rolling Action Plan." *Document*, 3 July 2001 (CEN ELEC: Brussels).

CEN Management Centre, CENELEC Secretariat and ETSI Secretariat (2.07.2002) "The contribution of European standardization to the eEurope Initiative: A Rolling Action Plan" (CEN ELEC: Brussels).

CEN/ISSS (2002) "Initiative on Privacy Standardization in Europe." *Document*, published 13 February 2002 (CEN/ISSS: Brussels).

CEN Technical Committee website (2006) at http://www.cen.eu/cenorm/businessdomains/technicalcommitteesworkshops/centechnicalcommittees/index.asp (accessed May 2006).

CEN/ISSS website (2006) at http://www.cen.eu/cenorm (accessed May 2006).

CEN/ISSS (2007) "Business Plan for CEN/ISSS Workshop Data Protection and Privacy." *Document* (CEN/ISSS WS/DPP: Brussels).

CESG website (2012) at http://www.cesg.gov.uk/policyguidance/IAMM/Pages/index.aspx and http://www.cesg.gov.uk/ServiceCatalogue/IAMM-SA/Pages/IAMM-SA.aspx (accessed August 2012).

Chadwick, Andrew; May, Christopher (2003) "Interaction between States and Citizens in the Age of the Internet: 'e-Government' in the United States, Britain and the European Union", *Governance*, Vol. 16, No. 2 (April), pp. 271-300.

Chadwick, Andrew (2006) *Internet Politics: States, Citizens, and New Communication Technologies* (Oxford University Press, Oxford).

Charmaz, Kathy (2006) *Constructing grounded theory: a practical guide through qualitative analysis* (SAGE: London).

Christiansen, Thomas; Kirchner, Emil (2000) *Europe in Change – Committee Governance in the European Union* (Manchester University Press: Manchester).

Chryssochoou, Dimitris N. (1998) *Democracy in the European Union* (Tauris Academic Studies: London/ New York).

CobiT website (2007) at http://www.itgi.org (accessed February 2007).

Codex Alimentarius website (2007) at http://www.codexalimentarius.net (accessed June 2007).

Coen, David (1997a) "The evolution of the large firm as a political actor in the European Union", *Journal of European Public Policy*, Vol. 4, No. 4 (March)(Routledge: London), pp. 91-108.

Coen, David (1997b) The European Business Lobby", *Business Strategy Review*, Vol. 8, No. 4, pp. 17-25.

Coen, David (1998) "The European business interest and the nation state : Large-firm lobbying in the European Union and member states", *Journal of Public Policy*, Vol. 18, No. 1, pp. 75-100.

Coen, David; Doyle, Chris (1999) "Designing Economic Regulatory Institutions for European Network Industries", *Current Politics and Economics of Europe*, Vol. 6, No. 4, pp. 83-106.

Coen, David; Dannreuther, Charles (2003) "Differentiated Europeanization: Large and Small Firms in the EU Policy Process", in Featherstone, Kevin; Radaelli, Claudio, eds. *The Politics of Europeanization* (Oxford University Press: Oxford), pp. 255-275.

Coen, David; Grant, Wyn (2006) "Managing Business and Government Relations", in Coen, David; Grant, Wyn (eds.) *Business and Government: Methods and Practice* (Barbara Budrich: Farmington Hills, MI), pp. 13-108.

Coen, David (2007a) "Empirical and theoretical studies in EU lobbying", *Journal of European Public Policy*, Vol. 14, No. 3, pp. 333-345.

Coen, David (2007b) *Lobbying in the European Union*, Briefing Paper PE 393.266 for the European Parliament's Committee on Constitutional Affairs (Brussels).

Coen, David; Richardson, Jeremy (2009a) "Learning to Lobby the European Union: 20 Years of Change", in *Lobbying the European Union: Institutions, Actors, and Issues* (Oxfords: Oxford University Press), pp 3-15.

Coen, David (2009b) "Business Lobbying in the European Union", in *Lobbying the European Union: Institutions, Actors, and Issues* (Oxfords: Oxford University Press), pp 145-168.

Cohen, Galit; Salomon, Ilan; Nijkamp, Peter (2002) "ICT and transport: does knowledge underpin policy?", *Telecommunications Policy*, Vol. 26, Nos. 1/ 2 (Feb./March), pp. 31-52.

Cohen, Louis; Manion, Lawrence (2000) *Research methods in education*, 5th edition (Routledge: London).

Colasanti, Fabio; Director General Information Society, European Commission. (2003) "The Communications Industry - The Next Phase: Communications and E-Commerce Forum." *Conference* on 12 November 2003, Wilmer, Cutler & Pickering, London (Whitehall).

Colasanti, Fabio; Director General of DG Information Society (30.01.2007) to Mr Roberto Viola (Chairman of the ERG), Mr Kip Meek and Mr Daniel Pataki, Document(2007)9-3380, *Letter* from Fabio Colasanti (Brussels).

Colomer, Josep Maria (2002) "The European Union: federalism in the making", in Colomer, Josep Maria, ed. *Political Institutions in Europe*, 2nd edition (Routledge: London), pp. 279-306.

Committee on the Internal Market and Consumer Protection (2006) "Report on the Implementation, Consequences and Impact of the Internal Market Regulation in Force", *Report*, A6-0083/2006, March 2006.

Committee of Sponsoring Organisations, COSO(2004) *Enterprise Risk Management Framework* (COSO).

Communication & Information Resource Centre Administrator website (2008) at http://circa.europa.eu/public/irc/infso/home/main (accessed August 2008).

Conservative Party (November 2009) *Regulation in the post-bureaucratic age* (London).

Cordis website (2012) at http://cordis.europa.eu (accessed July 2012).

Cordis focus website (2006) at http://cordis.europa.eu/news/focus (accessed August 2006).
COSO website (2007) at http://www.coso.org/publications/executive_summary_integrated_framework.htm (accessed February 2007).
Council Decision (1999a) (276/1999/EC) "Adopting a multi-annual Community action plan on promoting safer use of the Internet by combating illegal and harmful content on global networks", 25 January 1999 (Official Journal L 033 , 06/02/1999, Brussels).
Council Decision (1999b) (1999/468/EC) "procedures for the exercise of implementing powers conferred on the Commission (the Comitology Decision)", 28 June 1999, replaced the Council Decision of 13 July 1987 (OJ L 184/23 of 17.7.1999, Brussels).
Council Decision (1999c) (1999/193/CFSP) "on the joint action adopted by the Council on the basis of Article J.3 of the Treaty on European Union concerning the control of export of dual-use goods" (Brussels).
Council Decision (2003) (2003/793/EC) of approving "the accession of the European Community to the Protocol relating to the Madrid Agreement concerning the international registration of marks, adopted at Madrid on 27 June 1989", 27 October 2003 (Brussels).
Council Recommendation (1984) (84/549/EEC) "concerning the implementation of harmonisation in the field of telecommunications", 12 November 1984 (OJ L 298/49, Brussels).
Council Regulation (2000) (2000/2887/EC) on "unbundled access t the local loop", Official Journal, 30 .December 2000 (OJ L 336: Brussels).
Council Regulation (2002) (2002/792/EC) "amending temporarily Regulation (EEC) No 218/92 on administrative cooperation in the field of indirect taxation (VAT) as regards additional measures regarding electronic commerce", 7 May 2002 (European Council, Brussels).
Council Resolution (2003) (2003/5197/EC) on "the implementation of the eEurope 2005 Action Plan", 28 January 2003 (Brussels).
Council of the European Union (2000) "Presidency Conclusions - Brussels European Council 23 and 24 March 2000", 24 March 2000 (Brussels).
CEC (2000) "Presidency Conclusions: Lisbon European Council, 23 and 24 March 2000." *European Commission Press Release*, 24 March, no Conseil/00/900 (Lisbon).
Council of the European Union (2001) at Göteborg "Presidency Conclusions", 15 and 16 June 2001 (Göteborg).
Council of the European Union (2002) "Presidency Conclusions - Barcelona European Council 15 and 16 March 2002", SN 1000/1/02 (Barcelona).
Council of the European Union (2004a) "Presidency Conclusions - Brussels European Council 5 and 26 March 2004", 19 May 2004 (Brussels).
Council of the European Union (2004b) "Presidency Conclusions - Brussels European Council 4 and 5 November 2004", 8 December 2004 (Brussels).
Council of the European Union (2005a) "Presidency Conclusions - Brussels European Council 22 and 23 March 2005", DOC/05/01, 7619/1/05, 23 March 2005 (Brussels).
Council of the European Union (2005b) "Inter-Institutional Common Approach to Impact Assessment", Paper 14901/05, Annex C, November 2005 (Brussels).
Council of the European Union (2006) "Presidency Conclusions - Brussels European Council 23 and 24 March 2005", DOC/07776/106, 18 May 2006 (Brussels).

Council of the European Union (2008) Regulation "establishing the European Institute of Innovation and Technology", DOC 15647/07, 11 January 2008 (Brussels).

Cowhey, Peter F. (1990) "The International Telecommunications Regime", *International Organization*, No. 44 (Spring), pp. 169-200.

Cowles, Maria Green (1995) "The European Round Table of Industrialists: The Strategic Player in European Affairs", in Greenwood, Justin, ed. *European casebook on business alliances* (Prentice Hall International: Hemel Hempstead, Herts UK), pp. 225-236.

Cowles, Maria Green; Caporaso, James; Risse, Thomas, eds. (2001) *Transforming Europe: Europeanization and Domestic Change* (Cornell University Press: Ithaca NY/London).

Cram, Laura (1995) "Business Alliances in the Information Technology Sector", in Greenwood, Justin, ed. *European casebook on business alliances* (Prentice Hall International: Hemel Hempstead, Herts UK), page 23-37.

Cram, Laura (1997) "The EU institutions and collective action: Constructing a European interest?", in Greenwood, Justin; Aspinwall, Mark, eds. *Collective action in the European Union: interests and the new politics of associability* (Routledge: London), pp. 63-80.

Cram, Laura; Dinan, Desmond; Nugent, Neill (1999) "Reconciling Theory and Practice", in Cram, Laura; Dinan, Desmond; Nugent, Neil, eds. *Developments in the European Union* (Macmillan: London), page 3-19.

Creative Research Systems website (2009) at http://www.surveysystem.com/sscalc.htm (accessed October 2009).

Currie, Wendy (2000) *The global information society* (John Wiley & Sons: Chichester, UK).

Cutler, Claire; Haufler, Virginia; Porter, Tony (1999a) "Private Authority and International Affairs", in Cutler, Claire; Haufler, Virginia; Porter, Tony, eds. *Private Authority and International Affairs* (State University of New York Press: Albany), pp. 3-28.

Cutler, Claire; Haufler, Virginia; Porter, Tony (1999b) "The Contours and Significance of Private Authority in International Affairs", in Cutler, Claire; Haufler, Virginia; Porter, Tony, eds. *Private Authority and International Affairs* (State University of New York Press: Albany), pp. 333-376.

Cutler, Claire (2002) "Private international regimes and interfirm corporation", in Bruce Hall, Rodney; Biersteker, Thomas, eds. *The Emergence of Private Authority in Global Governance* (Cambridge University Press: Cambridge).

Data Protection Working Party Article 29 (1999) Recommendation 3(99)3/final WP25 on th "Preservation of traffic data by Internet Service Providers for law enforcement purposes", 7 September 1999 (Brussels).

Data Protection Working Party Article 29 (2000) Opinion 1/2000 on "certain data protection aspects of electronic commerce"; presented by the Internet task force on 3 February 2000 (Brussels).

David, Paul; Shurmer, Mark (1996) "Formal standards setting for global and telecommunications services: towards an institutional regime transformation?", *Telecommunications Policy*, Vol. 20, No. 10, pp. 789-811.

de Greene, Kenyon B. (1993) "Policy Challenges in a World of Nonlinearity and Structural Change", in Greene, Kenyon B. De, ed. *A Systems-Based approach to policymaking* (Kluwer Academic Publishers: Boston/London), pp. 1-38.

Delbridge, Rick; Kirkpatrick, Ian (1994) "Theory and Practice of Participant Observation", in Wass, V. J.; Wells, Peter E. (eds.) *Principles and Practice in Business and Management Research* (Dartmouth Publishing: Aldershot, UK), pp 35-61.

deLeon, Peter (1988) *Advice and Consent: The development of the Political Sciences* (Russell Sage Foundation: New York).

deLeon, Peter (1997) *Democracy and the policy sciences* (State University of New York Press: Albany NY).

deLeon, Peter (1999) "The Stages Approach to the Public Policy Process: What Has It Done? Where Is It Going?", in Sabatier, Paul A., ed. *Theories of the Policy Process* (Westview Press: Oxford), pp. 19-32.

Denzin, Norman K. (1978) *The Research Act: A Theoretical Induction to Sociological Methods* (Aldine Transaction: New Brunswick).

Deutsches Institut für Normung (DIN) website (2007) at http://www.din.de (accessed June 2007).

Dillman, Don A.; Salant, Priscilla (1994) *How to conduct your own survey?: Leading professionals give you proven techniques for getting reliable results* (John Wiley & Sons: New York).

Dillman, Don A. (2000) *Mail and Internet Surveys: The Tailored Design Method* (John Wiley & Sons: New York).

Docksey, Christopher; Williams, Karen (1994) "The Commission and the Execution of Community Policy", in Edwards, G. and Spence, D., eds. *The European Commission* (Lagman: London), pp. 117-145.

Douglas, Jack D. (1976) *Investigative Social Research: Individual and Team Field Research* (SAGE: Beverly Hills).

Dougal, Jim; Head, Representation of the European Commission in the UK (2004) "Enlightening the debate on good governance: European Union Enlargement." *Conference* on 28 April 2004, The Federal Trust for education & research, European Parliament UK Office, London.

Dowding, Keith (1995) "Model or Metaphor? A Critical Review of the Network Approach", *Political Studies*, No. 43, pp. 136-158.

Downs, Anthony (1957) *An economic theory* (Harper & Row: New York).

Dryden, John (2003) Deputy Director, Directorate Science, Technology and Industry (STI), *Personal interview* on 11.12.2003 at the OECD (Paris).

DTI/Ofcom (May 2006) "UK Response to the Call for Input on the forthcoming review of the EU regulatory framework for electronic communications and services" (London).

DTI website (2006) at http://www.dti.gov.uk (accessed July 2006 [suspended 2007]).

DTI website – eCommunications Review (2006) at http://www.dti.gov.uk/sectors/telecoms/2006review/page26449.html (accessed May 2006).

DTI website – ICT Policy (2006) at http://www.dti.gov.uk/sectors/ictpolicy/index.html (accessed June 2006).

DTI website – Telecoms (2006) at http://www.dti.gov.uk/sectors/telecoms/index.html (accessed June 2006).

Ducatel, Ken; Webster, Ken; Herrmann, Werner (2000) "Information Infrastructures of Society", in Ducatel, Ken; Webster, Ken; Herrmann, Werner, eds. *The Information Society in Europe: Work and Life in an Age of Globalisation* (Rowman & Littlefield Publishers: Lanham MD, USA), pp. 1-20.

Dunford, Michael; Perrons, Diane (1993) "Regional inequality as a cause and consequences of slower growth", in Getimis, Panagiotis and Kafkalas, Grigoris, eds. *Urban and Regional Development in the New Europe* (TOPOS: Athens), pp. 9-35.

E-Business, IT and Telecoms (EBITT) website (2006) at http://www.iccwbo.org/policy/ebitt/ (accessed May 2006).

Einstein, Albert (2001) *Relativity – The Special and General Theory*, first published in 1916. (Routledge: London).

Encyclopaedia Britannica website (2006) at http://concise.britannica.com (accessed May 2006).

ENISA website at (2006) http://enisa.europa.eu/ (accessed August 2006).

Enticknap, Nicholas (2004) "Making History – 40 years of the mainframe", *Computer Weekly*, 6 April 2004, p. 30.

ERP (European Recycling Platform) website (2012) at http://www.erp-recycling.org/ (accessed August 2012).

ERT (2007) European Round Table of Industrialists website (2007) at http://www.ert.be (accessed August 2007).

ETCA website (2012) at http://www.ectaportal.com (accessed July 2012).

EU Convention/Laeken Declaration on the Future of the EU website (2007) at http://www.euconvention.be/static/LaekenDeclaration.asp (accessed July 2007).

EU ICT Task Force (2006) "Fostering the Competitiveness of Europe's ICT Industry", *final report*, 27 November 2006 (European Commission: Brussels).

Eurofound – Comitology website (2012) at http://www.eurofound.europa.eu/areas/industrialrelations/dictionary/definitions/comitology.htm (accessed September 2012).

Europa Glossary – White Paper website (2008) at http://europa.eu/scadplus/glossary/white_paper_en.htm (accessed August 2008).

EuroISPA (2006) "Response to the Call for Input from DG Information Society & Media on the review of the EU regulatory framework for electronic communications" (Euro ISPA: Brussels).

EuroISPA website (2012) – official position papers and presentations at http://www.euroispa.org/23.htm (accessed July 2012).

Europa website – 1998 Regulatory Package at http://ec.europa.eu/information_society/topics/telecoms/regulatory/98_regpack/text_en.htm (accessed January 2008).

Europa website – Article 29 Data Protection Working Party (2006) at http://europa.eu.int/comm/justice_home/fsj/privacy/workinggroup/index_en.htm (accessed August 2006).

Europa website – Civic Society website (2007) http://ec.europa.eu/civil_society/index_en.htm (accessed May 2007).

Europa website – Cordis (2006) at http://cordis.europa.eu.int/marketplace (accessed May 2006). CORDIS focus and CORDIS RTD Results Supplement and is published by the Office for Official Publications of the European Communities, Luxembourg.

Europa website – Comitology (2012) at http://europa.eu/legislation_summaries/glossary/comitology_en.htm (accessed September 2012).
Europa website – Comitology Register (2012) at http://ec.europa.eu/transparency/regcomitology/index.cfm (accessed August 2012).
Europa website – Cordis FP7 (2006) at http://cordis.europa.eu/fp7/art171_en.html (accessed May 2006).
Europea website – Council of the European Union – Transport, Telecommunications and Energy (2007) at http://www.consilium.europa.eu/cms3_applications/applications/newsRoom/loadBook.asp?BID=87&LANG=1&cmsid=354 (accessed March 2007).
Europa website – Documentation (2006) at http://europa.eu.int/information_society/policy/ecomm/info_centre/documentation/index_en.htm (accessed May 2006).
Europa website – eCommunications Framework (2006) at http://europa.eu.int/information_society/policy/ecomm/index_en.htm (accessed August 2006). Also referred to as Framework for eCommunications Networks and Services.
Europa website – eCommunications Framework Reform (2006) at http://ec.europa.eu/information_society/policy/ecomm/tomorrow/index_en.htm (accessed May 2006).
Europa website – eCommunications Framework Review (2006) at http://europa.eu.int/information_society/policy/ecomm/info_centre/documentation/public_consult/index_en.htm#review (accessed August 2006).
Europa website – eCommunications Framework Review proposal (2007) at http://ec.europa.eu/information_society/policy/ecomm/library/proposals/index_en.htm (accessed November 2007).
Europa website – eCommunications Framework Review responses (2007) at http://ec.europa.eu/information_society/policy/ecomm/info_centre/documentation/public_consult/review_2/index_en.htm (accessed February 2007).
Europa website – eCommunications Framework Review responses on relevant markets (2007) at http://ec.europa.eu/information_society/policy/ecomm/info_centre/documentation/public_consult/relevant_mkts/index_en.htm (accessed February 2007).
Europa website – eCommunications Framework Review results (2006) at http://europa.eu.int/information_society/policy/ecomm/info_centre/documentation/public_consult/review/index_en.htm (accessed August 2006).
Europa website – eContent Plus (2006) at http://europa.eu.int/information_society/activities/econtentplus/index_en.htm (accessed May 2006).
Europa website – eEurope (2005) at http://europa.eu.int/information_society/eeurope/index_en.htm (accessed May 2005).
Europa website – eEurope 2005 TRUST (2006) at http://europa.eu.int/information_society/eeurope/2005/all_about/security/index_en.htm (accessed August 2006).
Europa website – Enterprise and Industry – ICT Task-Force (2012) at http://ec.europa.eu/enterprise/sectors/ict/competitiveness/task-force/ (accessed August 2012).
Europa website –EU Portal (2006) at http://europa.eu.int (accessed April 2006).
Europa website – European Commission, Information Society and Media Directorate-General (2006) at http://europa.eu.int/comm/dgs/information_society/index_en.htm (accessed April 2006).

Europa website – European Information Society (2006a) at http://europa.eu.int/information_society/ (accessed August 2006).

Europa website – European Information Society (2006b) i2010 at http://ec.europa.eu/information_society/eeurope/i2010/index_en.htm (accessed May 2006).

Europa website – European Institute of Innovation and Technology (EIT) (2008) at http://ec.europa.eu/eit/ (access February 2008).

Europa website – European Research Area (2007) at http://ec.europa.eu/research/era/index_en.html (accessed June 2007).

Europa website – European Transparency Initiative (2007) at http://ec.europa.eu/transparency/eti/index_en.htm (accessed May 2007).

Europa website – eTEN (2006) at http://europa.eu.int/information_society/activities/eten/index_en.htm (accessed May 2006).

Europa website – Framework Programme Experts (2007) at http://cordis.europa.eu/experts/fp6_candidature.htm (accessed January 2007).

Europa website – Green Papers (2006) at http://ec.europa.eu/comm/off/green/index_en.htm (accessed May 2006).

Europa website - ISPO (2006) at http://europa.eu.int/ISPO/intcoop/g8/i_g8conference.html (accessed May 2006).

Europa website – Lisbon Strategy (2006a) at http://ec.europa.eu/lisbon_strategy/intro_en.html and http://ec.europa.eu/growthandjobs/. (accessed August 2006).

Europa website – Lisbon Strategy (2006b) on European Councils at http://ec.europa.eu/growthandjobs/councils_en.htm (accessed September 2006).

Europa website – New Roaming Consultation (2007) at http://ec.europa.eu/information_society/activities/roaming/roaming_regulation/consultation/index_en.htm (accessed March 2007).

Europa website – New Roaming Regulation (2006) at http://ec.europa.eu/information_society/activities/roaming/roaming_regulation/index_en.htm (accessed December 2006).

Europa website – Radio Spectrum Policy (2006) at http://europa.eu.int/information_society/policy/radio_spectrum/index_en.htm (accessed May 2006).

Europa website – Safer Internet Forum (2007) at http://ec.europa.eu/information_society/activities/sip/si_forum/index_en.htm (accessed May 2007).

Europa website – Safer Internet Plus (2006) at http://europa.eu.int/information_society/activities/sip/index_en.htm (accessed May 2006).

Europa website – Safer Internet Plus Call for Independent Experts (2007) at http://ec.europa.eu/information_society/activities/sip/call/experts_2005/index_en.htm (accessed January 2007).

Europa website – Safer Internet Work Programme (2004) Self-Regulation website at http://ec.europa.eu/information_society/activities/sip/programme/workprogramme/wp2004_selfregulation/index_en.htm (accessed May 2007).

Europa website – Summaries of EU Legislation (2012) at http://europea.eu/legislation_summaries/index_en.htm (accessed August 2012).

Europa website – The Committee of the Regions website (2007) at http://www.cor.europa.eu/ (accessed June 2007).

European Business Summit (2007) "European Technology Platforms: developing lead markets", 16 March 2007 (Brussels).

European Business Summit website (2007) at http://www.ebsummit.org (accessed May 2007).

European Cable Communications Association (ECCA) website (2006) at http://www.ecca.be (accessed August 2006).

European Commission Environment website (2007) at http://ec.europa.eu/environment/policy_en.htm (accessed May 2007).

European Committee for Standardization (CEN) website (2006) at http://www.cenorm.be (accessed May 2006).

European Competitive Telecommunications Association (2006) "Delivering competition and innovation for next generation of consumers and businesses." *ECTA Response to the 2006 eCommunications Review* (Brussels).

European Competitive Telecommunications Association (ECTA) website (2006) at http://www.ectaportal.com (accessed July 2006).

European Convention website (2008) at http://european-convention.eu.int (accessed June 2008).

European Economic and Social Committee website (2007) at http://eesc.europa.eu (accessed May 2007).

European Governance Team (2001) 8533/01 "Consultations conducted for the preparation of the White Paper on Democratic European Governance", June, Report to the Commission (Brussels).

European Governance website (2007) at http://ec.europa.eu/governance/ (accessed May 2007).

European Parliament's website – eCommunications Framework (2008) at http://www.europarl.europa.eu/news/expert/event_by_week/05-2008/default_en.htm (accessed April 2008).

European Parliament's website – Legislative Observatory (2007) at http://www.europarl.europa.eu/oeil (accessed March 2007).

European Public Telecommunications Network Operator's Association (ETNO) website (2006) at http://www.etno.be (accessed August 2006).

European Regulators Group website (2006) at http://erg.eu.int (accessed August 2006).

European Research Council website (2007) at http://www.erc.europa.eu (accessed February 2007).

Eurostat website (2012) at http://epp.eurostat.ec.europa.eu (accessed July 2012).

Falkner, Gerda (2002) "How intergovernmental are Intergovernmental Conferences? An example from the Maastricht Treaty reform", *Journal of European Public Policy (Special Issue: EU Treaty Reform as a Three-Level Process)*, Vol. 9, No. 1 (Taylor & Francis Ltd.: London), pp. 98-119.

Farrell, Marie (2003) Policy Manager, e-Business, IT and Telecoms, *Personal interview* on 12.12.2003 at the ICC (Paris).

Featherstone, Kevin (2003) "Introduction: In the Name of Europe", in Featherstone, Kevin; Radaelli, Claudio, eds. *The Politics of Europeanization* (Oxford University Press: Oxford), pp. 3-26.

Ferrero-Waldner, Benita (2007) "Commissioner's statement: Patentability of computer-implemented inventions", *presentation*, 6 July 2007 (Strasbourg).

Financial Reporting Council (2006) "The Combined Code on Corporate Governance", published July 2003, up-dated on June 2006 (FRC: London).

Financial Reporting Council website (2007) at http://www.frc.org.uk/corporate/combinedcode.cfm (accessed June 2007).

Fouloy, Christian de (2000) *Glossary of EC terms* (Butterworth & Co (Publishers) Ltd., London).

Framework Programmes Website (2006; 2007) FP4 website at http://europa.eu.int/comm/research/fp4.html (accessed May 2006); FP5 website at http://europa.eu.int/comm/research/fp5.html; http://www.cordis.lu/fp5 (accessed May 2006); FP6 website at http://europa.eu.int/comm/research/fp6.html; http://cordis.europa.eu/fp6/ist.htm; http://cordis.europa.eu/ist/(accessed May 2006); FP7 website at http://europa.eu.int/comm/research/future/index_en.cfm (accessed February 2007) and http://cordis.europa.eu/fp7/home_en.html (accessed February 2007.

Francis, John G. (1993) *The Politics of Regulation: A Comparative Perspective* (Blackwell: Oxford).

Friedman, Milton (1953) *Essays in Positive Economics* (University of Chicago Press: Chicago).

Fuchs, Doris (2004) "Channels and Dimensions of Business Power in Global Governance", Paper presented at the annual meeting of the International Studies Association, March 17-21 (Montreal).

Fuchs, Doris (2005) *Understanding Business Power in Global Governance* (Nomos Publishers, Baden-Baden).

Fuchs, Doris (2007) *Business Power in Global Governance* (Lynne Rienner Publishers: Boulder).

Fuchs, Doris; Lederer, Markus (2007) "Business Power and Global Governance: The Power of Business", *Business and Politics*, Vol. 9, Issue 3 (The Berkeley Electronic Press), pp. 1-17.

G-8 DOT Force (2001) "Digital Opportunities for All: Meeting the Challenge", Report including a proposal for a Genoa Plan of Action, May 2001 (Digital Opportunity Task Force).

G-8 DOT Force (2002) "Report Card: Digital Opportunities for All", Report, June 2002 (Digital Opportunity Task Force).

G-8 DOT Force (2007) website (2007) at http://www.g8.utoronto.ca/summit/2001genoa/dotforce1.html (accessed July 2007).

G-8 Information Centre (2007) website (2007) at http://www.g8.utoronto.ca/summit/1994naples (accessed January 2007).

GAID (2006) "Global Alliance for Information and Communication Technologies and Development: Business Plan for 2006-2007".

GAID (2007) Global Information Society Watch 2007 report website (2007) at http://www.globaliswatch.org (accessed May 2007).

Galileo website (2006) at http://ec.europa.eu/dgs/energy_transport/galileo (accessed August 2006).

Gartner Group (2005) "IT Management Process Maturity Model".

Garrett, Geoffrey; Tsebelis, George (1996) "An Institutional Critique of Intergovernmentalism", *International Organisation*, Vol. 50, No. 2 (Spring), pp. 269-299.

Garrett, Geoffrey; Tsebelis, George (2000) "Legislative Politics in the European Union", *European Union Politics*, Vol. 1, No. 1, pp. 9-36.

Garrett, Geoffrey; Tsebelis, George (2001) "The Institutional Foundations of Intergovernmentalism and Supranationalism in the European Union." *International Organizations*, (Cambridge University Press), volume 55, part 2, pp. 357-390.

Gates, Bill (2000) *Business @ the Speed of Thought: Succeeding in the Digital Economy* (Penguin Books: New York).

GBDe (2002) Global Business Dialogue on eBusiness "Fourth Annual Conference of the GBDe" (Brussels, 29 October 2002).

GBDe (2004) Global Business Dialogue on eBusiness website (2004) at http://www.gbde.org/memberlinks.html (accessed May 2004).

Germain, Gilbert (2003): European Public Affairs team at PricewaterhouseCoopers, Practice Leader, meeting (Brussels).

Gerston, Larry N. (1997) *Public Policy-making: Process and Principles* (M. E. Sharpe Inc.: New York).

Gill, Stephen (1992) "The Emerging World Order and European Change", in R. Miliband and L. Panitsch (eds.) *The New World Order: Socialist Register 1992* (Merlin Press: London).

Gill, Stephen (1993) "Gramsci and Global Politics: Towards a Post-hegemonic Research Agenda", in S. Gill (ed.) *Gramsci, Historical Materialism and International Relations* (Cambridge University Press: Cambridge), pp. 1-18.

Glaser, Barney; Strauss, Anselm (1967) *The Discovery of Grounded Theory* (Aldine: Chicago).

Global Alliance for ICT and Development (2007) website (2007) at http://www.un-gaid.org (accessed May 2007).

Global Digital Divide Initiative (2007) website (2007) at http://www.weforum.org (access July 2007).

Grant, Wyn (1993) *Business and politics in Britain* (Macmillan: Basingstoke).

Grant, Wyn (2000) *Globalisation, Big Business and the Blair Government*, CSGR [Centre for the Study of Globalisation and Regionalisation], Working Paper No. 58/00 (University of Warwick: Warwick).

Greenwood, Justin (1997) *Representing interests in the European Union*, The European Union series (Macmillan: Basingstoke/London).

Greenwood, Justin (2000a) "Conclusions", in Greenwood, Justin; Jacek, Henry, eds. *Organised Business and the New Global Order* (Macmillan/International Political Science Association: Basingstoke).

Greenwood, Justin (2000b) "Organized Business and the European Union", in Greenwood, Justin; Jacek, Henry, eds. *Organised Business and the New Global Order* (Macmillan/ International Political Science Association: Basingstoke), pp. 77-98.

Greenwood, Justin; Aspinwall, Mark (1997) "Conceptualising collective action in the European Union", in Greenwood, Justin; Aspinwall, Mark, eds. *Collective action in the European Union: interests and the new politics of associability* (Routledge: London), pp. 1-30.

Greenwood, Justin; Grote, Jürgen; Ronit, Karsten (1994) "Introduction: Organized Interests and the Transnational Dimension", in Greenwood, Justin; Grote, Jürgen, Ronit, Karsten, eds. *Organized Interests and the European Community* (SAGE: London), pp. 1-41.

Greenwood, Justin; Westgeest, Alfons (2001a) "Introduction: Conference Issues and Themes", in Greenwood, Justin, ed. *The effectiveness of EU business associations* (Palgrave/Ernst & Young Association Management: New York, pp. 1-11.

Greenwood, Justin; Westgeest, Alfons (2001b) "Conclusions", in Greenwood, Justin, ed. *The effectiveness of EU business associations* (Palgrave/Ernst & Young Association Management: New York, pp. 223-233.

GSM Europe website (2006) at http://www.gsmworld.com/gsmeurope/index.shtml (accessed May 2006).

Haas, Ernst B. (2004) *The Uniting of Europe: Political, Social, and Economic Forces, 1950-1957* (University of Notre Dame Press: Notre Dame IN, USA).

Haas, Peter M. (1992) "Introduction: epistemic communities and international policy coordination", *International Organization*, Vol. 49, No. 1, pp. 1-54.

Haas, Peter M. (1997) "Epistemic Communities and International Policy Coordination", in Haas, Peter M., ed. *Knowledge, power, and international policy coordination* (University of South Carolina Press: Columbia SC), page 1-35. Originally published in *International Organization*, Vol. 46, No. 1, 1992.

Haas, Peter M.; Adler, Emanuel (1997) "Epistemic Communities, world order, and the creation of a reflective research program", in Haas, Peter M., ed. *Knowledge, power, and international policy coordination* (University of South Carolina Press: Columbia SC), pp.367-390 Originally published in International Organization, volume 46, no 1, 1992.

Hahn, Robert W.; Litan, Robert E. (2005) "Counting Regulatory Benefits and Costs: Lessons for the U.S. and Europe", *Journal of International Economic Law*, Vol. 8, No. 2, pp. 473-508.

Hampton, Philip (2005) "Reducing administrative burdens: Effective inspection and enforcement (The Hampton Review)". *Report*, March 2005(HM Treasury: London).

Harlow, Carol; Rawlings, Richard (1997) Law and Administration, 2nd edition (Butterworth: London).

Hassan, Ayesha (2003) Senior Policy Manager, e-Business, IT and Telecoms, *Personal interview* on 12.12.2003 at the ICC (Paris).

Healey, John: HM Treasury (2006)"Budget 2006: A strong and strengthening economy: Investing in Britain's future; Economic and Fiscal Strategy Report and Financial Statement and Budget Report." *UK Fiscal Report*, HC 968, March 2006 (HM Treasury: London).

Heclo, Hugh (1978) "Issue Networks in the Executive Establishment", in King, A., ed. *The New American Political System* (American Enterprise Institute: Washington, DC).

Heinelt, Hubert (1996) "Multilevel Governance in the European Union and the Structural Funds", in Heinelt, Hubert; Smith, Randall, eds. *Policy networks and European structural funds*, (Ashgate Publishing Ltd.: Hants, UK), page 9-25.

Heisenberg, Dorothee (2005) "The institution of 'consensus' in the European Union: Formal versus informal decision-making in the Council", *European Journal of Political Research* No. 44, pp. 65–90.

Héritier, Adrienne (2002) "New Modes of Governance in Europe: Policy-Making without Legislating?", in Héritier, Adrienne, ed. *Common Goods: Reinventing European and International Governance,* Governance in Europe series (Rowan Littlefield: Oxford), pp 185-206.

Higgs, Derek (2003) "Review of the role and effectiveness of non-executive directors (Higgs Review)", A *report* commissioned by the Department of Trade & Industry, January 2003 (DTI: London).

High Level Group (2004) "Facing the Challenge. The Lisbon strategy for growth and employment", *Report from the High Level Group chaired by Wim Kok*, November 2004(Office for Official Publications of the European Communities: Luxembourg).

Hix, Simon (1994) "The Study of the European Community: The Challenge to Comparative Politics", *West European Politics*, Vol. 17, No. 1, pp. 1-30.

Hix, Simon (1998) "The study of the European Union II: The 'new governance' agenda and its rival", *Journal of European Public Policy*, Vol. 5, No. 1 (March), pp. 38-65.

Hix, Simon (2005) *The Political System of the European Union* (Macmillan: Basingstoke).

HM Treasury (2006) "Implementing Hampton: from enforcement to compliance." November 2006 (HM Treasury, Cabinet Office, Better Regulation Executive: London).

Hobson, Claire (2007) "New EU regulatory framework for eComms." *BERR Presentation* to UK stakeholders, 19 November 2007 (London).

Home Office website (2007) at http://www.homeoffice.gov.uk/about-us/working-for-us/ (accessed February 2007).

Hood, Jane C. (2007) "Orthodoxy vs. Power: The defining traits of Grounded Theory", in Bryant, Antony; Charmaz, Kathy, eds., *The SAGE Handbook of Grounded Theory* (SAGE: London).

Hooghe, Liesbet (1995) "Subnational mobilisation in the European Union", *West European Politics*, Vol. 18, No. 2, pp. 175-198.

Hopkins, Paul (2012) *Fundamentals of Risk Management: Understanding, Evaluating and Implementing Effective Risk Management*. 2nd Edition (Institute of Risk Management-Kogan Page: London).

House of Lords Select Committee on European Communities (2 February 1999) Third Report on "Delegation of Powers to the Commission: Reforming Comitology" (United Kingdom).

Huber, Nick (2004) "Auditors working on cyber-risk standard", *Computer Weekly*, April 2004, p. 10.

Hull, Robert (1993) "Lobbying Brussels: A view from Within", in Mazey, Sonia; Richardson, Jeremy John, eds. *Lobbying in the European Community* (Oxford University Press, Oxford/ New York), pp. 82-92.

Hussey, Jill; Hussey, Roger (1997) *Business Research: a practical guide for undergraduate and postgraduate students* (Palgrave: Basingstoke).

Hutton, Rt. Hon. John, MP (2007a), Secretary of State for Business, Enterprise & Regulatory Reform (9 July 2007) "Speech to CBI President's Dinner." *Speech* (London, 9 July 2007).

Hutton, Rt. Hon. John, MP (2007b) "Better Regulation Reception." *Speech* at the Royal Society of Arts (London, 25 July 2007).

Hutton, Rt. Hon. John, MP (2007c) BERR (July 2007) Manufacturing, Materials, and Environment Newsletter, "Hot Issues" Issue 29 (BERR: London).

i2010 High Level Group (2006a) "The Challenges of Convergence: Discussion Paper", published 12.12.2006 (European Commission: Brussels).

i2010 High Level Group (2006b) "i2010 Work Programme for 2006/2007 – Information Space, Innovation & Investment in R&D and Inclusion", published 20.04.2006 (European Commission: Brussels).

ICC (2012) Factsheet: "Participation in ICC commissions for International Business Associations" (ICC: Paris).

ICC (2002a), International Chamber of Commerce, "ICC Arbitration: The World's most Trusted Arbitration System", *brochure* (ICC: Paris).

ICC (2002b), International Chamber of Commerce "Making Rules for Businesses", *information brochure* (ICC: Paris).

ICC (2003), International Chamber of Commerce, Commission on E-Business, IT and Telecoms *ICC compendium on ICT and E-Business policy and practice*, presented at the World Summit on the Information Society (Paris).

ICO (Information Commissioner's Office) website (2012) at http://www.ico.gov.uk (accessed July 2012).

ICT Task Force website (2007) at http://ec.europa.eu/enterprise/ict/taskforce.htm (accessed January 2007).

ICT4D Platform (ICT for Development Platform) website (2007) at http://www.ict-4d.org/about.htm (accessed July 2007).

Information Commissioner's Office website (2006) at http://www.ico.gov.uk (accessed May 2006).

Information Society Forum (1996) "Networks for People and their Communities: Making the Most of the Information Society in the European Union", *First Annual Report to the European Commission from the Information Society Forum* (Brussels: European Commission).

Information Society Forum website (2007) at http://www.securityforum.org (accessed July 2007).

Intellect UK website (2006) at http://www.intellectuk.org (accessed May 2006).

ISO (International Organisation for Standardisation) website (2007) at http://www.iso.org (accessed February 2007).

ITU website – Cybersecurity (2006) (International Telecommunications Union) at http://www.itu.int/osg/spu/cybersecurity/ (accessed July 2006).

ITU website – events (2007) (International Telecommunications Union) at http://www.itu.int/events/upcomingevents.asp (accessed May 2007).

ITU website – members (2007) (International Telecommunications Union) at http://www.itu.int/members/index.html (accessed June 2007).

ITU website – High Level Expert Group (2008) (HLEG) at http://www.itu.int/osg/csd/cybersecurity/gca/hleg/members.html (accessed May 2008).

ITU website – SPAM (2006) (International Telecommunications Union) at http://www.itu.int/osg/spu/spam/ (accessed July 2006).

ICANN website (2007) (Internet Corporation for Assigned Names and Numbers) at http://www.icann.org/ (accessed July 2007).

ITGI (2005) (Information Technology Governance Institute), *CobiT 4.0: Control Objectives, Management Guidelines, Maturity Models* (ITGI: Rolling Meadows IL, USA).

Jenkins-Smith, Hank; Clair, Gilbert K. (1993) "The Politics of Offshore Energy: Empirical Testing the Advocacy Coalition Framework", in Sabatier, Paul A.; Jenkins-Smith, Hank, eds. *Policy Change and Learning: An Advocacy Coalition Approach* (Westview Press: Oxford), pp. 149-176.

John, Peter (1998) *Analysing public policy*, Critical Political Studies (Pinter: London).

Jones, Charles O. (1977) *An Introduction to the Study of Public Policy* (Duxbury Press: Belmont CA, USA).

Jordan, Andrew (2001) "The European Union: an evolving system of multi-level governance … or government", *Policy & Politics*, Vol. 29, No. 2, (The Policy Press: Bristol), pp. 193-208.

Jordan, Grant (1999) "Sub-Governments, Policy Communities and Networks: Refilling the Old Bottles?", *Journal of Theoretical Politics*, Vol. 2, No. 3, pp. 319-338.

Jordan, Grant; Richardson, Jeremy (1982) "The British Policy Style, or the Logic of Negotiation", in Richardson, Jeremy, ed. *Policy Styles in Western Europe* (Allen and Unwin: London), pp. 80-110.

Josephson, John R.; Josephson, Susan G. (1994) Abductive Interference: Computation, Philosophy, Technology (Cambridge University Press: New York).

Kassim, Hussein (1994) "Policy Networks and European Policy Making: a Sceptical View." West European Politics, Vol. 17, Issue 4, October, pages 15-27.

Katholieke Universiteit Leuven, Interdisciplinary Centre for Law & Information Technology, "Legal and market aspects of the application of Directive 1999/93/EC and practical applications of electronic signatures in the Member States, the EEA, the Candidate and the Accession countries", *Study for the European Commission* (Leuven, Belgium).

Kelly, Kevin (1998) *New rules for the new economy* (Penguin Books: London/ New York).

Kilgour, Adam (2003) Manager, Competition Policy, Competition and Regulation, *Personal meeting* at Ofcom in May 2003.

Kimber, Carolyn (2004) "Ofcom accused of not focusing on business." *Computer Weekly*, 24 February 2004, p. 14.

King, Gary; Keohane, Robert; Verba, Sidney (1994) *Designing Social Inquiry: Scientific Inference in Qualitative Research* (Princeton University Press: Princeton NJ).

Knill, Christoph (2001) "Private governance across multiple areas: European interest associations as interface actors", *Journal of European Public Policy*, Vol. 8, No. 2, (Taylor & Francis Ltd.: London), pp. 227-246.

Knoke, David (1990a) *Organizing for collective action: the political economies of associations* (Aldine de Gruyter: New York).

Knoke, David (1990b) *Political networks: a structural perspective* (Cambridge University Press: New York).

Knoke, David (2001) *Changing organizations: business networks in the new political economy* (Westview Press: Boulder CO, USA).

Knott, Jack H.; Miller, Gary J. (1987) *Reforming Bureaucracy: The Politics of Institutional Choice* (Prentice Hall: New Jersey).

Konings, Marika (2007) "Bridging the reality gap", *Computer Weekly*, 17 April 2007, p. 38.

KPMG (1996) (Klynveld Peat Main Goerdeler), "Public Policy Issues Arising from Telecommunications and Audiovisual Convergence", *study* commissioned by the European Commission (Brussels).

Kohler-Koch, Beate; Eising, Rainer (1999) "Introduction: Network governance in the European Union", in Kohler-Koch, Beate; Eising, Rainer, eds. *The Transformation of Governance in the European Union* (Routledge: London), page 1-13.

Krugman, Paul R.; Obstfeld, Maurice (1991) International economics: theory and policy (Pearson: Cambridge).

Lannoo, Karel; Khachaturyan, Arman (2004) "Reform of Corporate Governance in the EU", *European Business Organization Law Review*, Vol. 5, No. 1 (Cambridge University Press: Cambridge UK), pp. 37-60.

Lasswell, Harold D. (1951) "The Policy Orientation", in Lerner, Daniel; Lasswell, Harold D., eds. *The Policy Science* (Stanford University Press: Stanford CA, USA).

Laumann, Edward O.; Knoke, David (1987a) *The organizational state* (University of Wisconsin Press: Madison WI, USA/London).

Laumann, Edward O.; Knoke, David (1987b) *Social Choice in National Policy Domains* (University of Wisconsin Press: Madison WI, USA/London).

Laumann, Edward O.; Pappi, Franz U. (1976) *Networks of collective action: a perspective on community influence system* (Academic Press: New York/London).

Lave, Charles; March, James (1997) *An Introduction to Models in the Social Sciences* (Harper & Row: New York).

Lawton, Thomas C. (2000) "Uniting European Industrial Policy: A Commission Agenda for Integration", in Nugent, Neill, ed. *At the Heart of the Union: Studies of the European Commission* (Macmillian Press Ltd.: London), pp. 131-146.

Leandri, Susan (2003) Global Best Practices at PricewaterhouseCoopers, Managing Director, telephone interview (Chicago).

Lecours, André (2005) "New Institutionalism: Issues and Questions", in Lecours, André, ed. *New Institutionalism: Theory and Analysis, Studies in Comparative Political Economy and Public Policy* (University of Toronto Press: Toronto).

Lee, Norman; Kirkpatrick, Colin (2004) *A pilot study on the quality of European Commission extended impact assessment* (University of Manchester: Manchester).

Li, Quan (2001) "Commitment Compliance in G-7 Macroeconomic Summit Policy Coordination", *Political Research Quarterly* (June) (The University of Utah: Salt Lake City UT, USA), pp. 355-377.

Liikanen, Erkki (2003) "Helping the World Communicate" - Keynote Speech opening. International Telecoms Union Conference (Geneva,12 October 2003).

Liikanen, Erkki (2004) Opening Remarks for OECD Workshop on Spam in Brussels on 2.2.2004 (Brussels).

Lindblom, Charles E. (1977) *Politics and Markets: The World's Political Economic System* (Basic Books: New York).

Lindblom, Charles E. (1980) *The Policy-Making Process*, 2nd edition (Prentice-Hall: New Jersey).

Lindblom, Charles (2001) *Why Government Must Cater to Business?* (Simon Fraser University: Vancouver).

Lloyd, Ian (2000a) *Information technology law* (Butterworths: London).

Lloyd, Ian (2000b) *Legal aspects of the information society* (Butterworths: London).

Locke, Karen (2001) *Grounded theory in management research* (SAGE: London).

Locke, Karen (2007) "Rational control and irrational free-play: dual-thinking modes as necessary tension in Grounded Theorizing", in Bryant, Antony; Charmaz, Kathy, eds., *The SAGE Handbook of Grounded Theory* (SAGE: London), pp. 565-579.

Lofstedt, Ragnar (2004) "The swing of the regulatory pendulum in Europe: From precautionary principle to (regulatory) impact analysis", *The Journal of Risk and Uncertainty*, Vol. 28, No. 3, pp. 237-260.

Lofstedt, Ragnar (2006) "The Plateau-ing of the European Better Regulation Agenda: An Analysis of Activities Carried Out by the Barroso Commission", *AEI-Brookings Joint Centre for Regulatory Studies* (July), pp. 1-30.

MacRae, Duncan; Whittington, Dale (1997) *Expert Advice for Policy Choice* (Georgetown University Press: Washington, DC).

Majone, Giandomenico (1997) "From the Positive to the Regulatory State: Causes and Consequences of Changes in the Mode of Governance", *Journal of Public Policy*, Vol. 17, No. 2, pp 139-167.

Majone, Giandomenico (2001) "A European regulatory state?", in Richardson, Jeremy John, ed. *European Union: power and policy-making* (Routledge: London), page 263-277.

Majone, Giandomenico (2005) *Regulating Europe*, European Public Policy Series (Routledge: London).

March, James G.; Simon, Herbert A. (1958) *Organizations* (Wiley: New York).

Marks, Gary (1993) "Structural Policy and Multilevel Governance in the EC", in Cafury, A. W.; Rosenthal G. G., eds. *The State of the European Community: The Maastricht Treaty and Beyond*, Vol. 2 (Longman: London), pp. 391-410.

Marks, Gary; Hooghe, Liesbet; Blank, Kermit (1996) "European integration from the 1980s: State-Centric v. Multi-level Governance", *Journal of Common Market Studies*, Vol. 34, No. 3, pp. 341-377.

Marsden, Christopher T. (2000) "Information and communication technologies, globalisation and regulation", in Marsden, Christopher T., ed. *Regulating the global information society* (Routledge: London), pp. 1-40.

Martin, William J. (1995) *The global information society*, 2nd edition (ASLIB/Gower: Aldershot).

Mather, Graham; Vibert, Frank (2005) *Rebalancing UK and European Regulation* (European Policy Forum: London).

Mattli, Walter (2001) "The politics and economics of international standards on international standards setting", *Journal of European Public Policy (Special Issue: Governance and International Standards Setting)*, Vol. 8, No. 3 (Taylor & Francis Ltd.: London), pp. 328-344.

Mazey, Sonia; Richardson, Jeremy (1993) "Introduction: Transference of Power, Decision Rules, and Rules of the Game", in Mazey, Sonia; Richardson, Jeremy, eds. *Lobbying in the European Community* (Oxford University Press: Oxford/ New York).

Mazey, Sonia; Richardson, Jeremy (2001) "Interest groups and EU policy-making: organisational logic and venue shopping", in Richardson, Jeremy, ed. *European Union: power and policy-making* (Routledge: London), pp. 217-238.

McClave, James; Benson, George; Sincich, Terry (1997) *Statistics for Business and Economics*, 7th edition (Prentice Hall: New Jersey).

McCormick, John (2001) "Policy Performance in the European Union", in Zeff, Eleanor; Pirro, Ellen, eds. *The European Union and the Member States: Cooperation, Coordination, and Compromise* (Lynne Rienner Publishers Inc.: London), pp. 7-26.

McKinsey & Company (2002) "Comparative Assessment of the Licensing Regimes for 3G Mobile Communications in the European Union and their Impact on the Mobile Communications Sector", *Report for European Commission/DG Information Society and Media*, June 2002 (European Commission: Brussels/Luxembourg).

McPherson, A.; Raab, Charles (1988) *Governing Education: a Sociology of Policy Science* (Edinburgh University Press: Edinburgh).

Meek, Kip (2006) "Review of the Regulatory Framework", *EuroISPA Newsletter*, Spring 2006 (EuroISPA: Brussels).

Meltsner, Arnold J. (1986) *Policy analysts in the bureaucracy* (University of California Press: Berkeley CA).

Meltsner, Arnold J. (1990) *Rules for rulers: the politics of advice* (Temple University Press: Philadelphia).

Michalowitz, Irina (2007) "What determines influence? Assessing conditions for decision-making influence of interest groups in the EU", *Journal of European Public Policy*, Vol. 14, No. 1, January 2007 (Routledge: London), pp. 132-151.

Mohamed, Arif (2004) "Microsoft and Sun's settlement will yield web services benefits and support for Java." *Computer Weekly*, 13 April 2004, p. 12.

Mohamed, Arif (2006) "RFID privacy guidelines established", *Computer Weekly*, 9 May 2006, p. 8.

Monteiro, Eric (2001) "Actor-Network Theory and Information Infrastructure", in Ciborra, Claudio; Braa, Kristin; Cordella, Antonio, eds. *From Control to Drift: The Dynamics of Corporate Information Infrastructures* (Oxford University Press: Oxford), pp. 71-83.

Moravcsik, Andrew (1991) "Negotiating the Single European Act: National Interests and Conventional Statecraft in the European Community", *International Organization*, Vol. 45, No. 1 (Winter), pp. 19-56.

Moravcsik, Andrew (1993) "Preferences and Power in the European Community: A Liberal Intergovernmentalist Approach", *Journal of Common Market Studies*, Vol. 31, No. 4, pp. 473-524.

Moravcsik, Andrew (1999) "Explaining the Treaty of Amsterdam: Interests, Influence, Institutions", *Journal of Common Market Studies*, Vol. 37, No. 1 (March) (Blackwell Synergy), pp. 59-85.

Moussis, Nicholas (2001) *Access to European Union: law, economics, policies*, 10th edition (European Study Services: Rixensart, Belgium).

Nachmias, David; Chava Nachmias (1976) *Research Methods in the Social Sciences* (St. Martin's Press: London).

Nahrath, Stéphane (1999) "The Power of Ideas in Policy Research: A Critical Assessment", in Braun, Dietmar; Busch, Andreas, eds. *Public Policy and Political Ideas* (Edward Elgar: Cheltenham, UK), pp. 41-58.

Nakamura, Robert (1997) "The Textbook Process and Implementation Research", *Policy Studies Review*, Vol. 1, pp. 142-154.

Nash, Richard (2004) "Combating Spam: ISP Industry Initiatives." *European Commission Workshop*, 15 November 2004 (EuroISPA: Brussels).

Naurin, Daniel (2008) *Deliberation behind closed doors: Transparency and Lobbying in the European Union* (ECPR Press Monographs: Colchester).

Nelson, Robert H. (1987) "The Economic Profession and the Making of Public Policy", *Journal of Economic Literature*, Vol. 25, No. 1 (March), pp. 49-91.

New Approach Standardisation in the Internal Market website (2006) at http://www.newapproach.org (accessed May 2006).

NewGov website (2007) (New Modes of Governance Project) at http://www.eu-newgov.org (accessed April 2007). Website of the Integrated Project on New Modes of Governance, co-ordinated by the European University Institute and its Robert Schuman Centre for Advanced Studies.

NGO Discussion paper website (2007) at http://ec.europa.eu/civil_society/ngo/ (accessed May 2007).

NHS website – Connecting for Health (2012) at http://www.connectingforhealth.nhs.uk/systemsandservices/nimm/ (accessed September 2012).

Niblett, Jim (2007) "ERG and ETMA - a comparative assessment." *Ofcom Presentation* to UK stakeholders, 19 November 2007 (London).

North, Douglass C. (1990) *Institutions, Institutional Change and Economic Performance: Political Economy of Institutions and Decisions* (Cambridge University Press: Cambridge UK).

North, Douglass C. (2005) *Understanding the Process of Institutional Change* (Princeton University Press: Princeton NJ).

Nugent, Neill (1994) *The Government and Politics of the European Union*, 4th edition (Macmillian, Basingstoke UK).

Nugent, Neill (1999) "Decision-Making: Key Characteristics of EU Decision-Making", in Cram, Laura; Dinan, Desmond; Nugent, Neil, eds. *Developments in the European Union* (Macmillan: London), pp. 130-150.

Nugent, Neill (2002) "The Commission's Services", in Peterson, John; Shackleton, Michael (eds.) *The institutions of the European Union* (Oxford University Press: Oxford), page 141-163.

O'Donoghue, T. & Punch, K. (2003) *Qualitative Educational Research in Action: Doing and Reflecting* (Routledge: London), p.78.

OECD (1980) "Guidelines Governing the Protection of Privacy and Transborder Flows of Personal Data", September 1980 (OECD: Paris).

OECD (1999a) "OECD Guidelines for Consumer Protection in Electronic Commerce", December 1999 (OECD: Paris).

OECD (1999b) "Principles of Corporate Governance", Ad-Hoc Task Force on Corporate Governance, 27 May 1999 (OECD: Paris).

OECD (1999c) "Regulatory Reform and International Standardisation" (OECD Working Party of the Trade Committee: Paris).

OECD (2001a) "Codes of Conduct: Data", DSTI/ICCP(2001)8, 6 February 2001 (OECD: Paris).

OECD (2001b) "First Report: Government and Private Sector Initiatives to Promote and Implement the OECD Guidelines for Consumer Protection in the Context of Electronic Commerce", DSTI/CP(2000)7/Final, 5 March 2001 (OECD: Paris).

OECD (2001c) "A Proposal for work on codes of conduct for electronic commerce", DSTI/ICCP/RD(2001)1, 7 March 2001 (OECD: Paris).

OECD (2002a) "OECD Guidelines on the Protection of Privacy and Transborder Flows of Personal Data", 23 September (OECD: Paris).

OECD (2002b) "OECD Guidelines for the Security of Information Systems and Networks: Towards a Culture of Security." Adopted as a Recommendation of the OECD Council at its 1037th Session on 25 July 2002 (OECD: Paris).

OECD (2002c) "OECD Reviews of Regulatory Reform: Regulatory Reform in UK – Regulatory Reform in the Telecommunications Industry." (OECD: Paris).

OECD (2002d) "Alliance for Global Business - Global Action Plan for Electronic Commerce", Third Edition, *GIIC Policy Paper* (OECD: Paris).

OECD (2003a) "Directory of Bodies 2003", I-22/181 P (OECD: Paris).

OECD (2003b) "Inventory of Instruments and Mechanisms contributing to the Implementation and Enforcement of the OECD Privacy Guidelines on Global Networks", DSTI/ICCP/REG(98)12/FINAL, January 2003 (OECD: Paris).

OECD (2003c) "OECD Reviews of Regulatory Reform: Regulatory Reform in France – Enhancing Market Openness through Regulatory Reform." (OECD: Paris).

OECD (2005a) "Anti-Spam Law Enforcement Report", DSTI/CP/ICCP/ SPAM(2004)3/Final, 26 May 2005 (OECD: Paris).

OECD (2005b) "Economic Policy Reforms: Going for Growth." (OECD: Paris).

OECD (2005c) "OECD Work on Science, Technology and Industry", *brochure* (OECD: Paris).

OECD (2005d) "SPAM issues in developing countries", DSTI/CP/ICCP/ SPAM(2005)6/Final, 26 May 2005 (OECD: Paris).

OECD (2005e) "Task Force on Spam background paper: Anti-Spam Regulation", DSTI/CP/ICCP/SPAM(2005)10/Final, 16 November 2005 (OECD: Paris).

OECD (2006) "Economic Policy Reforms: Going for Growth." (OECD: Paris).

OECD (2007) "Economic Policy Reforms: Going for Growth." (OECD: Paris).

OECD (2012) "ICT database and Eurostat: Community Survey on ICT usage in enterprises", June 2012 (OECD: Paris).

OECD website – Anti-SPAM toolkit (2006) at http://www.oecd-antispam.org (accessed July 2006).

OECD website – Key ICT indicators (2012) at http://www.oecd.org/internet/broadbandandtelecom/oecdkeyictindicators.htm (accessed September 2012).

OECD website – SPAM task force (2006) at http://www.oecd.org/sti/spam (accessed July 2006).

OECD website – SPAM task force, industry driven initiatives (2006) at http://www.oecd-antispam.org/article.php3?id_article=240 (accessed June 2006).

OECD website – STI directorate (2007) at http://www.oecd.org/sti (accessed May 2007).

Ofcom website (2006) at http://www.ofcom.org.uk (accessed June 2006).

Ofcom website – spam (2006) at http://www.ofcom.org.uk/telecoms/ioi/g_a_regime/sce/ori/osys/ (accessed July 2006).

Ofcom (2005) "ITC Guidance on Competition Procedures" (Ofcom: London).

Office of Fair Trading website (2006) at http://www.oft.gov.uk/News/Press+releases/2005/208-05.htm (accessed July 2006).

OGC Prince 2 website (2007) (Office of Government Commerce) at http://www.ogc.gov.uk/methods_prince_2.asp (accessed February 2007).

OPTEM (2001) "Perceptions of the European Union: A qualitative study of the public's attitude to and the expectations of the European Union in the 15 Member States and the 9 Candidate Countries", *Report*, June 2001 (OPTEM S.A.R.L.: Brussels).

Ormala, Erkki (2005) "Revisiting strategic thinking", *RTD info – Magazine on European Research*, No. 46 (August) (European Commission: Brussels), p. 22ff.

Ostrom, Elinor (1999) "Institutional Rational Choice: An Assessment of the Institutional Analysis and Development Framework", in Sabatier, Paul A., ed. *Theories of the Policy Process* (Westview Press: Oxford), pp. 35-71.

Ostrom, Elinor (2007) "Challenges and Growth: The development of the interdisciplinary field of institutional analysis", *Journal of Institutional Economics*, Vol. 3, pp. 239-264 (Cambridge University Press).

Ostrom, Elinor; Gardner, Roy; Walker, John (1994) *Rules, games & common-poll resources* (University of Michigan Press: Ann Arbor MI).

Ostrom, Elinor; Schroeder, Larry; Wynne, Susan (1993) *Institutional Incentives and Sustainable Development* (Westview Press: Boulder CO, USA/Oxford).

Pedler, Robin (1994) "Some Lessons from EU Lobby Cases", in Pedler; R. H.; Schendelen, Marinus van, eds. *Lobbying the European Union: Companies, Trade Associations and Issue Groups* (Dartmouth Publishing Company: Aldershot UK), pp. 303-311.

Pedler, Robin (1996) "Opening Brussels to Business", in Randall, Heather, ed. *Business Guide to Lobbying in the EU* (Cartermill International, London), pp 3-36.

Peirce, Charles Sanders (1902), "Application for support for his logic", from Memoir 19, Draft E: "On Arguments" (courtesy Peirce Telecommunity Project website, Texas Tech University).

Pelkmans, Jacques (2001) "The GSM standard: explaining a success story", *Journal of European Public Policy (Special Issue: Governance and International Standards Setting)*, Vol. 8, No. 3 (Taylor & Francis Ltd.: London), pp. 432-453.

Peters, Guy (2001) "Agenda-setting in the European Union", in Richardson, Jeremy, ed. *Policy Making in the European Union* (Routledge: London), pp. 77-94.

Peters, Guy (2002) "Contracts and Resource Allocation: Markets and Law at the Basis of Policy Instruments", in Héritier, Adrienne, ed. *Common Goods: Reinventing European and International Governance,* Governance in Europe series (Rowan & Littlefield: Oxford), pp 263-277.

Peters, Guy; Wright, Vincent (2001) "The national co-ordination of European policy-making: negotiating the quagmire", in .Richardson, Jeremy, ed. *Policy Making in the European Union* (Routledge: London), pp. 155-178.

Philip, Alan Butt; Gray, Oliver (1996) *Directory of Pressure Groups in the EU*, 2nd edition (Catermill Publishing: London).

Pierce, Roy (1994) "Fresh Perspectives on a Developing Institution", in Mesquita, Bruce Bueno de; Stokman, Frans N., eds. *European Community Decision Making: Models, Applications and Comparisons* (Yale University Press: New Haven CT/London), pp. 1-14.

Popper, Karl (1994) *The Myth of the Framework: In defence of science and rationality* (Routledge: London).

Portnoy, Brian (2000) "Alliance capitalism as industrial order: Exploring new forms of interfirm competition in the globalising economy", in Higgott, Richard; Underhill, Geoffrey; Bieler, Andreas, eds. *Non-state actors and authority in the global system* (Routledge: New York).

Price, Monroe; Verhulst, Stefaan G. (2005) *Self-Regulation and the Internet* (Kluwer Law International).

Prodi, Romano (2004) "A constitution for Europe." *Presentation* on 19 January 2004, LSE, London (Peacock Theatre).

PMI website (2007) (Project Management Institute) at http://www.pmi.org (accessed February 2007).

Raab, Charles (2001) "Understanding Policy Networks: a Comment on Marsh and Smith", *Political Studies*, Vol. 39, No. 4 (August), London School of Economics: Government Department & Political Studies Association (Blackwell Publishers: London), pp. 551-556.

Radaelli, Claudio M. (2003) "The Europeanization of Public Policy", in Featherstone, Kevin; Radaelli, Claudio, eds. *The Politics of Europeanization* (Oxford University Press: Oxford), pp. 27-56.

Radaelli, Claudio M. (2005) "What Does Regulatory Impact Assessment Mean in Europe?", *AEI-Brookings Joint Centre for Regulatory Studies*, January 2005, pp. 1-25.

Radaelli, Claudio; De Francesco, Fabrizio (2007) *Regulatory quality in Europe: concepts, measures and policy processes* (Manchester University Press: Manchester UK).

RSPG website (2006) (Radio Spectrum Policy Group) at http://rspg.groups.eu.int (accessed August 2006).

Reding, Viviane (2006a) "Request for advice of the European Regulators Group (ERG) in the context of the Review of the Regulatory Framework for Electronic Communications Networks and Services (Articles 3 and 7 of the Commission Decision 2002/627/EC, as amended by Commission Decision 2004/641/EC)", *Document* (2006)2685, Letter from Viviane Reding, published 30 November 2006 (Brussels).

Reding, Viviane (2006b) "The Review 2006 of EU Telecom rules: Strengthening Competition and Completing the Internal Market", *Speech*/06/422, Annual Meeting of BITKOM (Brussels).

Redwood, Rt. Hon John and Wolfson, Simon (August 2007) "Freeing Britain to Compete: Submission to the Shadow Cabinet", Economic Competitiveness Policy Group, Report (Westminster, London).

Reichertz, Jo (2007) "Abduction: the logic of discovery of Grounded Theory", in Bryant, Antony; Charmaz, Kathy, eds., *The SAGE Handbook of Grounded Theory* (SAGE: London), pp. 214-228.

RFID standards website (2007) at http://www.aimglobal.org/standards/rfidstds/RFIDStandard.asp (accessed May 2007).

Reinke, Guido (2009) *The European Information Society: Governance and the Decision-Making Process for ICT Policy and Standards* (Royal Holloway College, University of London, London).

Rhinard, Mark (2002) "The Democratic Legitimacy of the European Union Committee System", *Governance*, Vol. 15, No. 2 (April), University of Wisconsin (Blackwell Publishers: Madison), pp. 185-210.

Rhodes, R. A. W. (1985) "Power, Dependence, Policy Communities and Intergovernmental Networks", *Public Administration Bulletin*, No. 49, pp. 4-29.

Rhodes, R. A. W. (1990) "Policy Networks: A British Perspective", *Journal of Theoretical Politics*, Vol. 2, No. 3, pp.292-316.

Rhodes, R. A. W.; Marsh, David (1992) "New Directions in the Study of Policy Networks", *European Journal of Political Research*, Vol. 21, No. 1, pp.181-205.

Richardson, Jeremy (1994a) "Doing Less by Doing More? British Government 1979-1994", *West European Politics*, pp. 178-107.

Richardson, Jeremy (1994b) "EU Water Policy-Making: Uncertain Agendas, Shifting Networks and Complex Coalitions", *Environmental Politics*, Vol. 4, No. 4, pp. 139-167.

Richardson, Jeremy (1996a) "Actor-based models of national and EU policy-making", *Essex papers in politics and government*, No. 103 - April 1996 (University of Essex: Colchester UK).

Richardson, Jeremy (1996b) "Policy-Making in the EU: Ideas, Interests and Garbage Cans", in Richardson, Jeremy, ed. *Policy Making in the European Union* (Routledge: London).

Richardson, Jeremy (1996c) "Policy Actor-based models of national and EU policy-making", in H. Kassim and A. Menon (eds.), The European Union and National Industrial Policy (Routledge: London), pp. 26-51.

Richardson, Jeremy (2001a) "Policy-Making in the EU: Ideas, Interests and Garbage Cans", in Richardson, Jeremy, ed. *Policy Making in the European Union*, 2nd edition (Routledge: London), pp. 3-26.

Richardson, Jeremy (2001b) *European Union*, 2nd edition (Routledge: London).

Robert, Michael (2005) "Combating Spam: What can the ISP Industry do?" *Presentation at OECD Workshop*, 10 March 2005 (EuroISPA: Paris).

Robertson, David (1993) *A Directory of Modern Politics*, 2nd edition (New European Publications Ltd.: Rochester UK).

Root, Steven J. (2000) *Beyond COSO: internal control to enhance corporate governance*. (Wiley & Sons Australia).

Rosell, Steven A., ed. (1992) *Governing in an information society* (Institute for Research on Public Policy: Montreal).

Ross, William David (1928) (ed.), *The Works of Aristotle* (Clarendon Press: Oxford).

Rossmeissl, Lisbeth (1996) Telephone list for Unit A1 – Telecommunications Regulation, released on status 28 April 1996 (European Commission: Brussels).

Sabatier, Paul (1988) "An advocacy coalition framework of policy change and the role of policy-oriented learning therein", *Policy Science*, Vol. 21, pp. 129-168.

Sabatier, Paul A. (1993) "Policy Change over a Decade or More", in Sabatier, Paul A.; Jenkins-Smith, Hank, eds. *Policy Change and Learning: An Advocacy Coalition Approach* (Westview Press: Oxford).

Sabatier, Paul A. (1999a) "Fostering the Development of Policy Theory", in Sabatier, Paul A., ed. *Theories of the Policy Process* (Westview Press: Oxford), pp. 261-275.

Sabatier, Paul A. (1999b) "The Need for Better Theories", in Sabatier, Paul A., ed. *Theories of the Policy Process* (Westview Press: Oxford), pp. 1-17.

Sabatier, Paul A.; Jenkins-Smith, Hank (1993a) "The Advocacy Coalition Framework: Assessment, Revisions, and Implications for Scholars and Practitioners", in Sabatier, Paul A.; Jenkins-Smith, Hank, eds. *Policy Change and Learning: An Advocacy Coalition Approach* (Westview Press: Oxford), page 211-235.

Sabatier, Paul A.; Jenkins-Smith, Hank (1993b) *Policy Change and Learning: An Advocacy Coalition Approach* (Westview Press: Oxford).

Sabatier, Paul A.; Jenkins-Smith, Hank (1993c) "The Study of Public Policy Process", in Sabatier, Paul A.; Jenkins-Smith, Hank, eds. *Policy Change and Learning: An Advocacy Coalition Approach* (Westview Press: Oxford), pp. 1-9.

Sabatier, Paul A.; Jenkins-Smith, Hank (1999) "The Advocacy Coalition Framework: An Assessment", in Sabatier, Paul A., ed. *Theories of the Policy Process* (Westview Press: Oxford), page 117-166.

Sabatier, Paul A.; Mazmanian, Daniel A. (1981) "The Implementation of Public Policy: A Framework of Analysis", in Sabatier, Paul A.; Mazmanian, Daniel A., eds. *Effective Policy Implementation* (D. C. Heath and Company: Toronto), pp. 3-35.

Sait, Edward M. (1938) *Political Institutions – A Preference* (Appleton-Century-Crofts: Boston).

Salter, Liora (1999) "The Standards Regime for Communication and Information Technology", in Cutler, Claire; Haufler, Virginia; Porter, Tony, eds. *Private Authority and International Affairs* (State University of New York Press: Albany), pp. 97-127.

Samuelson, Pamela (2000) "Five challenges for regulating the Global Information Society", in Marsden, Christopher T., ed. *Regulating the global information society* (Routledge: London), page 316-330.

Sandholtz, Wayne (1998) "The Emergence of a Supranational Telecommunications Regime", in Sandholtz, Wayne; Sweet, Alec Stone, eds. *European integration and supranational governance* (Oxford University Press: New York), pp. 134-163.

Sandholtz, Wayne; Sweet, Alec Stone (1998) "Integration, Supranational Governance, and the Institutionalization of the European Polity", in Sandholtz, Wayne; Sweet, Alec Stone, eds. *European integration and supranational governance* (Oxford University Press: New York), pp. 1- 26.

Sandholtz, Wayne; Zysman, John (1992) "Recasting the European Bargain", *World Politics*, Vol. 42, pp. 95-128.

Saran, Cliff (2007) "Microsoft ruling to boost user choice", *Computer Weekly*, 25 September 2007, p. 10.

Schaefer, Guenther F. (1996) "Committees in the EC Policy Process: A First Step Towards Developing a Conceptual Framework", in Pedler, Robin; Schaefer, Guenther, eds. *Shaping European Law and Policy: The Role of Committees and Comitology in the Political Process* (European Institute of Public Administrations, Maastricht), pp. 3-24.

Scharpf, Fritz Wilhelm (1988) "The Joint-Decision Trap: Lessons from German Federalism and European Integration." *Public Administration*, Vol. 66, pp. 239-278.

Scharpf, Fritz Wilhelm (1994) "Community and Autonomy: Multilevel Policy-Making in the European Union", *EUI Working Paper*, no 94/1 (European University Institute, Robert Schuman Centre, Florence).

Scharpf, Fritz Wilhelm (1996) "Negative and positive integration in the political economy of European welfare states", in Marks, Gary; Scharpf, Fritz W.; Schmitter, Philippe C. and Streeck, Wolfgang, eds. *Governance in the European Union* (SAGE: London), pp. 15-39.

Scharpf, Fritz Wilhelm (1997) *Games Real Actors Play: Actor-Centred Institutionalism in Policy Research* (Westview Press: Boulder CO, USA).

Scharpf, Fritz Wilhelm (1999) *Governing in Europe: Effective and Democratic?* (Oxford University Press: New York).

Schiavone, Guiseppe (1997) *International Organizations: A Directory*, 4th edition (Macmillian Direct: Basingstoke UK).

Schlager, Edella (1995) "Policy Making and Collective Action: Defining Coalitions Within the Advocacy Coalition Framework", *Policy Science*, No. 28, pp. 243-270.

Schmidt, Suzanne and Werle, Raymund (1998) *Coordinating Technology: Studies in the International Standardization of Telecommunications* (MIT Press: Cambridge MA, USA).

Schmitter, Philippe; Karl, Terry Lyn (1991) "What Democracy Is … and Is Not", *Journal of Democracy*, Vol. 3, No. 3, pp. 75-88.

Schneider, Volker (2006) "Business in Policy Networks: Estimating the Relative Importance of Corporate Direct Lobbying and Representation by Trade Associations", in Coen, David; Grant, Wyn (eds.) *Business and Government: Methods and Practice* (Barbara Budrich: Farmington Hills, MI), pp109-127.

Senate and House of Representatives of the United States of America (2002) "Sarbanes-Oxley Act of 2002", 107th Congress, 116 STAT 745-810, 30 July 2002 (US Congress: Washington).

Sewell, Granville (1999) "Advocacy Coalitions and the Implementation of the Framework Convention on Climate Change: A Preliminary Analysis" in Sabatier, Paul, ed. *An Advocacy Coalition Lens on Environmental Policy* (MIT Press: Cambridge, USA).

Shafritz, Jay M. (2004) Directory of public policy and administration (Westview Press: Boulder CO, Oxford UK).

Shepsle, Kenneth A. (1989) "Studying Institutions: Some Lessons from the Rational Choice Approach", *Journal of Theoretical Politics*, Vol. 1, No. 2, pp. 131-147.

Shepsle, Kenneth A.; Weingast, Barry A. (1981) "Structure-Induced Equilibria and Legislative Choice", *Public Choice*, 37, pp. 503-519.

Shepsle, Kenneth A.; Weingast, Barry A. (1982) "Institutionalizing Majority Rule: A Social Choice Theory with Policy Implications", *American Economic Review*, pp. 367-72.

Simon, Herbert A.; Thompson, Victor A.; Smithburg, Donald W. (1991) *Public Administration*.

Smith, Martin J. (1994) "Policy Networks and State Autonomy", in Brooks, Stephen; Gagnon, Alain-G., eds. *The Political Influence of Ideas: Policy Communities and the Social Sciences* (Praeger Publishers: Westport CT, USA/London), page 33-55.

Snyder, Francais (2004) "Globalisation, Regulation and Governance", *London School of Economics lecture*, Course No. LSE EU 401, Spring 2004, London.

Soanes, Catherine; Hawker, Sara (2005) *Oxford English Directory* (Oxford University Press: Oxford).

Spamhaus Project website (2007) at http://www.spamhaus.org (accessed May 2007).

Stanford University Encyclopaedia of Philosophy website – Charles Sanders Peirce (September 2009) http://plato.stanford.edu/entries/peirce/#bio.

Strange, Susan (1988) *States and Markets* (Pinter Publishers: London).

Strange, Susan (1996) *The Retreat of the State: The Diffusion of Power in the World Economy* (Cambridge University Press: Cambridge).

Strange, Susan (1999) "The Westfailure system", *Review of International Studies*, 25, 345–354.

Strauss, Anselm; Corbin, Juliet M. (1994), "Grounded Theory Methodology: An Overview", in Denzin, Noemal K.; Lincoln, Yvonna S., eds., *Handbook of Qualitative Research* (SAGE: Thousand Oaks, CA), pp. 273-285.

Streeck, Wolfgang; Schmitter, Philippe C. (1985) "Community, market, state – and associations? The prospective contribution of interest governance to social order", *European Sociological Review*, Vol. 1 No. 2 (September 1985), pp. 119-138.

Streeck, Wolfgang; Schmitter, Philippe C. (1991) "From national corporatism to transnational pluralism: Organized interests in the Single European Market", *Politics and Society*, Vol. 19, No. 2 (June 1991), pp133-164.

Steinberg, Richard M. (2011) *Governance, Risk Management, and Compliance: It Can't Happen to Us – Avoiding Corporate Disaster While Driving Success* (John Wiley & Sons: Hoboken NJ).

Strumpf, Uli; Cave, Martin; Valletti, Tommaso (2006) "Experts' report in relation with the Review of the Recommendation on markets subject to *ex ante* regulation", *Report* (Publisher?: Brussels).

Symantec website (2012) at http://www.symantec.com/threatreport/ (accessed August 2012).

Thatcher, Mark (1997a) "The Development of European Regulatory Frameworks: The Expansion of European Community Policy Making in Telecommunications", in Stavridis, Stelios; Mossialos, Elias; Morgan, Roger and Machin, Howard, eds. *New Challenges to the European Union* (Dartmouth Publishing Company: Aldershot), pp. 297-327.

Thatcher, Mark (1997b) *Regulation and Regulators: Is the current system working or is there a need for rationalisation and reform?* (LSE Pubic Policy Group: London).

Thatcher, Mark (1999a) "The Europeanisation of regulation: The case of telecommunication", *working paper* RSC, No. 99/22 (European University Institute (EUI): Florence, Italy).

Thatcher, Mark (1999b) *The Politics of Telecommunications: national institutions, convergence, and change in Britain and France* (Oxford University Press: New York).

Thatcher, Mark (2001a) "The Commission and national governments as partners – EC regulatory expansion in telecommunications 1979-2000", *Journal of European Public Policy*, Vol. 8, No. 4 (Taylor & Francis Ltd.: London), pp. 558-583.

Thatcher, Mark (2001b) "European regulation", in Richardson, Jeremy, ed. *European Union: power and policy-making* (Routledge: London), pp. 303-320.

Thatcher, Mark (2002a) "Analysing regulatory reform in Europe", *Journal of European Public Policy (Special Issue: Regulatory Reform in Europe)*, Vol. 9, No. 6 (December) (Taylor & Francis Ltd.: London), pp 859-872.

Thatcher, Mark (2002b) "Regulation after delegation: independent regulatory agencies in Europe", *Journal of European Public Policy (Special Issue: Regulatory Reform in Europe)*, Vol. 9, No. 6 (December) (Taylor & Francis Ltd.: London), pp. 945-972.

Thatcher, Mark (2003) "Network Regulation." *Lecture and workshop* in spring 2003, LSE (GV 403), London.

Thatcher, Mark (2005a) "The Third Force? Independent Regulatory Agencies and Elected Politicians in Europe", *Governance*, Vol. 18, No. 3 (July) (Blackwell Publishing: Malden, Oxford), pp. 347-373.

Thatcher, Mark (2005b) "Winners and Losers in Europeanisation: Reforming the National Regulation of Telecommunications", in Radaelli, Claudio M.; Schmidt, Vivien A., eds. *Policy change and discourse in Europe* (Routledge: London), pp. 102-127.

Thatcher, Mark; Coen, David (2008) "Reshaping European Regulatory Space: An Evolutionary Analysis", in West European Politics, Vol. 31, No. 4, July, pp. 806-836.

The Anti-Abuse Project website (2008) at http//www.anti-abuse.org/category/internet-abuse (accessed August 2008).

Thomas, Daniel (2003) "Governments under pressure to beef up anti-spam legislation to protect business", *Computer Weekly*, 14 October 2003, p. 28.

Thompson, Richard (2003) Investigation Manager, Competition and Regulation for Telecoms, *Personal meeting* at Ofcom in May 2003.

Timms, Stephen (2007) "EU Framework Review Stakeholder Meeting." *Speech at BERR*, 19 November 2007 (London).

Tofan, Claudia (2008) International Law (Wolf Legal Publishers).

Torriti, Jacopo (2007) "Impact Assessment in the EU: A Tool for Better Regulation, Less Regulation or Less Bad Regulation?" *Journal of Risk Research.*, volume 10, March (Routledge: London), pages 239 – 276.

Trade Association Forum website (2007) at http://www.taforum.org (accessed August 2007).

Treaty of Amsterdam (1997) "Protocol (N° 7) on the application of the principles of subsidiarity and proportionality", Section 2: The Union and the Citizen (Amsterdam).

Tsebelis, George (1990) *Nested Games: Rational Choice in Comparative Politics* (University of California Press: Berkeley CA).

Turlea, Geomina et al. (2011) *The 2011 Report on R&D in ICT in the European Union* (Joint Research Centre, Institute for Prospective Technological Studies: Luxemburg), p. 28.

Tyson, Laura D'Andrea (2003) "The Tyson Report on the Recruitment and Development of Non-Executive Directors", A *report* commissioned by the Department of Trade & Industry following the publication of the Higgs Review of the Role and Effectiveness of Non-Executive Directors in January 2003, published in June 2003 (London Business School: London).

UNCITRAL (1998) (United Nations Commission on International Trade Law), "Draft Uniform Rules on Electronic Signatures", *Guidance* (Vienna).

UNECE (1998) (United Nations Economic Commission for Europe), "Convention on access to information, public participation in decision-making and access to justice in environmental matters ('Aarhus Convention')", 25.06.1998 (UNECE, Aarhus).

UNESCO (2006) (United Nations, Economic and Social Council), "Follow-up to the World Summit on the Information Society and review of the Commission on Science and Technology Development", *resolution* (2006/46), 43rd plenary meeting, 28 July 2006 (UN: New York).

UNESCO (2007a) (United Nations, Economic and Social Council), "Participation of business sector entities including the private sector in the work of the Commission on Science and Technology for Development", *Draft decision* submitted by the Vice-President of the Council, Léo Mérorès (Haiti), on the basis of informal consultations (E/2007/L.5), 20 April 2007 (UN: New York).

UNESCO (2007b) (United Nations, Economic and Social Council), "Participation of non-governmental organizations and civil society entities in the tenth and eleventh sessions of the Commission on Science and Technology for Development", *Draft decision* submitted by the Vice-President of the Council, Léo Mérorès (Haiti), on the basis of informal consultations (E/2007/L.4), 18 April 2007 (UN: New York).

UNESCO (2007c) United Nations Economic and Social Council, "Commission on Science and Technology for Development" 21-25 May 2007, E/2007/31.

United Nations (1945) *Charter of the United Nations and Statute of the International Court of Justice*, amended in 1963 and 1973 (United Nations: San Francisco).

United Nations ICT Task Force (2001) RESEARCH: A/56/3, chapter V, agreed conclusions 2001/I, para. 7.

United Nations ICT Task Force website (2007) at http://www.unicttaskforce.org/ (accessed July 2007).

United Nations General Assembly (2002) "Resolution adopted by the General Assembly on the report of the Second Committee (A/56/558/Add.3)." 56/183, *World Summit on the Information Society*, 90th plenary meeting, 31 January 2002 (UN: New York).

United Nations (2007) "Panel in Geneva calls for massive investments in information and communications technology for development." *Press Release* PI/1780, 30 May 2007 (Department of Public Information, News and Media Division: New York).

UN Commission of Science and Technology for Development (2007a) "Draft Decision to be brought to the attention of ECOSOC: Multi-year work programme of the Commission on Science and Technology for Development", *draft decision*, 21-25 May 2007 (UN: Geneva).

UN Commission of Science and Technology for Development (2007b) "Draft Resolution recommended to ECOSOC for adoption: Flow of Information for the Follow Up of the World Summit on the Information Society (WSIS)", *draft resolution*, 21-25 May 2007 (UN: Geneva).

van den Bos, Jan (1994) "The European Community, Decision Making, and Integration", in Mesquita, Bruce Bueno de; Stokman, Frans N., eds. *European Community Decision Making: Models, Applications and Comparisons* (Yale University Press: New Haven CT, USA/London), page 17-32.

van Schendelen, Marinus (1994a) "From National State Power to Spontaneous Lobbying", in Schendelen, Marinus van, ed. *National Public and Private EC Lobbying* (Dartmouth Publishing Company: Aldershot UK), pp. 283-301.

van Schendelen, Marinus (1994b) "The Relevance of National Public and Private EC Lobbying", in Schendelen, Marinus van, ed. *National Public and Private EC Lobbying*, (Dartmouth Publishing Company: Aldershot UK), pp. 1-19.

van Schendelen, Marinus (1994c) "Studying EU Public Affairs Cases: Does it Matter?", in Pedler; R. H.; Schendelen, Marinus van, eds. *Lobbying the European Union: Companies, Trade Associations and Issue Groups* (Dartmouth Publishing Company: Aldershot UK), page 3-20.

van Schendelen, Marinus (1998) "Prolegomena to EU Committees as Influential Policymakers", in Schendelen, Marinus van, ed. *EU Committees as Influential policymakers* (Ashgate Publishing: Aldershot), pp. 3-22.

Verdun, Amy (1996) *The Role of the Delors Committee in the Creation of EMU: An Epistemic Community* (European University Institute: Florence, Italy).

Verheugen, Günter (2004) "Enterprise Commissioner makes pledge to cut red tape." *Press Release*, 10 December 2004 (CEC: Brussels).

Verheugen, Günter (2005a) "Better Regulation", Keynote Speech. In Better Regulation Executive, Cabinet Office (eds.) *Competitiveness and Consultation: Business at the Heart of Europe-Better Regulation Conference*, 22 -23 September 2005, Edinburgh (Cabinet Office: London).

Verheugen, Günter (2005b) "Less red tape = more growth." *Press conference* on Better Regulation, 16 March 2005 (CEC: Brussels).

Verheugen, Günter (2005c) "A new industrial policy." *Speech*, Meeting with Confindustria, 18 November 2005 (Bologna).

Verrue, Robert (2002) "EU Policy for electronic commerce and the rights of the individual." *EEMA European Annual Conference* , 11 June 2002 (Amsterdam).

Vogel, Steven K. (1997) "International Games with National Rules: How Regulations Shape Competition in 'Global' Markets", *Journal of Public Policy*, Vol. 17, No. 2, pp. 169-193.

Waddington, David (1994) "Partcipant Observation", in Cassell, Catherine; Symon, Cill (eds.) *Qualitative Methods in Organizational Research: A Practical Guide* (SAGE: London).

Wagner, Ray (2003) "Lack of web security limit trading partnerships." *Computer Weekly*, 18 November 2003, p. 1.

Walden, Ian (2001) "Regulating electronic commerce: Europe in the global E-conomy", *European Law Review*, Vol. 26, No. 6 (December) (Sweet & Maxwell: London), pp. 529-547.

Walden, Ian (2003) "Telecommunications Law" and "Legal Regulation of Information Technology." *Lectures* at Queen Mary, University of London, London.

Walden, Ian; Angle, John, eds. (2001) *Telecommunications Law* (Blackstone Press: London).

Warleigh, Alex (2002) *Understanding European Union Institutions* (Routledge: London).

Webb, Eugene J.; Campbell; Donald T.; Schwartz, Richard D.; and Sechrest, Lee (1966) *Unobtrusive Measures: Nonreactive Research in the Social Science* (Rand McNally: Chicago).

Weiler, Joseph H.; Wind, Marlene, eds. (2003) *European Constitutionalism beyond the State* (Cambridge University Press: New York).

Werle, Raymund (2001) "Institutional aspects of standardization – jurisdictional conflicts and the choice of standardization organisations", *Journal of European Public Policy (Special Issue: Governance and International Standards Setting)*, Vol. 8, No. 3 (Taylor & Francis Ltd.: London), pp. 392-410.

Wessels, Wolfgang (1997) "An Ever Closer Fusion? A dynamic macropolitical view on integrtation process", Journal of Common Market Studies, Vol. 35, No. 2 (Blackwell Publishing: Oxford), pp. 267-299.

Wessel, Wolfgang (2009) "The making of the EU system: Reflections and suggestions for academic contributions". Contribution to the conference of the Jean Monnet network, December 2009.

Wessel, Wolfgang; Regelsberger, Elfriede (2004) "The evolution of the Common Foreign and Security Policy. A case of an imperfect ratchet fusion", in Verdun, Amy; Croci, Osvaldo (eds.) *Institutional and Policy-making Challenges to the EU in Wake of Enlargement* (Manchester University Press: Manchester).

Westlake, Martin (1998) "The European Parliament's Emerging Powers of Appointments", *JCMS: Journal of Common Market Studies*, Vol. 36, No 3, September 1998, p 431-444.

Wiener, Jonathan B. (2006) "Better Regulation in Europe", September 2006 (AEI-Brookings Joint Centre for Regulatory Studies), pp. 1-69.

Williams, Paul (2006) "A helping hand with governance", *Computer Weekly*, 19 September 2006, pp. 26-28.

WiMAX Forum website (2003) at http://www.wimaxforum.org (accessed June 2003).

Winter, Jaap (2002) "Report of the High Level Group of Company Law Experts on a Modern Regulatory Framework for Company Law in Europe (Winter Report)", prepared by the High Level Group of Company Law Experts, published November 2002.

WIPO website (2006) (World Intellectual Property Organisation) at http://www.wipo.org (accessed August 2006).

WSIS (2002) (World Summit on the Information Society), Working Group 1 on Civil Society Participation in the WSIS "Civil Society Participation in the World Summit on the Information Society: Issues and Principles", April. Discussion document. Also available at http://www.comunex.net/wsis/docs/wg108c.pdf (accessed August 2007).

WSIS (2005) (World Summit on the Information Society), *Tunis Agenda for the Information Society*, Second Phase of the WSIS, WSIS-05/TUNIS/DOC/6 (rev. 1), 18 November 2005 (WSIS: Tunis).

WTO website (2007) (World Trade Organisation) at http://www.wto.org (accessed July 2007).

WTO (1994) "Agreement on Technical Barriers to Trade (TBT)." Uruguay Round Agreement (WTO: Uruguay).

Yin, Robert K. (1994) *Case study research: design and methods* (SAGE: London).

Yin, Robert K. (1994) *Case Study Research: Design and Methods*, 2nd ed. (SAGE: Thousand Oaks, CA).

Yin, Robert K. (2003) "A case study research: design and methods", *Applied Social Research Methods Series*, (SAGE: Thousand Oaks CA, USA).

Zacher, Lech W. (2000) "The Way Towards a Knowledge Society: Some Barriers not only four Countries in Transition", in Banse, Gerhard; Langenbach, Christian; Machleidt, Peter, eds. *Towards the Information Society – The Case of Central and Eastern European Countries* (Springer-Verlag: Berlin/New York), pp 53-59.

Zito, Anthony R.; Radaelli, Claudio M.; Jordan, Andrew (2003) "Introduction to the Symposium on New Policy Instruments in the European Union", *Public Administration*, Vol. 2003, No. 3, (Blackwell Publishing: Oxford), pp. 509-511.

APPENDICES

APPENDICES

Table of Contents

APPENDIX 1: DEFINITIONS OF TERMS

In this Appendix the relevant terms and concepts used in this book are defined. It is essential that the reader understands the author's basic concepts exactly. Without this, the author's results and his discussion of them might be interpreted differently by readers with different backgrounds and assumptions. This is particularly important in interdisciplinary research like that underlying this book, which is intended to interest readers from legal and regulatory backgrounds, policy practitioners to business schools scholars.

A1.1 Information Society and information and communication technologies

Chapter Four of this research deals with the Information Society and with Information and Communication Technologies (ICTs), also sometimes known as Information Technology (IT) or "telematics" in EU terminology. The term Information- or Knowledge Society has also been used, predominantly by the European Commission (*viz.* DG Information Society), to promote the development and use of ICT-based services for both citizens and businesses.

Before defining and discussing the Information Society concept, it is necessary to treat of its constituent concepts: knowledge, information and society. During the Renaissance, Francis Bacon famously wrote, "Knowledge, of itself, is power".[239] Today it has become a truism that knowledge or information is power (Lloyd, 200a:xxvii), and to assert that we now live in an "Information Society". In the literature "knowledge" and "information" are often used synonymously. In reality, the distinction between these two terms is of considerable significance.

Knowledge may be represented in the form of information – typically, when it is recorded on paper, on electronic media, or is expressed in speech. Nevertheless, knowledge means more than just information; it conveys in addition a sense that understanding of the information has been achieved and applied. Information may be considered a commodity readily transferable from one person to another, while understanding and therefore knowledge is less readily communicated. "Knowledge is regarded as a higher order concept that information, as information that has somehow stood the test of time and entered into the knowledge base" (Martin, 1995:24). For example, anybody can buy a copy of Albert Einstein's book "Relativity – The Special and General Theory" (Einstein, 2001), which

239 Francis Bacon (1561-1626), Knowledge is power - 'Nam et ipsa scientia potestas est' in Meditationes Sacræ. De Hæresibus. Note: Francis Bacon is one of the important thinkers of the Scientific Revolution of the 17th century. He exerted great influence on his contemporaries by introducing a method in which science is based on observation and experimentation.

sets forth his revolutionary theories, and thereby acquire the *information* contained therein; however, it may be doubted whether many buyers could acquire Einstein's knowledge of the subject by trying to follow his mathematical reasoning in, let us say, the chapter on "the space-time continuum of the special theory of relativity".

Information often implies a collection of facts, data, or instructions that need to be critically analysed and assessed. *The Dictionary of Government and Politics* defines information as "details, which explain something" (Anonymous, 1997:144). This leads to the conclusion that information may be considered the raw materials of the process of acquiring knowledge; and later of making decisions.

The realisation has been dawning on the EU that the proliferation of ICT applications will continue to impact the organisation and viability of businesses. ICT may well significantly impact the ways goods are sold and distributed; alter the methods of delivering public services; and dramatically transform other areas of society, such as learning and communication. These developments have variously been labelled the "information economy", the "networked economy" and the "information society" (*e.g.* Castells, 1996, Kelly, 1998:140ff). EU policy papers often refer also to the "information age" and "knowledge society". As mentioned above, information is a commodity good that lies at the centre of today's society. Although it is difficult to think of any aspect of life which has not been affected by the Information Society, a satisfactory definition of the term has proved elusive. One justification often put forward for avoiding too clear-cut a definition is that the technology shaping the Information Society advances so rapidly that to try and demarcate specific attributes would entail perpetual adjustments in light of new technical developments. Where definitions have been attempted, as in certain European directives (see below), these have been so vague as to be virtually useless for scientific purposes.

The concept of society is possibly less tricky; the *Oxford English Dictionary* defines it as "a self-reproducing grouping of individuals occupying a particular territory, which may have its own distinctive culture and institutions" (Soanes and Hawker, 2005). Another, corroborating definition is "the aggregate of people living together in a more or less ordered community" (Soanes and Hawker, 2005). Following up this notion, Luc Soete has attempted a definition of Information Society: "The Information Society is the society currently being put into place, where low-cost information and data storage and transmission technologies are in general use. This generalisation of information and data use is being accompanied by organisational, commercial, social and legal innovations that will profoundly change life both in the world and in the Information Society generally" (Soete, 1997:11). A definition that conceives the Information Society more as a society than an economy is provided by William Martin: "… a society in which the quality of life, as well as prospects for social change and economic development, depend increasingly upon information and its exploitation. In such a society, living standards, patterns of work and leisure, the education system and the market place are all influenced markedly by advantages in information and knowledge" (Martin, 1988:179).

In general the literature distinguishes three types of Information Society: (1) The Information Society as Information Economy, embracing an "industry approach" which seeks to measure the development of the "information sector" through indices (*e.g.* household spending on information, information consumption), and an "occupational approach" which chooses analysis of the economy's occupational structure as its starting point (Bechmann, 2000:37-52); (2) Information Society as a post-industrial society based on the paramountcy of the information sector in comparison with the production of goods, and on the primary dependency of production on information (instead of raw materials and energy) (Bell, 1976); and (3) Information Society as a Knowledge Society, which recognises the impact on a modern society of the growth in importance of theoretical and scientific knowledge.

Explaining the role of ICT policy-making requires definitions of ICT and ICT policies. The existing conceptualisations of ICT do not clearly address whether both components of ICT – the communications element and the data-processing element – are to be included definitionally. The present dissertation will adopt a flexible approach and view all information and communications technologies as part and parcel of the ICT sector.

ICT has been characterised as leading to dynamic technology changes; decreasing costs for new equipment; a rapidly increasing range of applications; and penetration into many areas of professional and personal life (Cohen, Salomon and Nijkamp, 2002). The ICT sector has become a cynosure of public policy due to its expected high economic benefits in the information age. Other scholars define ICT "as a family of electronic technologies and services used to process, store and disseminate information, facilitating the performance of information-related human activities, provided by and serving the institutional and business sectors as well as the public-at-large" (Cohen, Salomon and Nijkamp, 2002:35).

Cohen defines ICT policy as "any public-sector action taken to advance the development of ICT or to promote their use by constituents for the benefits of society" (Cohen, Salomon and Nijkamp, 2002:36). He distinguishes between two basic policy forms. In one, ICT policy is identified as a set of objectives, including incentives to achieve these; in the other, ICT is a step toward achieving higher-order policy goals. Defining the scope of ICT policy is complicated by two factors. First, as the definitions suggest, ICT itself varies in terms of both technologies and services; it is thus ambiguous in nature. Second, the nature of public policy is ambiguous as well, since the term "policy" relates to all norm-making processes and any implementing action.

Chapter Three of this book will analyse the concept of the European Information Society, reviewing the EU programme, its regulatory and legal background and its Action Plans, and policy initiatives to implement the Information Society.

A1.2 Industrial policy, policy-making, regulation and standards

Other important terms calling for definition include: industrial policy, policy-making, regulation, and standards. Industrial policy has been defined as "government regulation of industrial planning and production through law, tax incentives, and subsidies" (Shafritz, 2004:154). According to Krugman and Obstfeld, "industrial policy is an attempt by a government to shift the allocation of resources to promote economic growth" (1991:281). The European Commission and national governments consider ICT policy a subset of industrial policy. This book will present evidence for the increased importance of industry policy, and of the actuality and the desirability of industry involvement in making it.

Schmitter *et al.* defined policy-making as the natural purview of governments, adding that policy-making should be "democratic policy-making" involving in some manner private citizens and organisations (Schmitter *et al*, 1991:75-88). "In the most general sense, policy-making consists of a general set of concepts, assumptions, frames-of-reference, mental models, and activities directed toward some perceived problem area" (Greene, 1993:7).

Regulation is defined as "the totality of government controls on the social and economic activities of its citizens" (Shafritz, 2004:253). Shafritz's definition also stresses the importance of independent regulatory authorities (IRAs) by acknowledging that regulation comprises "the rulemaking process of administrative agencies charged with the official interpretation of laws" (Shafritz, 2004:253). Regulatory regimes may include rules made inside private organisations and public bodies which govern their internal affairs.

On the other hand, Baldwin *et al.* (1998) distinguish three different senses in which the word regulation is used: First, to designate a set of legally binding commands issued by a dedicated rule-making body. The eight Data Protection Principles and Data Protection Directive as applied by the Information Commissioner is a fair example. Second, to designate a broader concept embracing all deliberate acts of state aimed at influencing (industrial) behaviour, which might include a range of behavioural modifications like economic incentives (*e.g.* taxes or subsidies), provision of information, deployment of resources, and other measures. Third, to designate a comprehensive concept encompassing the totality of forms of social control or influence whether springing from the state or from private sources (*e.g.* consumers' associations). This broadest definition sweeps-in both deliberately designed regulation and "accidental regulation", or regulation incidental to other objectives.

Self-regulation characterises a situation where firms or individuals exert normative control over their own and/or their members' behaviour. (On self-regulation see Price and Verhulst, 2005; Black, January 1996:24-55; Baldwin and Cave, 1999:39-41; Badwin and McCrudden, 1987). An association may self-regulate in a purely private sense – in pursuit of the private ends of its membership – or it may act "governmentally" insofar as public policy tasks may be delegated to it as also to other private actors or institutions. Self-regulation is encountered in many professions and in sectors like on-line services, financial services, advertising, and the press.

EU regulation "is an especially important component of the law, in many aspects relevant to the Information Society, with data protection, electronic commerce and intellectual property laws all deriving from European initiatives" (Lloyd, 2000b:10). Under the Community treaty, the EU has power to enact Regulations in a variety of spheres. Article 249(1) of the EU Treaty states that "the European Parliament acting jointly with the Council and the Commission shall make regulations and issue directives, take decisions, make recommendations or deliver opinions." Article 249(2) further states that a Regulation "has general application, is binding in its entirety and directly applicable in all Member States". It is "a legal instrument which applies throughout the EU and becomes part of national law without the need for any further action by national authorities" (Lloyd, 2000b:10). Regulations undergird uniformity of legal norms throughout the EU. They are normative in character and apply "generally" or to entire groups of people identifiable in the abstract (Anonymous, 2004a:19). Examples of EU Regulations are fire safety standards, labelling of food and other products, safety standards for electrical appliances, and standards for IT hardware and software.

Article 249(2) goes on to provide that EU Directives shall be binding "as to the result to be achieved", implying that "an EC regulation has immediately the full force of law in each member country, and can be called upon by citizens in legal cases" (Robertson, 1993:413). Although binding and directly applicable to all Member States, EU legislation does not bind individuals until it has been "transposed" into national law, the method and form of which is left up to national authorities. Directives define common norms and policy goals for the Member States, who then choose the ways and means that are the most appropriate to their own legal systems for enforcing and achieving them.

EU Decisions enjoy similar status: Article 249(2) provides that a Decision "shall be binding in its entirety upon those to whom it is addressed". Decisions may be addressed to Member States, to companies, or even to private individuals.

Recommendations and Opinions are not legally binding, having persuasive authority only, yet their existence obliges Member States to take them into account. In *Grimaldi v. Fonds des Maladies Professionnelles* (1988), the European Court of Justice ruled that national courts are "bound to take recommendations into consideration in deciding disputes submitted to them, in particular where they clarify the interpretation of national provisions adopted in order to implement them or where they are designed to supplement binding EEC measures".[240] It follows that Recommendations can play an important role in defining the purport of ICT regulations, helping to clarify the goals of the regulator.

Standards are non-binding norms designed to support policy objectives. Technical standards are widely acknowledged to be fundamental to the Information Society vision. They may be formulated by "standards organisations" closely cooperating with the ICT (or other) industry and/or consumers. Standards-setting processes typically involve lengthy rounds of negotiation and revision, compromise and accommodation, as consensus is essential to their normative effect. The consensus-building process may be influenced as much by the internal politics of the standards-setting organisation as by the external political environment framing it. (On the problem of processes and rule-making procedures, see Baldwin, 1995:167-174).

Often commercial organisations set industry standards; some for internal usage only, others for use by groups of people, groups of companies, or by the industry or subsection of the industry. Collaborative industry groups constitute a kind of interest group obtaining mutual gains from coordinated action that promotes group-wide conformity in a measure, or uniformity in a technical reference level of quality or attainment. Even standards never authorised by a formal standards-setting organisation may become *de-facto* standards which achieve such predominance that everybody follows them just as if they had been formally

240 Salvatore Grimaldi v. Fonds des maladies professionnelles (Case C-322/88): Judgement of the Court (Second Chamber) of 13 December 1989, Reference for a preliminary ruling: Tribunal du travail de Bruxelles, Belgium.

authorised. *De-facto* standards may cover formats, (programming) languages, computer applications, designs, or protocols. Typical creators of *de-facto* standards include:

- individual companies, often with dominant market positions in their sectors (*e.g.* Windows operating systems from Microsoft, Oracle databases, JavaScript from Netscape, Flash from Macromedia, PDF from Adobe)
- consortia of companies that join-up to develop and enhance industry solutions (e.g. the Moving Picture Expert Group, which developed the MPEG standard; or the Wi-Fi Alliance, which is enhancing security and product interoperability); and
- the standards-setting "working groups" of industry associations (e.g. the Information Security Audit and Control Association, which developed Cobit; or the Payment Card Industry Security Standards Council [PCI SSC]], which created the Data Security Standard (PCI DSS), the Payment Application Data Security Standard (PA-DSS), and the PIN Transaction Security (PTS).

Examples of important standards that were developed by private standards-setting efforts include:

- TCP/IP v4 to v6 (Transmission Control Protocol/Internet Protocol, set by the Information Science Institute), the standard for converting messages into streams of packets and addressing and routing the packets
- various e-Communications standards; e.g. SMTP (Simple Mail Transfer Protocol), or MPLS (Multi-Protocol Labelling Switching)
- the X.500 standard for distributed maintenance of fields and directories, set by the ITU, or ISO 27001, the international standard for Information Security Management Systems
- MPEG, set by ISO/IEC (for coded representation of digital audio and video), or mobile communications standards such as GSM, GPRS and UMTS; and
- various WiFi standards (802.11a, 802.11b, 802.11g, 802.11.i, 802.16, 802.1x).

Examples of *de facto* standards include:

- operating systems and server architecture (viz. Windows DOS/95/97/98/2000/NT/XP/Vista 2007, the .NET Framework, Internet Explorer, UNIX, Linux, Apple Mac)
- software application standards (viz. Word, Adobe Acrobat, Excel, Power Point, Photoshop)
- video streaming standards (e.g. RealPlayer),
- web technology (e.g. JavaScript, Google browser); and
- financial software standards (e.g. SAP, Oracle).

A1.3 Actors, stakeholders, interest groups, lobbyists and decision-makers

Unusually, the theories in this book feature actors and stakeholders; thus, it is of prime importance to distinguish these two closely related concepts. The Venn diagram below graphically represents the logical relation between them.

An actor is a person, either natural or legal, who is participating, or who seeks to participate in the policy process. The concept of actor embraces both stakeholders and non-stakeholders (in particular, the regulator). An actor is understood as a "generic term for a unitary social entity, whether an individual person or a larger collectivity, such as a corporation or a nation state" (Knoke, 1990a:1). Actors may be formal policy decision-makers (*e.g.* regulators or regulatory authorities), or informal policy decision-influencers, *i.e.* both active stakeholders (*viz.* business organisations trying to shape public policies that affect them) and organisations such as consumer groups who represent non-actors or passive stakeholders like consumers. It is important to note the distinction between passive stakeholders and the activists who have appointed themselves to represented them, as such representation needs not accurately reflect the passive stakeholders true desires or interests.

"Policy stakeholder", a term often used by the European Commission, shall be used in this book to mean a person, either natural or legal, on whom regulation has had or is likely to have an impact, and who therefore has a genuine interest (a "stake") in influencing and shaping regulation, whether they act on this interest or not. Stakeholders may play either an active (*i.e.* participatory) or a passive role in the policy process. The diagram below illustrates in detail the relationship between actors and stakeholders.

Figure A1.1: Distinguishing between stakeholders and actors

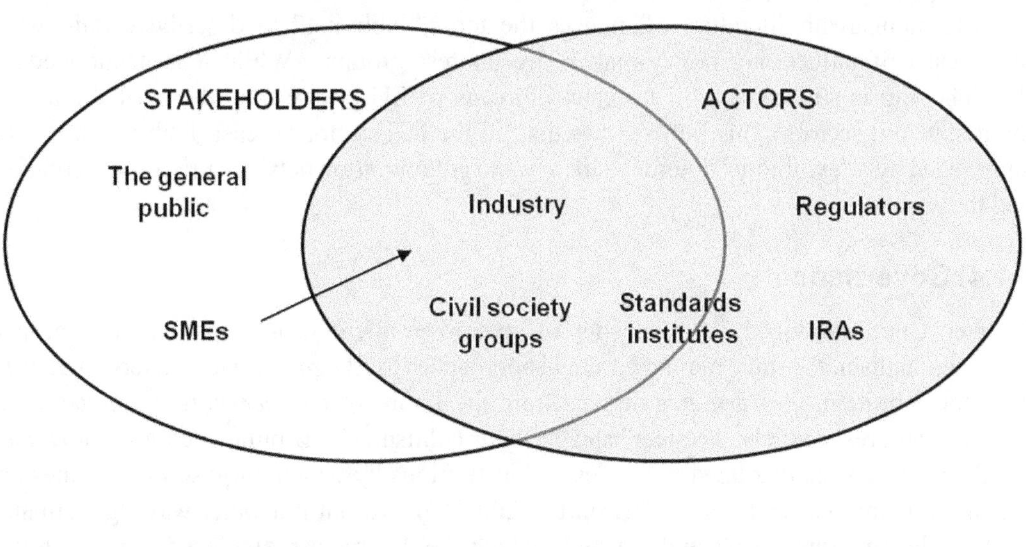

The scholarship that deals with policy processes inside the EU institutions defines "interest groups" (or "pressure groups") as "associations formed to promote a sectional interest in the political system" (Robertson, 1993:240). Such groups classically included trade unions, professional associations, and employers' organisations, all defending the common interests of their members. These interest groups have used a variety of tactics to pursue their goals at national level: trade unions typically threaten to strike (*e.g.* strikes between 1970 and 1990 in the coal and steel industry), whereas professional groups advance their causes by more indirect methods, like influencing bureaucratic decision-making processes, or developing close ties with political parties – not to mention generating publicity.

The interest groups that are the key focus of this book are mainly business, trade and professional associations, and may be defined as "a group of individuals and/or organisations from a specific industrial, commercial or service sector with a restricted membership". Professional associations offer "individuals with professional interests in common or associations of such individuals with a restricted membership based on professional qualifications and experience" (Philip and Gray, 1996:x).

Lobbying is the act of interested parties, whether individuals or organised groups to attempt to procure a decision of government in their own favour by persuasion or by applying behavioural incentives to political decision-makers; *viz.* "campaign contributions, public-relations campaigns, research supplied to legislative committees, and [even] formal testimony before such committees" (Encyclopaedia Britannica website, 2006; see also Fouloy, 2000:265). The term originated in the 19th century, when efforts to influence legislators in particular generally took place in the "lobby" outside legislative chambers. Lobbying in the contemporary sense, however, is not confined to legislative decision-maker but encompasses all significant political decision-makers, including high Executive officials and administrative agencies. It may be direct, that is, addressed to the decision-makers themselves, or indirect, e.g., through influencing public opinion.

The mainstream literature often uses the term "lobbying" to describe certain ways and means of influencing policy-makers by interest groups. While it is acknowledged that lobbying is still carried on in many domains of EU policy (*e.g.* the agricultural and environmental sectors), this book shows that, in the ICT sector at least, lobbying has been superseded by a "symbiotic" interdependency and collaboration between private stakeholders and the regulator.

A1.4 Governance

Chapter One introduced the concepts of intergovernmentalism, supranationalism, and neofunctionalism, the three main theoretical approaches to EU *governance* – a term that itself calls for definition. *Governance* derives from the Latin words *gubernare* and *gubernator* which meant, respectively, "to steer" and "pilot *or* helmsman". Bromley defines *governance* as "the relatively standardized processes and institutions by which purposeful outcomes are produced in any political system" (Bromley, 2001:10). To put it another way, "governance is about the structured ways and means in which the divergent preferences of independent actors are translated into policy choices to allocate values, so that the plurality of interests is transformed into co-ordinated action and the compliance of actors is achieved" (Kohler-

Koch and Eising, 1999:5). Rosell, who researches Information Society governance, defines "the process of governance [as] the process whereby an organization or society steers itself, and the dynamics of communication and control are central to that process"; and continuing, "While the role of government is and remains central to the process of governance, in the Information Society more and more players – voluntary organizations, interest groups, the private sector, the media and so on – become involved in this process" (Rosell, 1992:21).

Appendix 2: Participant observation (interlocutors, presentation, events)

This appendix incorporates the key influencers of this book and features a comprehensive list of organisations and associations. The reader should note that very many of the individuals listed below (if not the organisations) helped the author to shape the concepts he developed for this book.

I define the following terms: (a) an *interview* was a face-to-face communication, of limited duration (usually between half an hour and one-and-a-half hours), between myself and just one other person, wherein I asked a series of prepared questions and the person answered them without preparation; (b) a *(face-to-face) meeting* was a usually unplanned, informal encounter between myself and one other person, wherein I ask a limited number of questions spontaneously occurring to me, as suggested by the event in which context the "meeting" was taking place, and the other answers without preparation; (c) a *conference* is a meeting involving myself and many others, the time, venue and agenda of which was published in advance, and where information is communicated, formally by speeches and audio-visual presentations and informally by face-to-face meetings; (d) *correspondence* was any kind of communication other than the foregoing, between myself and one or more others, usually not face-to-face but by email or telephone, wherein I asked prepared questions to which the other(s) gave prepared answers; and (e) a *workshop* is an formally convoked brainstorming session involving myself participating with and observing experts who "work" to output recommendations and guidance for the organisation hosting the workshop.

A2.1 Face-to-face meetings, interviews, conferences and correspondence with individuals

Anselman, Norbert (9.5.2003): Head, Unit 'Standardisation' (G/2), DG Enterprise, European Commission. Meeting about the European Commissions initiatives in the standards-setting process. Brussels.

Astrup, Jonas (12.12.2003): Policy Manager, Commercial Law and Practice, Jurisdiction and Applicable Law in e-Commerce, ICC. Interview about E-Commerce and Incoterms. Paris.

Broster, David (9.5.2003): Head, Unit 'eTEN' (D/6), DG Information Society, European Commission. Meeting about eTEN programme, stakeholder participation and funding opportunities. Brussels.

Brower, Peter (5.2.2004): Policy Officer, Corporate Law and Governance, Confederation of British Industry (CBI), meeting about DTI Consultation on company law. London.

Bucher, Anne (9.5.2003): Head, Unit "eEurope and IS Strategy" (A/1), DG Information Society, European Commission. Meeting about eEurope programme, stakeholder participation and funding opportunities. Brussels.

Büscher, Reinhard (4.5.2003): Head, Unit 'ICT industries & services (D/4), DG Enterprise, European Commission. Meeting about DG Enterprise's role in ICT policy development. Brussels.

Carblanc, Anne (11.12.2003): Officer for Information Security and Privacy, OECD. Correspondence about OECD Guidelines about info security and privacy. Paris.

Carroll, Hilary (11.12.2003): Information Officer, OECD. Meeting about OECD Reports and other publications on economies. Paris.

Chadun, Yusuf (November 2003): Manager, Bailey Telecom. Interview about my Survey questionnaire. London.

Comyn, Gerard (9.5.2003): Head, Unit 'Strategies for IST Research' (A/2), DG Information Society, European Commission. Meeting about IST programme, stakeholder participation, and funding opportunities. Brussels.

Cunningham, George (April 2003): Head of EU Delegation to the UN, New York. Interview about how the EU is influencing the UN's ICT policies. New York.

Davis, Sue (March 2004): Executive Director, University Association for Contemporary European Studies (UACES), King's College London. Meeting about the UACES research agenda on EU ICT policy. London.

Dryden, John (11.12.2003): Deputy Director, Science, Technology and Industry (STI) Directorate, OECD. Correspondence about OECD involvement in defining global guidance on ICT policy. Paris.

Edrupt, Clive (12.10.2004): Deputy Head of Group, Company Affairs, Confederation of British Industry (CBI). Meeting about how the UK influences EU regulation. London.

Farrell, Marie (12.12.2003): Policy Manager, e-Business, IT and Telecoms (Data Protection), ICC. Interview about how ICC members are involved in defining industry standards. Paris.

Germain, Gilbert (December 2003): Practice Leader, European Public Affairs team, PricewaterhouseCoopers. Interview about PwC's involvement in EU-funded programmes. Brussels.

Hallentie, Timo (9.5.2003): European Commission DG Information Society, Scientific Officer, IST Programme. Interview about the IST Programme. Brussels.

Hassan, Ayesha (12.12.2003): Head of Commission on e-Business, IT and Telecoms (EBITT), ICC. Interview about ICC's involvement in the World Summit on the Information Society (WSIS) and in framing ICANN standards. Paris.

Houdt, Floor van (4.5.2003): DG Enterprise, Head of B/1 'Entrepreneurship'. Interview about DG Enterprise's involvement in making EU ICT policy. Brussels.

Ketchel, John (8.5.2003): Director, European Committee for Standardization (CEN). Interview about CEN's role in European standards-setting and about CEN's relationship with the European Commission. Brussels.

Kilgour, Adam (February 2004): Investigation Manager, Competition and Regulation, OFCOM. Meeting about OFCOM's competition policy. London.

Lee, Ray (28.10.2003): Professor, Royal Holloway College, University of London. Meeting about my Survey questionnaire methodology. Egham.

Mastrogiacomo, Giovanni (April 2003): Counsellor to Industry Policy & Economic Development Section, EU Delegation to the UN, New York. Meeting about the European Commission's collaboration with the UN. New York.

Mela, Chrissa (8.5.2003): Information Officer, Information Resource Centre (A/3), DG Information Society, European Commission. Meeting about EU dissemination of ICT policies and guidelines. Brussels.

Opteijnde, Sava (October 2001): Information Officer, Information Resource Centre (A/3), DG Information Society, European Commission. Meeting about EU ICT publications. Brussels.

Pelhate, Pierrette (9.5.2003): Head, 'Information and Communication' Unit (A/3), DG Information Society, European Commission. Interview about the Unit's information and communications policies. Brussels.

Powell, Ryan (January 2004): Datamonitor, Market Researcher. Meeting about my Survey questionnaire. London.

Schleck, Peter (4.11.2003): Head of Audit, O2. Interview about the impact of regulation and standards on O2. Slough.

Scott, Peter (8.5.2003): Head, 'Policy Development and Regulatory Framework' Unit (B/1), DG Information Society, European Commission. Meeting about the European Commission's Telecommunications Policy and Reviews. Brussels.

Sheehan, Jerry (11.12.2003): Head of Information Security and Privacy, OECD. Correspondence about OECD's global guidance on info security and privacy. Paris.

Styles, David (27.10.03): Assistant Director, DTI. Meeting about DTI Consultation on company law. London.

Teschner, Ralf (January 2004): Market Researcher, Gartner Group. Meeting about my Survey questionnaire. London.

Thompson, Richard (February 2004): Investigation Manager, Competition and Regulation for Telecoms Unit, OFCOM. Meeting about OFCOM's complaint procedures. London.

Tirler, Roman (October 2001): Head, 'Information Security' Unit (C4), DG Information Society, European Commission. Meeting about the EU's information security policy. Brussels.

Wyckoff, Andrew (11.12.2003): Head of 'Measuring the Information Economy' Unit, OECD. Correspondence about the OECD's e-Commerce statistical publications. Paris.

Ypsilanti, Dimitry (11.12.2003): Head of 'Telecommunications and Information Services Policy' Unit, OECD. Correspondence about OECD's ICT guidelines, project groups, and stakeholder involvement. Paris.

Zimmerman, Rainer (4.5.2003): Head, 'Electronic Components' Unit (C/1), DG Information Society, European Commission. Meeting about the EU's Fifth Framework Programme. Brussels.

A2.2 Observed presentations and speeches by individuals

Acemoglu, Daron (25-27.2.2004): Professor of Economics, MIT. LSE Lecture on "Understanding Institutions". London.

Allen, Martin (22.1.2009): Director, PricewaterhouseCoopers. Presentation on "Data Protection, Governance and Security". Information Systems and Audit Control Association (ISACA) Event, London.

Angell, Ian (27.11.2003): Head of Department of Information Systems, LSE. Presentation on "Security is a board-level issue – New regulations". "Enterprise Security – *Information Age*" Conference, London.

Archer, Quentin (22.06.2011): Partner, Hogan Lovells International LLP. Presentation on "The Future of the EU Data Privacy Directive and it's Global Impact". Lisbon.

Arora, Nikesh (12.10.2003): Chief Marketing Officer, T-Mobile International. Presentation on 'Industry roundtable: Reconnected'. "ITU Telecom World 2003" Conference, Geneva.

Barrington, Richard (11-13.6.2003): Director of Industry Unit, UK Office of e-Envoy. Keynote Speech on "UK online – Shaping the knowledge economy". "Internet World 2003" Conference, London.

Barroso, José Manuel (20.5.2005): President of the European Commission. Speech on "Response and Responsibility: the global partnership for aid and development". LSE Event, London.

Bassett, Paul (29.3.2006): Policy Officer, UK Office of Government Commerce (OGC). Presentation on "Data Protection and the Freedom of Information Act". Intellect UK offices, London.

Berry, Bradford (12.11.2003): Partner, Wilmer Cutler and Pickering, Washington and former Deputy Chief, Enforcement Bureau, FCC. Presentation on his firm's Communications and Electronic Commerce practice. London.

Bishop, Peter (25.2.2004): Deputy Chief Executive, Euro Info Centre, London Chamber of Commerce and Industry. Presentation on "EU enlargement and adoption of EU regulations by the accession candidates". "EU enlargement – opportunities for London businesses" Seminar, London.

Blyth, Andrew (7.7.2008): Head, Information Security Research Group, Glamorgan University. Presentation on "Effective Data Destruction – Does it Exist?". Intellect UK: "Security and Privacy" event, London.

Bootle, Roger (28.4.2004): Managing Director, Capital Economics (an economic advisor to Deloitte & Touche and a specialist advisor to the House of Commons Treasury Committee). Presentation on EU industrial policy in general. European Parliament's UK Office, London.

Bourne, Ian (27.7.2009): Head, Data Protection Projects, UK Information Commissioner's Office (ICO). Presentation on EU/UK data protection and privacy regulations. Intellect UK Roundtable on "ICO Personal Information: Online Code of Practice", London.

Bourne, Iain (28.11.2006): Head, Information Sharing, The Information Commissioner's Office (ICO). Presentation on "Information Sharing and Protection of Privacy – the Role of Technology". Intellect UK Workshop, London.

Boutros-Ghali, Boutros B. (1.4.2004): former UN Secretary General. Speech on "Reform of the United Nations". LSE event on "Intergovernmental Organisations", London.

Bradbury, Jonathan (19-20.11.2003): Head of Field Force Enablement, Accenture. Presentation on "Wireless technology as a critical aspect of corporate life – Introducing the mobile nature of today's nature". "European Wireless Technology" Conference, London.

Briault, Paul (13.6.2001): Policy Advisor, UK Office of the e-Envoy. Presentation on "Public Key Infrastructure". EEMA Members' Event on "eGovernment initiatives", Paris.

Broers, Lord (24.4.2007): Chairman of the Science and Technology Committee, House of Lords. Keynote Speech on "Internet Security". "Infosecurity Europe 2007" Conference, London.

Brunett, Peter (2.6.2003): Policy Officer, UK National Information Security Co-ordination Centre. Presentation on "Information security in the government sector". "eAwareness for Europe – Information Security Awareness and the Rule of Local Government" Conference, London.

Büscher, Reinhard (3.5.2003): Head of Unit 'ICT industries & services (D/4), DG Enterprise, European Commission. Presentation on "The European policy perspective". CEN Workshop, Brussels.

Bush, Nick (13.6.2001): Expert on Change Management, Government Unit, BT. Presentation on "Special Sessions: Introduction of New Technologies". EEMA Members' Event on "eGovernment initiatives", Paris.

Butler, John (11-13.6.2003): Director, Strategy and New Services, BTopenworld. Keynote Speech on "New telecommunications services". "Internet World 2003" Conference, London.

Campbell, Alan MP (23.2.2009): Parliamentary Under-Secretary of State, Home Office. Presentation on "e-Crime Reduction". Internet Services Providers' Association (ISPA): "Annual Parliamentary Advisory Forum on E-Crime Reduction", London.

Castells, Manuel (18.3.2004): Professor of the Information Society, Open University of Catalonia (UOC), Barcelona. LSE event on "The Information Age and Network Society", London.

Chalmers, Damian (Spring 2003): Senior Lecturer, LSE. Lecture on "The European Union: Government, Law and Policy". London.

Clark, John (13.10.2003): Secretariat to the High-Level Panel on UN-Civil Society Relations, Office of the General Secretary of the UN. Presentation on "The UN and Civil Society". LSE event on "Intergovernmental Organisations", London.

Clarke, Justin (25.6.2009): Director, Gothan Digital Services. Presentation on "Emerging Standards in Software Security Assurance". Information Systems Audit and Control Association (ISACA) event, London.

Cleveland, Alexis (21.5.2009): Chief Executive, The Pension Service, Department for Work and Pensions. Presentation on "Customer Service Oriented Government: The Challenge of Public Sector Service Transformation". British Computer Society event, London.

Colasanti, Fabio (12.11.2003): Director General, Information Society, European Commission. Presentation on the European Commission's ICT policy strategy. Conference on "The e-Communications Industry", London.

Cosgrave, Bridget (12.11.2003): President, Belgacom Carrier & Wholesales. Presentation on "Telecommunications services". Conference on "The e-Communications Industry", London.

Cowen, Tim (12.11.2003): General Counsel, BT Global Services. Presentation on "BT's e-Communications services and the regulatory challenges". Conference on "The e-Communications Industry", London.

Desai, Nitin (13.10.2003): Former UN Under-Secretary General for Economic and Social Affairs, currently Head, Centre for the Study of Global Governance, LSE. Presentation on "UN Governance". LSE event on "Intergovernmental Organisations", London.

Dickson, Jim (13.6.2001): Membership Director, EEMA. Keynote Speech on "The EEMA industry association". EEMA Members' Event on "eGovernment initiatives", Paris.

Dingwall, Colin (29.3.2006): Policy Officer, UK Department for Constitutional Affairs. Presentation on "The Dept. for Constitutional Affairs' Responsibilities under The Freedom of Information Act". Intellect UK offices, London.

Dirskovski, Robert (2.06.2003): Board Secretary, Trust UK. Presentation on "Consumer confidence online: Trustmark schemes, Codes of Practice and the development of eCommerce". "eAwareness for Europe – Information Security Awareness and the Rule of Local Government" Conference, London.

Dix, Alexander (23.06.2011): Commissioner for Data Protection & Freedom of Information, Germany. Presentation on "Data Privacy & Discovery". Lisbon.

Dixon, Colin (27.11.2003): Project Manager, Information Security Forum. Presentation on "Corporate Security Policies: Best Practices & Compliance". "Enterprise Security – *Information Age*" Conference, London. Presentation (27-29.4.2004) on "Corporate Governance and Basel II & CAD 3 – New Regulations and Driving Corporate Risk Management". "Information Security, Europe" Conference, London.

Dodd, James (12.11.2003): Vice-Chairman, European Telecommunications and Technology (ETT). Presentation on the "Competitiveness of the European Telecommunications Sector". "The Communications Industry – The next phase: Communications and e-Commerce Forum" Conference, London.

Dougal, Jim (28.4.2004): Head, the Representation of the European Commission in the UK. Presentation on "The European Commission's involvement in enlargement". Conference on "Enlightening the debate on good governance: European Union enlargement". London.

Eaton, Denis (19-20.11.2003): Chairman, WiFi Alliance. Presentation on "WiFi Standards – Delivering corporate effectiveness through interoperability". "European Wireless Technology" Conference, London.

Elgar, Stephen (8.3.2011): Information Governance and Security Manager, National Health Services (NHS), UK. Presentation on "Are my medical records safe?". BCS event, London.

English, Joe (13.10.2004): Engineering Manager, Intel and WiMAX Campaign Manager, WiMAX Forum. Presentation on "Information Security Standards for Wireless". "Wireless Enterprise World 2004" Conference, London.

Erroll, Lord Merlin Sereld Victor Gilbert Hay 24th Earl of (19.5.2009): Science and Technology Committee, House of Lords. Roundtable on "Intellect Data Breach Notification – Debate with the ICO and Lord Erroll". Intellect UK offices, London.

Evans, Bob (11-13.6.2003): Programme Director, UK Office of the e-Envoy. Presentation on "Digital Certificates – In Internet We Trust". "Internet World 2003" Conference, London.

Evans, Dave (19.5.2009): Senior Guidance Manager – Business and Industry, Information Commissioner's Office (ICO). Talk on "Guidance for Companies about Data Breach Notification". Roundtable on "Intellect Data Breach Notification – Debate with the ICO and Lord Erroll". Intellect UK offices, London. Presentation (7.6.2011) on "The Impact of EU Data Protection Legislation". Intellect UK offices, London.

Farina, Ana (25.2.2004): European Information Officer, European Information Centre, London Chamber of Commerce and Industry. Presentation on "EU funding and support for local businesses". "EU enlargement – opportunities for London businesses" Seminar, London.

Ferguson, Graeme (22.9.2004): Head of Content, O2 UK. Presentation on "The Universal Mobile Communications System". "Mobile Content World 2004" Conference. London.

Fiorina, Carly (12.10.2003): Chief Executive Officer, HP. Speech on "e-Inclusion". "ITU Telecom World 2003" Conference, Geneva.

Florini, Ann M. (15.1.2004): Senior Fellow at the Brookings Institution and Director, Global Governance Initiative, World Economic Forum. LSE event, London.

Garret, Charles (25.2.2004): Head, EU Enlargement Team, Foreign & Commonwealth Office, UK. Presentation on the UK government's involvement in enlargement. "EU enlargement – opportunities for London businesses" Seminar, London.

Gates, William (13.10.2003): Chairman, Microsoft Corporation. Presentation on "Software breakthroughs and a new generation of communications networks." "ITU Telecom World 2003" Conference, Geneva.

Graham, Christopher (1.12.2010): Information Commissioner, UK. Presentation on "The Development of a Global Standard". Conference, London.

Grant, Hazel (1.12.2010): Partner, Bristows Solicitors LLP. Presentation on "The Information Commissioner's New Powers – Audits and Money Penalties". Conference, London.

Green, Andy (13.10.2003): CEO, BT Global Services. Presentation on "Search for the killer application". "ITU Telecom World 2003" Conference, Geneva.

Gross, David (12.11.2003): Deputy Assistant Secretary, International Communications and Information Policy, US Department of State. "The Communications Industry – The next phase: Communications and e-commerce forum" Conference, London.

Hardman, Derek (6.4.2011): Director of Governance Systems, Fujitsu. Participant in "Panel Discussion – Policy Update: Bribery Act 2010". Intellect UK event, London.

Harrison, John (2.6.2003): Project Leader, Intellect UK. Presentation on "Understanding the role of government organisations in information security". "eAwareness for Europe – Information Security Awareness and the Rule of Local Government" Conference, London.

Hawes, Terry (11-13.6.2003): e-Business Programme Director, Inland Revenue, UK. Presentation on "Net Vision Session: Government & Public Sector". "Internet World 2003" Conference, London.

Hebson, Jane (13.6.2001): Project Manager, EEMA Supervisory Authority Group. Presentation on "EEMA European Certification Authority Forum (ECAF)". EEMA Members' Event on "eGovernment initiatives", Paris.

Held, David (13.10.2003): Professor of Political Science, LSE. Speech on globalisation. LSE event on "Globalisation". London.

Hobson, Claire (19.11.2007): Head, UK Telecoms Policy, BERR. Presentation on "Latest developments of the 2006 Review". eCommunications Framework Review Update, London.

Holland, John (15.5.2003): Senior VP of International Operations, TruSecure. Presentation on "Information Security". TruSecure event, London.

Innes, Abby (Autumn 2003; Spring 2004): Senior Lecturer, LSE. Doctoral Workshop on "European politics". European Institute at LSE, London.

Jafari, A. Reza (12.10.2003): Chairman, ITU Telecom Board, e-Development International. Presentation on "ITU e-Communications Initiatives". "ITU Telecom World 2003" Conference, Geneva.

Jay, Rosemary (28.10.2010 and 1.12.2010): Partner, Head of Information Law at Pinsent Masons LLP. Presentation on "The Government Agenda on Personal Data", BCS event, London. Presentation on "Data Transfer in an Interconnected World". Conference, London.

Jones, David (10.7.2012): CEO, Data Protection & Emerging Technologies, Autonomy/Hewlett Packard. Presentation on "Meaning-based Data Protection". Autonomy presentation, London.

Kaldor, Mary (13.10.2003): Co-Director, Centre for the Study of Global Governance, LSE. Speech on "Globalisation". LSE event on "Globalisation – where next?", London.

Kennedy, Caroline (14.3.2002): Legal Advisor, Harrier Zeuros. Presentation on "Legal issues that impact on information security". "The Costs and benefits of Compliance – Impact of Regulation on UK Companies" event, London.

Ketchel, John (3.5.2003): Director, European Committee for Standardization (CEN). Speech on "CEN Workshop agreement for privacy". CEN Workshop, Brussels.

Kopf, Wolfgang (12.11.2003): Executive Vice President, Public and Regulatory Affairs, T-Mobile International AG. Presentation on "WiFi hot-spots to connect local communities". "The Communications Industry – The next phase: Communications and e-Commerce Forum" Conference, London.

Kullman, Conny (12.10.2003): CEO, Intelsat Ltd. Speech on "Satellite communications". "ITU Telecom World 2003" Conference, Geneva.

Lambert, Sarah (25.2.2004): Head of Regional Affairs, European Commission Representation in London. Presentation on "EU enlargement". "EU enlargement – opportunities for London businesses" Seminar, London.

Layard, Richard (28.4.2004): Co-Director, Centre for Economic Performance, LSE and Chairman, Economic Council of Britain in Europe. Presentation on "Governance". LSE event on "Enlightening the debate on good governance: European Union enlargement", London.

Levin, Dave (19-20.11.2003): Head, Office of Strategy and Technology, HP. Presentations on "Mobile Enterprise – Accessing the True Costs of Going Mobile" and "Starbucks Hot-Spot implementation". "European Wireless Technology" Conference, London.

Liikanen, Erkki (12.10.2003), Commissioner, DG Enterprise and DG Information Society, European Commission. Speech on "European Telecoms Strategy". "ITU Telecom World 2003" Conference, Geneva.

Linda, Martin (13.6.2001): Technology Director, Siemens. Presentation on "Working Paper on the Position of Certificate Policies and Audit Schemes". EEMA Members' Event on "eGovernment initiatives", Paris.

Litvin, Gil (25.10.2007): Security Expert, Data Security Group, RSA. Presentation on "Managed Access to Data – the issues and risks". Information Systems Audit and Control Association (ISACA) event, London.

Lyons, John (27.11.2003): UK National High-Tech Crime Unit. Presentation on "High-Tech Crime: How to prevent it, how to react to it". "Enterprise Security – Information Age" Conference, London.

Macauley, Roderick (6.4.2011): Bribery Act Implementation Manager, Ministry of Justice. Participant in "Panel Discussion: Policy Update: Bribery Act 2010". Intellect UK event, London.

Mackay, Ronald (14.10.2003): Project Officer, "Innovation Policy Development" Unit (D1), DG Enterprise, European Commission. Speech on "Intellectual Capital – Intangible Investments: how much is your business worth?". "ITU Telecom World 2003" Conference, Geneva.

MacLeod, Andy (12.11.2003): CEO, MCI Europe. Presentation on "Telecoms innovation". "The Communications Industry – The next phase: Communications and e-commerce forum" Conference. London.

Mansfield, Nick (3.5.2003): Information Security Expert, Shell IT International B.V. and Chairman, Initiative for Privacy Standardisation in Europe (IPSE). Presentation on "Privacy in Practice – Implementation in a Global Company". CEN Workshop, Brussels.

Marsh, Stephen (29.4-1.5.2003): Director for Security Policy, Office of the e-Envoy UK. Keynote Speech on "UK Smart Card schemes". "InfoSecurity Europe 2003" Conference, London.

Martins, Emma (1.12.2010): Data Protection Commissioner, Jersey. Presentation on "Blogs and Privacy". Conference, London.

McCarthy, Sig (30-31.10.2003): Chairman, European Biometrics Forum (EBF). Presentation on "Security and biometrics standards". "Computer security and biometrics 2003" Conference, London.

McGlade, Dave (22.9.2004), CEO, O2 UK. Speech on "Content and O2". "Mobile Content World 2004" Conference, London.

McMurdie, Charlie (23.2.2009): Detective Superintendent, Central e-Crime Unit, London Metropolitan Police. Speech on "e-Crime and Identity Theft". ISPA event: "Annual Parliamentary Advisory Forum on e-Crime Reduction", London.

Meek, Kip (12.11.2003): Senior Partner, Competition and Content, OFCOM. Presentation on "UK e-Communications regulation". "The Communications Industry – The next phase: Communications and e-Commerce forum" Conference. London.

Michael, Alun MP (23.2.2009): Chairman, UK Internet Governance Forum and the EURIM e-Crime Working Group. Presentation on "The Government's Identity Card Scheme". Internet Services Providers Association (ISPA) event: "Annual Parliamentary Advisory Forum on E-Crime Reduction", London.

Minford, Patrick (28.4.2004): Professor of Economics, Cardiff University and Member, Panel of Forecasters, HM Treasury (1993-1996). Speech on "Should Britain join the Euro?". LSE event on "Enlightening the debate on good governance: European Union enlargement", London.

Murray, Andrew (Spring 2004): Senior Lecturer, LSE. Lecture for Module LL420 on "Legal Regulation of Information Technology". London.

Niblett, Jim (22.12.2005): International Policy Director, OFCOM. Presentation on "OFCOM's Position on the eCommunication Framework". BERR event on "The eCommunication Framework", London.

Nosella, Tom (13.10.2004): Director of Engineering, Internet Systems Business Unit, Cisco Systems Inc. Presentation on "A Holistic Look at SAN Security". "Wireless Enterprise World 2004" Conference, London.

Oliver, Adam (19-20.11.2003): Head of Information Access, BT. Presentation on "Wireless technology as a critical aspect of corporate life – Introducing the mobile nature of today's Internet". "European Wireless Technology" Conference, London.

Parapadakis, George (4.11.2010): ECM Strategy & Market Development, IBM. Presentation on "Business Process Management with Document and Content Management". Intellect UK offices, London.

Peacock, Matt (11.6.2003): Chief Communications Officer, AOL UK. Keynote Speech on "Internet access". "Internet World 2003" Conference, London.

Pepper, Bill (25.6.2006): Director, Security Risk Management, Computer Sciences Corporation (CSC). Presentation on "How to tackle data privacy and security issues in offshoring". Joint Meeting of the Security & Privacy and Outsourcing & Offshoring Groups. Intellect UK offices, London.

Pinder, Andrew (17.2.2004): e-Envoy, UK government. Presentation on "UK government's e-Envoy". LSE event on "The Future of the UK e-Government", London.

Pourquery, Pierre (21.4.2004): Global Head, Risk Management, IBM Business Consulting Services. Presentation on "Basel II & Regulatory Change: Business & Technology Impact". "e-World 2004" Conference, London.

Prodi, Romano (19.1.2004): President of the European Commission. Speech on "A constitution for Europe". LSE, London.

Raevens, Bénédicte (24.5.2012): Partner, Commercial and contract law, data privacy and EU regulatory issues, McGuire Woods LLP. Presentation on "International Transfer of Personal Data". Data privacy event, London.

Ramsey, John (18.10.2006): Head, Group Governance, Barclays. Presentation on "Governance, Responsibility and Liability". "Storage Expo" Conference, London.

Rapp, Peet (24.8.2010): Senior IT Consultant, Rapp Consulting. Presentation on "Personal Privacy Awareness during Social Networking" e-Symposium event.

Reedman, Clive (30-31.10.2003): Chairman, Association for Biometrics (AfB). Presentation on "Biometrics – law and order". "Computer security and biometrics 2003" Conference, London.

Rees, Phillip (24.5.2012): Partner, Technology & IP practice group, McGuire Woods LLP. Presentation on "Current Threat of Cybercrime and its Impact on Regulatory Requirements". Data privacy event, London.

Rifkind, Malcolm (18.11.2003): Foreign secretary, UK (1995-1997). Speech on "The Special Relationship". LSE event on "US-UK: The Special Relationship – is it special?", London.

Rivers, Graham (19-20.11.2003): Director, Business Development and Strategy, T-Mobile. Presentation on "Starbucks Hot Spot Implementation". "European Wireless Technology" Conference, London.

Robinson, Mary (1.4.2004): Former UN High Commissioner for Human Rights. Presentation on "Implementation of legal frameworks". LSE event on "Intergovernmental organisations", London.

Roger, Dean (13.6.2001): Executive Director, EEMA. Keynote Speech on "The EEMA industry association". EEMA Members' Event on "e-Government initiatives", Paris.

Roover, Bart De (12.11.2003): Director, Global Products and Services, Orange. Presentation on "Global Roaming and Interconnection". "The Communications Industry – The next phase: Communications and e-commerce forum" Conference, London.

Rudgard, Sian (15.5.2007): Senior Associate, UK Information Commissioner's Office (ICO). Presentation on "The UK Data Protection Act". Hunton & Williams LLP Seminar on "Security and Data Management Issues in Global Sourcing Transactions", London.

Ruggie, John (6.6.2002): Professor, LSE. Lecture on "Kofi Annan's Global Compact". London.

Rush, Terry (13.10.2004): Sales Manager, UK Enterprise, Sony. Presentation on "Understanding the Impact of Compliance Regulation on Achieving Infrastructure". "Wireless Enterprise World 2004" Conference, London.

Sahel, Jean-Jacques (27-29.4.2004): Deputy Head, e-Communications Policy, DTI. Presentation on "Anti-spam laws: Strengthening consumer confidence in electronic communication". "Information Security Europe 2004" Conference, London.

Samans, Richard (15.1.2004): Managing Director, World Economic Forum and former International Economic Policy Advisor to President Clinton. Presentation on "Global governance and global justice". LSE event on "World Economic Forum – Global Governance debate", London.

Scholtz, Tom (27.11.2003), VP Security & Risk Strategies, Meta Group. Presentation on "The Top 10 Issues Facing Information Security Staff". "Enterprise Security – *Information Age*" Conference, London.

Sembhi, Sarb (28.6.2012): Director of client services, Incoming Thought. Presentation on "The Risk Management and Information Governance Perspective of the EU Data Protection Directive". Information Systems and Audit Control Association (ISACA) event, London.

Servida, Andrea (29.4-1.5.2003): Head, 'Trust and Security' Unit (D4), DG Information Society, European Commission. Keynote Speech on "The European Initiatives on Network and Information Security". "Information Security Europe 2003" Conference, London.

Shannon, Kate (25.2.2004): Manager for Central Europe, UK Trade and Investment. Presentation on "Regional funding and support for local business". "EU enlargement – opportunities for London businesses" Seminar, London.

Skouma, Georgia (30-31.10.2003): Attorney, DLA Piper UK LLP, Brussels. Presentation on "The implementation of the Directive on Electronic Signatures (1999/93)". "Computer Security and Biometrics 2003". Conference, London.

Smedley, Christopher (12.11.2003): Managing Director, Hutchison Network Services. Presentation on "The UK's new optical fibre network". "The Communications Industry – The next phase: Communications and e-Commerce Forum" Conference, London.

Smith, David (2.7.2007): Deputy Commissioner, Information Commissioner's Office. Presentation on "The ICO's Position on Data Breaches". Intellect UK Security & Privacy Group Meeting on "Security Breach Notification: Making it work for Consumers". Intellect UK offices, London. Presentation (20.10.2012) on "Future Developments Regarding the Data Protection Act and Freedom of Information Requests". Intellect UK offices, London.

Snyder, Francis (Spring 2004): Professor, LSE. Lecture for Module LL422 on "Globalisation, Regulation and Governance". London.

Southgate, Roger (26.6.2008): Vice President, Information Systems Audit and Control Association (ISACA). Presentation "An Introduction to the ISO/IEC 38500 – The Corporate Governance of IT". ISACA event, London. Presentation (16.2.2010) "An Introduction to Risk IT and its Role in the Delivery of Good Governance". BCS event, London.

Szombati, Bela (28.4.2004): Ambassador of Hungary to the UK. Speech on "Hungary's accession to the EU". "Enlightening the debate on good governance: European Union Enlargement" Conference, London.

Tachikawa, Keiji (12.10.2003), CEO, NTT DoCoMo. Presentation on "Mobile networks and innovation". "ITU Telecom World 2003" Conference, Geneva.

Thatcher, Mark (Spring 2003): Senior Lecturer, LSE. Lecture for Module GV403 on "Network Regulation". London.

Thielemann, Eiko (Spring 2003): Senior Lecturer, LSE. Lecture for Module GV351 on "The European Union: Government, Law and Policy". London.

Thomas, Richard (6.6.2007): Information Commissioner, Information Commissioner's Office (ICO). Keynote Speech on "The importance of data protection law". Hunton & Williams and UK ICO's launch of the Second Edition of "European Data Protection Law – Corporate Compliance and Regulation", London.

Thorne, John (12.11.2003): Senior Vice President, Verizon. Speech on "e-Communications technologies". "The Communications Industry – The next phase: Communications and e-Commerce Forum" Conference, London.

Tippett, Peter (15.5.2003): Chief Technologist, TruSecure. Presentation on "Risk Management *vs.* IT Security". TruSecure event, London.

Tippett, Peter (23.10.2003): Chief Technologist, TruSecure. Presentation on "Costs and Benefits of New Technologies". TruSecure event on "Winning the right security budget", London.

Treacy, Bridget (18.11.2010): Partner, Privacy and Information Management Practice, Hunton & Williams LLP. Presentation on "Data Security and Data Protection Guidelines for Offshoring and Outsourcing". Hunton & Williams LLP offices, London. Presentation (9.2.2011) on "Data and Business Intelligence – Smarter Outsourcing". Bird & Bird LLP offices, London. Presentation (7.6.2011) on "The Impact of EU Data Protection Legislation". Intellect UK offices, London.

Turner, Adair (5.2.2003): Vice-Chairman, Merrill Lynch Europe. Presentation on "investments in new technologies". Centre for Economic Performance, LSE. Presentation (28.4.2004) on "The Role of ICT Technology". "Enlightening the debate on good governance: European Union Enlargement" Conference, London.

Utsumi, Yoshio (12.10.2003): Secretary-General, ITU. Keynote Speech on "Helping the World Communicate". "ITU Telecom World 2003" Conference, Geneva.

Van den Bulck, Paul (24.5.2012): Partner, Technology, IP and Data Privacy, McGuire Woods LLP. Presentation on "Data Privacy in the EU – Current Case Law and Findings". Data privacy event, London.

Venables, Tony (28.4.2004): Professor, The Centre for Economic Performance (CEP), LSE. Presentation on "What drives variances in economic performance across Europe". LSE event on "Productivity: understanding regional differences", London.

Walden, Ian (Spring 2003): Reader, Centre for Commercial Law Studies, Queen Mary, University of London. Lectures on "Telecommunications Law" and "Technology Law". London.

Wall, Stephen (28.4.2003): EU Adviser to the UK Prime Minister. Speech on "Britain and the European Union". Public debate at LSE, London.

Walter, Norbert (29.1.2004): Chief Economist, Deutsche Bank Group. Speech on "Europe: Pillar of the World Economy – or just an appendix?". LSE, London.

Watkins, Kevin (15.1.2004): Head of Policy, Oxfam. Speech – "Rigged Rules, Double Standards". LSE event on "Global governance and global justice", London.

Watts, Jonathan (11-13.6.2003): Managing Director, Colt Telecom. Keynote Speech on "Mobile technology". "Internet World 2003" Conference, London.

Wheeler, David (12.11.2003): Vice Chairman, Credit Suisse First Boston (CSFB). Speech on "Investment in New Telecommunications Technologies". "The Communications Industry – The next phase: Communications and e-Commerce Forum" Conference, London.

Willey, Stuart (12.11.2003): General Counsel for Investment Business, FSA. Speech on "Supervision and regulation". "The Communications Industry – The next phase: Communications and e-Commerce Forum" Conference, London.

Wilson, George (11.2.2010): General Manager, Original Software. Presentation on "Five Easy Steps to Take Control of Your Data for Testing". BCS event, London.

Wilson, Roger (12.11.2003): Managing Director, European Competitive Telecoms Association. Speech on "Regulation, lobbying and business development". "The Communications Industry – The next phase: Communications and e-Commerce Forum" Conference, London.

Xercavins, Josep (1.4.2004): Co-ordinator, World Forum of Civil Society Networks – UBUNTU. Speech on "Civil Society". LSE event on "Reforming the UN and Other Institutions", London.

Yunus, Farid (19-20.11.2003): Analyst, Wireless/Mobile Europe, The Yankee Group. Presentation on "Exploring the full potential of wireless technology", "European Wireless Technology" Conference, London.

A2.3 Stakeholder events attended and observed

BCS event (17.11.2008) "Achieving an efficient and sustainable records management strategy", BCS Office, London.

BCS event (16.4.2009) "Intelligent Fraud Detection: Neural computing and artificial intelligence in the detection of payment fraud", BCS Office, London.

BCS event (21.5.2009) "Customer service oriented government: The challenge of public sector service transformation", BSC Office, London.

BCS event (11.2.2010) "Addressing Two Data Management Issues: The MIKE2.0 Open-source Standard for Information Management and Five Easy Steps to Take Control of Your Data for Testing", BCS offices, London.

BCS event (16.2.2010) "An Introduction to Risk IT and its Role in the Delivery of Good Governance", BBC offices, London.

BCS event (28.10.2010) "The Government Agenda on Personal Data", BCS offices, London.

BCS event (8.3.2011) "Are My Medical Records Safe?", NHS offices, London.

BERR stakeholder meeting (22.12.2005): "First Stakeholder Group on 2006 Review of the Electronic Communications Framework", London.

BERR stakeholder meeting (7.3.2006) "2006 Review of eCommunications", London.

BERR stakeholder meeting (11.5.2006) "UK Response to the 2006 EU Review of the regulatory framework for electronic communications and services". DTI Conference Centre, London.

BERR stakeholder meeting (27.7.2006) "2006 Review of eCommunications". London

BERR stakeholder meeting (19.11.2007) "2006 Review eCommunications Update". DTI Conference Centre, London.

Conference (23-25.4.2002): "InfoSecurity Europe 2002". Olympia, London.

Conference (29.4-1.5.2003): "InfoSecurity Europe 2003". Olympia, London.

Conference (24-26.4.2007): "InfoSecurity Europe 2007". Olympia, London.

Conference (2003): "Mediacast 2003". ExCel, London.

Conference (11-13.6.2003): "Internet World 2003". Earls Court, London.

Conference (13-15.11.2002): "Knowledge Management Europe 2002". Alexandra Palace, London.

Conference (21.5.2002): "Mediacast". ExCel, London.

Conference (30-31.10.2003): "Computer Security and Biometrics 2003". Queen Elizabeth II Conference Centre, London.

Conference (12.6.2003): "European Regulatory Compliance in IT". The London Capital Club, London.

Conference (12-14.10.2003): "ITU Telecom World 2003". Palexpo, Geneva. *This is a key meeting place for the global telecommunications policy makers, industry leaders and innovators. Exhibition features a comprehensive range of telecommunications-related products and services. I attended Seminars at the Forum (presentations by CEOs from the sector's key players, industry visionaries and top-level representatives from regulators, development agencies and governments around the globe).*

Conference (12.11.2003): "The Communications Industry – The Next Phase: Communications and E-Commerce Forum". Wilmer, Cutler & Pickering offices, Whitehall, London.

Conference (19-20.11.2003): "European Wireless Technology" (EWT 2003). Olympia, London.

Conference (27.11.2003): "Enterprise Security – Information Age" Conference. London.

Conference (25.2.2004): "EU Enlargement Seminar – opportunities for London businesses", Euro Info Centre, London Chamber of Commerce and Industry, London.

Conference (9-10.3.2004): "The Risk Management Expo 2004". ExCel, London.

Conference (21.4.2004): "eWorld 2004". The Russell Hotel, London.

Conference (28.4.2004): "Enlightening the debate on good governance: European Union Enlargement". The Federal Trust for Education and Research, European Parliament UK Office, London.

Conference (27-29.4.2004): "Information Security Europe". Olympia, London.

Conference (8.5.2004): "UACES Student Forum: Fifth Annual Southern Conference". St. John's College, University of Cambridge.

Conference (22.9.2004): "Mobile Content World 2004". ExCel, London.

Conference (13.10.2004): "Wireless Enterprise World 2004". ExCel, London.

Conference (18.10.2006): "Storage Expo". Olympia, London.

Conference (1.12.2010) Organised by JUSTICE: "The Privacy and the Law Conference 2010". Pinsent Masons LLP offices, London.

Conference (22-23 June 2011) "The 3rd Annual Sedona Conference on Cross-Border Discovery & Data Privacy". Lisbon.

DTI event (7.2.2003): "eContent Information Day". DTI Conference Centre, London.

DTI event (11.2.2003): "FP6 IST Information Day". Institute of Mechanical Engineers, Westminster, London.

DTI event (25.2.2003): "Technology-enhanced learning and access to cultural heritage – IST workshop". DTI Conference Centre, London.

DTI event (27.2.2003): "Towards a global dependability and security framework – IST workshop". DTI Conference Centre, London.

EEMA UK user group meeting (7.11.2000): "Experience of a PKI Infrastructure in a Corporate Environment". London.

EEMA Members Event (12-13.6.2001): EEMA Annual Conference, "e-Government & Public Sector Interest Group". Le Meridien, Montparnasse, Paris.

EEMA UK user group meeting (25.9.2001): Roundtable debate on the "European Electronic Signature Directive". Queen Elizabeth Conference Centre, London.

EEMA UK user group meeting (12.2.2002): "A legal information day for businesses and technology managers" – Presentation of eGovernance White Paper response. London.

EEMA UK user group meeting (10.9.2002): "Delivering High-integrity/Efficient e-Business Communications". hosted by Shell Information Technology, London.

EU Information Day (2.6.2003): "eAwareness for Europe – Information Security Awareness and the Role of Local Government". London.

Event (30.4.2007): "FS Regulatory Update". Ernst & Young offices, London.

Event (24.5.2012): "Mind the Gap: Navigating Data Privacy and Security Policies". McGuire Woods LLP offices, London.

Hunton & Williams LLP event (15.5.2007): "Security and data management issues in global sourcing transactions". Hunton & Williams LLP offices, London.

Hunton & Williams LLP and UK ICO event (6.6.2007): "European Data Protection law: Corporate compliance and regulation". Hunton & Williams LLP offices, London.

Hunton & Williams LLP event (18.11.2010): "Data Security and Data Protection Guidelines for Offshoring and Outsourcing". Hunton & Williams LLP offices, London.

Intellect UK stakeholder meeting (25.9.2006): "Security & Privacy Group: How to tackle data privacy and security issues in offshoring". Intellect UK Conference Suite, London.

Intellect UK stakeholder meeting (28.11.2006): "Information sharing and protection of privacy – the role of technology". Intellect UK Conference Suite, London.

Intellect UK stakeholder meeting (12.3.2007): "Data protection, surveillance and privacy in the workplace". Intellect UK Conference Suite, London.

Intellect UK stakeholder meeting (24.4.2007): "Security and Privacy, Offshoring and Outsourcing". Intellect UK Conference Suite, London.

Intellect UK stakeholder meeting (11.6.2007): "Privacy and Security Guidelines working group". Intellect UK Conference Suite, London.

Intellect UK stakeholder meeting (2.7.2007): "Security & Privacy Group: Security breach notification – Making it work for consumers". Intellect UK Conference Suite, London.

Intellect UK stakeholder meeting (24.9.2007): "Security and Privacy Group Meeting: Using computer forensics to prevent e-Crime". Intellect UK Conference Suite, London.

Intellect UK stakeholder meeting (12.11.2007): "Data breach notification scoping meeting". Intellect UK Conference Suite, London.

Intellect UK stakeholder meeting (20.6.2008): "Document Management and Collaborative Working Environments". Intellect UK Conference Suite, London.

Intellect UK stakeholder meeting (7.7.2008): "Security and Privacy Group: Effective Data Destruction – Does it exist?" Intellect UK Conference Suite, London.

Intellect UK stakeholder meeting (12.11.2008): "Document management seminar: Governance, Risk and Compliance". Intellect UK Conference Suite, London.

Intellect UK stakeholder meeting (27.11.2008): "Financial crime roundtable". Intellect UK Conference Suite, London.

Intellect UK stakeholder meeting (19.5.2009): "Data breach notification debate with the ICO and Lord Erroll". Intellect UK Conference Suite, London.

Intellect UK stakeholder meeting (27.7.2009): Information Sharing Group and Security & Privacy Group – "ICO Personal Information Online code of practice roundtable". Intellect UK Conference Suite, London.

Intellect UK stakeholder meeting (20.10.2010): "Future Developments Regarding the Data Protection Act and Freedom of Information Requests". Intellect UK Conference Suite, London.

Intellect UK stakeholder meeting (4.11.2010): Various Document & Content Management Group presentations. Intellect UK Conference Suite, London.

Intellect UK stakeholder meeting (9.2.2011): "Data and Business Intelligence – Smarter Outsourcing". Bird & Bird LLP offices, London.

Intellect UK stakeholder meeting (15.3.2011): "Information Management & Security: Government's Transparency & Privacy Review". Intellect UK Conference Suite, London.

Intellect UK stakeholder meeting (6.4.2011): "Panel Discussion – Policy Update: Bribery Act 2010". Intellect UK Conference Suite, London.

Intellect UK stakeholder meeting (7.6.2011), Information Management & Security Group: "The Impact of EU Data Protection Legislation". Intellect UK Conference Suite, London.

ICC event (12.12.2003): Interviews, Paris.

ISACA event (19.6.2007): "e-Symposium: Managing Enterprise Security Risk". RBS offices, London.

ISACA event (25.10.2007): "Managed access to data – the issues and risks". RBS offices, London.

ISACA event (22.5.2008): "CobiT Security Baseline Update". RBS offices, London.

ISACA event (26.6.2008): "An introduction to the ISO/IEC 38500:2008 – The corporate governance of information technology". RBS offices, London.

ISACA event (22.1.2009): "Data Protection and Security". RBS offices, London.

ISACA event (26.3.2009): "Risk and IT Risk Exposure". RBS offices, London.

ISACA event (23.4.2009): "An introduction to the Business Model for Information Security". RBS offices, London.

ISACA event (25.6.2009): "Emerging standards in software security assurance". RBS Offices, London.

ISACA event (24.8.2010): "e-Symposium: Security, Privacy, and eDiscovery in the Cloud". London.

ISACA event (28.6.2012): "The Risk Management and Information Governance Perspective of the EU Data Protection Directive". Moore Stephens LLP offices, London.

ISPA event (23.2.2009): "Annual Parliamentary Advisory Forum: e-Crime Reduction". Portcullis House, London.

IST conference (22-24.11.1999): European Commission-sponsored event. Helsinki.

LSE event (6.6.2002): "Global Economic Governance: the corporate connection". London.

LSE event (5.2.2003): "What's wrong with Europe's Economy". London.

LSE event (28.4.2003): Public Debate – "Should Britain join the Euro?" Centre for Economic Performance, London.

LSE event (13.10.2003): Politics and Economics Debates – "Globalisation – where next?" London.

LSE event (18.11.2003): Politics and Economics Debates – "UK-US: The special relationship – is it special?" London.

LSE event (15.1.2004): "Global governance and global justice". World Economic Forum, LSE, London.

LSE event (19.1.2004): Policy Presentation – "A constitution for Europe". London.

LSE event (29.1.2004): Economic Presentation – "Europe: Pillar of the World Economy – or just an appendix?" London.

LSE event (17.2.2004): Department of Media and Communications – "The Future of the UK e-Government". London.

LSE event (25-27.2.2004): Lionel Robbins Memorial Lecture – "Understanding Institutions", covering Institutions and the Prosperity of Nations, Towards a Theory of Institutions, and Institutional Persistence and Institutional Change. London.

LSE event (18.3.2004): Miliband Lecture – "Politics and power in the network society". London.

LSE event (1.4.2004): Debate – "Reforming UN and other Institutions". London.

LSE event (20.5.2005): "Response and Responsibility: the global partnership for aid and development". London.

Presentation (10.7.2012): "Harness a Next-generation Information Platform: Move Your Business Forward with Meaning-based Data Protection". Autonomy, The Ritz Hotel, London.

Presentation (16.5.2002): "Bringing Trust & Security to an Internet World". London.

Presentation (14.3.2002): "The Costs and Benefits of Compliance – Impact of Regulation on UK companies". Harrier Zeuros offices, London.

Shepherd & Wedderburn LLP event (12.10.2006): "Data Protection and Freedom of Information: Hand in Hand?" Shepherd & Wedderburn LLP offices, London.

TruSecure event (23.10.2003): "Winning the Right Security Budget". The Renaissance Chancery Court Hotel, London.

A2.4 Archival Searches

National Statistics Library, Office for National Statistics (ONS) (August 2003): 1 Drummond Gate, London.

Representation of the European Commission in the UK (March 2003): Meetings with Jeffry Lamb, Information Support Unit; Ian Barber, European Commission London; Jeremy O'Sullivan, Press Office, EC Representation in the UK to discuss the responsibilities of the UK's Commission representation and access to resources. London.

Appendix 3: Survey questionnaire

The survey questionnaire below was provided to the survey participants both in hardcopy and in electronic format. For further details refer to Chapter Six: "Data Analysis and Survey Results".

Survey on Stakeholder Participation in Information and Communication Technologies (ICT) Governance, Regulations and Standards

Topics covered:

- impact on organisations,
- compliance, and
- participation in the decision-making process.

SECTION A: Participation in Decision-Making Processes for Regulations and Standards

(1) How would you describe your and your organisation's attitude towards decision-making?	Strongly Agree ☺	Agree	Disagree	Strongly disagree ☹
I like to have responsibility.	☐	☐	☐	☐
I believe that decision-makers have a more stressful life.	☐	☐	☐	☐
I prefer to make private decisions instead of decisions on behalf of my organisation.	☐	☐	☐	☐

(2) What is YOUR organisation's active participation in the decision-making on ICT issues via associations, task forces, and committees? NOTE: Please tick all answers that apply to YOUR organisation	Policy Advice (Please specify if possible)	Submission of papers/ consultation responses	Joint hosting of events/ conferences	Participation in workshops
In your own country (at National Level), your organisation participates in:				
1. Industry associations such as chambers of trade and commerce, trade associations, telecom/Internet associations (please specify:)	☐	☐	☐	☐
2. National standard institutes (please specify:)	☐	☐	☐	☐
3. Government initiatives such as advisory groups/ steering committees for government/ national eCommerce Action Plan (please specify:)	☐	☐	☐	☐
4. National programmes and initiatives e.g. participation in consultations, funding for research and technological development (RTD)	☐	☐	☐	☐

(2 continued) What is YOUR organisation's active participation in the decision-making on ICT issues via associations, task forces and committees? NOTE: Please tick all answers that apply to YOUR organisation	Policy Advice (Please specify if possible)	Submission of papers/ consultation responses	Joint hosting of events/ conferences	Participation in workshops
At the European Level, your organisation participates in:				
1. Industry associations, such as Association of European Chambers of Commerce and Industry (EUROCHAMBERS)	☐	☐	☐	☐

(2 continued) What is YOUR organisation's active participation in the decision-making on ICT issues via associations, task forces and committees? NOTE: Please tick all answers that apply to YOUR organisation	Policy Advice (Please specify if possible)	Submission of papers/ consultation responses	Joint hosting of events/ conferences	Participation in workshops
2. **European Standards Institutes** a) European Telecommunications Standards Institute (ETSI) b) European Committee for Electronic Standardisation (CENELEC) c) European Committee for Standardisation (CEN-ISSS) d) Others (e.g. European Safety Federation)	☐	☐	☐	☐
3. Fora connected to EU institutions: advisory group/ task force/ committee, e.g. European Round Table of Industrialists, ICANN Government Advisory Committee	☐	☐	☐	☐
4. European programmes and initiatives, e.g. Framework Programmes (FP6)/ European Research Area (ERA), Eureka, eContent	☐	☐	☐	☐
At the International Level, your organisation participates in:				
1. Industry associations/ interest groups, a) Internet Security Forum, I-4, WiFi-Alliance, etc. (please specify:)	☐	☐	☐	☐
b) International Chamber of Commerce (ICC)	☐	☐	☐	☐
2. International Telecommunications Union (ITU)	☐	☐	☐	☐
Organisation for Economic Cooperation and Development (OECD)	☐	☐	☐	☐

(2 continued) What is YOUR organisation's active participation in the decision-making on ICT issues via associations, task forces and committees? NOTE: Please tick all answers that apply to YOUR organisation	Policy Advice (Please specify if possible)	Submission of papers/ consultation responses	Joint hosting of events/ conferences	Participation in workshops
UN organisations e.g. UN Commission on International Trade Law (UNCITRAL), ICT Task Force, World Summit on the Information Society (WSIS)	☐	☐	☐	☐
3 Global programmes and initiatives, e.g. Internet Engineering Task Force, World Wide Web Consortium	☐	☐	☐	☐

Please, could you tell us:

1. Who represents your organisation at these consultative for a (position of the person, not his/her name)?

2. What function does your representative have?

3. How/ Why were these individuals selected?

(3) How satisfied is your organisation with the activities of these stakeholders in the policy and standards-setting processes?	Strongly satisfied ☺	Satisfied	Dissatisfied	Strongly Dissatisfied ☹
I. At Sub-national Level				
Industry associations	☐	☐	☐	☐
Non-profit organisations (e.g. consumer associations)	☐	☐	☐	☐
II. At National Level				
Politicians/ Parliaments in the country of your organisation	☐	☐	☐	☐
III. At European/ Global Level				

European regulation/ standards institutes	☐	☐	☐	☐
International organisations that issue guidelines and recommendations, such as the International Telecommunications Union (ITU), OECD, WTO etc.	☐	☐	☐	☐
Comments: How could involvement in these processes be improved?				

(4) Given that existing and new legislation and standards are being rigidly enforced for corporate governance regulation and all forms of electronic communication...

How does your organisation participate in policy, regulatory and standards-setting activities at the EU level?	☐	participation in conferences/ workshops
	☐	response to consultations
	☐	joint hosting of events/ conferences (1-2 days)
	☐	sending experts to hearings/ participation in evalutions (1-5 days)
	☐	studies such as feasibility studies and research projects (3-6 months)
	☐	pilots that involve different companies accross Europe (1-2 years)
	☐	services contracts (e.g. secondment of experts for 1-2 years)
	☐	continued involvement in committees (e.g. European Round Table of Industrialists, Data Protection working group)
	☐	Other forms (please specify)

To stimulate growth and development in Europe, the EU has allocated EURO 17.5 billion for Research and Development. It is planned to raise this budget to EURO 30 billion for the next Framework Programme (FP7). Has your organisation requested and received support from your government or from EU-funded programmes?	☐	no
	☐	yes – we have been successful
	☐	yes – but our proposal was rejected
	☐	planned
What form of support has your organisation received?	☐	financial support
	☐	dissemination of results
	☐	RTD co-operation with other companies/ organisations
	☐	knowledge- exchange and networking

(5) Here are some statements that people often make when they talk about publicly funded programmes. To what extent do you agree or disagree?	Strongly Agree ☺	Agree	Disagree	Strongly Disagree ☹
"EU programmes give organisations/ industry the opportunity to actively influence the decision-making process."	☐	☐	☐	☐
"EU programmes are hidden subsidies for industries in trouble/ regions with economic problems."	☐	☐	☐	☐
"EU programmes are a waste of tax-payers' money."	☐	☐	☐	☐
"The same organisations/ people always participate in EU projects and activities."	☐	☐	☐	☐
"The money/ effort could be invested better."	☐	☐	☐	☐

"Not everybody has the same opportunity to participate in EU programmes or to participate in shaping the regulatory framework for EU ICT policy and standards."	☐	☐	☐	☐
In one sentence, what is your attitude toward European-funded programmes:				

(6) Thinking of the following reasons to participate in funded programmes, could you indicate how important each one is for your organisation:	Very Important	Important	Not very important	Not important
To secure funding for research, and development, and for new product/ service development	☐	☐	☐	☐
To generate revenue for your organisation	☐	☐	☐	☐
To make profits	☐	☐	☐	☐
To market the products and services of your organisation	☐	☐	☐	☐
To influence the policy-making process/ standards developments	☐	☐	☐	☐
To find partners with the same interests in knowledge exchange and network building	☐	☐	☐	☐
To understand regulations and standards and to get involved at a very early stage	☐	☐	☐	☐
To assist with rolling out our products and services EU-wide	☐	☐	☐	☐
Other reasons (please specify)				

SECTION B: Impact of Information and Communication Technology Regulations and Standards on your Organisation

(7) Please help us to assess the impact of ICT regulation and standards on your organisation:				
Some stakeholders feel that regulation has a negligible impact on their organisation. Others believe it has a very big impact. Which comes closest to your belief?	☐ very big impact	☐ big impact	☐ small impact	☐ no impact

(8) Compliance, Regulation and Industry Standards have become a major issue for many organisations. Non-compliance can lead to competitive disadvantage or penalties. In which areas is your organisation specifically interested?	very interested	Fairly interested	Slightly interested	Not interested at all
I. Corporate governance / competition law				
Sarbanes-Oxley, OECD Principles of Corporate Governance, etc.	☐	☐	☐	☐
Consumer protection	☐	☐	☐	☐
Contract law, incl. on-line contracts, distance contracts	☐	☐	☐	☐
Competition law (Protection of new market entrants from unfair trade practices of established companies)	☐	☐	☐	☐
Dispute resolution/ settlement	☐	☐	☐	☐
II. Communications and infrastructure				
Communications services (new framework for electronic communications services)	☐	☐	☐	☐
Networks standards and initiatives (Trans-European networks, networked businesses and governments)	☐	☐	☐	☐

(7) Please help us to assess the impact of ICT regulation and standards on your organisation:				
Internet regulation and activities (e.g. eEurope, security framework, e-working, e-accessibility, e-safety, e-commerce, broadband)	☐	☐	☐	☐
Digital content (eContent)	☐	☐	☐	☐
IT platforms/ operating systems, protocols (TCP/IP) and embedded systems	☐	☐	☐	☐
III. Security and intangible property rights				
Data protection and privacy rights	☐	☐	☐	☐
Copyright and related rights in the Information Society	☐	☐	☐	☐
Cybercrime	☐	☐	☐	☐
Electronic signatures/ digital certificates/ Trusted Third Parties	☐	☐	☐	☐
E-Business 'codes of conduct'/ trust seals (for websites)	☐	☐	☐	☐
Information Security Standards (BS7799/ ISO 17799, 'OECD Guidelines for the Security of Information Systems and Networks')	☐	☐	☐	☐
IV. Commercial use				
Taxation and electronic commerce	☐	☐	☐	☐
Payment systems (e.g. SET)	☐	☐	☐	☐
V. Sector-targeted activities (defined in eEurope)				

(7) Please help us to assess the impact of ICT regulation and standards on your organisation:				
e-learning, e-research and access to cultural heritage	☐	☐	☐	☐
e-government	☐	☐	☐	☐
e-health	☐	☐	☐	☐
e-transport	☐	☐	☐	☐
Other compliance areas in which you are interested:				
Which of these issues have caused your organisation to represent its views to EU institutions or the national government, or to encourage action by intermediary organisations and associations?				

(9) Who is involved in reviewing and assessing the potential threats or opportunities presented by regulatory initiatives for your organisation? We are interested in his/her position in your organisation.	
Chairman	☐
Board	☐
Head of Department	☐
Senior Manager	☐
Specialist – Legal Advisor	☐
Specialist – Internal Audit	☐
Specialist – Public Affairs or Government Affairs Representative	☐
Other (please specify)	☐

(10) Many organisations have difficulties following new regulatory developments, for instance electronic signatures, rules for conducting business online, data protection, or new technical standards. How do you keep yourself and your organisation informed (sources of information)?	Usually	Sometimes	Never
1. Talk directly to local authorities	☐	☐	☐
2. Talk directly to national regulator/ government institutions	☐	☐	☐
Read national government publications	☐	☐	☐
3. Talk directly to the EU institutions	☐	☐	☐
Read EU publications	☐	☐	☐
Influence the agenda through participation in EU workshops and committees	☐	☐	☐
Participate in conferences/ road shows/ Information days	☐	☐	☐
Use a contact point in Brussels	☐	☐	☐
4. Membership of (industry) associations	☐	☐	☐
5. Debate in workshops and events at international level	☐	☐	☐
6. Talk to other companies	☐	☐	☐
7. Get advice from professional law/ accountancy/ consultancy firms	☐	☐	☐
8. Read press and media coverage on a specific issue	☐	☐	☐
Other forms that you use to keep yourself updated			

SECTION C: Opinions on the Regulatory Framework for Electronic Communications

(11) The following are some opinions about EU ICT regulations and standards-setting. To what extent do you agree or disagree with the following statements?	Strongly agree ☺	Agree	Disagree	Strongly disagree ☹
"EU regulation and Europe-wide applicable standards strengthen the EU ICT industry in the world."	☐	☐	☐	☐
"EU ICT regulation is forcing European industry to adopt many detailed norms and regulations that we don't want or need."	☐	☐	☐	☐

"Telecoms liberalisation in Europe was a success."	☐	☐	☐	☐
"The European mobile phone market (GSM) has been a success story (as compared to the US) because of EU telecoms legislation and liberalisation."	☐	☐	☐	☐
"UMTS (3rd generation of mobile phones) will be as successful as GSM"	☐	☐	☐	☐
"My country has been successful in influencing EU regulations/ standards."	☐	☐	☐	☐
"My organisation/ company has been successful in influencing EU regulations/standards."	☐	☐	☐	☐
"Only large multinational organisations can really influence regulations."	☐	☐	☐	☐
"EU regulations and standards are industry oriented."	☐	☐	☐	☐

In one sentence, what is your opinion?

(12) As you may know, the EU adopted a New Regulatory Framework for electronic communications infrastructure and associated services, which was implemented EU-wide by 25 July 2003. How satisfied are you with the following aspects of the framework?

If you don't know anything about this subject, please skip this question.	Very satisfied ☺	Satisfied	Dissatisfied	Strongly dissatisfied ☹
Common Regulatory Framework Directive (2002/21/EC)	☐	☐	☐	☐
Access and Interconnection Directive	☐	☐	☐	☐
Authorisation Directive	☐	☐	☐	☐
Universal Service and User's Rights Directive	☐	☐	☐	☐

Data Protection and Privacy Directive	☐	☐	☐	☐
Directive on Competition in Communication Services Markets	☐	☐	☐	☐
Regulation on Unbundled Access to the Local Loop	☐	☐	☐	☐
Guidelines on Market Analysis of Significant Market Power	☐	☐	☐	☐
List of Standards and/or Specifications for eCommunications	☐	☐	☐	☐

We would appreciate any comments you have on this New Framework, such as: Have you participated in shaping this Framework? How? What are your views on this Framework?

If you feel that you are not familiar enough with the New Framework directive, you can find information at http://europa.eu.int/information_society/topics/telecoms/regulatory/new_rf/index_en.htm

SECTION D: FINAL COMMENTS If you have any further comments about the issues raised, please use the space provided below.

What should be regulated/ de-regulated in the future?

How could participation in ICT regulation and standards-setting be improved?

Further comments

SECTION E: PERSONAL DETAILS

(E.1) Please, could you provide some details about yourself?

Name (voluntary)

Age	☐ less than 20	☐ 20-30	☐ 31-40	☐ 41-50	☐ 51-60	☐ 61 -

What is your current job title/ role?

Email address		@
Website	www.	

(E.2) Please, could you provide some organisational information

What is the name of your organisation?						
In which country do you presently work?				In which city?		
Which best describes the sector you work in?	☐ business & industry		☐ administration & government		☐ non-commercial sector (NGOs)	
How many employees work for your organisation?	☐ 1-9	☐ 10-49	☐ 50-499	☐ 500-999	☐ 1,000-9,999	☐ 10,000 +
What is the focus?	☐ local	☐ regional	☐ national	☐ EU-wide	☐ international	
HQ location	☐ EU	☐ East Europe	☐ USA	☐ Asia	☐ Japan	☐ other

Appendix 4: Survey Report and Data Sheet

The survey report and data sheet below summarize the survey results and was provided to the survey participants. For further details refer to Chapter Six: "Data Analysis and Survey Results".

EU Regulatory Compliance Survey Final Report

EU Survey: Governance, Regulations,and Standards-setting

1. Methodology

Prior key initiatives

The research effort for this report comprised a number of key initiatives:

- Substantial desk research into national, European, and international (ICT) standards and regulations.
- A series of meetings and interviews held with leading corporate and regulatory figures, such as the European Commission, European standards institutes (CEN), national standards institutes (BSI), industry associations (ICC, CBI, EEMA) and international organisations (EU representation to the UN, ITU, OECD).
- The research-coordinator's 9 years of experience in working for and with the European regulator, as well as his practical experience in advising the industry on issues of corporate governance regulation and regulatory compliance audits, which he leveraged to design the survey questionnaire.
- A test survey in March 2004 to ensure that the questions addressed the interests of the stakeholders and the objectives of the research project.

The Survey

The survey was conducted between April and September 2004. The questionnaire was distributed to:

- Selected individuals that the researcher had met personally at EU workshops, corporate governance and compliance presentations, and other topic-related events;
- Selected participants in EU Framework Programme and European Standardisation Body initiatives; and
- Active participants in various European and international associations.

Response

In total, 224 questionnaires were returned, from which 202 were selected and assessed for this report. The remaining 22 questionnaires were either less than 50% completed or the respondents came from countries outside the 15 EU Member States (before April 1). However, responses to open questions were considered from all participants.

Survey objectives

This survey sought to identify compliance issues facing business organisations, specifically:

(a) How organisations perceive corporate governance and ICTs regulation
(b) How stakeholders influence regulation
(c) What their interests are, and
(d) Where the EU regulator and standards-bodies could improve regulation and the decision-making process (governance)

Presentation of results

Full survey results are available in an annexe to this report (data sheets).

Executive Summary

A raft of general and ICT-specific regulations have come into force in recent years. In 1998 the deregulation of the European telecommunications market led to a re-shaping of the whole industry, followed by cross-country mergers and acquisitions. The Internet forced the regulator to respond with new

2. Highlights: *Issues at a glance*

Most organisations participate/ influence regulation and standards via national and international ***industry associations***.

- 78% participate in national industry associations,
- 50% contribute to issues via European industry associations, and
- 30% are involved in activities of international industry associations and interest groups.

Stakeholders are most satisfied with activities of ***industry associations*** (66%), while only 33% are ***satisfied with politicians of their own countries***.

58% are (very) satisfied with the work of the ***European Regulator and Standards Institutes***, and 60% welcome the work of international organisations such as OECD and ITU.

Preferred participation is via ***conferences & workshops*** (82%).

65% of the respondents believe that "***the same organisations/ people always participate in EU projects and activities***", and 68% believe that "EU programmes give organisations/ industry the opportunity to ***actively influence the decision making process***".

A majority of 75% agreed that participation in ***funded programmes*** helps them to understand regulations and standards, and to get involved at a very early stage.

Nearly three respondents in four (71%) reported that regulations and standards have a big or very big impact on their organisation.

Participants in this survey were most interested in ***Internet regulation and security*** (83%), followed by ***data protection and privacy rights*** (80%) and ***digital content*** (74%).

83% believe that "EU regulation and Europe-wide applicable standards ***strengthen the EU ICT industry in the world***", but only 32% believe that "their organisation/company has been successful in influencing EU regulations/standards".

regulations, to strengthen competition, protect user and consumer rights (data protection, copyright, distance contracts, distance marketing), and to beef up Internet security. The Regulatory Framework for electronic communications infrastructure and associated services, which was implemented EU-wide by 25 July 2003, consolidates most of the regulation in the new economy.

After the Enron revelations surfaced, corporate governance dominated the political and business agenda. Europe has already prepared its answer, the modernised 8th Directive on "Reinforcing the statutory audit in the EU", to US-led governance regulation (Sarbanes-Oxley Act).

Regulations and new standards to support interoperability and new applications are going to stay at the top of directors' agendas for the foreseeable future; therefore, European organisations have not only to understand regulations and standards, they have to become actively involved in shaping them. If organisations refuse to participate in this process, they, consumers and users, and in the long-term Europe's economy, will pay the price.

This survey revealed concerns among stakeholders in regulations and standards, and answers how the process may be improved so as to develop "better regulation" and standards that strengthen European industry. We sincerely hope that the results of this survey will help the stakeholders and the regulators develop "good regulations", and encourage a wider participation in the decision-making process.

Our deepest thanks go to all the contributors to the design of the survey, and to the survey respondents for sharing their insights.

3. Detailed Results

SECTION D: Respondent Demographics

Business sector

66% of the respondents worked for the "business & industry" sector (incl. bluechip companies, telecoms operators, consultancies, law firms and Small and Medium-sized Enterprises (SMEs)), 13% for "administration and government", 9% for "universities" and 12% for "non-governmental organisations" (NGOs).

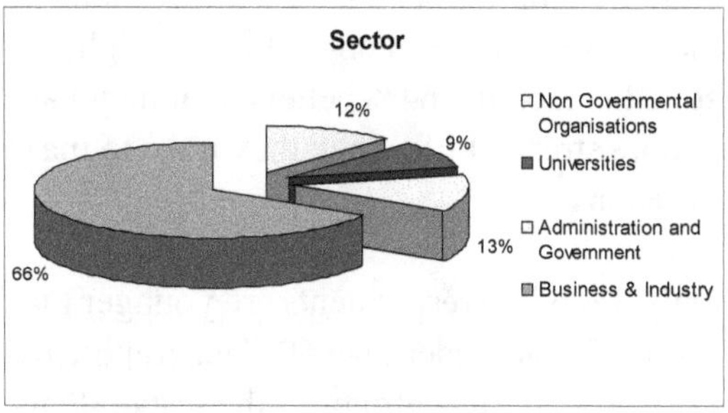

Profile of the organisations

39% of the organisations that participated in this survey had less than 49 employees, 24% had between 50-499 employees, and 37% had more than 500 staff. Over half (64%+) have a European and international focus, while only 13% described themselves as local and regional players. The majority of organisations had their headquarters in a Member State of the European Union (89%). With 7% of organisations having their headquarters in the US, American multinationals are the strongest influencer, outside the EU, over European policy and standards.

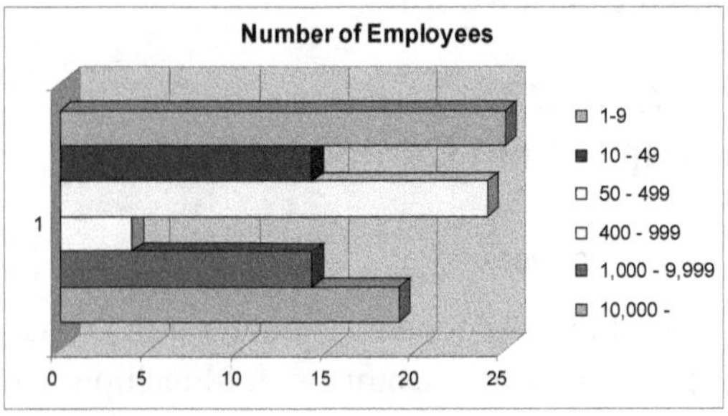

Profile of the respondents

96% of the respondents "like to have responsibility" and 76% prefer to make business decisions instead of private decisions. The commitment of our survey participants to their work and decision-making is high, despite the fact that 64% believe that they have a more stressful life when they have to make decisions.

Only 3% of the respondents are younger than 30 and 7% are older than 60. The graphic below shows the age groups of the respondents.

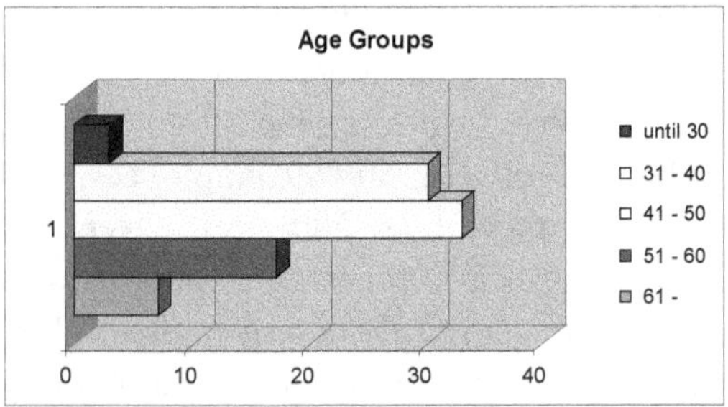

Geographical information

As one would expect most of the participants came from the largest EU countries – France, Germany, Italy, Spain and the United Kingdom. It should be noted that, with only 5% of the replies, Spain is underrepresented compared to an average 12% - 15% response from the other big EU countries. Belgium with many European and international organisations, reflects more a European than a national view, accounting for 14% of the total respondents. 202 responses from all 15 EU countries have been considered for this survey.

Assurance of representative results

The equal spread across countries (per size), age groups and business sectors justifies the conclusion that this survey is representative in its socio-demographic factors.

The response rate, too, is sufficient to base scientific conclusions on this survey. During assessment of the results, it was found that the last 50 responses changed the scale factor such as to allow a direct comparison of the grade of dis-/agreement for each question to within +/- 4.

SECTION A: Participation in Decision-Making Processes for Regulations and Standards

QUESTION 2: What is your organisation's active participation in decision-making on ICT issues via associations, task forces and committees?

The organisations surveyed expressed a clear preference for participating in regulations and standards discussions *via* national and international industry associations compared to other fora: 78% participate in national industry associations and 50% contribute to issues via European industry associations (*e.g.* Eurochambers). *Circa* 30% are involved in the activities of international industry associations and interest groups such as the

Internet Security Forum, the Wifi-Alliance, the International Telecommunications Union (ITU) or the International Chamber of Commerce (ICC).

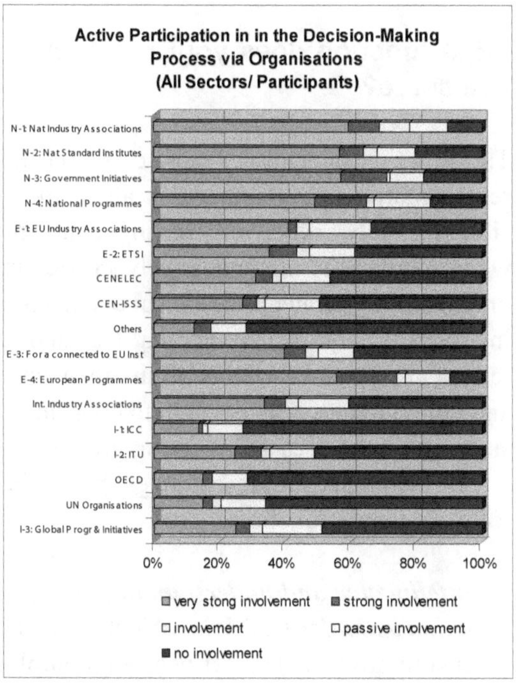

The data gathered by this survey also indicate that European programmes are considered an effective way to influence decision-making processes on ICT issues (80%). Even if the work of OECD and UN organisations is highly valued (see next question), participation is the lowest in these international organisations. The following diagram allows a direct comparison between the participation of business organisations (blue bar) and non-business organisations like public administration & government, universities and NGOs (red bar).

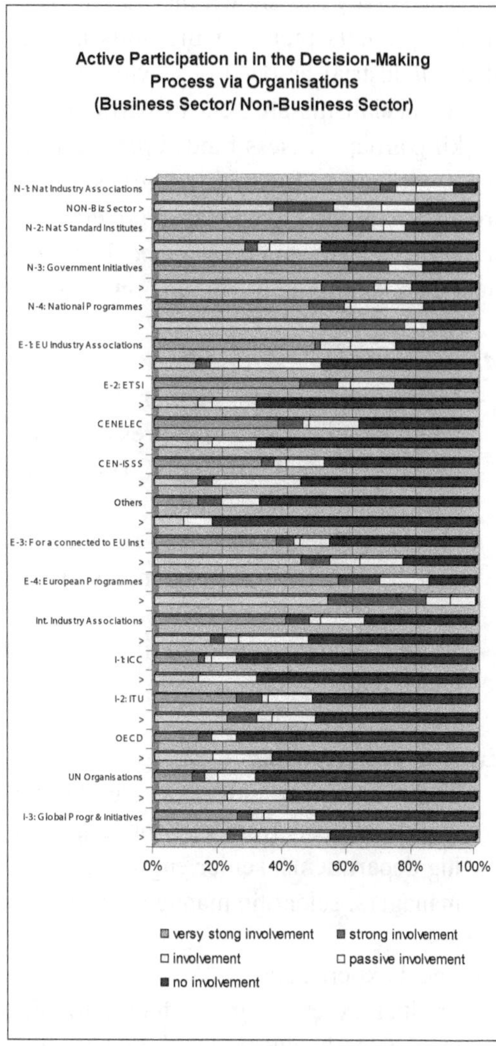

Who represents your organisation at these consultative forums?

Most organisations have no single person designated to represent their views at any of these fora. There is huge variation across the diverse departments and levels in organisations. The larger the organisation is, the more diverse the involvement.

The choice of whom to send is influenced by geography, the topic, and by the responsibilities of the representative.

The survey has shown that top management represents their organisations in most of the industrial associations, while experts in the specialisms are sent to participate in working groups, assess funded programmes, and contribute to focused initiatives. Larger organisations have designated government- or public- affairs managers who liase efficiently and continually with the regulator.

Management
- Managing Director/ Partner/ Chairman/ CEO/ President and Vice-President
- Chief Technical Officer (CTO), Chief Operational Officer (COO)
- Heads of Departments, *e.g.* Head of Research, Head of professional services, and
- Project managers and senior advisors/ consultants.

Experts in specialisms
- Technical expert advisors, *e.g.* IT network architects from software engineering departments, senior engineers, R&D managers, scientific managers, researchers
- Legal experts, and
- Product experts, *e.g.* product marketing managers, business development managers.

Specialists dealing with the regulator/ standards
- Public affairs managers, *e.g.* government relations managers, special interest group coordinators
- Product compliance managers, standards managers/coordinators, certification managers, and
- Legal and compliance officers, VP Technology Policy & Standards, regulation managers.

Others
- Senior civil servants/ officials
- Professors of academic departments, and
- Research fellows.

What function does your representative serve?

The function depends in most cases on the representative. (Top) managers are responsible for networking and raising concerns when regulations may negatively impact an organisation's strategy. Technical experts are involved in working groups that (re-)define technical standards. Global affairs managers and chief strategy officers help to coordinate steering committees and working groups.

In summary, representatives have the following main functions:

- ***Intelligence and understanding of regulations/standards***: Main objective is to ensure products and services are compliant with international standards, and getting ideas for additional product features for subsequent versions.
- ***Representation of the organisation's/ company's business interest***: Main aim is to articulate an organisation's position, stimulate discussion, raise concerns and initiate actions, and make worth-while proposals for improving regulations and standards in industry's and consumer's interests.
- ***Exchange of information***: This can have educational, research or know-how benefits.
- ***Lobbying and influencing decision-makers***: To persuade decision-makers to decide in ways aligned with a business organisation's strategy.

- ***Coordination of experts' activities***: This can include acting as an advisor or chairing working groups.

How/Why were these individuals selected?

Representatives were selected for a wide range of reasons. The most common are:

- ***Responsibility***: *e.g.* for delivery of product solutions internally and to end-users.
- ***Relevant knowledge and expertise***: in the subject matter field.
- ***Appointment***: by management/ the board, or election to this function, based on responsibility and expertise. In some cases seniority is relevant.
- ***Best individuals for representation***: due to personal networking, liaison experience, communications and language skills, and being most successful at making an impact on decision-making.

QUESTION 3: How satisfied is your organisation with the activities of these stakeholders in the diverse policy and standards-setting processes?

As the previous answer already implies, stakeholders are the most satisfied with the work of industry associations (66%). The degree of satisfaction is slightly higher when the responses of the business sector only are considered (71%).

60% of all the respondents are satisfied with the work of international organisations such as the ITU, OECD and WTO, compared to 24% who expressed dissatisfaction.

National politicians and parliaments are considered the worst conveyers of stakeholder interests. Only 33% of the organisations are satisfied, while a majority of 49% are dissatisfied with their elected parliamentarians. 18% had no view on the issue.

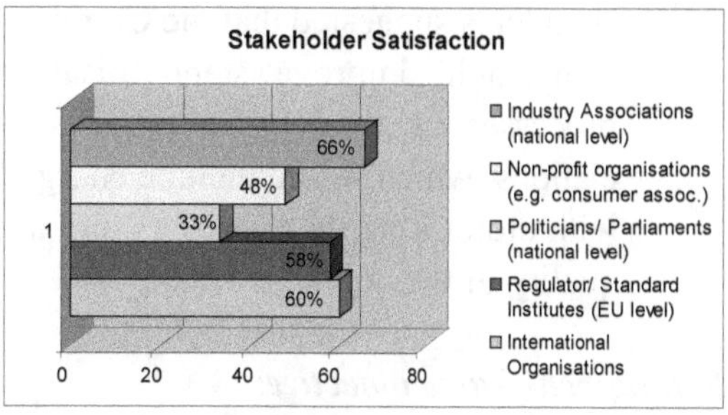

How could involvement in policy and standards-setting processed be improved?

Re-defining or clarifying the responsibilities of the regulator and stakeholders:

- The level of engagement of industry and standards bodies should be re-defined. This should include pre-defined selection criteria for deciding which organisations participate, *e.g.* representation of consumer interests or a track-record of launching new products in Europe.
- Respondents working for regulators and government bodies wished for the private sector, as contributor and driver of standards, to keep or even increase its influence, in order to guarantee that commercial needs will be met, benefiting consumers as well through the interoperability of products, greater choice, and reductions in prices.
- Civil society, which has limited resources, could play an advisory role through participation in consultations, like all other stakeholders.
- Many respondents believed that EU institutes are becoming less willing to be involved in standards-setting. They

also believed that these institutions transfer too much responsibility and funding to just three official European standards-setting bodies. Some respondents suggested that the Commission could improve standardisation processes by funding industry associations, which would then be charged with monitoring the processes and the quality of the output.

Setting achievable objectives:

The decisional processes that lead to new policies and standards could be improved by setting clearer objectives. The objective should be closely oriented to practical issues by considering real industry needs, which would help increase stakeholder buy-in and increase participation in standardisation processes.

As main objectives stakeholders mentioned:

(a) Harmonisation across Europe;

(b) Allowing needed flexibility, *i.e.* more attention to OPEN standards and codes of conduct (in lieu of formal regulations);

(c) Defining tangible output for stakeholders in the policy and standards-setting process, *e.g.* a targeted x% increase in private investment in RTD correlated with EU spending in RTD; and

(d) Improving project management components, such as timeframe, costs, and deliverables.

Stakeholder awareness campaign:

- Commercial pressures are not always understood by international civil servants. Often, stakeholder groups have a rather narrow view of the needs of other participants.
- The biggest obstacle to meeting the objectives of the working groups/committees is the fact that politicians, industry and other stakeholders often only pursue their own interests and seem to be more concerned with ensuring their mutual competitive advantage than with being cooperative. Cooperation is the foundation of standardisation and a speedy implementation of new rules/regulations for the new economy. If stakeholders hesitate to make compromises, then the deployment of standards often gets interrupted; therefore, the focus should be on identifying common goals and building a stronger relationship between all levels. Stakeholders should refrain from purely administrative attitudes. This would help to improve decisional processes as a whole.

Recognition of the international dimension of standards:

- Some respondents opined that there is an urgent need to become less "EU-egocentric" and to open-up to discussions with non-EU regulators and standards bodies. The global information society is borderless, only jurisdictions and lack of technical interoperability create virtual borders.
- Europe will be put at a disadvantage *versus* the US, Japan and Korea if Europe can't respond fast to new regulatory and standards requirements. Product lifecycles generally start in the US and the Far East, before the products enter the European market. Closer cooperation on an international level could speed up this process.

Funding and resources:

- Some groups, such as academic institutions and SMEs, consider lack of funding to be the main reason for their poor attendance of standards-setting workshops and committees.
- Examples of funding mentioned were better support for defraying travelling costs, *per diem* remuneration and investment in the dissemination of information.
- Some respondents stressed the importance of defining the criteria for funding. Currently one of the most important funding criteria are regional factors (structural funding), while other criteria such as industrial sectors and the size of companies are neglected. SMEs have needs different to large companies, which are often not sufficiently addressed.

Open dialogue and more flexibility in the implementation of regulations and standards:

- Greater flexibility in the attitude of the governmental delegates from Member States towards a more open stakeholder dialogue would speed up the process.
- Most important, for a broad acceptance of new regulations and standards a broader participation is needed. All industry players should have the opportunity to participate pro-actively in an open and transparent process.

Improving the communication and dissemination of information:

- In the view of many respondents improving accessibility and transparency has priority. A better understanding of the standardisation issues at national level and better information for all the stakeholders could improve the quality of participation. Also, some stakeholder groups such as academics feel that they are underrepresented in the consultation process. They wish to be invited to relevant workshops and kept better informed.
- Very important is the dissemination of results. Most of the reports and presentations of working groups are available on the Internet, but interested parties are often not aware of where to find this information.

Improving management processes:

- European business organisations are often diffuse and have divergent interests. Some believe that this has led to most proceedings being controlled by American and Asian lobbyists, which can be sometimes good, but not always.
- Leadership is necessary if the process is to become more efficient and the time-frame for implementation is narrowed.
- Many respondents believe the current process is time-consuming and that the need is urgent to reduce the time span from agenda-setting to consensus to implementation. Digitalisation and convergence have accelerated the speed of innovation, which demands new or revised regulations and standards. However, too many meetings and workshops are required to satisfy all stakeholders, and some stakeholders lack the resources for continual involvement. Sometimes it would even be better to conclude that no common standards are in range, than to dispute

endlessly with no certainty that an agreement will be ever reached.

QUESTION 4: How does your organisation participate in policy, regulation and standards-setting processes at the EU level?

88% of all respondents participate in conferences and workshops, 74% reply to public consultations, but only 24% have service contracts or expert secondments.

The diagram below shows the forms of participation at EU level.

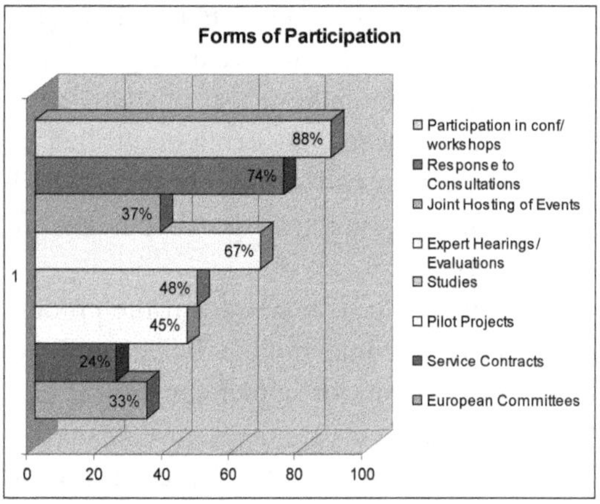

Has your organisation requested and received support from your government or from EU funded programmes?

49% of all participants have successfully bid for government or EU funding (44% of business sector, 59% of non-business sector), 6% have submitted proposals but have been rejected (6% of business sector, 7% of non-business sector), and 38% have not requested any public funding (43% of business sector, 28% of non-business sector).

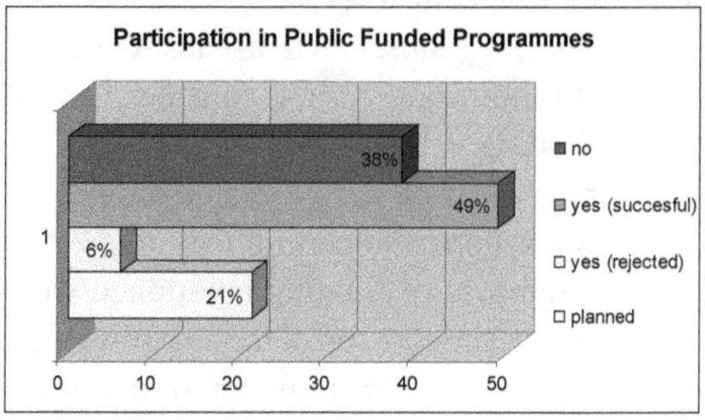

What form of support has your organisation received?

Survey participants could select several answers for this question. The answers are presented in the chart below.

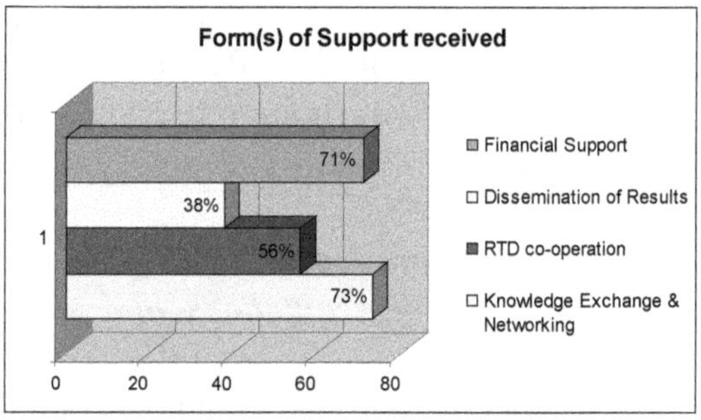

QUESTION 5: What is your opinion of publicly funded programmes? (Multiple choice of stock opinions)

The survey showed that 7 out of 10 believe that "Not everybody has the same opportunity to actively participate in shaping the regulatory framework for EU ICT policy and standards". However, only 1 out of 20 believe that "EU programmes are a waste of tax payers' money". Nevertheless, the need to revise and improve the publicly funded programmes is cited by half of all survey respondents.

A further observation is that stakeholders' interest in the Framework Programme is threatened by serious concerns. These centre on overly burdensome levels of bureaucracy, the high cost of bidding, insufficient support for SMEs, and the perception that the Framework Programme is more interested in using "stakeholder buy-in" to support European integration rather than to enhance international competitiveness.

In one sentence, what is your attitude towards European funded programmes?

The majority of respondents had a positive view. They stressed that EU/publicly funded programmes:

- Offer opportunities for all organisations to apply for funding;
- Add value by stimulating technological progress and pooling risks in highly innovative projects among a consortium of industry partners;
- Are believed to be necessary for developing European industry and supporting researchers;
- Have value that lies in supporting regional and local implementation of ICTs;
- Advertise the competence of the funded organisation at innovating products and professional services; and
- Are considered to be a good opportunity to develop collective action (*e.g.* bring subject matter experts together or establish joint research projects) and to develop trans-national cooperation and networks. These networks can include contacts with prospective customers, partners, and national/EU governments.

Across industry sectors, stakeholders believe that publicly funded programmes are key for the future competitiveness of European industry and research & development (R&D). They contribute to the economic, social, and cultural development of EU Member States and organisations. When allocated correctly, they can increase productivity, contributing to the strengthening of the Common Market.

Nevertheless, even if procedures have been changed and improvements made, most respondents are looking forward to seeing further improvements. The areas that have been mentioned are:

***European programmes profit larger organisations*:**
Some respondents, *e.g.* academic institutions, SMEs, and R&D centres, felt that it remains difficult for them to access funding, and participation is often difficult. They feel underrepresented and believe that the programmes favour large business organisations.

Often a consistent European approach is missing:

- Too much diffusion amongst countries lacking a clear view of how to help European industry become stronger and more competitive.
- Many respondents mentioned that R&D funding by the USA and Asia is much higher and much more focused.

The international dimension in EU programmes is inadequate:

It is difficult for participants to get accepted in consortia when coming from a "poor" country.

Big projects with unclear focus and benefits:

- Many believe that the EU supports too many "mega" projects with unclear results in the short term.
- Some respondents also suggested that funding should be provided primarily in areas where Europe can achieve real leadership positions, which automatically stimulate growth in research results and, subsequently, production.
- The international dimension (*e.g.* involving US or Asia) is often neglected.

Unequal chance for participation:

Many believe that due to project size not all organisations (public or private) have the same chances to participate in EU programmes. The 6th Framework Programme seems to put SMEs and innovators at a strategic disadvantage.

Review of cost model/ funding:

Most respondents believe that funded programmes do serve an important role; however, several felt that the shared-cost model is unworkable in practice. The entire system should be redefined and made more logical. Respondents who have received funding mentioned that, theoretically speaking, almost all participants in shared-cost programmes are engaged in some form of abuse.

Bureaucratic processes need to be addressed:

- Not enough direct contact with ongoing research.
- Insufficient "brainstorming" to take on board new ideas and follow up research clues.
- Too many administrators and not enough good project officers with requisite management skills.
- Often already the "language" used in tender specifications or programme descriptions and the size of documentation puts potential participants off.
- The Commission is often not reactive enough for fast moving fields such as ICT.
- The whole process is too slow.
- More new supportive initiatives are required, creating the right conditions for investment and growth by offering clarity, commitment, and a better environment for economic growth and innovation.
- Many commercial organisations, especially SMEs, complained about how costly it is to submit a proposal to the EU. The process from pre-proposal, proposal, negotiation and attached administrative activities are considered to be a big burden.
- However, due to the complexity of the issues and programmes involved, a moderate level of bureaucracy is unavoidable.

Lack of socio-economic components:

Programmes for technical R&D should be accompanied by socio-economic research into their objectives, targets, and likely outcomes and impacts.

Lack of transparency and implementation of results:

- It was suggested that one reference point (*e.g.* website) should be available that assembles all EU-funded initiatives before tenders are announced.
- The results must be made more transparent.
- Lack of which results in lack of knowledge-sharing, dissemination, and use of research results.

Lessons not learned by the regulator:
The intake of issues for policy-making on the EU level through results from research or obstacles encountered in projects under the Framework Programmes is considered to be limited.

As requirements for successful participation in EU funded programmes, the following qualities were mentioned:
- (High) motivation;
- A network of contacts;
- (Much) lobbying and intelligence gathering; and
- Investment in time and resources for becoming involved in the first instance (proposal preparation process).

QUESTION 6: What are the reasons for your organisation to participate in funded programmes? (Multiple choice of stock reasons)

This survey also found that the main driver of stakeholder involvement in publicly funded programmes is "to find partners with the same interests in knowledge exchange and network building" (82%) and "to understand regulations and standards and to get involved at a very early stage" (75%). Also, 77% hoped they could "influence the policy-making process/standards developments" through participation in publicly funded programmes. This implies that funding priorities should support these expectations. By contrast, "to generate revenue" (53%) or even "to make profits" (28%) were considered less important goals.

Other reasons?

In addition to the stock reasons, respondents wrote-in the following reasons why they participate in funded programmes:

Strengthening the European economy and policy through knowledge exchange:
- To engage in international networking and communication with other industry and policy experts;
- To communicate knowledge about national (industrial) requirements to the European level;
- To contribute with my (my organisation's) experience in ICT; and
- To contribute to European competitiveness.

Gaining knowledge:
- To participate in such EU programmes as are strongly linked with standardisation issues
- To gain experience in how European/international businesses think and operate
- To understand and be able to anticipate the different cultural habits of EU-companies; and
- To stimulate business development.

Participating in European research:
- To contribute to knowledge-sharing based on European research ambitions;
- To keep in touch with state-of-the-art research and developments in my (my organisation's) line of activity; and
- To lay a stronger foundation for European research.

Branding:
To being selected for EU funding, because it is a high-quality stamp that gives the company a good name.

SECTION B: Impact of Information and Communication Technology Regulations and Standards on your Organisation

QUESTION 7: How would you assess the impact of ICT regulations and standards on your organisation?

97% of the respondents reported that regulations and standards had some kind of impact on their organisation. Of these 71% stated that regulations and standards had a "big" or "very big" (22%) impact on their organisation.

QUESTION 8: In which areas of compliance, regulation and industry standards is your organisation specifically interested?

Respondents to this survey were most interested in Internet regulation and security (92%) and digital content (92%), followed by data protection and privacy rights (88%).

Interest in corporate-governance regulation (including International Accounting Standards, Basel 2) across all stakeholders groups seems to be low (58%). However, looking only inside the business & industry sector, interest increases to 79%. Interest is even higher (94%) amongst companies with more than 500 employees (representing 18% of all respondents).

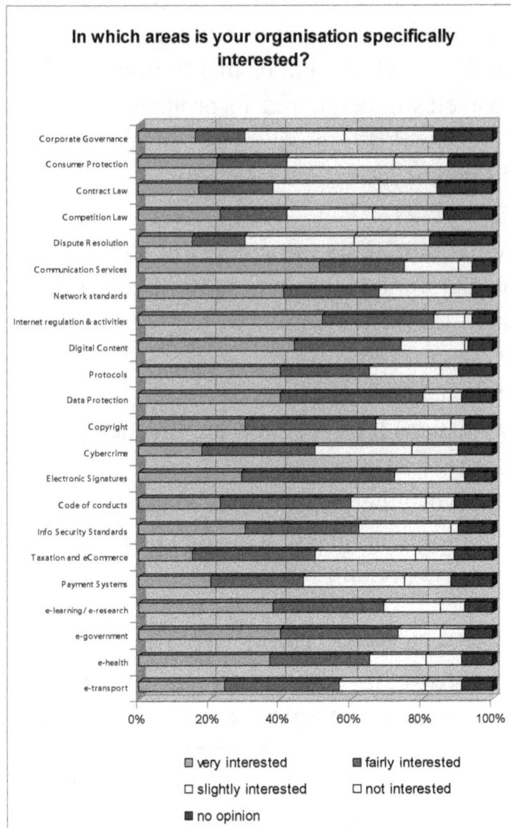

Other areas in which you are interested?

Respondents also expressed interest in the following regulatory, compliance, and standards issues:

- Industry-specific regulation, mainly for the financial and pharmaceutical industries and health sector;
- Health and safety;
- Environmental policy;
- Open sources (as an alternative to regulation);
- InfoMobility, *e.g.* mobile services in general, mobile content access; and
- Technical platforms for (*e.g.*) infotainment, consumer electronics, home networking, and mobile devices.

Which of these issues have caused your organisation to represent its views to EU institutions or thenational government, or to encourage action by intermediary organisations and associations?

Most of the respondents have actively contributed to the following issues:

- ***Corporate-governance regulation and company Law,*** taxation of internet and communication services, and digital contracts.
- ***Communications and infrastructure***, specifically access to e-content, interoperability questions, interoperability in digital interactive television.
- ***Security related areas***, *e.g.* through contributing guidelines for security standards, electronic signatures, security management, risk management, data protection, and copyright.
- ***public sector projects***, such as e-government, technology-enhanced learning (e-learning), e-research, cultural heritage, e-transport, telemedicine, and social inclusion for elderly and disabled persons.
- ***General contributions by providing knowledge and expertise,*** *e.g.* in project management and process modelling.

QUESTION 9: Who is involved in reviewing and assessing the potential threats and opportunities presented by regulatory initiatives for your organisation?

Senior Managers (52%) and Heads of Departments (49%) are mainly responsible for reviewing the implications of regulations. The diagram below provides an overview across the different grades.

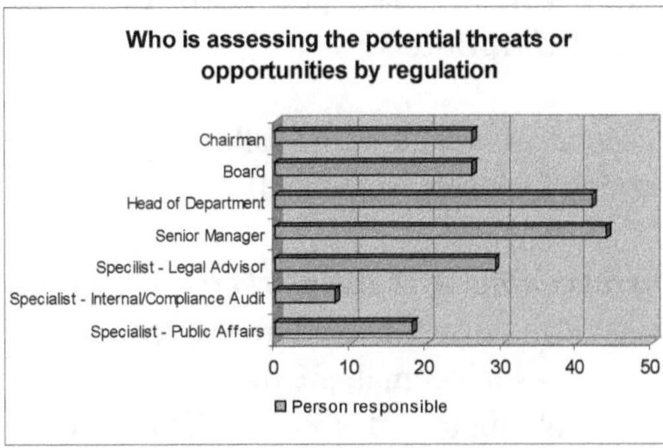

Other staff that assess implications of regulations on organisations

Other staff with regulatory compliance and standard responsibilities that were mentioned are:

Heads of Departments:

- Head of Human Resources
- Head of Taxation
- Head of Administration

Specialists:

- ICT specialists, *e.g.* IT architects
- Special interest group coordinators
- European policy specialists

QUESTION 10: How do you keep yourself and your organisation informed about new regulatory developments and standards initiatives?

The most common way is to read EU publications (scale factor 76), national government publications (scale factor 72) and to talk to other companies (scale factor 70). Less common is to take external advice (scale factor 41), to talk to local authorities (scale factor 43) and to use a contact point in Brussels (scale factor 44).

Other forms that you use to keep yourself updated?

Respondents wrote-in the following ways of keeping themselves updated:

Direct contact with the market:
- Running own conferences and inviting subject matter experts;
- Talking to and advising clients; and
- Conducting technical surveys.

Internet and webportals
e.g. Europa website, Euractive (www.euractiv.com), websites of standards institutes, and subscriptions to electronic newsletters.

Knowledge management
e.g. centres of excellence around compliance.

Participating in EU events
e.g. European (proposal) evaluations, brainstorming sessions, or meeting EU and standards-organisation representatives in Brussels.

SECTION C: Opinions on the regulatory framework for electronic communications

QUESTION 11: What is your opinion about EU ICT regulations and standards-setting? (Multiple choice of stock opinions)

Most respondents stated that "EU regulation and Europe wide applicable standards strengthen the EU ICT industry in the world" (83%), but only 32% believe that "my organisation/company has been successful in influencing EU regulation/standards". 68% believe that "only large multinational organisations can really influence regulations".

33% believe that "EU ICT regulation is forcing European industry to adopt many detailed norms and regulations that we don't want and need." And 70% are of the opinion that "EU regulations and standards are industry-oriented".

71% believe that "the European mobile market (GSM) has been a success story (as compared to the US) because of EU telecoms regulation and liberalisation", but only 36% believe that "UMTS (3rd generation of mobile phones) will be as successful as GSM".

We asked respondents to condense their opinion on this topic into one sentence.

Overview
- Standards are driven by industry and not technology. Big companies have a much stronger influence than SMEs, which can lead to a distortion of the representation of stakeholder interests. Sometimes SMEs wished that large companies had less influence.
- It costs stakeholders much effort and investment, but regulation and standards are considered by most as a necessity for successful business and research.
- EU policy reflects very strong influence by the industry. However, industry-controlled service providers and administrative interests are not always helpful for innovation and growth.
- The industry needs to improve its understanding of the requisites and benefits of international engagements. International standards are crucial to the successful implementation and operation of eCom-

merce and other emerging solutions. Thus, the EU should cooperate more strongly with North America and Japanese regulatory bodies.
- European regulation should be a means to support the EU ICT industry, but sometimes it appears to be an end in itself.

Positive

- Most respondents believe that good work has been done on ICT regulations and standards so far. EU standardisation is considered by many to be well balanced. Nevertheless, due to the nature of the matter frequent reviews are necessary.
- Unfortunately the same quality of work has not been done on the "social" side of Europe.
- European joint actions support national activities in global competition.
- Consensus is considered by many to be good.

Negative

- Several respondents complained about the lack of industry vision at EU level. This dearth of "hands on" knowledge has led to mistakes on the EU level, but also on the national governmental level. As examples of mistakes respondents mentioned *e.g.* UMTS and fibre versus ADSL.
- Many respondents demanded that the decision-making process should be speedier and more transparent.
- EU ICT regulation and standards-setting are matters for specialists. SMEs complained that it is very difficult to understand happenings and keep themselves updated.
- Respondents suggested that regulatory policy should pay more attention to achieving more transparent competitiveness and innovation.
- The EU should offer stronger guidelines for better business practice.

QUESTION 12: How satisfied are you with the several aspects of the New Regulatory Framework for electronic communications infrastructure and associated services, which was implemented EU-wide as of 25 July 2003?

Surprisingly, only half of the respondents were in a position to answer this question. This implies that the New Regulatory Framework is mostly unknown, even within the industry.

However, a majority of the respondents who were familiar with this new regulation seemed to be satisfied.

The charts below present the answers to three of the nine questions about the New Regulatory Framework.

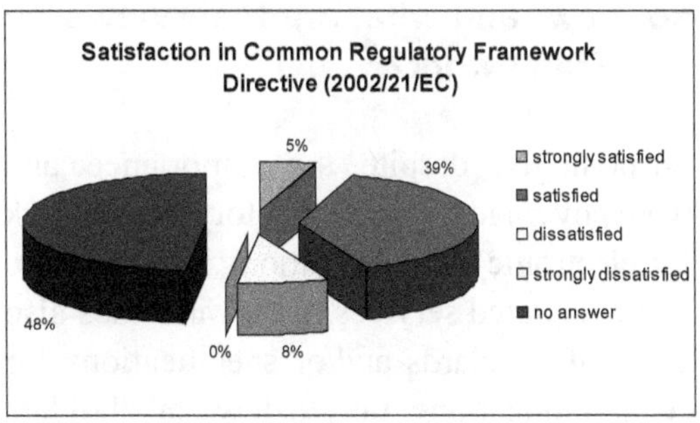

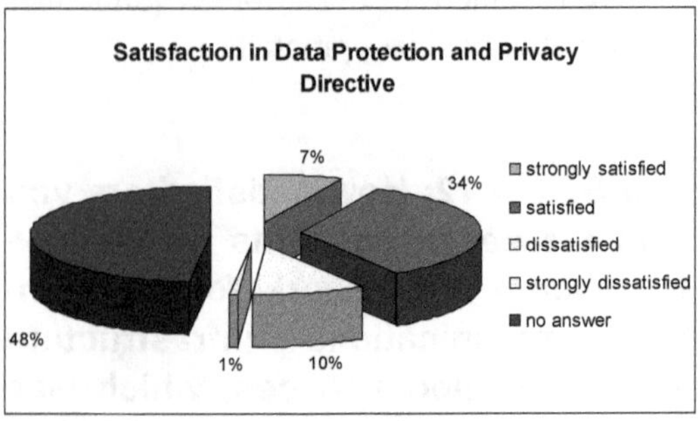

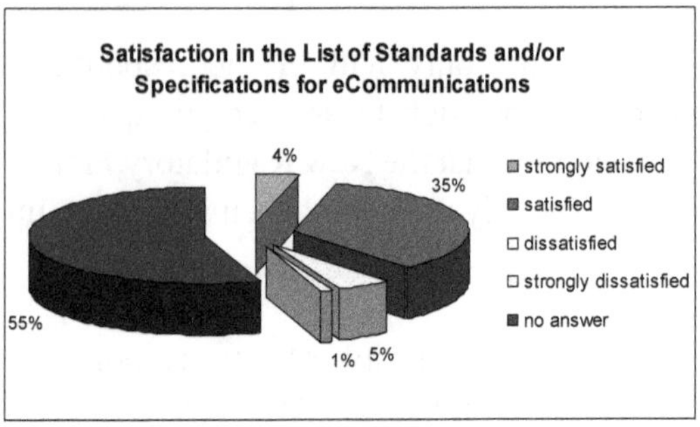

We asked for further comments on this Framework, such as whether the survey respondents had actively participated in shaping the Framework; if so, how; and what are their views on this Framework?

Surprisingly, despite the importance and wide coverage of the Regulatory Framework for electronic communications infrastructure and associated services, which includes also a list of standards and/or specifications for eCommunications, only a few stakeholders have participated in shaping the Framework. Common answers to this question were:

- I am not familiar with this regulation;
- I know too little to give my opinion on this regulation; or
- My organisation was only marginally involved.

Reasons given for non-participation were:

- Commercial pressures and lack of available relevant personnel; and
- It is not highly relevant for my organisation.

Views on the Framework:

- The framework does not apply in the same way for activities as it does for operators, *e.g.* installers (programmes that can re-route traffic and change tariffs without the users' knowledge);
- It is too bureaucratically oriented, with little focus on market needs; and
- The Framework is a very useful instrument to boost interoperability and ICT in general, although frequent updates are necessary.

SECTION D: Final Comments

What should be regulated/ de-regulated in the future?

Answers to this question were:

Corporate governance/ competition/ company law:

- Recent corporate governance regulation, which has been enforced on publicly listed companies, is beneficial for shareholders, employees, and customers (*e.g.* bank account holders, mobile phone users). More regulation is required, *e.g.* a percentage-increase cap on director's *per-annum* basic remuneration.
- Competition regulation is adequate.

ICT services:

- Ensure that unbundling of the local loop does actually take place. Also broadband take-up is vital for eCommerce uptake;

regulators should ensure that there is no hyper profit-taking by subsidised state monopolies.
- Radio frequencies should not be service-specific.
- Security standards and practices are needed for each business, at least for organisations with critical infrastructure.
- On-line identity must be regulated. However, this requires that biometric authentication is brought forward faster.
- Infrastructure, management, and trust should be regulated, but content should be deregulated.
- GSM roaming needs more regulation.
- Mobile-commerce needs more attention from the regulator.

Industry regulation:
- Communications within banking and health care should be standardised, allowing users to access services all over Europe as if in one country.
- Internet Registrars should be regulated.
- On-line gaming, on-line gambling, and on-line identity needs to be more closely monitored.
- Other markets that need regulation are the utility market and cable operators.

General views on how much regulations/ standards should be implemented/enforced, respondents answered that:
- Regulation should proceed in areas where there is a strong public interest, but should cover only the most necessary parts, leaving things open for new ideas and innovative development.
- Regulation should be phased out as soon as effective competition is achieved, and the scope of regulation should be extended to new areas.
- There should be as little regulation as possible.
- Regulations should be structural and not detailed.
- Regulations can be made, but the user makes ICT work.
- Ongoing monitoring of regulations is essential to ensure "better" regulation.
- In general, my organisation is very pleased with current progress.

In summary, many respondents believe that the question is not so much what should be regulated, but how it should be regulated. With several hundreds of bodies developing ICT standards and a lot of overlap worldwide, the question is, how will Europe ensure that devices, services, and content remain interoperable? This will probably be the main challenge for regulation in future: not setting the standards themselves, but defining models, architecture, codes of conduct, best practice guidelines on how solutions and technology can be applied and deployed.

How could participation in ICT regulation and standards-setting be improved?

General issues

In general, it is considered that participation in standardisation processes could and should be improved. The main reasons for stakeholders' lack of interest are the costs of participation, a lack of tangible results, and the complexity of the process (who is doing what?). These issues can be addressed either by additional third party funding (public sector, industry, or private investors), better project management, and more transparency.

Recommendations given by survey respondents about how participation in regulation and standards-setting could be improved are as follows:

Granting financing and funding:

- More research contracts would support the development of *e.g.* codes of practice, standards position papers, *etc.*
- Funding for a broad based forum of European stakeholders in the Information Society.
- More funding for national governments, academic research institutes, and SMEs to cover their costs of participating in workshops and committees. Many of these organisations have difficulties assigning people to follow the evolution of regulations/standards on an ongoing "cost" basis.
- Support for a variety of activities, including proof-of-concept.
- EU-funded projects and activities should be eligible for and encouraged to use public funding for participation in international fora. Moreover, it was suggested that Europe should support these fora financially.

Improving project management:

- Force the workshops and committees to take a stand in shorter time, then open the discussion up to associations or industry partners and other stakeholders for comment, and finalise the debate after another short discussion round. In the current situation we have endless rehashings, and the process becomes obscure and uninteresting for many stakeholders.
- Measurement of the effectiveness of regulations and standards should be based on timely and complete implementation of the content, and user success/satisfaction.
- Open up to new forms of participation, *e.g.* on-line participation (like for e-democracy).

Ensuring more transparency of activities:

- Proper advertising of meetings and events on national and European level.
- More communication and better information for stakeholders.
- Better dissemination of results.

Re-defining the responsibilities of standards-setting bodies, the regulators, and stakeholders:

- The current proliferation of standards-setting organisations is a concern for European business. With more than 400 fora and consortia active in ICT (see www.standardmedia.com), companies no longer have the capacity even to monitor the progress of the work, and even less to gain any significant level of influence.
- Use industry associations as a vehicle to communicate needs and requirements to the regulator and the industry.

Re-defining the focus:

- Europe should ensure a better link between technology-oriented standards and content-/ service-oriented standards.
- The very word "standard" is becoming more and more meaningless, nearly synonymous with "any commercial solution interoperable with itself". It is expected by some experts that vendors will eventually acknowledge that this situation has overall negative consequences on the market and that they will authorise to some extent a return to the consolidation of meaningful standards in truly open standard-setting organisations, to ensure a reasonable degree of consensus and coherence.

Attracting the best/right people:

- More user-oriented regulation would lead to more user involvement.
- Often the Commission and standardisation bodies work with consolidated lobbies instead of integrating all affected stakeholders, *e.g.* universities, professionals, non-profit organisations.
- Regulation and standardisation should be industry-driven, which will subsequently benefit users/consumers (good and affordable solutions), employees (full employment), and society as a whole.
- It is key to involve business as well as to interest government in public policy issues.

Further comments on these issues...

Requirement for simplification: EU institutions and decision-making are confusing, particularly for small businesses. The whole system needs to be simplified.

Understand the benefits of participation: Companies should heed the disadvantages of non-participation; *e.g.* "quarterly outlooks" often avoid the implications of standards-setting initiatives.

Have a bigger picture of regulation: It is crucial to be aware of regulatory issues beyond governance and ICT policy, such as social policy or the internal market.

Understand the main issues of ICT policy: The main issue of ICT policy is how it enhances an information and knowledge society. Core elements are providing mobility, ubiquitous access, and granting all citizens access to important information. Challenges include bridging the digital gap; access by minorities; privacy rights; intellectual property rights; security; and many more caused by the eEconomy and eSociety.

Re-think the processes of regulations and standards-setting: The need for a truly independent European organisation is now greater than ever, so that the rights, security, and privacy of European citizens are protected in the modern Global Information Society.

Innovative forms of participation/encouragement in the standards-setting process: International and national bodies should introduce transparent possibilities with associated benefits for stakeholder engagement. In a nutshell, currently the stakeholders agree on standards, the industry "produces" them, and people use them. If users do not like the outcome, they will not use the technology and the standard will fail (*e.g.* Betamax,VHS).

Consider alternatives to regulations and standards: EU must promote open source software: it helps development and diffusion of local competencies and reduces external monopoly strengths.

Appendix: Data Sheet

A.	Participation in Decision-Making Processes for Regulations and Standards

1.	How would you describe your and your organisation's attitude towards decision-making?						
	Question	Scale Factor (mean)	Strongly Agree	Agree	Disagree	Strongly Disagree	N/A	---
	Scale		*100*		*50*	*0*		
(a)	I like to have responsibility.	86	57%	39%	1%	0%	3%	---
(b)	I believe that decision-makers have a more stressful life.	62	21%	43%	21%	6%	9%	---
(c)	I prefer to make private decisions instead of decisions on behalf of my organization.	29	2%	13%	48%	28%	9%	---

2.	What is YOUR organisation's active participation in the decision-making on ICT issues?

	Question	Scale Factor	Very strong involvement	Strong involvement	Involvement	Passive involvement	No involvement	N/A
	Scale		*100*	*75*	*50*	*25*	*0*	
N-1	Industry associations.	74	52%	8%	8%	10%	9%	13%
N-2	National standard institutes	59	40%	5%	3%	8%	24%	20%
N-3	Government initiatives.	71	46%	11%	1%	8%	14%	20%
N-4	National programmes and initiatives	67	41%	13%	2%	14%	13%	16%
E-1	Industry associations (*e.g.* EUROCHAMBERS)	49	31%	2%	3%	14%	25%	24%

	Question	Scale Factor	Very strong involvement	Strong involvement	Involvement	Passive involvement	No involvement	N/A
E-2	(a) ETSI	47	26%	6%	3%	10%	28%	27%
	(b) CENELEC	40	23%	4%	2%	11%	34%	26%
	(c) CEN-ISSS	36	20%	3%	2%	12%	36%	26%
	(d) Others	19	9%	4%	0%	8%	53%	26%
E-3	Fora connected to EU Institutions	50	30%	5%	3%	8%	29%	25%
E-4	European programmes and initiatives	74	46%	15%	2%	11%	8%	18%
I-1	Industry associations/ interest groups (a) Internet Security Forum	44	26%	5%	3%	12%	31%	23%
	(b) ICC	18	10%	1%	1%	8%	53%	27%
I-2	(a) ITU	36	18%	6%	2%	10%	37%	27%
	(b) OECD	20	11%	2%	0%	8%	52%	27%
	(c) UN organisations	22	11%	2%	2%	10%	48%	27%
I-3	Global programmes and initiatives (Internet Engineering TF, www-Cons)	35	18%	3%	3%	13%	35%	26%

2.1	Who represents your organisation at these consultative fora?
	Open Question: see comments above

2.2	What function does your representative have?
	Open Question: see comments above

2.3	How/ Why were these individuals selected?
	Open Question: see comments above

3.	How satisfied is your organisation with the activities of these stakeholders?							
	Question	Scale Factor	Strongly satisfied	Satisfied	Dissatisfied	Strongly Dissatisfied	N/A	---
	Scale		*100*	*66*	*33*	*0*		
I.	**At Industry level**							
	1. Industry associations	61	7%	59%	15%	2%	17%	---
	2. Non-profit organizations (*e.g.* consumer associations)	54	2%	46%	22%	4%	26%	---
II.	**At national level**							
	1. Politicians/ Parliaments in the country of your organisation	42	0%	33%	38%	11%	18%	---
III.	**At European/ International level**							
	1. European regulations/ standards institutes	58	6%	52%	18%	4%	10%	---
	2. Guidelines and recommendations from international organisations such as the International Telecommunications Union (ITU), OECD, WTO etc.	59	4%	56%	16%	3%	21%	---

3.1	How could involvement in these processes be improved?
	Open Question: see comments above

4.	How does your organisation participate in policy, regulation, and standards-setting activities at the EU level?							
	Question	Scale Factor	Yes	No	N/A	---	---	---
I.	**Forms of Participation**							
	1. participation in conferences/ workshops	88	82%	11%	7%	---	---	---
	2. response to consultations	74	68%	24%	8%	---	---	---
	3. joint hosting of events/ conferences (1-2 days)	37	34%	57%	9%	---	---	---
	4. sending experts to hearings/ participation in evaluations (1-5 days)	67	61%	30%	9%	---	---	---

	Question	Scale Factor	Yes	No	N/A	---	---	---
	5. studies such as feasibility studies and research projects (3-6 months)	48	44%	47%	9%	---	---	---
	6. pilots that involve different companies across Europe (1-2 years)	45	41%	50%	9%	---	---	---
	7. services contracts (*e.g.* secondment of experts for 1-2 years)	24	22%	70%	8%	---	---	---
	8. continued involvement in committees (*e.g.* European Round Table of Industrialists, Data Protection working group)	33	30%	60%	10%	---	---	---
II.	**Has your organisation requested and received support from your government or from EU-funded programmes?**							
	no	38	35%	57%	8%	---	---	---
	yes – we have been successful	49	45%	47%	8%	---	---	---
	yes – but our proposal was rejected	6	6%	87%	7%	---	---	---
	planned	21	19%	73%	8%	---	---	---

III.	**Has your organisation requested and received support from your government from EU funded programmes?**							
	financial support	71	39%	16%	45%	---	---	---
	dissemination of results	38	21%	34%	45%	---	---	---
	RTD co-operation with other companies/ organisations	56	31%	24%	45%	---	---	---
	knowledge- exchange and networking	73	41%	15%	44%	---	---	---

5.	Here are some statements that people often make when they talk about publicly funded programmes. To what extent do you agree or disagree?

	Question	Scale Factor	Strongly Agree	Agree	Disagree	Strongly Disagree	N/A	---
	Scale		*100*	*50*		*0*		

	Question	Scale Factor	Strongly Agree	Agree	Disagree	Strongly Disagree	N/A	---
(a)	"EU programmes give organisations/ industry the opportunity to actively influence the decision making process."	59	10%	58%	24%	3%	4%	---
(b)	"EU programmes are a hidden subsidies for industries in trouble/ regions with economic problems."	40	1%	30%	53%	11%	4%	---
(c)	"EU programmes are a waste of tax-payers' money."	23	1%	4%	55%	36%	4%	---
(d)	"The same organisations/ people always participate in EU projects and activities."	60	13%	52%	25%	2%	8%	---
(e)	"The money/ effort could be invested better."	50	8%	41%	38%	7%	4%	---
(f)	"Not everybody has the same opportunity to participate in EU programmes and participate in shaping the regulatory framework for EU ICT policy and standards."	63	18%	55%	20%	4%	3%	---

5.1	In one sentence, what is your attitude toward Europeen funded programmes:
	Open Question: see comments above

6.	Thinking of the following reasons to participate in funded programmes, could you indicate how important each one is for your organisation.

	Question	Scale Factor	Very Important	Important	Not very important	Not important	N/A	---
	Scale		*100*		*50*	*0*		
(a)	To secure funding for research, development and new product/ service development	72	39%	35%	14%	5%	7%	---
(b)	To generate revenue for your organisation	51	13%	40%	28%	14%	4%	---
(c)	To make profits	34	7%	21%	35%	31%	6%	---
(d)	To market the services and products of your organisation	58	15%	50%	16%	10%	8%	---

	Question	Scale Factor	Very Important	Important	Not very important	Not important	N/A	---
(e)	To influence the policy-making process/ standards developments	65	22%	55%	10%	8%	5%	---
(f)	To find partners with the same interests in knowledge exchange and network building	72	33%	49%	8%	4%	6%	---
(g)	To understand regulations and standards and to get involved at a very early stage	69	29%	46%	17%	2%	6%	---
(h)	To assist with rolling out our products and services EU-wide	57	22%	36%	26%	11%	5%	---

6.1	Other reasons
	Open Question: see comments above

B.	**Impact of Information and Communication Technology Regulations and Standards on your Organisation**

7.	Please help us to assess the impact of ICT regulation and standards on your organisation.							
	Question	Scale Factor	Very big impact	Big impact	Small impact	No impact	N/A	---
	Scale		*100*	*66*	*33*	*0*		
	Some stakeholders feel that regulation has a negligible impact on their organisation. Others believe it has a very big impact. Which comes closest to your belief?	64	22%	49%	26%	1%	2%	---

8.	Compliance, Regulation and Industry Standards have become a major issue for many organisations. Non-compliance can lead to competitive disadvantage or penalties. In which areas is your organisation specifically interested?							
	Question	Scale Factor	Very interested	Fairly interested	Slightly interested	Not interested at all	N/A	---
	Scale		*100*	*66*	*33*	*0*		
I.	**Corporate governance / competition law**							
(a)	Sarbanes-Oxley, OECD Principles of Corporate Governance, etc.	42	16%	14%	28%	25%	17%	---
(b)	Consumer protection	52	22%	20%	30%	15%	13%	---

	Question	Scale Factor	Very interested	Fairly interested	Slightly interested	Not interested at all	N/A	---
(c)	Contract law, incl. on-line contracts, distance contracts	49	17%	21%	30%	16%	16%	---
(d)	Competition law (Protection of new market entrants from unfair trade practices of established companies)	51	23%	19%	24%	20%	14%	---
(e)	Dispute resolution / settlement	43	15%	15%	31%	21%	18%	---
II.	**Communications and infrastructure**							
(a)	Communications services (new framework for electronic communications services)	76	51%	24%	15%	4%	6%	---
(b)	Networks standards and initiatives (Trans-European Networks, networked businesses and governments)	70	41%	27%	20%	6%	6%	---
(c)	Internet regulation and activities (*e.g.* eEurope, security framework, e-working, e-accessibility, e-safety, e-commerce, broadband)	80	52%	31%	9%	2%	6%	---
(d)	Digital content (eContent)	75	44%	30%	18%	1%	7%	---
(e)	IT platforms/ operating systems, protocols (TCP/IP) and embedded systems	70	40%	25%	20%	5%	10%	---
III.	**Security and intangible property rights**							
(a)	Data protection and privacy rights	76	40%	40%	8%	3%	9%	---
(b)	Copyright and related rights in the Information Society	67	30%	37%	21%	4%	8%	---
(c)	Cybercrime	53	18%	32%	27%	13%	10%	---
(d)	Electronic signatures/ digital certificates/ Trusted Third Parties	68	29%	43%	16%	4%	8%	---
(e)	E-Business "codes of conduct"/ trust seals (for websites)	61	23%	37%	21%	8%	11%	---
(f)	Information Security Standards (BS7799/ ISO 17799, "OECD Guidelines for the Security of Information Systems and Networks")	66	30%	32%	26%	2%	10%	---
IV.	**Commercial use**							
(a)	Taxation and electronic commerce	53	15%	35%	28%	11%	11%	---

	Question	Scale Factor	Very interested	Fairly interested	Slightly interested	Not interested at all	N/A	---
(b)	Payment systems (*e.g.* SET)	53	20%	26%	28%	13%	12%	---
V.	**Sector-targeted activities (defined in eEurope)**							
(a)	e-learning, e-research and access to cultural heritage	69	38%	31%	16%	7%	8%	---
(b)	e-government	71	40%	33%	12%	7%	8%	---
(c)	e-health	67	37%	28%	16%	10%	9%	---
(d)	e-transport	59	24%	32%	25%	10%	9%	---

8.1	Other compliance areas in which you are interested
	Open Question: see comments above

8.2	Which of these issues have caused your organisation to represent its views to EU institutions or the national government, or to encourage action by intermediary organisations and associations?
	Open Question: see comments above

9.	Who is involved in reviewing and assessing the potential threats or opportunities presented by regultory initiatives for your organisation? We are interested in his/her position in your organisation.

	Question	Scale Factor	Yes	No	N/A	---	---	---
(a)	Chairman	31	26%	59%	15%	---	---	---
(b)	Board	31	26%	59%	15%	---	---	---
(c)	Head of Department	49	42%	43%	15%	---	---	---
(d)	Senior Manager	52	44%	41%	15%	---	---	---
(e)	Specialist – Legal Advisor	34	29%	56%	15%	---	---	---
(f)	Specialist – Internal Audit	9	8%	77%	15%	---	---	---
(g)	Specialist – Public Affairs or Government Affairs Representative	22	19%	66%	15%	---	---	---

9.1	Other
	Open Question: see comments above

10.	Many organisations have difficulties following new regulatory developments, for instance electronic signatures, rules for conducting business online, data protection, or new technical standards. How do you keep yourself and your organisation informed (sources of information)?							
	Question	Scale Factor	Usually	Sometimes	Never	N/A	---	---
	Scale		*100*	*50*	*0*			
1.	Talk directly to local authorities	43	13%	50%	25%	12%	---	---
2. (a)	Talk directly to national regulator/ government institutions	59	34%	40%	16%	9%	---	---
(b)	Read national government publications	72	44%	45%	4%	7%	---	---
3. (a)	Talk directly to the EU institutions	53	29%	41%	23%	7%	---	---
(b)	Read EU publications	76	52%	41%	2%	5%	---	---
(c)	Influence the agenda through participation in EU workshops and committees	50	26%	38%	26%	10%	---	---
(d)	Participate in conferences/ road shows/ Information days	64	32%	51%	7%	10%	---	---
(e)	Use a contact point in Brussels	44	24%	32%	35%	9%	---	---
4.	Membership of (industry) associations	62	39%	33%	18%	10%	---	---
5.	Debate in workshops and events at international level	58	17%	55%	12%	6%	---	---
6.	Talk to other companies	70	42%	44%	5%	9%	---	---
7.	Get advice from professional law/ accountancy/ consultancy firms	41	14%	44%	30%	11%	---	---
8.	Read press and media coverage on a specific issue	67	36%	51%	4%	8%	---	---

10.1	Other forms that you use to keep yourself up-dated
	Open Question: see comments above

C.	**Opinions on the Regulatory Framework for Electronic Communications**

11.	The following are some opinions about EU ICT regulations and standards-setting. To what extent do you agree or disagree with the following statements?							
	Question	Scale Factor	Strongly Agree	Agree	Disagree	Strongly Disagree	N/A	---
	Scale		*100*		*50*	*0*		
(a)	"EU regulation and Europe-wide applicable standards strengthen the EU ICT industry in the world."	70	27%	56%	11%	2%	4%	---
(b)	"EU ICT regulation is forcing European industry to adopt many detailed norms and regulations that we don't want or need."	44	5%	28%	57%	6%	4%	---
(c)	"Telecoms liberalisation in Europe was a success."	63	13%	61%	17%	2%	6%	---
(d)	"The European mobile phone market (GSM) has been a success story (as compared to the US) because of EU telecoms legislation and liberalisation."	67	22%	49%	18%	1%	9%	---
(e)	"UMTS (3rd generation of mobile phones) will be as successful as GSM"	46	5%	31%	43%	7%	13%	---
(f)	"My country has been successful in influencing EU regulations/ standards."	50	4%	42%	34%	6%	14%	---
(g)	"My organisation/ company has been successful in influencing EU regulations/ standards."	38	5%	27%	30%	25%	13%	---
(h)	"Only large multinational organisations can really influence regulations."	64	22%	46%	23%	3%	6%	---
(i)	"EU regulations and standards are industry-oriented."	61	9%	61%	21%	1%	8%	---

11.1	In one sentence, what is your opinion?
	Open Question: see comments above

12.	As you may know, the EU adopted a New Regulatory Framework for electronic communications infrastructure and associated services which was implemented EU-wide by 25 July 2003. How satisfied are you with the following aspects of the framework?							
	Question	Scale Factor	Very satisfied	Satisfied	Dissatisfied	Strongly Dissatisfied	N/A	---
	Scale		*100*	*66*	*33*	*0*		---
1.	Common Regulatory Framework Directive (2002/21/EC)	64	5%	39%	8%	0%	48%	---
2.	Access and Interconnection Directive	63	2%	41%	7%	0%	50%	---
3.	Authorisation Directive	66	4%	38%	4%	0%	45%	---
4.	Universal Service and User's Rights Directive	61	4%	33%	9%	0%	53%	---
5.	Data Protection and Privacy Directive	62	7%	34%	10%	1%	48%	---
6.	Directive on Competition in Communication Services Markets	61	4%	33%	9%	1%	53%	---
7.	Regulation on Unbundled Access to the Local Loop	56	3%	29%	13%	2%	53%	---
8.	Guidelines on Market Analysis of Significant Market Power	61	6%	26%	11%	1%	56%	---
9.	List of Standards and/or Specifications for eCommunications	64	4%	35%	5%	1%	55%	---

12.1	We would appreciate any comments you have on this New Framework, such as: Have you participated in shaping this Framework? How? What are your views on this Framework?
	Open Question: see comments above

D.	**Final Comments**

	What should be regulated/ de-regulated in the future?
	Open Question: see comments above

	How could participation in ICT regulations and standards-setting be improved?
	Open Question: see comments above

	Further comments
	Open Question: see comments above

E.	Personal Details

13.	Please, could you provide some details about yourself?				
	Question	In %		Question	In %
1.	**Country**		4.	**Number of employees**	
	AT - Austria	1%		1 – 9	25%
	BE - Belgium	14%		10 – 49	14%
	DE - Germany	15%		50 – 499	24%
	DK - Denmark	4%		500 – 999	4%
	EL - Greece	3%		1,000 – 9,999	14%
	ES – Spain	5%		10,000 +	19%
	FI - Finland	2%		**Total**	**100%**
	FR - France	12%		Average	3,000 +
	IE - Ireland	2%			
	IT – Italy	15%	5.	**What is the focus?**	
	LU - Luxembourg	1%		Local	3%
	NL - Netherlands	6%		Regional	10%
	PT - Portugal	1%		National	23%
	SE – Sweden	7%		EU-wide	26%
	UK – United Kingdom	14%		International	38%
	Total	**100%**		**Total**	**100%**
2.	**Age groups**		6.	**Location of organization's headquarters**	
	-30 years	3%		European Union	89%
	31-40 years	30%		USA	7%
	41-50 years	33%		Japan	3%
	51-60 years	27%		Other Asia	0%
	61- years	7%		Other	1%

	Total	**100%**
	Average	44

3.	**In which business sector do you work?**	
	business & industry	66%
	administration & government	13%
	universities	9%
	Non-Commercial Organisations (NGOs)	12%
	Total	**100%**

	Total	**100%**

Legal Disclaimer

The findings and views expressed in this report do not necessarily reflect the views of the researcher. All information provided by the respondents will be treated in CONFIDENCE. Answers can be released only as summaries in which no respondent's answer can be identified.

Appendix 5: Regulatory Compliance Matrix

A5.1. Summary of Regulatory Compliance Matrix

The following table lays out the principal domains of legislative and regulatory acts at all levels of governance applicable to the regulation of ICT together with other relevant general regulations, with all of which (business) organisations must comply.

A. General laws and regulations, and supporting standards, frameworks and guidance

- A.1 Business regulation (corporate governance, finance, accounting and contract law)
  - A.1.1 Corporate governance and accounting
  - A.1.2 Anti-bribery and corruption
  - A.1.3 Public procurement
  - A.1.4 Contract law
  - A.1.5 Finance and taxation law
- A.2 Consumer protection and employment law
  - A.2.1 Consumer protection and alternative dispute resolution
  - A.2.2 Work and employment
- A.3 Information security
  - A.3.1 Electronic signatures
  - A.3.2 Network security and security products
  - A.3.3 Cybercrime
  - A.3.4 Security for passports and visas
- A.4 Data protection and privacy rights
  - A.4.1 General data protection and data retention
  - A.4.2 Pan-European data transfer
  - A.4.3 Data protection and investigations
- A.5 Copyright and related rights
  - A.5.1 Intellectual property rights
  - A.5.2 Copyright
  - A.5.3 Patents
  - A.5.4 Trade marks and designs
  - A.5.5 Legal protection of hardware
  - A.5.6 Legal protection of software

A.5.7 Domain names
A.6 Electronic commerce
A.6.1 e-Commerce regulation
A.6.2 e-Government
A.6.3 Payment systems

B. Specific ICT Law and regulations, and supporting standards, frameworks and guidance

B.1 The Information Society
B.1.1 Market liberalisation and regulation framework
B.1.2 The New Regulatory Framework
B.2.3 Trans-European Networks (TEN)
B.2 Internet regulation and activities
B.2.1 Safer Internet Use
B.3 Telecommunication regulations
B.3.1 Wireless policy
B.3.2 Access and interconnection
B.3.3 Satellites
B.4 Digital media and content
B.4.1 Digital interactive television
B.4.2 Digital content
B.5 Radio services and equipment
B.5.1 Radio interference
B.5.2 Compatibility
B.5.3 Radio equipment
B.6 Audiovisual services
B.6.1 The audiovisual service industry
B.7 Environment ("Green IT")
B.7.1 Green IT
B.8 Other ICT-specific norms (sectoral hardware sector)
B.8.1 Wireless and fixed line
B.8.1 Data storage and power management

A5.2. Detailed regulatory compliance matrix

The following matrix provides a compendium of international and European as well as UK regulations and standards as one instance of ICT regulation at national level. These were the main laws, regulation and norms, and supporting standards, frameworks and guidance applicable to ICT at the time of publication. Section A of the Matrix contains general norms applicable to all industry sectors. Section B contains norms specific to the ICT sector.

Domain	Laws, Regulations and Norms	Standards, Frameworks, and Guidance
A. General laws and regulations, and supporting standards frameworks and guidance		
A.1 Business regulation (corporate governance, finance, accounting and contract law)		
A.1.1 Corporate governance and accounting	**EU corporate governance and auditing** • Decision No 716/2009/EC "Establishing a Community programme to support specific activities in the field of financial services, financial reporting and auditing" (16 September 2009). • Recommendation 2008/362 on "External quality assurance for statutory auditors and audit firms auditing public interest entities" (6 May 2008). • Directive 2006/43/EC on "Statutory audit of annual accounts and consolidated accounts, amending Council Directives (78/660/EEC) and (83/349/EEC) and repealing Council Directive (84/253/EEC)" (8th Company Law Directive on statutory audit)" (17 May 2006). • COM(2003/286/EC) on "Reinforcing the statutory audit in the European Union" (21 May 2003). • Regulation No 1606/2002 on "The application of international accounting standards" (19 July 2002). • "Winter Report": Report of the High Level Group of Company experts (2002) on "A modern regulatory framework for company law in Europe" (Brussels). • Recommendation (2002) "Statutory auditors' independence in the EU: a set of fundamental principles" (16 June 2002). • Recommendation (2000) "Quality assurance for the statutory auditor in the EU". • COM(2001/428/EC) "European governance: a White Paper (25 July 2001). • COM(1998) "The statutory audit in the European Union: the way forward". • Regulation (2137/85/EC) on "the European Economic Interest Grouping (EEIG)", (25 July 1985). • 8th Council Directive (84/253/EEC) on the "approval of persons responsible for carrying out the statutory audits of accounting documents" (10 April 1984) [repealed].	**EU corporate governance and auditing** • Guidelines of the European Group of Auditors' Oversight Bodies (EGAOB) and Public Interest Oversight Board (PIOB). • COSO (The Committee of Sponsoring Organizations of the Treadway Commission): 1. COSO Internal Control – Integrated Framework, and 2. COSO Enterprise Risk-Management Framework. • COBIT Framework (Control Objectives for Information and related Technology), IT Governance Institute, ISACA. • ITIL (IT Infrastructure Library, Office of Government Commerce/OGC). ITIL Configuration management database. • CICA CoCo [Criteria of Control] Framework. • Rules and standards defined by the International Chamber of Commerce (ICC), for example: International Commercial Terms (Incoterms 2000) – standard trade definitions for international sales contracts. • Standards of the International Auditing Practices Committee (IAPC) and the International Accounting Standards Committee (IASC). • "Guidelines on Auditing Quality" of EuroSAI (29 October 2004). • **General Practice Guidance** • PRINCE (Project In Controlled Environment), Office of Government Commerce/OGC. • MSP (Management Successful Programmes); Office of Government Commerce/OGC. • Capability Maturity Model Integration (CMMI), Software Engineering Institute. • Project Management Body of Knowledge (PMBOK).

Domain	Laws, Regulations and Norms	Standards, Frameworks, and Guidance
Global Regulation and Standards (Examples)	• Sarbanes-Oxley Act (2002) "to rebuild public trust in corporate business and reporting practices", 15 USC Chapter 98 §§ 7201-7266, Public Law 107-204 (30 July 2002;), USC § 7262 (Pub. L. Sec. 404) – Management assessment of internal controls. • International Accounting Standards Committee (IASC, 2001) "Guidelines for International Financial Reporting Standards".	**Corporate Governance and Accountancy** • Public Company Accounting Oversight Board (PCAOB) Rules approved by the US Securities and Exchange Commission (SEC). • OECD (2004) "Principles of Corporate Governance" (supersedes the OECD Principles of 1999, endorsed by the member states at the OECD Council meeting at ministerial level on 26-27 May 1999). • American Institute of CPAs (AICPA): SSAE No 16 for Service Auditors ("Reporting on Controls at a Service Organization") and Clarified Auditing Standard for User Organizations ("Audit Considerations Relating to an Entity Using a Service Organization"). (supersedes SAS70, Standards on Services Organisations). • Institute of Chartered Accountants in England and Wales (ICAEW), Faculty of Information Technology: FIT 1/94 "Audit Information Systems". • ICAEW, Audit and Assurance Faculty: AAF 1/06 "Assurance reports on internal controls of services organisations made available to third parties" (supersedes FRAG 21/94) International Accounting Standards (IAS) of the International Accounting Standards Board (IASB) and the International Financial Reporting Standards (IFRS) Foundation. • ISO 9000/ISO14000 "Quality Management and Quality Assurance standard".
UK National Regulations and Standards	**Regulation** • Companies Act 2006 (Chapter 46). • Companies (Audit, Investigations and Community Enterprise) Act 2004 (Chapter 27), Part 1. • FSA (July 2007) "Treating customers fairly" (TCF), the FSA's principles-based approach to regulation.	**Corporate Governance Reporting** • The Financial Reporting Council (2010) "The UK Corporate Governance Code" (The Combined Code). • Higgs Report: "Review of the role and effectiveness of non-executive directors" (January 2003). • Institute of Chartered Accountants in England & Wales (September 1999): The Turnbull Report – "Internal Control: Guidance for Directors on the Combined Code". • London Stock Exchange, Confederation of British Industry, Institute of Directors, Consultative Committee of Accountancy Bodies, National Association of Pension Funds, Association of British Insurers (January 1998): Hampel Committee, Final Report on Corporate Governance. • Confederation of British Industry (17 July 1995): Greenbury Report on Directors' Remuneration • ICAEW (December 1994): Rutteman Report on Internal Control and Financial Reporting: Guidance for directors of listed companies registered in the UK. • Financial Reporting Council and London Stock Exchange (December 1992): Cadbury Report on Financial Aspects of Corporate Governance.

Domain	Laws, Regulations and Norms	Standards, Frameworks, and Guidance
A.1.2 **Anti-Bribery and corruption**	**EU Anti-Fraud and Anti-Corruption initiatives** • Directive 2005/60/EC on "the prevention of the use of the financial system for the purpose of money laundering and terrorist financing" (26 October 2005). • Amsterdam European Council 2000/C124/01: "The prevention and control of organised crime: a European Union strategy for the beginning of the new millennium" (27 March 2000). • Brussels European Council 97/C251/01: "Action plan to combat organized crime" (28 April 1997).	**Guidance** The European Anti-Fraud Office (OLAF), EUROJUST and the European Police Office (Europol) provide some guidance, including tools, information exchange and FAQs on their respective websites.
Global Regulation and Standards (Examples)	**OECD** • OECD Convention on Combating Bribery of Foreign Public Officials in International Business Transactions (Adopted by the Negotiating Conference on 21 November 1997). • OECD Recommendation of the Council on Tax Measures for Further Combating Bribery of Foreign Public Officials in International Business Transactions (25 May 2009). • OECD Recommendation of the Council on Bribery and Officially Supported Export Credits (14 December 2006). • OECD Recommendation on Anti-Corruption Proposals for Aid-Funded Procurement: Follow-up report. **United Nations** • Convention against Corruption (UNCAC) (14 December 2005): United Nations, Treaty Series, vol. 2349, p. 41; Doc. A/58/422.	**OECD** • OECD Guidelines for Multinational Enterprises – Section VII (2008). • OECD Recommendation of the Council for Further Combating Bribery of Foreign Public Officials in International Business Transactions (Adopted by the Council on 25 May 2009 and 26 November 2009). including Annex 1 (Good Practice Guidance on Implementing Specific Articles of the Convention on Combating Bribery of Foreign Public Officials in International Business Transactions) and Annex II (Good practice guidance on internal controls, ethics, and compliance). **United Nations** • UN Office on Drugs and Crime (2009) "Technical Guide to the United Nations Convention against Corruption".
UK National Regulations and Standards	• Money Laundering Regulations (2007), Statutory Instrument 2007 No 2157. • Proceeds of Crime Act 2002 (Chapter 29), Part 7. • Fraud Act 2006 (Chapter 35). • Bribery Act 2010 (Chapter 23). • Civil Evidence Act 1995 (Chapter 38). • Theft Act 1968 (Chapter 60).	• Ministry of Justice "Guidance about procedures which relevant commercial organisations can put into place to prevent persons associated with them from bribing (section 9 of the Bribery Act 2010)". • HM Revenue and Customs (July 2010), Anti-money laundering guidance for trust or company service providers • Consultative Committee of Accountancy Bodies (August 2008), Anti-money Laundering guidance for the accountancy sector • Prevention of money laundering / combating terrorist financing – guidance for the UK financial sector Parts I & II, Joint Money Laundering Steering Group (JMLST) Guidance (December 2007).

Domain	Laws, Regulations and Norms	Standards, Frameworks, and Guidance
A.1.3 **Public procure-ment**	• Directive 2007/66/EC "amending Council Directives 89/665/EEC and 92/13/EEC with regard to improving the effectiveness of review procedures concerning the award of public contracts" (11 December 2007). • Directive 2004/18/EC (31 March 2004) on "the coordination of procedures for the award of public works contracts, public supply contracts and public service contracts" (31 March 2004), "Public Sector Directive". • Directive 97/52/EEC European Parliament and Council Directive 97/52/EC "amending Directives 92/50/EEC, 93/36/EEC and 93/37/EEC concerning the coordination of procedures for the award of public service contracts, public supply contracts and public works contracts respectively" (13 October 1997). • Directive 92/13/EEC "coordinating the laws, regulations and administrative provisions relating to the application of Community rules on the procurement procedures of entities operating in the water, energy, transport and telecommunications sectors" (25 February 1992). • Directive 89/665/EEC on "the coordination of the laws, regulations and administrative provisions relating to the application of review procedures to the award of public supply and public works contracts" (21 December 1989). • EC Decision 87/95/EEC on "standardization in the field of information technology and telecommunications" (22 December 1986).	

Domain	Laws, Regulations and Norms	Standards, Frameworks, and Guidance
Global Regulation and Standards *(Examples)*	• Agreement on Government Procurement (GPA) (15 April 1994) [a WTO Uruguay Round agreement] 1915 UNTS 103.	
UK National Regulations and Standards	• The Public Procurement (Miscellaneous Amendments) 2011, Regulations Statutory Instrument 2011 No 2053. • The Public Contracts (Amendment) 2009, Regulation Statutory Instrument 2009 No 2992. • The Utilities Contracts (Amendment) Regulations Statutory Instrument 2009, No 3100. • The Public Contracts Regulation 2006, Statutory Instrument 2006 No 5.	
A.1.4 **Contract law**	• Directive 2001/115/EC "amending Directive 77/388/EEC with a view to simplifying, modernising and harmonising the conditions laid down for invoicing in respect of value added tax" (Electronic Invoicing Directive) (20 December 2001). • Directive 2000/31/EC on "certain legal aspects of information society services, in particular electronic commerce, in the Internal Market" (E-Commerce Directive) (8 June 2000). • Directive 1997/7/EC on "the Protection of Consumers in respect of Distance Contracts" (Distance Selling Directive) (20 May 1997).	• COM(2001)398 on "European Contract Law" (11 July 2001). • Standards for interoperability of e-invoice systems (*e.g.* sharing electronic files between companies, complying with Member States' different book-keeping standards). International Chamber of Commerce • ICC (2012) "Model Contracts and Clauses". • ICC (2011) "ICC Model International Franchising Contract". • ICC (2011) "ICC Model Subcontract". • ICC (2011) "ICC Legal Handbook on Global Sourcing Contracts". • ICC (2002) "Model Commercial Agency Contract".
UK National Regulations and Standards	• Companies Act 2006 (Chapter 46). • Competition Act 1998 (Notification of Excluded Agreements and Appealable Decisions) Regulations 2000, Statutory Instrument 2000 No 263. • Unfair Terms in Consumer Contracts Regulations 1999, Statutory Instrument 1999 No 2083. • Sale and Supply of Goods Act 1994 (Chapter 35). • Supply of Goods and Services Act 1982 (Chapter 29). • Sale of Goods Act 1979 (Chapter 54). • Unfair Contract Terms Act 1977 (Chapter 50).	• The Corporate Responsibility Coalition (2007), "The Companies Act 2006: Director's Duties Guidance". • DTI (June 2007), "Companies Act 2006: Duties of company director – Ministerial statements". • Institute of Chartered Secretaries & Administrators (2007), "ICSA Guidance on Directors' General Duties".

Domain	Laws, Regulations and Norms	Standards, Frameworks, and Guidance
A.1.5 **Finance and taxation law**	**Tax Regulation** **Value added Tax (VAT)**: "The common system of VAT applies to the production and distribution of goods and services bought and sold for consumption within the European Union (EU). To ensure that the tax is neutral in impact, irrespective of the number of transactions, taxable persons for VAT may deduct from their VAT account the amount of tax which they have paid to other taxable persons." The EU VAT agreements are only temporary, as Member States are unwillingly to cede their sovereign powers of taxation to the EU. Most EU tax agreements aims to harmonize the Single Market for a competitive e-Commerce tax regime. • Directive 2006/58/EC "amending Council Directive 2002/38/EC as regards the period of application of the VAT arrangements applicable to radio and television broadcasting services and certain electronically supplied services" (27 June 2006). • Directive 2002/38/EC "amending ... Directive 77/388/EEC as regards the value added tax arrangements applicable to ... certain electronically supplied services" (2 May 2002). • Directive 1999/59/EC "amending Directive 77/388/EEC as regards the value added tax arrangements applicable to telecommunications services" (17 June 1999). **Financial sector-specific regulations** • Regulation No 1287/2006 "implementing Directive 2004/39/EC as regards record-keeping obligations for investment firms, transaction reporting, market transparency, admission of financial instruments to trading, and defined terms for the purposes of that Directive" (short Markets in Financial Instruments Directive - MiFID), (10 August 2006). • Directive 2006/31/EC "amending directive 2004/39/EC on markets in financial instruments, as regards certain deadlines" (5 April 2006). • Directive 2005/60/EC on "the prevention of the use of the financial system for the purpose of money laundering, including terrorist financing (Third Anti-Money Laundering Directive) (26 Oct 2005). • Directive 2004/39/EC "on markets in financial instruments *etc.*" (Markets in Financial Instruments Directive - MiFID) (21 April 2004). • New Basel Capital Accord (Basel II)/ Capital Requirements Directive (CRD; "International Convergence of Capital Measurement and Capital Standards - A Revised Framework" (June 2004).	• COM(2000)349 on "administrative cooperation in the field of indirect taxation (VAT), as regards the VAT arrangements applicable to certain services supplied by electronic means" (7 June 2000). • COM(1998)374 on "Electronic Commerce and Indirect Taxation" (17 June 1998). [NB: As taxation is considered by Member States to be within their exclusive competence, guidance is primarily available from member States national tax offices.] Enterprise Resource Planning (ERP) software standards providing multiple application modules for business in the areas of Financial Management, Logistics, Manufacturing, Human Resources and extended supply chain operations; *e.g.*: • SAP • Oracle Financials • PeopleSoft • Hyperion Enterprise

Domain	Laws, Regulations and Norms	Standards, Frameworks, and Guidance
A.2 Consumer Protection and Employment Law		
A.2.1 **Consumer protection and alternative dispute resolution**	**Consumer Protection** • COM(2001)531 "Green Paper on European Union Consumer Protection" (2 October 2001). • Directive 2002/65/EC on "distance marketing of financial services and amending Council Directive 90/619/EEC and Directives 97/7/EC and 98/27/EC" (23 September 2002). • Directive 98/27/EC on "injunctions for the protection of consumers' interests" (Injunctions Directive) (19 May 1998). • Directive 97/7/EC on "the Protection of Consumers in respect of Distance Contracts" (Distance Selling Directive) (20 May 1997).	Recommendation (2001)310 on "Principles for out-of-court bodies involved in the consensual resolution of consumer disputes" (4 April 2001). Guidance on contract law from international organisations such as the International Chamber of Commerce. The European Social Charter (signed by the members of the Council of Europe in Turin, 18 October 1961) provides a framework for social rights in order to improve the standard of living and social well-being. It was intended to fill a gap left by the Convention for the Protection of Human Rights and Fundamental Freedoms, which essentially covers only civil and political rights.
Global Regulation and Standards (Examples)	• COM(98)50 "Globalisation and the Information Society: The Need For Strengthened International Coordination" (14 February 1998).	• UN (1985) "United Nations Guidelines for Consumer Protection". • OECD "Guidelines for Consumer Protection in the Context of Electronic Commerce" (9 December 1999).
UK National Regulations and Standards	• The Consumer Protection from Unfair Trading Regulations 2008, Statutory Instrument 2008 No 1277. • Financial Services (Distance Marketing) Regulation 2004, Statutory Instrument 2004 No 2095. • Consumer Protection: The Enterprise Act 2002 (Part 8 Domestic Infringements) Order 2003, Statutory Instrument 2003 No 1593. • The Unsolicited Goods and Services Act 1971 (Electronic Communications) Order 2001, Statutory Instrument 2001 No 2778. • Consumer Protection (Distance Selling) Regulations 2000, Statutory Instrument 2000 No 2334. • Unfair Terms in Consumer Contracts Regulations 1999 (UTCCRs), Statutory Instrument 1999 No 2083. • Consumer Credit Act 1974 (Electronic Communications) Order 2004, Statutory Instrument 2004 No 3236. • Management of Health and Safety at Work and Fire Precautions (Workplace) (Amendment) Regulations 2003, Statutory Instrument 2003 No 2457. • Trade Descriptions Act 1968 (Chapter 29).	• Department for Business Enterprise and Regulatory Reform (May 2008) "Guidance on the UK Regulations implementing the Unfair Commercial Practices Directive". • BIS (2008) "The Consumer Protection from Unfair Trading Regulations: a basic guide for business". • Office of Fair Trading (OFT), complaints evidence checklists. • OFT, Business to business promotions and comparative advertisements - A quick guide to the Business Protection from Misleading Marketing Regulations 2008 • DTI Consumer White Paper "Modern Markets: Confident Consumers" (1999).

Domain	Laws, Regulations and Norms	Standards, Frameworks, and Guidance
A.2.2 **Work and employment**	• Directive 2009/104/EC concerning "the minimum safety and health requirements for the use of work equipment by workers at work (second individual Directive within the meaning of Article 16(1) of Directive 89/391/EEC)" (16 September 2009). • Directive 2003/88/EC on "certain aspects of the organisation of working time" (2003 Working Time Directive) (4 November 2003). • Directive 90/270/EEC on "the minimum safety and health requirements for work with display screen equipment (fifth individual Directive within the meaning of Article 16 (1) of Directive 89/391/EEC) (29 May 1990). • Directive 89/391/EEC on "the introduction of measures to encourage improvements in the safety and health of workers at work" (12 June 1989).	(General employment law, health and safety regulations are primarily defined at national level.)
UK National Regulations and Standards	• Equality Act 2010 (Chapter 15). • Corporate Manslaughter and Corporate Homicide Act 2007 (Chapter 19). • Control of Lead at Work Regulations 2002, Statutory Instrument 2002 No 2676. • Race Relations (Amendment) Act 2000 (Chapter 34). • National Minimum Wage Regulations 1999, Statutory Instrument 1999 No 584. • Workplace (Health Safety and Welfare) Regulations 1992, Statutory Instrument 1992 No 3002, esp. §§ 5 & 11. • Health and Safety (Display Equipment) Regulations 1992, Statutory Instrument 1992 No 2792. • Race Relations Act 1976 (Chapter 74). • Sex Discrimination Act 1975 (Chapter 65). • The Equal Pay Act 1970 (Amendment) Regulations 2003, Statutory Instrument 2003 No 1656. • The Employment Equality (Age) Regulations 2006, Statutory Instrument 2006 No 1031.	Guidance produced by the Equality Commission for Northern Ireland: • Equality Act 2010 Statutory Code of Practice. • Quick-start guide to providing equal pay. • Code of Practice on Equal Pay (February 1999). • Employment Practice Data Protection Code (2002).

Domain	Laws, Regulations and Norms	Standards, Frameworks, and Guidance
A.3 Information security		
A.3.1 **Electronic signatures**	• Commission Decision 2003/511/EC on "the publication of reference numbers of generally recognised standards for electronic signature products in accordance with Directive 1999/93/EC *etc.*" (14 July 2003). • Directive 1999/93/EC on "a Community Framework for Electronic Signatures" (13 December 1999). Annexe I: Requirements for qualified certificates Annexe II: Requirements for CSPs issuing qualified certificates Annexe III: Requirements for secure signature-creation devices Annexe IV: Recommendations for secure signature verification • Commission Decision 2000/709/EC on "the minimum criteria to be taken into account by Member States when designating bodies in accordance with Article 3(4) of Directive 1999/93/EC of the European Parliament and of the Council on a Community framework for electronic signatures (6 November 2000). • Council Decision 1999/468/EC "laying down the procedures for the exercise of implementing powers conferred on the Commission" (28 June 1999). • COM(97)503 "Ensuring Security and Trust in Electronic Communication: Towards A European Framework for Digital Signatures and Encryption" (8 October 1997).	**Guidance** • COM(2006) 120 final "Report on the operation of Directive 1999/93/EC on a Community framework for electronic signatures" (15 March 2006). **SIGNATURE STANDARDS** **European Commission** • Official recognition of EESSI (European Electronic Signature Standardisation Initiative) standards in OJ, 14.07.03 – Qualified Signatures, Qualified Certificates. **European Telecommunications Standard Institute (ETSI)** • ETSI TS 101 733 "Electronic Signature Formats" for usage of X.509. • ETSI TS 101 456 "security management and policy requirements". **ITU standards** • X.400 standard for "electronic mail transfer (ITU-T standard)". • X.509 Public key certificate [ITU standard]. • X.500 standard for "distributed maintenance of files and directories (ITU-T standard)". • Lightweight Directory Access Protocol (LDAP) standard [for reading X.500 directories]. **Encryption Technologies - Industry Standards** • SSL-128B (Secure Sockets Layer), AES (Advanced Encryption Standard), DES (Data Encryption Standard), 3DES, RC4, RSA (Redundant Acronym Syndrome), Hashing (MD5, SHA). • Secure VPNs with IP Security Protocols (Ipsec).
UK National Regulations and Standards	• Electronic Communications Act 2000 (Chapter 7), Statutory Instrument 2000 No 1798. • The Communications Act 2003 (Consequential Amendments) Order 2003, Statutory Instrument 2003 No 2155.	**NATIONAL STANDARDS** • Self Regulatory body and standards for trust services tScheme (www.tscheme.org.uk). • Alliance for Electronic Business (tScheme) "HMG Public Key Infrastructure - High Level Processes and Procedures".
Global Regulation and Standards (Examples)	• UNCITRAL Model Law on Electronic Signatures (2001).	

Domain	Laws, Regulations and Norms	Standards, Frameworks, and Guidance
A.3.2 **Network security and security products**	**Network Security** • Council Framework Decision 2005/222/JHA on "attacks against information systems" (24 February 2005). • Council Resolution 2003/C 48/01 on "a European approach towards a culture of Network and Information Security" (18 February 2003). **Encryption** • N/A no specific encryption law exist within the EU. **Standardised and secured system of registries** • Regulation No 2216/2004/EC for "a standardised and secured system of registries pursuant to Directive 2003/87/EC of the European Parliament and of the Council and Decision No 280/2004/EC" (21 December 2004). **Information Systems** • Decision 2005/222/JHA on "attacks against information systems" (24 February 2005).	**EU GUIDANCE** • COM(2006)688 on "Fighting spam, spyware and malicious software" (15 November 2006). • COM(2006)251 "A strategy for a Secure Information Society – "Dialogue, partnership and empowerment"" (31 May 2006). • Council Resolution 2003/C 48/01 on "a European approach towards a culture of network and information security" (18 February 2003).

Domain	Laws, Regulations and Norms	Standards, Frameworks, and Guidance
Global Regulation and Standards (Examples)	• United Nations Convention on the Use of Electronic Communications in International Contracts (2005) [enters into force 1 March 2013].	**ISO Standards** • ISO/IEC 27001:2005 "Information Security Management System - Requirements. (Replacing BS7799-2, ISO/IEC 27001). ISO27001 is designed to harmonise with ISO9001:2000 (The Quality Management Process) and ISO14001:1996 (environmental management system - EMS). • ISO/IEC 27002:2005 (17799) Information technology. Security techniques. "Code of practice for information security management". • ISO/IEC 17799:2005 establishes guidelines and general principles for initiating, implementing, maintaining, and improving organizational information security management. • ISO 20000 (BS15000/BS 15000) "IT Service Management (ITSM) Standard". (Based on ITIL (IT Infrastructure Library) which was sponsored by the UK Government). • ISO 15292 "Information Security – Security techniques - Protection Profile registration procedures". **Other global standards** • UNCITRAL (Working Group on Electronic Commerce) Draft "Uniform Rules on Electronic Signatures" (12 November 98). • OECD (2002) "OECD Guidelines for the Security of Information Systems and Networks: Towards a Culture of Security" (25 July 2002). • OECD "Guidelines for Cryptographic Policy" (27 March 1997). • BIAC and ICC "Information Security Assurance for Executives – An international business companion to the 2002 OECD Guidelines for the security of networks and information systems: Towards a culture of security" (November 2003). • IETF (Internet Engineering Task Force) Internet-3125 "Electronic Signature Policies" (March 2001. • Information Security Forum (ISF) "Standard of Good Practice for Information Security" (2011). • US Federal Information Processing Standards (FIPS): FIPS 140-1 level2/3/4 "Crypto Module Evaluation", FIPS 186-1 "Standard for DSA", FIPS 180-1 "Standard for SHA-1", FIPS 46-3 "Standard for 3-DES". • ITSEC (Information Technology Security Evaluation Criteria) E1, E2, E3, E4, E5 and E6 (ratings) • US National Institute of Standards and Technology "Advanced Encryption Standard" (AES).

Domain	Laws, Regulations and Norms	Standards, Frameworks, and Guidance
UK National Regulations and Standards	• Civil Contingencies Act 2004 (Chapter 36), esp. §§5, 6, 12 & 17. • Courts Act 2003 (Chapter 39). • [Electronic] Communications Act 2003 (Chapter 21). • Mobile Telephone (Re-Programming) Act 2002 (Chapter 31). • Private Security Industry Act 2001 (Chapter 12), Schedule 2. • Contempt of Court Act 1981 (Chapter 49). • Computer Misuse Act 1990 (Chapter 18). • Official Secrets Act 1989 (Chapter 6).	**British Standard Institute (BSI)** • BS25999 "Business Continuity Management" (1:2006 Code of Practice, 2:2007 Specification). • BS 60950-1:2006 "Requirements for ensuring safety of IT equipment". • BS ISO/IEC 18028:2006 "Information technology. Security techniques". • PD ISO/IEC TR 18044:2004 "Information Technology. Security Techniques (Information Security Incident Management)". • BS ISO/IEC 15408-1:2005 "Information technology. Security techniques". • PD ISO/IEC TR 15443:2005 "Information technology. Security techniques. A framework for IT security assurance. Overview and framework". • PD ISO/IEC TR 15446:2004 "Information technology. Security techniques. Guide for the production of Protection Profiles and Security Targets". • BS7799/ ISO 17799 (British Standard Institute, UK government standard).
A.3.3 **Cybercrime**	**Cybercrime** • Council Framework Decision 2005/222/JHA on "attacks against information systems" (24 February 2005). • Council of Europe Convention on Cybercrime CETS No 185 (23 November 2001).	See also security standards.
UK National Regulations and Standards	• Computer Misuse Act 1990 (Chapter 18). • Police and Justice Act 2006 Part 5 (Chapter 48). • (Commencement No 9) Order 2008 No 2503 (C. 107). • Serious Crime Act 2007 (Chapter 27) Police and Justice Act 2006 (Chapter 48), esp. §§ 35-40. • Serious Organised Crime and Police Act 2005 (Chapter 15). • Police and Criminal Evidence Act 1984 (Chapter 60).	• Cabinet Office "The UK Cyber Security Strategy: Protecting and promoting the UK in a digital world" (November 2011). • Department for Business, Innovation and Skills (BIS): "Cyber Risk Management: A Board Level responsibility" (2012). • CESG "Executive Companion: 10 Steps to Cyber Security" (2012).
A.3.4 **Security for passports and visas**	**Standards for security features and biometrics in passports** • Council Regulation No 2252/2004 on "standards for security features and biometrics in passports and travel documents issued by Member States" (13 December 2004). **Visa Information** • Council Decision 2004/512/EC "establishing the Visa Information System (VIS)" (8 June 2004).	**Biometrics Standards** • BS ISO/IEC 19794-3 "Information technology. Biometric data". • BS ISO/IEC 19784-1:2006 "Information technology. Biometric application programming interface. BioAPI specification". • BS ISO/IEC 19794-1:2006 "Information technology. Biometric data interchange formats. Framework". • BS ISO/IEC 19795-1:2006 "Information technology. Biometric performance testing and reporting. Principles and framework". • BS ISO/IEC 19794-2:2005 "Information technology. Biometric data interchange formats. Finger minutiae data". • BS ISO/IEC 19794-4:2005 "Information technology. Biometric data interchange formats. Finger image data". • BS ISO/IEC 19794-5:2005 "Information technology. Biometric data interchange formats. Face image data". • BS ISO/IEC 19794-6:2005 "Information technology. Biometric data interchange formats. Iris image data". • BS ISO/IEC 19785-1 "Information technology. Common biometric exchange formats framework. Data element specification". • BS ISO/IEC 19785-2 "Information technology. Common biometric exchange formats framework. Procedures for the operation of the Biometric Registration Authority".

Domain	Laws, Regulations and Norms	Standards, Frameworks, and Guidance
A.4 Data protection and privacy rights		
A.4.1 **General data protection and data retention**	**Data Protection Directive** • COM(2012/11/EC) final "on the protection of individuals with regard to the processing of personal data and on the free movement of such data (General Data Protection Regulation)" (25 January 2012). • COM(2012/9/EC) "Safeguarding Privacy in a Connected World – A European Data Protection Framework for the 21st Century" (25 January 2012). • Directive 97/66/EC on "processing of personal data and the protection of privacy in the telecommunications sector" (15 December 1997). • Directive 95/46/EC on "the protection of individuals with regard to the processing of personal data and on the free movement of such data" (Data Protection Directive) (24 October 1995). **Protection of personal data in relation to electronic communications networks and Data Retention** • Directive 2006/24/EC on "the retention of data generated or processed in connection with the provision of publicly available electronic communication services or of public communications networks amending Directive (2002/58/EC)" (15 March 2006). • Directive 2002/58/EC on "processing of personal data and protection of privacy in the electronic communications sector" (Privacy and electronic communications Directive) (12 July 2002).	**Data Protection Standards:** • *Data Protection Working Party* [established by Article 29 of Directive 95/46/EC as an independent EU Advisory Body on Data Protection and Privacy]: • *Art.* 29 Working Party (10054/03-WP68) "Working Document on on-line authentication services" (29 January 2003). • Art. 29 WP "Opinion 2/2000 concerning the general review of the telecommunications legal framework", presented by the Internet Task Force (3rd February 2000). • Art. 29 WP Opinion (2000)5009final Opinion 1/2000 on "certain data protection aspects of electronic commerce"; presented by the Internet task force (3 February 2000). • Art. 29 WP Recommendation 3(99)3/final WP25 on "the preservation of traffic data by Internet Service Providers for law enforcement purposes" (7 September 1999). • Chartered Accountants of Canada (CICA) and the American Institute of Certified Public Accountants (AICPA) - AICPA/CICA Privacy Task Force "Generally Accepted Privacy Principles (GAPP)".. **Data Retention/ Information Management Standards** • ISO TC 46 "Information and Documentation". • ISO TC 171 "Document Management Applications". • ISO 15489:2001 "Records Management". • ISO 23081-1:2006 "Information and documentation, Records management process, Metadata for records (Paer 1: Principles) ". • ISO 15801 "Authenticity of electronic information". • ISO 17799 "Information Security Management". • ISO 19005:2005 "PDF/A electronic archiving format". **Information and Records Management** • BS ISO 15489:2001 "Information and documentation. Records management". • BS 5454:2000 "Recommendations for the storage and exhibition of archival documents". • BS ISO/IEC 10918-4:1999 "Information technology. Digital compression and coding of continuous-tone still images". [Registration of JPEG profiles, SPIFF profiles, SPIFF tags, SPIFF colour spaces, APPn markers, SPIFF compression types, and Registration Authorities (REGAUT)] • PD 0006:1995 "Technical guide to JPEG. Digital compression of photographic images". **Storage Devices/Interfaces** • Fibre Channel, Serial ATA (SATA), Serial Attached SCSI (SAS), parallel SCSI. • DAS (Direct-Attached Storage) and FAS (Fabric-Attached Storage). • Virtual Tape Libraries (VTL).

Domain	Laws, Regulations and Norms	Standards, Frameworks, and Guidance
UK National Regulations and Standards	• Data Protection Act 1998 (Chapter 29). (Eight key principles for European data protection in appendix). • Freedom of Information Act 2000 (Chapter 36). • The Data Retention (EC Directive) Regulations 2009, Statutory Instrument 2009 No 859.	See also A.4.3 Data Protection and investigations. **UK Information Commissioners Office (ICO)** **ICO Data Protection Good practice notes, *e.g.*:** • "Buying and selling customer databases" • "Checklist for handling requests for personal information (subject access requests.)" • "Collecting personal information using websites" • "Outsourcing and Provide personal info to 3rd parties" • "Security of personal information" • "Notification of Data Security Breaches to the Information Commissioner's Office". **Freedom of Information Good practice notes, *e.g.:*** • "Advice on using the procedural codes of practice" • "ICO policy on publication schemes" • "Time constraints on considering the public interest".
A.4.2 **Pan-European data transfer**	**Protection from misuse of individuals' personal data by Community bodies** • Council Decision (2004/644/EC) adopting implementing rules concerning Regulation (EC) No 45/2001 on "the protection of individuals with regard to the processing of personal data by the Community institutions and bodies and on the free movement of such data" (13 September 2004). • Regulation (EC) No 2001/45 on "the protection of individuals with regard to the processing of personal data by the institutions and bodies of the Community and on the free movement of such data" (18 December 2000). **Transmission of data to the Commission** • Commission Regulation 9 (EC) No 179/2005 amending Regulation (EC) No 1917/2000 with regard to the transmission of data to the Commission (2 February 2005). **Alternative set of standard contractual clauses for transfer of personal data to third countries** • Commission Decision (2004)915 "amending Decision (2001/497/EC) as regards the introduction of an alternative set of standard contractual clauses for the transfer of personal data to third countries" (27 December 2004). • Commission Decision (2000)2441 "pursuant to Directive 95/46/EC of the European Parliament and of the Council on the adequacy of the protection provided by the safe harbour privacy principles and related frequently asked questions issued by the US Department of Commerce" (26 July 2000). • Resolution (2000)0177 "European Parliament Resolution: Safe Harbour Privacy Principles", developed by the U.S. Department of Commerce in consultation with the European Commission (22 June 2000).	See also A.4.1 General data protection and data retention and A.4.3 Data protection and investigations.

Domain	Laws, Regulations and Norms	Standards, Frameworks, and Guidance
UK National Regulations and Standards	• The Privacy and Electronic Communications (EC Directive) Regulations 2003, Statutory Instrument 2003 No 2426. • The Telecommunications (Data Protection and Privacy) Regulations 1999, Statutory Instrument 1999 No 2093. • The Telecommunications (Data Protection and Privacy) (Direct Marketing) Regulations 1998, Statutory Instrument 1998 No 3170.	
A.4.3 **Data protection and investigations**	**Transfer of air passenger name record data** • Council Decision 2007/551/CFSP/JHS on "the signing, on behalf of the European Union, of an Agreement between the European Union and the United States of America on the processing and transfer of Passenger Name Record (PNR) data by air carriers to the United States Department of Homeland Security (DHS) (2007 PNR Agreement) (23 July 2007). • Commission Decision 2006/253/EC on "the adequate protection of personal data contained in the Passenger Name Record of air passengers transferred to the Canada Border Service Agency" (6 September 2005). • Data Protection Working Party Advisory Opinion 6/2004 on "the implementation of the Commission Decision of 14 May, 2004 and Council decision of 17 May, 2004 on the adequate protection of PNR of air passengers transferred to the United States Bureau of Customs and Border Protection and the Department of Homeland Security" (22 June 2004). • Council Decision 2004/496/EC on "the conclusion of the Agreement between the EU and the USA on the processing and transfer of PNR data by Air Carriers to the US Department of Homeland Security" (17 May 2004), referring to COM/2004/0190final. • Commission Decision 2004/535/EC on "the adequate protection of personal data contained in the PNR of air passengers transferred to the United States' Bureau of Customs" (14 May 2004).	See also A.4.1 General data protection and data retention. **Card fraud protection databases** • Guidelines by the EU Committee of Data Protection Authorities on "the collection and processing of data on merchants whose contracts to accept payment cards have been terminated" (2 March 2005).
Global Regulation and Standards (Examples)	• United Nations "Universal Declaration of Human Rights" (10 December 1948) • The European Convention on Human Rights and its five protocols (20 January 1966)., • EU 2000/C363/01 Charter of Fundamental Rights of the European Union (Article 8 "Protection of personal data") (18 December 2000).	• U.S. Department of Commerce "Safe Harbour Privacy Principles" (21 July 2000). • OECD Recommendation "Guidelines on the Protection of Privacy and Transborder Flows of Personal Data" (23 September 1980). • OECD DSTI/ICCP/REG(98)12/FINAL, Working Party on Information Security and Privacy, "Inventory of Instruments and Mechanisms contributing to the Implementation and Enforcement of the OECD Privacy Guidelines on Global Networks" (11 July 1999) . • OECD DSTI/ICCP/REG(98)6/FINAL, Directorate for Science, Technology and Industry – Committee for Information, Computer and Communications Policy, "Practices to implement the OECD Privacy Guidelines on global networks" (23 December 1998). • International Working Group on Data Protection in Telecommunications "Working Paper on data protection aspects of digital certificates and public-key infrastructures", (28 August 2001).

Domain	Laws, Regulations and Norms	Standards, Frameworks, and Guidance
UK National Regulations and Standards	• Protection of Freedoms Act 2012 (Chapter 9). • The Privacy and Electronic Communications (EC Directive) (Amendment) Regulations 2011, Statutory Instrument 2011 No 1208. • Electronic Communications: The Data Retention (EC Directive) Regulations 2009. • Coroners and Justice Act 2009 (Chapter 25), Part 8. • Counter-Terrorism Act 2008 (Chapter 28). • Data Retention (EC) Regulation 2007, Statutory Instrument 2007 No 859. • Terrorism Act 2006 (Chapter 11). • Children Act 2004 (Chapter 31), esp. § 63. • [Electronic] Communications Act 2003 (Chapter 21). • The Privacy and Electronic Communications (EC Directive) Regulations 2003, Statutory Instrument 2003 No 2426. • Anti-Terrorism, Crime and Security Act 2001 (incl. Data Retention regulation). • Freedom of Information Act 2000 (Chapter 36). • Regulation of Investigatory Powers Act (RIPA) 2000 (Chapter 23). Part 1 (communications, ePrivacy in Article 5.1) Part 2 (surveillance and covert human intelligence sources) Part 3 (disclosure of information). • Terrorism Act 2000 (Chapter 11). • Telecommunications (Lawful Business Practice) (Interception of Communications) Regulation 2000, Statutory Instrument 2000 No 2699 [implementing ePrivacy Article 5.2]. • Data Protection Act 1998 (Chapter 29). Incl. Schedule 1 "The Data Protection Principles". • Human Rights Act (HRA) 1998 (Chapter 42). • Public Interest Disclosure Act 1998 (Chapter 23). Environmental Information (Amendment) Regulations 1998, Statutory Instrument 1998 No 1447. • Environmental Information Regulations 1992, Statutory Instrument 1992 No 3240. • Public Records Act 1958 (Chapter 51).	**UK Information Commissioners Office (ICO)** • Employment Practices Code (November 2011). • CCTV Code of practice (January 2008). • Guidance for marketers on the Privacy and Electronic Communications (EC Directive) Regulations 2003 (2007). • A strategy for data protection regulatory action (November 2005). • Employment Practices Code, Supplementary Guidance, (June 2005). • Data Protection Audit Manual (June 2001). **Ofcom** • Oftel Code of Practice on "Telecommunications Directory Information Covering the Fair Processing of Personal Data" (21 December 1998). **UK-specific Information Management Standards (examples)** • BIP 0008-1 "Legal Admissibility of stored information". • BIP 0008-2 "Legal Admissibility of communicated information". • BIP 0008-3 "Legal Admissibility of electronic identity". **Business associations** • Intellect UK (2010) "Data Protection and Data Security Guidelines for Offshoring and Outsourcing"

Domain	Laws, Regulations and Norms	Standards, Frameworks, and Guidance
A.5 Copyright and related rights		
A.5.1 **Intellectual property rights**	• COM(2012)372 on "collective management of copyright and related rights and multi-territorial licensing of rights in musical works for on-line uses in the internal market" (11 July 2012). • Statement by the Commission 2005/295/EC "concerning Article 2 of Directive 2004/48/EC of the European Parliament and of the Council on "the enforcement of intellectual property rights" (13 April 2005). • Directive 2004/48/EC on "the enforcement of intellectual property rights" (29 April 2004).	For example, guidance issued by the Intellectual Property Rights (IPR) Helpdesk and national IRAs . • Recommendation 2005/737/EC on "collective cross-border management of copyright and related rights for legitimate online music services" (18 May 2005). • The European Commission's IPR (Intellectual Property Rights) Helpdesk provides manifold guidance, a helpline and training.
Sub-national Regulation and Standards		• European Charter for the Development and the Take-up of Film Online, agreed on 23 May 2006 at the Europe Day of the 59th Cannes Film Festival. • OMA DRM 1.0 including forward lock for content protection, combined delivery, separate delivery and super distribution.
Global Regulation and Standards	• Decision of the EEA Joint Committee (No 110/2004) amending Annex XVII (intellectual property) to the EEA Agreement (9 July 2004).	
A.5.2 **Copyright**	• Directive 2006/115/EC on "rental right and lending right and on certain rights related to copyright in the field of intellectual property" (12 December 2006). • Directive 2001/84/EC on "the resale right for the benefit of the author of an original work" (27 September 2001). • Directive 2001/29/EC on "the harmonisation of certain aspects of copyright and related rights in the information society" (22 June 2001). • Directive 93/83/EEC on "the coordination of certain rules concerning copyright and rights related to copyright applicable to satellite broadcasting and cable retransmission" (27 September 1993).	• IPR Helpdesk (2012) "Fact Sheet: How to deal with IP-related issues in transnational negotiations". • Intellectual Property Rights (IPR) Helpdesk provides guidance, a Helpline and training on European IP.
UK National Regulations and Standards	• Legal Deposit Libraries Act 2003 (Chapter 28). • Copyright (Visually Impaired Persons) Act 2002 (Chapter 33). • Copyright, etc. and Trade Marks (Offences and Enforcement) Act 2002 (Chapter 25). • Copyright, Design and Patents Act 1988 (Chapter 48). • Patents, Designs, Copyright and Trade Marks (Emergency) Act 1939.	See Intellectual Property Office (IPO) website.

Domain	Laws, Regulations and Norms	Standards, Frameworks, and Guidance
A.5.3 **Patents**	• Directive 2009/24/EC on "the legal protection of computer programmes" (23 April 2009).	For example, the Intellectual Property Rights (IPR) Helpdesk provides guidance, a Helpline and training for European IP. *e.g.* IPR Helpdesk (2012) "Fact Sheet: How to deal with IP-related issues in transnational negotiations".
UK National Regulations and Standards	• Patents Act 2004 (Chapter 16). • Patents Act 1977 (Chapter 37).	See Intellectual Property Office (IPO) website.
A.5.4 **Trade marks and designs**	**Trade Marks** • Regulation (EC) No 355/2009 "amending Regulation (EC) No 2869/95 on the fees payable to the Office for Harmonization in the Internal Market (Trade Marks and Designs) and Regulation (EC) No 2868/95 implementing Council Regulation (EC) No 40/94 on the Community trade mark" (31 March 2009). • Regulation (EC) No 1687/2005 "amending Regulation (EC) No 2869/95 on the fees payable to the Office for Harmonization in the Internal Market (Trade Marks and Designs) with regard to adapting certain fees" (14 October 2005). • Decision 2003/793/EC "approving the accession of the European Community to the Protocol relating to the Madrid Agreement concerning the international registration of marks" (27 October 2003). • Regulation (EC) No 2869/95 on the fees payable to the Office for Harmonization in the Internal Market (Trade Marks and Designs) (13 December 1995). • Regulation (EC) No 40/94 (20 December 1993). • Directive 89/104/EEC for "the harmonisation of the substantive law of validity and infringement of trade marks" (21 December 1988). **Designs** • Regulation No 1891/2006 amending Regulations (EC) No 6/2002 and (EC) No 40/94 to give effect to the accession of the European Community to the Geneva Act of the Hague Agreement concerning the international registration of industrial designs (18 December 2006). • Directive 1998/71/EC on "the legal protection of design" (13 October 1998).	Trade Marks are primarily defined at national level by the national patent offices.

Domain	Laws, Regulations and Norms	Standards, Frameworks, and Guidance
Global Regulation and Standards (Examples)	• Madrid Protocol Relating to the International Registration of Marks (27 June 1989). • Paris Convention for the Protection of Industrial Property (20 March 1883). • World Trade Organisation Agreement "Agreement on Trade-Related Aspects of Intellectual Property Rights ("TRIPs").	See World Intellectual Property Organization (WIPO) website.
UK National Regulations and Standards	• Trade Marks Act 1994 (Chapter 26).	See Intellectual Property Office (IPO) website.
A.5.5 **Legal protection of hardware**	**Semiconductors** • Decision 1994/828/EC on "the extension of the legal protection of topographies of semiconductor products to persons from certain territories" (19 December 1994).	
A.5.6 **Legal protection of software**	**Databases** • Directive 1996/9/EC on "the legal protection of databases" (11 March 1996).	
A.5.7 **Domain names**	• Regulation (EC) No 874/2004 "laying down public policy rules concerning the implementation and functions of the .eu Top Level Domain and the principles governing registration" (28 April 2004). • Regulation (EC) No 2002/733 on "the Implementation of the Internet Top Level Domain .eu" (22 April 2002).	• Internet Corporation for Assigned Names and Numbers (ICANN). • EURid (European Registry of Internet Domain Names). • Nominet-DRS (Register of all .UK domain names). • Verisign Global Registry Services. • Internet Engineering Task Force (IETF) and the Internet Architecture Board. • Technical guidance by Internet Engineering Task Force (IETF) and the Internet Architecture Board.
Global Regulation and Standards (Examples)	• US Department of Commerce (June 1998) US Policy Statement on "Management of Internet Names and Addresses.	

Domain	Laws, Regulations and Norms	Standards, Frameworks, and Guidance
A.6 Electronic commerce		
A.6.1 **e-Commerce regulation**	**e-Commerce regulation** • Directive 2000/31/EC on "certain legal aspects of information society services, in particular electronic commerce in the Internal Market" (Electronic commerce directive) (8 June 2000). • Directive 2009/110/EC on "the taking up, pursuit and prudential supervision of the business of electronic money institutions amending Directives 2005/60/EC and 2006/48/EC and repealing Directive 2000/46/EC" (16 September 2009). (Electronic Commerce regulation is covered in other thematic sections of this Matrix, including consumer protection (A.2) information security (A.3) and data protection and privacy rights (A.4). This section lists only regulations that define the scope of the EU jurisdiction over e-Commerce.)	
Global Regulation and Standards (Examples)	• OECD (16.11.2005) "Task Force on Spam background paper: Anti-Spam Regulation", DSTI/CP/ICCP/SPAM(2005)10/Final. • OECD (26.05.2005) "Anti-Spam Law Enforcement Report", DSTI/CP/ICCP/SPAM(2004)3/Final. • OECD (26.05.2005) "SPAM issues in developing countries", DSTI/CP/ICCP/SPAM(2005)6/Final. • OECD (25.7.2002) "OECD Guidelines for Information Security on Information Systems and Networks: Towards a Culture of Security".	• OECD DSTI/CP(2000)7/Final "First Report: Government and Private Sector Initiatives to Promote and Implement the OECD Guidelines for Consumer Protection in the Context of Electronic Commerce" (5 March 2001). • OECD (December 1999) "OECD Guidelines for Consumer Protection in Electronic Commerce". • OECD (16.11.2005) "Task Force on Spam background paper: Anti-Spam Regulation", DSTI/CP/ICCP/SPAM(2005)10/Final. • OECD (25.7.2002) "OECD Guidelines for Information Security on Information Systems and Networks: Towards a Culture of Security".
UK National Regulations and Standards	• Electronic Commerce (EC Directive) Regulations 2002, Statutory Instrument 2002 No 2013. • Misrepresentation Act 1967 (Chapter 7).	

Domain	Laws, Regulations and Norms	Standards, Frameworks, and Guidance
Sub-national Regulation and Standards	N/A – EU Regulation is standard neutral. Standards are developed by standards institutes, industry associations or/and often innovative or market dominant market players.	**Software standards for documents, images, video and music (examples)** • Documents: MS Windows (.doc), MS-DOS Text (.txt), Adobe Acrobat (.pdf), Word Macintosh (.mcw), Word Perfect (.doc). • Images: TIFF (.tif), JPEG (.jpg, .jpe), photoshop (.eps), Bitmap (.bmp), Macromedia Flash. • Video: Real Player, Windows Media Player. • Music: MP3 (MPEG-1 Audio Layer 3, more commonly referred to as MP3). **Internet Software and Web Technology (examples)** • JavaTM – Java Scripts, Java Enterprise Edition (JEE), Java Management extension (JMX), Joram (Java Open Reliable Asynchronous Messaging), J2EE Development, MIDP 2.0, CLDC (Connected Limited Device Configuration (J2ME)), Ajax (Asynchronous Javascript and XML). • Google browser technology (incl. Google Apps Premier Edition web-based office suite). • HTML 4.0 etc, HTTP. • WAP 2.0 XHTML/HTML multimode browser (Wireless Application Protocol). **Operating Systems/ Server Architecture (examples)** • Microsoft OS: Windows DOS/95/97/98/2000/NT/XP/Vista (previously Longhorn)/ Office 2007, .NET Framework, Internet Explorer, Exchange Server 2007; Microsoft Communication Protocol Program (MCPP). • Windows Mobil OS (v. 6.0, using MS SharePoint collaboration server). • UNIX and AIX (advanced Interactive Execution). • Apple Macintosh. **Database/ Enterprise Resource Planning (ERP) standards (examples)** • Oracle Database/ Management System (Procedural language (SL) and Structured query language (SQL), MySQL, relational databases). • JD Edwards. • SAP Enterprise Resource Planning (ERP)/ Service Oriented Architecture (SOA) system: SAP NetWeaver, MySAP ERP, SAP xApp Composite Applications, SAPDB. **Electronic Communications – Internet and email (examples)** • Simple Mail Transfer Protocol (SMTP, defined in RFC 821 (STD 10) as amended by RFC 1123 (STD 3) chapter 5). • Local Area Networks (LANs): IEEE802 LAN standards, Ethernet 802.3, Switched LANs. • Wide Area Networks (WANs): T1/CEPT-30(E1), Fractional T1, SONET/8DH, Transparent LAN service.
A.6.2 **e-Government**	eGovernment regulation is covered in other thematic sections of this Matrix, including consumer regulation, information security and VAT taxation.	

Domain	Laws, Regulations and Norms	Standards, Frameworks, and Guidance
A.6.3 **Payment systems**	• Regulation (EC) No 924/2009 on "cross-border payments in the Community and repealing Regulation (EC) No 2560/2001" (16 September 2009). • Directive 2007/64/EC on "payment services in the internal market amending Directives 97/7/EC, 2002/65/EC, 2005/60/EC and 2006/48/EC and repealing Directive 97/5/EC" ("Payment Services Directive") (13 November 2007). • Directive 2000/46/EC on "the taking up, pursuit of and prudential supervision of the business of electronic money institutions" (18 September 2000). • Directive 2000/28/EC on "amending Directive 2000/12/EC relating to the taking up and pursuit of the business of credit institutions" (18 September 2000). **Encryption/conditional access** • Directive 98/84/EC on "the legal protection of services based on, or consisting of, conditional access" (20 November 1998).	• European Commission "The Payment Services Directive: What it means for consumers". • Payment Card Industry Data Security Standards (PCI DSS, Dec 2004) "Data Security Standards".
Global Regulation and Standards (Examples)	• United Nations Commission on International Trade Law (UNCITRAL) "Model Law on Electronic Commerce with Guide to Enactment" (1996).	
B. Specific ICT Law and regulations, and supporting standards, frameworks and guidance		
B.1 The Information Society		
B.1.1 **Market liberalisation and regulation framework**	**Liberalisation of the Market** • Directive 2002/77/EC on "competition in the markets for Electronic Communications Services" (Liberalisation Directive) (16 September 2002). **Regulation of the Framework** • Decision 2010/299/EU "repealing Decision 2002/627/EC establishing the European Regulators Group for Electronic Communications Networks and Services" (10 May 2010). **European Initiative and Policy Papers** • Directive 2004/38/EC on "the right of citizens of the Union and their family members to move and reside freely within the territory of the Member States" (29 April 2004); "Citizen rights Directive".	**European Information Society Framework** • COM(97/623) Green Paper on "the Convergence of the Telecommunications, Media and Information Technology Sectors, and the Implications for Regulation. Towards an Information Society Approach" (3 December 1997). • COM(96/359) "Standardization and the Global Information Society: The European Approach" (24 July 1996). • Recommendation (1994) "Europe and the global information society - Recommendations to the European Council", (Bangemann Report) (30 November 1994). • COM(2003)567final "The role of eGovernment for Europe's future" (26 September 2003).
UK National Regulations and Standards		Examples: • BS 8419-1:2005 "Interoperability between metadata systems used for learning, education and training. Code of practice for the development of application profiles". • BS 8426:2003 "A code of practice for e-support in e-learning systems".

Domain	Laws, Regulations and Norms	Standards, Frameworks, and Guidance
B.1.2 **The New Regulatory Framework**	**The Harmonisation Directives (2009 updates)** • Directive 2009/140/EC "amending Directives 2002/21/EC on a common regulatory framework for electronic communications networks and services, 2002/19/EC on access to, and interconnection of, electronic communications networks and associated facilities, and 2002/20/EC on the authorisation of electronic communications networks and services" (eCommunications Framework)(25 November 2009). • Directive 2009/136/EC "amending Directive 2002/22/EC on universal service and users' rights relating to electronic communications networks and services, Directive 2002/58/EC concerning the processing of personal data and the protection of privacy in the electronic communications sector, and Regulation (EC) No 2006/2004 on cooperation between national authorities responsible for the enforcement of consumer protection laws" (EU Cookie or ePrivacy Directive) (25 November 2009). **Electronic Communications Services** The Harmonisation Directives: 1. Directive 2002/21/EC on "a common regulatory framework for electronic communications infrastructure and associated services" (Framework Directive) (7 March 2002). 2. Directive 2002/19/EC on "access to, and interconnection of, electronic communications networks and associated facilities" (Access Directive) (7 March 2002). 3. Directive 2002/20/EC on "authorisation of electronic communications networks and services" (Authorisation Directive) (7 March 2002). 4. Directive 2002/22/EC on "Universal service and users' rights relating to electronic communications networks and services" (Universal Service Directive) (7 March 2002). (a) Decision 2003/548/EC on "minimum set of leased lines with harmonised characteristics and associated standards referred to the Universal Services Directive" (23 July 2003). 5. Directive 2002/58/EC "concerning the procession of personal data and protection of privacy in the electronic communications sector" (ePrivacy Directive) (12 July 2002). **Framework related Regulations**: • Regulation (EC) No 531/2012 on "roaming on public mobile communications networks within the Union" (13 June 2012). • Regulation (EC) No 717/2007 on "roaming on "public mobile telephone networks within the Community and amending Directive 2002/21/EC" (27 June 2007). • COM(2004)28 on "unsolicited commercial communications or 'spam'" (22 January 2004) • Decision 676/2002/EC on "a regulatory framework for radio spectrum policy in the European Community" (Radio Spectrum Decision) (7 March 2002). • Regulation (EC) No 2887/2000 on "unbundled access to the local loop" (18 December 2000). **Standards-setting procedures in support of harmonization** • Directive 98/34/EC "laying down a procedure for the provision of information in the field of technical standards and regulations and of rules on Information Society services (22 June 1998). • Directive 98/48/EC "amending Directive 98/34/EC laying down a procedure for the provision of information in the field of technical standards and regulations" (20 July 1998). **Telecoms Licences** • Directive 97/13/EC on "a common framework for general authorizations and individual licences in the field of telecommunications services" (10 April 1997).	**NRA Framework Authority under the Harmonisation Directives** • COM(2006)28final on "Market Reviews under the EU Regulatory Framework – Consolidating the internal market for electronic communications" (6 February 2006). • (a) Recommendation 2003/311/EC on "relevant product and services markets within the electronic communications sector susceptible to regulation in accordance with the Framework Directive" (11 February 2003). OJ L 114/45 • (b) Recommendation 2003/497/EC on "relevant product and service markets within the electronic communications sector susceptible to ex ante regulation in accordance with Directive 2002/21/EC on a common regulatory framework for electronic communication networks and services" (11 February 2003). • (c) Recommendation 2003/561/EC on "notifications, time limits and consultations under art. 7 of the Framework Directive" (23 July 2003). OJ L190 • Commission's Information Society Directorate-General Commission Staff Working Document on "the Treatment of Voice over Internet Protocol (VoIP) under the EU Regulatory Framework" (14 June 2004). • Notice (98/C 6/04) Status of voice communications on Internet under Community law and, in particular, pursuant to Directive 90/388/EEC (10 January 1998).

Domain	Laws, Regulations and Norms	Standards, Frameworks, and Guidance
UK National Regulations and Standards	• The [Electronic] Communications Act 2003 (Chapter 21). (Implementation of the EU Communications Directives on 25 July 2003). • Companies Act (Electronic Communications) Order 2000. • Telecommunications (Fraud) Act 1997 (Chapter 4). • Telecommunications Act 1984 (Chapter 12).	**Guidance provided by Ofcom** • Ofcom (September 2005) "Telecommunications Strategic review". • Ofcom (23 June 2005) "telecommunications: A new regulatory approach". • Ofcom (2011) "Electronic Communications Code". **Guidance by the Information Commissioners Office** • ICO (7/09/2011) "The Guide to Privacy and electronic communications" • ICO (may 2012) "Guidance on the rules on use of cookies and similar technologies". • ICO (17/07/2012) "Notification of personal data breaches". Various standards are defined by international, European and national standards organisations.
B.1.3 Trans-European Networks (TEN)	**Trans-European [Telecommunications] Networks (TEN)** • Decision No 2002/1376/EC "amending Decision No 1336/97/EC on a series of guidelines for trans-European telecommunications networks" (12 July 2002).	
B.2 Internet regulation and activities		
B.2.1 **Safer Internet Use**	Safer Internet Use is covered in other thematic sections of this Matrix, including information security, data protection and privacy rights and electronic commerce. . **The Internet: Safer Internet Use** • Decision No 854/2005/EC "establishing a multi-annual Programme on promoting safer use of the Internet and new online technologies" (11 May 2005). • Decision No 1151/2003/EC "amending Decision No 276/1999/EC adopting a multiannual Community action plan on promoting safer use of the Internet by combating illegal and harmful content on global networks" (16 June 2003). • Decision No 276/1999 "adopting a multiannual Community action plan on promoting safer use of the Internet by combating illegal and harmful content on global networks" (25 January 1999).	• Communication COM(2002) 152 "Follow-up to the multiannual Community action plan on promoting safer use of the Internet by combating illegal and harmful content on global networks – Proposal for a Decision final amending Decision No 276/1999/EC adopting a multiannual Community action plan on promoting safer use of the Internet by combating illegal and harmful content on global networks" (22 March 2002). **New internet protocol** • COM(2002)96final "Next Generation Internet – priorities for action in migrating to the new internet protocol Ipv6" (21 February 2002).

Domain	Laws, Regulations and Norms	Standards, Frameworks, and Guidance
B.3 Telecommunication regulations		
B.3.1 **Wireless policy**	**Radio Spectrum Policy** • Directive 2006/28/EC "amending, for the purposes of their adoption to technical progress, Directive 72/245/EEC relating to the radio interference (electronic magnetic compatibility) of vehicles and amending Directive 70/156/EEC on the approximation of the laws of the Member States relating to the type-approval of motor vehicles and their trailers" (6 March 2006). • COM(2005/361 final) Proposal for a Directive repealing Directive 90/544/EEC on "the frequency bands designated for the coordinated introduction of pan-European land-based public radio paging in the Community" (3 August 2005). • Directive 2005/82/EC repealing Council Directive 90/544/EEC on "the frequency bands designated for the co-ordinated introduction of pan-European land-based public radio paging in the Community" (14 December 2005). • Directive 2005/49/EC "amending, for the purposes of their adaptation to technical progress, Council Directive 72/245/EEC relating to the radio interference (electromagnetic compatibility) of vehicles and Council Directive 70/156/EEC on the approximation of the laws of the Member States relating to the type-approval of motor vehicles and their trailers" (25 July 2005). • Decision 2005/513/EC on "the harmonised use of radio spectrum in the 5 GHz frequency band for the implementation of wireless access systems including radio local area networks (WAS/RLANs)" (11 July 2005). • Decision 2005/50/EC on "the harmonisation of the 24GHz range radio spectrum band for the time-limited use by automotive short range radar equipment in the Community" (17 January 2005). • Decision No 676/2002/EC on "a regulatory framework for radio spectrum policy in the European Community" (Radio Spectrum Decision). **Radio and Telecommunications Equipment Liberalisations** • Commission Decision on "the application of Article 3(3)(e) of Directive 1999/5/EC to radio equipment intended to participate in the Automatic Identification System (AIS)" (25 January 2005). • Directive 1999/5/EC on "radio equipment and telecommunications terminal equipment and the mutual recognition of their conformity" (9 March 1999). • Agreement on mutual recognition between the European Community and the United States of America (18 May 1998). **Interfaces and technical design** • Directive 1999/5/EC on "radio equipment and telecommunications terminal equipment and the mutual recognition of their conformity" (9 March 1999).	Standards defined by ITU Radiocommunication Sector (ITU-R): The Radio Regulations incorporates the decisions of the World Radiocommunication Conferences, including all Appendices, Resolutions, Recommendations and ITU-R Recommendations incorporated by reference (http://www.itu.int/en/ITU-R/). **Radio Spectrum Policy** The Radio Spectrum Policy Group (RSPG) provides guidance and opinions on *e.g.* • "Opinion on Digital Switchover" (document RSPG04-55). • "Opinion on Multimedia Services" (document RSPG06-143). • "Report and Final Opinion Scientific use of Spectrum" (document RSPG06-144). • "Final Opinion on EU Spectrum Policy Implications of the Digital Dividend" (document RSPG07-161). • "Final Revised Opinion on WRC-07" (document RSPG07-162). **Third-Generation Mobile Communications** • COM(2002/301final) "Towards the Full Roll-Out of Third Generation Mobile Communications" (20 March 2002). • COM(2001/141final) "The introduction of third generation mobile communication in the European Union: State of play and the way forward" (20 March 2001). **Radio and Telecommunications Equipment Liberalisation** • Decision No 31/2005 of the Joint Committee established under the Agreement on Mutual Recognition between the European Community and the United States of America of 14 February 2005 related to the listing of a Conformity Assessment Body under the Sectoral Annex on Telecommunication Equipment 2005/251/EC (22 March 2005). **Technical Standards that require licencing** • WCDMA 2100 with simultaneous voice and package data (PS max speed UL/DL 128/384kbps, CS max speed 64kbps). • EGPRS, class B, multislot class 10 (UL/DL = 118.4/238.8kbps). • GPRS, class B, multislot class 10. • Speech codecs: FR, EFR, WCDMA, GSM AMR.

Domain	Laws, Regulations and Norms	Standards, Frameworks, and Guidance
UK National Regulations and Standards	• Wireless Telegraphy Act 2006 (Chapter 36).	
B.3.2 **Access and interconnection**	• Regulation (EC) No 2887/2000 on “unbundled access to the local loop” (30 December 2000).	Notice (2002/C 165/03) “Commission guidelines on market analysis and the assessment of significant market power under the Community regulatory framework for electronic communications networks and services” (11 July 2002).
B.3.3 **Satellites**	• Regulation (EC) No 683/2008 on “the further implementation of the European satellite navigation programmes (EGNOS and Galileo)” (9 July 2008). • Regulation (EC) No 1943/2006 “amending Regulation (EC) No 876/2002 setting up the Galileo Joint Undertaking” (12 December 2006). • Regulation (EC) No 876/2002 on the establishment of Galileo Joint Undertaking (21 May 2002).	Key institutes involved in technical guidance: • The European Telecommunications Satellite Organisation (EUTELSAT) to guarantee certain standards and parameters in order to guarantee high quality reception and the safety of the overall system • Green Paper COM(2006)769final on “Satellite Navigation Applications” (8 December 2006).
B.4 Digital media and content		
B.4.1 **Digital interactive television**	• Directive 2007/65/EC “amending Council Directive 89/552/EEC on the coordination of certain provisions laid down by law, regulation or administrative action in Member States concerning the pursuit of television broadcasting activities” (11 December 2007). • Directive 97/26/EC on “the coordination of certain provisions laid down by law, regulation or administrative action in Member States concerning the pursuit of television broadcasting activities” (30 June 1997). • Directive 89/552/EC on “the coordination of certain provisions laid down by Law, Regulation or Administrative Action in Member States concerning the pursuit of television broadcasting activities” (Television without Frontiers Directive) (3 October 1989).	• Notice (2004/C 102/02) “Commission interpretative communication on certain aspects of the provisions on televised advertising in the ‘Television without frontiers’ Directive” (28 April 2004). • COM(2003)784final on “the future of European regulatory audiovisual policy” (15 December 2005). **Technical Protocols** • Internet Protocol TV (IPTV). Industry standards, *e.g.* Microsoft’s IPTV. • Single Programme Transport Stream (SPTS). • Formats for MPEG-2, MPEG-4 HD, MPEG-4 AVC, MPEG-7 (metadata) (Moving Picture Experts Group; ISO working group). • Multimedia Home Platform (MHP) and set-top boxes (STB). • Video Networks. • Fibre-to-home (FTTH) technology. • Video-on-demand (VOD). • VGA camera. • Resolution “standards”: 176x208 pixels, 640x460 pixels, 1600x1200 pixels, etc. • 3GPP video streaming. • Digital Video Broadcasting (DVB-SH). •

Domain	Laws, Regulations and Norms	Standards, Frameworks, and Guidance
UK National Regulations and Standards	• Broadcasting Act 1996 (Chapter 55), esp. §§ 18-31.	
B.4.2 **Digital content**	• Recommendation 2006/952/EC on "the protection of minors and human dignity and on the right of reply in relation to the competitiveness of the European audiovisual and on-line information services industry" (20 December 2006). • Recommendation 2005/865/EC on "film heritage and the competitiveness of related industrial activities" (Protection of film heritage of European significance) (9 December 2005). • Council of Europe: Additional Protocol to the Convention on Cybercrime, Concerning the Criminalisation of Acts of a Racist and Xenophobic Nature Committed through Computer Systems CETS No.: 189" (28 January 2003).	• Decision 456/2005/EC "establishing a multi-annual Community programme to make digital content in Europe more accessible, usable and exploitable" (of 9 March 2005).
UK National Regulations and Standards	Obtaining, use and dissemination of illegal content is covered in the UK by: • The Equality Act (Disability) Regulations 2010 (DDA), Statutory Instrument 2010 No 2128. • Coroners and Justice Act 2009 (Chapter 25), Part 2 §§ 62-69. • Criminal Justice and Immigration Act 2008 (Chapter 4), Part 5 §§ 63-71. • Sexual Offences Act 2003 (Chapter 42) esp. §§ 45-46. • Criminal Justice and Police Act 2001 (Chapter 16), § 42. • Protection of Children Act 1999 (Chapter 14). • The Defamation Act 1996 (Chapter 31). • Disability Discrimination Act 1995 (Chapter 50). • Criminal Justice and Public Order Act 1994 (Chapter 33), Part VII §§ 84-87 • Criminal Justice Act 1988 (Chapter 33), Part XI §§ 160, 160A & 161. • Civic Government (Scotland) Act 1982 (Chapter 45), esp. § 52. • Protection of Children Act 1978 (Chapter 37). • Obscene Publications Act 1959 (Chapter 66) and 1964 (Chapter 74). Children and Young Persons (Harmful Publications) Act, 1955 (Chapter 28). • Protection from Harassment Act (PHA) 1997 (Chapter 40). • Malicious Communications Act 1988 (Chapter 27). • Public Order Act 1986 (Chapter 6). • Offences Against the Person Act 1861 (Chapter 100) esp. § 16.	• House of Lords (2012) "1st Report of Session 2012-13: Broadband for all – an alternative vision" (24 July 2012). • BIS (2010) "Digital Radio" and "Vehicles sold with digital radios by 2013". • IPO (2010) "Copyright policy (inc. artist's resale rights)" and (2011) "Extending Copyright Exceptions for Educational Use" • ICO (2011) "Personal information online – code of practice"

Domain	Laws, Regulations and Norms	Standards, Frameworks, and Guidance
Sub-national Regulation and Standards		• European Charter for the Development and the Take-up of Film Online, agreed on 23 May 2006 at the Europe Day of the 59th Cannes Film Festival. • OMA DRM 1.0 including forward lock for content protection, combined delivery, separate delivery and super distribution.
B.5 Radio services and equipment		
B.5.1 **Radio interference**	**Radio Interference (electromagnetic compatibility) of vehicles** • Directive 2009/19/EC on "amending, for the purposes of its adaptation to technical progress, Directive 72/245/EC relating to the radio interference (electromagnetic compatibility) of vehicles" (12 March 2009). • Directive 2006/28/EC on "amending, for the purposes of their adaptation to technical progress, Directive 72/245/EEC relating to the radio interference (electromagnetic compatibility) of vehicles and Directive 70/156/EEC on the approximation of the laws of the Member States relating to the type-approval of motor vehicles and their trailers" (6 March 2006).	
B.5.2 **Compatibility**	**Electromagnetic Compatibility** • Directive (2004/108/EC) of the European Parliament and of the Council on "the approximation of the laws of the Member States relating to electromagnetic compatibility and repealing Directive" (89/226/EEC)	ISO standards, *e.g.* • ISO 33.100 "Electromagnetic compatibility (EMC)"; • ISO 33.100.10 "Emission"; • ISO 33.100.20 "Immunity" and • ISO 33.100.99 "Other aspects related to EMC" BSI standards *e.g.* • BS EN 55011 "Industrial, scientific and medical equipment. Radio-frequency disturbance characteristics. Limits and methods of measurement". • BS EN 55022 "Information technology equipment. Radio disturbance characteristics. Limits and methods of measurement".
B.5.3 **Radio equipment**	**Radio Equipment intended to participate in the Automatic Identification System (AIS)** □ Commission Decision on "the application of Article 3(3)(e) of Directive (1999/5/EC) to radio equipment intended to participate in the Automatic Identification System (AIS)" (25 January 2005). [Adopted by the Commission on 25.01.2005, Published on 26.01.2005, OJ L22/14 C(2005) 110].	

Domain	Laws, Regulations and Norms	Standards, Frameworks, and Guidance
B.6 Audiovisual services		
B.6.1 **The audiovisual services industry**	• Directive 2010/13/EU on "the coordination of certain provisions laid down by law, regulation or administrative action in Member States concerning the provision of audiovisual media services" (Audiovisual Media Services Directive) (10 March 2010).	• Technical media formats (decoding): MP3, AAC, Real Audio, WAV, Nokia Ring Tones, AMR, AMR-WB, AMR-NB, AU, MIDI, H.263, JPEG, JPEG2000, EXIF 2.2, GIF 87/89, PNG, BMP (W-BMP), MBM, MPEG-4, eAAC+. • Decision No 1718/2006/EC concerning "the implementation of a programme of support for the European audivisual sector" (MEDIA 2007) (15 November 2006). **European Audiovisual Observatory** • Council of Europe Resolution (92) 70 establishing a European Audiovisual Observatory.
B.7 Environment ("Green IT")		
B.7.1 **Green IT**	**Energy Efficiency** • COM(2011)370final Proposal for a Directive on "energy efficiency and repealing Directives 2004/8/EC and 2006/32/EC" (22 June 2011). • Directive 2006/32/EC on energy end-use efficiency and energy services and repealing Council Directive 93/76/EEC" (5 April 2006). • Directive 2004/8/EC on "the promotion of cogeneration based on a useful heat demand in the internal energy market and amending Directive 92/42/EEC" (11 February 2000). **Waste Electrical and Electronic Equipment (WEEE)** • Directive 2012/19/EU on "waste electrical and electronic equipment (WEEE)" (4 July 2012). • Directive 2008/112/EC "amending Directives 76/768/EEC, 88/378/EEC, 1999/13/EC and Directives 2000/53/EC, 2002/96/EC and 2004/42/EC in order to adapt them to Regulation (EC) No 1272/2008 on classification, labelling and packaging of substances and mixtures" (16 December 2008). Directive 2003/108/EC "amending Directive 2002/96/EC on waste electrical and electronic equipment (WEEE)" (8 December 2003). • Directive 2002/95/EC on "the restriction of the use of certain hazardous substances in electrical and electronic equipment" (27 January 2003). • Directive 2002/96/EC on "waste electrical and electronic equipment (WEEE)" (27 January 2003).	**Waste Electrical and Electronic Equipment (WEEE)** • European Recycling Platform (ERP): Europe's leading WEEE compliance scheme. • ISO14001:2004 "Environmental Management Standard" (replaces the old ISO14001:1996 standard).

Domain	Laws, Regulations and Norms	Standards, Frameworks, and Guidance
UK National Regulations and Standards	• **Climate Change** • Climate Change Act 2008 (Chapter 27). **Waste Electrical and Electronic Equipment** • The Waste Electrical and Electronic Equipment (Amendment) Regulations 2007, Statutory Instrument 2007 No 3454 • The Waste Electrical and Electronic Equipment Regulations 2006, Statutory Instrument 2006 No 3289. . • The Environmental Information Regulations 2004, Statutory Instrument 2004, No 3391. • The Control of Substances Hazardous to Health Regulations 2002, Statutory Instrument 2002 No 2677. • The Control of Lead at Work Regulations 2002, Statutory Instrument 2002 No 2676. • The Environmental Information (Amendment) Regulations 1998, Statutory Instrument 1998, No 1447.. • The Environmental Information Regulations 1992, Statutory Instrument 1992, No 3240.	**Green IT** • Government Offices of Sweden, Ministry of Enterprise, Energy and Communications (September 2009) "A Green Knowledge Society: An ICT policy agenda to 2015 fro Europe's future knowledge society". **Waste Electrical and Electronic Equipment** • UK Environment Agency "Waste electrical and electronic equipment: A guide to when electrical and electronic equipment is considered waste and the controls that apply" (March 2012). • BSI BIP 2117 "The Waste Electrical and Electronic Equipment Directive. Requirements and Implementation" (July 2008). • Code of Practice on the discharge of the obligations of public authorities under the Environmental Information Regulations 2004, Statutory Instrument 2004 No 3391. (February 2005).

Domain	Laws, Regulations and Norms	Standards, Frameworks, and Guidance
B.8 Other ICT-specific norms (sectoral hardware norms)		
B.8.1 **Wireless and fixed line**	(Sectoral norms are also covered in other thematic sections of this Matrix). • Directive 1999/5/EC on "radio equipment and telecommunications terminal equipment and the mutual recognition of their conformity" (9 March 1999).	The following lists examples of standards especially applicable to ICT manufacturers: **Wireless Standards** • Universal Mobile Telecommunications Services (UMTS) • UMTS High Speed Downlink Packet Access (HSDPA, speeds up to 3.5Mbps, Mobile Broadband).. • General Packet Radio Services (GPRS) – 2.5G cellular technology. • General System of Mobile Communications (GSM) – 2G cellular technology: 900/ 1800/ 1900 MHz GSM. • EDGE (Enhanced Data Rates for Global Evolution) – emerging 3G technology, 3 times faster data transfer as with GSM/GPRS. • Wideband Code-Division Multiple Access (WCDMA) – Europe's 3G cellular technology; WCDMA 2100 networks with simultaneous voice and package data (PS max speed UL/ DL 128/384kbps, CS max speed 64kbps). • EGPRS, class B, multislot class 10 (UL/DL = 118.4/238.8kbps). **Wireless protocols (incl. security)** • Virtual Private Networking (VPN) – to secure end-to-end communication. • Private Mobile Networks (PMN), Private Mobile Exchange (PMX). • Media Access Control (MAC). • Visitor Based Network (VBN). • Wireless Application Protocol (WAP). • Wireless Encryption/Equivalent Privacy (WEP) protocol (Wlan standard, Institute of Electrical and Electronics Engineers, old standard). • WiFi Protected Access (WPA and WPA2) security protocol (Wi-Fi Alliance). • Radio Frequency Identification (RFID) Standard, RFID Security. • Temporal key integrity protocol (TKIP). • WI-Fi Protected Setup standard (WPS). • Wireless Mark-up Language (WML). • Wireless Fidelity (WiFi) – wireless local area networking technology Standards: **Emerging standards to address Internet security** • High-Speed Uplink Packet Access (HSUPA, 5.8Mbps). • High Speed Downlink Packet Access (HSDPA, 14Mbps). • 3G LTE (Long-Term Evolution) standard, *a.k.a.* Super 3G' (enhance the capabilities of 3G networks from 2009, 20Mbps). • Very high bit-rate DSL (VDSL, xDSL technology providing data transmission, 20-50 Mbps). • Worldwide Interoperability for Microwave Access (WiMax, up to 75Mbps). • Fiber-to-the-X (FTTx, 10-100Mbps).

Domain	Laws, Regulations and Norms	Standards, Frameworks, and Guidance
B.8.1 **Wireless and fixed line**	(Sectoral norms are also covered in other thematic sections of this Matrix). • Directive 1999/5/EC on "radio equipment and telecommunications terminal equipment and the mutual recognition of their conformity" (9 March 1999).	**Frequency Spectrum** • 802.15 or XDA – Bluetooth. Ulta wide broadband (IEEE 802.15.3a, 2gbps within 4ms). • 802.11a (54 MB sec, 5GHz band, 300 feet range, licensed spectrum) • 802.11b (11 MB sec, 2.4GHz, 200 feet range, unlicensed spectrum) • 802.11g (54 MB sec, 2.4 GHz, unlicensed spectrum) • 802.11i (Forthcoming, security-hardened version of WiFi standard) • 802.16 – WiMAX, wide-radius, high-bandwidth wireless coverage • 802.1X - certificates or per-user passwords (IEEE protocol) • 802.11n (wireless network broadband) • WiMAX (Alvarion, Intel, 5GHz 802.n mesh and 2.4 GHz 902.11 access). • Direct Sequence Spread Spectrum (DSSS) (complies with 802.11b). • Remote Authentication Dial-In User Service (Radius). **Network connection** • X.25 Network connections between DTE and DCE, data link layer protocol (ITU-T standard). • X.121 International Data Numbers (ITU-T standard). • X.21 serial communications over synchronous digital lines [ITU-T standard). • X.28 terminal-to-PAD interface [ITU-T standard]. • X.75 specification for signalling system between two PDNs (ITU-T standard). **Voice Features** • Speaking Independent Name Dialling (SIND). • Stereo Handset HS-3. • Stereo Handset HS-3. **Fixed line internet connection** • Fixed Broadband: ADSL2+, VDSL (speeds up to 55Mbps). **Network Cables** • Connectivity Cable (USB): CA-53 • USB 2.0 full speed via Pop-PortTM (Nokia standard) interface

Domain	Laws, Regulations and Norms	Standards, Frameworks, and Guidance
B.8.2 **Data storage and power management**		**Memory** • Multi Media Card (MMC), reduced size Mul; (RS-MMC). • 64 MB Reduced Size Dual Voltage (1.8/3V) Multi Media Card (MMC). **Storage Devices/Interfaces** • Fibre Channel, Serial ATA (SATA), Serial Attached SCSI (SAS), parallel SCSI. • DAS (Direct-Attached Storage) and FAS (Fabric-Attached Storage). • Virtual Tape Libraries (VTL)[**Power Management** • General Battery Standards (IEC 60086-1 BS 387, ANSI C18.1M, ERR 1625,); • Lithium Standards (BS EN 60086-4:2000, IEC), • Nickel Metal Hydride Standards, Nickel Cadium Standards, Lead Acid Standards, Photovoltaic Standards, Safty Standards, etc. • Charger: AC-4.

Appendix 6: Stakeholders Directory

The following is a compendious list of ICT stakeholders that was compiled in order to identify and categorise the main stakeholders engaged in shaping ICT regulations, polices, and standards. Chapter Five above discusses Sub-national, National, European and Global stakeholders in detail and assesses their importance. Chapter Seven analyses the interaction between these stakeholders and their individual and collective influence on the eCommunications Regulatory framework. Groups of participants for the survey (Chapter Six) were selected from this list, which was also used to develop the Four-Level model (Chapter One). Due to the numerous stakeholders at National Level, the list samples that level primarily by drawing on stakeholders from the United Kingdom.

Due to the vast number of stakeholders operating at the different levels, this list provides only examples of certain categories, which are therefore marked with the symbol *). Please note that the field of ICT regulation is dynamic and the identities of actively engaged stakeholders is subject to change over time.

A6.1 Level 1: Sub-national Stakeholders

Level 1: Individual advocates

1. Management and Employees/Specialists of Companies*)

1.1 Individuals

- **Management** comprises those who lead and direct all or part of any organization, often a business, through the deployment and control of resources human, financial, material, and intellectual or intangible.
- **Specialists** comprises those who are widely recognized as reliable sources of knowledge, techniques and/or skills, and whose judgment is accorded authority by the public or by their peers. Specialists have prolonged or intensive experience through practice and education in a particular field.

1.2 Telecommunications and Network Operators*)

1.2.1 Austria

- A1 Austria [http://www.a1.net]
- TELE2 Austria (UTA) [http://www.tele2.at]
- T-Mobile Austria (*ex* Max.mobile) [http://www.t-mobile.at]
- Orange Austria [http://www.orange.at]

1.2.2 Belgium

- Belgacom [http://www.belgacom.be]
- BT Belgium [http://www.bt.be]

- KPN Belgium [www.kpngroup.be]
- Belgacom Mobile/ Proximus [http://www.proximus.be]
- Mobistar [http://www.mobistar.be]
- BASE (*ex* KPN Orange) [http://www.base.be]

1.2.3 Denmark
- Telecom Denmark/ TDC [http://www.tdc.dk]
- TDC Mobile [http://www.tdcmobil.dk]
- Telenor [http://www.telenor.dk]
- Telia Denmark [http://www.telia.dk]
- Orange (*ex* Mobilix) [http://orange.dk]

1.2.4 France
- France Telecom Orange (formerly France Telecom S.A.) [http://www.orange.fr]
- SFR [http://www.sfr.fr]
- Bouygues Telecom [http://www.bouygues.fr]

1.2.5 Finland
- Sonera [http://www.sonera.fi]
- Finnet Group [http://www.finnet.fi]
- Elisa Telecommunicatios [http://www.elisa.fi]
- Sonera [http://www.sonera.com]
- Telia Finland [http://www.teliasonera.com]

1.2.6 Germany
- Deutsche Telekom [http://www.telekom.de]
- Mannesmann Arcor [http://www.arcor.de]
- MobilCom [http://www.mobilcom.de]
- BT Ignite [http://www.btignite.de; http://www.ignite.com]
- T-Mobile [http://www.t-mobile.de]
- Vodafone (*ex* Mannesmann D2) [http://www.vodafone.de]
- E-Plus [http://www.eplus.de]
- Telefonica [http://www.telefonica.de]

1.2.7 Greece
- OTE – Hellenic Organization of Telecommunications [http://www.ote.gr]
- Vodafone (*ex* Panafon) [http://www.vodafone.gr]
- Cosmote [http://www.cosmote.gr]
- Stet Hellas/ TELESTET [http://www.telestet.gr]

1.2.8 Ireland
- Eircom [http://www.eircom.ie]
- Esat BT [http://www.esat.net]
- Vodafone (*ex* Eircell) [http://www.vodafone.ie]
- Meteor [http://www.meteor.ie]

1.2.9 Italy
- Telecom Italia [http://www.telecomitalia.it]
- Wind Infostrada [http://www.wind.it/it]
- Telecom Italia Mobil [http://www.telecomitalia.com]

- Vodafone (*ex* Omnitel) [http://www.vodafone.it]
- Wind [http://www.wind.it]
- Libero (*ex* Blu) [http://www.libero.it]

1.2.10 Luxembourg

- EPT [http://www.pt.lu/portal]
- LUXGSM [http://www.luxgsm.lu]
- Tango GSM [http://www.tango.lu]

1.2.11 Netherlands

- KPN Telecom [http://www.kpn.nl; http://www.kpn-corporate.com]
- Versatel [http://www.versatel.nl]
- Safenames [http://www.safenames.net]
- Vodafone (*ex* Libertel) [http://www.vodafone.nl; http://www.libertel.nl]
- Telfort [http://www.telfort.nl]
- T-Mobile [http://www.t-mobile.nl]

1.2.12 Portugal

- Portugal Telecom [http://www.telecom.pt; http://www.portugaltelecom.pt]
- Vodafone [http://www.vodafone.pt]
- TMN [http://www.tmn.pt]
- Optimus [http://www.optimus.pt]

1.2.13 Spain

- Telefónica, S.A. [http://www.telefonica.es]
- RIPE NCC [http://www.ripe.net]
- BT Telecoinicaciones [http://www.bt.es]
- Movistar [http://www.movistar.es]
- Vodafone [http://www.vodafone.es]
- Amena [http://www.amena.es]

1.2.14 Sweden

- Telia [http://www.telia.se]
- Tele2 [http://www.tele2.se]
- Telia Mobitel [http://www.telia.se]
- Comviq/Tele2 [http://www.comviq.se]
- TDC [http://tdc.se]

1.2.15 United Kingdom

- British Telecom [http://www.bt.co.uk; http://www.bt.com]
- C&W [http://www.cw.com]
- NTL [http://www.ntl.co.uk]
- Virgin [http://www.virginmediabusiness.co.uk]
- Kingston Communications [http://www.kc.co.uk]
- Vodafone UK [http://www.vodafone.co.uk]
- O2 [http://www.o2.co.uk]
- Orange [http://www.orange.co.uk]
- T-Mobile [http://www.t-mobile.co.uk]

1.2.16 European-wide/ Global*)
- Cable & Wireless [http://www.cw.com]
- Sprint [http://www.sprint.com]
- NTT Communications [http://www.ntteurope.com]

1.3 Internet Service Providers (ISPs)*)
- AOL – America Online [http://www.aol.com]
- Orange [http://www.orange.co.uk/]
- Easynet Connect [http://www.easynetconnect.net/]
- Virgin Media [http://www.virginmedia.com/]
- Sky [http://www.sky.com]
- TalkTalk [http://sales.talktalk.co.uk/]
- Plusnet [http://www.plus.net/]
- Eclipse [http://www.eclipse.net.uk]

1.4 Equipment and Infrastructure Suppliers*)
- Alcatel [http://www.alcatel.com]
- Bull [http://www.bull.com]
- Dell [http://www.dell.com]
- Ericsson [http://www.ericsson.com]
- Hewlett-Packard [http://www.hp.com]
- Motorola [http://www.motorola.com]
- Nokia [http://www.nokia.com]
- Nortel Network [http://www.nortelnetworks.com]
- Siemens Nixdorf [http://www.siemens.com]
- Toshiba [http://www.toshiba.com]

1.5 Software developers and vendors of IT goods and services, including applications, operating systems, and databases*)
- Apple Macintosh [http://www.apple.com]
- Cisco [http://www.cisco.com]
- IBM [http://www.ibm.com]
- Microsoft [http://www.microsoft.com]
- Oracle [http://www.oracle.com]
- SAP [http://www.sap.com]

1.6 Professional Firms/ Business Advisory Service firms (Examples)
- Consultancies and Advisory firms (system integration, IT effectiveness, IT security)
- Accountancy and tax firms (Deloitte and Touche, Ernst & Young, KPMG, PwC)
- Legal firms (Clifford Chance, Linklaters, Allen & Overy, DLA Piper)

1.7 Further Categories of Decision Makers

1.7.1 Lobbyists

Those who are engaged in public affairs, usually representative of businesses, non-profit organisations or special interest groups, who attempt to influence public opinion as well as legislation. Lobbying is the practice of private advocacy with the goal of influencing a public body, to ensure that an individual's or organization's point of view is adequately represented to the government.

1.7.2 Think tanks

In effect a subcategory of lobbyists, who aim to influence public opinion and governing bodies through regular publicity, such as releases to the media, for further dissemination of detailed reports and supporting research.

1.7.3 Journalists (and Public Relations Officers)

Those who gather and disseminate information about current events, trends, issues and people.

1.7.4 Representatives of Employees

These include trade unions, which represent workers in a particular industry (industrial unionism) or crafts (craft unionism).

1.7.5 Public Interest Advocates

This comprises a broad range of stakeholders, including musicians, artists and media personalities, who can influence consumers' acceptance of new technologies (*e.g.* music download sites, on-line auctions for the arts, official websites of new channels, *etc.*).

Level 1: Public sector & non-profit organisations

1. Council/ Government

- City Councils
- Local and Regional governments

2. Trades Unions

- Representatives of workers in a particular industry (industrial unionism) or craft (craft unionism).

3. Consumer Associations

National consumer associations in EU member-States, such as:
In the United Kingdom:

- Office of Fair Trading (OFT): protecting consumers by preventing abuse; empowering consumers by giving them access to information and redress; and promoting competitive and responsive supply. [http://www.oft.gov.uk]
- Citizens Advice Bureaux: quasi-public bodies offering free, confidential, impartial and independent advice. [*e.g.* https://www.citizensadvice.org.uk]

In Germany:

- Verbraucherzentrale Bundesverband: an organisation of 37 German consumer associations lobbying for consumer interests. [http://www.vzbv.de]

Level 1: Industry-focused associations

1. Local and Regional Associations*)

- London Chamber of Commerce and Industry, which includes The Euro Info Centre: this is the voice of London business, representing some 3,500 business-

es, with a broad-based membership across the capital. It facilitates presentations, seminars, assistance and advice. [http://www.londonchamber.co.uk/Europe]
- North Kent Chamber of Commerce: aims to build and support an environment that enables business growth; it is run and owned by its membership, the business community. [http://www.kentinvictachamber.co.uk]

2. **Other industry associations**
   - This includes activities on company level, such as writing of white papers, responding to consultations or hosting of events for members of the association.

Level 1: Project groups

1. **Research and Technological Development (RTD) Departments within companies**
   Industry-financed RTD projects.
2. **Strategic Joint Projects**
   Team-ups between ICT companies, which profit from knowledge-sharing and collaboration, 'economies of scale' on European/ global level.
3. **Project Managers of EU Programmes**
   Those who carry out EU-funded programmes, such as FP6, eContent, eEurope *etc.*
4. **Business Conferences**
   Seminars, presentations and other network events, which most large business organisations and associations organise for their partners, clients and members.

A6.2 Level 2: National Stakeholders

Level 2: Individual advocates

1. **Politicians, Political Parties, Ministers of Telecommunications**
   - Political organisations that politicians associate with in EU Member States, which operate on the national level, including: Socialist/ Labour parties; Conservative parties; Liberal parties and Green parties.
2. **Lobbyists**
   - Those who representing major stakeholders.
3. **Press**
   - The national and regional press.
4. **Advisory Groups (Government Initiatives)**
   - Ad hoc/ permanent groups which advise national governments and parties on specific ICT issues.
5. **Steering Committees (Government Initiatives)**
   - Governing bodies set up inside national parliaments and local/Federal assemblies/ councils/ upper houses.

Level 2: Public-sector and non-profit organisations

1. Regulators in Europe, eCommunications

- ICT Independent Regulatory Authorities (IRAs) exist in each EU member-State, such as:

1.1 Austria

- Rundfunk & Telekom Regulierungs-GmbH (RTR) [http://www.rtr.at]

1.2 Belgium

- Belgisch Instituut voor postdiensten en telecommunicatie (BIPT) (Belgian Institute of Postal Services and Telecommunications) [http://www.ibpt.be]

1.3 Denmark

- Digitaliseringsstyrelsen (Danish Agency for Digitisation) [http://www.digst.dk/da/Servicemenu/English]

1.4 France

- Autorité de Régulation des Communications Électroniques et des Postes (ARCEP) [http://www.arcep.fr/]

1.5 Finland

- Viestintävirasto (Finnish Communications Regulatory Authority)
- Ministry of Transportation and Communications [http://www.mintc.fi/]

1.6 Germany

- Bundesnetzagentur [http://www.bundesnetzagentur.de/cln_1911/DE/Home/home_node.html]

1.7 Greece

- Εθνική Επιτροπή Τηλεπικοινωνιών και Ταχυδρομείων (National Telecommunications and Postal Commission, EETT) [http://www.eett.gr]

1.8 Ireland

- Coimisiún um Rialáil Cumarsáide (Commission for Communications Regulation, ComReg) [http://www.comreg.ie]

1.9 Italy

- Autorità per le Garanzie nelle Comunicazioni (Italian Communications Authority) [http://www.agcom.it]

1.10 Luxembourg

- Institut Luxembourgeois de Régulation, Secteur Télécom (ILR) [http://www.etat.lu/ILR]

1.11 Netherlands

- Onafhankelijke Post en Telecommunicatie Autoriteit (OPTA) [http://www.opta.nl]

1.12 Portugal

- Autoridade Nacional de Comunicações (ANACOM) (National Authority of Communications) [http://www.anacom.pt]

1.13 Spain

- Comision del Mercado de las Telecomunicaciones (CMT) [http://www.cmt.es]

1.14 Sweden

- Post- och Telestyrelsen (PTS) [http://www.pts.se]

1.15 United Kingdom

- Office for Communication (Ofcom) (formerly the Office of Telecommunications/Oftel, BSC, ITC, Radio Authority or RA) [http://www.ofcom.org.uk]
- PhonepayPlus is the organisation that regulates phone-paid services in the UK [http://www.phonepayplus.org.uk/]

2. Regulators in Europe, Data Protection/ Privacy

Data Protection/ Information Commissioners exist in each EU Member State

2.1 Austria

- Österreichische Datenschutzkommission [http://www.dsk.gv.at]

2.2 Belgium

- Commission de la protection de la vie privée [http://www.privacycommission.be]

2.3 Denmark

- Datatilsynet [http://www.datatilsynet.dk]

2.4 France

- Commission Nationale de l'Informatique et des Libertés [http://www.cnil.fr]

2.5 Finland

- Office of Data Protection – Ombudsman [http://www.tietosuoja.fi]

2.6 Germany

- Der Bundesbeauftragte für den Datenschutz und die Informationsfreiheit [http://www.bfdi.bund.de]

2.7 Greece

- Αρχη Προστασιας Δεδομενων Προσωπικου Χαρακτηρα – Hellenic Data Protection Authority [http://www.dpa.gr]

2.8 Ireland

- Data Protection Commissioner – An Coimisineir Cosanta Sonraí [http://www.dataprotection.ie]

2.9 Italy

- Garante per la Protezione dei Dati Personali [http://www.garanteprivacy.it]

2.10 Luxembourg

- Commission Nationale pour la Protection des Données [http://www.cnpd.lu]

2.11 Netherlands

- College Bescherming Persoonsgegevens (CBP) - Dutch Data Protection Authority [http://www.cbpweb.nl]

2.12 Portugal

- Comissão Nacional de Protecção de Dados [http://www.cnpd.pt]

2.13 Spain

- Agencia de Protección de Datos [http://www.agpd.es]

2.14 Sweden

- Datainspektionen [http://www.datainspektionen.se]

2.15 United Kingdom

- Information Commissioner – The Office of the Information Commissioner Executive Department (ICO) [http://www.ico.gov.uk]

3. Government departments and ministries of EU Member States*)

3.1 Austria

- Bundesministerium füf Verkehr, Innovation and Technology (Federal Ministry for Transport, Innovation and Technology)

1.2 Belgium

- Federale Overheidsdienst Mobiliteit en Vervoer / Service public fédérale Mobilite et Transports (Federal Public Service Mobility and Transport)

3.3 Denmark

- Ministeriet for Forskning, Innovation og Videregående Uddannelser (Ministry for Science, Innovation and Higher Education)

3.4 France

- Ministère du Redressement Productif (Ministry of Productive Recovery)

3.5 Finland

- Likenne- ja Viestintäministeriö (Ministry of Transport and Communications)

3.6 Germany

- Bundesministerium für Wirtschaft und Technologie (Federal Ministry of Economics and Technology)

3.7 Greece

- Υπουργειο Αναπτυξης Ανταγωνιστικοτητας Υποδομων, Μεταφορων & Δικτυων (Ministry of Infrastructure, Transport and Networks)

3.8 Ireland

- Roinn Cumarsáide, Fuinnimh agus Acmhainnií Nádúrtha (Department of Communications, Marine & Natural Resources)

3.9 Italy

- Ministero dello Sviluppo Economico (Ministry of Economic Development)

3.10 Luxembourg

- Ministère d'Etat, Service des Médias et des Communications (Ministry of Media and Communications)

3.11 Netherlands

- Ministerie van Economische Zaken (Ministry of Economic Affairs)

3.12 Portugal

- Ministério da Economia e do Emprego (Ministry of Economy and Employment)

3.13 Spain

- Ministerio de Industria, Energía y Turismo
(Ministry of Industry, Energy and Tourism)

3.14 Sweden

- Näringsdepartementet (Ministry of Information Technology and Energy)

3.15 United Kingdom

- Department for Business, Innovation and Skills (BIS)

4. National Governmental Supporting Bodies and Ministries in EU Member States; for example in the United Kingdom:*)

4.1 Other Central Governmental Departments

- Cabinet Office (responsible for Information Assurance, 'Get Safe Online and ITsafe')
- Home Office, *e.g.* Computer Crime Policy Team
- Department for Business, Innovation and Skills (BIS); formerly Department for Business, Enterprise and Regulatory Reform (BERR) and before that the Department of Trade and Industry (DTI)
- Government Offices, *e.g.* Office of the eEnvoy (suspended)
- House of Lords, Science and Technology Committee

4.2 Central Government programmes

- Information Security Focus: National Infrastructure Security Coordination Centre (NISCC)
- Serious Organised Crime Agency (SOCA)
- Critical National Infrastructure (CNI)
- Computer Emergency Response Team (CERT)
- Serious and Organised Crime Agency (SOCA), and National Hi-Tech Crime Unit (NHTCU)
- Communications-Electronics Security Group (CESG)
- New standards, such as ITIL (IT Infrastructure Library) [http://www.itil-itsm-world.com] and PRINCE [http://www.ogc.gov.uk/prince2]. Although the UK Government created these standards, they have rapidly been adopted across the world as the standard for best practice in the provision of IT Service.

4.3 Local Government

Sub-national level initiatives

5. Trades Unions

Organisations representing employee interests on national level (e.g. minimum wage, hours of work, social benefits).

6. Non-profit issue-groups

Non-profit groups/ Non-governmental organisations (NGOs) operating on national level.

7. National Scientific Organisations

At EU Member State-level these are organisations that aim to:

- Provide an open forum for debate on science and technology
- Strengthen the links between science and society
- Contribute to the creation of an integrated space for science and technology in Europe,

and

- Influence science and technology policies

  (For more detailed information, follow the links of the European Scientific Organisations to be found on Level 3: Government & Non-profit Organisations: European Scientific Organisations.)

Level 2: Industry-focused associations

These associations and lobbying groups for Small and Medium Sized Enterprises (SMEs), for large organisations and for other stakeholders include:

1. Chambers of Trade and Commerce*)

1.1 United Kingdom

- British Chambers of Commerce (BCC) [http://www.britishchambers.org.uk]
- Confederation of British Industry UK (CBI) – 'The Voice of Business' [http://www.cbi.org.uk]

1.2 Germany

- Die deutschen Auslandshandelskammern (AHK) [http://www.ahk.de]
- Deutsche Industrie- und Handelskammertag (DIHK), an umbrella organisation of all 82 chambers of trade and commerce [http://www.dihk.de]
- Industrie- und Handelskammer (IHK) [http://www.ihk.de]

1.3 France

- Assemblée des Chambres Françaises de Commerce et d'Industrie (ACFCI) [http://www.acfci.cci.fr]
- L'Union des Chambres de Commerce et d'Industrie Françaises à l'Etranger (UCCIFE) [http://www.uccife.org/en]

2. National ISP Associations (Members of EuroISPA)

2.1 Austria

- Internet Service Providers Austria (ISPA Austria) [http://www.ispa.at]

2.2 France

- Association des Fournisseurs d'Accès et de Services Internet (AFA) [http://www.afa-france.com]

2.3 Germany

- Verband der deutschen Internetwirtschaft (ECO Forum) [http://www.eco.de]

2.4 Ireland

- Internet Service Providers Association of Ireland (ISPAI) [http://www.ispai.ie]

2.5 Italy

- Associazione Italiana Internet Providers (AIIP) [http://www.aiip.it]

2.6 Netherlands

- Nationale Beheersorganisatie Internet Providers (NBIP; *ex* Branchevereniging van Nederlandse Internet Providers) (NLIP) [http://www.nbip.nl]

2.7 UK

- Internet Services Providers Association UK (ISPA UK) [http://www.ispa.org.uk]

3. National Telecoms Services Association (ETSA)

ETSA: a group of 13 European national telecommunications trade associations (10 EU countries and Switzerland and Norway) representing approximately 2500 telecom companies. ETSA's mission is the promotion of common interests through the development of cooperation, the exchange of information and the continued liberalisation of the telecommunications market. [http://www.etsa.org]

3.1 Denmark
- Elinstallatørernes Landsforening (TEKNIQ-ELFO) [http://www.tekniq.dk]

3.2 France
- Fédération Interprofessionnelle de la Communication d'Entreprise (FICOME) [http://www.ficome.fr]

3.3 Germany
- Bundesverband Telekommunikation (VAF) [http://www.vaf-ev.de]

3.4 Italy
- Associazione Nazionale Costruttori di Impianti (ASSISTAL) [http://www.assistal.it]

3.5 Luxembourg
- Fédération Luxembourgeoise des Entreprises en Télécommunications, Téléinformatique et Systèmes d'Alarme (FLETTA) [http://www.fletta.lu]

3.6 Netherlands
- Unie van elektronische ondernemers (UNETO-VNI) [http://www.uneto-vni.nl]

3.7 Spain
- Federación Nacional de Instaladores de Telecomunicación (FENITEL) [http://www.fenitel.es]

3.8 Sweden
- Elektriska Installatörsorganisationen (EIO) [http://www.eio.se]

3.9 UK
- The Electrical Contractors' Association (ECA) [http://www.eca.uk]

4. National Manufacturers of Insulated Wires and Cables

Members of EUROPACABLE [http://www.europacable.com/members/member-companies.html]

4.1 Austria
- SKB Gruppe [http:// www.skb-gruppe.at]

4.2 Belgium
- Kabelwerk Eupen [http://www.eupen.com]

4.3 Denmark
- Nexas – Global Expert in cables and cable systems [www.nktcables.com]
- Ntk cables [http://www.nktcables.com]

4.4 Finland
- Reka Cables [http://www.reka.fi]

4.5 France
- ACOME [http://www.acome.com]
- Nexans [http://www.nexans.com]
- SIPD [http://www.sipd.fr]

3.6 Germany
- LEONI Kerpen [http://www.leoni-kerpen.com]
- OFS [http://www.ofsoptics.com]
- Waskönig+Walter [http://www.waskoenig.de]

4.7 Great Britain

- British Cables Association (BCA) [http://www.bcauk.org]

4.8 Greece

- CABLEL Hellenic Cables S.A. [http://www.cablel.com]

4.9 Italy

- Italian Cable Company (ICC) [http://www.icc.it]
- Prysmian Group [http://www.prysmiangroup.com]
- Tratos Cavi [http://www.tratos.eu]

4.10 Netherlands

- TKF [http://www.tkf.nl]

4.11 Norway

- Europacable Norge AS

4.12 Spain

- General Cable [http://www.generalcable.es]

4.13 Sweden

- Ericsson [http://www.ericsson.com]

4.14 Poland

- TELE-FONIKA Kable [http:// www.tfkable.com]

5. National Industry Associations – for example in the UK:*)

- Society of Information Technology Management (SOCITM): "Socitm is the association for ICT and related professionals in the public and third sectors. We offer networking and peer support, professional development, and access to research and consultancy on a wide range of policy and technology issues." [http://www.socitm.net/]
- IBM Computer Users Association (IBM CUA UK): "We are an independent non-profit making association run exclusively for our members." [http://www.ibm-cua.org.uk/]
- British Computer Society (BCS): "Through our IT training and professional development services, we are raising the levels of competence and professionalism within the industry." [http://www.bcs.org]
- Communications Management Association (CMA): "CMA supports businesses delivering services online. As part of BCS, the Chartered Institute for IT, CMA offers members access to good practice, knowledge networks and government representation in communications, collaboration and cloud services."
- [http://www.thecma.com]
- Intellect: "Intellect is the voice of the UK's technology industry. We believe that a vibrant and successful technology sector is vital to the long term economic well-being of the country. Our business services help companies of all sizes compete and innovate in a dynamic global market. We represent the views of industry to government and regulators and also provide opportunities for government and regulators to interact with industry on key policy and market issues." [http://www.intellectuk.org]

- European Information Society Group (EURIM) "EURIM is the expert group for internet and information society policy. EURIM brings together industry experts, observers from the civil service, professional bodies, charities and trade associations to help identify solutions to policy, regulatory and legislative problems impacting UK competitiveness. Our technical working groups produce consensus based reports and recommendations, launched and disseminated at high profile events attended by our members both in the UK and Brussels." [http://www.eurim.org.uk/].

6. Standards Institutes – National Standardisation Bodies

(N.B.: every EU country has national standards organisations)

6.1 Austria

- Austrian Standards Plus [http://www.as-plus.at/]
- Österreichischer Verband für Elektrotechnik (ÖVE) [http://www.ove.at]

6.2 Belgium

- Bureau de Normalisation / Bureau voor Normalisatie (NBN) [http://www.nbn.be]
- Comité Electrotechnique Belge/ Belgisch Elektrotechnisch Comité (CEB/BEC) [http://www.ceb-bec.be]

6.3 Denmark

- Dansk Standard (DS) [http://www.ds.dk]
- Telestyrelsen/ National Telecom Agency (NTA) [http://www.itst.dk]

6.4 Finland

- Suomen Standardisoimisliitto SFS r.y. (SFS) [http://www.sfs.fi]
- Telehallintokeskus (THK/TFC) [http://www.telehallintokeskus.fi]
- Suomen Sähköteknillinen Standardisoimisyhdistys (SESKO ry)/ Finnish Electrotechnical Standards Association [http://www.sesko.fi]

6.5 France

- Association Française de Normalisation (AFNOR) [http://www.afnor.fr]
- Union Technique de l'Electricité et de la Communication (UTE) [http://www.ute-fr.com]

6.6 Germany

- Deutsches Institut für Normung e.V. (DIN) [http://www.din.de]
- Deutsche Kommission Elektrotechnik Elektronik Informationstechnik im DIN und VDE (DKE) [http://www.dke.de]
- 6.7 Greece
- Ελληνικός Οργανισμός Τυποποίησης (ΕΛΟΤ)/ Hellenic Organization for Standardization (ELOT) [http://www.elot.gr]

6.8 Ireland

- National Standards Authority of Ireland (NSAI)/ Údarás um Chaighdeáin Náisiúnta na hÉireann [http://www.nsai.ie]
- Electro Technical Council of Ireland (ETCI) [http://www.etci.ie]

6.9 Italy

- Ente nazionale italiano di unificazione (UNI) [http://www.uni.com]

- Comitato Elettrotecnico Italiano (CEI) [http://www.ceiweb.it]

6.10 Luxembourg

- Inspection du Travail et des Mines (ITM) [http://www.itm.lu]
- Institut Luxembourgeois de la Normalisation, de l'Accréditation, de la Securité et Qualité des Produits et Services (SEE) [http://www.ilnas.public.lu]

6.11 Netherlands

- Nederlands Normalisatie-Instituut/ Nederlands Elektrotechnisch Comité (NEN) [http://www.nen.nl]

6.12 Portugal

- Instituto Português da Qualidade (IPQ) [http://www.ipq.pt]

6.13 Spain

- Asociación Española de Normalización y Certificación (AENOR) [http://www.aenor.es]

6.14 Sweden

- Standardiseringen i Sverige/ Swedish Standards Institute (SIS) [http://www.sis.se]
- Svenska Elstandard SEK [http://www.elstandard.se]
- Informationstekniska Standardiseringen (ITS) [http://www.its.se]

6.15 United Kingdom

- British Standards Institution (BSI) [http://www.bsi-global.com]

<u>Level 2: Project groups</u>

1. **National RTD Programmes**
   Funded by the public sector or private investors, *e.g.* National eCommerce Action Plans (Government Initiatives) – similar to the eEurope Action Plan.
2. **Research at Universities and Institutes**
   University RTD programmes and laboratories that, for example, develop semiconductors, software, network protocols, *etc.*
3. **National Contact Points (NCPs)**
   EU NCPs for 'science and society' – information dissemination and discussion of RTD on national level.
4. **Structural Programmes for the Regions:** – for example, up until March 2012 eight Regional Development Agencies (RDAs) in England were strategic drivers of sub-national regional economic development. Since March 2012, their functions have been taken over either by larger, nationwide agencies or by smaller Local Enterprise Partnerships:
   - Homes and Communities Agency (HCA) took over East of England RDA [http://www.homesandcommunities.co.uk]
   - Department for Business, Innovation and Skills took over Advantage West Midlands RDA [http://www.advantagewm.co.uk]
5. **National Conferences** – in the UK for example:*)
   - The IT Directors' Forum (UK): a business event that provides common ground for senior IT executives, service providers and industry specialists to create stra-

tegic business alliances in an environment that is conducive to discussion, debate and advancing corporate goals. [http://www.itdf.com]

- Business Continuity Forum (UK): provides independent advice, information and support to the private and public sectors covering business continuity management, disaster recovery, crisis management, emergency planning and security. [http://www.continuityforum.org/]
- Information Security Specialist Group (BCS-ISSG) (UK): The BCS-ISSG was formed in 1984 as a specialist sub-group of the British Computer Society. The annual conference covers presentations and discussions on Information Security. [http://www.bcs-issg.org.uk/conference.html]
- GC Expo (UK): the UK's leading technology event for the public sector.
- eWorld Purchasing & Supply (UK): the UK's most comprehensive business forum for eProcurement, eSourcing and Supply Chain Technologies. [http://www.eworld-purchasing.com]
- Storage Expo (UK): the UK's largest dedicated data-storage event. Bringing together over 3000 end users and over 90 exhibitors, this event is a key event in the calendar for anyone challenged with the movement, management, storage, back-up, recovery and archiving of data. It offers a keynote programme alongside streamed business and technical seminars. [http://uk.linkedin.com/pub/storage-expo/14/535/7b8]
- VoIP for Business Event (UK): this exhibition includes educational seminars, briefings and presentations. [http://www.voip-info.org/wiki/index.php?page_id=5371]
- ICT2day (Netherlands): a conference that discusses the perception of ICT and of the ICT department, the added value and opportunities offered by ICT and the relationship between the ICT department and other services. [http://www.ict2day.nl]
- CBI Annual Conference (UK): Receiving extensive coverage on every major news channel, it features keynotes by cabinet ministers and by business leaders of some of the world's biggest companies, as well as a line-up of business and political panellists. The event offers an opportunity to make new business contacts and to question Government ministers about policy decisions that affect your business. [http://www.cbi.org.uk/events]
- Enterprise Architecture Conference Europe (UK): engages practitioners from leading companies and thought leaders in the field of Enterprise Architecture, to uncover strategies for success in delivering world-class systems, products and services. [http://www.irmuk.co.uk/eac2012]
- Complitech (UK): Europe's leading regulatory technology exhibition and conference tailored to the financial services market.
- eGov Summit (UK): transforming the relationship between citizen and state. Government, engaged citizens, strategists, and IT professionals can learn about the challenges of transforming the processes, culture and bottom lines of the

business of local and central government. [http://www.webitexpo.com/en/eGov/2010/index.html]

A6.3 Level 3: European Stakeholders

Level 3: Individual advocates

1. **Lobbyists**
   Individual representatives of major stakeholders, who shape governmental and public opinion at EU level.
2. **Press**
   European press and media (*e.g.* CNN Europe, RTL, Reuters)
3. **Individual investors**
   Oligarchs, venture capitalists and entrepreneurs.
4. **European Associations Representing Professions**

4.1 Secrétariat Européen des Professions Libérales, Indépendantes et Sociales (SEPLIS) – the European umbrella organisation of the professions in Brussels (formed in 1974).

4.2 Council of European Professional and Managerial Staff (EUROCADRES): formed in 1993, it represents more than 5 million professional and managers throughout Europe in all branches of industry, private and public services, and administrative departments. [http://www.eurocadres.org/]

4.3 Confederation Européenne des Cadres (CEC)/ European Confederation of Executives and Managerial Staff: formed in 1989, it is a network of 1.5 million employed executives, managers and professional staff in Europe. It represents independent organisations of managerial staff primarily in industry and commerce [http://www.cec-managers.org]

Level 3: Public-sector and non-profit organisations

1. **European Politicians and Parties**
   In EU Member States most politicians are members of the following parties: Socialist/ Labour party; Conservative party; Liberal party; Green party.
2. **Advisory Groups on Specific Member State Initiatives (at European Level)**
   Ad hoc/ permanent groups to advise the national governments and parties collectively on specific ICT issues.
3. **Steering Committees of Specific Member State Initiatives (at European Level)**
   In national parliaments and local/federal assembly/ council/ upper house.
4. **European Committees and Councils – Stakeholders** (Collective European Fora – Connected to the EU Institutions)

4.1 e-Inclusion/e-Accessibility+AAL Research & Innovation

4.2 e-Inclusion/e-Accessibility R&D Projects administered by EC / DG Information Society & Media [http://circa.europa.eu/irc/infso/e-inclusion/info/data/home_page.html]

4.3 EC-Candidate Countries Joint High Level Committee on the Information Society (JHLIS): formerly comprising high level government representatives from the erstwhile 13 candidate countries (acceded 2004 or 2007) and the European Commission, it is responsible for providing political guidance to the eEurope+ initiative launched by the governments of the candidate countries, and outlining progress regarding the overall implementation of the information society in these countries.

4.4 Group to Promote Digital Public Data: a co-ordination platform and sounding board for activities related to digital public sector information, mainly exploitation issues. It comprises representatives from the Member States, but other stakeholders, for instance representatives from consumers organisations and the information industry, may be involved at dedicated sessions.

4.5 IST ERA Portal Study Interaction Forum: hosts interaction between EC staff, National Representatives and Study Contractor for the IST ERA Portal feasibility study.

4.6 Safer Internet Action Plan: combats illegal and harmful content on the global networks.

4.7 Trans-European Telecommunications Networks Financial and Guidelines Committee: advises the Commission on issues relating to the eTEN (*e.g.* TEN-Telecom) programme.

4.8 eEurope+ Statistical Working Group (SWG): comprises officials from the National Statistical Offices of the Candidate Countries, who provide and discuss data collected for the 'monitoring and benchmarking' exercise as outlined in the eEurope+ Action Plan.

4.9 ICANN Government Advisory Committee (GAC): in which the European Commission participates, together with representatives of several Member States, in the work of the Governmental Advisory Committee to ICANN. [https://gacweb.icann.org/display/gacweb/Governmental+Advisory+Committee]

4.10 The European Research Council (ERC): stimulates scientific excellence by supporting and encouraging creative scientists, engineers and scholars to be adventurous and take risks. The scientists should go beyond established frontiers of knowledge and the boundaries of their discipline. The ERC complements other funding activities in Europe, such as those of the national research funding agencies, and is a flagship component of the "Ideas Programme" of the European Union's Seventh Framework Programme (FP7). [http://erc.europa.eu]

4.11 European Institute of Innovation and Technology (EIT): a public-private partnership for scientific research and development that should be set-up by 2008, and operational in 2009.
[http://ec.europa.eu/education/policies/educ/eit/index_en.html]

5. European Scientific Organisations

5.1 Scientific InformAtion for Policy Support in Europe (SINAPSE) e-Network: offers a set of essential tools to promote and encourage effective exchange of information between all stakeholders concerned in the application of science to European governance. Current membership consists of universities, national academies of sciences, scientific associations, several national research/ health/ ethics councils, various other research organisations and advisory bodies covering different policy areas, and a miscellany of other organisations (NGOs, industrial companies/ associations) interested in the application of science in policy-making. [http://europa.eu/sinapse]

5.2 European Science Foundation (ESF): promotes high-quality science at European level, and catalyses scientific development by bringing together leading scientists and funding agencies to debate, plan and implement pan-European initiatives. [http://www.esf.org]

5.3 Joint Institute for Innovation Policy (JIIP): an initiative of four of the major public research organisations in Europe, TNO (Netherlands), VTT (Finland), Joanneum Research (Austria), and Tecnalia (Spain), it focuses on research-based support. [http://jiip.eu]

5.4 European Research Forum (ERF): the single forum that by Commission Decision 98/611/EC/Euratom superseded and streamlined ESTA and IRDAC, the previous high-level consultation instruments. It has two chambers – the academic and scientific chamber, and the industrial services and users chamber.
[http://ec.europa.eu/research/erf.html]

5.5 European Research Advisory Board (EURAB): a high-level independent advisory committee set up to advise the Commission on the design and implementation of EU research policy. EURAB is made up of 45 top experts from EU countries and beyond, nominated in a personal capacity and coming from a wide range of academic and industrial backgrounds. They focus their attention on realising the European Research Area and applying policy instruments such as the Community RTD Framework Programmes.
[europa.eu.int/europ/research/eurab/index_en.html]

5.6 All European Academies (ALLEA): the Federation of 52 Academies of Sciences and Humanities in 39 European countries, whose Member Academies are self-governing communities of scientists and scholars. ALLEA seeks to: (a) promote the exchange of information and experience between Academies; (b) offer European science and society advice from its Member Academies; and (c) strive for excellence in science and scholarship, reaching high ethical standards while maintaining independence from political, commercial and ideological interests.
[http://www.allea.org]

5.7 European Academies Science Advisory Council (EASAC): provides a forum for Europe's national Academies to work together to insert high quality science into EU policy-making. They translate science into policy at EU level by providing independent, expert, credible advice about the scientific aspects of public policy issues to those who make or influence policy for the European Union. Their ambition is for EASAC to be recognised by EU policy-makers as *the* place to go for reliable, timely advice reflecting the best that the European scientific community can deliver. [http://www.easac.org]

5.8 European Association of Research and Technology Organisations (EARTO): the trade association of Europe's specialised research and technology organisations. EARTO represents the views of its members to European decision-makers, publishing policy papers and organising briefings. Its members sit on the influential European Research Forum and Programme Advisory Committees. EARTO provides its members with information about European policies and programmes, obtains official documents, and arranges meetings with European officials. [http://www.earto.org]

5.9 European Patent Office (EPO): the patent granting authority for Europe, supporting innovation, competitiveness and economic growth for the benefit of the citizens of Europe. In carrying out its mission, the EPO strives to: (a) set patent protection standards which respond to the needs of the system's users maintain its position as a global player in the international patent world; (b) set a benchmark for best patent practice as one of the world's leading providers of technical information; (c) help to promote a knowledge-based society in Europe; and (d) stand out as a model international public-service organisation. [http://www.epo.org]

5.10 The Academy of Europe (Academia Europæa): a non-governmental association acting as an Academy. Their members are scientists and scholars who aim to promote learning, education and research. The Academy has over 2000 members from thirty-five European countries and eight non-European countries, including leading experts from the physical sciences and technology; biological sciences and medicine; mathematics; letters and humanities; social and cognitive sciences; economics; and the law. [http://www.acadeuro.org]

5.11 European University Association (EUA): the representative organisation both of European universities and their national rectors' conferences, it is the main voice of the higher education community in Europe. In serving its membership, both individual and collective, EUA's main focus is: (a) strengthening the role universities play in the emerging European Higher Education and European Research Areas (EHEA and ERA) through contributing to and influencing policy debate and developing projects in the interest of its members; (b) working with member institutions, through the implementation of projects, on key issues to improve quality overall while strengthening individual universities' European profiles; (c) enhancing the European dimension within higher education and promoting the flow of information through regular meetings and conferences and the publication of studies; and (d) providing advocacy on behalf of its members, both at European level to promote common policies, and at the international level to promote increased cooperation and enhance the visibility of European higher education in a global context. [http://www.eua.be]

5.12 Network of Universities from the Capitals of Europe (UNICA): a network of 41 universities from the capital cities of Europe, with a combined strength of over 120,000 staff and 1,500,000 students. Its role is to promote academic excellence, integration and co-operation between member universities throughout Europe. It seeks also to be a driving force in the development of the Bologna Process and to facilitate the integration of universities from Central and Eastern Europe into the European Higher Education Area. [http://www.ulb.ac.be/unica]

5.13 European Council of Applied Sciences, Technologies and Engineering (Euro-CASE): an organisation of national Academies from nineteen European countries, Euro-CASE has access to top-level European experience and provides impartial, independent, balanced advice on technological issues with a clear European dimension. The members are elected from the Euro-CASE Academies for their excellence and knowledge in specific fields and for their contributions to technological, scientific, economic and social progress. This unique resource of experts, numbering 5,500 individual Fellows from 19 national Academies, is the core of Euro-CASE. [http://www.euro-case.org]

5.14 European Cooperation in Scientific and Technology (COST): an intergovernmental framework for international co-operation amongst nationally funded research activities. It is the longest-running European networking system in research, established in 1971, and now has 35 member countries. It supports co-operation amongst scientists and researchers across Europe, enabling them to collaborate on a broad spectrum of activities in research and technology. [http://www.cost.eu]

5.15 European Association of Research Managers and Administrators (EARMA): hosts public and private research organisations from over 30 countries across Europe. It aims to provide a voice for research managers in European policy-making. [http://www.earma.org]

5.16 European Industrial Research Management Association (EIRMA): an independent non-profit which promotes innovation through more effective market-oriented research and development. Through being member-focused and providing a forum for discussing ideas and exchanging practical experience, EIRMA is up-to-date with the ways managers think and operate. It supports companies with benchmarking and improving their innovation processes, ensuring well-managed and well-organised research and development. These activities also establish EIRMA as a natural first point of contact for policy-makers and others seeking the business community's insight. EIRMA has some 150 member companies based in over twenty countries, which collectively fund the major portion of business enterprise investment in R&D in Europe. [http://www.eirma.org]

5.17 Science Europe: sees to the collective interests of the Research Funding and Research Performing Organisations of Europe. It supports its member organisations in their efforts to foster European research. It will strengthen the European Research Area through its direct engagement with key partners. In doing so it will be informed by direct representation of all scientific communities in its reflections on policies, priorities and strategies. [http://www.scienceeurope.org]

5.18 Euroscience: a pan-European association of individuals interested in constructing a scientific Europe "from the bottom-up". It provides an open forum for debate on science and technology; strengthening the links between science and society, contributing to the creation of an integrated space for science and technology in Europe, and influencing science and technology policy. It represents European scientists of all disciplines in the public sector, universities, research institutes as well as in business and industry. [http://www.euroscience.org]

5.19 The University Association for Contemporary European Studies (UACES): an independent forum for debate and information about European affairs. It is directly involved in promoting research and establishing teaching- and research networks. UACES has a regular programme of Conferences, Workshops and Study Groups throughout the year. Other initiatives include support for the UACES Student Forum and financial assistance for graduates doing research on Europe. [http://www.uaces.org]

6. European Organisations with stronger links to European institutions

6.1 Committee of Permanent Representatives of the Member States (COREPER): a forum for ambassadors from the Member States (or "permanent representatives"), who meet weekly in the Permanent Representatives Committee. The role of this committee is to prepare the work output of the European Council.
[http://europa.eu/legislation_summaries/glossary/coreper_en.htm]

6.2 Association pour la Normalisation Européenne pour les Consommateurs (ANEC)/ European Association for the Co-operation of Consumer Representation in Standardization: the European consumer voice in standardisation, it defends consumer interests inside the processes of standardisation and certification. ANEC was set up in 1985 by national consumer bodies from EU and EFTA Member States to coordinate consumer representation in response to the Mew Approach. [http://www.anec.eu]

6.3 European Trade Union Confederation (ETUC): a trade union counterbalance to the economic forces of European integration, ETUC has in its membership 78 national trade union confederations from a total of 34 European countries, plus 11 European industry federations, making a total of 60 million members. [http://www.etuc.org]

6.4 Other European Consumer Associations
EU-wide consumer associations – for ICT-related issues – such as:
- Assembly of Consumer Associations in Europe [http://ec.europa.eu/consumers/cons_org/assembly/assembly_en.htm]
- European Consumer Centres Network (ECC-Net) [http://ec.europa.eu/consumers/ecc/index_en.htm]

See also the Commission's consumer protection webpages [http://europa.eu/consumers/index_en.htm]

6.5 Bureau Européen des Unions de Consommateurs (BEUC)/ European Consumers' Organisation: a federation of independent national consumer organisations from all of the Member States of the EU and other European countries. Their job is to influence, in the consumer interest, the development of EU policy, while promoting and defending the interests of all European consumers. [http://www.beuc.org]

6.6 European Free Trade Association (EFTA): an inter-governmental organisation set up by countries of Western and Northern Europe that wished to create a larger market for their manufactured goods through the liberalisation of mutual trade, without taking-on the far-reaching political and economic obligations stemming from membership of the European Economic Community (EEC), it consists of only four countries: Iceland, Liechtenstein, Norway and Switzerland. [http://www.efta.int]

Level 3: Industry-focused associations

1. Sectoral (Sector-specific) European Industry Associations

1.1 European IT Roundtable [Direct Membership]
IT Roundtable: established by 12 leading IT companies in the EU – ICL, GEC and Plessy of the UK; Thompson, Bull and CGE from France; AEG, Nixdorf and Siemens from Germany; Olivetti and STET from Italy; and Philips from the Netherlands, it played a critical role in the establishment of the EU ESPRIT programme.

1.2 European Confederation of National Associations of Manufacturers of Insulated Wires and Cables (Europacable): the European forum for cable manufacturers and the industry's voice to the European Commission. Promoting the use of cables, and wire and cable technology which embodies the state of the art in safety and ecological care, it represents approximately 90% of the European industry and, through its National Associations, more than 200 individual cable manufacturers. [http://www.europacable.com]

1.3 The association of the European space industry (EUROSPACE): the organisation of the European space industry. It is an international non-profit association whose members represent 90% of the total turnover of the European space industry. The objective of Eurospace is to promote European space activities and to present the views and opinions of the European space industry to the European space authorities, mainly regulatory agencies, the EU, and relevant ministries. [http://www.eurospace.org]

1.4 Committee of Associations of Transformer Manufacturers in the Common Market (COTREL): promotes common professional interests of the European transformer manufacturing industry. [http://www.cotrel.com]

1.5 Association of European Accumulator Manufacturers (EUROBAT): with 37 member companies, represents more than 85% of the battery industry in Europe. It acts as a unified voice and reference source promoting the interests of the European battery industry to consumers, the EU institutions, and national governments.
[http://www.eurobat.org]

1.6 European Portable Battery Association (EPBA): represents approximately 98% of portable battery manufacturers, importers and assemblers in Europe. To further develop the EU Battery Directive, EPBA provides information about the battery market, the experience of recycling batteries around Europe, and consumer behaviour.
[http://www.epba-europe.org]

1.7 European Public Telecommunications Network Operator's Association (ETNO): the principal policy group for European electronic communications network operators. ETNO's primary purpose is to establish for the benefit of users a constructive dialogue between its member companies and decision-makers and other actors involved in the development of the European Information Society. Forty of Europe's largest and most established telecoms groups are members of ETNO, which also provides a forum for the exchange of views on telecom policy among its members. Most of its detailed discussions and studies occur in its working groups. [http://www.etno.be]

1.8 The European Association of Information Services (EUSIDIC): a channel of communication for professionals in the information industry, both suppliers and users. The association is fully independent, funded by its members and activities, receiving no subsidy. Membership includes around 100 organisations from 16 European countries. [http://www.eusidic.org]

1.9 European Telecommunication Services Association (ETSA): a focal point for quality and standards in the supply and support of telecoms equipment and services in Europe, it is a collective voice for the European telecoms service industry. It has influenced liberalisation of the European telecoms market, and is involved in developing European telecoms engineering, vocational and process standards, and disseminating regulatory, technical and commercial information to members. [http://www.etsa.org]

1.10 European Telecommunications Satellite Organisation (EUTELSAT): an organisation promoting design, conduct, establishment, operation, and maintenance of the European outer-space telecommunications satellite systems that provide international public telecommunications. Its membership now comprises 26 national telecommunications administrations in Western Europe. [http://www.eutelsat.com]

1.11 Cable Europe (formerly known as European Cable Communications Association, ECCA): uniting all the leading European broadband cable communications operators and their national trade associations throughout Europe, it has 35 member organisations in 20 countries, and is dedicated to fostering cooperation between cable operators, and promoting and presenting their interests at European and international levels. Cable Europe promotes a level playing field between the various infrastructures, and harmonised telecom regulations throughout the European Union; while supporting a realistic approach to the management of copyright issues in the European context; and encouraging the development of market-driven standards. [http://www.cable-europe.eu]

1.12 European Venture Capital Association (EVCA): the European Private Equity and Venture Capital Association representing the European private equity and venture capital industry since 1983 and promoting private equity investment to investors, policy makers, entrepreneurs and industry. With over 925 members in Europe, EVAC's role includes representing the interests of the industry and standards-setters; developing professional standards and providing industry research. It also promotes professional development and holds forums to facilitate interaction between its members and key industry participants such as institutional investors, entrepreneurs, policymakers and academics. [http://www.evca.com]

1.13 European Internet Services Providers Association (EuroISPA EEIG): an association of Internet service providers associations in the EU member states. It the largest association of ISPs in the world.
[http://www.euroispa.org]

1.14 Federation of Telecommunications Engineers of the European Union (FITCE): founded by telecommunications engineers from France and Belgium in 1962, FITCE has over 3,500 members across Europe. It promotes the development of science in the field of telecommunications, enabling each member to benefit from the experience of the other members across all telecommunications fields, developing cultural ties, and encouraging networking between telecommunications professionals. FICTE organises (*e.g.*) the European Telecommunications Congress, which covers topics from Mobility, Corporate/Carrier Services to Residential Services. [http://www.fitce.org]

(National FITCE associations exist *e.g.* in Belgium [http://www.fitce.be/].)

1.15 GSM Europe (GSME): the public face of European mobile operators and the key representative forum for the European wireless industry. It seeks to enhance and protect investments in network infrastructure and to drive innovation and growth, expanding consumer choice. It represents around 147 operators in 50 countries/areas in Europe, serving around 558 million subscribers. GSM Europe Working Groups: Regulatory, Interconnection, Frequencies, M-Commerce and Health & Environment. [http://www.gsmworld.com/gsmeurope/index.shtml]

1.16 European Telecommunications Resilience & Recovery Association (ETR²A): a forum for discussion, research, debate and information-sharing based in the UK, it aims to understand the relation between telecommunications, information security, business continuity, disaster management and information assurance/governance. ETR²A has the backing of government, business and academia. [http://www.etr2a.org]

1.17 Organisme de Liaison des Industries Métalliques Européennes (ORGALIME): a European engineering industries association founded in 1954 to promote the industry and to defend its interests at EU level. It has 34 member trade federations representing some 130,000 companies in 23 European Countries, which generate over €1,200 billion per year. [http://www.orgalime.org]

1.18 European Electronic Component Manufacturers Association (EECA): an association of electronic manufacturers set up in 1973 to promote their vital interests and support their competitive position in the global marketplace. It is composed of 4 industry associations: (1) European Semiconductor Industry Association (ESIA); (2) European Display Industry Association (EDIA); (3) European Passive Components Industry Association (EPCIA); and (4) European Packaging and Interconnection Industry Association (EPIA). [http://www.eeca.org]

1.19 European Information & Communications Technology Industry Association (EICTA): representing more than 10,000 companies all over Europe with more than 1.5 million employees and revenues of more than €190 billion, it is a merger of (a) The Association of the European Telecommunications and Professional Electronics Industry (ECTEL), the telecoms specialist federation with (b) The European Association of Manufacturers of Business Machines and Information Technology Industry (EUROBIT), the ICT specialist federation. EICTA merged with the European Association of Consumer Electronics Manufacturers (EACEM), the national consumer electronic association, in 2001. [http://www.eicta.org]

1.20 European Competitive Telecommunications Association (ECTA): the leading pan-European trade association serving the telecommunications industry, it encourages market liberalisation and competition and represents the telecommunications industry to key government and regulatory bodies, helping new market entrants through pro-competitive policies. [http://www.ectaportal.com]

1.21 Centre for European Policy Studies (CEPS): an independent policy research institute dedicated to developing constructive solutions to the challenges facing Europe today. Its goals are to achieve high standards of academic excellence and maintain unqualified independence; to provide a forum for discussion amongst all stakeholders in the European policy process; to build collaborative networks of researchers, policy-makers and businesses across the whole of Europe; and to disseminate findings through a regular flow of publications and public events. [http://www.ceps.be]

1.22 European Broadcasting Union (EBU): an independent, non-governmental commercial body which promotes cooperation in international radio and television broadcasting. [http://www.ebu.ch]

2. Cross-sectoral (general) European Industry Associations

2.1 ICT-focused Industry Associations

2.1.1 European Forum for Electronic Business (EEMA), formerly the European Electronic Messaging Association: the premier European forum for electronic business, formed in March 1987. It is an international, non-profit organisation providing an independent forum for all participants in electronic business. EEMA's membership includes users, hardware- and software vendors, and government ,bodies, public and private systems, and service providers. focusses on IT Security, including trusted service provision, digital certificates & PKI; EDI and XML; e-mail; directories; the internet and the world wide web; e-commerce best practice; wireless messaging; unified messaging. [http://www.eema.org]

2.1.2 European Recycling Platform (ERP): set up in 2002 to respond to the European Union's Waste Electronic and Electrical Equipment (WEEE) Directive. Its mission is to aid cost-effective implementation of the WEEE Directive, for the benefit of participating companies and their customers, by developing and operating a common waste management procurement platform. [http://www.erp-recycling.org]

2.2 Not exclusively ICT-focused Industry Associations

2.2.1 European Round Table of Industrialists (ERT): forum of European industrial leaders promoting competitiveness and European economic growth. Since 1983 ERT has contributed to the improved dialogue between industry and governments, at both national and European levels. Every six months ERT endeavours to meet the government holding the EU Presidency to discuss priorities. At national level each member communicates ERT's views to his own national government and parliament, business colleagues and industrial federations, other opinion-formers, and the press. ERT members may be found in 18 European countries, and have a combined turnover of around €1,600 billion, employing around 4.5 million people. They include major European ICT companies like Bosch, BP, Daimler Benz, Deutsche Telekom, Ericsson, Fiat, Nokia, Olivetti, Philips, Siemens, Telefónica and Volvo. [Formal Direct Membership] [http://www.ert.be]

2.2.2 Informal *ad hoc* organizations of industrial elites (as on European state visits abroad).

- Representatives from major multinationals in Europe and the USA.
- Representatives from major multinationals in Europe and Japan.

2.2.3 European Network of Business and Innovation Centres (BICs): the reference point for innovation, incubation and entrepreneurship in Europe, EBN offers services aimed at co-ordinating the activities of the BICs, while developing and promoting the BIC concept within and beyond the European Union. [http://www.ebn.be]

2.2.4 European Corporate Governance Institute (ECGI): an international non-profit association which provides a forum for debate and dialogue between academics, legislators and practitioners, focussing on major corporate governance issues and thereby promoting best practices. Its primary role is to undertake or commission, and disseminate research on corporate governance. [http://www.ecgi.org]

2.2.5 Union of Industrial Employers' Confederations of Europe, Brussels (UNICE): comprising national federations of employers, its priorities are (*e.g.*) a well-functioning internal market; less and better legislation; coherent competition rules and support for innovation. [http://www.unice.org] [http://www.businesseurope.eu]

2.2.6 The EU Committee of the American Chamber of Commerce (AMCHAM-EU): the organisation representing to the EU institutions the views of American companies committed to Europe. With over 600 active professionals producing *ca.* 60 position papers annually, AmCham-EU provides substantial input into the European legislative process. [http://www.eucommittee.be]

2.2.7 Association of European Chambers of Commerce and Industry (EUROCHAMBERS): representing 41 national associations of Chambers of Commerce and Industry, it is a pan-European network of 1,600 regional and local Chambers with over 15 million member enterprises in Europe. [http://www.eurochambres.be]

2.2.8 European Association of Craft, Small and Medium-sized Enterprises *or* Union Européenne de l'Artisanat et des Petites et Moyennes Entreprises (UEAPME): the voice of SMEs in Europe, it represents, at European level, the interests of crafts, trades, and SMEs in the European Union and in countries applying for accession to the European Union. It is non-profit and non-partisan with 75 member organisations, and recently merged with the European Committee for Small and Medium-sized Enterprises (EUROPMI).
[http://www.ueapme.com]

2.2.9 European Tech Investment Forum (ETIF): provides a platform where Europe's most promising or innovative information- and communication-technology companies can meet with venture capital investors, with leading corporate contacts scouting innovation, and with specialised intermediaries from outside their home countries. Formerly the European Investment Forum (EIF), it is supported by the European Commission's IST Programme. [http://www.e-unlimited.com]

2.2.10 JWG-IT: an independent think-tank that defines workable solutions for financial institutions to handle EU regulatory change. JWG contributes appropriate, affordable and advanced IT solutions. [http://www.jwg-it.eu]

3. European – Organisations with link to European Institutions

3.1 European Space Agency (ESA): promotes the vision of Europe's future in space and of the benefits of space (*e.g.* satellites) for Europeans on the ground. It develops strategies to fulfil this vision, through collaborative projects in space science and technology. [http://www.esa.int]

3.2 European Investment Bank (EIB): the European Union's investment bank, founded in 1958 under the Treaty of Rome, it contributes to the integration, balanced development, and economic and social cohesion of EU member states, raising substantial volumes of funds from the markets which it directs on most favourable terms to capital projects in line with EU objectives. Projects considered for EIB financing must contribute to (*e.g.*) developing transport, telecommunications, and energy-transmission infrastructure networks with a Community dimension. In partnership with the European Commission, EIB runs the European Investment Fund (EIF). [http://www.eib.org]

3.3 European Bank for Reconstruction and Development (EBRD): founded in 1991 when communism was crumbling in Central and Eastern Europe, it supports the liberated countries in nurturing a private sector in a democratic environment. [http://www.ebrd.com]

3.4 European Central Bank (ECB): the central bank for Europe's single currency, the euro, its main task is to maintain price stability and the euro's purchasing power in the 'euro zone' of the 12 EU member states that have joined the euro since 1999. [http://www.ecb.int]

3.5 European Investment Fund (EIF): invests equity in venture capital funds and business incubators that support SMEs, particularly early-stage and technology-oriented ones. [http://www.eif.org]

3.6 European Network and Information Security Agency (ENISA): founded under the authority of Regulation (EC) No 460/2004, its main role is to support the exchange of information and facilitate co-operation on issues of IT security in the Single Market. It aims to achieve a high level of security awareness amongst businesses; analyse risks; and follow up standardisation efforts in collaboration with suppliers. [http://www.enisa.eu.int]

3.7 The European Registry of Internet Domain Names (EURid): a Belgian non-profit that the European Commission chose to operate the new .eu top level domain. It will establish 4 additional regional offices to support registries (Brussels, Stockholm, Pisa, Prague). [http://www.eurid.eu]

4. European Standards Institutions (with some association with the EU)

4.1 New Approach to Standardisation in the Internal Market: joins up the efforts of CEN, CENELEC and ETSI (the three European standards organisations) to the European Commission and EFTA. [http://www.newapproach.org]

4.1.1 Comité Européen de Normatisation (CEN) [European Committee for Standardisation]: aids voluntary technical harmonization in Europe, coordinate with worldwide bodies and its European partners. [http://www.cenorm.be]

4.1.2 European Committee for Electronic Standardisation (CENELEC): creates voluntary electro-technical standards for Europe, having been converted in 1973 to a non-profit under Belgian law. It was officially recognised as *the* European standards organisation in its field by the European Commission in Directive 83/189/EEC. Its members have been collaborating in the interests of European harmonisation since the late Fifties, maturing alongside the European Economic Community. CENELEC works with 35,000 technical experts from 22 European countries to publish standards for the European market. [http://www.cenelec.org]

4.1.3 European Telecommunications Standards Institute (ETSI): founded in 1988 to collaborate internationally toward developing globally applicable standards meeting the needs of the telecommunication/ electronic communication community, while fulfilling its duty to support EU and EFTA regulation and initiatives. Membership by category as of 1 Feb 2003: manufacturers 51%, service providers and others 24%, network operators 14%, administrators 8%, users 3%. It has 786 members from 56 countries. [http://www.etsi.org]

4.2 Supporting Standards-Setting Initiatives

4.2.1 Information Society Standardization System (CEN-ISSS): provides market players with a comprehensive and integrated range of standardisation-oriented services and products, to contribute to the success of the Information Society in Europe. [http://www.cenorm.be/isss]

4.2.2 European Workshop for Open Systems (EWOS): set up in 1987 in CEN/CENELEC framework, participants are some of the most representative European federations of IT producers and organisations.

4.2.3 International Electrotechnical Commission (IEC): co-operation between the IEC and CENELEC is stipulated in what is known as 'the Dresden Agreement' of September 1996. [http://www.iec.ch]

5. European – Standards Institutes (with *no* EU link)

5.1 Standardising information and communication systems (ECMA): an industry association dedicated to information and communication systems standardisation. [http://www.ecma-international.org]

5.2 Confédération Européenne des Organismes de Contrôle technique, d'inspection, de certification et de prévention (CEOC): a confederation of independent private, semi-private or government organisations, or associations of such organisations, for testing, technically inspecting, and certifying products and Quality Management Systems, and for risk prevention. [http://www.ceoc.com]

5.3 European Organisation for Technical Approvals (EOTA): organises national Approval Bodies that issue European Technical Approvals (ETAs), nominated by EU and EFTA member states who belong to the European Economic Area Agreement. Monitoring and speeding the drafting of ETA Guidelines (ETAGs), and coordinating activities relating to issuing ETAs, it collaborates with European Commission, EFTA, CEN, European trade associations and industrial organisations, who are also present as observers at all EOTA levels. [http://www.eota.be]

5.4 European Federation of National Associations of Measurement, Testing and Analytic Laboratories (EUROLAB): created on the basis of a memorandum of understanding signed by delegations representing the private and public laboratories of 17 out of the 19 countries of the EEC and EFTA. [http://www.eurolab.org]

5.5 European Safety Federation (ESF): founded in 1991 to unite European manufacturers, suppliers, and distributors of Personal Protective Equipment (PPE), it represents them at all governmental levels of the European Union and before other European institutions. [http://www.european-safety-federation.org]

5.6 European Electrical Products Certification Association (EEPCA): European Certification Schemes for Electrical Products offer third-party certification of products in the Low Voltage Directive (LVD). [http://www.eepca.org/]

EEPCA collaborates with:

- ENEC Secretariat [http://www.enec.com]
- HAR Secretariat [http://www.har-cert.com/welcome.html]
- IECQ Secretariat [http://www.iecq.org]

Level 3: Project groups

Relevant Task Forces, Working Groups, Workshops, Industry Committees include:

1. **European Programmes**

1.1 EU Framework programmes (FP)

The Framework Programmes are the EU's main platforms for supporting leading-edge research and technological development.

- FP4 (1994-1998, budget of €13 billion): [europa.eu.int/europ/research/fp4.html]
- FP5 (1998-2002, budget of €15 billion):

[europa.eu.int/europ/research/fp5.html]
[http://www.cordis.lu/fp5]

- FP6 (2003-2006, budget of €19 billion): [europa.eu.int/europ/research/fp6.html]
- FP7 (2007-2013, budget of €53.3 billion): [europa.eu.int/europ/research/future/index_en.cfm] [http://cordis.europa.eu/fp7/home_en.html]

Regional Representations: *e.g.* in the UK 'Supporting UK applications to the EU's 6th FP. [fp6uk.ost.gov.uk/Default.aspx]

EU Research Projects

Sample of Research Projects hosted by CORDIS (Community Research and Development Information Service):

- Co-operation Platform for Research and Standards: FP6-IST 2002 (Accompanying Measures) [http://www.w3.org/2004/copras/]
- Enterprise Next Generation Network Vision 2010: FP6-IST 2005 (ICT for Environmental Risk Management) [http://www.u-2010.eu]
- Pan European laboratory for next generation networks and services (PANLAB): FP6 2005 (Research networking testbeds)
- Connecting Excellence on European Governance (CONNEX): FP6 2006 (citizens and governance) [http://www.connex-network.org]

1.2 Joint Research Centre (JRC): an essential element of the European Research Area (ERA), the Institute for Prospective Technological Studies (IPTS), its subsidiary, carries out and supports scientific and technical research in areas such as Information Society technologies, cybersecurity, research policy, economic and technical change. [http://www.jrc.cec.eu.int]

1.3 Eureka: European network for market-oriented R&D which aims to strengthen European competitiveness through collaborative research, it has 34 members. [http://www.eureka.be]

2. Various Initiatives at European level

- **IRC (Innovation Relay Centres)** facilitate innovative technology transfer to and from European companies and research departments. [irc.cordis.lu; http://www.innovationrelay.net]
- **CORDIS Technology Marketplace** connects people to technology, featuring research results and business opportunities related to emerging technologies. [http://www.cordis.lu/marketplace] [http://www.cordis.lu/results]
- **EIC (Euro Info Centres)** more than 320 centres in 42 countries inform, advise, and assist businesses on all EU issues, including policies, legislation, and R&D programmes. Its Research & Development Working Group helps EICs increase their level of service in the field of R&D and innovation. [europa.eu.int/europ./enterprise/networks/eic/eic.html]
- **EBN (European Business and Innovation Centre Network)** brings together 160 Business and Innovation Centres (BICs) and similar organisations, such as incubators, and innovation and entrepreneurship centres. [http://www.ebn.be]
- **IRP (Intellectual Property Rights) Helpdesk**: first-line assistance for IP issues. [http://www.ipr-helpdesk.org]
- **EIT (European Institute of Innovation and Technology)**: set up in 2006 as a flagship research university for excellence in higher education, research and innovation. [http://ec.europa.eu/education/policies/educ/eit/index_en.html]

JTI (Joint Technology Initiatives) long-term public-private partnerships that advance technology in specific fields, they receive funding from the European Commission under FP7 (*q.v.*), as well as from the European Investment Bank (EIB). [http://cordis.europa.eu/fp7/jtis]

3. **European Business Summit (EBS)**: an initiative of the Belgian Business Federation together with UNICE and the European Commission, the annual event promotes dialogue between leading European businessmen and policy makers, and provides thousand of participants from the world of business, politics and academia, and NGOs the opportunity to meet for an exchange of views and to exert their joint influence to build a better, more competitive Europe. [http://www.ebsummit.org]

4. **EU Academies' Science Advisory Council (EASAC)**: a means for the national Academies of Europe to work together to inject high-quality science into EU policy-making. EASAC's task is to build science into policy at the EU level by providing independent, expert, credible advice about the scientific aspects of public policy issues to those who make or influence policy for the European Union. [http://www.easac.org]

5. **European Conferences*)**

- **CEPT (European Conference of Postal and Telecommunications Administrations)**: founded in 1959 by 19 countries, expanded to 26 in its first ten years, CEPT is a forum for discussing sovereignty and regulatory issues in the postal/telecommunications fields, and exerts influence over the goals and priorities in this sector by forging common positions and facilitating ties between European regulators. Members are mainly national government ministries. [http://www.cept.org]
- **InfoSec Europe** (InfoSecurity Europe): Europe's most inclusive forum of information security professionals. [http://www.infosec.co.uk]
- **EEMA UK (European Electronic Messaging Association)**: now European Forum for Electronic Business, it hosts user-group meetings. [http://www.eema.org]
- **EuroCACS (European Computer Audit, Control and Security Conference)**: sponsored by ISACA®, it includes training streams focusing on business IT management, IS audit, IS security, and core competencies. Sessions are designed to meet the educational needs of CIOs, audit directors, IS audit and security managers, and other audit, security and control professionals. [http://www.isaca.org/eurocacs]
- **EWC (European Wireless Conference)**: promotes technologies, protocols, services, applications enabling a full, seamless, nomadic access to new classes of multimedia services with a user-centric focus.
[http://www.european-wireless2005.de]
- **The Wireless Event**: the world's biggest wireless broadband conference, it attracts hundreds of CEOs and senior executives from the most important, innovative players in the market, from mobile operators to WISPs to cable operators. [http://www.thewirelessevent.com]
- **ETIF (European Tech Investment Forum)**: organised by Europe Unlimited and promoted by the European Commission's IST Programme, its mission is to facilitate the growth of Europe's most promising innovative information and communication technology companies by providing a European forum where entrepreneurs can meet with active venture capital investors and with leading corporate contacts scouting innovation. [http://www.e-unlimited.com/etif]
- **Mediacast**: the leading technology show for digital media, it showcases cutting-edge technologies that allow one to manage, secure, and make money from digital content. Held in the UK. [http://www.mediacast.net]
- **Complitech (Compliance Technology)**: Europe's leading regulatory technology exhibition and conference, tailored to the financial services market. Held in the UK. [http://www.complitech.co.uk]
- **WiCon (Wireless Connectivity World)**: held in the Netherlands, the world's largest showcase of wireless connectivity solutions, Bluetooth, DECT, GPS,

IrDA, OSGI, RFID, UWB, WiMedia, Wireless 1394, WLAN, Zigbee, proprietary wireless systems, and more besides. [http://www.wiconworld.com]

- **Internet World**: covers New Media Marketing, Internet Security and Payments, Web Content Management, Hosting and Connectivity, Mobile/ Wireless Technologies. Held in the UK. [http://www.internetworld.co.uk]
- **Mobile Enterprise**: held in the UK, it covers everything that matters to enterprise decision makers on mobile and wireless solutions, security, and integrating across networks. [http://www.mobileenterpriseevent.com]
- **Enterprise Network (EN)**: held in the UK, it is an interactive event specially designed for Communications, ICT, Network and Corporate Managers, and an opportunity to learn about the next generation of network solutions. [http://www.enterprisenetworks.co.uk]
- **Information Technology & Telecommunications (IT&T) Conference**: it is attended by leading academic and industrial researchers nationally and internationally. [http://www.ittconference.ie]
- **eChallenges**: sponsored by the European Commission, it brings together leading enterprises, professionals, researchers, academics and public authorities to share their experiences, visions and projects, and to increase mutual awareness of exploitable technologies and applications. Its thematic priorities are: eBusiness; Future forms of organisations; Technology and Applications, eGovernment; Services to Citizens and Business; Organisational Transformation; eWork – New Working Environments; eEurope 2005; ICT take-up by SMEs, and International Collaboration on IST. [http://www.echallenges.org]
- Annual Cable Congress (formerly known as the ECCA Congress): the annual conference of the Cable Europe association. [http://www.cable-europe.eu]

A6.4 Level 4: Global Stakeholders

Level 4: Individual advocates

1. Global Summits

1.1 Group of Eight (G8), formerly G-7 before Russia joined in 1994: an international forum for the governments of Canada, France, Germany, Italy, Japan, Russia, the United Kingdom and the United States, which represent 65% of the world economy. Each year, member states take turns at the G-8 presidency, setting its annual agenda and hosting the summit of the year. They agree on co-ordination of strategies, stimulation of research, information, knowledge exchange, security policy, *etc.* [http://g8live.org]

1.2 Group of Twenty (G-20): with Argentina, Australia, Brazil, Canada, China, France, Germany, India, Indonesia, Italy, Japan, México, Russia, Saudi Arabia, South Africa, South Korea, Turkey, the United Kingdom, the United States, and the EU as members the G-20 is an informal forum that promotes an open and constructive dialogue between finance ministers and central bank governors of systemically significant industrial and emerging market economies. Representing around two-thirds of the world's population and 90% of world gross domestic product, the G-20 is uniquely placed to tackle issues of significance for the international economy and monetary system. [http://www.g20.org]

2. Global Fora and Conferences

2.1 World Economic Forum (WEF): an independent international organization committed to improving the state of the world, it provides a collaborative framework for world leaders to address global issues, engaging particularly its corporate members in global citizenship. [http://www.weforum.org]

2.2 World Radio Communications Conference (WEC): organised by the US Federal Communications Commission and periodically convened to consider a regulatory framework to manage the international use of radio-frequency spectrum in a rational and equitable manner. [http://www.fcc.gov/wrc-12]

2.3 World Summit on the Information Society (WSIS): held in two phases, with 175 countries participating, the first took place in Geneva, 10-12 December 2003, hosted by Switzerland, and the second in Tunis, 16-18 November 2005, hosted by Tunisia. Four documents were adopted:

- Geneva Declaration of Principles
- Geneva Plan of Action
- Tunis Commitment, and
- Tunis Agenda for the Information Society.

The ITU took the lead in organizing the Summit.
[http://www.itu.int/wsis] [http://groups.itu.int/wsis-forum2012/Home.aspx]

2.4 ITU Telecom and ITU World Telecom: part of the ITU (*q.v.*), it organizes events for the world's ICT community, providing a unique global networking forum where great minds, companies and new technologies connect. One ITU Telecom event is held each year, with ITU World Telecom events held every three years.
[http://www.itu.int/ITUTELECOM] [http://world2012.itu.int]

2.5 GSMA Mobile World Congress, formerly 3GSM World Congress: a world congress with exhibition, speakers and workshops. [http://www.mobileworldcongress.com]

2.6 The Internet Governance Forum (IGF): helps the UN Secretary-General carry out the WSIS mandate to convene a permanent forum for multi-stakeholder policy dialogue, through the UN ICT Task Force and non-governmental stakeholder participation. [http://www.intgovforum.org]

Level 4: Public-sector and non-profit organisations

1. International Organisations

1.1 World Trade Organisation (WTO): the only international organization dealing with the rules of international trade, at its heart are the WTO agreements negotiated, signed and ratified by the bulk of the world's trading nations. Its goal is to help producers, exporters and importers of goods and services do business. It has 151 members, and is the successor to GATT (*q.v.*). [http://www.wto.org]

1.2 Organisation for Economic Co-operation and Development (OECD): 30 member countries sharing a commitment to democratic government and market economy, it has relationships with 70 other countries and civil society and global reach. Its work covers economic and social issues from macroeconomics to trade, education, development, and science and innovation. Its Directorate for Science, Technology and Industry (STI) "provides governments with analytical basis for policy formulation and advice on the scientific, technological and industrial environment and its relation to growth, employment and well-being", and its Statistics Directorate (STD) provides statistics on a comparable basis for the OECD's analytical work, develops international statistical standards and co-ordinates statistical activities both within the Organisation and with other international agencies. [http://www.oecd.org]

1.3 Business and Industry Advisory Committee to the OECD (BIAC): an independent advisory committee officially recognised by the OECD as representative of the OECD business community, it advises the OECD on business issues. Its members are the major industrial and employers' organisations in the 30 OECD member countries. Its 34 standing committees and policy groups mirror all economic policy issues the OECD covers, as well as their impacts on members and, increasingly, on non-members like Russia and China. Every year over 1000 business representatives get actively involved in the work of the OECD through BIAC, whose main objectives are to:

- influence OECD policies to reflect business priorities
- influence government representatives participating in OECD committees; and
- provide members with information on OECD policies and their implications for business.

[http://www.biac.org]

1.4 United Nations (UN): established in 1945 by 51 countries committed to keeping peace through international cooperation and collective security, today, nearly every nation in the world belongs to the UN: membership totals 191 countries. It has six main organs: General Assembly, Security Council, Economic and Social Council, Trusteeship Council and the Secretariat (all based at UN Headquarters in New York), and the International Court of Justice (at The Hague). [http://www.un.org]

- General Assembly (GA; UNGA): the deliberative body of the United Nations, it comprises all United Nations member states and meets in regular yearly sessions. [http://www.un.org/ga]
- Economic and Social Council (ECOSOC): the central forum for discussing international economic and social issues, and for recommending policy to member states and the UN. [http://www.un.org/en/ecosoc]

1.4.1 UN Conference on Trade and Development (UNCTAD): has two divisions directly relevant to ICT affairs:

a) Commission for Science and Technology for Development (CSTD): a subsidiary of the Economic and Social Council (ECOSOC). It provides the General Assembly and ECOSOC with high-level advice on relevant science and technology issues. [http://unctad.org/cstd]

b) Investment, Technology and Enterprise Development (DITE): analyses trends in foreign direct investment and their impact on development; helps countries to promote international investment and to understand the issues involved in international investment agreements; devises strategies for development of small and medium-sized enterprises; identifies policy options and implements capacity-building programmes to encourage the use of new technologies. [http://unctad.org/dite]

1.4.2 Global Alliance for Information and Communication Technologies and Development (GAID): once a subgroup and now a continuation of the Information and Communication Technologies (ICT) Task Force set up by Secretary-General Kofi Annan to find creative means to spread the benefits of the digital revolution and avert a two-tiered information society, it responds to the need for an inclusive global forum for cross-sectoral policy dialogue on the use of ICT for the achievement of internationally agreed development goals, notably reduction of poverty. [http://www.un-gaid.org]

1.5 Relevant Specialized UN Agencies (only ICT relevant agencies are listed)

The United Nations is central to global efforts to solve problems that challenge humanity. Cooperating in this effort are more than 30 affiliated organizations, known together as the UN system.

1.5.1 International Telecommunications Union (ITU): fosters international cooperation on telecommunications of all media, coordinates use of radio and TV frequencies, promotes safety measures and conducts research. Its membership represents a cross-section of the telecommunications and information technology industry, and includes 189 member states and over 650 sector members. ITU is divided into three core sectors:

- Radiocommunication Assembly (ITU-R)
- Telecom Standardization Sector (ITU-T), and
- Telecom Development (ITY-D).

Reform calls for a common vision of the ITU's future as a public/private partnership, to preserve and strengthen its international credibility. The respective roles in this partnership must be better defined, so that both sides have rights and duties. The ITU's decision-making must reflect the modern, competitive telecommunications environment in which the private sector plays the leading role while the regulatory agencies act as an arbitrator for the wider public interest. [http://www.itu.int]

1.5.2 United Nations Commission on International Trade Law (UNCITRAL): the core legal body of the UN system in the field of international trade law, it formulates modern, fair, and harmonized rules on commercial transactions. [http://www.uncitral.org/uncitral/en]

1.5.3 World Bank Group, New York: gives loans and technical assistance to developing countries to reduce poverty and advance sustainable growth. A vital source of these goods to the world's developing countries, it comprises two unique development institutions owned by 185 member countries: the International Bank for Reconstruction and Development (IBRD) and the International Development Association (IDA). [http://www.worldbank.org]

1.5.4 International Bank for Reconstruction and Development (IBRD): aims to reduce poverty in middle-income and creditworthy poorer countries by furthering sustainable development through loans, guarantees, risk management products, and analytical and advisory services. Established in 1944 as the original institution of the World Bank Group, IBRD is a cooperative operated for its 185 member countries' benefit. [http://www.worldbank.org/ibrd]

1.5.5 International Development Association (IDA): the World Bank unit that lends to the world's poorest countries, it aims to reduce poverty by providing interest-free loans and grants for Programmes; boost economic growth; and reduce inequalities and improve living conditions. [http://www.worldbank.org/ida]

1.5.6 International Monetary Fund (IMF): facilitates international monetary cooperation and stability, providnig a permanent forum for consultation, advice and assistance on financial issues. [http://www.imf.org]

1.5.7 World Intellectual Property Organization (WIPO): promotes international protection of intellectual property and promotes cooperation on copyrights, trademarks, industrial designs and patents. It is dedicated to helping ensure that the rights of creators and owners of intellectual property are protected worldwide, and that inventors and authors are recognized and rewarded for their ingenuity. [http://www.wipo.org]

1.5.8 United Nations Educational, Scientific and Cultural Organization (UNESCO): promotes universal education and cultural development, protection of the world's natural and cultural heritage, international cooperation in science, press freedom and communication. [http://www.unesco.org]

1.6 UN Special Interest Groups and Conferences

1.6.1 ICT for Development Platform (ICT4D Platform): aims to enrich the political core of the World Summit on the Information Society (WSIS). The Platform brings together ICT4D specialists, best practices, innovations, and international experience and raises awareness of the importance of ICT for development.
[www.edwebproject.org/wsis03/ict4d.html]

1.6.2 UN Working Group on Internet Governance (WGIG): set up by the Declaration of Principles and Action Plan, its main activity is "to investigate and make proposals for action, as appropriate, on the governance of Internet by 2005". The WGIG was asked to present the result of its work in a report "for consideration and appropriate action for the second phase of the WSIS in Tunis 2005". [http://www.wgig.org]

1.6.3 UN Conference on Trade and Development (UNCTAD): its activities include trade, commodities; investment, technology, enterprise development; macroeconomic policies, debt, development financing; transport, customs and information technology. [http://www.unctad.org]

1.6.4 United Nations Economic Commission for Europe (UNECE): fosters sustainable economic growth among its 55 member countries, providing a forum for communication among States; brokes international legal instruments addressing trade, transport, the environment; and supplies statistics and economic and environmental analysis. [http://www.unece.org]

1.6.5 United Nations Centre for Trade Facilitation and Electronic Business (UN/CEFACT): aims to better the ability of business, trade and administrative organizations from developed, developing and transitional economies to exchange products and relevant services effectively. [http://www.unece.org/cefact]

1.6.6 UN Development Programme (UNDP): the UN's global development network, an organization advocating for change and connecting countries to knowledge, experience and resources. [http://www.undp.org]

1.6.7 The Council of Europe: an organization of 47 member states in the European region (also including Azerbaijan, Armenia, Turkey, Georgia and Cyprus). Its most enduring legacy is the European Convention on Human Rights, adopted in 1950. "The aim of the Council of Europe is to achieve a greater unity between its members for the purpose of safeguarding and realising the ideals and principles which are their common heritage and facilitating their economic and social progress" (Article 1(a)) TEU). [http://www.coe.int]

1.7 Global Business Dialogue on e-Society, formerly Global Business Dialogue on e-Commerce (GBDe): a CEO-led, worldwide business initiative established to help create a policy framework for development of a global online economy. [http://www.gbd-e.org]

1.8 International Telecommunications User Group (INTUG): an international association of users of communication technology and applications founded in 1974. Its members include national user groups and individual members from major multinational enterprises, academia, law and other relevant industry sectors. [http://intug.org]

1.9 Global Information Infrastructure Commission (GIIC): fosters private-sector leadership and private- and public-sector cooperation in the development of information networks and services to advance global economic growth, education and quality of life. It is an independent, non-governmental initiative involving leaders from developing and industrialized countries. GIIC's goals are to:

- strengthen the leadership role of the private sector in the development of a diverse, affordable and accessible information infrastructure
- promote involvement of developing countries in the building and utilization of truly global and open information infrastructure
- facilitate activities and identify policy options which foster effective applications of telecommunications, broadcasting and information technologies and services.. [http://www.giic.org]

1.9 World Information Technology and Services Alliance (WITSA): a consortium of 53 information technology (IT) industry associations from economies around the world. WITSA members represent over 90 percent of the world IT market. As the global voice of the IT industry, WITSA is dedicated to:

- advocating policies that advance the industry's growth and development
- facilitating international trade and investment in IT products and services

- strengthening WITSA's national industry associations through the sharing of knowledge, experience, and critical information
- providing members with a vast network of contacts in nearly every geographic region of the world
- hosting the World Congress on IT, the premier industry-sponsored, global IT event
- hosting the Global Public Policy Conference; and
- hosting the Global Information Security Summit.

Founded in 1978 and originally known as the World Computing Services Industry Association, it has increasingly assumed an active role in international public policy issues affecting the creation of a robust global information infrastructure, including advocacy for:

- increasing competition through open markets and regulatory reform
- protecting intellectual property
- encouraging cross-industry and government cooperation to enhance information security
- bridging the education and skills gap
- reducing tariff and non-tariff trade barriers to IT goods and services; and
- safeguarding the viability and continued growth of the Internet and electronic commerce.

[http://www.witsa.org/v2]

1.10 Alliance for Global Business: comprehending ICC, INTUG, BIAC, WITSA and GIIC, it holds discussion events and hosts a platform for publications (*e.g.* "A Global Action Plan for Electronic Business") prepared by business with recommendations for governments [http://www.witsa.org/agb.htm]

1.11 International Communications Round Table (ICRT): a cross-sectoral forum for the exchange of information and views on the convergence of the telecommunications, entertainment, computer and publishing industries, and the regulatory issues that this will present. Its members, 25 leading communications companies, analyse regulatory developments and prepare innovative approaches to the public policy issues they raise. It is global in perspective, covering Europe, the United States and Japan. [http://www.icrt.org]

1.12 International Telecommunications Satellite Organisation (INTELSAT): the world's largest commercial satellite communications services provider. On July 18, 2001 Intelsat became a private company, 37 years after being formed as an intergovernmental consortium owning and managing a constellation of communications satellites (Intelsats) to provide international broadcast services. [http://www.intelsat.com]

2. International Scientific Organisations

Some international scientific organisations that offer a platform for stakeholders interested in science include:

2.1 International Council for Science (ICSU): a non-governmental organization representing a global membership that includes 104 national scientific bodies and 29 international scientific unions. Through this extensive international network, it hosts discussions of issues relevant to international science policy and makes known the importance of international science for policy issues. It undertakes the following core activities:

- Planning and coordinating interdisciplinary research to address major issues of relevance in both science and society
- Actively advocating for freedom in the conduct of science, promoting equitable access to scientific data and information, and facilitating science education and capacity building
- Acting as a focus for the exchange of ideas, the communication of scientific information and the development of scientific standards; and
- Supporting in excess of 600 scientific conferences, congresses and symposia per year all around the world, as well as the production of a wide range of newsletters, handbooks, learned journals and proceedings. [http://www.icsu.org]

2.2 UNESCO
See also: United Nations Educational, Scientific and Cultural Organization. (UNESCO) [http://www.unesco.org]

Level 4: Industry-focused associations

1. Cross-sectoral International Industry Associations

1.1 International Chamber of Commerce (ICC): the voice of world business championing the global economy as a force for economic growth, job creation and prosperity. Founded in 1919, it sets rules and standards, promotes growth and prosperity, spreading business expertise and advocating for international business. Dedicated to the expansion of cross-border trade, ICC champions liberalisation of telecoms and the development of infrastructures that support global online trade.
The ICC Commission on e-Business, IT and Telecoms (EBITT) comprises a group of experts on the public policy aspects of ICTs, divided into the following Task Forces: TF on Telecoms Policy, TF on Protection of Personal Data, TF on IT Services, TF on Jurisdiction and Applicable Law in e-Commerce, TF on Consumer Policy for e-Business, TF on Security and Authentication, TF on Electronic Contracting. Headquartered in Paris it has national committee staff in some 64 countries. [http://www.iccwbo.org]

1.2 World Chambers Network (WCN): a global virtual network of over 12,000 registered Chambers of Commerce & Industry and Boards of Trade, representing tens of millions of businesses worldwide, it provides an electronic platform for Chambers worldwide to participate in eCommerce. [http://www.worldchambers.com]

1.3 International Corporate Governance Network (ICGN): an unincorporated, non-profit association having 4 primary purposes: (1) to host an investor-led network for exchanging views and information about corporate governance issues internationally; (2) to examine corporate governance principles and practices; (3) to develop and promote adherence to corporate governance standards and guidelines; and (4) to promote good corporate governance. Membership is open to those committed to the development of good corporate governance. [http://www.icgn.org]

1.4 Global Corporate Governance Forum (GCGF): a multi-donor trust fund co-founded by the World Bank Group and the Organisation for Economic Co-operation and Development (OECD) to promote global, regional, and local initiatives to improve the institutional framework and practices of corporate governance. Its activities promote sustainable economic growth and poverty reduction within the framework of agreed international development targets. With input from the Private Sector Advisory Group (PSAG), its work program encompasses: (1) raising awareness and building consensus for implementation of reform through meetings, briefings, policy papers, and conferences; (2) supporting institution and capacity building, and giving technical assistance to implementation at the field level through training programmes, toolkits and other direct assistance; (3) supporting research fitted to the needs of developing countries to underpin reform efforts, and building sustainable networks for academics in developing countries; and (4) disseminating best-practices materials, publications and guidelines developed with leading global specialists and practitioners.
[http://www.gcgf.org/wps/wcm/connect/Topics_Ext_Content/IFC_External_Corporate_Site/Global+Corporate+Governance+Forum]

1.5 The Committee of Sponsoring Organizations of the 'Treadway Commission' (COSO): a voluntary, private-sector organization dedicated to improving the quality of financial reporting through business ethics, effective controls, and corporate governance. [http://www.coso.org]

1.6 International Compliance Association (ICA): a professional non-profit furthering regulatory compliance and anti-money laundering best practices, it educates and supports compliance and anti-money laundering professionals globally through the provision of internationally recognised qualifications, information exchange, and training. It also sets standards of technical knowledge and professional competence. [http://www.int-comp.org]

1.7 World Bank: one of the world's largest sources of development assistance, in 2002 it provided $19.5 billion to developing countries and worked in more than 100 developing economies, bringing finance and/or technical expertise (incl. for telecoms). [http://www.worldbank.org]

1.8 Privacy International (PI): a human rights watchdog on surveillance and privacy invasions by governments and corporations. Based in London with offices in Washington, PI has conducted campaigns and research throughout the world on issues from wiretapping and national security to ID cards, video surveillance, data matching, medical privacy, and freedom of information and expression. [http://www.privacy-international.org]

1.9 International Association of Privacy Professionals (IAPP): the world's largest privacy professionals association, it has 4000 business, government and academic members from 32 countries. [https://www.privacyassociation.org]

1.10 Anti-Phishing Working Group (APWG): a global pan-industrial and law-enforcement association focused on eliminating the fraud and identity theft that results from phishing, pharming and email spoofing of all types. [http://www.antiphising.org]

2. ICT Sector Specific International Industry Associations

2.1 International Organisation for Standardisation (ISO): a worldwide federation of national standards bodies of 147 countries promoting standardization with a view to facilitating the international exchange of goods and services.
[http://www.iso.ch]

2.2 Organization for the Advancement of Structured Information Standards (OASIS): an international consortium that drives the development, convergence, and adoption of e-business standards. The consortium produces more Web services standards than any other organization, including for security and e-business, and assists standardization efforts in the public sector and for application-specific markets. Founded in 1993, OASIS counts more than 5,000 participants representing over 600 organizations in 100 countries. [http://www.oasis-open.org]

2.3 Institute of Electrical and Electronics Engineers – Standards Association (IEEE-SA): the leading developer of a broad range of global industry standards including: power and energy, biomedical and healthcare, information technology, telecommunications, transportation, nanotechnology and information assurance. IEEE has over 20,000 members from corporations, organizations, universities, and government agencies around the globe. [http://standards.ieee.org]

2.4 Internet Corporation for Assigned Names and Numbers (ICANN): responsible for technical coordination of the assignment of parameters in identifier spaces used on the Internet, including MIME media types, port numbers, private-enterprise numbers, and protocol numbers. It is also responsible for technical aspects of assigning top-level domains (including ccTLDs) within the Internet's domain name system, and for coordinating the IP-address allocation system operated in conjunction with Regional Internet Registries. [http://www.icann.org]

2.5 Wi-Fi Alliance, formerly Wireless Ethernet Compatibility Alliance: an international non-profit that certifies the interoperability of wireless Local Area Network products based on the IEEE 802.11 specification. Currently the Wi-Fi Alliance has 205 members, and 915 products have received Wi-Fi certification since certification began in March of 2000. Its goal is to enhance user experience through product interoperability. [http://www.wi-fi.org]

2.6 Payment Card Industry (PCI) Security Standards Council: a global forum for ongoing development, enhancement, storage, dissemination and implementation of security standards for account data protection, its mission is to enhance payment account data security by promoting broad adoption of the PCI Security Standards. It owns, develops and distributes the PCI Data Security Standard (DSS), and was founded by American Express, Discover Financial Services, JCB, MasterCard Worldwide, and Visa International. [https://www.pcisecuritystandards.org]

Level 4: Project groups

Task Forces, Working Groups, Workshops, Industry Committees include:

1. Global

1.1 Internet Engineering Task Force (IETF): an international community of network designers, operators, vendors, and researchers concerned with the evolution of Internet architecture and its smooth operation. IETF has more than 60 working groups whose activities include anti-spam research, IPv6 development, and application- and network standard development. [http://www.ietf.org]
On European Level: European IPv6 Task Force and National IPv6 Task Forces.

1.2 Internet Protocol version 6 Forum (IPv6 Forum):- a consortium of Internet vendors, industry subject matter experts, and research and education networks, with a clear mission to advocate IPv6 by dramatically improving technology, market, and deployment user and industry awareness of IPv6, creating a secure New Generation Internet allowing world-wide equitable access to knowledge and technology. It is a non-profit organisation with head office in Luxembourg. [http://www.ipv6forum.org]

1.3 World Wide Web Consortium (W3C): pursues its mission through the creation of Web standards and guidelines, called W3C Recommendations, of which it has published more than ninety since 1994. It engages in education and outreach, develops software, hosts an open forum for discussion about the Web, and developed a Platform for Internet Content Selection (PICS), which enables labels to be associated with Internet content. [http://www.w3.org]

1.4 Internet2: the foremost US advanced networking consortium, led by the research and education community since 1996. It promotes the missions of its members by providing both leading-edge network capabilities and unique partnership opportunities facilitating the development of revolutionary technologies. [http://www.internet2.org]

1.5 Internet Systems Consortium (ISC): a non-profit corporation supporting the infrastructure of a universal-connect, self-organizing Internet, and the autonomy of its participants, by developing and maintaining core production quality software, protocols, and operations. ISC is the renowned producer and distributor of Critical Internet Infrastructure software. Its commercial quality open source software, including BIND and DHCP, is deployed by over 80% of Internet providers worldwide. [http://www.isc.org]

1.6 G8 Digital Opportunity Task Force (G8 DOT Force): created by the G8 Heads of State at their Kyushu-Okinawa Summit in July 2000, it brought together 43 teams from government, the private sector, non-profit organizations, and international organizations. Representing developed and developing countries, its objective was to identify ways the digital revolution can benefit all the world's people, especially the poorest and most marginalized. [http://www.g8.utoronto.ca/summit/2001genoa/dotforce1.html]

2. International Conferences (examples)

- TVConnect, formerly IPTV World Forum: integrating media to monetise the multiplatform environment, its events feature over 20 worldwide Telcos and ISPs discussing IPTV service deployment issues. The name change reflects the changing "ecosystem", which has converged and is focussed more on a strategic vision. New players from the world of apps, advertising, content and new media are having a greater influence on the industry's evolution. [http://www.tvconnectevent.com/]
- CeBit: The world's largest trade fair showcasing digital IT and telecommunications solutions for home and work environments. The key target groups are users from industry, the wholesale/retail sector, skilled trades, banks, services, government agencies, science and users passionate about technology. [http://www.cebit.de]
- World Congress on Information Technology (WCIT): The WCIT is a biennial meeting attracting leading ICT personalities, top corporate executives, distinguished academics and researchers, and government officials and policy makers from all over the world, whose interaction and decisions shape the future of the ICT world. [http://www.wcit2012.org]
- World Wide Web Conference (WWW): Organised by the International World Wide Web Conference Committee (IW3C2) since 1994, the annual WWW Conference has played the fundamental role of gathering the trail-blazers from the international community to discuss, debate and explore how to shape and develop the future direction of the World Wide Web. [http://www2012.org]
- IGrid Events: The community-driven biennial International Grid event is a coordinated effort to accelerate the use of multi-10Gb international and national networks, to advance scientific research, and to educate decision makers, academics and industry researchers on the benefits of these hybrid networks. [http://www.startap.net] [http://www.igrid2005.org]]

Arbitrators and mediators (Examples)

1. European Independent Regulatory Authorities*)

1.1 European Data Protection Working Party (Article 29 Working Party): established by Article 29 of Directive 95/46/EC, it is the independent EU Advisory Body on Data Protection and Privacy. Its tasks are laid down in of Directive 95/46/EC (Article 30) and Directive 2002/58/EC (article 15).
[http://ec.europa.eu/justice/policies/privacy/workinggroup/index_en.htm]
[http://ec.europa.eu/justice/data-protection/article-29/index_en.htm]

1.2 Body of European Regulators for Electronic Communications (BEREC), formerly the European Regulators Group (ERG): established by the Regulatory Framework Directive to assist the Commission in developing the Internal Market for electronic communications and services and in ensuring the consistent application of the regulatory framework. [http://berec.europa.eu]

1.3 Radio Spectrum Policy Group (RSPG): adopts opinions assisting and advising the Commission on radio spectrum policy issues; on co-ordination of policy approaches; and, where appropriate, on harmonisation with regard to the availability and efficient use of radio spectrum as necessary for the establishment and functioning of the internal market. [http://rspg.groups.eu.int]

2. European Committees and Councils – Mediators
(Collective European Fora – Connected to the EU Institutions)

2.1 Advisory Committees of Directorates General within the Commission: representing the ICT industry on all relevant committees: Communication & Information Resource Centre Administrator (CIRCA).
[http://forum.europa.eu.int/Public/irc/infso/Home/main]

2.1.1 Communication Committee (COCOM-CIRCA): established under the new regulatory framework for electronic communications, in order to replace the ONP Committee and the Licensing Committee (instituted under the 1998 regulatory package for telecommunications). The committee assists the Commission in carrying out its executive powers under the new regulatory framework and the Regulation on the .eu Top Level Domain.
[https://circabc.europa.eu/faces/jsp/extension/wai/login.jsp]

2.1.2 Radio Spectrum Committee (RSC-CIRCA): established under the Radio Spectrum Decision 676/2002/EC as part of the new regulatory framework for electronic communications, it assists the Commission in developing and adopting technical implementation measures aimed at ensuring harmonised conditions for the availability and efficient use of radio spectrum, as well as the availability of information related to the use of the radio spectrum. [http://ec.europa.eu/information_society/policy/ecomm/radio_spectrum/eu_policy/rsc/index_en.htm]

2.1.3 Advisory Committee on the Implementation of Open Telecommunications Network Provision (ONP-CIRCA): established under the ONP Framework Directive 90/387/EC, it also deals with issues arising from the other ONP Directives (*e.g.* on Leased Lines, Voice Telephony and Interconnection). The ONP Committee meetings are attended by representatives of the Member States and the EEA countries as well as any candidate countries, including the independent national regulatory authorities. Exercising both advisory and regulatory functions, the Committee plays a key role in encouraging co-operation between Member States at the working level, helping them seek guidance and clarification from the Commission on particular Directives-implementation issues. The Committee is closely involved in preparing important elements of market regulation such as the Commission Recommendations on Interconnection, the annual Leased Line Report, and the implementation of the Regulation on Local Loop Unbundling. It has been superseded by Cocom.

2.1.4 Licensing Committee (CIRCA): established under the Licensing Directive 97/13/EC, the Committee meetings are attended by representatives of the Member States and the EEA countries, including the independent national regulatory authorities. Exercising both advisory and regulatory functions, its principal task is to harmonise the conditions for licensing so as to establish a "one-stop shopping" procedure; as well as to discuss the need for harmonisation of spectrum. It has been superseded by Cocom.

2.2 European Regulators Group: for European Regulators only
At national level the UK example is: e-Business Regulatory Alliance

2.3 i2010 High Level Group, formerly the "Bangemann Group": the expert group that produced "Europe's Way to the Information Society: An Action Plan", a report requested by the European Council to be prepared by a group of prominent persons on the specific measures to be taken into consideration by the Community and the Member States concerning infrastructure in the sphere of information.
[http://ec.europa.eu/information_society/eeurope/i2010/high_level_group/index_en.htm]

2.4 Committee on Industry, Research and Energy (ITRE) of the European Parliament: responsible for monitoring and reporting on the EU's industrial policy and the application of new technologies, including measures relating to SMEs; research policy, including the dissemination and exploitation of research findings; the activities of the Joint Research Centre; the information society and information technology, including the establishment and development of trans-European networks in the telecommunication infrastructure sector. It also coordinates European space policy, and as such, has ties with the European Space Agency. It has oversight duties on the Joint Research Centre and the Central Office for Nuclear Measurements, and similar projects.
[http://www.europarl.europa.eu/committees/itre_home_en.htm]

This list of ICT stakeholders has been compiled and updated with the help of EU magazines (*viz.* CORDIS, CORDIS focus) and weekly on-line newsletters (*viz.* the "Europe's Information Society Newsroom Update" provided by DG Information Society; "Enterprise News" by DG Enterprise and Industry; "Europe in the UK" by the European Commission Representation in the UK; and "EU News" by the Euro Info Centre, hosted by the London Chamber of Commerce).

Additionally, the following literature was consulted in compiling this list:

Anonymous (2001) *Lobbying in the European Union: Explanatory guide and contacts*, 2nd edition (Euroconfidential S.A.: Genval/Belgium).

Anonymous (2000) *The Europa Directory of International Organizations*, 2nd edition (European Publications Ltd.: London).

CEC (2001) *EURO-GUIDE: Yearbook of the institutions of the European Union and the other European organisations*, 18th edition (Editions Delta: Brussels).

Philip, Alan Butt; Gray, Oliver (1996) *Directory of Pressure Groups in the EU*, 2nd edition (Catermill Publishing: London).

Schiavone, Guiseppe (1997) *International Organizations: A Directory*, 4th edition (Macmillian Direct, Basingstoke, UK).

Seingry, Georges-Francais (1998) *Euro-Lobbying: Directory of the pressure groups in the EU, Vol. I: trade and professional associations*, 6th edition (Editions Delta, Brussels).

Appendix 7: Regulatory Compliance Maturity Model

The Regulatory Compliance Maturity Model is a tool for specifying the current state of an organisation (whether internationally or restricted to certain jurisdictions) or a department in its progress toward meeting those regulations or sets of regulations, out of all those presented in the Regulatory Compliance Matrix, that apply to that organisation. Once drafted, the model is supposed to measure (and flag up) the current level of regulatory *non-compliance*, after having defined the desired, fully compliant end-state and mapped a pathway (*a.k.a.* roadmap) identifying the steps already taken or yet to be taken to achieve that end-state. The roadmap specifies which policies, procedures, processes and controls, in four pillars of Governance, People, Controls, Technology, if installed or improved, would move the organisation to higher levels of compliance maturity.

The model defines the following maturity levels, which are *de facto* industry standards used in many other maturity models.

Level	LEVEL 1	LEVEL 2	LEVEL 3	LEVEL 4	LEVEL 5
	Nascent [Naive/ *ad hoc*/ Sub-standard]	**Initiative** [Basic/ Self-started/ Under construction]	**Established** [Developed/ Formal/ Essential]	**Advanced** [Competent/ Validated/ Proactive]	**Perfected** [Excellent/ Monitored/ Transformational]
Description	➢ Policies and processes not documented ➢ No organised approach ➢ Processes are executed in an *ad hoc*, uncontrolled or reactive manner	➢ Minimal documentation ➢ Approach lacks stability and discipline ➢ Processes are executed irregularly and/or are not standardised	➢ Clearly defined and documented policies and processes ➢ Consistent approach across the organisation ➢ Processes are consistently executed	➢ Policies and processes are reviewed for effectiveness and regular improvement ➢ Processes get independently scrutinised by independent assessors or auditors	➢ Policies and processes are monitored and benchmarked by a formal procedure ➢ Frequent assessments or audits are undertaken

Abbreviations used below:
RC = regulatory compliance
SM = Senior Management
GRC = Governance, Risk management and Compliance

Dimensions	LEVEL 1	LEVEL 2	LEVEL 3	LEVEL 4	LEVEL 5
	Nascent	Initiative	Established	Advanced	Perfected
Governance					
G1: Senior Management sponsorship	SM is not aware of any RC programmes. Ownership of RC programmes lies with departments only.	SM has issued some vague guidance on RC.	SM has an understanding of relevant regulations and is initiating new programmes whenever they believe that there is a need for this.	SM has a deep understanding of applicable regulations and is executing the new programmes, but is not monitoring.	SM has a deep understanding of applicable regulations, is committed to approving and monitoring RC programmes.
G2: Responsibilities and Accountability	Responsibilities for RC not specifically assigned. Incident-reporting and escalation procedures are undeveloped.	Roles and responsibilities for RC strategy, prevention, detection, reporting and communication defined. Escalation procedures not defined.	Organisational structure reflects responsibility for RC. A detailed escalation policy has been communicated, outlining procedures in case of an incident (*e.g.* data leakage).	Organisational structure reflects responsibility for RC and is linked to the strategy, compliance approach and (internal and external) communication procedure.	Organisational structure and RC approach is joined-up with other departments and programmes, such as Information Security and Financial Crime.
G3: Strategy	No documented RC strategy or approach.	A documented RC plan, but no detailed procedures.	A documented RC strategy, detailed procedures and guidance.	A documented, approved, communicated RC strategy that is actually being implemented.	A documented, approved, communicated and implemented RC strategy, which includes IT security policies and reporting requirements to external parties.

Dimensions	LEVEL 1	LEVEL 2	LEVEL 3	LEVEL 4	LEVEL 5
	Nascent	Initiative	Established	Advanced	Perfected
G4: Risk Assessment	The organisation has not formally established any RC risk assessment. The mounting risks of legal liability or reputation loss are unknown or ignored.	Identification of generic RC risks. A risk-based approach exists; however, this process has not been formally documented or is not centrally managed.	Full RC risk assessment is conducted to identify generic and specific RC risks, mitigating controls and likely business impact. Monitoring of non-compliance covers the breadth of operations.	Centrally managed RC risk assessment is operative. Proactive identification of emerging RC risks through proactive scanning of new regulations. Use of tools (*e.g.* Maturity model, heatmaps) for comparing changes in risk environment over time.	Risk appetite for RC is part of the compliance planning review. Information from external stakeholder events and other intelligence sources is input into an ongoing RC risk assessment approach.
G5: Monitoring	No monitoring of compliance.	An informal process of monitoring compliance with key regulatory controls, as part of a general monitoring function; *i.e.* through internal audit reviews or risk self-assessments.	Compliance monitoring reviews specifically map compliance efforts to key regulations.	A centrally managed process requiring all staff to sign annual declarations of compliance with key policies, such as ethics, money laundering, and IT security.	Assurance and monitoring system integrated into the organisation, including regular internal audits, risk self-assessments and regular reports (listing non-compliance issues) to SM.
G6: Quality Reviews and Audits (QR&A)	No RC QR&A has been performed for the last 12 months. SM is unaware of any issues.	A few *ad hoc* RC QR&A have been performed, but SM is unaware of any issues.	Enhanced QR&A activities, and issues are escalated to SM.	QR&A results are analysed with tools (*e.g.* Maturity model, heatmap). Active plans (*e.g.* roadmaps) to address RC issues exist.	QR&A results are analysed with RC tools. Proactive plans to address RC issues are implemented and progress is monitored.

Dimensions	LEVEL 1	LEVEL 2	LEVEL 3	LEVEL 4	LEVEL 5
	Nascent	Initiative	Established	Advanced	Perfected
People					
P1: Training and Awareness	No training or awareness programme exists. Some RC (*viz.* data protection, AML and fraud prevention) may be covered briefly during the corporate introduction training.	*Ad hoc* training and uncoordinated awareness initiatives are made, but inconsistent and not customised for key operational areas. Online training courses available for staff.	An appropriate and proportionate training and awareness regime is in place, customised to the several business units as required.	Staff is sufficiently trained to detect and prevent non-compliance events. The training and awareness regime is measured.	The training and awareness regime is measured and improved constantly. Refresher training courses are offered. Compliance officers and other key staff attend external stakeholder events.
P2: Stakeholder Activities	Responsible staff do not participate in any industry association or other stakeholder activities.	Some stakeholder interaction and attendance of industry events, although this is left to SM at their discretion.	Stakeholder interaction and communication with external subject matter experts. Staff involved in shaping regulations and guidance, but reactively.	Regular attendance of stakeholder meetings as well as participation in policy consultations so as to shape upcoming regulations.	Regular meetings with various advocacy coalitions (set forth in the Four-Level model), in particular with own-industry stakeholders and regulators. All future law and regulations on all levels are considered and their possible impacts, benefits and problems.
P3: Ethics and Compliance	Ethics and compliance are not part of the employment and evaluation process.	Some consideration is given to ethics screening and reference checking at the employment stage.	Dedicated procedures in place for non-compliance prevention and detection applicable to staff who work at highly regulated functions.	Bonus structures and rewards based not only on financial performance, but also on ethics and compliance with policies and procedures; ethical misconduct leads to reduction or cancellation of bonuses and rewards	Ethics and compliance are fully embedded in employment, performance management, and disciplinary policies and practices. Standards are consistently applied and compliance monitored. Rewards are firmly linked to compliance.

Dimensions	LEVEL 1	LEVEL 2	LEVEL 3	LEVEL 4	LEVEL 5
	Nascent	Initiative	Established	Advanced	Perfected
Control through Policy and Processes					
C1: Policy ("Compliance Statement")	No formal organisational compliance control policy formalised or fitted to the scope of the organisation's actual liabilities.	A formal policy fitted to the scope of actual organisational liability exists (on paper). However, it is ineffectively communicated and only partially followed.	The full set of internal policies documented, communicated and understood by all staff concerned.	A policy statement intermittently reviewed to check compliance with internal procedures, and applicable laws and regulations.	A policy statement frequently (at least annually) reviewed to check compliance with internal procedures, applicable laws and regulations, service-level agreements, other contracts.
C2: Procedures and Processes	No established written procedures or processes formulated to fit the scope of the organisation's actual liabilities.	Established written procedures and processes s to fit the scope of actual liability. The procedures, however, are not enforced and compliance may be coincidental.	Established written procedures and controls with established monitoring of the effectiveness of procedures and controls. However, this is not consistent across the whole organisation.	Established written procedures and controls, with monitoring of their effectiveness across the whole organisation.	Established written procedures and controls, with monitoring of their effectiveness across the whole organisation. Process levels are monitored and reported as well.
C3: RC Methodology	A few policy documents exist (*viz.* Data Protection Policy), but no processes (*e.g.* Subject Access Requests) to support the policy.	Policies, procedures and processes are defined and communicated to staff (as required).	An RC methodology or approach is developed with appropriate resources (*e.g.* in form of a handbook). An inventory/register of all main policies and processes exists.	The RC methodology/ approach, policies, procedures and processes are reviewed and updated regularly.	A robust RC methodology/ approach is implemented. Key individuals tasked with RC issues participate regularly in external stakeholder events as part of the intelligence and innovation process.

Dimensions	LEVEL 1	LEVEL 2	LEVEL 3	LEVEL 4	LEVEL 5
	Nascent	Initiative	Established	Advanced	Perfected
C4: Incident Response Plan	No incident-response plan exists at all, whether formally defined or not.	An incident response plan and process does exist; however, it has not been formally defined or documented.	An incident response plan is formally defined and documented, and processes and steps respecting incidents are specified.	An effective incident plan is validated/ tested. Roles and responsibilities in case of an incident are in place to contain the incident and remedy it.	An effective incident response plan is tested, and roles and responsibilities defined. But in addition, this is regularly updated, and timely, controlled reports to regulators, shareholders, customers and public published as necessary.
C5: Third Party Compliance Management	Limited compliance checks of external service providers, if they support existing RC policies, RC procedures and laws.	Some arrangements in place with certain key service providers; however, no controls over the selection of providers exists.	Controls in place to check that key service suppliers meet existing RC policies, RC procedures and laws.	Key service providers an integral part of host organisation's RC approach and RC programmes.	Key service providers are fully integrated in RC processes, and are monitored.
C6: System Support	Paper based manual processes.	Most information keep on paper, but some stored electronically on shared drives.	Much information is captured on IT systems. Some information is captured and available through a GRC software application.	Most information is captured and available through a GRC software application, which is used organisation-wide. Non-compliance prevention and detection decisions are system-based and easily accessible. SM can request any system report at any time.	All information is captured and available through a GRC software application. The GRC is regularly updated with new content (*viz.* regulatory requirements).

Dimensions	LEVEL 1	LEVEL 2	LEVEL 3	LEVEL 4	LEVEL 5
	Nascent	Initiative	Established	Advanced	Perfected
Technology					
T1: Automated Tools (Software Applications)	RC issues captured on Excel spreadsheets and reports in Word. Templates and documentation stored on laptops/desktops.	No GRC application likely used. RC information stored on shared drives and accessible by appropriate staff.	GRC application installed, which stores all results in a central database.	GRC application installed, which stores all results in a central database, and allows customised reporting and manual updating. SM can request reports to be produced within 24 hrs.	An external or internal resource frequently updates the GRC application with regulations, regulatory requirements, controls *etc.*
T2: Methodological Tools (Process and Content Management)	RC not seen as a major risk. Little or no investment made in any methodological tool.	A few key regulations identified as critical (*viz.* data protection regulation, data retention, IP law), and appropriate steps taken to comply with these regulations.	A basic inventory used to monitor legal and regulatory requirements, but not shared with the wider organisation.	A sophisticated inventory used (*viz.* the Regulatory Compliance Matrix herein presented, which gives guidance on RC). Risk assessments conducted and *ad hoc* QR&As performed to measure compliance.	A set of tools regularly used; *viz.* sophisticated inventories, maturity models, RCM, heatmaps and roadmaps (as presented in Chapter Eight), and linked by an RC methodology.
T3: Analysis and Business Intelligence	Limited or no use of GRC systems and compliance databases, or other external data sources.	Some compliance databases used; however, no data/ information shared with other organisations.	Some compliance databases available to appropriate staff.	Some compliance databases available to appropriate staff, and some data/ information shared with other organisations.	Access to organisation-wide, industry-wide compliance-relevant external data source(s) as integral part of compliance monitoring, and Information shared both with other organisations and with stakeholders.

Index

The letters f, d, and t following entries denoted footnote, diagram and table, respectively.

www.ingramcontent.com/pod-product-compliance
Lightning Source LLC
LaVergne TN
LVHW082015200926
848481LV00010B/2861
9781908585028